CRISIS IN
AMERICAN INSTITUTIONS

CRISIS IN
AMERICAN INSTITUTIONS

Fifth Edition

JEROME H. SKOLNICK
University of California
Berkeley

ELLIOTT CURRIE
University of California
Berkeley

LITTLE, BROWN AND COMPANY
Boston • *Toronto*

PREFACE

For this fifth edition, the plan of the book remains basically the same as in earlier editions, but with important additions and deletions. The first part, "Systemic Problems," considers basic processes within American society that affect the way all other institutions work—the nature of the corporate economy and the patterns of class, racial, and sexual inequality. For this edition, we have split our former chapter on capitalism into two— "Corporate Power" and "Economic Crisis" — because we felt that the importance of economic issues today required more attention than we could give it in a single chapter.

The second part, "Institutions in Crisis," considers several key institutions in the light of these basic processes. We have added a chapter on the issue of national security, increasingly a pressing concern in an age of growing military budgets and rising international tensions. We have collapsed our earlier chapters on health care and social services into one, combining the best articles from both. Finally, we have dropped our separate chapter on education, though articles partly dealing with educational issues appear in several other chapters, including those on racism, the family, and the workplace.

Each edition has offered an opportunity to review contemporary writings on America and its social problems; and with each we have regretted dropping old favorites and omitting promising new writings. The distinctions we make are scarcely invidious. We generally find far more worthwhile writing than we are able to reproduce. After all, we survey a range of topics—from capitalism through racism, to the family and criminal justice—each of which could profitably generate a lifetime of study and writing.

Only one article has made it through five editions— "Keeping the Poor Poor," by Paul Jacobs, who died of cancer in 1977. Paul was a rare man of both the old left and new left, a tenacious social critic, a compassionate observer, a generous friend, and a damned good analytical journalist. He was particularly good at making an issue come alive, especially when it arose from exploitation of other human beings. We dedicate this edition to his memory.

Paul would not mind if we also thanked others. Our editors at Little, Brown and Company have surveyed the book's users over the years, and the responses and comments have proven helpful in guiding our selection of articles. The Center for the Study of Law and Society at the University of California, Berkeley, once again offered facilities and a supportive environment. Christina Miller and Viki Merrick provided important administrative assistance. Ingrid Barclay pitched in to launch the manuscript. Rod Watanabe, the center's administrative assistant, as always, made the operation go. We appreciate their assistance and friendship. Finally, we are most grateful to the students who taught their teachers and us about each edition's strengths and weaknesses.

Jerome H. Skolnick
Elliott Currie

CONTENTS

INSTITUTIONS IN CRISIS

CRISIS IN
AMERICAN INSTITUTIONS

INTRODUCTION: APPROACHES TO SOCIAL PROBLEMS

Inflation. Unemployment. Energy crises. Tax revolt. Bankrupt cities. Political corruption and business bribery as routine news items. In the 1980s it is no longer a secret that the American system has not worked the way we were taught it should. When we first put this book together in the late sixties, most people who wrote about "social problems" still thought of the United States as a society whose basic economic and political problems had been solved. It is hard to find anyone who still seriously believes that—even among professional social scientists. Americans express continuing dissatisfaction and mistrust about the major institutions that affect their lives. The important question is no longer *whether* American institutions are in crisis, but *why*—and what can be done about it?

Today virtually every institution in American life—from the economy, to the family, to the welfare system—is the focus of intense debate. We can better understand the context of these debates if we look at the ways in which social science has approached the study of social problems in the past.

DEFECTIVES AND DELINQUENTS

The earliest writers on social problems in this country were straightforward moralists, staunch supporters of the virtues of thrift, hard work, sexual purity, and personal discipline. Writing at the end of the nineteenth century, they sought ways of maintaining the values of an earlier, whiter, more Protestant,

1

and more stable America in the face of the new challenges of industrialization, urbanization, and immigration.[1]

This early social science usually concentrated on the problems of what one nineteenth-century textbook described as the "defective, dependent, and delinquent classes."[2] The causes of social problems were located in the physical constitution or the moral "character" of the poor, the criminal, the insane, and other "unfortunates." For these theorists, the solution to nineteenth-century social problems lay in developing means of transforming the character of these "defective" classes, in the hope of equipping them better to succeed within a competitive, hierarchical society whose basic assumptions were never questioned. Social reformers working from these theories created, in the last part of the nineteenth and the first part of the twentieth centuries, much of the modern apparatus of "social control" in the United States: reformatories, modern prisons, institutions for the mentally ill, and the beginnings of the modern welfare system.

THE RISE OF "VALUE-FREE" SOCIAL PROBLEMS

During the first decades of this century this straightforward moralism was increasingly discarded in favor of a more subtle, ostensibly "neutral" approach to writing about social problems. By the 1930s, the idea that the social sciences were—or could be—purely "objective" or "value-free" had come to be widely accepted. From that point until the present, social problems theory has been characterized by a tortuous attempt to prove that theories and policies which serve to support the status quo are actually scientific judgments arrived at objectively. In this view, social scientists do not try to impose their own values in deciding what kinds of things will be defined and dealt with as social problems. Instead, the "scientific" student of social problems simply accepts "society's" definition of what is a problem and what is not. This approach is apparent in these statements, taken from major textbooks, on what constitutes a social problem:

Any difficulty or misbehavior of a fairly large number of persons which we wish to remove or correct.[3]

What people think they are.[4]

Whenever people begin to say, isn't it awful! Why don't they do something about it?[5]

Conditions which affect sizable proportions of the population, which are out of harmony with the values of a significant segment of the population, and which people feel can be improved or eliminated.[6]

Any substantial discrepancy between socially shared standards and actual conditions of social life.[7]

These definitions share the common idea that social problems are popularly defined. No condition is a problem unless a certain number of people in a society say it is. Since we are merely taking, as our starting point, the definitions of the problem that "other people," "society," or "significant segments of the population" provide, we are no longer in the position of moralizing about objective conditions.

The basic flaw in this happy scheme is that it does not make clear *which* segments of the population to consult when defining problems, or how to decide between conflicting ideas about what is problematic and what is not. In the real world, societies are divided along class, racial, sexual, and other lines, and the sociologist who proposes to follow "people's" definitions of social problems in fact generally adopts one of several competing ideologies of social problems based on those divisions. In practice, the ideology adopted has usually been not too different from that of the "unscientific" social problems writers of the nineteenth century.

These points are not new; they were raised as early as 1936 in an unusually perceptive paper called "Social Problems and the Mores," by the sociologist Willard Waller. Waller noted, for example, that discussions of poverty in the social problems literature of the 1930s were shaped by the unquestioning acceptance of the ideology of competitive capitalism:

A simpleton would suggest that the remedy for poverty in the midst of plenty is to redistribute income. We reject this solution at once because it would interfere with the institution of private property, would destroy the incentive for thrift and hard work and disjoint the entire economic system.[8]

Waller's question is fundamental: What has been left out in a writer's choice of what are to be considered as problems? What features of society are going to be taken for granted as the framework *within* which problems will be defined and resolved? In this case, the taken-for-granted framework is the principle of private property and individual competition. In general, Waller argued, "social problems are not solved because people do not want to solve them";[9] they *are* problems mainly because of people's unwillingness to alter the basic conditions from which they arise. Thus:

Venereal disease becomes a social problem in that it arises from our family institutions and also in that the medical means which could be used to prevent it, which would unquestionably be fairly effective, cannot be employed for fear of altering the mores of chastity.[10]

For Waller the definition of social problems was, in the broadest sense, a political issue involving the opposed ideologies of conflicting groups.

Waller's points still ring true. Most social problems writers in the United States still tacitly accept the basic structure of American society, and restrict their treatment of social problems to maladjustments *within* that structure.

SOCIAL PROBLEMS IN THE 1950s: GRADUALISM AND ANTICOMMUNISM

This is not to say that the literature on social problems since the 1930s has all been the same. Books on social problems, not surprisingly, tended to reflect the preoccupations of the time when they were written. Those conceived in the 1950s, for example, reflected social and political concerns that now seem bizarre. The shadow of McCarthyism and the general national hysteria over the "Communist menace" pervaded this literature. Consider the discussion of "civil liberties and subversion" in Paul B. Horton's and Gerald R. Leslie's textbook, *The Sociology of Social Problems*.[11] Horton and Leslie saw the "American heritage of liberty" being attacked from both left and right, from both "monolithic communism" and overzealous attempts to defend "our" way of life from it. Their position was resolutely "moderate." They claimed a scientific objectivity; yet, they were quite capable of moral condemnation of people whose politics were "extreme," whether right or left:

Most extremists are deviants. Most extremists show a fanatical preoccupation with their cause, a suspicious distrust of other people in general, a disinterest in normal pursuits, recreations, and small talk, and a strong tendency to divide other people into enemies and allies.[12]

The preference for "normal pursuits," even "small talk," over social criticism and action was common in an age noted for its "silent generation," but it was hardly "scientific." Among the other presumably objective features of the book were the authors' "rational proposals for preserving liberty and security," including these:

An adequate national defense is, needless to say, necessary in a world where an international revolutionary movement is joined to an aggressive major power. This is a military problem, not a sociological problem, and is not discussed here.

Counterespionage is essential. Highly trained professional agencies such as the FBI and the Central Intelligence Agency can do this efficiently and without endangering personal liberties of citizens. If headline-hunting congressmen, Legion officials, or other amateurs turn G-men, they merely scare off any real spies and destroy the counterespionage efforts of the professionals.[13]

The military and intelligence services themselves were not considered as problems relevant for social science. Questions about the operation of these agencies were viewed as internal and technical, military rather than sociological issues.

In a section on "Questions and Projects," the authors asked: "How have conservatives or reactionaries sometimes given unintentional assistance to the Communists? How have liberals sometimes given unintentional assistance to the Communists?"[14]

In the introduction to their book, Horton and Leslie considered the possibilities of social change and the proper role of social scientists in promoting it. They carefully adopted a middle ground between conservatives, to whom social problems were primarily problems of individual character, and "extremists" hoping for sudden or radical changes in social structure. ✳ They argued that the resolution of social problems "nearly always involves sweeping institutional changes"; but also that such changes are "costly" and "difficult," and that therefore:

it is unrealistic to expect that these problems will be solved easily or quickly. . . . Basic solutions of social problems will come slowly, if at all. Meanwhile, however, considerable amelioration or "improvement" may be possible.[15]

Social change, according to these authors, must be gradual and realistic; it must also be guided by experts. The authors insisted that their own role, and that of social experts in general, was merely to show the public how to get what they already valued. But in this role it was folly for the "layman" to question the expert. Horton and Leslie wrote that "when experts are agreed upon the futility of one policy or the soundness of another, it is sheer stupidity for the layman to disagree."[16]

An elitist, cold-war liberalism and gradualism, a fear of extremism and of an international Communist conspiracy—all these were presented not as moral and political positions but as fundamental social scientific truths. The sturdy entrepreneurial and Protestant values described in Waller's paper of the 1930s gave way, in Horton and Leslie's book of the 1950s, to a general preference for moderation, anticommunism, and "normal pursuits."

THE 1960s: AFFLUENCE AND OPTIMISM

A different imagery dominated the social problems literature of the next decade. Robert K. Merton's and Robert M. Nisbet's *Contemporary Social Problems*[17] was a product of the beginning of the 1960s, the period of the "New Frontier," which saw a significant shift, at least on the surface, in the focus of social concern. Americans were becoming aware of an "underdeveloped" world abroad and a "disadvantaged" world at home, both unhappily excluded from the benefits of an age of general "affluence" and well-being. New agencies of social improvement were created at home and abroad. A critique of old-style welfare efforts began to develop, along with the notion of "helping people help themselves," whether in Latin America, Harlem, or Appalachia. The idea of inclusion, of participation, in the American way of life became a political metaphor for the age. From a slightly different vantage, the idea emerged as "development" or "modernization." The social problems of the 1960s would be solved by extending the technological and intellectual resources of established American institutions into excluded, deprived, or underdeveloped places and groups. An intervention-minded government combined with an energetic social science on a scale unprecedented in this country.

In this period—very brief, as it turned out—social problems were often seen as problems of being *left out* of the American mainstream: "left behind," as the people of Appalachia were described; "traditional," like the Mexican-Americans; or "underdeveloped," like most Africans, Asians, and Latin Americans. In social problems theory, these ideas were manifested in a conservative ideology that celebrated American society as a whole, coupled with a liberal critique of the conditions hindering the extension of the American way to all.

One variant of this view was given in Nisbet's introduction to *Contemporary Social Problems*. For Nisbet, social facts become problematic when they "represent interruptions in the expected or desired scheme of things; violations of the right or the proper, as a society defines these qualities; dislocations in the social patterns and relationships that a society cherishes."[18]

Nisbet's assessment of the American situation was in keeping with the exaggerated optimism of the early 1960s:

In America today we live in what is often called an affluent society. It is a society characterized by imposing command of physical resources, high standards of private consumption, effective maintenance of public order and security, freedom from most of the uncertainties of life that plagued our ancestors, and relatively high levels of humanitarianism. There are also, of course, squalid slums, both urban and rural; occasional epidemics of disease; sudden eruptions of violence or bigotry, even in the most civilized of communities; people for whom the struggle for food and shelter yet remains obsessing and precarious. Thus, we are not free of social problems, and some of them seem to grow almost in direct proportion to our affluence.[19]

Nisbet was aware that America had not yet solved all its problems; indeed, that some seem to come with the generally glittering package that is America in the twentieth century. Yet, the problems were viewed as peripheral, as occasional eruptions in the backwaters of society where modern institutions had not fully penetrated.

Like earlier theorists, Nisbet sharply separated the role of the scientific student of social problems from that of other concerned people. The social scientist, as a scientist, should not engage in moral exhortation or political action, but should concentrate on understanding. At the same time, the scientist is

as interested as the next citizen in making the protection of society his first responsibility, in seeing society reach higher levels of moral decency, and when necessary, in promoting such legal actions as are necessary in the short run for protection or decency.[20]

Here the scientific stance masked a preference for vaguely defined values—"societal protection" and "moral decency"—which, in turn, determine what will be selected as social problems. In this instance, problems were selected according to whether they offended the values of social stability—that is, values associated with the conservative tradition in social thought.

Thus, problems were repeatedly equated with "dislocations and deviations";[21] they were problems of "dissensus," as if consensus might not also be a problem. Indeed, the entire book was divided into two sections, one of which dealt with "deviant behavior" and the other with "social disorganization." The articles in the text were not all of a piece. A paper by Robert S. Weiss and David Riesman on the problems of work took a different view on what constitutes a problem; the authors declared that "social forms which tend toward the suppression or frustration of meaning and purpose in life are inferior forms, whether or not they tend toward disorganization."[22] But many of the articles simply accepted the purposes of existing institutions and defined problems in terms of combating disorganization *within* those institutions. Perhaps the clearest illustration of this tendency appeared in an essay by Morris Janowitz dealing with problems of the military establishment:

It is self-evident that the military establishment, the armed forces, and their administrative organizations have become and will remain important institutions of United States society. The distinctive forms of military organization must be analyzed in order to understand the typical sources of personal and social disorganization found in military life.[23]

The existence of a large military establishment was defined as outside the critical concern of the sociologist. The focus was not on the effect of the military on national or international life, but on the problems of maladjustment within the military apparatus. The increasing scope of military activities was noted, but simply accepted as a fact of modern life:

The armed forces have also become involved in a wide variety of logistical, research, and training activities. In the current international scene, they must take on many politico-military duties, including military assistance of allied powers. . . .[24]

The implication was that the militarization of American society is not itself a problem for social analysis. And the acceptance of the place of the military in American society leads to the enlistment of social science in the service of military ends. Thus, in discussing changes in the requirements of military discipline, Janowitz noted that, in the 1960s, instead of employing "shock technique" to assimilate the recruit into the military, the problem had become how to foster "positive incentives and group loyalties through a team concept."[25] Janowitz didn't ask *what* the recruit is being assimilated *into*. The effect of primary-group relations on morale under cold-war conditions was extensively discussed, but the cold war itself was not.

Robert Merton's epilogue to *Contemporary Social Problems*, called "Social Problems and Sociological Theory," represented a major attempt to give theoretical definition to the "field" of social problems. Merton was well aware that different interests were present in society and therefore that definitions of social problems are likely to be contested—"one group's problem will be another group's asset"—and more specifically that "those occupying strategic positions of authority and power of course carry more weight than others in deciding social policy and so, among other things, in identifying for the rest what are to be taken as significant departures from social standards."[26]

According to Merton, however, this diversity of perspectives did not mean that sociologists must succumb to relativism or abandon their position as scientific students of society's problems. The way out of the dilemma was to distinguish between "manifest" and "latent" social problems—the latter are problems also "at odds with the values of the group," but not recognized as such. The task of the sociologist is to uncover the "latent" problems or unrecognized consequences of existing institutions and policies; in this way, "sociological inquiry does make men increasingly accountable for the outcome of their collective and institutionalized actions."[27]

The demand that social science make people accountable for their actions was a healthy departure from the false relativism of some earlier theorists. But the distinction between manifest and latent problems did not do what Merton claimed for it: it did not make the choice of problems a technical or neutral one. Actually, Merton's approach is best seen as providing a rationale for evaluating and criticizing particular policies and structures within a presumably consensual society whose basic values and institutions are not seen as problematic.

We could easily agree with Merton that "to confine the study of social problems to only those circumstances that are expressly defined as problems in the society is arbitrarily to discard a complement of conditions that are also dysfunctional to values held by people in that society."[28] But what about those values themselves? Shouldn't they be examined and, if necessary, criticized? It seems obvious to us, for example, that it is part of the sociologist's task to study and criticize the values held by people in German society during the Nazi era, or by slaveholders in the antebellum American South, rather than

to confine ourselves to studying those conditions that might be
"dysfunctional" in terms of those values. To do otherwise
amounts to an acceptance by default; the social scientist becomes an expert at handling problems within the confines of
an assumed consensus on basic goals and values.

The division of social problems into the two categories of
deviant behavior and *social disorganization* reflected this acceptance, for both categories were defined as "disruptions" of
an existing social order and did not question the adequacy of
that social order itself. Thus:

> Whereas social disorganization refers to faults in the arrangement
> and working of social statuses and roles, deviant behavior refers to
> conduct that departs significantly from the norms set for people in
> their social statuses.[29]

It is not, as some critics have suggested, that this kind of analysis suggests that whatever is, is right. But it does imply that
whatever *disturbs* the existing social system is the primary
problem.

The sociologists' "expert" judgment, of course, may conflict
with what people themselves feel to be their problems, and if
so, according to Merton, the expert should prevail. Merton argued that:

> We cannot take for granted a reasonably correct public imagery of
> social problems; of their scale, distribution, causation, consequences
> and persistence or change. . . . Popular perceptions are no safe
> guide to the magnitude of a social problem.[30]

The corollary, presumably, is that the sociologist's imagery of
social problems is at least "reasonably correct," even, perhaps,
where segments of the public strongly object to having their
problems defined, or redefined, for them. We seem back again
to the same condescending attitude toward the public expressed by Horton and Leslie and other sociologists of the
1950s.

This kind of attitude wasn't, of course, confined to writers
on social problems. It was a major theme in the social thought
and government policy of the sixties, a decade characterized
by an increasing detachment of governmental action from
public knowledge and accountability—as exemplified in the
growth of a vast intelligence apparatus, the repeated attempts
to overthrow popularly elected governments overseas, and the
whole conduct of the Vietnam War. This process was often ex-
cused on the ground that political decisions involved technical
judgments that were out of the reach of ordinary people.

The conception of social problems as technical, rather than moral and political, issues was explicit in Merton's and Nisbet's text. Thus, Merton suggested that "the kind of problem that is dominated by social disorganization results from instrumental and technical flaws in the social system. The system comes to operate less efficiently than it realistically might. . . ."[31]

If the problems are technical ones, then it was, of course, reasonable to view social scientists as technicians and to regard their intervention into social life as free from partisan interest. It is this, apparently, that renders the social scientist a responsible citizen, rather than a "mere" social critic or ideologue:

Under the philosophy intrinsic to the distinction between manifest and latent social problems, the social scientist neither abdicates his intellectual and professional responsibilities nor usurps the position of sitting in judgment on his fellow men.[32]

It is apparent, however, that this kind of "philosophy" lends itself all too easily to an alignment of expertise and "professionalism" with dominant values and interests masquerading as societal consensus. This is apparent in the choice of topics offered in most textbooks. Merton and Nisbet—whose widely used textbook has gone through several editions—characteristically dealt with mental disorders, crime and delinquency, drug use, alcoholism, suicide, sexual behavior, the population crisis, race relations, family disorganization, work and automation, poverty, community disorganization, violence, and youth and politics. The book did not deal with (to take some examples from our own table of contents) corporate power, sexism, health care, the criminal justice system, and so on. The pattern of these differences is obvious: Merton and Nisbet focused most heavily on those who have, for one reason or another, failed to "make it" within the American system—delinquents, criminals, the mentally ill, drug users—and on disorganization *within* established institutions. Even when individual authors in their book attempted to analyze the system itself, the effort was usually relegated to a peripheral, or merely symbolic, place.

In spite of its claim to political neutrality, the social science of the 1960s typically focused on the symptoms of social ills, rather than their sources: criminals, rather than the laws; the mentally ill, rather than the quality of life; the culture of the poor, rather than the decisions of the rich; the "pathology" of the ghetto, rather than the problems of the economy. What "socially shared standards" dictated this choice of emphasis? In the introduction to a newer edition of *Contemporary Social*

Problems, Nisbet tried to answer this question. "It may well be asked," he writes, "why these problems have been chosen by the editors," rather than others, which "for some persons at least might be regarded as even more pressing to national policy."

The answer is that this is a textbook in sociology. Sociology is a special science characterized by concepts and conclusions, which are based on analysis and research, yielding in turn perspectives on society and its central problems. For many decades now, sociologists have worked carefully and patiently on these problems. In other words this book is concerned not only with the presentation of major social problems but with the scientific concepts and procedures by which these problems have been, and continue to be, studied.[33]

Nisbet seems to be explaining that these problems were selected by the editors because sociologists have studied them, and not others, in the past. Such an argument is hardly compelling.

Even the Merton and Nisbet view of contemporary social problems has changed somewhat with the times. Their latest editions include some chapters and revisions far more critical of the prevailing social system than was evident in previous editions. Still, as the preface points out, ". . . the fundamental character of this book has remained constant through all editions."

THE SEVENTIES: DEEPENING CRISIS AND DECLINE OF OPTIMISM

The social problems literature of the 1960s—and the official policies that paralleled it—assumed that the problems of American society could be solved by piecemeal measures. If people could be given enough training, there would be no unemployment and no "social dynamite" in the ghettoes. If criminals and drug addicts could be "rehabilitated," there would be no more crime and social disintegration. This approach, like those before it, although giving considerable lip service to the idea that "society" was to blame for social problems, ultimately laid the burden of change on individuals. And when in the seventies things began to get worse instead of better, many social scientists could only conclude that there was something fundamentally wrong with people.

The new, gloomy social science of the 1970s rediscovered, and made respectable, some of the old theories of degeneracy and defectiveness. Writers like William Shockley and Arthur Jensen resurrected long-discredited hereditary theories of racial inferiority to "explain" why blacks still were not succeeding in America, in spite of all that had been "done for them" in the 1960s. Other theorists concluded that the reason there was still considerable poverty in the United States was that poor people either really *liked* living in slums or were sunk in a "culture of the lower class" that prevented them from thinking ahead, accumulating savings, or staying on the job.[34] The persistence of crime and urban violence was increasingly held to be the result of a "subculture of violence" among the black poor (as opposed, say, to mainstream white culture, which presumably eschewed violence and aggression) or, in even more pessimistic fashion, was attributed to the "innate" aggressiveness of the human species or to chemical imbalances in the brain. In a real sense, conventional social science in the United States had come full circle, shedding even the limited optimism and social activism of the 1960s to focus once again on the "defective" classes and the remedy of containment through punishment. Much the same was true of government, which, during the 1970s, whether Democratic or Republican, stressed the need for "limits" in our expectations, for lowered aspirations for the quality of life, and for tightening our belts in the face of economic decline.

THE EIGHTIES: THE DEMAND FOR CHANGE

These appeals to lowered expectations didn't hold for long. The 1980s were ushered in on a wave of popular demands for change, and a new administration came to power on a program purporting to restore life to the economy and bring new vigor to American values. Often, however, the political expression of this quest for change seems to be a call to move rapidly backward, to return to traditional institutions and roles, whether real or imagined—the spirit of "free enterprise," the traditional relations between men and women, and American military domination of the rest of the world.

There have also been more positive expressions of the sense of crisis and the desire for change. Among them is an encouraging renewal of a more flexible and critical understanding of social problems. When we first wrote this introduction in 1969, we commented that there were virtually no serious studies of the American business system, or of the police, courts, military, and other key institutions. Today, this statement, happily, could not be made. A new school of economists is effectively challenging the conventional images of the affluent economy; and the amount of serious critical writing on the health-care system, the workplace, human services, and other institutions is much greater than we anticipated a few years ago and is growing all the time.

It is out of this emerging body of critical work that we have taken our selections for this reader. As in earlier editions, the selections represent a diversity of opinions, styles, and perspectives, but all within a common general framework: a critical, democratic approach to social institutions that sees them as changeable and accountable and that emphasizes human potential and the possibility of meaningful social change. Our emphasis is on the economic and political structures that are shaped by the imperatives of profit and power—not on the supposed flaws of the people victimized by these structures.

Within this admittedly very broad perspective there is room for much controversy over particular theories of social structure and strategies of institutional change as well as particular definitions of human and social priorities. The editors of this book do not necessarily agree with each other on more than the most basic themes. Both of us would describe ourselves as to the left of center politically; both of us have been participants in many of the movements for social change of the past two decades. Yet we find ourselves in a continuing debate over many of the issues covered in this book—for example, the proper response by workers to automation or the prohibition of pornography. We think this tension is fruitful, however, and we have tried to reflect it in our selection of readings, which represent a fairly wide spectrum of political opinion and theoretical perspective.

We see this book as an introductory work, useful for beginning courses in sociology, social problems, or political science. Its purpose is to raise issues, to provide students with the beginnings of a critical approach to the society they live in and will hopefully help change. It provides few definitive answers and it leaves unresolved many basic theoretical and practical questions about the sources and solutions of the American crisis. But its purpose will be accomplished if it helps lead students to begin their own process of confronting those questions.

REFERENCES

1. C. Wright Mills, "The Professional Ideology of the Social Pathologists," in Irving L. Horowitz, ed., *Power, Politics and People:*

The Collected Essays of C. Wright Mills (New York: Ballantine, 1963).

2. Charles Richmond Henderson, *An Introduction to the Study of Defective, Dependent and Delinquent Classes* (Boston: Heath, 1906).

3. Lawrence K. Frank, "Social Problems," *American Journal of Sociology*, 30 (January 1925), p. 463.

4. Richard C. Fuller and Richard R. Myers, "The Natural History of a Social Problem," *American Sociological Review*, 6 (June 1941), p. 320.

5. Paul B. Horton and Gerald R. Leslie, *The Sociology of Social Problems* (New York: Appleton-Century-Crofts, 1955), p. 6.

6. Arnold M. Rose, "Theory for the Study of Social Problems," *Social Problems*, 4 (January 1957), p. 190.

7. Robert K. Merton and Robert M. Nisbet, *Contemporary Social Problems* (New York: Harcourt, Brace and World, 1961), p. 702.

8. Willard Waller, "Social Problems and the Mores," *American Sociological Review*, 1 (December 1936), p. 926.

9. *Ibid.*, p. 928.

10. *Ibid.*, p. 927.

11. Horton and Leslie, *Sociology*. We refer here to the original edition in order to place the book in its historical context.

12. *Ibid.*, p. 517.

13. *Ibid.*, p. 520.

14. *Ibid.*, p. 523.

15. *Ibid.*, p. 12.

16. *Ibid.*, p. 19.

17. Merton and Nisbet, *Contemporary Social Problems*. Here, too, we refer to the first edition in order to consider the book in historical perspective. The general theoretical perspective in the book has changed little if at all, as we will note later; there have been some substantive changes, however—for example, the chapter by Janowitz has been dropped, and new chapters added.

18. Robert A. Nisbet, "The Study of Social Problems," in *ibid.*, p. 4.

19. *Ibid.*, p. 5. The reader might compare C. Wright Mills' notion, developed during the same period, that the United States should be seen as an "overdeveloped" society; see Irving L. Horowitz, "Introduction," in Horowitz, *Power, Politics, and People*, p. 8.

20. Nisbet, "The Study of Social Problems," p. 9.

21. *Ibid.*, p. 12.

22. Robert S. Weiss and David Riesman, "Social Problems and Disorganization in the World of Work," in Merton and Nisbet, *Contemporary Social Problems*, p. 464.

23. Morris Janowitz, "The Military Establishment: Organization and Disorganization," in Merton and Nisbet, *Contemporary Social Problems*, p. 515.

24. *Ibid.*, p. 516.

25. *Ibid.*, pp. 533–534.

26. Robert K. Merton, "Social Problems and Sociological Theory," in Merton and Nisbet, *Contemporary Social Problems*, p. 706.

27. *Ibid.*, p. 710.

28. *Ibid.*, p. 711.

29. *Ibid.*, p. 723.

30. *Ibid.*, pp. 712–713.

31. *Ibid.*, p. 723.

32. *Ibid.*, p. 712.

33. Robert M. Nisbet, "The Study of Social Problems," in *ibid.*, p. 2.

34. For Jensen's perspective and some criticisms of it, see *Harvard Educational Review*, May 1968; for another influential work in this vein, see Edward Banfield, *The Unheavenly City* (Boston: Little, Brown and Co., 1968).

SYSTEMIC PROBLEMS

I
CORPORATE POWER

The myth of American capitalism is individual "free enter-prise"; the vision of the hard-working, thrifty entrepreneur competing with others and constrained by the forces of the market. But the reality of American capitalism is what Ralph Nader once called "corporate collectivism": the domination of economic life by a relative handful of giant corporations—cor-porations whose size and power enable them to control mar-kets rather than be controlled by them.

Since the late 1960s, the 500 largest industrial corporations in America have consistently accounted for about two-thirds of all industrial sales, four-fifths of all industrial profits, and three-fourths of all industrial employment. The largest 50 of those corporations alone account for about a fourth of the value of all manufactured goods in the country and employ about one in five industrial workers. Similar concentration ex-ists in other areas of business as well—banking and finance, transportation, utilities, and communications. All told, about a thousand corporations now produce roughly half of all pri-vately produced goods and services in the United States, and those corporations are deeply entwined with government in a multitude of ways—from long-term defense contracts to mas-sive federal "bail-outs" of big corporations in trouble.

The real issue, then, is not whether we have a "free enter-prise" economy in any meaningful sense; we don't. Instead, the important questions have to do with the performance and control of the modern corporate version of capitalism: How has the concentration of corporate power affected such key economic problems as inflation and recession? How has it changed the terms on which business relates to the public and to political authorities? And how, more generally, does the growing power of the giant corporation affect the quality of social life?

For years after World War II, when the American economy was expanding and bringing unheard-of-levels of consumption, such questions were rarely heard, and almost never voiced by social scientists. The ability of the corporate economy to provide material abundance and social enrichment was taken for granted.

By the 1970s, that casual acceptance disintegrated. With the economic recession of the mid-decade, Americans from all walks of life suddenly were faced with the threat of unemployment, shortages of food and gasoline, skyrocketing prices, and real doubts about whether they could provide for themselves and their families. Meanwhile, dramatic instances of business corruption, dangerous consumer products, and corporate intervention in overseas governments helped create a mood of mistrust and skepticism about the fundamental character of economic life in America.

The articles in this section probe some of the reasons why that mistrust has grown.

Mark Dowie's story of the Ford Motor Company's refusal to make minor changes in its Pinto that would have saved hundreds of lives shows, in stark relief, the insulation of the giant corporations from public accountability or social control. At the time the article was written, Ford was the fifth largest industrial corporation in the world; its total sales exceeded the gross national products of all but thirty of the world's countries. Ford's enormous economic power enabled it to operate with military-like secrecy, open defiance of government safety standards, and a near-total disregard for the well-being of its consumers.

Some of American industry's products are dangerous; most are also increasingly overpriced. For most Americans, the pinch of rising prices—especially in housing, fuel, health care, and food—has become a constant source of anxiety. Why do prices rise? Who's to blame? Daniel Zwerdling's analysis of the food industry offers an explanation of the rising costs at the supermarket counter. Contrary to industry's claim that price increases reflect "natural" problems such as frosts or crop failures, Zwerdling shows that the real source of escalating food costs is the growing concentration of the multibillion-dollar food business—a concentration that allows the food giants to raise prices almost at will, without suffering the effects of competition. In the past several years, food industry concentration has become much worse as food corporations have

indulged in a "takeover binge," swallowing up smaller businesses and sinking vast sums into advertising campaigns—
which, ultimately, are paid for by consumers in higher food
prices.

Zwerdling argues that food corporations are in business not
to produce food, but to make money. The article by Lappé
and Collins on the marketing of infant formula in the Third
World confirms this point. In this case, the need for the food
product was unclear from the start. Food was *already* available
to the potential consumers of infant formula—mothers' milk,
which was far better, nutritionally, than the manufactured formula that the international food corporations sought to substitute for it. Lacking the facilities to prepare the formula
properly and the money to buy enough of it, poor families in
the underdeveloped countries were the victims of a massive
sales effort that opened new markets for the food companies—
but often led to tragic damage to children's health. (In the
latest chapter of this story, successful pressure by the concerned
groups mentioned by Lappé and Collins led to congressional
hearings on the infant formula problem in the United States
and to an international declaration against the unscrupulous
marketing of formula in the Third World, which was signed
by every major country—except the United States.)

1
PINTO MADNESS

Mark Dowie

One evening in the mid-1960s, Arjay Miller was driving home from his
office in Dearborn, Michigan, in the four-door Lincoln Continental that
went with his job as president of the Ford Motor Company. On a crowded
highway, another car struck his from the rear. The Continental spun
around and burst into flames. Because he was wearing a shoulder-strap
seat belt, Miller was unharmed by the crash, and because his doors didn't

From *Mother Jones*, Vol. II, No. VIII, September/October 1977. Reprinted by permission.

jam he escaped the flaming wreck. But the accident made a vivid impression on him. Several months later, on July 15, 1965, he recounted it to a U.S. Senate subcommittee that was hearing testimony on auto safety legislation. "I still have burning in my mind the image of that gas tank on fire," Miller said. He went on to express an almost passionate interest in controlling fuel-fed fires in cars that crash or roll over. He spoke with excitement about the fabric gas tank Ford was testing at that very moment. "If it proves out," he promised the senators, "it will be a feature you will see in our standard cars."

Almost seven years after Miller's testimony, a woman, whom for legal reasons we will call Sandra Gillespie, pulled onto a Minneapolis highway in her new Ford Pinto. Riding with her was a young boy, whom we'll call Robbie Carlton. As she entered a merge lane, Sandra Gillespie's car stalled. Another car rear-ended hers at an impact speed of 28 miles per hour. The Pinto's gas tank ruptured. Vapors from it mixed quickly with the air in the passenger compartment. A spark ignited the mixture and the car exploded in a ball of fire. Sandra died in agony a few hours later in an emergency hospital. Her passenger, 13-year-old Robbie Carlton, is still alive; he has just come home from another futile operation aimed at grafting a new ear and nose from skin on the few unscarred portions of his badly burned body. (This accident is real; the details are from police reports.)

Why did Sandra Gillespie's Ford Pinto catch fire so easily, seven years after Ford's Arjay Miller made his apparently sincere pronouncements—the same seven years that brought more safety improvements to cars than any other period in automotive history? An extensive investigation by *Mother Jones* over the past six months has found these answers:

Fighting strong competition from Volkswagen for the lucrative small-car market, the Ford Motor Company rushed the Pinto into production in much less than the usual time.

Ford engineers discovered in pre-production crash tests that rear-end collisions would rupture the Pinto's fuel system extremely easily.

Because assembly-line machinery was already tooled when engineers found this defect, top Ford officials decided to manufacture the car anyway—exploding gas tank and all—*even though Ford owned the patent on a much safer gas tank*.

For more than eight years afterwards, Ford successfully lobbied, with extraordinary vigor and some blatant lies, against a key government safety standard that would have forced the company to change the Pinto's fire-prone gas tank.

By conservative estimates Pinto crashes have caused 500 burn deaths to people who would not have been seriously injured if the car had not burst into flames. Burning Pintos have become such an embarrassment to Ford that its advertising agency, J. Walter Thompson, dropped a line from the end of a radio spot that read "Pinto leaves you with that warm feeling."

Ford knows the Pinto is a firetrap, yet it has paid out millions to settle damage suits out of court, and it is prepared to spend millions more lobbying against safety standards. With a half million cars rolling off the assembly lines each year, Pinto is the biggest-selling subcompact in America, and the company's operating profit on the car is fantastic. Finally, in 1977, new Pinto models have incorporated a few minor alterations necessary to meet that federal standard Ford managed to hold off for eight years. Why did the company delay so long in making these minimal, inexpensive improvements?

Ford waited eight years because its internal "cost-benefit analysis," *which places a dollar value on human life,* said it wasn't profitable to make the changes sooner.

Before we get to the question of how much Ford thinks your life is worth, let's trace the history of the death trap itself. Although this particular story is about the Pinto, the way in which Ford made its decision is typical of the U.S. auto industry generally. There are plenty of similar stories about other cars made by other companies. But this case is the worst of them all.

The next time you drive behind a Pinto (with over two million of them on the road, you shouldn't have much trouble finding one), take a look at the rear end. That long silver object hanging down under the bumper is the gas tank. The tank begins about six inches forward of the bumper. In late models the bumper is designed to withstand a collision of only about five miles per hour. Earlier bumpers may as well not have been on the car for all the protection they offered the gas tank.

Mother Jones has studied hundreds of reports and documents on rear-end collisions involving Pintos. These reports conclusively reveal that if you ran into that Pinto you were following at over 30 miles per hour, the rear end of the car would buckle like an accordion, right up to the back seat. The tube leading to the gas-tank cap would be ripped away from the tank itself, and gas would immediately begin sloshing onto the road around the car. The buckled gas tank would be jammed up against the differential housing which contains four sharp protruding bolts likely to gash holes in the tank and spill still more gas. The welded seam between the main body frame and the wheel well would split, allowing gas to enter the interior of the car.

Now all you need is a spark from a cigarette, ignition, or scraping metal, and both cars would be engulfed in flames. If you gave the Pinto a really good whack—say, at 40 mph—chances are excellent that its doors would jam and you would have to stand by and watch its trapped passengers burn to death.

This scenario is no news to Ford. Internal company documents in our possession show that Ford has crash-tested the Pinto at a top-secret site more than 40 times and that *every* test made at over 25 mph without special structural alteration of the car has resulted in a ruptured fuel tank. Despite this, Ford officials denied having crash-tested the Pinto.

Eleven of these tests, averaging a 31-mph impact speed, came before Pintos started rolling out of the factories. Only three cars passed the test with unbroken fuel tanks. In one of them an inexpensive light-weight metal baffle was placed so those bolts would not perforate the tank. (Don't forget about that baffle which costs about a dollar and weighs about a pound. It plays an important role in our story later on.) In another successful test, a piece of steel was placed between the tank and the bumper. In the third test car the gas tank was lined with a rubber bladder. But none of these protective alterations was used in the mass-produced Pinto.

In preproduction planning, engineers seriously considered using in the Pinto the same kind of gas tank Ford uses in the Capri. The Capri tank rides over the rear axle and differential housing. It has been so successful in over 50 crash tests that Ford used it in its Experimental Safety Vehicle, which withstood rear-end impacts of 60 mph. So why wasn't the Capri tank used in the Pinto? Or, why wasn't that baffle placed between the tank and the axle—something that would have saved the life of Sandra Gillespie and hundreds like her. Why was a car known to be a serious fire hazard deliberately released to production in August of 1970?

Whether Ford should manufacture subcompacts at all was the subject of a bitter two-year debate at the company's Dearborn headquarters. The principals in the corporate struggle were the then-president Semon "Bunky" Knudsen, whom Henry Ford II had hired away from General Motors, and Lee Iacocca, a spunky young turk who had risen fast within the company on the enormous success of the Mustang. Iacocca argued forcefully that Volkswagen and the Japanese were going to capture the entire American subcompact market unless Ford put out its own alternative to the VW Beetle. Bunky Knudsen said, in effect: let them have the small-car market; Ford makes good money on medium and large models. But he lost the battle and later resigned. Iacocca became president and almost immediately began a rush program to produce the Pinto.

Like the Mustang, the Pinto became known in the company as "Lee's car." Lee Iacocca wanted that little car in the showrooms of America with the 1971 models. So he ordered his engineering vice president, Bob Alexander, to oversee what was probably the shortest production planning period in modern automotive history. The normal time span from conception to production of a new car model is about 43 months. The Pinto schedule was set at just under 25.

Design, styling, product planning, advance engineering and quality assurance all have flexible time frames, and engineers can pretty much carry these on simultaneously. Tooling, on the other hand, has a fixed time frame of about 18 months. Normally, an auto company doesn't begin tooling until the other processes are almost over. *But Iacocca's speed-up meant Pinto tooling went on at the same time as product development.* So when crash tests revealed a serious defect in the gas tank, it was too late. The tooling was well under way.

When it was discovered the gas tank was unsafe, did anyone go to Iacocca and tell him? "Hell no," replied an engineer who worked on the Pinto, a high company official for many years, who, unlike several others at Ford, maintains a necessarily clandestine concern for safety. "That person would have been fired. Safety wasn't a popular subject around Ford in those days. With Lee it was taboo. Whenever a problem was raised that meant a delay on the Pinto, Lee would chomp on his cigar, look out the window and say 'Read the product objectives and get back to work.' "

The product objectives are clearly stated in the Pinto "green book." This is a thick, top-secret manual in green covers containing a step-by-step production plan for the model, detailing the metallurgy, weight, strength and quality of every part in the car. The product objectives for the Pinto are repeated in an article by Ford executive F. G. Olsen published by the Society of Automotive Engineers. He lists these product objectives as follows:

1. TRUE SUBCOMPACT
   - Size
   - Weight
2. LOW COST OF OWNERSHIP
   - Initial price
   - Fuel consumption
   - Reliability
   - Serviceability
3. CLEAR PRODUCT SUPERIORITY
   - Appearance
   - Comfort
   - Features
   - Ride and Handling
   - Performance

Safety, you will notice, is not there. It is not mentioned in the entire article. As Lee Iacocca was fond of saying, "Safety doesn't sell."

Heightening the anti-safety pressure on Pinto engineers was an important goal set by Iacocca known as "the limits of 2,000." The Pinto was not to weigh an ounce over 2,000 pounds and not to cost a cent over $2,000. "Iacocca enforced these limits with an iron hand," recalls the engineer quoted earlier. So, even when a crash test showed that that one-pound, one-dollar piece of metal stopped the puncture of the gas tank, it was thrown out as extra cost and extra weight.

People shopping for subcompacts are watching every dollar. "You have to keep in mind," the engineer explained, "that the price elasticity on these subcompacts is extremely tight. You can price yourself right out of the market by adding $25 to the production cost of the model. And nobody understands that better than Iacocca."

Dr. Leslie Ball, the retired safety chief for the NASA manned space program and a founder of the International Society of Reliability Engineers, recently made a careful study of the Pinto. "The release to production of the Pinto was the most reprehensible decision in the history of American engineering," he said. Ball can name more than 40 European and Japanese models in the Pinto price and weight range with safer gas-tank positioning. Ironically, many of them, like the Ford Capri, contain a "saddle-type" gas tank riding over the back axle. *The patent on the saddle-type tank is owned by the Ford Motor Co.*

Los Angeles auto safety expert Byron Bloch has made an in-depth study of the Pinto fuel system. "It's a catastrophic blunder," he says. "Ford made an extremely irresponsible decision when they placed such a weak tank in such a ridiculous location in such a soft rear end. It's almost designed to blow up—premeditated."

A Ford engineer, who doesn't want his name used, comments: "This company is run by salesmen, not engineers: so the priority is styling, not safety." He goes on to tell a story about gas-tank safety at Ford:

Lou Tubben is one of the most popular engineers at Ford. He's a friendly, outgoing guy with a genuine concern for safety. By 1971 he had grown so concerned about gas-tank integrity that he asked his boss if he could prepare a presentation on safer tank design. Tubben and his boss had both worked on the Pinto and shared a concern for its safety. His boss gave him the go-ahead, scheduled a date for the presentation and invited all company engineers and key production planning personnel. When time came for the meeting, a total of two people showed up—Lou Tubben and his boss.

"So you see," continued the anonymous Ford engineer, "there *are* a few of us here at Ford who are concerned about fire safety." He adds: "They are mostly engineers who have to study a lot of accident reports and look at pictures of burned people. But we don't talk about it much. It isn't a popular subject. I've never seen safety on the agenda of a product meeting and, except for a brief period in 1956, can't remember seeing the word safety in an advertisement. I really don't think the company wants American consumers to start thinking too much about safety—for fear they might demand it, I suppose."

Asked about the Pinto gas tank, another Ford engineer admitted: "That's all true. But you miss the point entirely. You see, safety isn't the issue, trunk space is. You have no idea how stiff the competition is over trunk space. Do you realize that if we put a Capri-type tank in the Pinto you could only get one set of golf clubs in the trunk?"

Blame for Sandra Gillespie's death, Robbie Carlton's unrecognizable face and all the other injuries and deaths in Pintos since 1970 does not rest on the shoulders of Lee Iacocca alone. For, while he and his associates fought their battle against a safer Pinto in Dearborn, a larger war against safer cars raged in Washington. One skirmish in that war involved Ford's successful eight-year lobbying effort against Federal Motor Vehicle Safety Standard 301, the rear-end provisions of which would have forced Ford to redesign the Pinto.

But first some background:

During the early '60s, auto safety legislation became the *bête-noire* of American big business. The auto industry was the last great unregulated business, and if *it* couldn't reverse the tide of government regulation, the reasoning went, no one could.

People who know him cannot remember Henry Ford taking a stronger stand than the one he took against the regulation of safety design. He spent weeks in Washington calling on members of Congress, holding press conferences and recruiting business cronies like W. B. Murphy of Campbell's Soup to join the anti-regulation battle. Displaying the sophistication for which today's American corporate leaders will be remembered, Murphy publicly called auto safety "a hula hoop, a fad that will pass." He was speaking to a special luncheon of the Business Council, an organization of 100 chief executives who gather periodically in Washington to provide "advice" and "counsel" to government. The target of their wrath in this instance was the Motor Vehicle Safety Bills introduced in both houses of Congress, largely in response to Ralph Nader's *Unsafe at Any Speed*.

By 1965, most pundits and lobbyists saw the handwriting on the wall and prepared to accept government "meddling" in the last bastion of free enterprise. Not Henry. With bulldog tenacity, he held out for defeat of the legislation to the very end, loyal to his grandfather's invention and to the company that makes it. But the Safety Act passed the House and Senate unanimously, and was signed into law by Lyndon Johnson in 1966.

While lobbying for and against legislation is pretty much a process of high-level back-slapping, press-conferencing and speech-making, fighting a regulatory agency is a much subtler matter. Henry headed home to lick his wounds in Grosse Pointe, Michigan, and a planeload of the Ford Motor Company's best brains flew to Washington to start the "education" of the new federal auto safety bureaucrats.

Their job was to implant the official industry ideology in the minds of the new officials regulating auto safety. Briefly summarized, that ideology states that auto accidents are caused not by *cars*, but by people and highway conditions.

It is an experience to hear automotive "safety engineers" talk for hours without ever mentioning cars. They will advocate spending billions educating youngsters, punishing drunks and redesigning street signs. Listening to them, you begin to think that it is easier to control 100 million drivers than a handful of manufacturers. They show movies about guardrail design and advocate the clear-cutting of trees 100 feet back from every highway in the nation. If a car is unsafe, they argue, it is because its owner doesn't maintain it properly.

In light of an annual death rate approaching 50,000, they are forced to admit that driving is hazardous. But the car is, in the words of Arjay Miller, "the safest link in the safety chain."

Before the Ford experts left Washington to return to drafting tables in Dearborn they did one other thing. They managed to informally reach an agreement with the major public servants who would be making auto safety decisions. This agreement was that "cost-benefit" would be an acceptable mode of analysis by Detroit and its new regulators. And, as we shall see, cost-benefit analysis quickly became the basis of Ford's argument against safer car design.

Cost-benefit analysis was used only occasionally in government until President Kennedy appointed Ford Motor Company President Robert McNamara to be Secretary of Defense. McNamara, originally an accountant, preached cost benefit with all the force of a Biblical zealot. Stated in its simplest terms, cost-benefit analysis says that if the cost is greater than the benefit, the project is not worth it—no matter what the benefit. Examine the cost of every action, decision, contract, part, or change, the doctrine says, then carefully evaluate the benefits (in dollars) to be certain that they exceed the cost before you begin a program or pass a regulation.

As a management tool in a business in which profits count over all else, cost-benefit analysis makes a certain amount of sense. Serious problems arise, however, when public officials who ought to have more than corporate profits at heart apply cost-benefit analysis to every conceivable decision. The inevitable result is that they must place a dollar value on human life.

Ever wonder what your life is worth in dollars? Perhaps $10 million? Ford has a better idea: $200,000.

Remember, Ford had gotten the federal regulators to agree to talk auto safety in terms of cost-benefit. But in order to be able to argue that various safety costs were greater than their benefits, Ford needed to have a dollar value figure for the "benefit." Rather than coming up with a price tag itself, the auto industry pressured the National Highway Traffic Safety Administration to do so. And in a 1972 report the agency determined that a human life lost on the highway was worth $200,725 [Table 1]. Inflationary forces have recently pushed the figure up to $278,000.

Furnished with this useful tool, Ford immediately went to work using it to prove why various safety improvements were too expensive to make.

Table 1 What's Your Life Worth? Societal Cost Components for Fatalities, 1972 NHTSA Study

Component	1971 Costs
Future productivity losses	
Direct	$132,000
Indirect	41,300
Medical costs	
Hospital	700
Other	425
Property damage	1,500
Insurance administration	4,700
Legal and court	3,000
Employer losses	1,000
Victim's pain and suffering	10,000
Funeral	900
Assets (lost consumption)	5,000
Miscellaneous accident cost	200
Total per fatality: $200,725	

Here is a chart from a federal study showing how the National Highway Traffic Safety Administration has calculated the value of a human life. The estimate was arrived at under pressure from the auto industry. The Ford Motor Company has used it in cost-benefit analyses arguing why certain safety measures are not "worth" the savings in human lives. The calculation above is a breakdown of the estimated cost to society every time someone is killed in a car accident. We were not able to find anyone, either in the government or at Ford, who could explain how the $10,000 figure for "pain and suffering" had been arrived at.

Nowhere did the company argue harder that it should make no changes than in the area of rupture-prone fuel tanks. Not long after the government arrived at the $200,725-per-life figure, it surfaced, rounded off to a cleaner $200,000, in an internal Ford memorandum. This cost-benefit analysis argued that Ford should not make an $11-per-car improvement that would prevent 180 fiery deaths a year.

This cold calculus [Table 2] is buried in a seven-page company memorandum entitled "Fatalities Associated with Crash-Induced Fuel Leakage and Fires."

The memo goes on to argue that there is no financial benefit in complying with proposed safety standards that would admittedly result in fewer auto fires, fewer burn deaths and fewer burn injuries. Naturally, memoranda that speak so casually of "burn deaths" and "burn injuries" are not released to the public. They are very effective, however, with

Table 2   *Benefits and Costs Relating to Fuel
Leakage Associated with the Static
Rollover Test Portion of FMVSS 208*

Benefits

Savings: 80 burn deaths, 180 serious burn injuries, 2,100
  burned vehicles.
Unit cost: $200,000 per death, $67,000 per injury, $700
  per vehicle.
Total benefit: 180 × ($200,000) + 180 × ($67,000) +
  2,100 × ($700) = $49.5 million.

Costs

Sales: 11 million cars, 1.5 million light trucks.
Unit cost: $11 per car, $11 per truck.
Total cost: 11,000,000 × ($11) + 1,500,000 × ($11) =
  $137 million.

Department of Transportation officials indoctrinated in McNamarian cost-benefit analysis.

All Ford had to do was convince men like John Volpe, Claude Brinegar and William Coleman (successive Secretaries of Transportation during the Nixon-Ford years) that certain safety standards would add so much to the price of cars that fewer people would buy them. This could damage the auto industry, which was still believed to be the bulwark of the American economy. "Compliance to these standards," Henry Ford II prophesied at more than one press conference, "will shut down the industry."

The Nixon Transportation Secretaries were the kind of regulatory officials big business dreams of. They understood and loved capitalism and thought like businessmen. Yet, best of all, they came into office uninformed on technical automotive matters. And you could talk "burn injuries" and "burn deaths" with these guys, and they didn't seem to envision children crying at funerals and people hiding in their homes with melted faces. Their minds appeared to have leapt right to the bottom line—more safety meant higher prices, higher prices meant lower sales and lower sales meant lower profits.

So when J. C. Echold, Director of Automotive Safety (chief anti-safety lobbyist) for Ford wrote to the Department of Transportation—which he still does frequently, at great length—he felt secure attaching a memorandum that in effect says it is acceptable to kill 180 people and burn another 180 every year, *even though we have the technology that could save their lives for $11 a car.*

Furthermore, Echold attached this memo, confident, evidently, that the

Secretary would question neither his low death/injury statistics nor his high cost estimates. But it turns out, on closer examination, that both these findings were misleading.

First, note that Ford's table shows an equal number of burn deaths and burn injuries. This is false. All independent experts estimate that for each person who dies by an auto fire, many more are left with charred hands, faces and limbs. Andrew McGuire of the Northern California Burn Center estimates the ratio of burn injuries to deaths at ten to one instead of the one to one Ford shows here. Even though Ford values a burn at only a piddling $67,000 instead of the $200,000 price of life, the true ratio obviously throws the company's calculations way off.

The other side of the equation, the alleged $11 cost of a fire-prevention device, is also a misleading estimation. One document that was *not* sent to Washington by Ford was a "Confidential" cost analysis *Mother Jones* has managed to obtain, showing that crash fires could be largely prevented for considerably *less* than $11 a car. The cheapest method involves placing a heavy rubber bladder inside the gas tank to keep the fuel from spilling if the tank ruptures. Goodyear had developed the bladder and had demonstrated it to the automotive industry. We have in our possession crash-test reports showing that the Goodyear bladder worked well. On December 2, 1970 (*two years before* Echold sent his cost-benefit memo to Washington), Ford Motor Company ran a rear-end crash test on a car with the rubber bladder in the gas tank. The tank ruptured, but no fuel leaked. On January 15, 1971, Ford again tested the bladder and again it worked. The total purchase and installation cost of the bladder would have been $5.08 per car. That $5.08 could have saved the lives of Sandra Gillespie and several hundred others.

When a federal regulatory agency like the National Highway Traffic Safety Administration (NHTSA) decides to issue a new standard, the law usually requires it to invite all interested parties to respond before the standard is enforced—a reasonable enough custom on the surface. However, the auto industry has taken advantage of this process and has used it to delay lifesaving emission and safety standards for years. In the case of the standard that would have corrected that fragile Pinto fuel tank, the delay was for an incredible eight years.

The particular regulation involved here was Federal Motor Vehicle Safety Standard 301. Ford picked portions of Standard 301 for strong opposition back in 1968 when the Pinto was still in the blueprint stage. The intent of 301, and the 300 series that followed it, was to protect drivers and passengers *after* a crash occurs. Without question the worst postcrash hazard is fire. So Standard 301 originally proposed that all cars should be able to withstand a fixed barrier impact of 20 mph (that is, running into a wall at that speed) without losing fuel.

When the standard was proposed, Ford engineers pulled their crash-

test results out of their files. The front ends of most cars were no problem—with minor alterations they could stand the impact without losing
fuel. "We were already working on the front end," Ford engineer Dick
Kimble admitted. "We knew we could meet the test on the front end."
But with the Pinto particularly, a 20-mph rear-end standard meant redesigning the entire rear end of the car. With the Pinto scheduled for
production in August of 1970, and with $200 million worth of tools in
place, adoption of this standard would have created a minor financial
disaster. So Standard 301 was targeted for delay, and, with some assistance
from its industry associates, Ford succeeded beyond its wildest expectations: the standard was not adopted until the 1977 model year. Here is
how it happened:

There are several main techniques in the art of combating a government safety standard: a) make your arguments in succession, so the feds
can be working on disproving only one at a time; b) claim that the real
problem is not X but Y (we already saw one instance of this in "the
problem is not cars but people"); c) no matter how ridiculous each argument is, accompany it with thousands of pages of highly technical asser-
tions it will take the government months or, preferably, years to test.
Ford's large and active Washington office brought these techniques to
new heights and became the envy of the lobbyists' trade.

The Ford people started arguing against Standard 301 way back in
1968 with a strong attack of technique b). Fire, they said, was not the real
problem. Sure, cars catch fire and people burn occasionally. But statistically auto fires are such a minor problem that NHTSA should really
concern itself with other matters.

Strange as it may seem, the Department of Transportation (NHTSA's
parent agency) didn't know whether or not this was true. So it contracted
with several independent research groups to study auto fires. The studies
took months, often years, which was just what Ford wanted. The completed studies, however, showed auto fires to be more of a problem than
Transportation officials ever dreamed of. A Washington research firm
found that 400,000 cars were burning up every year, burning more than
3,000 people to death. Furthermore, auto fires were increasing five times
as fast as building fires. Another study showed that 35 per cent of all fire
deaths in the U.S. occurred in automobiles. Forty per cent of all fire department calls in the 1960s were to vehicle fires—a public cost of $350
million a year, a figure that, incidentally, never shows up in cost-benefit
analyses.

Another study was done by the Highway Traffic Research Institute in
Ann Arbor, Michigan, a safety think-tank funded primarily by the auto
industry (the giveaway there is the words "highway traffic" rather than
"automobile" in the group's name). It concluded that 40 per cent of the
lives lost in fuel-fed fires could be saved if the manufacturers complied

with proposed Standard 301. Finally, a third report was prepared for NHTSA. This report indicated that the Ford Motor Company makes 24 per cent of the cars on the American road, yet these cars account for 42 per cent of the collision-ruptured fuel tanks.

Ford lobbyists then used technique a)—bringing up a new argument. Their line then became: yes, perhaps burn accidents do happen, but rear-end collisions are relatively rare (note the echo of technique b) here as well). Thus Standard 301 was not needed. This set the NHTSA off on a new round of analyzing accident reports. The government's findings finally were that rear-end collisions were seven and a half times more likely to result in fuel spills than were front-end collisions. So much for that argument.

By now it was 1972; NHTSA had been researching and analyzing for four years to answer Ford's objections. During that time, nearly 9,000 people burned to death in flaming wrecks. Tens of thousands more were badly burned and scarred for life. And the four-year delay meant that well over 10 million new unsafe vehicles went on the road, vehicles that will be crashing, leaking fuel and incinerating people well into the 1980s.

Ford now had to enter its third round of battling the new regulations. On the "the problem is not X but Y" principle, the company had to look around for something new to get itself off the hook. One might have thought that, faced with all the latest statistics on the horrifying number of deaths in flaming accidents, Ford would find the task difficult. But the company's rhetoric was brilliant. The problem was not burns, but . . . impact! Most of the people killed in these fiery accidents, claimed Ford, would have died whether the car burned or not. They were killed by the kinetic force of the impact, not the fire.

And so once again, the ball bounced into the government's court and the absurdly pro-industry NHTSA began another slow-motion response. Once again it began a time-consuming round of test crashes and embarked on a study of accidents. The latter, however, revealed that a large and growing number of corpses taken from burned cars involved in rear-end crashes contained no cuts, bruises or broken bones. They clearly would have survived the accident unharmed if the cars had not caught fire. This pattern was confirmed in careful rear-end crash tests performed by the Insurance Institute for Highway Safety. A University of Miami study found an inordinate number of Pintos burning on rear-end impact and concluded that this demonstrated "a clear and present hazard to all Pinto owners."

Pressure on NHTSA from Ralph Nader and consumer groups began mounting. The industry-agency collusion was so obvious that Senator Joseph Montoya (D-N.M.) introduced legislation about Standard 301. NHTSA waffled some more and again announced its intentions to promulgate a rear-end collision standard.

Waiting, as it normally does, until the last day allowed for response, Ford filed with NHTSA a gargantuan batch of letters, studies and charts now arguing that the federal testing criteria were unfair. Ford also argued that design changes required to meet the standard would take 43 months, which seemed like a rather long time in light of the fact that the entire Pinto was designed in about two years. Specifically new complaints about the standard involved the weight of the test vehicle, whether or not the brakes should be engaged at the moment of impact and the claim that the standard should only apply to cars, not trucks or buses. Perhaps the most amusing argument was that the engine should not be idling during crash tests, the rationale being that an idling engine meant that the gas tank had to contain gasoline and that the hot lights needed to film the crash might ignite the gasoline and cause a fire.

Some of these complaints were accepted, others rejected. But they all required examination and testing by a weak kneed NHTSA, meaning more of those 18-month studies the industry loves so much. So the complaints served their real purpose—delay; all told, an eight-year delay, while Ford manufactured more than three million profitable, dangerously incendiary Pintos. To justify this delay, Henry Ford II called more press conferences to predict the demise of American civilization. "If we can't meet the standards when they are published," he warned, "we will have to close down. And if we have to close down some production because we don't meet standards we're in for real trouble in this country."

While government bureaucrats dragged their feet on lifesaving Standard 301, a different kind of expert was taking a close look at the Pinto— the "recon man." "Recon" stands for reconstruction; recon men reconstruct accidents for police departments, insurance companies and lawyers who want to know exactly who or what caused an accident. It didn't take many rear-end Pinto accidents to demonstrate the weakness of the car. Recon men began encouraging lawyers to look beyond one driver or another to the manufacturer in their search for fault, particularly in the growing number of accidents where passengers were uninjured by collision but were badly burned by fire.

Pinto lawsuits began mounting fast against Ford. Says John Versace, executive safety engineer at Ford's Safety Research Center, "Ulcers are running pretty high among the engineers who worked on the Pinto. Every lawyer in the country seems to want to take their depositions." (The Safety Research Center is an impressive glass and concrete building standing by itself about a mile from Ford World Headquarters in Dearborn. Looking at it, one imagines its large staff protects consumers from burned and broken limbs. Not so. The Center is the technical support arm of Jack Echold's 14-person anti-regulatory lobbying team in World Headquarters.)

When the Pinto liability suits began, Ford strategy was to go to a jury.

Confident it could hide the Pinto crash tests, Ford thought that juries of solid American registered voters would buy the industry doctrine that drivers, not cars, cause accidents. It didn't work. It seems that citizens are much quicker to see the truth than bureaucracies. Juries began ruling against the company, granting million-dollar awards to plaintiffs.

"We'll never go to a jury again," says Al Slechter in Ford's Washington office. "Not in a fire case. Juries are just too sentimental. They see those charred remains and forget the evidence. No sir, we'll settle."

Settlement involves less cash, smaller legal fees and less publicity, but it is an indication of the weakness of their case. Nevertheless, Ford has been offering to settle when it is clear that the company can't pin the blame on the driver of the other car. But, since the company carries $2 million deductible product-liability insurance, these settlements have a direct impact on the bottom line. They must therefore be considered a factor in determining the net operating profit on the Pinto. It's impossible to get a straight answer from Ford on the profitability of the Pinto and the impact of lawsuit settlements on it—even when you have a curious and mildly irate shareholder call to inquire, as we did. However, financial officer Charles Matthews did admit that the company establishes a reserve for large dollar settlements. He would not divulge the amount of the reserve and had no explanation for its absence from the annual report.

Until recently, it was clear that, whatever the cost of these settlements, it was not enough to seriously cut into the Pinto's enormous profits. The cost of retooling Pinto assembly lines and of equipping each car with a safety gadget like that $5.08 Goodyear bladder was, company accountants calculated, greater than that of paying out millions to survivors like Robbie Carlton or to widows and widowers of victims like Sandra Gillespie. The bottom line ruled, and inflammable Pintos kept rolling out of the factories.

In 1977, however, an incredibly sluggish government has at last instituted Standard 301. Now Pintos will have to have rupture-proof gas tanks. Or will they?

To everyone's surprise, the 1977 Pinto recently passed a rear-end crash test in Phoenix, Arizona, for NHTSA. The agency was so convinced the Pinto would fail that it was the first car tested. Amazingly, it did not burst into flame.

"We have had so many Ford failures in the past," explained agency engineer Tom Grubbs, "I felt sure the Pinto would fail."

How did it pass?

Remember that one-dollar, one-pound metal baffle that was on one of the three modified Pintos that passed the pre-production crash tests nearly ten years ago? Well, it is a standard feature on the 1977 Pinto. In the Phoenix test it protected the gas tank from being perforated by those four bolts on the differential housing.

We asked Grubbs if he noticed any other substantial alterations in the rear-end structure of the car. "No," he replied, "the [baffle] seems to be the only noticeable change over the 1976 model."

But was it? What Tom Grubbs and the Department of Transportation didn't know when they tested the car was that it was manufactured in St. Thomas, Ontario. Ontario? The significance of that becomes clear when you learn that Canada has for years had extremely strict rear-end collision standards.

Tom Irwin is the business manager of Charlie Rossi Ford, the Scottsdale, Arizona dealership that sold the Pinto to Tom Grubbs. He refused to explain why he was selling Fords made in Canada when there is a huge Pinto assembly plant much closer by in California. "I know why you're asking that question, and I'm not going to answer it," he blurted out. "You'll have to ask the company."

But Ford's regional office in Phoenix has "no explanation" for the presence of Canadian cars in their local dealerships. Farther up the line in Dearborn, Ford people claim there is absolutely no difference between American and Canadian Pintos. They say cars are shipped back and forth across the border as a matter of course. But they were hard pressed to explain why some Canadian Pintos were shipped all the way to Scottsdale, Arizona. Significantly, one engineer at the St. Thomas plant did admit that the existence of strict rear-end collision standards in Canada "might encourage us to pay a little more attention to quality control on that part of the car."

The Department of Transportation is considering buying an American Pinto and running the test again. For now, it will only say that the situation is under investigation.

Whether the new American Pinto fails or passes the test, Standard 301 will never force the company to test or recall the more than two million pre-1977 Pintos still on the highway. Seventy or more people will burn to death in those cars every year for many years to come. If the past is any indication, Ford will continue to accept the deaths.

According to safety expert Byron Bloch, the older cars could quite easily be retrofitted with gas tanks containing fuel cells. "These improved tanks would add at least 10 mph improved safety performance to the rear end," he estimated, "but it would cost Ford $20 to $30 a car so they won't do it unless they are forced to." Dr. Kenneth Saczalski, safety engineer with the Office of Naval Research in Washington, agrees. "The Defense Department has developed virtually fail-safe fuel systems and retrofitted them into existing vehicles. We have shown them to the auto industry and they have ignored them."

Unfortunately, the Pinto is not an isolated case of corporate malpractice in the auto industry. Neither is Ford a lone sinner. There probably isn't a car on the road without a safety hazard known to its manufacturer. And though Ford may have the best auto lobbyists in Washington, it is not alone. The anti-emission control lobby and the anti-safety lobby usually work in chorus form, presenting a well-harmonized message from the country's richest industry, spoken through the voices of individual companies—the Motor Vehicle Manufacturers Association, the Business Council and the U.S. Chamber of Commerce.

Furthermore, cost-valuing human life is not used by Ford alone. Ford was just the only company careless enough to let such an embarrassing calculation slip into public records. The process of willfully trading lives for profits goes back at least as far as Commodore Vanderbilt, who publicly scorned George Westinghouse and his "foolish" air brakes while people died by the hundreds in accidents on Vanderbilt's railroads.

The original draft of the Motor Vehicle Safety Act provided for criminal sanction against a manufacturer who willfully placed an unsafe car on the market. Early in the proceedings the auto industry lobbied the provision out of the bill. Since then, there have been those damage settlements, of course, but the only government punishment meted out to auto companies for non-compliance to standards has been a minuscule fine, usually $5,000 to $10,000. One wonders how long the Ford Motor Company would continue to market lethal cars were Henry Ford II and Lee Iacocca serving 20-year terms in Leavenworth for consumer homicide.

This article was published in September of 1977, and in February 1978 a jury awarded a sixteen-year-old boy, badly burned in a rear-end Pinto accident, $128 million in damages (the accident occurred in 1973 in Santa Ana, Calif.). That was the largest single personal injury judgment in history.

On May 8, 1978, the Department of Transportation announced that tests conducted in response to this article showed conclusively that the Pinto was defective in all respects described in the article and called for a recall of all 1971 to 1976 Pintos—the most expensive recall in automotive history.

2
THE FOOD MONSTERS

Daniel Zwerdling

Why does food cost so much? It's easy to understand once you understand the logic of the food corporations, and understanding the logic is easy once you recall why they are in business. Food corporations, whether General Mills or Nestle or Continental Grain, are *not* in business to produce food, any more than Exxon is in business to produce oil. Food corporations are in business to produce *money*—and food, like oil, is merely one vehicle for making it. To put it bluntly, the major corporations that produce food—the most precious resource, the sustainer of life—have one overriding purpose, and that is to amass all the riches and power they possibly can.

Is this interpretation too strident?

"Ours is a simple objective," declares Philip Morris-Miller Beer executive John Murphy; the legs of his desk dig into a red-and-white carpet bearing the seal of arch-competitor Anheuser-Busch. "It's to become Number One." "We'll earn every share of the market we can," declares a top executive at Kellogg, which has already wrestled a controlling grip on the cereals market. "I'm not satisfied," Kellogg Vice President Arnold Langbo adds, "with a 42 per cent share."

With such corporate motives as the backdrop, simple logic dictates why food prices are rising and why food quality is getting worse. Close your eyes, lean your head back, take some deep breaths, and relax. Now fantasize: Suppose *you* were the leader of a food corporation. How would you accomplish your corporate mission—and double profits in the next five years?

If you've reached into the Machiavellian shadows of your mind, you might recall that when nations have lusted after riches and power, they have invaded weaker countries which possess the resources they want. Spain invaded Mexico for its gold. U.S. troops seized Puerto Rico and Cuba for their sugar. In political history, they call the strategy imperialism; in the world of corporate finance, it's called diversification through merger.

When you pay at the checkout counters, you're financing the food conglomerates' takeover campaigns.

Corporate strategists at Pillsbury yearn, they tell *Business Week*, "to do combat with multibillion-dollar giants such as General Foods and General Mills." So they plunk down $152 million and take control of Green Giant—and overnight grab a nationwide processed-vegetables market plus an extra half-billion dollars in annual sales.

R. J. Reynolds, the $4 billion cigarette, transportation, and petroleum empire, decides to branch out into food. Reynolds does not buy a few hundred acres and plant some seeds; it comes up with $621 million and seizes Del Monte, itself the archetypal multinational octopus that plundered banana plantations in the Philippines, pineapple plantations in Kenya, asparagus farms in Mexico, plus ranches, fisheries, and factories in two dozen other countries to build a billion-dollar-a-year empire as the most powerful producer of processed fruits and vegetables in the world.

"The Great Takeover Binge," *Business Week* calls it. While consumers paid record prices at the supermarkets, the food megacorporations were gobbling up—and being gobbled by—other huge corporations in the most ferocious corporate takeover wars in U.S. history. As the imperialists of the Seventeenth and Eighteenth Centuries knew so well, taking control of another power—whether a country or corporation—buys instant market expansion, instant diversification, instant rivers of cash. Especially in today's schizoid economy, where the prices of corporate stocks tumble while every other price soars, taking over existing firms has become far cheaper than building new ones from scratch. For many major food corporations—and other corporations, as well—takeovers have become the single most important strategy for building market power.

The quintessential food imperialist is probably the nation's least known, at least to consumers—Beatrice. Corporate executives like to reminisce about the company's humble beginnings as a butter-and-egg firm in Beatrice, Nebraska. The firm started to acquire a string of dairies, the oil wells of the food industry, milked for their steady stream of cash. While soldiers fought the Axis overseas, Beatrice picked up LaChoy Chinese foods—and since then, humble Beatrice has seized more than 400 companies, many of them small regional firms that the conglomerate has muscled into national brands. Names that are household words to American eaters—Canada Dry and Schweppes, Dannon Yogurt, Aunt Nellie's vegetables, Louis Sherry ice cream, RC Cola, Sunbeam Bread and Clark Bars, Martha White Flour, Eckrich Sausage and Brookside Wines—are to the Beatrice conglomerate just so many "profit centers," along with Airstream Trailers, Miracle White Fabric Softener, and Samsonite Luggage, that funnel the incomprehensible torrents of cash—$7 billion last year—to fuel the expanding conglomerate nation.

At a convention for Beatrice employes in Nashville, *Fortune* tells us, corporate executives leaped to the stage and led 700 employes "lustily in the chorus of a song. . . . 'We're Number One,' they sang, thrusting their fingers into the air. The theme of the convention, registered in placards,

banners and speeches, as well as the song, was 'Number One,' i.e., Beatrice now makes more money than any other food processor."

But more money is not enough money. Beatrice executives say their
goal is to double sales before 1984. To kick off their latest expansion campaign, they've declared war against Coca-Cola—and plunked down half
a billion dollars to take control of Tropicana, a firm that already controls
up to half the bottled orange juice market in some Eastern states.

Beatrice executives' grab to double their power stems from more than
their reflex lust for more bucks. They know, as all corporate executives do,
that if they *don't* expand their market power *another giant* like Nestle
will—because Nestle knows that if it doesn't expand, another giant will
. . . and Beatrice will lose its markets, perhaps forever. And so, individual
executives and corporations have become both perpetrators and victims
of an irrational system. Trapped in its crazy momentum, the corporate
grab for power appears not only rational but necessary.

You help finance these expansion crusades at the supermarket, as conglomerates raise prices to nourish their bank accounts with takeover cash.
When Beatrice seized Tropicana and Reynolds seized Del Monte, they
paid $1 billion—$1 billion not to build new factories, not to hire thousands of unemployed workers, not to create new socially useful products,
but merely to change the name on some ownership deeds. While these
takeovers were more expensive than most, they were just two of several
hundred food company takeovers recorded in the past few years.

But the biggest consumer cost of these takeovers doesn't come directly
from the purchase price; it stems from the future market power they give
the conglomerate imperialists. With 400 separate profit centers under its
control, for instance, Beatrice is like a massive bank that collects money
from all over the globe and then shuffles and redistributes the profits
wherever they will do the most good. The rising price you pay for Dannon Yogurt has less to do with the state of the nation's udders than with
the cash-flow needs of Samsonite Luggage.

In this conglomerate scheme, how much of the premium price you
paid last week for Minute Maid orange juice—it costs 30 per cent more
than the store brand at my local Safeway—was dictated by the sun and
the bugs on Coca-Cola's orange groves in Florida? And how much of the
premium was dictated by the conglomerate's far-flung political and financial manipulations? How much of the premium was tacked on to
finance Coca-Cola's "free" soccer games and clinics for children in Africa
and the Middle East, to build the brand name abroad? How much to
help Coca-Cola finance its subsidiary, Aqua-Chem, Inc., which is struggling to get a grip on water desalination technologies in the Third World?
How much to help finance Coke's chief executive as he shuttled back and
forth between Arab potentates, secretly negotiating like a corporate Kis-
singer to grab a monopoly on their cola markets? How much to finance

Coca-Cola's recent joint purchase, with Japan's Mitsui Sugar Co. and England's Tate & Lyle, the world's largest sugar producer, of a sugar mill in Swaziland? How much to nourish Coca-Cola's massive new "money, muscle, and marketing" blitz on the U.S. wine market, including $110 million worth of recent vineyard takeovers and more than $13 million in wine ads last year alone?

Back to your fantasy: You've been amassing resources and potential clout by taking control of other corporations. Now how do you begin to harvest those resources, and make them pay off? Governments have always consolidated power by building mass loyalty with such tactics as controlling education in the schools, manipulating information in the media, and occasionally passing out direct bribes (tax cuts before elections). In government circles they call it propaganda; in the corporate world it's advertising.

Consumers are paying rising prices at the supermarkets to finance the corporate ad campaigns.

In the consumer-conscious 1970s, it became almost fashionable to berate the evils of corporate advertising; there's always at least one Congressional hearing in Washington, it seems, where activists are warning how Kellogg "brainwashes" children to lust after cereals spun half from sugar (and not just in the United States—the latest beneficiaries of Kellogg's sugar propaganda are children in the Middle East and South America). But activists seldom pinpoint the critical strategic role that advertising plays in the corporate control of the economy and the inexorably soaring price of food. Advertising is not just an expensive and annoying tactic that corporations use *after* they have acquired wealth and power: Advertising has become a critical *cause* of the corporate drive to amass wealth and power.

Procter & Gamble understands the connection. This $7 billion conglomerate helped write the rules of mass advertising as it built the world's most powerful empire devoted to satisfying the oral and anal needs of the public. Procter & Gamble executives learned that the key to corporate power is to become the Number One or Number Two brand in a market—at least half the shoppers in the supermarket, industry studies show, choose mainly the top brand products, even though they are the most expensive (and reap the highest profits). And P&G executives also learned they could virtually buy control of the market if only they bought enough advertising.

Today, P&G products are in control at virtually every stage between kitchen and toilet. When you open your mouth for a fix of sugar and fat, Pringles will be first choice for potato chips and Duncan Hines will likely be your cake (P&G controls almost 40 per cent of the nation's cake-mix market); when you cook dinner, Crisco will be one of your two main choices for fat, and when you clean the grease off your dishes you'll squirt leading brands Joy or Ivory Liquid; when you brush your teeth after a meal, you'll use the king of toothpastes, Crest (which alone accounts for 35 per cent of the toothpaste on the nation's shelves); when you defecate, White Cloud or Charmin will be at your side (they dominate the toilet paper market) while your little ones will be protected by Luvs or Pampers (70 per cent of the nation's disposable diapers). Procter & Gamble controls the shampoos in your shower, and the deodorants you squirt under your arms—and when your clothes come out of the washer, chances are fifty-fifty they'll smell like P&G Tide or Cheer or one of the other P&G detergents that together have grabbed half the nation's sales. Just to make sure it gets good television ad time, the P&G productions unit produces five leading soap operas, including "Search for Tomorrow" and "As the World Turns."

But Procter & Gamble has other markets to conquer, and some years ago the conglomerate targeted coffee. There were only two obstacles: General Foods was by far the most powerful coffee marketer in the nation—in fact, in the world—and P&G didn't own a single coffee bean. But those weren't obstacles that a conglomerate ad budget could not surmount. Procter & Gamble picked up a Southwest regional coffee company named J. A. Folger, and starting about eight years ago—using this coffee producer as its base—P&G's marketing forces unleashed one of the most intensive ad and promotion wars the food industry has ever known.

Like Sherman's army ravaging its way across the nation, Procter & Gamble hit city by city in the industrial heartlands of the East—launching Folger ad blitzes and discount campaigns against General Foods' Maxwell House and crushing any small independent producers that stood in the way. P&G struck Cleveland in 1972: "A horrible time was had by all," the staid *Tea and Coffee Trade Journal* reported. P&G invaded Philadelphia in 1973: "We're all bleeding to death," a local coffee company executive moaned, as the conglomerate saturated television with ads, mailed free samples to 1.5 million homes and twenty-five-cent discount coupons to a million more. In 1974 P&G ravaged Pittsburgh: By the time the "memorable bloodbath" was through, as *Fortune* put it, the $12 million local Breakfast Cheer company had been forced to sell out. "We were raped," a company official said.

And next the conglomerate blasted Syracuse, flooding the market with so many discount coupons and special deals that it reportedly slashed the price of Folger's coffee to less than fifty cents per pound. General Foods followed suit—and within three years, retail sales of the local Paul de Lima coffee company plunged 80 per cent and Folger had exploded out of nowhere to grab 25 per cent of the market. "We simply could not set our wholesale prices to the grocers as low as these companies were selling," Paul de Lima, Jr. told U.S. Senate investigators. This year, Folger's marketing forces are pushing into the Northeast as the new Number One coffee producer in the nation.

The cost of the Procter & Gamble war against General Foods has been awesome. Last year alone, according to *Advertising Age*, the two giants spent a combined $80 million on coffee advertising as they grappled like overgrown schoolyard bullies to be biggest on the coffee heap; the P&G conglomerate has spent so much money buying ads and slashing coffee prices to woo consumers that in 1977 it "lost" $60 million on the Folger subsidiary. I put "lost" in quotes because P&G didn't really lose money— you financed the coffee war when you paid inflated prices for Duncan Hines cake mix and other dominant P&G products, and the conglomerate merely shifted its profits to subsidize the coffee war.

If you live in one of the cities where Procter & Gamble and General Foods are dueling, don't be fooled by the bargain prices they are stamping on the coffee cans. Like most megacorporations attempting to take control of a market, the two conglomerates have slashed prices—temporarily—to win shoppers to their side. In Chicago and Cleveland, some industry officials charge, General Foods and P&G have been selling coffee for less than it costs to produce it.

But both P&G and General Foods know their battles, no matter how expensive in the short run, are worth the long-term payoffs. For they are seizing an economic system and mass loyalty: The two conglomerates already control about 60 per cent of the U.S. coffee market, and industry analysts expect their monopoly control will expand in the next few years. And unless the imperatives of history go haywire, consumers will see rapidly rising prices on the coffee cans—just as coffee buyers in Pittsburgh paid 70 per cent more during a recent period for the same coffee than their relatives did in Chicago, where the giants are still battling for control of the market.

As megacorporations discover that massive ad campaigns can buy the nation's markets, they are launching a Cold War in foods. Each corporation frenetically tries to outadvertise the competition by a few more million dollars, just as the United States and the Soviet Union grapple to build one more warhead or missile or tank. When Philip Morris bought Miller Brewing Company in 1972, Miller was an ailing firm holding seventh place in the beer market. But Philip Morris, the $3 billion conglomerate that built its empire selling nicotine addiction abroad, knew that an ad fortune could do for beer what it did for the Marlboro Man: Half a dozen years and tens of millions of dollars later ("If you've got the time, we've got the beer") Miller had quintupled sales and become the nation's second leading brewery, fast approaching the mighty leader, Anheuser-Busch. During its struggle to the top, according to economist Willard Mueller, the Philip Morris conglomerate paid $120 million more promoting its beers than it got back in sales—proving once again, as Mueller puts it, this "unique and awesome power of the conglomerate" to buy entire markets almost at will.

Consumers probably don't care which firm is Number One, or Number Two, or Number Six—when I gave six beer-loving friends a blind taste-test recently, not one of them could distinguish the difference between Budweiser, Miller, Pabst, and Schlitz—and the cheapest beer on the Washington market, Yeungling. But to conglomerate executives, it's a matter of utmost gravity. "'We will remain Number-One.'" August Busch III told *Newsweek*, "speaking very slowly . . . with an icy stare." Philip Morris reportedly targeted $75 million on beer ads last year, so Busch retaliated with $100 million.

As the megacorporations battle it out, grappling to launch preemptive strikes with their booming ad budgets, all the competitors must follow— at least, "everyone who can afford the raised ante," as *Business Week* puts it. But to afford the raised ante, the corporations must amass greater financial resources, and to amass the necessary resources, they must merge. When food corporations merge, government studies show, one of the first tangible results is that their advertising budgets explode to almost double the former size, which raises the ante again. Food advertising, which consumed a record $12 billion in social resources last year, has become the catalyst in a vicious chain of corporate control—the prime cause of corporate takeovers as well as the result.

What happens to the firms that can't afford the raised ante? Like Pittsburgh's Breakfast Cheer coffee company, they drop out of the market, or out of business. The beer industry used to be one of the nation's most decentralized industries, dominated by hundreds of feisty independents, rooted in cowboy towns and the old brick factories of gritty cities from Hartford to Milwaukee to San Francisco—producing such brands as Lone Star, Pearl, Buckhorn, Iron City. But more than 300 breweries have been gobbled up or wiped out in the past three decades; now that the mightly nationals have raised the ante, says Coors President Bill Coors, "We . . . have to stay in the top five to survive."

As the economy crumbles, you can expect the advertising wars to become even more fierce—and far more expensive. The megacorporations have learned that when consumers are feeling most economically insecure, it's time to hit them hardest. In the worst years of food inflation, between 1973 and 1977, food industry strategists did not relax their ad campaigns; they doubled them. And shoppers' loyalty to the most heavily advertised expensive brands—call it brainwashing, call it masochism— this loyalty became so ingrained that as consumers screamed about doubling food bills they did not shun the most expensive brands in favor of cheaper products. Rather, they flocked to the most expensive brands like lambs skipping to slaughter. And the most expensive three brands in most processed foods actually tightened their grip on the market.

The 1980s promise to be a thrilling decade, if my industry sources are right—as Nabisco launches a massive ad attack to challenge Pepsico's Frito-Lay bagged snacks; as General Foods, R. J. Reynolds, and Coca-Cola duke it out to be Number One in powdered soft drinks; as Quaker, General Mills, Pillsbury, and Nestle grapple on the networks to dominate the booming market for frozen pizzas.

How much will you pay at the supermarket checkout counters to finance these inane advertising wars? On the average, six cents of every dollar you spend on processed foods will go directly to buy ad time on television and other promotion—but when you buy one of industry's hot-selling brands you'll pay far, far more. In a recent year, breakfast eaters who bought Kellogg's Country Morning, a so-called "natural cereal" that better resembles crumbled cookies, paid thirty-five cents of every dollar merely to finance Kellogg's ads persuading them to buy it again. And every gullible beer drinker who bought a six-pack of Philip Morris Lowenbrau shelled out about fifty-five cents just to finance the conglomerate's ad hypes—persuading consumers to pay a premium price for a pretentiously bottled beer that tastes like all the rest.

Having decided to build market power with ad campaigns, you come to another critical decision in your power fantasy: What *kinds* of products will your ad dollars sell best? Like Pentagon generals trying to sell Congress on a new tank or candidates running for President, you must persuade your potential buyers that you are selling something different. As the marketing lingo goes, you'll need to differentiate your products.

The easiest way to differentiate foods, of course, is to process them. Give them a new color. Or texture. Or shape. Or flavor. That's why almost 80 per cent of the additives in foods, according to a General Accounting Office study, are cosmetics. And super-processed foods also lend themselves, unlike fresh foods, to corporate assembly-line production and mass-marketing techniques.

Processed foods with artificial colors and flavors are less vulnerable to the whims of weather or of striking farmworkers; with push-button production lines, Procter & Gamble can guarantee that its twenty-billionth Pringle will look exactly like the first—a soothing element of stability and dependability that is essential to mass advertising appeals. With its Birds-Eye broccoli petrified in synthetic cheese sauce and encased in plastic, and its Country Time lemonade artificially colored against the ravages of the air, the centralized factories of General Foods can stockpile enormous quantities of products and ship them to distant corners of every supermarket shelf in the nation—never worrying that the broccoli might wilt or that the "lemonade" might lose its yellowish hue. At Campbell, engineers are inventing methods to keep foods "fresh"—presumably including their soups, Swanson frozen dinners, Franco-American ravioli, and Hungry Man pizzas—for more than two or three years.

Many consumers sense all this as they weave through the supermarket aisles. But few recognize the vital link that processed foods forge in the chain of corporate control: As food corporations merge, in part to amass the financial power they need to launch massive advertising campaigns, the ad campaigns in turn dictate the kinds of foods they must produce—*processed*. The statistics before me fit together like a battle plan: The fastest-growing segment of the food industry produces the most intensively processed foods, and the most intensively processed foods are the most heavily advertised and the most profitable.

And the corporations that produce most of these foods and the ads that sell them are those with the tightest monopolistic grip on their markets—such megagiants as General Foods, General Mills, Procter & Gamble, Kraft, Nestle, and Coca-Cola. "In my business," says Albert Clausi, vice president at General Foods, "commodity is sort of a bad word."

When we pay high prices at the checkout counters, we are financing the food industry campaign to differentiate and super-process foods.

"Consumer hot buttons"—that's what the food marketers call those soft areas of consumer vulnerability, those needs and desires just waiting to be tapped by the latest synthetic food. In their efforts "to get a tighter grip on their markets," as *Business Week* reports, the food corporations are ballooning budgets for "psychographic" market research and new-product development. General Foods has beefed up its new-product research, $70 million worth a year now, and is building a gleaming new research lab. At Standard Brands, executives have increased their research staff by 60 per cent in the past few years. "Research has become responsible for corporate growth," declares Robert Carbonnell, vice president of this $2 billion conglomerate that produces Sun Maid raisins, Fleischmann's margarines, Tender Leaf teas, Baby Ruth candies, and a dazzling number of spirits from Great Nun and Weibel wines to Pernod liqueur and Benedictine.

What kind of "new product thrusts," as food executives call them, is Standard Brands making to zap the hot buttons? Hold your breath: The conglomerate's "most important product trial" in twenty years, according to an industry magazine, is Smooth & Easy, a margarine-like stick that becomes gravy when heated. Pillsbury is making even bolder strides in its effort to "redefine convenience foods," according to Vice President David Ehlen—by inventing new boil-in-a-bag main dishes for *singles.*

When a series of major nationwide studies on "The American Family" appeared recently in the social research literature, the sponsors were not profound academic thinkers pondering the future of society—they were the research and development people at General Mills. One bold response to these six-year surveys is "High Protein Breakfast Squares," a vitamin-fortified candy breakfast designed for all those women, who, the study revealed, are going back to work and don't want to dally over toast and eggs but are still concerned with their family's health. Breakfast Squares are a concoction of sugar and saturated fats plus artificial colors, flavors, and a slew of other additives; they are "a terrible tasting product," according to General Mills' own president, H. Brewster Atwater, Jr. But at $2.18 per pound they should be earning hefty profits.

The corporate imperative to transform food into synthetics has virtually turned fresh commodities into a novelty item—fresh fruits and vegetables account for less than 10 per cent of supermarket sales. And now even those few surviving natural foods—natural, that is, if you disregard the pesticide residues and wax coatings—are rapidly approaching extinction. Ten years ago, for instance, the United Brands conglomerate of Chiquita bananas fame bought out six lettuce and celery growers in California, overnight becoming one of the two largest lettuce producers in the United States. Two years ago, arch competitor Castle & Cooke—which already controls half the nation's pineapples and 40 per cent of its bananas under the Dole label—took control of the other leading lettuce producer, Bud Antle, itself a multinational operation with far-flung ventures in Africa.

Now here's the interesting part: United Brands and Castle & Cooke are not interested in selling plain, unadulterated heads of lettuce; they know their conglomerate operations can't produce lettuce of as good quality as the smaller independents they are choking out. (Who said, "Monopoly is an enemy of good management"? Adam Smith did, in 1776.)

"If we fight with the little guys in the commodity markets, they're going to kill us," a top official at United Brands Interharvest in Salinas, California, told me, "because their costs are lower and they produce a better product. The only answer for a company our size is to really differentiate our product."

And so United Brands is channeling its massive capital into what executives predict will be "the next major breakthrough" in the lettuce industry—processed-prepared salads-in-a-pouch. Every day the conglomerate ships truckloads of its Sun World-brand prepared salads from its processing plants in Salinas, most of them destined for the fast food counters of McDonald's and Burger King. But United Brands' next big push will be alongside Chiquita bananas in the supermarkets. The conglomerate is already test marketing its salad-in-a-bag in Salt Lake City, Spokane, and Atlanta. The day is not too far away, some executives predict, when a head of gentle, green lettuce will virtually be a memory of the past. You'll buy a plastic pouch, marked with the Sun World or Dole label (or Betty Crocker, now that General Mills is raising hydroponic lettuce in nutrient-filled vats). Just before dinner you'll tear open the bag, with that hermetically-sealed whoosh; then you'll pour the ready-made salad, centrifugal-dried and vacuum preserved, into your best simulated wood-grain bowl.

The corporate imperative to process the diet locks two more costs into

rising prices. Processing demands packaging—and the corporate imperative to differentiate the packaging means ever-growing costs for the art of
embalming vegetables in a glossy pouch or potato chips in a stylish tennis-
ball can. If Procter & Gamble took away the glib package from Pringles,
you could slash the supermarket price by about 20 per cent—and that's
typical of super-processed foods.

But the next equation is even more disturbing: Processing and packaging mean expensive energy, lots of it. Pillsbury's grand strategy to "redefine convenience foods" will take the form of pouches fabricated from
polypropylene, polyester, and aluminum, three of the most energy- and
cost-intensive materials on the market. This year, U.S. Department of Agriculture researchers say, processing alone will consume 40 per cent of all
the energy devoted to food production. And that demand will mushroom
in an era when the United States—and the rest of the world—confronts
the most critical energy crisis in history.

The links between corporate power and processed foods and energy
explain why consumer campaigns against lousy food—ban Red No. 2
here, ban sodium nitrite there—are ultimately doomed to fail. Super-processed foods fabricated from food additives are not just the tasteless by-
product of corporate power, they are an imperative building block of it.
This was to be one of the most important revelations in Senator George
McGovern's historic Senate Nutrition Committee report, *Dietary Goals
for the United States*. But, under attack from fearful members of the
Committee, the warning never made it into the published report. "The
strong association of poor nutritional quality with both high and increasing [corporate] concentration remains irrefutable," wrote economist John
Connor, now at USDA, in a preliminary, pioneering study commissioned
by the Committee staff. "If past trends [toward corporate control] continue, the nation can expect a worsening situation. . . ."

It was an economist's passionless way of delivering the chilling news:
Until the nation's economic system changes, the quality of the food in this
country will not—*cannot*—improve significantly. It *must* get worse.

The final link in the corporate strategy for control of the food system is,
of course, the chain supermarket. It is curious how the supermarkets portray themselves as weak and impoverished victims of forces beyond their
control. I recall the spectacle of Safeway President William "Billy"
Mitchell, the most powerful spokesman for the megachains, sitting before
a Senate committee five years ago and deflecting charges that supermarket profits were too steep. Mitchell launched into the supermarkets'
favorite theme—that the average supermarket chain was earning only a
penny of profit on every dollar of sales. "If all those net profits were
handed back to grocery store customers at the end of each week,"
Mitchell told the committee, "they would not even have received enough
to pay for their postage to send a letter to their respective Senators, regu-

lar mail. The old nursery rhyme about a penny for a spool of thread certainly holds true for the grocer. 'A penny for the grocer.' "

Mitchell, like others speaking for the supermarket industry, neglected to explain that his grocer's penny is an *after-tax* penny; if you really want to know how much profit you're giving to the megachains, you have to examine their pre-tax figures, and those are far higher. In a recent year you were paying about three cents on every dollar you gave Safeway just to nourish its bank accounts, and as much as four cents at chains like Winn-Dixie. That means a family of four shelled-out up to $50 last year just to fuel the megachains' profits. Don't weep with Safeway's Mitchell. The major chains have been earning high profits in recent years—"well above the average of all but the most concentrated American industries," according to University of Wisconsin economists Willard Mueller and Bruce Marion.

It makes sense, because the major supermarkets *are* one of the nation's most concentrated industries. In most of the 200 leading cities and towns, a cartel of four or fewer supermarket chains already controls food sales, and the monopoly hold is fast increasing.

When we pay at the checkout counters, we are financing the mega-chains' city takeover campaigns.

One of the most expensive monopoly tactics is overstoring. Just as General Mills floods the shelves with breakfast cereals to ensure that whatever kind you buy, it's Betty Crocker, so Safeway saturates a target city with stores to make sure when you dash into the nearest supermarket, it's a Safeway. Overstoring jacks up supermarket costs as the chains build more stores on more high-priced parcels of land than a city's population—or economic efficiency—would justify. According to Canadian studies, which serve as a rough guide, you pay four cents on every supermarket dollar just to subsidize your supermarkets' overstoring tactics.

We pay rising prices in towns controlled by supermarket cartels to subsidize their takeover battles elsewhere.

As economists Marion and Mueller discovered in an investigation for the Congressional Joint Economic Committee, powerful chains pump up prices in cities where they have already achieved control. Then they shift those superprofits to subsidize operations in other cities where prices and profits are still low, in an effort to get a grip on the market. As Mueller and Marion put it in a flight of Biblical inspiration, the megachains "rob Peter to pay Paul." Suppose you were an employe in the Justice Department's Anti-Trust Division: You probably would have paid $400 more for your family's groceries last year in Washington—where Safeway and Giant Food control 70 per cent of the market—than your relatives paid in Phoenix, where the chains are still competing for control.

We're paying rising prices as the chains use expensive technologies to get a firmer grip on their markets.

The most infamous technological bogeyman is the Universal Product

Code system—those zebra stripes on almost every package that enable supermarkets to ring up groceries by computer. An industry-wide shift to computer checkouts could cost $5 billion, according to researcher Amanda Spake, and consumers will foot the bill. But the most painful expense of the computer systems won't be the costs of conversion: It will be the power the technology gives the chains that can afford it to analyze market patterns and manipulate prices better than ever before. The computer systems give supermarket executives instant, sophisticated market research information—"scanner intelligence," the industry calls it—that reveals exactly how many customers buy how many products at what prices at which stores.

When Ralph's supermarkets, one of the leading chains on the West Coast, installed its computer systems, it tried an experiment: Overnight, the chain raised the price of its "bargain" store-brand orange juice at just two stores. When the computer reported that shoppers hadn't noticed the difference, Ralph's executives raised their bargain-brand prices chain-wide. On the other side of the country, Giant Food executives will use scanner intelligence to tailor specific food products to specific neighborhoods, store by store. "We'll wind up with super-sophisticated mom-and-pop operations," Giant Executive Donald Buchanan says—helping this $1 billion chain wipe out the few remaining independents that survive on their ability to cater to ethnic neighborhood tastes.

How much are we overpaying for food? When we come to the ultimate question, we unlock the ultimate scandal: Nobody has the information. The Federal Government has never forced corporations to disclose how much their foods cost to produce and how much money they are earning. The Federal Trade Commission announced several years ago it was launching a major investigation of supermarket prices and profits, but the investigation died before it got off the ground—when the megachains announced they would refuse to cooperate. The most fundamental facts of human survival—how much money our nourishment costs to produce and how much we are overpaying for it—have been blessed by the Government as private corporate secrets.

And so the handful of economists who believe it is important to crack industry's secrets have been forced to become food industry sleuths. FTC economist Russell Parker and USDA economist John Connor sifted through Government documents and industry reports and business magazines, and amassed bits and pieces of data on corporate ad expenses and sales and profits. When they cranked them into a computer, they produced some interesting results: The nation's food manufacturers, Parker and Connor estimate, charge $15 billion more than they would if the industry were not so tightly controlled. Using similar computer wizardry, economists Mueller and Marion have produced data suggesting the supermarket monopolies have inflated prices another $1 billion. It all adds up to almost $300 per year for a family of four.

But these estimates, while clearly the best clues yet produced, don't come close to estimating the massive amounts of money that the food conglomerates are forcing consumers to overpay for their food. For they suffer a fatal flaw: The studies analyze price differences within the U.S. corporate food system as a given. They compare how much you pay for Hamburger Helper produced by corporate monopolies that spend exorbitant amounts of money on advertising, to how much you'd pay for Hamburger Helper produced by less powerful corporations that spend somewhat less on ads.

The studies don't challenge the corporate food system itself: How much are we overpaying for a national system of foods that are processed and synthesized and energy-intensive and propagandized in the mass media in the quest for booming corporate profits—and how much would we pay for a system of foods that are fresh and energy-conserving, and produced by decentralized firms with the aim of providing Americans with the most satisfying, healthful, and reasonably priced diet possible?

Ask that question, and the corporate overcharges become awesome. How much are consumers paying in dollars—and anguish—as they succumb to such degenerative illnesses as hypertension, heart disease, and cancer that conglomerate diets cause? How much do they pay as the megacorporations consume billions of dollars that could be spent on solving critical social problems—housing, mass transportation, health care, new energy sources—and divert the wealth instead to their inane struggle to produce the nation's best-selling powdered soft drink or frozen pizza crust?

As I write this, the conglomerate takeovers quicken—*The New York Times* arrived this morning: "Nestle to Acquire Beech-Nut Foods." In some ways, warnings about the impending conglomerate takeover of our food supply come too late, for conglomerates already control the nation's food supply far more extensively than most Americans understand. In most food products—not many, *most*—two to four corporations already have seized control of the market. In this vast nation of 220 million people, only fifty manufacturing firms now control the means of food production. Sitting at his desk in his cramped cubicle, surrounded by stacks of papers and economic reports, Russell Parker tries to assess the enormity of what this means: "When you have only fifty firms accounting for 64 per cent of all the industry assets—remember, food is about 20 per cent of all consumer expenditures, which is a pretty damned big chunk—then I'd say that's pretty tight control by a few firms. And if we project what's happening into the future," Parker says glumly, "things only look worse."

Tight control by a few firms. The phrase has a weary ring to it, wrung out and overused by a decade of activists. But how many Americans really comprehend just how tight that handful of corporations is? When you go to the checkout counter next time, how will you sort out the implications of these facts: that in a recent year, corporate directors of Standard Brands, Procter & Gamble, Del Monte, H. J. Heinz, General Mills, Kraft, and Pepsico all sat together on the board of directors of General Motors; that one of the two controlling stockholders of Pepsico was New York's mighty Bankers Trust, which in turn was controlled by corporate directors from General Foods, Heinz, Campbell, Philip Morris, Kraft, and Nabisco; that the other leading stockholder of Pepsico, along with Bankers Trust, was the titan Morgan Guaranty Trust, which was also a leading shareholder of arch-competitor Coca-Cola as well as super-rivals Anheuser-Busch and Philip Morris; that the corporate board of J. P. Morgan was steered by directors from Procter & Gamble, from Campbell, Coca-Cola, and Standard Brands, while Morgan's stocks were controlled in part by Bankers Trust and Citibank; that the corporate directors of Citibank and its parent Citicorp came from Procter & Gamble, Kraft, Pepsico, Beatrice, and Philip Morris; and that Morgan Guaranty in turn was the top controlling stockholder of Bankers Trust and Citicorp, as well as the second-largest controlling stockholder of—we're back where we began—General Motors.

There's no way to understand the full implications of this economic Mobius strip—we can only add it to the other pieces of the food price puzzle. And as the pieces begin to fall into place, they form a rough picture of the food dilemma that Americans confront: No FTC investigations will ever break up the conglomerates—the FTC started its anti-trust effort against the cereal manufacturers back in 1968, and Government officials predict a final ruling is still at least five to ten years off. And that affects just one of hundreds of food product industries. No Congress beholden to business interests will pass tough laws striking at conglomerate power: The latest move in Congress, in fact, is to gut the meager powers of the FTC, not to strengthen them. No zealous prosecutors will halt conglomerate manipulations of the market: When the state of Colorado convicted Beatrice recently of bribing giant retailers to sell its dairy products, the criminal fine—"the biggest in state history," an assistant attorney general told me—hit Beatrice like a mosquito, stinging it for about fifteen minutes' worth of sales.

The pieces add up: No conventional Government actions will make a significant dent in the inexorable inflation and deterioration of the nation's food supply.

Economist Parker has made a career of sorts in recent years of testifying before various Congressional committees on the need for this bill restricting corporate mergers, or that bill strengthening anti-trust laws, or the need for new regulations forcing corporations to disclose at least some financial information. But in those gloomy moments of reflection that come at the end of a day, Parker is changing his tune: "Recent events make me think that public policy *isn't* going to be an effective instrument to change all this," he says. "But if public policies can't stop the corporate take-overs," I asked Parker, "what's left?"

There was a long silence. Suddenly, Parker started to laugh. He was silent again. "You want me to say, 'Take to the streets,' " Parker said, quietly. He paused. "But I *can't* say that."

Even as conglomerate power rolls like thunderheads over a cornfield, there is a stirring, a rustling of citizens starting to fight back, like a seed struggling to sprout. Food co-op networks are spreading in Minnesota, and consumers and farmers are launching direct-marketing projects in Tennessee. Small farmers are banding together in South Dakota, and working-class citizens are raising food on patches of land in the center of Boston.

These aren't answers, they are beginnings—first steps toward a national food system in which citizens and their elected representatives decide what foods and other vital natural resources should be produced in their communities and regions.

It was a coincidence, perhaps, that a new film premiered last year in Crosby, North Dakota. *Northern Lights* is a rough-hewn, flawed but moving epic documenting the struggles of the Nonpartisan League, a populist alliance of angry small-town citizens and farmers that came from nowhere in 1916—and took control of the state political machine, and founded the nation's first public-controlled grain elevators and banks. As *Northern Lights* portrayed it, the flashpoint for the citizens—the moment they stopped wringing their hands against the abuses of the Eastern monopolies and decided to struggle—came at the moment of understanding.

They understood that an economic and political system erected by humans, no matter how powerful, could be toppled and rebuilt by humans. At the dawn of the 1980s, understanding *why* we pay too much for our food is the first step—a small but critical step—toward forging the solution.

3
DO THEY REALLY KILL BABIES?

Frances Moore Lappé and Joseph Collins

When the birth rate in industrial countries started to decline in the 1960s, articles in business magazines proclaimed the crisis: "The Baby Bust" and "The Bad News in Babyland." One response of baby food corporations was to diversify into other products. Another was to market to the fast-growing population of infants in underdeveloped countries. Sales of infant formula in underdeveloped countries by Abbott Laboratories, American Home Products, and Bristol Myers (through its Mead Johnson Division) began to increase faster than sales at home. Nestlé, with 81 plants in 27 underdeveloped countries and 728 sales centers throughout the world, intensively promotes its Lactogen, Nan, and Cerelac. Borden and Carnation are also in on the growing business.

Most people would assume that sales of baby formula stand in dramatic contrast to the pushing of nonnutritious processed food. Why is it then that over five years ago international agencies such as the World Health Organization (WHO) began to look upon the increased sales of infant formula in underdeveloped countries as a serious health *problem?* Indeed, a public interest group in England, War on Want, in 1974 launched an international campaign claiming that the promotion of infant formula in underdeveloped countries was contributing to severe malnutrition and even to the death of infants. When their pamphlet was translated into German as "Nestlé Kills Babies," Nestlé sought $5 million in damages in the Swiss courts. Nestlé charged that the accusations in the pamphlet—that its efforts were unethical and immoral, that its marketing techniques resulted in infant death, and that it disguised its representatives as medical personnel—were all defamatory. At the last minute Nestlé decided to drop these three claims of defamation. The only charge which Nestlé pressed was that the pamphlet's title "Nestlé Kills Babies" was defamatory. Although the judge ruled in favor of Nestlé on this count, he declared, "This verdict is no acquittal [of Nestlé]."

What did the judge mean? What is the evidence that links the marketing of bottled formula to increased infant death?

In underdeveloped countries the mortality rate for bottle-fed infants is about double that of breast-fed. A recent Inter-American Investigation of Mortality in Childhood, checking on the causes of 35,000 infant deaths,

From *Food First: Beyond the Myth of Scarcity* by Frances Moore Lappé and Joseph Collins. Copyright © 1977 by Institute for Food and Development. Reprinted by permission of Ballantine Books, a Division of Random House, Inc.

has determined that "nutritional deficiency" as an underlying or associated cause of death was "less frequent in infants breast fed and never weaned than in infants who were never breast fed or only for limited periods." In rural Punjab, India, according to a 1974 report in the medical journal, *The Lancet*, "in the study population virtually all infants died who did not receive breast milk in the first months of life." Two decades ago when breast-feeding was widespread among the poor, severe malnutrition was usually held off beyond the absolutely crucial first year of a child's life. But now, according to World Bank nutritionist Alan Berg, the rapid decline in breast-feeding over the past two decades has caused the average age of the onset of malnutrition to drop from eighteen months to a more critical eight months in several countries studied.

Baby formula displaces mother's milk. But because, as scientific research indicates, mother's milk has changed and evolved along with the human race, it, like nothing else, can sustain the newborn. It contains not the "highest amounts" but the *proper* amounts of proteins and fats for the human baby. Human milk contains only 1.3 percent protein; cow's milk, 3.5 percent. The protein, mineral and fat levels in mother's milk, notes Dr. Hugh Jolly, a prominent London pediatrician writing in the London *Times*, suits the capacity of a human baby's kidney perfectly. Calves need and can handle more protein because they grow much faster. A six-week calf is, after all, already a small cow. These are just some of the reasons why pediatrics professor Paul Gyorgy of the University of Pennsylvania likes to say, "Cow's milk is best for baby cows and human breast milk is best for human babies."

If you still need to be convinced that nature knows what it is doing, please note that human milk comes complete with infection immunizers for humans, especially critical in unsanitary living conditions. Scientists hypothesize that the immunity probably results from the initial dose of antibodies in the colostrum (the yellowish fluid that comes from the mother's breast a few days after birth). Apparently colostrum protects the child against locally common infections, particularly those of the intestinal tract, and against food allergies. "This might explain why allergies are more common in artificially fed babies," comments Dr. Alan Berg. "Gastroenteritis is almost unknown in breast-fed babies, whereas it may be lethal in those fed on cow's milk, especially where sterilization of bottles may be impossible," notes Dr. Jolly. Diarrhea, which can prevent the absorption of any nutrients at all, is rare among breast-fed babies. A mother can adequately feed her infant for at least six months. Even mothers who are themselves malnourished can adequately breast-feed—although partially at the expense of their own tissues. Physiologists agree that the first months of life are crucial for normal brain development. The negative effects of later malnutrition, though highly undesirable, are far more remediable.

Actually a child can be well nourished on breast milk for two years or

more if a few other foods are added—and they certainly need not be
from a can. In some cultures children are breast fed much longer. As
recently as forty years ago, Chinese and Japanese mothers nursed their
children as long as five and six years; Caroline Islanders up to ten years;
and Eskimoes up to fifteen years.

Several multinational companies, however, have not been satisfied with
nature—or at least, not satisfied that nature seemed to leave no room for
commercial exploitation. But to create a market where none seemed to
exist, multinational corporations found they could play upon another aspect of human nature—the natural desire of parents to ensure a healthy
baby. Exposed to countless billboards, newspaper advertisements, and
color posters, parents in underdeveloped countries come to equate a
happy, healthy baby with a bottle or can of Lactogen. They learn that
educated and upper-class families use feeding bottles. They, too, want the
best for their baby. The tragic irony, however, is that for most parents in
underdeveloped countries, formula feeding actually endangers their
baby's life.

First, most families simply cannot afford to buy the necessary amount.
To feed one four-month-old infant in Guatemala would require almost 80
percent of the per capita income. To feed such a baby in Lima, Peru,
adequately by bottle would take almost 50 percent.

These cost estimates do not include bottles, artificial nipples, cooking
utensils, refrigeration, fuel, and medical care (often ten times more
needed for the formula-fed than for the breast-fed child). How can a
family devote over half or more of its income to food for their youngest
and totally unproductive member? The answer is that it cannot.

The seeming solution is to "stretch" the formula with water. Reports of
dilution are commonplace. A 1969 survey in Barbados found that 82 percent of the families using formula as the sole food for two- or three-
month-old babies were making a four-day can last five days to three
weeks. Dr. Adewale Omololu, a professor of nutrition in Nigeria, reported
treating a severely malnourished baby whose mother had switched from
breast-feeding to a bottle. For a month the child had nothing but water
from the bottle because there was only enough money for the *bottle;* it
took a month to save up to buy the can of formula!

On diluted formula, a baby loses weight and deteriorates progressively
into the malnourished condition called marasmus. The child becomes increasingly susceptible to infection, a problem compounded by bottle-
feeding, as we will see.

Second, formula-feeding requires clean water and conditions for sanitary preparation that often do not exist even for the middle classes in
underdeveloped countries. "Wash your hands thoroughly with soap each
time you have to prepare a meal for baby," reads the Nestlé's *Mother
Book* distributed by the company in Malawi. But 66 percent of the house-

holds even in the capital city have no washing facilities. "Place bottle and lid in a saucepan of water with sufficient water to cover them. Bring to the boil and allow to boil for 10 minutes," is the counsel of the Cow and Gate Company in its Babycare Booklet for West Africa. The text is accompanied by a photo of a gleaming aluminum saucepan on an electric stove. But you have to go far to find an electric stove in West Africa. Most West African mothers have to cope with a "three-stone" kitchen, that is, three stones supporting a pot above a wood fire. There is only one pot. One pot for sterilizing the baby's bottle and for cooking the family meal. To the mother's eye, putting the bottle in boiling water doesn't seem to do much, anyway; so sterilizing is probably forgotten.

The bottle, the nipple, and the formula are invariably found in the context of illiteracy, a contaminated water supply and the lack of washing, refrigeration or cooling facilities, and household hygiene. The combination, then, of malnutrition and exposure to bacteria sets up a vicious circle. The infant gets chronic diarrhea and therefore is unable to assimilate even the diluted formula. The infant's nutritional state worsens and it becomes even more vulnerable to respiratory infection and gastroenteritis. This is the state of millions of children who could have been adequately nourished by their mother's milk.

The companies like to argue that they are *fulfilling* and not creating a need. "Just think what the situation would be if we were to say, all right, we think these people [the critics] are right. What would the result be?" asks Ian Barter of Cow and Gate Company. "It would be the death of thousands of children because there are tens of thousands of mothers in these countries who have got to have some substitute for their milk in order to feed their babies."

Let's look at the facts. Nutritionists recognize that there are some women who cannot feed for physiological reasons. But even the companies admit that at most such mothers are fewer than 5 percent. Dr. David Morley surveyed a rural Nigerian village and found less than 1 percent of mothers had serious breast-feeding problems.

Indeed, confidence—lack of anxiety—seems to be the key to breast-feeding without difficulties. Several doctors now believe that the typical company advertising does more than anything else to undermine the mother's confidence. By just mentioning "women who do not have milk" and "poor quality" milk, the companies place not so subtle doubts in a mother's mind about her ability to breast-feed.

The companies also stress that their products are needed by women who work. In fact, the percentage of Third World women who work away from their families is very low. (Countries where there is far greater employment for women, such as the Soviet Union and Cuba, provide extensive paid maternity leaves and day care centers at the workplace, which allow working mothers to breast-feed several times a day.)

But even if there is a need for artificial feeding, does it follow that a country needs a half dozen profit-oriented multinational firms? Is this the only alternative that you, say, as a minister of health, could think of for your country? Is the technology of making an equivalent baby food really so difficult? The United Nations Protein Advisory Group has recommended that underdeveloped countries come up with a product *better* than the expensive, easily contaminated products of the world's largest companies. Various nutritionists have designed, for mothers who cannot breast-feed, nourishing artificial feeding regimes suitable to low-income homes with minimum hygiene, no refrigeration, and limited cooking facilities—and several would cost only a quarter of the current high-priced formulas.

Finally, the companies try to defend themselves by claiming that they really aim their products only at the rich. According to Ross Laboratories' president David O. Cox, only "coincidentally" do his company's promotional activities reach the poor.

This claim again does not fit the facts. The companies have actually devised sophisticated and often ingenious promotion strategies specifically for expanding sales down the income ladder. To begin with, colored wall posters of a healthy baby clutching a feeding bottle greet women, both rich and poor, who enter hospitals and clinics. The companies also employ milk nurses, women who commonly are fully trained nurses. In Nigeria 96 percent of mothers who used bottle-feeding thought they had been so advised by impartial medical personnel, mainly nurses. In fact, these nurses were company representatives. Nestlé employs 4000 to 5000 such "mothercraft advisors" in underdeveloped countries. Dressed in crisp white uniforms, they visit new mothers, no matter what their income level is. In many countries these nurses are allowed to enter maternity wards. Often they receive a commission in addition to salary. Moreover, higher pay offered by the companies diverts nurses trained at public expense from basic full-time health work.

In addition, the companies provide free samples, often through the hospitals. Surveys have shown that just as many illiterate mothers as literate ones receive samples, indicating there was no attempt to select mothers who were able to afford the product. Companies often supply hospitals with free fomula supplies, hoping that mothers will feel they must keep on using the products. Abbott Laboratories recently sold $300,000 worth of Similac to the New York City hospitals for only $100,000. A city spokesperson said, "For the company, it's an investment. They hope to get the future business."

Another device clearly aimed at the poor are "milk banks," usually in hospitals and clinics. They sell the commercial formulas at discount prices to mothers who can prove they are really poor. In this way they can expand sales among the really poor without lowering the price in the normal commercial market. Milk banks in their hospitals just serve to convince women that they need something that they really don't. But even at discount prices (usually 30 to 40 percent), the formulas are too expensive for parents to buy enough. In Guatemala City, fifty mothers buying at a milk bank were questioned. Despite the discount, they could not afford enough so they "prepared the bottles with less milk and more water and in this way the milk lasted longer." Tea or chocolate drink is often substituted.

Radio is also an advertising vehicle to reach the poor. A typical day in Sierra Leone sees fifteen 30-second radio advertisements for Nestlé: "Now Lactogen a better food cos it don get more protein and iron, all de important things dat go make pikin strong and will. . . . Lactogen and Love." The use of the common dialect of the poor makes it hard for Nestlé to convince us that they are directing their advertising at only those who can afford it.

Under the pressure of unfavorable publicity, the companies say they have modified their advertisements. Now the commercial product is pushed as "the next best thing to mother's milk," for cases in which "you find you need a substitute or a supplement to breast milk." Nestlé now recommends "an occasional bottle-feed—if you cannot breast-feed Baby entirely yourself."

The tactic is ingenious. As a Consumers' Union-funded study comments, "By openly recommending breast feeding, the companies can earn their public relations credits. At the same time, the companies can undermine breast feeding by implying repeatedly that a mother may not have enough milk and may need supplementary bottles of formula." La Leche League International, an organization devoted to helping women breast-feed, comments, "This 'supplementary' formula is one of the greatest deterrents to establishing a good milk supply, and frequent nursing is one of the greatest helps."

Such ingenious modification of tactics serves to emphasize how the solution to this grave situation is not simply another "code of conduct" for the companies. One such code, already drawn up, would have company milk nurses wear the company insignia on their uniform. The companies must really think their critics are simple-minded! All the codes condone the use of medical facilities to market their products.

Nestlé hoped to get some public relations mileage out of its claim that it no longer would dress its salespeople in white uniforms. White uniforms obviously gave the impression of medical authority. What Nestlé neglected to say is that its salespeople now are wearing blue and yellow uniforms. Now really. Doesn't a uniform, any uniform, still carry authority?

Not only is the decline in breast-feeding a personal tragedy for babies who suffer malnutrition and disease, but it can be calculated as a loss to the natural resources of the country. In Kenya, notes Alan Berg, "The estimated $11.5 million annual loss in breast milk is equivalent to two-thirds of the national health budget, or one-fifth of the average annual economic aid." In the Philippines $17 million was wasted on imported milk in 1958; by 1968, the number of mothers breast-feeding their babies dropped by 31 percent, and the national dollar loss had doubled. As breast-feeding declined sharply in the 1960s, Colombian milk imports soared; in 1968 they were seven times greater than the 1964–1967 average. Berg concludes that "losses to the developing countries more likely are in the billions."

An attack on the bottle-baby tragedy is now underway in some under-developed countries. Here are only a few examples. In Papua, New Guinea, the director of public health is enlisting the support of all health workers to persuade storekeepers not to display formula company advertisements. Dar es Salaam University in Tanzania has put out a new guide on baby care for paramedical workers warning of the dangers of formula feeding. In Segbwena, Sierra Leone, a Nutrition Rehabilitation Unit is feeding malnourished children on locally available foods and showing mothers how to prepare well-balanced and inexpensive meals for their families. The Nairobi City Council, Kenya, has banned milk nurses. Some African governments have even instructed rural health workers to destroy formula ads wherever they find them.

In contrast to the private multinational companies, a state-owned company in Zambia announces on its can of milk: "BREAST FEED YOUR CHILD." The label goes on to persuade the potential buyer not to buy the product unless the purchaser can afford to buy enough for many months.

Public action in the industrial countries to halt the ongoing tragedy did not stop with the Nestlé trial in the summer of 1976. Later that summer, groups from eight countries working on infant formula malnutrition met in Bern to plan and coordinate their efforts. That fall in New York the Sisters of the Precious Blood, working with the Interfaith Center for Corporate Responsibility (ICCR), brought suit against Bristol Myers. The Sisters charged Bristol Myers with committing fraud in its proxy statement to shareholders. In its statement Bristol Myers claimed to have been "totally responsive" to the concerns of the earlier stockholder resolution. Moreover, the company claimed that it does not promote its products to people who cannot afford to use them safely, that it does not sell directly to the consumer at all but only through professional medical personnel. The Sisters, working with ICCR, gathered over 1000 pages of testimony and other evidence from around the world that directly contradict these claims. This documentation demonstrated that Bristol Myers does use many techniques to reach the poor, including selling its products in poor people's stores, distributing free samples through health clinics, and using sales personnel dressed as nurses.

Even though the suit was not successful—the Sisters' appeal was dismissed by the U.S. District Court in 1977—the publicity of the suit, combined with the earlier Nestlé trial, launched the concern over infant formula malnutrition into an international campaign. The Infant Formula Action Coalition (INFACT, 1701 University Avenue, SE, Minneapolis, MN 55414) formed to coordinate the campaign. Its first move was to launch a boycott of Nestlé until the corporation agrees to stop all promotion of infant formula in the Third World. Many groups such as Clergy and Laity Concerned and Church Women United immediately backed INFACT and the Nestlé boycott. In addition, a Senate subcommittee held hearings on the problem in May of 1978. Thus news of the bottle baby tragedy is spreading rapidly. Church and community groups around the country are educating their constituencies using the film "Bottle Babies" (available from INFACT). The crisis of infant formula malnutrition is thus becoming for more and more people an example of how corporate economic motives not only can fail to serve the interests of people, but can directly contribute to their suffering.

We hope that by now we have given you an understanding of what the judge in the Swiss trial meant when, after ruling in favor of Nestlé, he added: "This verdict is no acquittal [of Nestlé]."

In an interview on West German radio in 1975 a pediatrician on the staff of Nairobi's Kenyatta National Hospital, Dr. Elizabeth Hillman, told this story:

A short while ago . . . the Nestlé's representatives came to visit us at Nairobi's hospital to ask if we had any opinion about the publication "Nestlé Kills Babies." They really wanted us to say that Nestlé did not kill babies.

We discussed this at length with them and were not able to say of course that Nestlé either does kill or does not kill, statistically speaking. But, to illustrate the point, I mentioned that there was a child over in our emergency ward . . . who was very near to death, because the mother was bottle-feeding with the Nestlé's product (Lactogen, a milk preparation), and out of interest I asked whether they would like to see the baby. I took the two representatives over into our emergency ward and as we walked in the door the baby collapsed and died. I had to leave these two non-medical gentlemen for a moment . . . and help with the resuscitation procedure. It was unsuccessful. And, after the baby was pronounced dead, we all watched the mother turn away from the dead baby and put the can of Nestlé's milk in her bag before she left the ward. . . . In a sense . . . it was a vivid demonstration of what bottle-feeding can do because this mother was perfectly capable of breast-feeding. The two gentlemen walked out of that room, very pale, shaken and quiet and there was no need to say anything more.

II

ECONOMIC CRISIS

In the 1980s, economic troubles have come to be an expected part of American life. We don't any longer question whether we'll have high unemployment—only whether this year's rate will be fractionally above or below last year's. We congratulate ourselves if the rate of inflation falls much below double digits. And we grasp with a certain desperation at any one of a variety of schemes to reorganize or "revitalize" an economy that, by common agreement, is failing us in several ways at once—especially when compared with the more successful economies of some of our foreign competitors.

These expectations mark a sharp departure from most of the post–World War II era, when an expanding and bountiful economy was largely taken for granted. According to many social theorists in the 1950s and 1960s, most major economic problems had been solved in the "affluent" society that had emerged from World War II. But by the 1970s those problems had obviously returned with a vengeance.

The articles in this chapter explore, in various ways, the nature and causes of the present economic crisis. In "Beyond Boom and Crash," Robert Heilbroner points out that the sense of crisis is not at all new; capitalism's history is one of "alternating euphoria and despair," especially in the minds of business people. To Heilbroner, the fears and anxieties generated by economic crises can't be explained on economic grounds alone. They represent a recognition that the deeper dangers of a crisis are social and political ones. Crises are threatening to business primarily because they threaten to expose the entire happy vision of equality and affluence that ensures the loyalty of working people to the economic system as a whole. The hardships and inequalities the crisis produces create the possibility that capitalism "will be recognized for what it is, with who knows what consequences."

62

Heilbroner's underlying theme is that there is a fundamental tension in modern capitalism—a contradiction between the system's social and political ideals and its economic realities. The next two articles explore the same theme in more specific ways.

Our culture, for example, places a very high value on the "work ethic." Yet the lack of work—unemployment—is a built-in feature of the modern capitalist economy. As Robert Lekachman shows in "The Specter of Full Employment," one of the most important reasons for the devastating persistence of unemployment is that it is a useful device—from the point of view of business—for controlling the work force. A pool of workers without jobs puts a damper on the expectations and demands of employed workers, frightens people into staying in jobs that are demeaning and badly paid, and therefore helps keep wages low and profits high.

John Logue's portrait of the destruction of the Youngstown, Ohio steel industry powerfully illustrates how the drive for maximum profit can undermine an entire industry and the communities that depend on it. The shutdown of the Mahoning Valley steel mills did not result primarily from foreign competition or declining productivity—two problems most often cited as responsible for industrial decline in America. Instead, Logue shows, the mills were deliberately drained of their resources by their new owners—conglomerate corporations less interested in making steel than in finding other, more immediately profitable places to invest the steel companies' money. The Youngstown story shows clearly how the twin problems of corporate power and the crisis of the economy are often one and the same.

4
BEYOND BOOM AND CRASH

Robert L. Heilbroner

The psychological history of capitalism is a tale of alternating euphoria and despair. We tend to think of the late nineteenth century as a period of huge self-confidence and ebullience, but the diaries of the captains of industry reveal another mood just below the surface, a mood described by economic historian E. C. Kirkland as "panic and pain." When recessions struck with their never-quite-predictable regularity, the latent mood surfaced, and businessmen tore their collars and feared for the end. "All the fortune I have made has not served to compensate for the anxiety of that period," wrote John D. Rockefeller, looking back on forty years of a career that we think of as an unbroken series of triumphs.

The labile business state of mind was no doubt the consequence in the first place of the continual buffeting to which business was subject. But I suspect there was another reason as well. It was—and is—that capitalism never found a rationale that entirely dispelled the anxieties of the business world as to the viability of the capitalist mechanism, again and again teetering at the edge of what seemed like collapse; nor did capitalism ever gain a credo that rescued it, once for all, from the doubts and criticisms of its moral critics. The economics profession, writing at an Olympian level of abstraction after the 1870s, and concerning itself more and more with problems of "equilibrium" and "pure competition" that had no visible counterpart in the real world, could not convince businessmen that the rocking economic system was an unsinkable ship with a foolproof self-righting mechanism. And the moralists of the system (many of them also economists) never quite explained away the tendency of the system to create poverty alongside riches and squalor along with success. Here the problem was that the culture that produced the economic values embodied in a capitalist system also produced the political and social values embodied in a bourgeois democracy. Thus, unlike previous economic systems, capitalism has always been exposed to an egalitarian countercurrent that undermined the simple endorsement of inequality characteristic of precapitalist societies.

As a result, the state of mind of the capitalist class has always been insecure and defensive during a crisis—insecure because it was never entirely convinced that the economic vehicle would not tip over, defensive because it could never entirely square the results of the economic system with the values of its social and political beliefs. It is interesting, from this point of view, to reflect on the number of businessmen (and the even greater number of their widows) who turned into reformers of one kind or another, usually trying to temper the raw workings of the marketplace to bring its results into closer consonance with their moral beliefs. What other system has produced such a show of uneasy conscience?

It is, I think, this uneasy conscience, quite as much as the unsettled questions regarding the stability of the system, that accounts for the swings in mood that have always assailed the system. For periods of crisis not only test the operational capabilities of the system, but also the ultimate granite on which it rests—the loyalty, or at least the acquiescence, of the labor force on which it depends. The cooperation of that labor force is no longer won, as it was in Marx's time, by a reliance on the lash of sheer need, or by the limitation of its suffrage, or the steadying hand of venerable traditions of the natural superiority of the rich. The cooperation of the work force today is secured by the systematic misrepresentation of the system as a kind of large, hearty, and cheerful family. Corporations that command immense wealth and make strategic decisions of global importance portray themselves as "just folks," personified by the ordinary people who are featured in their institutional advertisements. Consciously or otherwise, the media present an image of the capitalist world as a great cornucopia of commodities available to all, where laughing young women and energetic young men make their serious, playful determinations as to what car to buy, soap to use, bank to borrow from. The "problems" of the system are presented as detached from, and in no way connected with, its "successes." The central facts of the system are ignored so that it becomes almost a radical statement when Paul Samuelson writes in his famous text that a pyramid of personal incomes in the United States, constructed with children's blocks each representing $1000, would soar far higher than the Eiffel Tower, although most of the population would be within a yard of the ground.

A vast hypocrisy is thus characteristic of the self-advertisement of capitalism, a hypocrisy that threatens the system in moments of crisis because there is always the risk that it will be recognized for what it is, with who knows what consequences. Thus when confidence wanes, it is not only because the omnipresent danger of a collapse is again experienced, but because the social and political legitimacy of the system must again be put to the test. I suspect that all capitalist nations experience this unease because of the inescapable conflict between their extreme economic privileges and their social and political egalitarian tendencies and commitments, but perhaps in America this tension is greatest and the ensuing insecurity most keenly felt.

I raise these speculative considerations because one must search for some explanation of the black mood that haunted the financial and business world in late 1977 and early 1978. As with the international economic picture, one could not explain the heavy tone of the stock market, that traditional barometer of confidence, merely in terms of a calculus based on realistic projections. When the stocks that made up the Dow Jones Average could be bought for an aggregate price that was less than their book value, the market was predicting some terrible occurrence. What could that occurrence have been? A minor dip in the rate of economic growth—the worst that anyone expected for the next year or so? An increase in the rate of inflation by a percentage point, or even by two percentage points? A failure to write a stringent energy bill—or perhaps the opposite, the achievement of such a bill? None of these and similar eventualities, endlessly discussed in the business pages, warranted the kind of determined pessimism that Wall Street showed . . .

The answer must have been, I believe, that The Street was predicting something far more serious. It was predicting that behind the manifest not-too-serious crisis lurked the possibility of a profound, even catastrophic crisis, a crisis from which the system could not recover, at least in anything like its present shape. As with the international financial world, the domestic financial community was weighing the future of the system in its mind. The crisis was not one of present realities but of expected developments, not one of economics alone but of belief. . . .

As Marx was the first to point out, not only does the capitalist system unfold through a more or less regular succession of booms and crises, but the crises themselves exert lasting and cumulative effects on the system. The business cycle, in other words, is not just a wavelike movement of production, but a movement of the whole socioeconomic order through history; and the measure of the cycle therefore requires that we pay heed not alone to its quantitative effects on production or prices or employment, but also to its qualitative impact on the organization of the society itself.

Two such changes seemed to Marx of central importance. One was the tendency of repeated crises to bring into being an economy of giant enterprises. Each crisis encouraged the formation of large enterprises because smaller and weaker firms were the typical victims of economic hesitations and downturns, while stronger and larger firms survived to buy up and integrate the assets of their competitors. "Capital grows to a huge mass in a single hand in one place," Marx wrote in *Capital*, "because it has been lost by many in another place." This process, which was only in its incipient stage in Marx's time, has changed the world of "competitive capitalism" of the 1860s into that of the "monopoly capitalism" of the present day.

At a deeper level the effect is even more dramatic, and certainly more important, than the rise of large-scale production. Enormous enterprises require extensive internal planning, as John Kenneth Galbraith has repeatedly pointed out. At the same time, the rise of a vast, integrated core of industrial firms—the five hundred largest of which produce a value of output almost as big as that of the remaining 400,000-odd industrial enterprises—brings into being a structural organization of capitalism that differs very little in technology or organization from that of the ministries of a socialist economy. Thus, while capitalism clings tenaciously to its beliefs in the "privateness" of property, it has in fact created an economic milieu in which property has become ever more social. This unintended socialization of the productive forces of the system was felt by Marx to be the "contradiction" that above all else directed the long-term development of capitalism toward socialism.

A second textural change envisaged by Marx affected the social rather than the technological or organizational aspects of capitalism. He saw the hammer blows of successive crises altering the class structure of the system in ways that he also felt to be ultimately incompatible with the legal privileges of a capitalist order. One of these alterations—again stunningly confirmed by history—was the elimination of petty proprietorships and independent artisanships as dominant forms of social being. The competitive powers of capitalist production, he felt, were unchallengeable by the small producer. All would be forced eventually to become sellers of their wage-labor—proletarians—rather than sellers of their own products.

The prediction is again fully confirmed by events. In the early 1800s, for example, about four-fifths of all American working people were self-employed as farmers, artisans, small businessmen, and the like. Only about ten percent of the labor force is self-employed today, and one-third of the labor force works for the central core of the great Five Hundred Firms.

The political consequences of this "proletarianization" of capitalism have not, however, accorded with Marx's general expectations. Although more and more of the work force has become drawn into the capital-wage relationship, the newly created proletarians have not developed a unitary class consciousness nor experienced a welling up of revolutionary will. Instead, a process of "bourgeoisification," already foreseen and lamented by Engels, has forestalled the militancy and insurgency on which the revolutionary prognosis ultimately hinged. Veblen, perhaps more clearly than Marx, anticipated the consequences of a system of high productive powers and democratic views: The lower orders would look to the upper classes as models to be aped, not as masters to be dethroned. Thus the hypocritical and biased self-advertisement of capitalism has been received not with skepticism but faith, embraced by a working class that wanted to believe in the benign workings and accessible heights of the business world.

Only recently have we had disturbing evidences of a turning away from the system, most dramatically played out in the terrorist tactics of European revolutionary gangs, but perhaps more significantly manifested in the anticapitalist mood of student bodies throughout the world. No one knows, of course, whether these movements will become full-fledged threats to the stability of the system. That depends, probably, on whether the working class can be won from its conservative views to a "genuinely" proletarian perspective. Although that has not yet been the case in any capitalist nation, the advent of a crisis always raises the spectre of such a revolutionary "awakening." Thus crisis comes not only as a test to the working order of the economy, but also to the reliability of its moral order and its traditional observances and obeisances. It is this test, I think, that troubles the sleep of the guardians of the system today far more than the economic damage that has been suffered or that seems likely to come. . . .

5
THE SPECTER OF FULL EMPLOYMENT

Robert Lekachman

Men and women want to work. Work, private and public, is there to be done. How come, a wandering rationalist might ask, the work and the workers are not happily married? Well, as the radicals of my youth were wont to intone, it is no accident that we tolerate as a nation years of 7, 8, even 9 percent general unemployment and horrifying rates of teenage joblessness which among urban blacks exceed, by some estimates, 50 percent.

The brutal fact is that unemployment at "moderate" rates confers a good many benefits upon the prosperous and the truly affluent. If everyone could be employed, extraordinarily high wages would have to be paid to toilers in restaurant kitchens, laundries, filling stations, and other humble positions. Whenever decent jobs at living wages are plentiful, it is exceedingly difficult to coax young men and women into our volunteer army. Without a volunteer army, how can the children of the middle and upper classes be spared the rigors of the draft?

Unemployment calms the unions and moderates their wage demands. . . . When people are scared about losing their jobs, they work harder and gripe less. In more dignified language, absenteeism declines and productivity ascends.

Better still, factory and office workers, alert to potential layoffs and plant shutdowns, are unlikely to nag unions and employers to make work more interesting, and less menacing to health and personal safety. It cannot be mere coincidence that in Sweden, where job enrichment and plant democracy have had their greatest success, unemployment is practically zero and astute management of their economy protected Swedes even from the worldwide economic crisis of 1973–75. The new government, elected on the fortuitous issue of nuclear safety, has promised to extend even further the social benefits for which Sweden has become celebrated. American employers preserve themselves from Swedish experiments in good part by keeping the industrial reserve army plentifully manned.

Nor is this quite the end of the tale. The hunger of communities and regions for jobs and tax revenues has allowed large corporations to extort an endless assortment of valuable concessions from local and state governments, either as blackmail to keep existing installations or bribes to lure new ones. Few major corporations pay their fair share of property taxes. Propaganda by oil, steel, chemical, and paper industries has noticeably slowed the pace of regulation to protect the environment. . . .

By contrast, full employment on a sustained and assured basis (the system can stand a spell of full employment so long as all parties understand that it is temporary) presents an embarrassment to the movers and shapers of American plutocracy. To begin with, full employment is the most efficient agent of equitable income redistribution which is at all politically feasible in the United States. Full employment sucks into the labor force men and women who now struggle on welfare, food stamps, Social Security, and unemployment compensation. It pushes up the wages of low-paid people whose position is scarcely less precarious than that of the unemployed. It is an especial boon to blacks, Hispanics, teen-agers, and women—last hired and first fired in expansion and recession alike. A long spell of full employment would substantially narrow existing wide differentials between the earnings of these groups and those of white males. In a time of layoff and business contraction, affirmative action is a mockery, but when there is full employment the cry for justice is heard more sympathetically by members of [the] majority whose own security is not threatened.

These repercussions are severe enough to alarm gentlemen in their

clubs and boardrooms. The threat, I suspect, is still more grave. For men
of property the charm of the 1970s lies in the way economic adversity . . .
cooled the campuses and shoved American politics, already the most conservative in the developed world, still further right; one only has to look
at Gerald Ford of all people, after Watergate and the Nixon pardon, and
in the middle of a messed-up economy, very nearly winning the Presidential election. This could not have happened without general apprehension
and dampened expectations of the efficacy of action by any national administration. As one comedian commented upon the stock-market decline which preceded the election, investors were selling out of deadly
fear that one of the candidates would win. Lift the burdens of apprehension and apathy from the psyches of ordinary folk and—who knows?—
they might entertain radical thoughts of inviting the rich to share rather
more of their capital gains and inheritances.

It goes without saying that it is scarcely respectable for the rich and their
mercenaries, lawyers, economists, politicians, public-relations types, and
so on, to openly proclaim their affection for unemployment, although
among friends they tend to be more candid. One requires a respectable
rationale, a convenient theory that combines apparent concern about the
sufferings of the unemployed with actual capacity to avoid any action
realistically calculated to alter their status.

My colleagues (I am an economist, but I am confessing, not boasting)
have risen to the challenge. As their apologetic runs, we can't proceed
sensibly toward universal job guarantees, even in the cautious, timid
shape of the Humphrey-Hawkins Full Employment Bill, a revival of the
1945 original effort to write a serious job guarantee into law, because of
the horrifying menace of more inflation. That menace is among economists embodied in a marvelous construction interred in the textbooks under the rubric of the Phillips curve.

The provenance of this notion that democratic societies must choose
between inflation and unemployment deserves a paragraph. The late
A. W. Phillips, a British economist who taught for much of his career in
Australia, published in 1958 an article catchily entitled "The Relationship
between Unemployment and the Rate of Change in Money Wage Rates
in the United Kingdom, 1862–1957." Phillips's data appeared to demonstrate that, as unemployment rose, wages increased less and less rapidly.
The man said nothing at all about prices, price inflation, or the manner in
which rising wages might or might not be translated into commensurate
increases in the cost of living. Nevertheless, his findings were rapidly extended in statements like this typical textbook pronouncement: "Low
rates of unemployment tend to be associated with high rates of inflation
and, conversely, price stability or low rates of inflation tend to be associ-

ated with high rates of unemployment." Triumphant conclusion: "There seems to be a trade-off between employment and the price level."

Economists shifted from Phillips's cautious conclusions about unemployment and wage rates to the words just cited very simply. After all, wages and salaries, including those of executives and other overpriced folk, amount to about 70 percent of business costs. Wherever competition reigns, employers have no choice except to pass along plumper labor costs to their customers in the shape of higher prices. The line of causation is direct: low unemployment stimulates wage demands, higher wages enlarge business costs, and these in turn lead to higher prices. It's an indisputable pity, but if we are to restrain demand inflation, we simply must operate the economy at what an MIT economist, Robert Hall, has recently labeled the "natural" rate of unemployment. A bit hard on those selected to serve their country by losing their jobs, but their patriotic sacrifice is nothing less than a valuable public service.

Let us absolve A. W. Phillips of blame for the intellectual sins committed in his name and look calmly, on its merits, at the Phillips curve in its modern guise. It is to start with an embarrassingly inaccurate explanation of recent stagflation—the malignant combination of persistent inflation and high unemployment. To those untutored in economics, the causes of a good part of current inflation have nothing at all to do with the Phillips curve. Out there in a world mostly beyond American control, OPEC has been busy quintupling petroleum prices, the Russians have been bidding up the cost of food in American supermarkets by vast grain purchases, and the world market for American farm products, temporary fluctuations aside, has been exerting steady upward pressure upon domestic food supplies.

These external shocks initiated in inflationary surge in 1973 and 1974. In spite of the sharpest recession (1974–75) since the 1930s, that inflation continued, somewhat abated in 1976, and gave ominous signs of spurting once more by the end of that year. Here is the real embarrassment for Phillips curve groupies. Their mechanism has simply failed to work. Unemployment has escalated and stuck at the highest recorded levels since the Great Depression. Wages have risen more slowly than the cost of living. Productivity is improving. Nevertheless, prices continue to rise. It has proved perfectly possible to suffer simultaneously from severe inflation and still more severe unemployment and factory under-utilization.

As it happens, there is a reasonable explanation at hand for events so baffling to partisans of inflation-unemployment trade-offs. Clearly, inflation is not a simple matter of translation of higher wages into higher prices. Rather, it is an aspect of the distribution and concentration of market power among suppliers and sellers, abroad and here at home, who are in a position, within generous limits, to set their own prices for the goods and services that they sell. In both recession and expansion, sellers with market power have chosen to charge more, even if, as a result, they sell less. Businessmen and respectable mainstream economists who judge full employment to be inflationary are utterly correct. It is only their reasons that are wrong.

Prices rise during both phases of the business cycle because in recession businessmen who enjoy monopoly or quasimonopoly power over their markets push prices upward in order to maintain their profit margins. When better times come, businessmen seize the opportunity to improve their profit margins. As fair example, recall that during 1974 and 1975, two of the auto industry's worst years since the 1950s, General Motors and its amiable rivals marked up auto sticker charges an average of $1,000 per car, even though the customers were reluctant to buy. The rarer the customers, the larger the profit that needed to be attached to the selling price of each unit. Now that sales are behaving more wholesomely, prices continue to rise. Why not get more when the customers are willing to pay more? As in autos, so in steel, aluminum, and a long list of other industries in which one, two, three, or four dominant corporations set prices and conduct orderly markets unblemished by unseemly price rivalry. The manufacturers have company. In the delivery of health services, a pleasant cartel of health insurers, hospitals, medical societies, and complaisant federal authorities has propelled medical costs higher at twice the pace of general inflation. The television monopolies have raised the charges for network time, and the university professors who lecture and consult have done rather better than the inflation rate. Lawyers have long judged advertising and price competition two serious breaches of legal ethics. Food prices rise partly because of the widening profit margins of food processors.

WORSE THAN THE DISEASE

The diagnosis dictates the choice of remedies. One is as old as the 1890 Sherman Antitrust Act: break up the monopolies and end price-fixing in restraint of trade. The remaining true believers in antitrust would cheerfully fragment the large corporations, which, either by themselves or in combination with one or two peers, dominate many markets. Alas, the nonprogress of former Sen. Philip Hart's oil divestiture bill in the last Congress and its dim prospects in the new one are the latest evidence of the political futility of this tactic. Although no technical reasons justify the size of Exxon or General Motors, the public is yet to be persuaded that small is beautiful.

The only feasible alternative is control of key prices and profit margins in the very large proportion of the economy where old-fashioned competition is celebrated only by banquet speeches. Such controls were imposed during World War II and the Korean War. It is a historical curiosity that John Kenneth Galbraith, who was a price administrator, and Richard Nixon, who briefly served as a compliance attorney, drew diametrically opposite conclusions from their respective experience. Galbraith continues to believe that price control is both necessary and feasible. Nixon preached the wickedness of interference with private markets, but nevertheless suddenly froze prices August 15, 1971, and followed the ninety-day freeze with a year or so of more flexible but astonishingly successful wage- and price-hike limitations. As the Nixon experience suggests, wage controls generally accompany price controls. There recently has been the rub. The wage controls in 1972 and 1973 were considerably more effective than the price controls, for two excellent reasons. The Nixon controllers, pro business to a man, were far more eager to check union demands than to interfere with business earnings, and employers gladly cooperated with Washington to police the wage-rise limits. Seldom did patriotism pay better.

The fact is that in the United States (England is, of course, quite a different matter) mandatory price controls over concentrated industries and the health sector, together with voluntary wage guidelines, would probably work very well for a time. American unions are, after all, both weak and conservative. The path to full employment without inflation is impossible without a firm incomes policy and the statutory authorization of price controls administered by individuals who believe in what they are doing.

Does the political will to shape a national full employment policy exist? It is difficult to answer yes to that question. . . . For, as has been noted, full employment means diminishing long-standing inequalities of income, wealth, and power; inviting the black, brown, young, and female to the American celebration; and controlling the rapacity of doctors, lawyers, giant corporations, and other reputable extortionists. After full employment who will iron Russell Long's shirts, clean up after the Lutèce diners, and do the world's dirty work? Settle the job issue once and for all, and even American unions will begin to entertain dangerous thoughts about job redesign, codetermination, and similarly radical Swedish and German nonsense.

The fine Christian (and occasionally Jewish) men whom the good Lord has placed in the seats of authority and the halls of the mighty know that there are far worse phenomena than unemployment. One of them is full employment. . . .

A genuine commitment to sustained full employment demands a good deal more than a temporary tax cut or a brief loosening of the federal purse strings. The United States will move toward a coherent high-employment economy at the same time as it becomes politically feasible to diminish the power of great wealth and reduce inequalities of income and wealth.

The fate of George McGovern in 1972 and Fred Harris in 1976, two brave souls who rose to the perils of open discussion of such political dynamite, makes it depressingly plain that Americans continue to admire the people and institutions that make life harder for them than it need be. As Prof. Walter Burnham of MIT pointed out last year, the missing 45 percent of the American electorate who don't turn up on Election Day in Europe vote Labor, Socialist, or Communist.

All my life my country has suffered from the absence of significant political Left. As I trudge through middle age toward the golden years of senior citizenship, I glimpse even less hope of the emergence of a democratic socialist party than I did during the late 1930s and early 1940s when, at least in Manhattan, revolution was in the air.

Until a credible left rises in the United States, unemployment will be a little higher when the Republicans are in the White House, a little lower when the Democrats take their turn. Genuine full employment, decent jobs at decent wages for every man, woman, and youth interested in working, has been a myth, is a myth, and will stay a myth so long as every four years voters choose between one party minimally to the right of dead center and a second minimally to the left.

6
WHEN THEY CLOSE THE FACTORY GATES: HOW BIG STEEL SCRAPPED A COMMUNITY

John Logue

Just west of the Pennsylvania border lies the Mahoning Valley, once the second-leading steel producing area in the United States. In Youngstown and in its industrial suburbs, mills line both sides of the river. For generations their noise has muted the Mahoning, but in recent times the fur-

Reprinted by permission from *The Progressive*, 409 East Main Street, Madison, Wisconsin 53703. Copyright © 1980, The Progressive, Inc.

naces have gradually been banked, and one by one the mills have closed. In a matter of months, the sounds of the river will be audible again.

Youngstown is a microcosm of the problems of the aging industrial towns of the Northeast: the predatory conglomerate, systematic disinvestment, the flight south, the trained labor force suddenly unemployed, the collapse of the community tax base, and the obsolescence of the rusting mills that once employed thousands. The names of the mills are a litany of despair:

- The Campbell works, abandoned in September 1977 with the loss of 5,000 jobs.
- The Brier Hills works, which employed 3,300 a few years ago, shut in December 1979 with the loss of 1,250 jobs.
- U.S. Steel's McDonald and Ohio works, which once employed 10,000—final shutdown now under way, with the loss of the remaining 3,500 jobs.
- Republic's one remaining blast furnace in Youngstown, scheduled for shutdown in 1981, as is the coke battery that still employs about 700 at the remnants of the Campbell works.

Ten years ago, the steel industry employed 25,000 directly in the Mahoning Valley; today there are 12,000; by the end of next year, there may well be fewer than 10,000. The valley and its steel towns have lost their reason for being.

Youngstown's symptoms of decline—aging industrial plants, a decision at some distant corporate headquarters not to reinvest, and finally the closing of the mills—are not a product of a corporate conspiracy but of the facts of American economic life.

In the United States, economic power has become increasingly concentrated. The 200 largest firms controlled 45 per cent of manufacturing assets at the end of World War II; they control 60 per cent today. The 2,000 largest firms—about 1 per cent of all the manufacturers—control 88 per cent of manufacturing assets and make 90 per cent of the manufacturing profits; the other 99 per cent share 10 per cent of the profits. The U.S. economy is hardly the preserve of home-owned small business.

There is no reason to be sentimental about size in business. Scale is vital to efficiency, particularly in the capital-intensive steel industry. The price tag for a major modernization program at a medium-sized steel works starts at about $200 million. But there is good reason to be concerned about the lack of worker and community influence on the decisions of corporate giants. That is what the Youngstown story is all about.

The Youngstown mills were antiquated. Their blast furnaces were small. All of them used open-hearth furnaces for steel making, less efficient than the more modern Basic Oxygen and Electric Arc furnaces. Some of the finishing mills are run by the original steam engines installed before World War I. "Hell, they belong in the Smithsonian," says Ed Mann, president of the Brier Hill steelworkers' local.

Despite the equipment, the Ohio works set production record after production record in the months before the shutdown. Among U.S. Steel's oldest plants, it outperformed the company's new Baytown, Texas, facility in head-on competition in 1978. Improvements in productivity rested on the creativity and dedication of the labor force, aware that saving their plants and jobs depended on increasing production. They succeeded, but the gates still closed.

In the long run, labor force dedication cannot replace modernization. And modernization simply did not occur in Youngstown. The steel companies took millions out of the valley over the last decades and returned little to the plants.

The lack of reinvestment in the Mahoning Valley had a variety of causes. One is geographic: Inland mills lack cheap water transportation, a notable handicap for traditional mills (though not for those with modern electric furnaces which use a higher proportion of scrap). More crucial was the changing industrial structure. Merger activity hit steel—and Youngstown—hard. Lykes, the New Orleans-based shipping conglomerate, acquired Youngstown Sheet and Tube in the late 1960s. Sheet and Tube was more than six times the size of Lykes at the time of acquisition but the smaller fish swallowed the bigger. Lykes was less interested in Sheet and Tube's dies and presses than in its large cash flow, which could be diverted into financing other acquisitions. Plant maintenance diminished from the day Lykes took over, and investment in modernizing steel facilities slowed notably. Similarly, Jones and Laughlin Steel (J&L) was absorbed by the LTV corporation, a Dallas-based conglomerate.

Systematic disinvestment by the conglomerates is a symptom of the deeper problem: International competition in steel is intense, and profits are lower than in other industries. Emerging from World War II with its facilities intact, the American steel industry prospered while its foreign competition was prostrate. In time, the German and Japanese mills were reconstructed with more advanced technology, but American management rested on its laurels, in large measure because of the conviction that the new technology being pioneered abroad (derived, ironically, from foreign studies of American plants) was inappropriate for the huge scale of the American domestic market. New investment went instead into advanced versions of technologically antiquated production processes. By the late 1960s, foreign steel companies were making major inroads into the American market, while American investment had lagged so far behind the growth in demand that American producers were no longer able to meet peak domestic requirements.

Wages play a subsidiary role to investment. American steelworkers are among the best-paid industrial workers in the country, but the same can be said of Western European steelworkers. Japanese wage rates, long below those in other industrial countries, have moved up rapidly. But new plants now coming on line in such Third World countries as Brazil and South Korea will benefit not only from a low-wage labor force but also from the anti-union policies of those governments.

The obvious answer is to encourage unionization, and efforts to aid union organizers in Third World countries have met limited success. The principal problem is pressuring Third World governments to permit union organizing. Unions in western nations have had occasional successes: The threat of a boycott on unloading Chilean exports wrung a few concessions from that government in allowing union activity in Chile. But what is really needed is governmental pressure, and for all the human rights campaign, the Carter Administration has done little in this area.

Not all American steel firms have been slow to modernize. Some smaller companies, like Armco's Western Steel division, which has installed electric furnaces in all its plants, are fully modern, highly competitive, and profitable. But the industry giant, U.S. Steel—which last year grossed $12 billion, equal to the gross national product of Egypt—has lagged so far behind that cynical outsiders suspect it of deferring capital spending and allowing foreign inroads into its market in order to compel the Government to provide tax breaks for the industry.

Instead of modernizing their mills, many American steel firms are diversifying—diverting profits from steel into investment in other areas. The conglomerates that now own Youngstown Sheet and Tube and J&L do this as a matter of course. But even U.S. Steel is turning its back on the industry, channeling an increasing portion of its investment dollars into the chemical industry, oil, gas, and uranium exploration, and real estate development. U.S. Steel's latest annual report is illustrated with pictures of a company-developed shopping mall.

If Youngstown's problems were typical of the industry's, its response was not: Workers and community have fought stubbornly and imaginatively to save the valley's economic backbone. It is this struggle that has projected Youngstown into the national consciousness.

The fight began with Lykes's surprise shutdown of Sheet and Tube's Campbell works. Campbell local union presidents first learned of the impending disaster when they were called into management offices one Monday morning in September 1977 to receive the press release announcing the closure; the first layoffs began three days later. Initially accepting management's explanation that the plant was a victim of pollution control rules and Japanese imports, tens of thousands signed petitions asking the Government to invoke import restrictions and relax environmental protection standards.

But public outrage grew as the real reasons for the closure became clear: New Orleans executives had plundered Sheet and Tube to invest elsewhere, leaving Youngstown with a silent mill and 5,000 unemployed. The formation by religious leaders of the Ecumenical Coalition of the Mahoning Valley provided a focal point for organization. Its goal quickly became a worker-community run steel mill—a suggestion first made by Gerald Dickey, a steelworker at the Brier Hill works and recording secretary of the union local. The proposal called for a community corporation that would combine worker, community, and private investment. After a study by Gar Alperovitz and the Center for Economic Alternatives established that a community mill was potentially viable, the Ecumenical Coalition asked the Federal Government for $245 million in loan guarantees—guarantees of the sort provided to other steel producers, such as Wheeling-Pittsburgh, for modernizing aging plants. Reaction was initially favorable, but in March 1979 the Government rejected the request, killing the Campbell plan. (See "Must Youngstown Roll Over and Die? How 'Big Steel' Got to Jimmy Carter," *The Progressive*, October 1979.)

By this time, the Justice Department had compounded Youngstown's problems by suspending antitrust rules that would probably have prevented the merger of Lykes, the owner of Youngstown Sheet and Tube (the nation's eighth-largest steel producer), and LTV, which owned Jones and Laughlin (the seventh-largest). Overruling staff recommendations, Attorney General Griffin Bell approved the merger under an imaginative application of the "failing business doctrine," otherwise reserved for firms in or near bankruptcy. Bell cited a desire to save jobs at Sheet and Tube, but that wasn't one of the results of the merger. Sheet and Tube's Brier Hill mill was superfluous to the integrated company and was closed in December 1979.

The U.S. Steel shutdown, announced November 27, 1979, was less surprising than the earlier closures. The Ohio and McDonald works were among the most marginal facilities the company owned; they had been close to getting the ax before. Yet to a community organized on the issue of plant closings, the shutdown was the final straw: Keeping the plants open or selling them to the employes was an issue to be pushed in the streets as well as in the courts. Irate steelworkers seized U.S. Steel's district headquarters on January 28 to underline their view.

The aborted plan for a community takeover of the Campbell works was readily adapted to U.S. Steel's Youngstown works. This time the plan called for a small infusion of local capital, a $60 million Federally guaranteed loan, and a substantial reduction in labor costs by deferring incentive payments and writing off accumulated pension and vacation benefits. Plans called for running the mills "as is" until the regular capital market could be tapped—possibly with Government loan guarantees—for modernization funds. The plan called for cutting labor costs by 21 per cent, but this time it was hoped that labor's sacrifice would save the mill jobs permanently.

"We have a much better chance than ever existed for reviving the Campbell works," said Bob Vasquez, chairman of the Ohio Works local. "The labor force is in place. The management is in place. Our customers have not turned to other suppliers yet."

There was just one problem: U.S. Steel refused to sell the mills to any group which sought Federal loan guarantees—a proviso that would exclude sales to several of U.S. Steel's competitors as well as to former employes. Ironically, the company's stand was announced at a press conference in conjunction with the steel industry's request for new tax deductions which would cost other taxpayers some tens of billions of dollars.

The leadership of the steelworkers' locals at U.S. Steel's McDonald and Ohio Works in Youngstown are not radicals. They seemed more discomfited than the company itself by the temporary occupation of U.S. Steel's Youngstown headquarters, preferring to place their hopes in reviving the mills under community ownership. That required the cooperation of the Carter Administration, not notable for its enthusiasm for plant occupations. They sought redress in the courts, suing U.S. Steel for breaking what they alleged was an oral agreement to keep the mills open as long as they broke even, and for anti-trust violations in refusing to sell the mills to Community Steel.

"We are not talking about a local bakery shop, a grocery store, a tool-and-die shop, or a body shop in Youngstown that is planning to close and move out," Federal District Judge Thomas Lambros declared in granting the restraining order that prevented the planned March 10 shutdown. "U.S. Steel cannot leave the Mahoning Valley and the Youngstown area in a state of waste." In agreeing to hear the case, the judge said he chose to "view the law not as something static but in terms of modern-day conditions." And he moved the trial to Youngstown to enable the plaintiffs to subpoena U.S. Steel executives from Pittsburgh.

William Roesch, president of U.S. Steel since April 1979, told the crowded courtroom of studies that had been undertaken to determine whether there was a "viable fit" between Jones and Laughlin and Youngstown Sheet and Tube, and whether a merger would improve the profitability of the two.

What about the "fit" between Sheet and Tube's Brier Hill works in Youngstown and J&L's seamless operation at Aliquippa, Pennsylvania? asked Staughton Lynd, attorney for the steelworkers.

"I didn't see that as a problem," Roesch responded. There were murmurs from the audience, most of whom were free to attend the trial because of what the "fit" had done to the Brier Hill works in December.

David Roderick, chairman and former president of U.S. Steel, making his first trip to Youngstown since 1977, testified that when the decision was made to shut down the Youngstown works on November 27, 1979, U.S. Steel officials had performance figures for Youngstown showing profitable operation in the first half of the year and a cumulative loss of only $300,000 for the first ten months (Roderick's salary in 1979 was $360,000). It was on the basis of future projections that U.S. Steel acted, Roderick said.

What projections? Lynd demanded. He said U.S. Steel's own figures, from plant management, showed a projected 1980 *profit* on fixed expenses. Roderick said he had no knowledge of that report.

Roderick's answers seemed surprisingly thin on facts, but he spoke categorically on policy topics. U.S. Steel would not sell the plants to its employes or any other group with a Government-guaranteed loan.

"Are you closing the door?" Lynd asked. Roderick affirmed his belief in free enterprise and the market place.

"Is there anything that the USW locals and the community can do to reopen U.S. Steel's consideration of the closures?" Lynd asked. "I cannot foresee such circumstances," the company chairman replied. His answer had a ring of finality.

The judge also heard from William Kirwan, general superintendent of the Youngstown works. Kirwan did not talk of free enterprise but of producing steel profitably—of the fact that the Youngstown works turned a $10 million profit on fixed expenses in 1978 and $4 million in 1979, with the projection of a tiny profit in 1980. He recalled how, in February 1979, Youngstown had produced half the profits in U.S. Steel's Eastern Division, and how production records were broken time and time again despite the antiquity of the equipment.

Kirwan spelled out the details of his "Kirwan plan," which he had pushed on the unreceptive U.S. Steel hierarchy, for massive new investment in the Youngstown works, and for building a new mill on the site of the old works. The audience applauded this glimpse of what community control is all about.

Judge Lambros's decision favored the company. The last heat of iron was tapped at the Ohio works within hours after the decision was handed down. Judge Lambros dismissed the employes' antitrust case three weeks later, ruling that despite Community Steel's offer of $20 million for the Youngstown works, the steelworkers had not demonstrated "any ability to purchase, [and] therefore no one has denied them anything."

A legal victory by the steelworkers might have brought a delay of one or two years in the shutdown. But the Youngstown issue goes deeper than that: What is a corporation's responsibility to employes and the community and what influence should employes have on investment decisions?

The Youngstown shutdowns and community opposition to them have drawn national attention. The United Steel Workers, whose national leaders have done little to help save the Youngstown mills, have now introduced plant shutdowns as a national bargaining issue.

Pending before the Ohio legislature is a bill requiring advance notification, severance pay, and payment to a community readjustment fund in the event of closures of major plants. Similar legislation has been proposed in Oregon, Michigan, Massachusetts, Pennsylvania, and New York, and in Congress. Milder plant closing laws are already on the books in Maine and Wisconsin.

FROM FAMILY FIRM TO MINI-CONGLOMERATE

Small, family-owned companies have been hit hard by the merger wave of the 1960s and 1970s, with countless hundreds of locally owned firms falling into new hands. The A. C. Williams Company in Ravenna, Ohio, about thirty miles west of Youngstown, is a case in point.

Founded in 1844, A. C. Williams is among the oldest foundries in the country, and until 1976 it was still owned and managed by the family that founded it. The firm's two plants in Ravenna—together the town's second-largest private employer—had been unionized since the mid-1930s, and while wages were hardly munificent, the atmosphere was decent, the work steady, and the stress less than at the higher-paid assembly line jobs in the region. Union local president Jim Boyle described labor relations as average to good; in the twenty-one years he had worked at A. C. Williams, there had been only one strike, and that had lasted less than a day.

Four years ago, a group of investors bought the firm, and quickly used the assets to acquire three other Ohio foundries. As it happened, two of the new plants were non-union. So it was hardly surprising that the new management was willing to take a strike at A. C. Williams when the old contract expired in January 1980. Management did not even appear at the bargaining table; it sent only its attorney.

In the third week of the strike, the company bought a non-union foundry in Tennessee and announced its intention to move machinery from one of the struck plants to the new one, where production could be resumed. What followed could have been a scene out of a Grade B 1930s strike film.

Shortly after midnight on Thursday, February 14, a convoy of eleven trucks drove full speed through the picket line, along with a car and a van carrying twelve men equipped with pistols, shotguns, mace, nightsticks, and riot helmets. The pickets were forewarned of the arrival of the "movers" (who, according to Boyle's queries, specialize in such operations and have moved 192 plants under comparable circumstances) because the convoy got lost and radioed the police for directions. The police charged the eight pickets with aggravated riot, but they did not search the trucks for armaments. Only after the trucks were on the road did the police have a look in the remaining vehicle—the van—to find some disassembled shotguns and a fully assembled pistol.

The story has a happy ending. Although production did begin at the Tennessee plant, a decent contract was finally signed in Ravenna, raising wages, improving pensions, and leading to the rehiring of three employes previously fired. The old machinery stayed in Tennessee, but new machinery was brought in from yet another plant bought during the strike. The union chalked it up as a victory.

But the nature of the company and its relations with the employes had been fundamentally changed. Four years ago, A. C. Williams was part of the community; today, it is free to shift work among union and non-union plants, or even out of state.

"When I went to work there twenty-one years ago," Boyle says, "the manager was Harry Beck. He knew the wife's name, the names of your children, whether they played baseball or football, when they were sick. All that's gone now. This president don't give a damn whether he operates in Ravenna or someplace else."

A few months after the end of the strike, the company proved Boyle right by shutting one of its two Ravenna plants indefinitely for economic reasons and laying off half the work force. It was the first shutdown within memory; A. C. Williams had weathered other recessions and the Great Depression by reducing the work week rather than shutting down.

As in Youngstown, the power has moved out of the community, and with it has gone the old sense of security. Community loyalty and 130 years of tradition mean little in the new world of the mini-conglomerate.

—J. L.

Such moves deal with effects, not causes. Employe influence on investment decisions is more crucial; it was the decision not to reinvest in Youngstown, made in the 1960s and early 1970s, that led to the shutdown. Employes now have some influence in other countries—in Sweden and in Germany, for example—and few would maintain that the plants are the worse run for it. Swedish employers are required to provide full information to their employes and to negotiate all major investment decisions with the union. Full disclosure requirements would probably improve the quality of information in the hands of managers when they make important decisions. Perhaps the most astonishing point in Roderick's testimony in the Youngstown trial was the paucity of his company's knowledge of the profitability of the Youngstown works when the decision was made to shut them. He had never heard of the "Kirwan plan" to modernize the works.

Though the plant closing legislation under consideration confers no powers on employes or communities, it does raise the cost of shutting marginal facilities rather than modernizing them. Currently the tax law weights the balance on the other side. The economics of massive closures are more attractive to corporate executives because the public pays most of the tab. The company takes a one-year bath of tax losses (which can be written off against future income) and ends the drain on current earnings. Its executives gain a reputation for acting decisively to "turn the company's profits around."

But the cost to the taxpaying public for shutting marginal mills is heavy. Of the roughly $200 million loss, charged against future taxable income, that U.S. Steel took in the Youngstown shutdown, other taxpayers will eventually pick up 46 per cent, or almost $100 million. In addition, the direct cost in unemployment compensation, retraining, and other benefits for workers idled by the shutdown is estimated at $70 million over the next three years. Add in the state and Federal governments' losses in taxes, the waste in underutilization of Youngstown schools, roads, water and sewage plants, and the sum of losses absorbed by the public would far exceed $200 million—about the cost of Kirwan's modernization program.

Perhaps the greatest irony is that Youngstown employes were unable to use their considerable financial clout. The assets of U.S. Steel's manual employes pension plan are *double* the value of the corporation's stock. Were the equity of the fund subdivided, Youngstown workers would be entitled to about $100 million. But far from following the interests of its nominal owners, the company-controlled pension fund has sunk (as of 1976) a half billion dollars into the stock of predominantly non-union and, in some cases, blatantly anti-union firms. Conceivably, many of the beneficiaries would have preferred to see some of that fund invested in saving jobs by modernizing the mills instead of being pumped into non-union companies investing in the South or farther afield in Taiwan, South Korea, or Brazil. But the company controls the fund.

At issue in Youngstown, then, was the question of economic power. Do the rights of property ownership include the right to scrap jobs, mills, an

entire town? The answer of the Youngstown community was a resound-
ing No. While community control has been invoked as a last resort, Community Steel could have provided the vehicle to save Youngstown's steel
industry by taking over the mills as Sheet and Tube, J&L, and U.S. Steel
shut them down. Stabilizing the Youngstown steel industry under community control would also have cost jobs, but nothing like the 10,000 that
now have disappeared.

The decision was not up to Youngstown. It rested with the steel companies and the courts, which ruled, albeit reluctantly, that the privileges
of ownership included the right to scrap a community and its people.

III
INEQUALITY

In the 1950s and 1960s most social scientists believed that we were living in an "affluent" society—a society in which most people could expect steady improvement in their living standards, in which income disparities were diminishing, and in which real poverty was fast becoming a thing of the past.

This vision of American affluence was based on some undeniable facts. The incomes of the American people did rise substantially after World War II, and during the 1960s millions of the formerly poor were lifted above the official poverty lines. It was natural to believe that the process would continue.

The experience of the past decade has, however, shattered the myth of affluence and its accompanying myth of declining income inequality. We discovered, first of all, that even the progress made in raising the overall standard of living through the 1950s and 1960s made virtually no impact on the *distribution* of income and wealth in America—the gap between rich and poor. Thirty years ago, the upper fifth of income earners received roughly 40 percent of all income, the bottom fifth about 5 percent. Today, the same proportions hold. And in the 1970s, under the impact of slowing economic growth, the "real" incomes—income adjusted for rising taxes and costs of living—of many Americans began a slow but steady decline.

That decline has been most severe for working people. As the article by Currie, Dunn, and Fogarty shows, the combination of inflation and economic stagnation—"stagflation"—that has plagued the American economy in recent years has had a complex and often devastating impact on the way people live. This impact is especially clear when we look beneath the standard statistics on trends in income. The economic crisis has profoundly changed the nature of work and family life in the

United States. It has deeply altered, sometimes in subtle ways, what most Americans can expect from their future. And since the changes have struck some groups much harder than others, they have also brought new and deeper forms of inequality to American life. Currie, Dunn, and Fogarty argue that currently fashionable panaceas for boosting the overall economy will not restore the "American Dream" of equality in affluence. If anything, they will worsen inequality and aggravate the impoverishment and desperation of millions of Americans.

Currie, Dunn, and Fogarty see new kinds of poverty emerging in the 1980s, along with new forms of affluence and wealth. And despite many years of an official national commitment to ending poverty, there is grim evidence that the "War On Poverty" is, at best, a stalemate. There were more poor people in 1979 than in 1969, and the size of the poverty population has remained depressingly unchanged for a decade.

Why is poverty so hard to eradicate? Part of the reason is that, as Paul Jacobs shows, the poor are confronted with a special economic system of their own—the "poverty market"—that helps ensure that the poor are kept poor. Jacobs' article was written in the mid-1960s, before the impact of most of the "antipoverty" programs. Some of the figures have changed; the latest official poverty count, for 1979, included about 25 million people. The "poverty line" moved up from $4,000 to $7,412 for a nonfarm family of four, to take account of the rising cost of living. And interest rates have gone up dramatically since Jacobs wrote (new car loans, as of 1981, usually began at around 17%). But the substance of Jacobs' analysis, tragically, still holds true.

Jacobs shows compellingly that middle-class people enjoy many subtle economic advantages that make all the difference between security and insecurity, well-being and constant anxiety. Poverty is a self-perpetuating system, making economic life very different for the poor and much more difficult—a fact often ignored by those social scientists who smugly explain poverty as the result of "lower-class culture" or lack of motivation.

Another way the structure of inequality is maintained, in spite of efforts at reform, is through the tax system. In capitalist societies, the "progressive" income tax is usually considered the great leveler—the agency through which a society based on individual competition and private profit softens the inequalities it creates. But as Brandon, Rowe, and Stanton demonstrate in "Tax Politics," the tax system is rigged to offer even more advantages to those who have the most. Through a bewildering variety of loopholes and dodges, the rich in America get what amounts to a vast and costly welfare program all their own. While the share of the total tax bill paid by working people is steadily rising, that of the corporations is steadily declining. As a result, the egalitarian idea of a tax system based on people's ability to pay has been steadily subverted.

7
THE FADING DREAM: ECONOMIC CRISIS AND THE NEW INEQUALITY

Elliott Currie, Robert Dunn, and David Fogarty

In the 1980s, no one any longer doubts that the United States is in the midst of a deep crisis in expectations. In the 1950s and 1960s, most Americans were led to believe in a future of indefinite economic expansion. Rising living standards, it was said, had made most people feel part of the "middle class." Real economic deprivation, to the extent that it was acknowledged at all, was presumed to be confined to the margins of the "affluent" society.

The combination of economic stagnation and high inflation—"stagflation"—in the 1970s replaced that rosy vision with the sense that the United States was slipping rapidly into economic decline. Suddenly the celebrated American standard of living seemed to be falling precipitously, and the easy optimism was quickly displaced by gloom and anxiety about the future. Faith in the "American Dream" disintegrated with dizzying speed, bringing fear, resentment, and a widespread demand to "turn the country around" at whatever cost. Today, some variant of a program for economic "revitalization" is on everyone's agenda, at all points on the political spectrum.

But beyond the sense of crisis and the urgent call for change, there is remarkably little agreement about the degree to which the era of "stag-

Revised from Elliott Currie, Robert Dunn, and David Fogarty "The New Immiseration—Stagflation, Inequality, and the Working-Class," *Socialist Review* No. 54, November/December 1980. Reprinted by permission.

flation" has actually damaged American standards of living or clouded the prospects for the future. *Fortune* magazine recently described, with considerable accuracy, the national pessimism about the state of the economy:

Of all the changes in American society during the Seventies, none was more fundamental than the erosion of faith in the future. By the end of the decade, the conviction that the material aspects of life will get a little bit better each year had given way to the bleakness of spirit known as diminishing expectations. It seems that most people nowadays aspire to little more than holding on to what they've already got, and many become downright despondent when they contemplate the world their children will inherit.

Fortune hastened to assure us, however, that such "dour resignation" was "out of phase" with the "upbeat outlook" for family income in the 1980s and also exaggerated what really happened during the 1970s. Many groups "did a lot better in the 1970s than is generally appreciated." The real problem, *Fortune* insisted, was psychological: people's expectations had been too high to begin with, so they "didn't *think* they were doing particularly well."

The disagreement has been sharpest over the impact of inflation. The business-oriented Committee for Economic Development, for example, describing inflation as a "pernicious addiction," declared that "the damage inflation does to the fabric of both our economic system and our society is so great that it must not be allowed to proceed unchecked." On the other hand, others have argued, with the economist Robert Heilbroner, that whatever dangers inflation may hold for the future, its impact on current living standards has been "much less than we commonly believe." "Despite our sense of being impoverished by inflation," Heilbroner writes, inflation has not "substantially" affected the "national standard of well-being and comfort."

Which of these views is accurate? As with so many social issues, the answers we get depend greatly on the kinds of questions we ask. In what follows, we want to delve beneath the conventional statistics on income and earnings to ask a different, and broader, set of questions about the way the economic crisis has affected social life and living standards in the United States.

In particular, we want to address two crucial problems in the usual statistics and the debates based on them: (1) They tell us nothing about the measures people have had to take in order to cope with recession and inflation, and (2) they are *averages* that tell us nothing about how *different groups* have fared under the impact of economic crisis.

The answers to these questions are crucial to an understanding of the social impact of the current economic crisis and, consequently, for evaluating policies that claim to confront it. We will look at the way inflation and recession have affected work and family life, patterns of saving and debt, and the availability of housing and jobs, and will argue that neither the relatively optimistic view—that the crisis has had only a mild effect on living standards—nor the more drastic vision of a massive economic decline adequately conveys what has happened to American life under the impact of "stagflation."

The real picture is more complicated. Developments in the economy have brought a complex sorting of the population into "winners" and "losers"—a recomposition, or reshuffling of the deck, rather than a uniform decline. On the one hand, many American families have maintained living standards, if at all, only by working harder, sacrificing leisure and family life, and/or mortgaging their futures and those of their children. Those hardest hit by the economic crisis, and with the least resources to cope with it, have suffered real decline; poverty-level styles of life have appeared among people who once thought of themselves as part of the "middle class." Some of the basics of the "American Dream"—the home of one's own, the successful job as the reward for education and effort—have moved, for all practical purposes, beyond their reach. At the same time, at the other end of the scale is a new affluence for the relative "winners" in the restructuring of social and economic life in America.

Increasingly, one's chances of affluence or poverty, comfort or insecurity, are crucially determined by a complex web of conditions that includes not only one's sex, color, and age, but also family composition, position in the housing market, and much more. One implication of this complex trend—as we will see—is that policies of economic "renewal" designed to stimulate the economy as a whole through such means as cuts in taxes and social spending may only accelerate the resorting of the American population into affluent "winners" and impoverished "losers." And the destruction of the social programs that have traditionally cushioned the blows suffered by those "losers" can only hasten the process.

THE PLIGHT OF THE THREE-JOB FAMILY

How we define the contours of a problem depends crucially on the way we choose to measure it. Measured in terms of overall family income, the rapid growth in living standards that fed rising expectations throughout postwar America came to an abrupt halt in the early 1970s. The median income for all American families approximately doubled (in constant dollars) between 1950 and 1973. But it fell—by over a thousand dollars—during the recession of the mid-1970s and by 1979 had inched back no further than its level of six years before.

Some economists dispute the relevance of these figures, arguing that real living standards actually *rose* even at the height of the mid-1970s "stagflation." This view is based on the argument that *per capita* income—total personal income divided by the number of people—is a much better measure, since it allows us to take account of the statistical impact of population changes. For example, since families are smaller, on the average, than they used to be, measures of overall family income will give a misleading picture of trends in how well-off families are: What we need to know is the income available per person, which may have increased even while total family income has stagnated. As Lester Thurow argues, "from 1972 to 1978, real per capita disposable income rose 16%. After accounting for inflation, taxes, and population growth, real incomes have gone up, not down. The average American is better off, not worse off."

What this argument ignores is that behind the soothing figures on per capita income is the grinding reality that, for many families, that income has been achieved only by sending more people to work. The clearest evidence of this fact comes when we look not simply at income per family or per person, but per *worker.* Thus discretionary income—basically, disposable income minus expenditures for necessities and transfer payments—declined by about 5 percent between 1973 and 1979. But this figure ignores one of the most striking features of the 1970s—the great increase in the number of people working. As *Business Week* points out, "Adjusting discretionary income for the huge recent increases in employment, to reflect the sweat that goes into producing that income, shows that discretionary income per worker over the past six years declined by 16%." These figures show that families increasingly need two—or more—workers just to keep up, much less to "get ahead." Statistics on the trend of family incomes in the 1970s bear this out: the incomes of families with only one earner fell about 7 percent behind the cost of living from 1969 to 1978; those of two- (and three-) earner families came out about 6 percent above it.

This trend has given the family a crucial—and somewhat paradoxical—role in the contemporary economy. On the one hand, the material support of other family members is often all-important as a protection against the erosion of living standards. Such support is especially crucial for women, given the pervasive discrimination they face in the labor market. This difference is most apparent in what has been called the "feminization of poverty"; single women, especially those with young children, have become the most predictably impoverished group in America. But at the same time, increased labor places severe strains on many dual-earner families. The need for two incomes in such families means that three jobs are now being done for the price of one—two in the paid labor force, one unpaid—the household and childrearing tasks done in the home. As the work time needed to keep up with living costs increases, something has to give. And there is considerable evidence that often what is "giving" is the quality of family life.

On the one hand, the tasks of child-rearing and housework are often being pushed out of the home—usually to the private sector—as working people, if they can afford to, consume more and more day care, fast food, and even paid housekeeping. (A result is the rapid growth of low-wage, quasi-domestic "service" occupations that both cater to the needs of the multiearner household and often supply what passes for job opportunities for the second earner.) On the other hand, especially for those who cannot afford outside services, modern family life often means a decline in the possibility of real leisure—or, what amounts to the same thing, an increase in the pace of life, a kind of social "speedup" resembling the deliberately increased pace of an industrial assembly line. With an extra job to do and little public provision for domestic services, many people wind up routinely cutting corners, compressing their lives, and feeling "hassled" much of the time they are supposedly "off the job." While this situation has always been the fate of many lower-income working families, it is now becoming a predictable aspect of the lives of many who once saw themselves as part of the "middle class."

But—like other effects of the rising cost of living—the burden of this "social speedup" has not been evenly distributed among working people. Instead, it has served to widen the gap between men and women and between income groups, in ways that are obscured by the conventional statistics on income and earnings.

Most of the extra work brought by the "speedup" has fallen on women—both because they are most of the second earners in the paid labor force and because paid work has not freed most women from unpaid work in the home. Instead, the extra job that women do has most often been coupled with continuing responsibility for running the household. As Willard Wirtz, head of the National Commission on Working Women, puts it,

For a great many women, taking a job outside the home isn't a matter of substituting one kind of work for another; what it means is double duty. . . . If limited opportunities on the new job away from home are part of the problem, the rest of it is the unchanging terms and conditions of the job at home. When all the old duties still have to be performed, body and mind sag under the double burden.

Much of that burden involves child care. A 1978 study by the University of Michigan's Survey Research Center found that nearly half of women working in the paid labor force, versus only 13 percent of men, reported spending 3½ hours or more—*on working days*—with their children. Forty-four percent also reported spending an additional 3½ hours on other household chores.

It is remarkable, in fact, how closely the overall working time of typical two-earner families matches the time requirements of three full-time jobs—and what a large proportion of the "third job" falls to women. Another recent study found that among working couples, the men spent an average of about 9 hours a week on family care, the women an average of about 29 hours. At the same time, the men averaged 44, to the women's 40, hours of paid work (because men were more often in jobs with frequent overtime). Put together, this amounts to an average of 69 hours of work a week for women, 53 for men, or 122 altogether for a family—the equivalent of three full-time jobs.

For many women, then, entering the labor force to keep the family standard of living intact has meant more work, less leisure, and a more harried family life. What one critic has called the "overwhelming poverty of time" in these families is given abundant testimony in a national survey of women wage-earners undertaken by the National Commission on Working Women. An astonishing 55 percent of the women surveyed reported having *no* leisure time; 39 percent had no time to pursue education. Only 14 percent were able to say that job and family life did not seriously interfere with each other.

There is, of course, another side to this increase in women's work. It is doubtless true that moving into the paid labor force has provided many women with wider options and may have helped undermine the traditional subordination of women in many families. But because of the persistence of the sexual division of labor in the home and the lack of adequate public support services, it has also meant that women have shouldered a disproportionate—though often hidden—share of the burdens imposed by the economic crisis. And the potential benefits in greater independence for women have also been constrained by the rising cost of living—especially in housing—which, in some areas, has made "coupling" almost an economic requirement.

Obviously, the effects of entering the labor force are different for the grocery clerk's wife who gets a job as a telephone operator than for the lawyer's wife who becomes a stockbroker or psychotherapist. And this difference illustrates one of the most striking trends of the stagflation era. For women who have the resources to enter well-paying and rewarding jobs, and to afford the costs of the private-sector "industrialization" of domestic services, the "two-paycheck" family can represent an enviable and liberating way of life. At the other end of the scale, it can mean a virtually unrelieved round of dull, rote work, in and out of the home. And the distance between these two ways of life is growing—in part because an increasing proportion of the wives entering the paid labor force comes from more affluent families, with the result that, as a Labor Department study puts it, "the gap between above-average income families and below-average income families will widen" in the coming years.

As access to extra work becomes more and more important in maintaining or improving standards of living, we can expect this gap to widen for another reason as well. Not everyone has the *opportunity* to take on more work—even relatively unrewarding work—in response to threats to their living standards. In a survey of how different kinds of families coped with recession and inflation, David Caplovitz found that about two out of five tried to handle inflation by working more—either sending more family members to work or taking on overtime or an extra job. But poorer people, often lacking access to even *one* job, were less often able to exercise those options.

The "new impoverishment"—of time as well as income—of many American families, then, is only one side of the coin; the other is the growing affluence of some families. Between 1970 and 1977, when average family incomes barely improved at all and many families' living standards fell sharply, the proportion of families with incomes above $25,000 (in constant dollars) jumped by about 23 percent. The rise in the number of relatively affluent families was even sharper for blacks, at the same time as many blacks suffered even greater stagnation or decline in living standards.

At one end of the new scale of living standards is what *Fortune* has gushingly termed the "superclass"; those two-income families with the additional "formidable advantages of connections, intelligence, and education," whose incomes may reach six figures. At the other end is a broad stratum of the poor and nearly poor—single parents, one-earner families with low incomes, and people on fixed incomes. Somewhere in the middle are the broad ranks of two-earner families with middling incomes who must cope with the escalated costs of necessities and the increased need for domestic services, for whom even two paychecks barely cover expenses from one week to the next.

MORTGAGING THE FUTURE

Conventional data on living standards, then, obscure the enormous increases in labor—and the resulting changes in family life—that have gone into keeping up with the rising cost of living. Something similar happens with the conventional picture of working people's consumption. The fact that levels of buying and spending have, on the whole, remained remarkably high in the stagflation era is often taken as evidence that things can't be as bad as we might think. Again, though, this conclusion ignores what working people have *done* in order to maintain consumption. For many families, stagflation has meant sacrificing the future to pay for the present, making the future a source of anxiety and dread—a situation most clearly visible in the changing patterns of savings and debt.

As recently as the fourth quarter of 1975, the rate of personal saving—the proportion of people's income put away for the future—stood at 7.1 percent. By the fourth quarter of 1979, it had dropped to 3.3 percent, less than half its level only four years before. This general figure masks much lower rates of saving at the lower levels of the income ladder and among younger people, but the inability to save afflicts even many middle-class families that have otherwise been able to weather inflation's attack fairly well. As Caplovitz's survey discovered, "Even if they are able to maintain their standard of living within limits, many white collar families find for the first time that they are unable to save money."

Along with reduced saving has come rising consumer debt. The average American consumer now holds only about $3 in assets for every dollar of debt owed, compared with about $5 in the 1950s. Installment credit as a proportion of disposable income rose by about 42 percent between 1960 and 1978.

Like the increase in labor, the growth of debt has struck some people much more severely than others—in this case, particularly lower-income and younger people. Debt repayments as a percentage of disposable income were 25 percent for the lowest income fifth in 1977, only 6 percent for the highest fifth. And that disparity has been increasing steadily; the proportion rose from 19 percent for the lowest-income fifth since 1970, while it dropped slightly for the most affluent.

The result is that low-to-moderate income families have become ever more highly "leveraged," in financial jargon, and hence ever more precarious financially. As a leading student of debt patterns in the United States notes, "As measured by the ratio of debt payment commitments to income, vulnerability to recession has increased, especially among the lowest 20 percent of the income distribution." Debt use is also most frequent among the young—especially younger families.

Why has debt grown—and savings evaporated—so rapidly while average family incomes have remained relatively stable? Part of the answer is that, as research by the National Center for Economic Alternatives has shown, costs for the necessities—food, energy, housing, health care—have risen much faster than the Consumer Price Index as a whole in the past few years. This rise in the cost of necessities seriously undermines the value of income even when it is measured in "real" terms—that is, adjusted for rises in the overall cost of living. Hence the sharp rise in the debt burden of families at the lower end of the income scale, where necessity costs already take a larger chunk of total income.

But there is a more subtle and less measurable reason for the growth of debt: more expenses become necessary as inflation creates its own set of escalated needs. Thus sharply rising housing prices may force a family out of easy commuting range to jobs and services, raising transportation and energy costs, perhaps requiring a second car. Paying for the extra car and the extra gas may require a second job. The second job in turn increases transportation costs still further; it may also create the need for more paid day care, and probably changes eating habits in a vastly more expensive direction—more eating out, less careful food shopping and less economical food preparation. Thus the changes in family living patterns we noted above lead not only to increased labor, but to escalating expenses as well. At the extreme, the new expenses may cancel out most of the benefits of increased work, in an inflationary "Catch 22."

Greater "leveraging" of family income to cope with these inflation-induced "needs," as well as the rising cost of necessities, is hard to avoid, given the insufficiency of public services that could cushion the need for ever-higher individual expenditures. But this "leveraging" means that some families—again, especially younger and poorer ones—may not be able to provide for a reasonably secure future. They won't be able to send their kids to college, cope with emergencies like major illnesses or deaths, or add savings to their pensions to help ensure a decent retirement.

These issues have become especially keen because of the specter of disintegration of the traditional systems of support for old age. Although Social Security benefits have so far kept up with inflation, the entire system's funding is increasingly in jeopardy—and reduction in benefits is now on the political agenda. Living on Social Security benefits alone, in any case, is a sure ticket to poverty; and private pensions, the most common alternative support, are rarely adjusted for increases in the cost of living.

The need to sacrifice security to keep up with essentials can only have a devastating psychological impact on the quality of life. It not only makes the present more frightening, but is one reason why many can no longer look forward to the ideal of a decent old age as the reward for a lifetime of labor—and why opinion polls show that Americans, for the first time in memory, think that their children will live in conditions worse than the present. In 1979, according to a *Washington Post*/ABC News poll, 66 percent of respondents still believed that their children would be "better off" than they were, whereas 18 percent thought their children would be worse off. By March 1981, only 47 percent thought their children would be better off, and 43 percent now believed their children would lead worse lives than their own.

THE VANISHING PROSPECT FOR HOME OWNERSHIP

Coping with "stagflation," then, has meant cutting deeply into savings and going further into debt, as well as greatly increasing labor—for some people much more than others. But even with these adaptations, there are aspects of the traditional American Dream that many working people—

especially the young—may never achieve, given the peculiar contours of the economic crisis. One of them, as we'll see in a moment, is the good job with reasonable chances for achievement—or at least good pay. Another is a home of one's own.

What has happened to housing represents a drastic change from traditional expectations. Decent housing, even rental housing, is fast becoming an unrealistic goal for all but a dwindling fraction of young Americans. Between 1972 and 1978, the price of an average one-family new home increased 72 percent nationally, 86 percent in the West, and much more in some high-demand metropolitan areas, while median family income increased only 40 percent. The Department of Housing and Urban Development estimates that in 1970 half of the American people could have afforded a median-priced new house (then costing $23,400), using the standard rule of thumb that no more than a fourth of pretax income should be spent on mortgage costs. In 1979, by the same standard, only 13 percent could afford new-home ownership (the median price then being $62,000), and 38 percent of all actual new-home buyers were ignoring the prudent rule of thumb.

The "affordability crisis" has hit renters as well, and today both owners and renters are overspending in order to put a roof over their heads. American families are now paying an average of almost 36 percent of disposable income for housing and housing-related expenses, double the average of only ten years ago. For low-income households the situation is much worse; by 1977, some 5.8 million households—4.2 million renters and 1.6 million owners—were paying over half of their incomes for shelter, and the problem has worsened considerably since then.

For many of these families, the cost of housing has meant stretching their budgets beyond the point where they can pay for other necessities and has made them terribly vulnerable to recession-caused disasters—either forced sale, default, or learning to live with poverty-level habits in all other realms of life.

Rising housing costs, moreover, have priced some groups out of the housing market altogether—notably low-income families, young couples, singles, and minorities. In 1975, a couple earning $16,650 could have bought a median-priced California home for $41,000. They would have made a 20 percent down payment of $8,000, and their monthly mortgage payment—including insurance, interest and taxes—would have been $347. By the end of 1979, the same home cost $88,300. A buyer had to earn over $35,000 to qualify for a loan, put down $17,750 as a 20 percent down payment, and pay out $878.42 per month.

At those rates, a broad segment of American working people—especially those now coming of age and those who, for whatever reasons, have delayed entry into the housing market for too long—may never have a chance to own a home. The fading dream of home ownership represents a crucial change in living standards—not only because it condemns some people to inferior housing, but perhaps even more importantly, because it eliminates one of the only tangible assets traditionally available to people without high incomes. The fact that roughly two-thirds of American families own their own homes today suggests how far down the income scale home ownership has extended in postwar America. Without the home as asset, the material security of these people will drop precipitously, again suggesting that ordinary income and wealth data greatly underestimate the real "losses" stagflation has caused for some groups.

Meanwhile, those who already have a strong foothold in the housing market have seen their homes appreciate wildly in value and their relative mortgage costs decline, often dramatically, because of inflation. The benefits of inflation for people who already own their homes should not be exaggerated, however, for other costs—maintenance and taxes, particularly—have risen dramatically in the past decade. For people with limited or fixed incomes, these costs can tip the balance between being able to keep a home or being forced back into the rental market. Still, the crisis in housing has created one of the deepest and most powerful divisions between "winners" and "losers" in the stagflation era.

THE OUTLOOK FOR JOBS

The divisions between winners and losers multiply and deepen when we look at what recent changes in the American economy have meant in terms of the kinds of jobs that will be available in the future. For, like housing, the job outlook is changing—in ways that will mean intensified competition for a shrinking proportion of good jobs. The losers in that competition may face a lifetime of poorly-paid, dull, and unstable work.

Some point to the rapid growth of overall employment, even during the recessionary 1970s, as evidence of the fundamental health of the economy. Nearly 13 million new jobs were created between 1973 and 1979. The American economy, in fact, produced new jobs at a rate much faster than its chief economic competitors, West Germany and Japan. What is striking, however, is that the economy stagnated, and living conditions flattened, in *spite* of all those new jobs. Why, with all those people newly at work, did only a minority of families see their standard of living rise?

The answer lies partly in the nature of the new jobs themselves—and it bodes ill for the future. For the new jobs have overwhelmingly been in those parts of the economy that offer the poorest pay, the fewest chances for advancement, and the least possibility of providing an adequate livelihood. And it is precisely these jobs that are expected to continue to grow in the future, while those that have traditionally offered a ticket to higher living standards will correspondingly decline.

By the end of the 1970s, well over two-fifths of all American workers in the private, nonagricultural economy were employed in just two sectors: retail trade and "services." More significantly, over 70 percent of all *new* jobs created in the private economy between 1973 and 1980 were in those two sectors. What kinds of jobs are these? Labor Department economists estimate that by 1990 there will be over 4 million new jobs in various private medical-care services—nursing homes, hospitals, blood banks, and medical laboratories. Another fast-growing sector is "miscellaneous business services," including janitorial, photocopying, and temporary office help. Over 5 million new jobs are expected in retail trade, mainly in fast-food restaurants, department stores, and food stores.

The jobs in these expanding fields are notoriously low-paying. In 1979, workers in manufacturing industries averaged about $232 a week in spendable earnings. Workers in service industries averaged $162, and in wholesale and retail trade, $155. Part of the reason for these low average earnings is that these jobs are often part-time, as is illustrated by the short—and declining—work weeks in service and retail trade. The average work week in retail trade was almost 40 hours in 1959, had dropped to 33 hours by 1977, and is expected to drop to 30 hours by 1990. Workers in manufacturing, as Emma Rothschild points out, had an average work week (in 1979) of about 40 hours, while workers in eating and drinking places, one of the fastest-growing sectors of the economy, averaged just 26 hours a week.

In the 1950s and 1960s social critics often worried that technological changes in the economy were on the verge of eliminating work. A whole literature about the "postindustrial" society emerged, in which the problem of what to do with the predicted increase in leisure was a primary concern. But the reality today is not quite what these critics expected. Technological change has not so much eliminated jobs, in the aggregate, as it has changed the mix of jobs available—and with it, the relative chances that work will bring economic security. The prediction of a "postindustrial" or "service" economy has been partly realized—and will become even more so during the remainder of this century. But—as we've already seen—the rise of the "service society" has not brought greater leisure—but, in many cases, the opposite; not increased freedom from toil—but, often, an ever-faster race to stay in one place.

The impact of these changes is already ensuring that youth are one of the greatest casualties of the economic crisis. Men and women under twenty-four are earning less today, in real terms, than their counterparts did in 1967. Even *Fortune* magazine, in its generally "upbeat" rendering of the income picture during the 1970s, notes that the combination of the "bulge" of baby-boom workers and a declining job market has played havoc with youth's life chances. Men aged fifty-five to sixty-four, the magazine points out, enjoyed a real income increase of nearly 18 percent between 1969 and 1977; those twenty-five to thirty-four saw their incomes rise less than 3 percent, while men eighteen to twenty-four suffered a slight decline. The cumulative effect has been dramatic: "By the end of the Seventies," *Fortune* notes, "the baby boomers had effectively lost about ten years' income growth relative to the group just ahead of them. One of the biggest uncertainties about income in the Eighties is whether they will be able to make up that lost ground." The division between those with a clear shot at the dwindling proportion of good jobs, and those who may never rise out of the poorly paid, unstable work force in the spreading retail and service sectors will become increasingly important in the coming years.

That division will probably be intensified by the wholesale destruction of many blue-collar jobs under the impact of the decline and restructuring of key industries like auto, steel, and rubber. Traditionally, these industries provided high-wage jobs that often offered a path into relative affluence (though that affluence was always threatened by job instability). Until the late 1970s workers in these industries (as well as certain others, like coal mining) fared best in terms of real income. By 1977, nearly a third of all American families making between $25,000 and $50,000 a year were officially classified as "blue collar." But these jobs, of course, are threatened with elimination as those industries either shut down, move away, or automate in response to intense competition. According to recent estimates, for example, by late 1980 the crisis in the American auto industry had cost the jobs of close to 300,000 workers in the industry itself and another 600,000 in related industries. And it is clear that—even if the industry does ever regain its past level of production—it will do so with a work force that is considerably smaller, replaced as much as possible by new, superefficient "robots."

To the extent that these and other well-paying blue-collar jobs are obliterated, the result will be a still greater split between a relatively few high-level professional and technical jobs on the one hand, and a growing array of poorly paid, rote jobs on the other. This split will strike hardest at younger workers' expectations for a decent job in the future, especially young minority workers, for whom industrial blue-collar jobs have long been a main route to a decent standard of living.

THE NEW INEQUALITY AND ECONOMIC POLICY

Two themes stand out most strongly from the strands of evidence on changes in work and family life, expectations for jobs and housing, and patterns of spending, saving, and debt.

First, it is true that—as *Business Week* magazine puts it—"the American credo that each generation can look forward to a better life than its predecessor has been shattered." What's more, it has been shattered in particularly threatening ways, for what have been most powerfully assaulted by the changes in the economy are the most fundamental expectations and most basic sources of stability and security—the quality and character of home and family life, the security of one's future, and the fate of one's children.

At the same time, these burdens have been felt very differently by different groups. The lineup of "winners" and "losers" in this redistribution of life-chances is complicated and sometimes unexpected. Traditional differences, like sex, race, and age, have been widened and redefined, while newer ones based on family composition, position in the housing market, or—increasingly—participation in specific industries have arisen or become more important. The brunt of stagflation's impact on living standards, patterns of labor and family life, and job prospects has been borne by a few especially hard-hit groups. Others, better endowed with the appropriate resources, have coped more than adequately, carving out new kinds of affluence in the midst of economic "decline."

What do these trends tell us about the social and economic policies that could reverse the harshest effects of the new inequality? It would take another article to do justice to such a large, and freighted, question. But a few general points seem clear.

Most importantly, our analysis suggests that the kind of economic "revitalization" so fashionable among the legions of the "New Right"—and given political momentum by the Reagan administration—is more likely to aggravate the trends we've outlined than to alter them. At the core of the "conservative" program is a set of incentives designed to fuel economic expansion by stimulating private investment. These incentives include across-the-board tax cuts, "deregulation" of industry, and drastic reductions in public spending on social programs (coupled, of course, with massively increased spending for defense). According to the new conventional wisdom of "supply-side" economics, these policies would both fight high inflation and "get America moving again" by "unleashing" private enterprise.

At bottom, the "supply-side" vision is the most recent (and most drastic) variant of the longstanding argument that the way to increase jobs, income, and well-being throughout the society is to allow them to "trickle down" from an expanding private economy. By shifting the balance of social resources upward and improving the "business climate," society as a whole—including its poorest members—should benefit.

Whether such a program can, in fact, cause a spurt of economic growth—as measured by a rising Gross National Product or a higher rate of productivity—is a question we won't venture to answer. For our purposes, it is the wrong question. The more important one is not whether we can generate *some* kind of economic growth—but whether the growth we produce will be translated into better lives and greater opportunities across all sectors of society. And this is where the "supply-side" program seems badly out of touch with the reality of modern society.

The "supply-side" program assumes, at least implicitly, that the problem we face is a general economic decline—a decline that can be reversed by providing sufficient lures to ever-greater investment. But the notion of a *general* economic decline, as we've demonstrated, is misleading. Something far more complex has been taking place. Rather than a simple, overall stagnation, we are witnessing a complicated process of recomposition and "restratification," bringing new sources of affluence along with new forms of poverty. Economic shifts have been translated into complex changes in work, family, and other social institutions. Policies of "revitalization" that fail to take account of those changes—of the institutional structure that necessarily forms the context of economic life—will only deepen present inequalities, worsening the situation of those "losing" and accelerating the advance of those already "winning" in the social and economic reshuffling we've described.

Illustrations are not hard to come by. How will an economic "boom," fueled by tax cuts for the wealthy, help an unskilled single mother find economic security—especially when the same policies are, with the other hand, taking away public funds for child care that would enable her to take a job—if a job were there? How will growth in nursing homes and hamburger stands help a skilled blue-collar worker whose $20,000-a-year job has been lost to a more "productive" industrial robot? How will the expansion of defense industries in the Southwest help a young minority couple facing the runaway housing market in New York? Or an unemployed 18-year-old in Chicago's ghetto?

Dealing effectively with the new forms of impoverishment will require policies targeted directly to those groups most at risk in the modern economy—and to those sectors of the economy where inflation and recession have taken their worst toll. A program to confront the new inequality cannot simply bank on the "trickling down" of jobs and income from expanding private investment, but must involve active intervention in economic life toward explicit social goals.

Addressing these problems will require *more* "government intervention," not less; a larger (if more efficient) public sector, not a diminished one; more "planning," not less. We know that these strategies go strongly against the stream. But we believe that without them the alternative scenario is clear: a sharper division between the newly affluent and the newly poor; for the young, fast-vanishing opportunities for good jobs and decent housing; and continued inflation with its devastating pressures on home and family. The choice is clear. We will either decide to engage in serious, democratic public planning to redress the social imbalances generated by economic development or we will watch helplessly as an uncontrolled "revitalization" brings greater insecurity, desperation, and misery in its train.

STAGFLATION, INEQUALITY, AND
THE POLITICAL CULTURE

What are the prospects for that kind of democratic social planning? At first glance, the outlook seems less than hopeful. In the face of the injuries inflicted by the economic crisis, there have been some encouraging expressions of public mobilization and concern. But, at least as often, the crisis has seemed to generate cynicism and political withdrawal, epitomized by the fact that the winner of the 1980 presidential election came into office on only 26 percent of the potential popular vote. Contemporary politics—and contemporary American culture as a whole—often seem mired in narrow interest-group concerns and a spirit of individual indulgence.

And these responses—negativism, cynicism, withdrawal from social concern—are themselves partly rooted in the changes we have already described. The heightened insecurity that economic crisis has brought to personal life in America—the receding prospects for decent jobs and housing, the looming threat of downward mobility and of a pauperized old age—helps explain the resurgence of broader cultural themes of competition and individual survival. ("Tomorrow only the fit will survive," declares an ad for a new magazine for "entrepreneurs," "and only the *very* fit will flourish.") And it also offers fertile soil for the desperate focus on the "self" that Barbara Ehrenreich has aptly called a "psychological version of the 'lifeboat ethic' "—the "me-first" character of life lived mainly in the present because the future seems less and less certain or worth building toward. Given the particularly harsh effects of the economic crisis on family life, it isn't surprising that political campaigns narrowly focused on the "defense" of the traditional family—like the campaign against the Equal Rights Amendment—have enjoyed especially wide appeal in the era of "stagflation."

All of these tendencies have been reinforced by the increasing *fragmentation* we have described. When relative prosperity or impoverishment may hang on the timing of a house purchase or the fact of working in (say) the aerospace rather than the auto industry or having been born in 1940 rather than 1950, the sense of commonality of experience and needs disintegrates. Individual (or, at best, familial) solutions to social and economic problems can easily come to seem the only alternatives available, the only visible avenues to security and well-being.

This individualization is aggravated by the growing split between the newly affluent and other working people—what we might call the "Brazilianization" of the American class structure. Working people see some enjoying considerable success—"making it" in highly visible ways—while others sink; some buying second homes in the mountains, speedboats, and Cuisinarts, while others descend into the ranks of the welfare poor. Those differences act both as a spur to individual striving and as a demonstration that the proper management of personal life can bring significant rewards—that it can put you, as *Fortune* pants, on "a fast track to the good life." And for those at the upper reaches of the scale, it provides a sharp and nagging incentive to hold on more tightly to what they have.

These trends—fragmentation, individualization, the narrowing of political concern to family and personal life—are not the only ones now evident in the United States. As Michael Harrington has pointed out, the American people seem to be moving in several different ideological directions at once. There is a new theme of narrow self-seeking in American culture; but there is also—as public opinion polls reveal—a growing support for guaranteeing jobs through public programs and for accepting wage and price controls in response to runaway inflation. There is, in some quarters, a new reverence for private gain and the forces of the "market"; but there is also evidence of a growing concern for what the psychologist Urie Bronfenbrenner has called the "human ecology"—a recognition of the connectedness of the fabric of social life and a rejection of the periodically fashionable idea that human life should be left to the not-so-tender mercies of the "free market." Which trend will prevail depends crucially on the seriousness and energy with which we build a broad movement for democratic planning and control of economic life.

8
KEEPING THE POOR POOR

Paul Jacobs

Let me begin with a true story about how, for some poor people, pineapple juice tasted not sweet, but salty. At regular intervals, pineapple juice canneries must clean out the pipes that carry the juice from the crushing to the canning rooms. To do this, a salt solution is forced through the pipes and then flushed out before the new canning process starts again. A few years ago, one large cannery went through this cleaning operation and began running juice again before it was discovered that the pipes had not been totally purged of the salt solution. But, by that time, thousands of gallons of pineapple juice, all of it slightly salty, had already been processed and canned.

The cans, unlabeled, were sold at a very low price to a food distributor who specializes in handling offbrand and reject merchandise for sale in poor neighborhoods and communities. The distributor put a label on the cans and retailed them for about half the usual price for that size, making a very good profit for himself. Across the label was printed "No Sweetener Added," certainly an accurate statement of the juice's condition.

In both a real and symbolic sense, this otherwise trivial incident involving the sale of salty pineapple juice is characteristic of the relationships of the poor to society. The merchandise would have had little or no monetary value outside the poverty market. It seemed cheap to those who purchased it, although in reality, considering its actual value, it was very expensive. No complaints about the saltiness of the juice were recorded, and its sale was justified by the distributor on the basis that, even though the merchandise was imperfect, it was at least available to the poor who might not otherwise have been able to buy any.

Precisely the same set of characteristics are true for most of the life of the poor. As David Caplovitz has clearly demonstrated in his study, *The Poor Pay More*, not only do the poor pay more proportionately for what they get, but what they get for more money is often of inferior quality. Thus, the poverty market can be an extremely profitable one for those who specialize in selling to it, although the rewards are tempered by high risks.

The overall dimensions of the poverty market are reasonably well es-

From Leonard H. Goodman, ed., *Economic Progress and Social Welfare*, pp. 159–184. Copyright © 1966 National Conference on Social Welfare, Columbus, Ohio. Reprinted by permission of Columbia University Press and the Estate of Paul Jacobs.

tablished. It includes approximately 35,000,000 people divided into seven million families and four million unrelated individuals. Their total income is estimated at $28,000,000,000. (Oscar Gass in *Commentary*.) But the poor dispose of this income in their own distinctive ways.

To begin with, those who constitute the poverty class spend different proportions of their income for food, shelter, clothing, and medical care than are spent by the remaining four-fifths of the population. Nearly 29 percent of the average poor person's income goes into food expenditures, while those whose income exceeds $4,000 a year spend less than 24 percent of it for food. The cost of shelter for the poor is more than 29 percent of their incomes, in contrast to the 17 percent expended by those in the higher income brackets. Ironically, too, although the poor spend a higher proportion of their income for housing, what they get in exchange is always worse than similarly priced—or even lower-priced—middle-income housing.

The differences between the expenditures of the poor and other income groups on clothing and medical care are even sharper: the poor spend one-half as much of their income on clothing as do their economic betters, but a higher proportion on medical care, which, in accordance with the iron law of poverty, is almost always bad. And because the poor have far less money to spend, they are at the same time in much greater debt relative to their income than the middle and upper income brackets. (Interestingly enough, the only items on which both the poor and the rich spend the same proportion of their respective incomes are gifts and contributions.)

The food the poor eat is different from that purchased by the other segments of the population, even taking into account regional preferences; they seek recreation in different ways; they buy in different kinds of stores, although the prices they pay may be just as high or higher, and they buy some items, such as cockroach powder, rarely used by the rest of the consumers. Their overriding economic concerns are short-term rather than long-range ones, for they must worry about whether or not they will have enough money tomorrow rather than after retirement.

Yet these statistical differences do not adequately reflect the fact that poverty creates not only a different life style but a different emotional set as well. Anxiety and uncertainty, derived from their economic situation, dominate the orientation of the poor to the world.

Because of their anxiety and uncertainty certain social types unknown to us become prominent in the lives of the poor. The "mouse man" or the "six-for-fiver," for example, are familiar characters in many poor neighborhoods, just as the "mouse house" (loan company) is an important part of the appliance- and automobile-buying pattern of the poor. And although the "policy" industry is estimated to take in a quarter of a billion dollars annually in New York City alone, the "collectors" who can be found on every Harlem street corner will rarely be seen on the quiet streets of Riverdale. "Collectors" and "mouse men" live on the economic anxiety of the poor, without whom they could not thrive.

How large this anxiety factor looms in the lives of the poor is illustrated in almost all the problems they face. As we all know too well from our daily lives, the automobile is one of the most ubiquitous features of American material culture, and the quiet humming of its engine a great source of pride to its owner. But the battered old cars of the poor are noisy, and the sound of a loud engine rattle, an increasingly noisy rod, or a grinding bearing strikes panic in the hearts of the poor. If their car breaks down on the highway, or if it will not start in the morning, they cannot call the auto club. What may be merely a nuisance to others is a major disaster to them; they are caught in a trap from which they cannot escape without paying a great price. Generally, they cannot afford to have their cars fixed, but without a car many of them cannot go to work or look for employment, the two primary functions for which they need a car. And so, after they have found a relative or friend who will tow their disabled car back to their homes, they are forced to try fixing it themselves. (Public libraries get much less use in poor neighborhoods than in other areas, but what little use is made of them includes the frequent borrowing of do-it-yourself repair manuals.)

However, unlike the Model T or Model A Ford, the modern car is not likely to be fixed by anyone except a skilled mechanic. Indeed, if I have no other criterion by which to judge the character of a strange neighborhood, the number of junked cars on the streets or in yards serves as an accurate measure; the more abandoned cars, the poorer the area. After a while, the rusty and broken-down monuments of junk become so much a part of the landscape of poverty that no one even notices their presence.

When the poor must somehow face up to purchasing another car, the magnitude of the problem is likely to be overwhelming. Since approximately 60 percent of all the cars purchased in the United States are bought on time, automobile financing is a big business. And, as might be expected, the poor buy far more used than new cars: in 1962, only 9 percent of the new cars purchased on installment payments were bought by people whose income was below $3,000, but 40 percent of all the used cars were sold in the poverty market, 75 percent of them at less than $500. (University of Michigan Survey Research Center, Survey of Customer Finances.)

The cheapest way to buy a car—by means of a personal bank loan—is rarely open to the poor. In order to secure such a loan, at a simple interest rate, the prospective borrower must put up some collateral, such as stocks, a savings account, or property—assets rarely held by the poor as a matter of definition.

The next cheapest method is to get a bank loan on the car. For this, the bank usually requires a down payment of one-third to one-fourth in cash; then it will finance the car, holding a chattel mortgage on it until all the payments have been completed. The interest rates for such loans vary from 4 to 6 percent, depending on whether the bank also purchases paper from dealers, in which case the dealers must be protected. (The dealer will normally try to get 6 percent interest from buyers, although he will bargain about these rates and settle for 5.5 percent or even 5 percent. Then he will sell the sales contract to the banks for 4 percent, keeping the balance in his own reserve funds.)

Recently, I purchased a new car, and the contrast between the way in which that transaction was carried on and what happens when a poor person does the same thing was most revealing. After I picked out the car I wanted, I called a bank for some information about their low-cost loans. But instead of getting merely information, I got the loan, by telephone, in the space of about five to seven minutes. The bank official asked me where I lived, and after I gave him the address, which is in a "good" section of the city, he asked me if I owned my house. When I replied in the affirmative, he then inquired where I held charge accounts. After I named the stores, which were obviously all "good" ones by his standards, he asked the purchase price of the car and how much I was going to pay in cash. When I told him I would be paying between a quarter and a third down, he informed me I could have the loan without even having to come to the bank. And not once did he ask me what my income was, for my economic position—indeed my entire life pattern—was evident from my residential location and my choice of stores and my tone of voice.

The pattern of life for the poor is equally clear to him; and so poor people are rarely able to get car loans directly from banks, even if they apply in person. Banks don't like to make small loans, for the administrative costs are too high; and they are reluctant to make loans to people whose income is uncertain or whose credit rating is less than exemplary. To the poor, a bank is the place where the teller scowls as he cashes a welfare check and charges 25¢ for the service.

In Los Angeles recently, 8,067 interviews were conducted among all income groups to obtain data concerning the use of banks. Almost 18 percent of the families questioned refused to reveal their income, but 9.1 percent of those who did said they earned less than $250 a month; of this group 47 percent had checking accounts and 51 percent had savings accounts—somewhat higher percentages than the national average for this income level. (The bank that made the survey believes the reason for this was that the sample included a large proportion of retired people whose cash income may be below $250, but whose real income is higher.) Seventy-three percent of those in the $250–$650-a-month group and 91 percent in the $650–$1,000-a-month group had checking accounts.

Quite apart from the wide gap in the use of checking accounts between the poor and other groups, the data also revealed that the bank is not a place in which the poor conduct much business. For instance, 24 percent of all the families in the sample had obtained a loan within the two years prior to the survey, but only 8 percent of the poor had received such loans.

Whatever business the poor do have in banks is likely to involve savings accounts: branch banks located in poor neighborhoods usually have many more savings accounts than checking accounts. Indeed, the poor use their savings accounts as others use their checking accounts; their frequent withdrawals and deposits distinguish branch banks in poor neighborhoods from those located elsewhere.

But for many of the poor, a bank is far too intimidating a place even when they can afford to patronize it. I suspect, too, that the notion that some impersonal agency is keeping a permanent record of one's residence and of how much money one has, keeps away those who are worried about being found by the skip tracers who work for collection or welfare agencies.

The practice of paying bills by check as a matter of routine scarcely exists for the poor. Instead, more than half pay cash or use money orders, purchased either at the post office or, equally likely, from the liquor stores or gas stations which sell the commercial variety.

The commercial money-order business has developed in response to the peculiar need of the poverty market, where marginality is so dominant a theme. Unlike the money orders obtainable in the post office or the banks, commercial ones vary in price, depending on whether the location in which they are sold produces a high or low volume. But even if they are more expensive than bank or postal money orders, they are more convenient for the poor since they can be purchased in handy locations at night or on weekends. Moreover, they do not involve the permanent records associated with a checking account.

The commercial money-order business is a fairly simple one. The company maintains an account in a regular bank and the money order it sells is treated like a check; that is, the bank assumes no responsibility for the transaction beyond what is normal for bank and depositor. This fact is not usually clear to the poor; for the bank's name appears on the money order, which enhances the legitimacy of the transaction. Most of the companies operating in this field are legitimate, but occasionally one does go out of business, leaving the holder of the money order without recourse.

Commercial money-order companies are not regulated by state or federal agencies, and thus can charge whatever price they believe the market will bear. As a result, the rates vary; a company in a "good" location, one with a high volume of sales, can charge higher rates than one in an area where people rely upon post-office money orders or checking accounts. And since these commercial money orders are used almost ex- clusively to pay bills, they provide another illustration of the dictum that the poor, who can least afford it, pay more, even if only to pay their bills.

That basic principle operates throughout the lives of the poor, no mat- ter what other differences may exist among them. Thus, unless they be- long to credit unions, they must finance any substantial purchases through dealers or through finance companies whose rates vary enor- mously, depending upon what they find the traffic will bear.

Finance-company rates *are* incredible. There is no point in going into a detailed analysis of their operations, for these have been explored and documented by the Congress. (No action has been taken, incidentally, to reduce the exorbitant rates of interest exacted from the poor.) Instead, let me use but one example of the possible range. If a middle-class person borrows $2,500 from a bank on a 36-month personal loan, it will cost him $238.16; financing the purchase of a car at the usual rate of 6 percent will cost him $449.84 for the same period of time. At a loan company, a "mouse house," the normal charge is $674.84. Thus, for the privilege of borrowing the same sum of money, a man with savings or other assets pays $346.68 less than the one without resources.

Not only do the poor pay more for credit, they also run greater risk of losing their purchases. Dealers will normally extend credit to any pro- spective purchaser so long as he has no record of repossession, even though he may already be in debt to a number of finance companies, as are so many of the poor. So long as the buyer can make a down payment, either with his own money or by getting a loan from a "mouse house," the dealer will sell the commodity. However, if the buyer gets laid off or has an emergency drain on income and falls 30 days behind in payments without attempting to contact whoever is holding the contract, an inex- orable process starts. The contract holder hires a "recovery outfit," a com- pany which has the legal authority, under the terms of the contract, to simply repossess the car or television set in any way it can. Normally, in the case of a car, this is done either at the debtor's place of work or at home, late at night, while he is asleep. Appliances or furniture are simply removed from the home.

Once the property is back in the possession of the mortgage holder, the debtor is offered the opportunity to get it back by making up the pay- ments. If he cannot pay, he is sent a "5-day letter" which by law gives him five days to either pay up or refinance, at additional interest charges, of course.

If the debtor does neither, the property reverts to the mortgage holder, who then resells it. After the repossessed item has been sold, the mortgage holder will attempt to recover from the customer the difference between the unpaid balance and the price the property brought at resale. The recovery attempt is made by a collection agency which gets half of whatever is recovered. The agency goes to court, routinely, to obtain orders to attach the wages of debtors. Just as routinely, the court issues these orders merely on the presentation of the contract and the record of payments, but without notification to the buyer or his representative. The court order is then presented to the debtor's employer, who must go to the administrative expense of withholding the amount specified from the employee's wages and paying it over to the agency. Very often, the employer simply fires the employee rather than be bothered.

The same process operates regardless of the purchaser's income. Obviously, the chances are much greater that the poor, who are generally not well educated, and whose income is low and irregular, will get caught up in the endless series of credit traps. From the dealer or finance company's viewpoint, the justification for their very high interest rates lies in the risk that the purchaser will be unable to make his payments and will skip town.

Normally, if a credit manager has losses of more than 1 percent a year, he is in danger of losing his own job, for he is apparently using bad judgment about who represents a good credit risk. Yet in some parts of the poverty market, a credit manager who loses less than 10 percent or 12 percent of his customers is considered equally lacking in judgment; he, obviously, is setting too rigorous standards and is thus keeping away potential customers.

The 10 percent or 12 percent loss rate is taken into account when the retail price is established on an item to be sold within the poverty market. In the jewelry industry, for example, a normal markup is 100 percent, but for jewelry sold to the poor, this markup often goes to 300 percent and even higher. Thus, as a rule, a ring, for which a jewelry store pays a $50 wholesale price, is sold for $100 on a cash or short-term credit basis. That same ring will retail for $300 in the poverty market, where the credit jeweler will attempt to get as large a down payment as possible in order to protect himself against the possibility of default on future weekly payments. If the customer can be persuaded to make a $60 down payment, the retailer will have covered the price of the ring and made a modest profit. From then on everything he receives helps swell his profit rate.

The fact that the retailer wants a large number of customers who will enter into such credit arrangements requires that his credit standards be considerably lower than those established by the merchant who caters to middle- and upper-income families. The credit manager in the poverty market demands of his customer only a fixed place of residence and a fixed income, no matter how small, either from a job or from some government agency. In fact, what the retailer is selling is credit itself, and his efforts are bent on trying to keep the customer always in debt to him. He attempts, wherever possible, to draw the customer into the store to make the weekly payments so that he can continue to sell additional merchandise, often by displaying tempting "bargain" items close to the payment counter. In these transactions the price is quoted as a dollar a week rather than some fixed total sum, and the new purchases are urged on the customer on the basis that it will only mean continuing to pay the dollar a week. Every effort is expended to keep the customer on the books continuously in a state of delicate equilibrium in which the desire for goods will outweigh the anxiety associated with the perpetual need to keep up payments.

My own experience living among the poor has been a vivid demonstration of the axiom that the poor pay more, proportionately, in exchange for less. The food stores in poor neighborhoods are more monopolistic than stores in other areas. For one thing, the poor are simply less mobile than middle-class people; shopping around for bargains by bus is much more difficult than shopping by car. The poor are less likely to leave their own neighborhoods and less likely to make a large-scale expenditure on food at any one time. The amount of money they spend on food is the only nonfixed item in their budgets. Thus, they must buy it daily, and never in the larger amounts on which they save money; for what they spend on food may be the carfare they will need tomorrow to get their sick kids to the hospital. It is this need to keep the food budget in a fluid state that accounts, in part, for the low rate of participation in the food-stamp programs: families on welfare, or with uncertain income, cannot spend a sizable sum of money at one time, especially at the beginning of the month when rent, utilities, and other fixed-cost items must be paid.

The kinds of food they buy also reveal the great differences between their life styles and those of the other groups. The poor buy markedly less meat, poultry, eggs, dairy products, fruits, and vegetables than do those in higher income brackets. The only items which they buy in significantly greater amounts are grain products. Dried beans, bread, spaghetti, macaroni, and other starches are what the poor use to fill their stomachs, while their children drink far more soda pop than milk.

Those who specialize in selling in the poverty market can count on certain other characteristic patterns of behavior among their customers. Middle-income people tend to read advertising about sales and to take advantage of them; not so the poor. Nor do they readily buy secondhand merchandise: the Goodwill stores are patronized more by bohemians and the middle class than by the poor. They do not save trading stamps as avidly as middle-class families, and they do not participate in "giveaway" programs. They combine an inability to discern real value with a psychic need to buy something new and a financial incapacity to buy more than they require for their immediate purpose. Welfare recipients are often at the mercy of retailers who demand that a fixed amount of goods be purchased before they will cash a relief check. Even worse, they may insist, as a condition of cashing welfare checks, that their customers buy slow-moving items for which the hapless consumer may have little or no use. When that happens, the poor have no choice, for usually they require the cash as quickly as they can get it because some other pressing need is at their throats.

Vulnerability to exploitation of their pervasive anxiety is only one of many special characteristics of the economic situation of the poor. Their economic milieu is also marked by the fact that different kinds of goods and services are available to them than to those in other circumstances. This is, in part, a reflection of their distinctive value system, but to some extent their values are shaped, in turn, by their consumer choices. For instance, reading a morning newspaper (while drinking their nonsalty pineapple juice) is a commonplace, routine act for most Americans, but it is not a characteristic pattern of the poor. Instead, they watch television and listen to the radio, and these media, almost exclusively, mold their view of the world.

. . . Bad economic circumstances force the poor into seeking abnormal solutions to those economic problems which create far more anxiety for them than the same problems do for the rest of society. Indeed, pitifully few responses are available to what is the basic fact of economic life amongst the poor: that more money must go out each month to pay a myriad of bills from rent and utilities, to furniture payments, to automobile installments, than comes in from wages, salaries, or welfare payments. And since income is capricious while the monthly bills must constantly be met, anxiety is always present; by law, the consequences of nonpayment are inevitable: eviction, the gas shut off, the car or furniture repossessed. Thus, for example, a working mother, without a husband, may have to leave her job because of the unreliability of baby sitters. Once this happens, she and her children are caught in a whirlpool which will suck them all down into despair.

Many people—most, perhaps—who are not poor also go into debt for consumer items such as cars, furniture or appliances, medical care, clothing, jewelry, and so on. But if the low-wage earner is out of work for an extended period, or if his wife loses her job, the very delicate balance between wages and debts is upset and the family gets into real trouble.

When he falls behind in installment payments, a characteristic response of the low-income person is to go to a finance company to "consolidate" his debts and to undertake a series of single monthly payments, presumably according to his ability to pay. As we know, the interest rates are outrageous, but most people in these straits seem to have few alternatives indeed.

For those whose debts continue to escalate despite consolidation, or for those who cannot even get credit from the finance companies, only slender choices remain. One is to give their children away, a practice common among urban Negroes who have simply adapted a Southern rural custom—and out of the same economic motives. If a mother cannot support her children, she will "give" them to a relative, usually the child's grandparents, to raise. Usually, she is expected to provide some money for the child's upkeep, but frequently, of course, she cannot. . . .

More unique to the poor is a sense of gratitude for what others assume to be their natural due. For example, they view installment buying as a privilege to which they are not really entitled—because they do not feel worthy of receiving the fruits of the society. As a result, they are much less likely to grow indignant over the exploitive rates of interest and carrying charges they pay for the right to use merchandise which is not paid for in full. As a consequence of this attitude, the poor are much better customers than the rich from the retailer's point of view: they are not so quick to complain about the quality of the merchandise; they are much more easily intimidated; and they shop far less carefully. The notion of depending upon an organization such as Consumers Union to help protect their interests is completely meaningless to the poor; it assumes a degree of self-consciousness about themselves as consumers which they do not have as yet.

How can the poor become more self-conscious, self-interested consumers? It does little good to educate them about what foods make up a proper nutritional balance when their food budget fails to match the requirements, or when it remains the only item which gives them any financial flexibility. Indeed, the whole notion of a budget implies some ability to plan ahead, to project actions on the basis of a stable income which is enough to meet the reasonable demands put upon it. But the income of the poor is either capricious or inadequate—or both—and only the demands made upon it are stable, fixed by forces and institutions over which they have little or no measure of control.

Thus, I am somewhat pessimistic about the value of educational programs directed toward helping the poor become better consumers. What good will it do to convince the Indians of the Pima reservation in Arizona that their children should drink less pop and eat more meat when very few of the mud "sandwich" houses on the reservation have either electricity or water? Milk and meat spoil in the hot Arizona summer unless they are refrigerated; soda pop and beans do not. What the Pima Indians need is either to cease being poor or to become much more aware of their rights despite their poverty. Such an awareness can come, I believe, only as part of a *general* rise in their living standards, or of a *general* awakening to their rights through some form of political action. . . .

All of us are born into a state of anxiety, and many, or even most, of us must cope, throughout our lives, with deep-rooted feelings of personal inadequacy. For the poor, these feelings are continuously reinforced by the economic circumstances in which they live and by their relationships with the rest of society. In an egalitarian society where everyone is living in poverty, being poor generates neither much anxiety nor strong feelings of inadequacy. But in a society such as ours, which measures achievement primarily by financial and material standards, to be poor is to be scorned by others, and even worse, by one's own self. It is for this reason that in America the taste and smell of poverty are so sour.

9
TAX POLITICS

Robert M. Brandon, Jonathan Rowe, and Thomas H. Stanton

Broad based movements for reform are one of the oldest American traditions. They are older than the Declaration of Independence, the Constitution, the two-party system, and either of the major political parties today. From the colonial riots protesting the British Sugar and Stamp Acts, the Revolution itself, to the Whiskey Rebellion, the latter-nineteenth-century Populist agitation for progressive income taxes, and all the lesser-known but no less ardent battles in the states and localities, Americans have risen up against economic injustice imposed by established powers. Today, the need for reform impresses itself regularly. In June 1974, a poll by Louis Harris reported that 79 percent of the Americans surveyed agreed that the rich get richer and the poor get poorer (versus 45 percent in 1966); 78 percent agreed that special interests get more from the government than do ordinary people; and 75 percent felt that the tax laws are written to help the rich. Taxpayers have been swamping public meetings, marching and demonstrating, besieging their elected officials with letters and petitions to make known their view that the tax laws need reform.

We read in the newspapers of multinational oil companies and other major corporations enjoying record profits but paying little or nothing in taxes. We learn of well-heeled stalwarts of the expense-account set who pay a rate of tax close to, or even less than ours. The bewildering complexity of the tax laws states the case eloquently. As we try to puzzle out our federal income tax returns, or try to follow the explanations of our local assessor, it becomes very plain that whatever is in those thousands of pages of federal tax laws and regulations, and in their state and local counterparts, it wasn't put there for us. Taxes hurt, and they are hurting ordinary taxpayers increasingly. Between 1953 and 1972, the total tax bill of the typical family of four increased 70 percent as a percent of income.

People, sometimes well-meaning, sometimes not, often divert discussions of tax reform into debates over spending. Spending is indeed a crucial issue. Most people agree there is too much of it on the wrong things, and perhaps not enough of it on the right things, though they disagree on what these "right" and "wrong" things may be. The spending ploy is a tempting one. Staggered by the bulk and complexity of the tax laws, and confused by the sophisticated arguments by which special interests defend their loopholes, spending seems a much simpler and easier target on which to vent frustrations. But it misses the mark. Whether spending is large or small, the question is how the burden of paying for this spending will be allotted.

What Is Fair Taxation?

The principle for allocation of the tax burden that the authors choose is ability-to-pay. People and corporations should contribute to the commonwealth in the proportion that they are able. This view is neither radical nor novel. No less an apostle of free enterprise than Adam Smith argued in 1776 that "the subjects of every state ought to contribute toward the support of the government as nearly as possible in proportion to their respective abilities."

Smith pointed to a basis for the ability-to-pay principle that isn't always remembered. "The expence of government to the individuals of a great nation," he said, "is like the expence of management to the joint tenants of a great estate, who are all obliged to contribute in proportion to their respective interests in the estate." The more one has, Smith was saying, the bigger one's stake in the social order, and therefore the more expense of maintaining and protecting that order the taxpayer should bear.

Progressive taxes are a direct attempt to embody the ability-to-pay principle. The phrase arises constantly in discussions of tax reform. We should try to understand what it means.

A tax is progressive if it is larger on those who have a lot of the thing taxed than it is on those who have a little. The more the taxpayer has, the higher the rate becomes.

The reason for progressive taxes is simple and was well stated by the political philospher Montesquieu, writing about the tax system in ancient Athens:

It was judged that each had equal physical necessities, and that those necessities ought not to be taxed; that the useful came next, and that it ought to be taxed, but less than what was superfluous; and lastly, that the greatness of the tax on the superfluity should repress the superfluity.

In other words, as applied to income taxes, people need a certain amount to acquire their basic necessities, and this amount should not be taxed. The more they have above this amount, the less they need it, and thus the more heavily it can be taxed. It bears repeating that the intent of progressive taxes is not to afflict the rich, but rather to put the tax burden where it will cause the least suffering.

Progressivity should not just be measured in terms of income. A property tax is progressive if it taxes people with lots of property at higher rates than people with little. It is common, however, to rate the progressivity of taxes solely in terms of how the taxes affect taxpayers at different income levels. This is a major blind spot in our thinking about taxes and is a reason why wealth taxes have made so little headway in the United States.

The federal income tax illustrates a progressive rate structure. The rates on unmarried individuals (in 1974) rose from 14 percent on the first $500 of taxable income, to 15 percent on the next $500, 16 percent on the next $500, up to 70 percent on all income over $100,000. Note that the very rich do not pay the highest rates on all of their income, but only on the income above set levels.

The opposite of a progressive tax is a regressive tax, when the less a person has of the thing taxed, the higher is the rate he pays. The social security tax is a perfect example of a regressive tax. Workers making $15,000 a year pay $825, which is 5.5 percent of their income. Meanwhile an executive pulling in $100,000 a year pays the same $825, which is less than one-tenth of 1 percent of his or her income.

A tax which is neither progressive nor regressive is called proportional. This means that everyone, rich and poor alike, is taxed at the same rate. A tax rate which goes neither up nor down, but stays the same for everyone, is called a *flat rate.*

The income tax is not the only tax that can be progressive. A sales tax could be progressive, with rates increasing according to the size of the sale. A permit fee could be progressive if the fee increased according to the size of the business applying. A property tax could be progressive, with people paying a rate that was high or low according to how much property they owned. The Australians have such a progressive property tax, and in the United States it could be the most progressive tax of all, since property ownership in this country is more concentrated among a wealthy few than is income.

Similarly, progressive rates are not the only way to make a tax progressive. A tax can also be progressive or regressive according to what it taxes.

For example, a sales tax could be progressive in a rough sense if food and medicines were exempted but attorneys', real estate brokers', and other professional service fees were taxed. An income tax would be roughly progressive, even with flat rates, if workers' earnings were exempted but income from stocks, bonds, and sales of property were fully taxed.

By the same token, we should not be fooled by tax rate structures. They tell only half the story. Exemptions and loopholes are the other half. The most progressive rate structure in the world is not worth much if special provisions allow the most well-off to slip through untouched. The key is not the statutory tax rate, but the rates people actually pay, taking into account all exemptions, deductions, and other special provisions. This tax rate that people actually pay is called the "effective" tax rate. As we shall see, there is a vast difference between the rates listed in the Internal Revenue Code and the effective rates that taxpayers end up paying.

Despite the long tradition of the ability-to-pay principle, the lip service we pay to it, and its supposed embodiment in the federal income tax, the tax system we have today falls far short of this ideal. Nationwide, and all taxes considered, the very wealthy pay taxes at virtually the same rate as that imposed on people far less well-off.

THE TAX SYSTEM TODAY

Our present tax system is the product of a continuing move away from the ideals of progressive taxation. It is important to understand that there are three basic ways in which the ability-to-pay principle has been undermined.

First, more reliance on taxes which tend to be regressive and proportional rather than on those which tend to be progressive makes the whole tax system less fair. For example, a state may have a progressive income tax and a general sales tax which includes food and medicine and is highly regressive. The over-all tax burden may be proportional, rich and poor paying about the same percentage of their income in taxes. If the same state is facing financial difficulties and must raise added revenues, the two most apparent choices would be to raise the income tax rates or to add a penny to the sales tax. By relying more heavily on the income tax, the state's burden would fall more heavily on those most able to afford it—taxes would become more progressive. Raising the sales tax would increase the tax burden on low income groups, making the state's over-all tax burden more regressive and further eroding the ability-to-pay principle.

Unfortunately, most states have chosen this latter course. The 1974 New Jersey State Legislature, for example, rejected a proposed progressive income tax to reduce the burden of the property tax and to help equalize school financing. The people of New Jersey and their representatives apparently resisted the new income tax even though the vast majority of taxpayers (low and moderate income people) would have had a lighter over-all tax burden.

In similar fashion, the federal government has been placing greater and greater reliance on the highly regressive payroll tax to fund social security benefits instead of financing these through the income tax.

The second major source of erosion of the ability-to-pay principle is the eating away of the tax base itself through exemptions and deductions. A state, for example, might have adopted long ago a comprehensive property tax on a person's total wealth—real, personal, and intangible property. This same state later might have exempted personal and intangible property such as stocks and bonds. As a result, the tax originally designed to tax total wealth would now fall more lightly on wealthy individuals and be less progressive.

The erosion of the tax base, and therefore of progressivity, in the federal income tax structure is striking. As set forth at the beginning of the Internal Revenue Code, the legal tax rates on individuals range from 14 percent on the first $500 of income, up to 70 percent on income over $100,000. These rates originally were designed to apply to "all income from whatever source derived." But the Congress, in the following hundreds of pages, has exempted an ever-growing number of items from the definition of taxable income. They have excluded one half of all capital gains income (gains from selling property), 22 percent of income from oil wells, all the income from interest on state and local bonds, and certain pension and retirement benefits. They have allowed deductions for mortgage interest and property tax payments, accelerated depreciation, oil drilling, cattle breeding, and child care. And finally, they have granted special tax rates for income splitting and heads of households. All of these erode the income tax base and do so much more for those with high incomes than for those less well-off. As a result, the federal income tax is much less progressive than the statutory rates seem to indicate [Table 1].

Careless administration is the third and probably least noted source of tax injustice. Local governments lose billions of property tax dollars each year through faulty assessing and collection practices. State governments miss perhaps one-half of the taxes corporations are supposed to pay, because audits are so weak. Even the federal government fails to collect significant revenues, especially from businesses and recipients of stock dividends. It is the largest taxpayers with the most complicated tax situations who benefit from this weak administration. The typical wage earner's taxes are withheld from the weekly paycheck, and that's the end of it.

One form of erosion can encourage another. If, for instance, exemptions or loopholes in the estate tax system substantially erode the tax base and

Table 1   High Erosions in the Tax
          Base Undermine the
          Ability-to-Pay Principle

Income Class° (Thousands of Dollars)	Effective Rate (%)
0–3	0.3
3–5	4.6
5–10	8.6
10–15	10.9
15–20	12.8
20–25	14.5
25–50	17.3
50–100	23.8
100–500	24.6
500–1,000	27.2
1,000 and over	29.8
All classes†	13.1

°Income is equal to adjusted gross income as
defined in the Internal Revenue Code, modified to include the full amount of capital
gains plus losses receiving special treatment.
†Includes negative income class not shown
separately.
Source: From Edward R. Fried and others,
*Setting National Priorities: The 1974 Bud-
get*, Tables 3–6 and 3–8. Copyright © 1973
by the Brookings Institution. Reprinted by
permission.

thereby cut down revenues, the government may make up the lost revenues by increasing the excise (sales) tax on gasoline.

Another example is the corporate income tax. This tax has been so deci-
mated by special tax breaks or subsidies since World War II that its contribution to the federal revenues dropped from 34 percent in 1944 to a
paltry 14 percent in 1974. This loss of revenues had to be made up somewhere, and a quick look at federal tax receipts shows where. During the
same thirty years the regressive payroll tax was rising from 3.9 percent of
federal revenues in 1944 to nearly 30 percent in 1974. As the corporate
tax base continues to erode, payroll taxes will continue to climb.

Federal Taxes Today

The federal tax burden is by far the largest for most taxpayers. About
two-thirds of all taxes are collected by the federal government, amount-

ing to some $300 billion in fiscal 1976. These revenues are collected through a variety of taxes, on individual incomes, corporate incomes, payrolls (for social security and unemployment), estates and gifts, excise or sales taxes on liquor, tobacco, gasoline, and other items, and duties on imports [Table 2].

Individual Income Taxes   The individual income tax is the most important source of federal tax revenues, contributing about 45 percent of total receipts. Reliance on the income tax has increased rapidly since the beginning of World War II. In 1939, the tax yielded about $1 billion, but by 1974 it was bringing in $118 billion. Lawmakers leaned on the income tax to this extent because of its supposed fairness—the close relationship between people's incomes and their taxpaying ability. Unfortunately, as the reliance on the income tax increased, its progressive nature was undermined.

The late Louis Eisenstein, a prosperous yet candid corporate tax lawyer, developed a wry perspective on our tax system. "Our taxes represent a continuing struggle among competing interests for the privilege of paying the least," he said. And, of course, some taxpayers are much better equipped than others to pass their burdens onto someone else.

Economists Joseph Pechman and Benjamin Okner calculate that if all of the special tax breaks were eliminated, we could cut the income tax rates by an average of 43 percent. Wealthy individuals who now effectively reduce their tax bills by more than 43 percent would then actually pay more, while the majority would pay less.

Though averages show how tax preferences have cut into the progressivity of the income tax, they do not show the great reduction in the tax burden that some individuals enjoy. In 1972, income tax breaks allowed an estimated 37,000 American families with incomes over $20,000 to get away without paying any federal income taxes. Moreover, 402 of those non-taxpayers actually made over $100,000 a year. Among them was multimillionaire Stewart Mott, heir to a large General Motors fortune, who told CBS-TV: "I paid about zero tax to the federal government" in 1972 on income of roughly $1 million.

Besides those who pay no taxes, many wealthy taxpayers manage to pay very little. Ed Riley, who paid only $300 federal income taxes on the $293,000 he made in 1971, tours the country telling people—for a fee— how to use tax preferences to do it themselves. That year, with or without Ed Riley's advice, almost 100,000 Americans reduced their taxes by an average of at least $62,000 each through federal income tax preferences. Their federal income taxes were an average of only $1,700 (about 2.5 percent) each.

The Corporate Income Tax   In most years prior to World War II, the corporate income tax was the major source of federal revenues. In 1944,

Table 2   Budget Receipts by Source (in Billions of Dollars)
This [table] shows the various sources of federal tax revenues (in billions of dollars) and their contribution to over-all federal budget receipts (in percentages).

	1974		1975		1976 (estimated)	
Individual income taxes	119.0	(45%)	122.4	(44%)	130.8	(44%)
Corporation income taxes	38.6	(15%)	40.6	(14%)	40.1	(13%)
Social insurance taxes and contributions	76.8	(29%)	86.4	(31%)	92.6	(31%)
Excise taxes	16.8	(6%)	16.6	(6%)	16.9	(6%)
Other receipts	13.7	(5%)	14.0	(5%)	17.2	(6%)
	264.9	(100)	281.0	(100)	297.5	(100)

Source: Report of the House Budget Committee, FY 1976 Budget.

corporate income tax revenues made up 34 percent of the federal receipts; since then they have steadily declined until they now account for only 14 percent of federal revenues, far behind individual income and payroll taxes. However, they are still an important source of revenues, amounting to $39 billion in 1974.

Should income taxes apply to corporations at all, or should they bypass corporations and focus on the shareholder? Business interests are not the only ones raising this question. Earnest tax reformers argue that in some ways the corporate income tax opens the floodgates to tax avoidance, providing the foundation for numerous corporate tax subsidies.

Supporters of the corporate income tax say that if corporations were not taxed, wealthy shareholders could avoid taxes by keeping the business from distributing the profits as dividends. Instead, the profits would stay in the corporation, pushing up the value of its stock. The shareholders would get their piece of these profits when they sold the stock, enjoying in the process the special capital gains rates that are one-half the ordinary rates.

Opponents reply that such avoidance could easily be curbed by limiting the amounts corporations could accumulate, or by attributing retained earnings to the shareholder. They also observe that many advantages would ensue from dumping the corporate tax and taxing the shareholders directly on corporate profits. This would wipe out at a stroke the plethora of loopholes that not only permit the corporations (and thus their shareholders) to escape taxes but also distort economic activity as the corporations plot intricate strategies to qualify for the loopholes.

Is the corporate tax progressive? It can be argued that any tax on corporations can be progressive to the extent that the tax is borne by the corporation, since the holders of corporate stock are in upper income brackets. In competitive industries, the tax is more often absorbed by the company than passed on to customers in the form of higher prices. In less competitive industries, taxes can more readily be passed on to customers through higher prices. Reducing taxes in the latter instance would only mean that all taxpayers would incur a great tax burden in order to subsidize the purchasers of the products of those industries. Because of the different assumptions as to who bears the burden of the corporate tax, there is no clear answer as to how progressive the present tax is.

Some economists argue that the tax is borne by the corporation and therefore by its shareholders. Others argue that the tax is passed forward to the consumers in the form of higher prices. Still others believe the tax is passed back to the workers in the form of lower wages. A large number hold that the tax is borne by all three groups, but primarily by the shareholders. Economist Joseph Pechman has concluded under this view that federal and state corporate income taxes are, in fact, more progressive than federal and state income taxes on individuals.

Given this high degree of progressivity, it is regrettable that the corporate income tax is bearing a diminishing share of the federal tax burden.

The idea of eliminating the corporate income tax and taxing shareholders directly for corporate profits is referred to as "integration" of the corporate and the individual income tax. This concept will be discussed in coming years as part of the tax-reform debate. As with many areas of taxation, integration can be good or bad depending on how it is accomplished. Unfortunately, most proposals that have been advanced tend simply to cut taxes for stockholders. They go only part way in integrating the two systems.

Ideally, corporate tax integration could be a progressive step that would tax stockholders at their high tax brackets, while eliminating current corporate subsidies such as capital gains tax rates and accelerated depreciation. However, one version of integration proposed by Treasury Secretary Simon in 1975 is really just a reduction in the taxes stockholders pay on dividends. It does not end capital gains treatment or the other subsidies. Since 50 percent of corporate stockholders are in the richest 1 percent of the country's population, lowering their taxes would be a highly regressive step that would give even more federal tax money to the rich. Even though integration is capable of making things better, the Simon version would only make them worse.

Profits are paid out to stockholders in two ways. About 40 percent of profits is usually paid out directly in the form of dividends. Dividends are included in a stockholder's regular income and are taxed at whatever tax rate he or she is ordinarily subject to.

The other 60 percent of a corporation's after-tax profits is paid to stockholders in an indirect way. The corporation holds these profits for expansion and investment. This makes the company richer, and the richer the company, the more valuable its stock becomes; therefore stockholders can readily regain these profits by selling their stock. The income they get in this way is treated as a capital gain and is taxed at only half the rate of dividends or wages.

Under full integration, all profits would be taxed at the stockholder level. The 60 percent of profits that is currently kept to generate capital gains would be taxed at progressive rates rather than at the special capital gains rates. Under Simon's partial integration plan, the capital gains loophole is kept, the only change being that one tax rather than two is imposed on dividends.

Of course, progressive full integration would require the elimination of capital gains rates and other preferences that reduce the actual tax rates shareholders currently pay. Without that, tax reformers should not support the idea of tax integration. It could simply lower taxes further on corporation stockholders at a time when the tax burden of corporations and their owners has already been reduced to unacceptable levels.

While tax preferences lower corporate tax rates, they do not provide uniform relief. Some corporations may pay a 40 percent tax on their profits while others pay 15 percent, 5 percent, or nothing. In 1974, for instance, G.M. paid taxes at a rate of 39 percent, while Westinghouse paid at a rate of only 16 percent. Typically, the tax laws favor one industry over another, producing wide variations in industry by industry effective tax rates [Table 3].

A study by Representative Charles Vanik (D-Ohio) of 143 of the nation's largest corporations showed an effective 1973 tax rate of only 27.1 percent, down from 29.6 percent in 1971. (The statutory corporate tax rate is 48 percent.) Vanik found ten corporations within combined profits of $976 million paying no federal income tax at all. These included companies such as Con Ed of New York, Chemical New York Corporation, and Bankers Trust. In fact, seven companies actually received credits to reduce past or future tax bills. Another twenty corporations with 1973 profits of $5.3 billion paid between 1 percent and 20 percent in taxes. McDonnell-Douglas, for instance, the giant aircraft corporation, paid only 3.2 percent on $200 million. (The company paid no federal income tax in 1971 and 1972 on yearly incomes over $100 million.) The list goes on: Chrysler Corporation, 7.5 percent; National Cash Register, 9 percent; Uniroyal, 6.5 percent, etc. ITT, one of the nation's largest corporations, paid only 10.1 percent on $470 million profit; in 1972 ITT had paid only 1 percent on profits of $376 million.

The nation's oil companies have been unusually adept at corporate tax avoidance even while they pull in record profits. For the nineteen largest oil companies, those profits surpassed an incredible $18.5 billion in 1973. Yet according to U.S. Oil Week, their 1973 U.S. income tax bill averaged only 6.5 percent: Exxon paid 5.4 percent, Texaco only 1.6 percent, Mobile 2.2 percent, Gulf 1.1 percent, and Standard of California 4.1 percent.

Table 3   Effective Corporate Tax Rates by Industry on Worldwide Income

The worldwide rate on worldwide income usually shows the real income tax burden for most industries. Their U.S. rate appears lower because foreign income taxes are credited against U.S. taxes. For the extractive industries, the U.S. rate represents their real income tax burden since their payments to foreign governments, though credited as income taxes, are actually royalty payments.

Industry	# of Co.'s	Worldwide Rate on Worldwide Income	Share to Foreign Government [# of Co.'s]	U.S. Rate on Worldwide Income
Beverages	6	39.9	(16.7) [3]	31.5
Chemical	12	36.2	(11.8) [12]	24.4
Commercial banks	12	16.1	(9.9) [12]	8.4
Conglomerates	10	29.3	(5.4) [9]	24.5
Drug companies	12	36.7	(14.5) [12]	22.4
Electronics	11	41.2	(9.1) [9]	33.7
Food processors	10	41.5	(14.6) [9]	28.3
Metals and mining	10	25.5	(8.2) [10]	17.7
Oil	10	37.0	(25.4) [10]	11.5
Paper	8	34.5	(11.2) [5]	27.5
Retailers	11	33.5	(14.9) [3]	29.4
Steel	13	39.9	(11.7) [1]	34.2
Timber	10	40.9	(4.9) [5]	34.5
Trucks and equipment	10	39.1	(10.4) [7]	31.7

Source: Compiled by Tax Analysts and Advocates from SEC filings.

Commercial banks also get high marks as students of applied tax avoidance. Through the use of a large array of tax breaks, commercial banks have been able to lower their effective tax rate, according to the Federal Deposit Insurance Corporation, from 38.3 percent in 1961 to less than 15 percent in 1973. Chase Manhattan, the nation's third largest bank, paid 2.5 percent in federal income taxes. First National City kicked in 14.1 percent of its $300 million profits to the U.S. Treasury, while Western Bancorp, Chemical New York, Bankers Trust, and Continental Illinois Bank paid no U.S. taxes at all on combined incomes of $330 million.

These corporations were not the great exception. Among all 143 companies, profits rose in 1973 nearly $7 billion, or 25.8 percent, while tax payments rose only $740 million, or 10 percent.

In presenting his report to Congress, Vanik said, "In 1974 during economic hard times, corporations are crying for tax relief. This study is a reminder that many giant corporations already pay little or nothing in federal income taxes and that across-the-board industry tax breaks will only add to the list of profitable corporate tax freeloaders."

Social Security Payroll Tax   The fastest growing and most regressive of federal taxes is the payroll tax. It is second only to the individual income tax as a revenue source, bringing in nearly $77 billion, or 29 percent of the entire federal budget in 1974. This share is up from only 4 percent in 1944, 10 percent in 1954, and 20 percent in 1964, and it will rise even higher as schedule increases in the tax take effect in future years.

Payroll taxes for social security were originally designed for a system in which workers would set aside funds for their retirement, receiving future benefits based on their past earnings. Retired people today, however, receive social security benefits far greater than were their "contributions" to the system. Benefits include, in addition, social security payments, retirement income credits, supplemental security; Medicare and Medicaid are included as well. Since social security is no longer an insurance-type system at all, but actually just another federal expenditure, payroll taxes should be viewed as simply another source of federal revenues contributing to the support of a number of federal programs. Relying on it to the extent that we have, under the guise of an "insurance system," has greatly eroded the ability-to-pay principle.

The present social security payroll tax is a flat 5.85 percent on the first $14,100 a worker earns, matched by another 5.85 percent from the employer. Although in theory only half the tax is deducted from the worker's paycheck and the other half is paid directly by the employer, economists generally agree that the whole 11.7 percent tax, in fact, comes out of wages or is reflected in lower fringe benefits. If there were no payroll tax, wages would rise by approximately the amount now paid by the employer.

This payroll tax appears to be a proportional or flat-rate tax. Why, then, is the payroll tax regressive? The reason is that while the payroll tax shows a striking lack of particular loopholes—all wages are taxed—it does have one very large loophole. All income above $14,100 is completely exempt from the tax. That, combined with the flat rate, makes the payroll tax very regressive—low-income families and individuals pay a much higher proportion of their income in payroll taxes than do higher income families [Table 4].

The present 5.85 percent rates will continue to rise automatically to 7.2 percent by the year 2000. The ever increasing yearly cost of social security benefits for retired persons will be paid more and more by present workers. Thus, the growing financial burden of the social security tax falls on the taxpayer, but not on all taxpayers. Instead, the wage earner alone will make up for the erosion in the social security trust fund every year at

Table 4   The Social Security
              Payroll Tax

Income (Thousands of Dollars)	Effective Rate (Percent)
0–3	4.6
3–5	4.8
5–10	7.4
10–15	8.7
15–20	7.8
20–25	6.7
25–50	5.3
50–100	2.4
100–500	0.6
500–1,000	0.1
1,000 and over	
All classes	6.3

Source: From Edward R. Fried and others, *Setting National Priorities: The 1974
Budget*, Tables 3–6 and 3–8. Copyright ©
1973 by the Brookings Institution. Reprinted by permission.

a painful regressive rate. On the other hand, if the increased costs of
social security and related benefits were paid out of general revenues
raised through the corporate and individual income tazes, the cost of supporting retirees would be shared by all taxpayers and through progressive
taxes.

Estate and Gift Taxes   Estate and gift taxes have a great deal of merit
on social, moral, and economic grounds. Early supporters of federal death
taxation came from all income classes. Theodore Roosevelt and Andrew
Carnegie, for example, saw death and gift taxes as properly limiting the
transfer of excessive accumulations of wealth. Carnegie wrote that "the
parent who leaves his son enormous wealth generally deadens the talents
and energies of the son, and tempts him to lead a less useful and less
worthy life than he otherwise would." Others have advocated the estate
tax as a levy on those who escape their share of income tax during their
lifetimes.

Finally, both estate and gift taxes most closely embrace the ability-to-
pay principle. Bequests and gifts, like income from work or investments,
represent a source of ability-to-pay. Unlike these other income sources,
however, the recipients of bequests and gifts did nothing to earn them;
they are windfalls.

Despite the compelling fairness of these taxes, they remain our most neglected source of federal revenues. Today's estate tax, enacted in 1916, and gift tax, enacted in 1932, have yielded only small amounts. By 1939, they accounted for only 6 percent of federal revenues, and even this small amount fell to 4.5 percent by 1941 and to 2 percent or less in the post-World War II period. In 1974, federal estate and gift taxes brought in about $5 billion, just under 2 percent of federal tax revenues.

The estate tax is imposed on property or money left at death. A rate schedule sets taxes that range from 3 percent on small estates to 77 percent on estates over $10 million. There are several exemptions: a $60,000 exemption for the estate itself, one-half the estate if left to a surviving spouse, and a 100 percent deduction for anything left to charity. The gift tax rates are three-fourths of those for estate taxes, reaching a top rate of 57.75 percent on gifts over $10,000 a year. The gift tax also has a number of exemptions and deductions including a lifetime $30,000 exemption, yearly $3,000 exemptions for each gift recipient, and deductions for charitable contributions and gifts to spouses.

All these exemptions and deductions account for a tremendous erosion in these otherwise progressive taxes. One main defect in the present estate and gift tax is that it allows wealthy individuals to give away part of their estate before they die and avoid a healthy portion of the tax. Not only do such maneuvers take advantage of the lower gift tax rates, the taxpayer gets to use the lower end of the rate schedule twice. It is as though a runner set a world's record for the mile by running a half-mile, resting up for a few days, and then running a half-mile again.

Two months before his death, industrial magnate Irénée duPont made a "gift" of about one-fifth of his $176 million estate, avoiding about $16 million in estate taxes in the process.

As with other taxes, such cases are not the exception. In 1970, forty-seven millionaire estates paid no estate tax whatsoever. In fact, people died leaving more than $50 billion that year, yet the federal estate tax collected amounted to a meager $3 billion, or 6 percent from 100,000 taxable estates—less than 5 percent of the total estates in that year.

The Treasury Department's 1969 estate tax figures show that millionaire estates paid federal estate taxes amounting to 21 percent of the net estates and 25 percent when state, foreign, and other death taxes were included. The vast accumulations in the $10 million and above category paid even less, averaging only 17 percent despite a statutory rate of 77 percent applicable to those estates.

Excise and Other Taxes   The excise tax (the federal government's name for a sales tax) is declining as a source of federal revenues. Many excises were eliminated with the Excise Tax Reduction Act of 1965 and others were scheduled to be phased out.

Table 5   Effective Rates of
           Federal Excise Taxes,
           1954

Income Class (Dollars)	Federal Excise Taxes (Percentages)
0– 1,000 } 1,000– 2,000	5.0
2,000– 3,000	4.5
3,000– 4,000	4.1
4.000– 5,000	3.9
5,000– 6,000 } 6,000– 7,500	3.6
7,500–10,000	3.3
10,000–15,000 } 15,000 and over	1.9
All classes	3.4

Source: Adapted from Richard S. Mus-
grove, "The Incidence of the Tax Structure and Its Effects on Consumption,"
Joint Committee on the Economic Report, 84th Cong., 1st Sess. (1965). Foot-
notes omitted.

Before the 1965 Act excises brought in about 12.5 percent of our tax revenues. Today, the excise tax share is about 6.5 percent, $17 billion in 1974. The 10 percent tax on automobile sales is gone and the 10 percent telephone tax is down to 6 percent, scheduled to end in 1982. The remaining federal excise taxes include: highway user taxes on gasoline; alcohol and tobacco taxes; a tax on truck parts and accessories; taxes on fishing equipment and firearms; aircraft user taxes; and regulatory taxes on phosphorus matches and gambling.

A tax whose burden falls primarily on consumers can be progressive or regressive, depending on what is taxed. For example, a tax on beer and cigarettes is highly regressive, while excise taxes on furs and jewelry would be progressive. On balance, the postwar excise tax system has been regressive [Table 5].

Given this regressivity, moves to reduce the reliance on excise taxes should be met with general approval by advocates of the ability-to-pay principle. While some regressive taxes have been eliminated, those on alcohol, tobacco, and gasoline remain.

Customs duties are another source of federal revenues, accounting for a little more than 1 percent. These duties are levied on imported items primarily to protect domestic industries and not to produce federal revenues. For this reason, this [article] will not discuss import duties further.

Table 6   Tax Revenues by Source

Fiscal Year	Total %	Individual Income	Corp. Income	Social Security°	Excise	Other†
1944	100	44.6	33.6	3.9	9.7	8.2
1949	100	43.8	27.0	5.8	17.7	5.7
1954	100	42.4	30.3	10.3	14.3	2.7
1959	100	46.4	21.8	14.8	13.3	3.7
1964	100	43.2	20.9	19.5	12.2	4.2
1969	100	46.5	19.5	21.3	8.1	4.6
1974	100	44.8	14.6	29.1	6.3	5.2

°Includes payroll taxes, federal employee contributions for retirement, and contributions for supplementary medical insurance.
†Includes estate and gift taxes, customs duties and deposits of earnings by Federal Reserve banks.

Our quick look at the federal tax structure shows several major trends. First, the fast rise in revenues from the regressive payroll tax closely matches the decrease in revenues collected from the corporate income tax. In 1954, the payroll tax (which is borne fully by the wage earner) supplied 10 percent of the revenue receipts, while corporations kicked in 30 percent. By 1974, these figures were almost reversed with the payroll tax bringing 29 percent of Uncle Sam's revenues, while corporations provided only 14 percent. [Table 6] illustrates this trend.

When we look at the individual tax burden by adding income and payroll tax and compare it to the corporate tax burden we get [Table 7].

While supplying an increasing share of total federal revenues, the tax burden on individuals has itself become more regressive. Those less able to pay have been hit the hardest to make up for taxes the corporations and the wealthy are not paying. It is true that income taxes were cut in

Table 7   Individual Tax Burden vs. Corporate Tax Burden as Percentage of Total Receipts, 1944–1974

Fiscal Year	Total	Individual Income	Corporation Income	All Other°
1944	100	48.5	33.6	17.9
1949	100	49.6	27.0	23.4
1954	100	52.7	30.3	17.0
1959	100	61.2	21.8	17.0
1964	100	62.7	20.9	16.4
1969	100	67.8	19.5	12.7
1974	100	73.9	14.6	11.5

°Includes excise, estate and gift and miscellaneous taxes.

1969 and 1971, so that in 1974 revenues were reduced by approximately $16 billion. But payroll taxes were raised at the same time by about $19 billion. Taking the combination of income and payroll taxes, the trend toward tax reductions for higher income families but higher taxes on middle and lower income families is evident. . . .

The individual income tax, itself, has become less progressive as a result of the many tax preferences that cast their greatest benefits on those with the greatest wealth. These trends, as well as a general failure to use the estate tax, have brought on the erosion of progressivity in the over-all federal tax system.

WHO BEARS THE TAX BURDEN?

What does it all mean? The most recent and comprehensive study, *Who Bears the Tax Burden?* by Joseph Pechman and Benjamin Okner of the Brookings Institution in Washington, D.C., testing various assumptions about who bears certain taxes, found that irrespective of income, most Americans pay roughly the same rate of tax. The evidence further suggests that historically the over-all tax system—federal, state, and local—is becoming less and less fair. A study by the Advisory Commission on Inter-governmental Relations showed that between 1953 and 1974, the tax burdens on average income families increased much more rapidly than the tax burdens on higher income families. In those twenty years, the tax burden on high-income families increased by 52 percent. But the tax burden on average families increased by 98 percent.

Most striking is the parallel erosion of the income tax and property tax and the way in which specific reductions in each tend to benefit similar special interests. Thus, today we find:

fast "write-offs" for industrial machinery under the income tax, and exemptions for machinery and often for entire industrial plants under the property tax;

income tax provisions allowing corporations and wealthy individuals to duck taxes through "tax-loss farming," and "farm-land assessment laws" enabling these same interests to avoid their share of property taxes;

"capital gains" provisions allowing investors profiting from stock and bond deals to pay only one-half the income tax rate paid by working people, and property tax exemptions for stocks, bonds, and other forms of so-called intangible property;

"depletion allowances" that shrink income taxes on profits from oil and other resources, and the notorious underassessment of these resources for property tax purposes;

accelerated depreciation for business real estate, and assessment techniques which result in lower assessments on business property than assessments placed on homes;

"capital gains" treatment for income from land speculation, and the underassessment of vacant land, cutting costs and increasing profits for the same speculators.

Nor do these arm-in-arm tax breaks stop with income and property taxes. For example, investors not only benefit from property tax exemptions and captial gains income tax rates. Stock and bond sales commonly are exempt from sales taxes as well. Similarly, industrial equipment often is exempt from sales taxes, in addition to the other tax breaks its owners receive. A thorough inventory of the entire tax system would show still further benefits converging from many directions upon business and the wealthy. This is not surprising when we examine who most influences the nation's tax laws.

Legislators have increasingly favored regressive over progressive taxes. They have undercut progressivity with numerous exemptions, deductions, and special preferences. And administrators have opted for convenience over fairness in formulating and applying tax laws. We can see that in all areas of taxation reforms are needed to overcome these three trends which undermine fairness and underlie the rising protest against unfair taxes.

IV
RACISM

Another legacy of America's postwar optimism was the idea that racial discrimination, like so many other social problems, was destined to disappear in the not-so-distant future. One reason for this belief was the tendency to see racism mainly as a problem of the denial of civil rights. The successful struggle for legislation enforcing equal opportunity for minorities—in jobs, housing, education, and other realms—gave rise to the hope that the most important barriers to racial progress would be steadily removed through government action. Similarly, the tendency to view racism as fundamentally a problem of "prejudice"—of bigoted attitudes in the minds of individual white people—often made it easy to ignore some other, deeper sources of racism in economic development and social organization. Finally, the expectation of an ever-expanding economy promised that there would be room for everyone to have a chance at good jobs, a good income, and a good education.

To some extent, these expectations were borne out—for a while. Blacks and other minorities made significant social and economic progress, especially during the 1960s, as a result of the combined effect of government policy, economic expansion, and changing attitudes. But the urban riots of the 1960s and the reversals of minority gains that took place in the 1970s showed that none of those mechanisms was sufficient to eliminate the deeper sources of racism in American life. In the 1980s, minorities have not only failed to "catch up" with whites; in many ways, they are falling further behind, as a result of sharp reversals in social and economic trends—a contracting economy, a less generous public policy, and a hostile backlash from whites, many of whom are themselves anxious

132

and resentful under the pressure of economic troubles. The articles in this chapter explore these themes.

In "Growing Up Black in America," Marian Wright Edelman shows that the impact of racism on the lives of children remains pervasive and tragic, despite decades of civil-rights legislation and attempts at affirmative action. In every area— income, work, health, schooling, and family stability—black children face multiple hardships and burdens. Edelman doesn't argue that there has been no progress for black children, but, rather, that progress has been painfully slow and that, in some ways, the gap between the chances of black and white children has widened.

The United States has traditionally been ambivalent about its role as a refuge for minority immigrants—welcoming them with open arms when their labor has been needed in farms and factories and often imposing harsh restrictions and even deportation when the economy slackened. Recently, high rates of unemployment and the pinch of rising taxes have brought out new and tougher demands for dealing with "illegal" immigrants, especially those from Mexico.

The facts about illegal Mexican aliens are explored in the article by Wayne Cornelius. Contrary to popular stereotypes, there is no evidence that illegal aliens take jobs away from American workers, and illegal aliens contribute far more in taxes than they consume in social services. Cornelius argues that harsh measures to restrict immigration—through closing the border with Mexico or tightening up enforcement efforts against aliens and their employers—will do more harm than good.

The first casualties of racism in the United States were the native Americans. In "American Indians: Struggling for Power and Identity," Howell Raines shows that Indians are still suffering from a legacy of hundreds of years of exploitation and neglect. Moreover, in the 1980s, Indians face a strong backlash by whites against the gains they have made in recent years in areas such as fishing rights. And at the same time, the rich energy reserves that lie beneath their once-neglected reservations are likely to be the source of a rough struggle for control over the fate of Indian lands and cultures, which may pit Indians against one another as well as against whites.

10
GROWING UP BLACK IN AMERICA

Marian Wright Edelman

I. OVERVIEW

I wouldn't want to be black in America, would you?—MIAMI MAYOR
MAURICE FERRE, COMMENTING ON REPORT ON THE CAUSES OF RACIAL VIO-
LENCE IN MIAMI LAST MAY.[1]

Despite progress in the battle against inequality, black children, youth,
and families are worse off than whites in every area of American life.
Twenty-seven years after *Brown v. the Board of Education*, most black
children still have not gained the opportunities that most white children
take for granted. In some areas the gap between black and white children's chances for success has actually widened rather than narrowed in
the past decade. For example, although black infants are twice as likely as
white infants to die within the first year of life, the infant mortality rate
fell faster during the 70s among white families than among black. Real
per capita income increased slightly for whites but fell for black families.
The disparity in school suspension and teenage unemployment rates between white and black children increased.

America's poor population includes a higher proportion of children,
minorities, and women than ever before. Children are the poorest group
in American society: one in six is poor in any one year; one in four is on
Aid to Families with Dependent Children (AFDC) at some time in his or
her lifetime.[2]

Today, 47 out of every 100 black babies are born into poverty, compared to fewer than one in eight white babies.[3] Between 1969 and 1977,
the rate of poverty among black families rose from 3.75 to 4 times that of
white families.[4] In 1977 the per capita family income among two-parent
black families was about equal to that among female-headed white families; female-headed black families had only half as much income per person as male-headed white families.

Despite the continuing and increasing poverty of blacks, many whites
are turning their backs on and resisting efforts to ensure equal oppor-

Reprinted with permission of the National Urban League, Inc., from *The State of Black America,
1981*, ed. James D. Williams, (New York: National Urban League, 1981).

tunities for black children. Although a black child still has a one in three chance of attending a racially isolated school, an anti-busing amendment that would make it even harder to achieve school desegregation was approved by the 96th Congress but later vetoed by President Carter. Racial isolation has shifted from the South, where it is lowest, to the Midwest, where it is higher than in the rest of the country. Indeed, a black child moving from the South to the Midwest (e.g., from Biloxi, Mississippi to Chicago) about doubles his or her chance of ending up in a 90% black public school.

From birth through young adulthood, blacks still face staggering obstacles as they struggle to achieve decency, dignity, and success in America.

Twice as many black as white women lack prenatal care at almost every stage of pregnancy. This imbalance persists despite high correlations between lack of prenatal care and infant mortality and illness.

Black mothers die in childbirth three times as often as white mothers. Of those who survive, one in 40 must then watch her baby die in the first year of life.

Growing up, black children are more likely to be sick because they are more likely to be poor. One out of seven black children under the age of 15 lacks a regular source of health care. Partly as a result, black children, aged one to four, die of heart disease 100% more often than white children and die from accidents 50% more often than white children. New tuberculosis cases occur five times as often among black as among white children.

Less than half of all black children live with both parents; the majority live within single-parent families or with other relatives. Black children are more likely than white children to live without or away from any family and are disproportionately represented in institutions that typically serve the young (e.g., children's homes, psychiatric facilities), where twice as many non-whites as whites have no families at all.

The black child's mother goes to work when her child is younger, works longer hours and earns less than a white child's mother. This means that black children need full-day child care more often than white children. But child care is still an inadequately supported service. Head Start serves only 20% of all eligible children and it may have to serve even fewer if funding fails to keep pace with the rate of inflation and as more budget cuts to social programs are threatened.[5]

Once a black child enters public school he or she is twice as likely as a white child to be held back a grade, three times as likely to be placed in classes for the educable mentally retarded, and twice as likely to be suspended from school. It should be no surprise, therefore, that in any year, for every two black students who graduate from high school, one drops out. Poor skills development and inadequate training of black children in school contributes to this high drop-out rate. Often these problems stem

from and/or are reinforced by the low expectations and negative attitudes many education officials hold for black children. Black children, in
turn, often internalize these expectations and label themselves as failures.
Sadly, the current national atmosphere, if combined with weakened
federal enforcement of civil rights, may encourage a revival of overt
negative attitudes and acts against black children in some public schools.

Even if he or she graduates from high school, a black youth is three
times as likely to be unemployed as a white youth. Black college graduates are employed at about the same rate as white high school dropouts.

Below is a summary of facts about the lives of black children in today's
America and what they mean in human terms. They add up, for many
millions of black children, to a societal condemnation to second-class citizenship.

II. FAMILY STRUCTURE

I will always love my mother. I would a never been here but my mother
birthed me.[6]

—Jerry, age 11

Q: What does your dad do?
A: He works in a restuarant. He's—I think in Ohio—or somethin' like that.
Q: Do you see him?
A: Well he sends money to us.
Q: He's working in Ohio, so I guess you don't really get to spend much time
   with him.
A: No.
Q: What's the best part of your life?
A: Bein' with my mother and brother.[7]

—Orlando, age 11

Having a stable family life is critical to the well-being of all children. Yet
black children are far more likely than white children to live with one or
neither parent.

• One black child in eight lives with neither parent.
• One black child in five lives in a family where the parents have sepa-
rated. This is seven times the white rate.
• Black children are three times as likely as white children to have their
father die; one black child in every 16 lives with a widowed mother.
• One black child in three is born to a teenaged mother.
• Black children live in families headed by someone other than their
parents at rates four times higher than those for white children.

From 1973 to 1974 the proportion of black children living with their mothers in the households of relatives jumped from 30 to 39%.[8]

The proportion of black children informally adopted or absorbed into the households of relatives rose from 13 to 15% between 1970 and 1978. Today about 1.4 million black children live in extended families. Many more live with relatives for short periods of time while their parents work, recover from illnesses, or reside in institutions.[9]

The educational process is still permeated by racial discrimination. This oath, which has circulated in different forms since desegregation of schools began, has resurfaced in Jackson, Mississippi since the November 4th election. Evidently it comes from the area of the East Baton Rouge Parish school district in Louisiana. A copy of the oath was brought to the Children's Defense Fund's Mississippi office by a local resident, who found it on a table in a fast food restaurant.

WHITE CITIZENS FOR E. B. R. P. SCHOOLS: *"ONLY"*

Oath of all white Teachers and Principals:

I. All white high schools will write up as many suspensions on Negroes as they occur, small or large.
I. All white high schools will bring about the suspensions of 25 supposed to be Negro graduates (15 boys and 10 girls).
I. All white high schools will send Negroes home for any little thing they do so that we may have on record their lack of interest in school.
I. Nigger is not a bad word to call Negroes, so use the name at will.
I. Be aware that all maids and yard boys will do as we tell them because in their eye sight white is still the best thing they have ever seen.
I. All white School Board Members are with us (except one).
I. K. K. K. are doing a thing too, so together we will have Niggers in a turmoil.
I. Junior high is the area where we get Niggers prepared for the 12th and 14th grades.
I. This paper is not to get in the hands of any Negro mothers (don't worry about the fathers, they don't show up for nothing) or Negro children. The good we are doing for the Negroes should never be talked about in their presence. Any reading of this na-

ture should be read and burned up before it get in the hands of your maids or yard boys.

I. Reappointment of the School Board (one man one vote to a single member district vote went like white supremecy is supposed to go?) Anyway, we feel that Negroes are getting more education now than they will ever use.

I. Our goal is to average 240 Negroes suspended per month to aid drop out-inferior education.

III. POVERTY

She won't go because she's ashamed that we ain't got anything, in the way of material things I mean. She's afraid that folks will find out just how poor she is, and she don't want them knowing anything about this. Girl has only got a couple of dresses and after she wore them day after day she thought she shouldn't go to school anymore. People would be laughing at her, she said, 'cause she always looked the same. Same goes for her shoes. She says they look like boys shoes, and the other kids are going to laugh at them. The children go to the cafeteria at lunchtime and she never has any money to buy things. She's always hungry and she doesn't have the nerve to ask them for money, otherwise like I told you, they'll see how bad off she is. Then another thing. She used to like to talk in class. But then the teacher started to ask the children about their homes and their families, and what it was like outside of school. She knew they'd get around to her and she's have to tell them about this house, and the street, and us too. She must have got scared, or ashamed, like I said before. She couldn't do it. I think that's when she stopped going.[10]

—Grandmother of Theresa, age 12

When you do it, you don't think about it. When you're poor and starving how are you gonna put yourself in the position to think about it? You are in the streets to get over. You don't think about what anybody else needs. You don't cut the streets: the streets cut you. You either make it or break it.[11]

—Gordon Andrews, age 16

Not all black children and youth react to poverty as Gordon did by turning to street life, but many black children do have to decide how they are going to adjust to a life spent without enough money to get by and the indignities associated with such a status.

Poverty is the most persistent and pressing problem facing black children today. Their poverty rate is about four times higher than that of white children.

• The median family income in constant dollars (that is, adjusted for inflation) for black families fell during the 1970s; for white families it rose.

• In 1979 the median family income of black children was almost exactly half that of white children.

• Although in 1977 there were more white children and families than black children and families on Aid to Families with Dependent Children (AFDC), a far higher proportion of all black families and children were on AFDC. Almost 41% of all black children are AFDC recipients.

• AFDC payments are intolerably low. The national average, which typically covers one mother and two children, is $241.35 per month or $2.74 a day per person. In Mississippi the per day payment is 93¢ per person. Despite rhetoric about the importance of maintaining families intact, many states deny support to families unless unemployed fathers leave home.

• Many of the differences in black and white families' poverty levels can be explained by the lower earnings of blacks, particularly black males. In 1977 the median income for black males was $9,035; for white males it was $13,482.

• Four out of every ten black children, compared to one out of eight white children, depend upon the income of their mother. Because the black mother faces discrimination both as a black and as a woman, she is the lowest paid and most unemployed worker in the nation. Black women heading families are three times more likely to be unemployed today than they were at the beginning of the 1970s.[12] Thus two out of every three black children in female-headed families live in poverty. Only two out of five white children living in female-headed families live in poverty.

IV. CHILD CARE

There is a real need right now for infant care. For example, we have a lot of mothers in high school who can't return to high school and are staying at home. After a year or two of this they are not going to want to go back to school. They will have just gotten out of the mood and then the rest of their lives are going to be harder because they have not graduated from high school. . . .

It seems to me that of our parents, a large majority of them have come off of the AFDC rolls when they found a job, because our center was available to them. And if that center is not available to them, the only option for most of them, I would say 75% of them, is to go back on the AFDC rolls. But they have in fact decided that life can be better than that: that they can be in control of their lives. I see women who, because that center is there, think, "I am about something that has some worth to it. I go to work every day, I can get a pay check, I can hold down this job, I can meet my family's needs. I have crises often when there's any extra expense, but I can in fact be in control of things."[13]

> —Mary Lynn Porter,
> Director of Auburn Day Care,
> Auburn, Alabama

My son has been in day care since he was about nine months old. Before that, my grandmother kept him, but she got sick and so she couldn't keep him for me anymore. . . . I need day care services because I need to work. My husband and I both work. We have to pay a fee for (our son to be in day care), but it is much less than what we would have to pay to a private day care center. . . . Day care services, private day care services, are very expensive in Auburn.[14]

> —Mrs. L., Auburn, Alabama

Child care services are still too scarce for the many families who want and need them at prices they can afford. A disproportionate number of children who need child care—children of working and single parents, children born to teenaged parents, children born into poverty, children at risk of abuse, neglect or institutionalization, and children with special needs who could benefit from preschool programs—are black.

• One out of every two black children under age six has a mother who is either working or seeking work.

• Black mothers participate in the labor force at their maximum rate as soon as their youngest child is three years old; white mothers reach their maximum labor force participation rate after their youngest child turns six, and even then only if they are divorced or separated. Three out of five black children attending pre-schools do so full time; three out of four white children attending pre-schools do so only part time. Although one in every four black three-year-olds attends pre-school full time, less than one in every 14 white three-year-olds does.

• While few black families can afford to pay for private pre-school programs, three out of four black 3 to 5-year-olds who are in private pre-schools attend full time; only about one in four white children in private pre-schools attends full time.

• Two-parent black families often earn too much to qualify for federally subsidized child care but too little to pay for private child care. As a result relatives often care for their children. One study found that the black extended family alone accounts for 40% of the black need for child care.[15]

• Poor black single mothers use federally subsidized child care for their children more than do any other parents. Approximately 40% of the children enrolled in centers that receive federal subsidies are black.[16] More than 40% of all black 3 to 5-year-old children are in public day care programs, while less than 30% of all white 3 to 5-year-olds are in such programs. Indications of similar disparities can be found in Head Start, WIN, Title XX of the Social Security Act, and whatever data on the race of the beneficiaries of day care are available.

V. Child Health

One night Wilson, a frail 12-year-old with a long standing cough, woke up vomiting blood. He and his mother arrived, by bus, at their local emergency room at 8 a.m., and were then forced to wait until 6:30 p.m. before seeing a doctor. Test results indicated Wilson had signs of tuberculosis and possible leukemia, and that he displayed symptoms of severe malnourishment. Had Wilson received basic health services such as routine checkups and prompt attention, there is little question that his problems could have been treated long before he became critically ill.[17]

Mrs. Carolyn Lewis, from Knoxville, Tennessee, is a divorced, working mother with three children. Her older daughter has an eye problem and needs to see the eye specialist at least twice a year. Her youngest daughter was born with the tube closed in her right ear. Recurring infections destroyed her right eardrum, so she is now partially deaf. When wax builds up in her left ear she has difficulty hearing. This happens because Mrs. Lewis can't afford to take her to the ear specialist to get her ears cleaned out when needed. Mrs. Lewis's son was born with a birth defect and is hyperactive. Last year, when he had a lesion on his chest, the Health Department provided free medical care. Now Health Department funds have been cut back, and Mrs. Lewis has to pay. Mrs. Lewis says of her children's situation:
"I was on welfare for three years, and that was how I found out about their problems, and that is how their medical bills were covered through Medicaid. . . . But now, I have to follow up their medical needs on my income ($419 a month), and I can't do it. . . . The only way that I could get health care now would be to quit work. I would have to quit work, go back home and sit down, and then have welfare tell me I need to get out and go to work. That is the only way I could get Medicaid."[18]

I am married and have a wife and three kids. I bring home at least $500 a month. That is not enough to pay expenses like light bills, oil, and stuff like that. For about the past four years, I was just trying to provide my family with health insurance . . . so I can just take them to the hospital and get them checked on. They have never had their teeth checked on, and I would like very much to have that. . . . Shawn (my son) had been sick for about three weeks, and I had to take him to the hospital. They told me that they would not take him unless they had a deposit of $60. . . . I went out, trying to find $60. . . . I borrowed it from my father. Shawn was in there for about three days.[19]

—Roger Glover, father of three,
Beaufort, S. Carolina

Mr. Glover, a Vietnam war veteran and day laborer, is still trying to pay the bill for his son's three days of hospital care. His other two children, both under five, have never seen a doctor. They are among the one in seven, or over 9 million American children who have no known regular source of primary health care. His children are also among the one in three, or 18 million, who have never seen a dentist. These children are disproportionately black.

In South Carolina, only if Mr. Glover left home would his family become eligible for Medicaid. Indeed, fathers who refuse to leave their families are ineligible for Medicaid benefits in over half the states—an anti-family discrimination that must be ended. Yet conservative Republicans blocked a bill, the Child Health Assessment Program (CHAP), in the 96th Congress, which would have enabled poor, working and intact families to get Medicaid benefits, and which would have invested more of the federal dollar on cost-effective preventive health services for children.

One black mother in seven receives less than the recommended minimum of five prenatal medical examinations; one in 16 receives no prenatal care until the last three months of pregnancy. Medicaid in 17 states does not cover prenatal care during the first pregnancy.

• On any given day, among 6 to 11-year-old black children, one in ten eats less protein than the amount set by established minimum standards. One in five black children does not get enough calcium; two in three do not get enough iron in their meals. Poor nourishment, except for iron, is twice as prevalent among black as among white children.
• Many black children are not protected against diseases we know how to prevent. Two out of every five black 5 to 9-year-olds in central cities are not immunized against polio, tetanus, diphtheria, or whooping cough.
• Black children lack a regular source of health care twice as often as do white children. Four out of every ten black children under age 15 depend upon hospital emergency rooms, out-patient clinics, or unknown sources for primary medical care. More than eight out of every ten white children receive care from private doctors in individual or group practice.
• For every black child who has private hospital or surgical insurance, another does not. Only one white child in five lacks such insurance.
• On the average, white children visit dentists one more time per year than black children.
• Black children who require mental health services are more likely

than white children to be treated on an inpatient rather than an outpatient basis. In fact, 22.8% of the residents in psychiatric facilities are
black; of these, half are under 18. Too many black children who do reach
outpatient mental health clinics receive only diagnostic services, and must
go elsewhere for actual treatment.

• Many poor black families are unaware of and fail to receive services
for which they are eligible. Approximately one out of every two black
AFDC families do not receive free school lunches for their children; more
than one in four do not get food stamps.[20]

Medicaid's Early and Periodic Screening, Diagnosis and Treatment
program (EPSDT) serves only about one-fourth of all eligible children. A
disproportionate number of those not being served are black.[21] Major and
systematic efforts must be expended within the black community, and
through health delivery institutions, to ensure that families are aware of
and take advantage of the benefits available under this existing program.
At present in many states, outreach and other support services to enable
parents and children to know about and use this and other federal and
state programs are poor.

Despite the fact that pregnancy and childhood are the times when
health care has the greatest preventive payoff, children and pregnant
women are covered particularly poorly by the present mix of public programs and private insurance. Less than 30% of American children are
covered through private insurance for out of hospital, physician visits.
Employment-based insurance plans shortchange coverage for children's
needs. Only 15% cover children's eyeglasses, 9%, preventive care, and
32% children's dental care.

It is time for those who profess to be concerned with escalating health
costs to invest far more of the public and private dollar on prevention.
This is not only cost effective, it is more humane. How many of us who
are parents would like to see our children suffer pain and impairment
because we did not have the money to pay for health care?

VI. EDUCATION

B. J. Harris was a 10-year-old black boy who lived with his parents, two brothers, and four sisters in Massachusetts. When the school year finished B. J.'s
parents were told he had done well enough to pass. Yet when B. J. returned to
school in September he had been placed in one of the school's classes for the
mentally retarded and children with learning disabilities. B. J. was disappointed and his mother felt ashamed. After two months in the special class B. J.
stopped going to school. Each day there was less and less for him to do. B. J.
found himself killing time. He sat in the same corner of the room watching the
teacher and the other children and began to believe that school was making

him act like the really retarded children in the class. His belief was reinforced by his friends in the regular classes, who now avoided him, assuming that if he had been put in a special class, there must be something wrong with him.

B. J. seemed as intelligent as any of the children in his regular class. A psychologist from the Children's Defense Fund was given access to B. J.'s official school folder. His I.Q. score was given as 85, which seemed too low for B. J.'s abilities, although it would have correctly placed him in the special class. After much investigation it was revealed that B. J. had been assigned an I.Q. score, but had never been given an I.Q. test. Additional searching turned up eight more children, all but one of them black boys, who had been placed in special classes because of "low I.Q. scores." Each of the children had been labeled a "problem case" by their teachers, but only one of them had been doing poorly enough to warrant placement in a special class. When I.Q. tests were administered, all but one did well enough to return to the regular classroom.[22]

CDF staff met Kenny when he was a 14-year-old black child in Mississippi. Because he was partially sighted, he had not been in school since 3rd grade. A teacher in the public school told his mother that she "didn't have the time or the patience to teach him." Kenny's mother took him out of school and tried to get help at The Blind Institute. The principal there said that he would have to put Kenny, then 13, in a class with five- and six-year-olds. Already embarrassed and behind in his classes, Kenny was not willing to go to classes with such young children. This was the last attempt his mother made to get Kenny enrolled in a school.

At the time no program existed to deal with his special needs in the local public schools. Said his mother, "I want the school to prepare a class or program to meet Kenny's needs without making him embarrassed. Most of all, I want him to have an education so that he will be able to get a job to support himself. I don't know what he's going to do when I'm no longer with him."[23]

Over one million school-aged children are not enrolled in school. Many are not out of school by choice, but because they have been excluded—expelled, repeatedly suspended, excluded because they are "different" by virtue of race, income, physical, mental or emotional handicap, pregnancy, marriage or age. Hundreds of thousands of others are not being provided the special services they need within schools.

• More than one out of every five black 14 to 17-year-olds from low-income families are not enrolled in school; among all black children between the ages of 14 and 17, one in six is out of school.
• Black children are disproportionately placed in classes for the educable mentally retarded (EMR). Too often these classes merely slow instruction down to the presumably lower learning rates of the children placed in them and do not vary or intensify instruction. One black child in 30 is placed in these classes.
• A white child is twice as likely to be placed in a class for gifted students as in an EMR class; a black child is almost three times as likely to be placed in an EMR class as in a class for gifted students.

• Half of all black children come from families where the head of the family did not graduate from high school. Only one black child in 20 comes from a family where the head of the household graduated from college; white children are four times as likely to come from a college graduate's family. A black child from an intact two-parent family is still less likely to have a college graduate as the head of that family than is a white child in a female-headed household.

• One out of every 16 black public school students (from grades kindergarten through 12) was corporally punished in 1977–1978; one in 13 was suspended from school. These are more than twice the rates for white students.

One black family in four reports that it has had at least one child suspended from school; one in 14 that it has had at least one child expelled from school. Among black families with incomes of $20,000 or more per year, almost one in five reported having had at least one child suspended.[24] Clearly suspensions are not just a problem of low-income black families.

• Many black children are not being adequately taught and are therefore not learning. Too many black youth are leaving school—drop-outs and graduates—unable to read, write, or compute well enough to get a job. Some 13% of all 17-year-olds are functionally illiterate, unable to do basic reading, writing, or counting, unable to understand want ads, fill out job applications or get the right change for a purchase at the supermarket.[25]

• Black children repeat grades more than twice as often as white children. Among 18 and 19-year-olds, fewer than one in ten white students is still enrolled below the college level, while more than one in five black students are. Despite repeating grades, fewer black students ultimately complete high school than do whites.

• For the smaller percentage of black students who do manage to complete high school, the odds of going on to college are almost equal to those of white students. But because of the smaller percentage of blacks completing high school, 20% fewer of them ultimately reach college.

VII. Youth Unemployment

So it seem like the sun is shinin. Feels good. Feels real good. Now I'm going down and talking to all the fellows out there. My main partner, I talked him into gettin' a job. I talked his brother into gettin' a job. I be walkin' in New York and don't be walkin' just to see what you could steal, but walkin' cause I got somewhere to go and somethin' to do. That's nice. I dig that.[26]

—Tom Burdette, age 18

I knew it was gonna be hard to find a job but I didn't know it was gonna be as hard as it is. 'Cause I've heard most people say to get your high school education and you can get a job. Well, you don't have to have no high school. You can have a eighth-grade education, and if the white man knows you, you got a job; you can have a college degree, and if he don't want you to work, you ain't gonna work. Not unless you go out of town. A white lady can be dumb and not know how to write her name, and I can fill out the application and spell everything right; but by her color being a little lighter than mine she gets the job. And I can go on back home and start all over again.[27]

—Karen Lewis, age 22

Contrary to the stereotype, many black youth do want to work, although they may be discouraged by the poor prospects of finding a job. A recent study of youth unemployment in New York State found that 20% of the more than 3,000 youth surveyed were "super youth" who worked full time and also went to school or trained for future employment. These "super youth" were predominantly from minority groups—Native Americans, Orientals, Hispanics, and blacks.[28] Unfortunately black youth who want jobs, particularly black males, face extremely high unemployment rates. Racial discrimination, lack of youth jobs, and lack of job skills all contribute to the severe jobless rate for black teenagers.

Too many black youth, even those who stay in school, know very little about how to look for a job or what an employer expects. Many employers fail to recruit inner-city youth, while publicly funded vocational education and employment services too seldom reach the most disadvantaged youth. When they do, they often track black youth into less desirable professions. For example, black public secondary school students are overrepresented in vocational education programs like consumer education, home economics, and homemaking, but are underrepresented in technical and modern industrial arts programs.[29] In vocational programs given in comprehensive high schools, black students are more than twice as likely to receive training to become custodians than they are to receive training to become candidates for law enforcement.[30]

Growing up, black children see far more unemployment around them than white children. Many question if they'll ever get the chance for a decent living even if they stay in school.

• A black child is about twice as likely as a white child to have at least one parent unemployed. Thirty percent of all black children have no parent in the labor force, primarily because black children are so much more likely than white children to live in single-parent households.

• Among 16 to 21-year-old black youth who are not in school, almost one in three is unemployed—a rate three times higher than the rate for whites.

• Recent black college graduates are almost three times as likely to be unemployed as recent white college graduates. More than one out of every five recent black high school graduates is unemployed. Thus while a black youth who graduates from high school has about the same chance of going on to college as does a white youth, neither completing high school nor completing college provides a black youth with the same chances that a white youth has in the labor market. College attendance rates for blacks improved over the past decade; unemployment rates worsened.

With the odds against their own employment and the widespread unemployment around them, it's no wonder that some black youth just give up and quit looking for work. As one teenager put it:

You just live with your mom until you get a job—that should be any time a job comes looking for you. Why should you bother to go look for it? Even your parents can't find work.[31]

VIII. Inadequate Housing and Housing Discrimination

I grew up in the projects. I was afraid to walk in the streets because of all the trouble that was outside waiting for me.[32]

—Gordon Andrews, age 16

Q: Do you like where you're living?
A: No—too many things be goin' on around there.
Q: What's going on?
A: Shootin', trouble . . . my friend—her mother told her to go to the store about 10 o'clock at night and they were shootin' out—and she went outside and they shot her . . . she got killed.[33]

—Ernestine, age 13

Black children are more than twice as likely as white children to be inadequately housed. Inadequate housing means [a] dwelling unit lacking one or more of the following: plumbing, kitchen, sewage system, heating (except in the South), access to toilets, or physical or electrical maintenance to a degree that threatens health or safety. Millions of black children live in housing projects and neighborhoods where they do not feel safe.

• One black child in four lives in inadequate housing; among black families who rent, one child in three lives in inadequate housing.
• Even among black children from two-parent families who own their own homes, over one in ten live in inadequate housing.
• Because of the black extended family structure, 15% of all black families living in federally financed housing for the elderly have children living with them.

Racial discrimination in housing [and] discrimination against families with children strongly [contribute] to the number of black children living in inadequate housing. According to a report from the U.S. Department of Housing and Urban Development (HUD), 26% of all rental units ban children; of those rental units with two or more bedrooms that do accept children, 55% have restrictions based on the number, age and sex of children. As a result, 47% of all two-bedroom rental units exclude families.[34]

The situation is particularly severe in large cities with disproportionately large black populations. In Los Angeles, 70% of all advertised rental housing excluded or restricted children. In Dallas, 52% of existing apartment buildings was for adults only. And in Atlanta, 75% of all new construction was limited to adults.[35]

Housing discrimination against families with children is often a smoke-screen for sexual and racial discrimination. Families headed by women and minorities particularly suffer. Black families, which generally have more children and less income than white families, have a harder time finding adequate housing. There is a severe shortage of family housing that low-income families can afford.

Several local studies have found that no-children policies are most prevalent in "white" areas of cities. Thus the restrictions tend to perpetuate segregated school systems. In addition the widespread association of public housing with black children and their families is often cited as the reason for community opposition to low-income multi-family housing.

IX. CHILDREN WITHOUT HOMES

Mary A. first enrolled in school at the age of seven. After one week the school sent her home to stay since she was not toilet-trained and "exhibited" some signs of retardation. When Mary was 12 years old she still had never had any kind of formal schooling or training. The school also considered her brother, James A. to be profoundly retarded; he was never permitted to attend school. The County Welfare Department recommended that both children be permanently institutionalized in the State's retardation center. When Mrs. A. objected, welfare officials obtained a neglect ruling in State court and removed Mary and James from their home anyway. (The Welfare Department did not remove Mrs. A's—the "unfit" parent's—three remaining children.) Mrs. A. did not understand why her children were taken; she was not properly informed that she was entitled to legal representation at this hearing. Neither the local school system nor any other government agency had offered to provide assistance and training in a less restrictive environment for the two children threatened with removal.[36]

I have an allocations worker. I have a caseworker, I have my caseworker's supervisor. None of them ever met me. They don't know what I look like. All they know is what my psychological test said. . . . The allocations worker is supposed to find a group home that is right for me, but she's never met me, she doesn't know what kind of a person I am. How can she find a group home. . . . And this is the same for all the people there . . . I'm not just one special case.[37]

—Thelma, age 15

Thelma is right; there are tens of thousands more children with similar problems. Black children are overrepresented among the more than 500,000 children growing up in foster homes, group homes, and other institutions, and black and other minority children are particularly vulnerable to public neglect once placed out of their homes.

Black children without homes are likely to receive few services, and to have a history of more than one out-of-home placement. Social Service agencies often write off these black children as "unadoptable," making only limited attempts to find them families. If public systems recognized or took more advantage of informal supports in the black community— relatives who are willing to take in their nieces, nephews, and cousins, and neighbors and local churches that can provide help to families— many black children now placed in institutions that are often too restrictive, inappropriate, and far from their home communities could remain at home or at least in their hometowns.

- Nonwhite children are placed in facilities for homeless, retarded, handicapped, and emotionally disturbed children at rates about 40% greater than white children.
- Black children live apart from relatives, in foster homes and in informal group quarters, at about three times the rate of white children.
- Minority youths in institutions for the mentally retarded are, on the average, much younger than white youths. The median age of nonwhite residents in institutions for the retarded is 17; for whites, 29.

The current anti-family child welfare system is on the verge of reform with the passage of the Adoption Assistance and Child Welfare Act of 1980. The new law holds out to the over half million children growing up in foster, group, and institutional care a chance to return home or be placed for adoption as appropriate. Until now, our child welfare system has had short-sighted, almost perverse fiscal incentives. At the federal level we have paid hundreds of millions of dollars a year to keep children in costly and impermanent foster and institutional care, and little or nothing to support them in permanent placements with adoptive families. For the first time federal reimbursement will be available for preventive services to families and for adoption subsidies. However, unless sound regulations are developed and implemented and adequate funding to implement the new legislation is appropriated, the new law will not work.

In states such as Alabama and Illinois not enough parents are found to take homeless black infants into their lives, largely due to poor outreach by public and private agencies responsible for these children. These infants will grow up, as will thousands of older homeless black youngsters and adolescents, without the psychological roots vital to their security.

X. CRIME AND ARRESTS

Q: Are you ever frightened?
A: Yeah. Cause my mother be sayin' when the garbage get full she don't want my sisters go out there cause some mens come out from the back, wait, and try to rape your daughter. And that's why she tell me or my older brother to take it out.
Q: And how do you feel when you take out the garbage?
A: Makes me a little—uh—frightened.[38]

> —Jerry, age 11

I shot craps; won a lot of money. Cracked niggers upside the head with pop bottles. I even started fights occasionally. I was a gang leader for little poohbut gangs who ran around and stuck up kids and took their money. I didn't get nothin' but education everyone should know.[39]

> —Gordon Andrews, age 16,
> later became captain of his school's wrestling team,
> and planned to continue on to college.

Many black children and adolescents grow up in fear of being victimized by crime.

• Out of every 32 nonwhite females between the ages of 16 and 19, one is a victim of serious crime each year (i.e., robbery or assault, with injury; assault with a weapon; and rape).
• Among 16 to 19 year-old nonwhite males, one out of 17 is a victim of serious crimes each year.
• Nonwhite males 15 to 19 years-old, are almost six times as likely to be murdered as white males of the same age; nonwhite females 15 to 19 years-old are over four times as likely to be murdered as white females.
• Shockingly, the murder rate among nonwhite preschoolers one to four years old is higher than the murder rate among white teenagers.
• Black children are far more likely to get arrested than white children. Between the ages of 11 and 17, a black teenager is seven times as likely as a white youth to be arrested for violent crimes, and is twice as likely to be arrested for serious property crimes. More than half of all arrests of black teenagers, compared with more than one-third of all arrests of white teenagers, are for serious violent or property crimes.

Whether a child is the victim of a crime or arrested for a crime, the impact of the event can permanently change his image of himself and his world. We must concentrate our efforts on preventive programs that lessen the probability that children will grow up feeling unsafe or alienated, with negative views of themselves and the society in which they live.

XI. CONCLUSION

The disparity in opportunity for black children is a blight on the nation's professed belief in and rhetoric about equal opportunity. In the 1980's, black children and families must become a major focus of black communities and of our political leaders and policymakers for moral as well as practical reasons. It is more humane and cost-effective to prevent and deal with the problems of black children before they occur or become serious and require costly remediation. Public and private sector policies must build on the considerable strengths of black families and enable them, to the extent possible, to stay together and become more self-sufficient. At present too many programs and policies undermine families' and children's well-being.

A specific set of programmatic goals to address the range of problems described here must be developed. With a relatively modest investment in fairly administered and preventive measures, children can grow into assets. To the extent that the skills and talents of our children and youth are developed, our productivity as a nation is enhanced and our burden to provide for them is decreased.

Every American child is entitled to a fair chance. Millions of black children are not getting theirs. Those white Americans who think that they are should ask themselves, like Miami's Mayor Ferre did, whether they'd care to trade places. That so many black families have helped their children survive and succeed despite the hurdles of unemployment, poor health care, and nutrition is a tribute to their strength and persistence.

REFERENCES

1. "Miami Riot Report Causes Little Stir," *New York Times* (December 7, 1980).

2. Children's Defense Fund, *America's Children and Their Families: Basic Facts* (Washington, D.C.: Children's Defense Fund, 1979), p. 6.

3. Children's Defense Fund, *Portrait of Inequality: Black and White Children in America* (Washington, D.C.: Children's Defense Fund, 1980). All statistics and facts included in this article which are not footnoted are based on data and sources used in this book.

4. United Press International, "Frightening Shift in Poverty Reported Toward Women and Minorities in U.S.," *Washington Post* (October 19, 1980).

5. Fifteenth Anniversary Head Start Committee, *Head Start in the 1980's: Review and Recommendations*, Publications Unit, Project Head Start, Health and Human Services Department, September 1980, pp. 28–34.

6. Pamela Blafer Lack, "For Bushwick Kids, 'Year of the Child'? Ha." *New York Times* (October 13, 1979).

7. Ibid.

8. Robert B. Hill, "Black Families in the 70's," in *The State of Black America: 1980*, ed. by James D. Williams (New York: National Urban League, Inc., 1980), p. 48.

9. Ibid., p. 49.

10. Children's Defense Fund, *Children Out of School in America* (Washington, D.C.: Children's Defense Fund, October 1974), p. 31.

11. Johnny Vaughn, "You don't cut the streets; they cut you," *New Expression* (September 1978).

12. Hill, op. cit., p. 45.

13. Excerpt from an unpublished interview with Mary Lynn Porter, Auburn, Alabama, October 29, 1980, Children's Defense Fund, Washington, D.C.

14. Excerpt from an unpublished interview with Mrs. L., Auburn, Alabama, October 29, 1980, Children's Defense Fund, Washington, D.C.

15. See, *The Status of Black Children in 1980* (Washington, D.C.: National Black Child Development Institute, Inc., October 30, 1980), p. 4.

16. Ibid. p. 6.

17. Children's Defense Fund, *Child Health Advocacy Is Everybody's Business* (Washington, D.C.: Children's Defense Fund, June 1979), p. 1.

18. Transcript of Proceedings, *Citizen's Panel on Child Health: Public Hearing on S. 1204*, Washington, D.C., November 12, 1980, Children's Defense Fund, Washington, D.C., pp. 42–44.

19. Ibid., pp. 16–19.

20. *The Myth of Income Cushions for Blacks* (Washington, D.C.: National Urban League, Research Department, 1980), p. 43.

21. Children's Defense Fund, *EPSDT: Does It Spell Health Care for Poor Children?* (Washington, D.C.: Children's Defense Fund, June 1977), pp. 29–30.

22. Children's Defense Fund, *Children Out of School in America* (Washington, D.C.: Children's Defense Fund, October 1974), pp. 25–26.

23. Ibid., pp. 20–21. After years of litigation, CDF and the State of Mississippi have entered into a consent decree guaranteeing the 40,000 handicapped children in the state a right to education suitable to their needs. See *Mattie T. v. Charles E. Holladay* (DC-75-31-S).

24. "Initial Black Pulse Findings," *Research Department Bulletin No. 1* (Washington, D.C.: National Urban League, Research Department, August 1980), p. 3.

25. Children's Defense Fund, *America's Children and Their Families: Basic Facts* (Washington, D.C.: Children's Defense Fund, 1979), p. 9.

26. Harry Maurer, *Not Working: An Oral History of the Unemployed* (New York: Holt, Rinehart and Winston, 1979), p. 204.

27. Ibid., p. 192.

28. Sheila Rule, "Federal Policies on Job Training Said to Harm the Disadvantaged," *New York Times* (November 19, 1980).

29. *The Condition of Vocational Education*, processed document, issued September 17, 1980, by the National Center for Education Statistics, U.S. Department of Education, pp. 103–104.

30. "National Summary of the Fall 1979 Vocational Education Civil Rights Survey," unpublished data from the Office for Civil Rights, U.S. Department of Education, Washington, D.C., 1980. Calculations by the Children's Defense Fund.

31. Dearich Hunter, "Ducks vs. Hard Rocks," *Newsweek* (August 18, 1980), pp. 14–15.

32. Vaughn, op. cit.

33. Lack, op. cit.

34. Children's Defense Fund, *Background Memorandum on Housing Discrimination Against Families With Children* (Washington, D.C.: Children's Defense Fund, June 1980).

35. Ibid.

36. Children's Defense Fund, Mississippi Project, *Special Education Advocacy Program: Progress Report* (Washington, D.C.: Children's Defense Fund, December 1976), pp. 7–8.

37. Children's Defense Fund, *Children Without Homes: An Examination of Public Responsibility to Children in Out-of-Home Care* (Washington, D.C.: Children's Defense Fund, 1978), p. 37.

38. Lack, op. cit.

39. Vaughn, op. cit.

11

MEXICAN MIGRATION TO THE UNITED STATES: CAUSES, CONSEQUENCES, AND U.S. RESPONSES

Wayne A. Cornelius

Perhaps the most revealing test of any society is the manner in which it deals with those who lack the political or economic power to achieve their just aspirations.—RAY MARSHALL, U.S. SECRETARY OF LABOR, MAY 11, 1978[1]

I have interviewed hundreds of persons that we have either deported or dealt with and, when you see the drive and ambition of someone who has walked two hundred miles across the desert to come here to take any job, you develop a great sense of respect for them and a great question about what this country is really doing.—LEONEL CASTILLO, COMMISSIONER, U.S. IMMIGRATION AND NATURALIZATION SERVICE, FEBRUARY 24, 1978[2]

The scenario is a familiar one in twentieth century U.S. history: Americans beset with rising unemployment (sometimes combined with high inflation), high taxes, and other problems over which they feel they have little control, begin searching for scapegoats. The search, feeding upon residual racial prejudice, as well as economic woes, leads quickly to the foreign migrant and, especially, the Mexican, who is not only the most numerous but the most visible among the foreign-born population. Politicians, journalists, organized labor, and other interest groups rush to blame him for every imaginable problem afflicting American society, from high unemployment to depressed wages, poor working conditions, lack of union organization among wage earners, high social service costs, international balance-of-payments deficits, rising crime rates, drug abuse, infectious disease, insect infestation, overpopulation, environmental pollution, energy shortages, and even Communist subversion.

Citizens demand that their elected officials "do something" about these problems by deporting the migrants and restricting future entries. Never

Excerpted from "Mexican Migration to the United States: Causes, Consequences, and U.S. Responses." Center for International Studies, Massachusetts Institute of Technology, 1978. Reprinted by permission.

mind that just a short time before, the migrants' labor was considered essential either to a national war effort or to economic growth, or both; now, the Mexican migrant is viewed as an economic threat, an intolerable burden on the U.S. taxpayer, and a cultural-racial contaminant. The presence of large numbers of Mexicans in the country is attributed either to a monstrous conspiracy of big business and its allies in Congress against the American working man, or to Mexican governments which prefer to export their problems rather than solve them. Most U.S. officials find such explanations convenient, since they divert public attention from their own failures of policy and performance. Responding to "popular demand," they proceed to deal with the "Mexican problem" through mass roundups and deportation ("repatriation") campaigns.

This general scenario has been played out no fewer than four times in the past 58 years: in 1920 to 1921, 1930 to 1935, 1953 to 1954, and 1973 to the present. The most recent episode has not yet culminated in mass roundups and deportations, although polls show that a majority of Americans would approve—once again—of this kind of "solution."

This paper represents an attempt to identify some of the basic factors underlying Mexican migration to the United States and U.S. responses to this migratory movement, primarily during the period since 1917. Particular attention is devoted to the role of the U.S. itself—including both public- and private-sector actors—in stimulating and institutionalizing migration from Mexico. The available evidence concerning the magnitude, characteristics, and socioeconomic impacts of the migration upon the United States and Mexico is summarized, and policy options for reducing or regulating the flow are discussed briefly.

Because of the clandestine existence that they must lead and their extreme geographic dispersion, it is impossible to estimate the total number of illegal Mexican migrants currently living in the U.S. with any degree of precision. Nevertheless, an inordinate preoccupation among U.S. officialdom with "counting the uncountable" has spawned a wide variety of "guess-timates" ranging from 2 to 12 million illegals, of whom two-thirds to three-quarters are assumed to be Mexicans. Perhaps the most widely cited estimate of the illegal Mexican population (5.2 million, in 1975) was produced by a private consulting firm under contract to the Immigration & Naturalization Service (INS) (Lesko Associates, 1975). This estimate was regarded by virtually all experts as excessively high, by several millions; and several detailed examinations have found the assumptions and methodology employed in producing it to be scientifically indefensible.

Indeed, if the stock of permanent-resident illegal Mexicans in the U.S. were as large as indicated by the Lesko estimate and those that exceed it, virtually all of the 15- to-44-year-old males enumerated in the 1970 Mexican census in the six principal "sending" states of Mexico would have to have migrated permanently to the U.S. by 1975, a rather unlikely occurrence.

The most basic flaw in such estimates is that they either ignore or grossly underestimate the volume of return migration to Mexico. For example, the Lesko estimation procedure assumed that only 2 percent of the illegals entering the U.S. in a given year do not settle permanently in the U.S.

But all field studies completed to date indicate that the reverse flow of migrants from the United States to Mexico is actually quite large. INS apprehension statistics indicate that the number of Mexican illegals entering the U.S. is also quite large.[3] But the *flow* of migrants must not be confused with the *stock* of permanent or long-term resident immigrants, which is likely to be expanding much more slowly than the number of migrants who simply attempt to enter the U.S. illegally. One researcher, using data from the U.S. Bureau of the Census, recently estimated the *net* flow of illegal Mexican migrants—i.e., the increment to the more-or-less permanent stock—at 82,000 to 130,000 per year, and even those estimates may be upwardly biased. The distinction between "flow" and "stock" is by no means a trivial one; the available evidence suggests that there are very important differences between the Mexican migrant who enters the U.S. occasionally for short-term employment and the migrant who seeks to establish permanent residence in the U.S., differences that are crucial to intelligent policy making. While it is quite likely that the number of *temporary* Mexican migrants to the U.S. has increased substantially in recent years largely in response to deteriorating economic conditions in Mexico, there is no evidence indicating that the number of new *permanent* additions to the illegal migrant population has risen dramatically.

It is unfortunate that recent discussions of the policy issues raised by illegal migration have been conducted mainly in terms of such numbers, which in themselves are meaningless. The key questions concern the *consequences* of the migration for both the United States and Mexico and other sending countries. Claiming to already have the answers to these "impact" questions, government officials and interest groups favoring a more restrictive immigration policy have seized upon the large increases in the number of apprehensions since the late 1960s to inflame public opinion. The public has been led to believe that there "must be" a substantial adverse impact on the U.S. economy and society, because there are so many millions of them "here"; that the situation is "out of control," with the outcome of the struggle for "containment" uncertain. While no constructive purpose can be served by such rhetoric, a political purpose is no doubt served, and that would be consistent with a well-established historical pattern of U.S. responses to Mexican migration.

Causal Factors: The U.S. Role in
Promoting Mexican Migration

Those with short memories find it easy to blame Mexico for the current state of affairs: that the "illegal alien problem" exists mainly because Mexico has failed to limit its population growth, failed to create enough jobs, etc. Even a superficial examination of the facts reveals this to be a gross oversimplification of the historical record.

Most Mexican and Chicano historians would begin a discussion of this topic with the U.S. annexation of Texas in 1845 and the Mexican war of 1846 to 1848. Undoubtedly the most sordid war of aggression in U.S. history (Ulysses S. Grant later called it "America's great unjust war"), the war enabled the U.S. to seize half of Mexico's national territory—disputed land in Texas, all of what is now California, most of New Mexico, Arizona, Nevada, and Utah, and part of Colorado and Wyoming. I shall begin the story some 40 years later, when the U.S. made its first serious efforts to recruit Mexican workers to meet the labor shortages being created by American economic expansion.

As early as the 1880s and 1890s, small groups of U.S. farmers were dispatching labor recruiters into northern Mexico. By 1911 or 1913, recruiting agents for U.S. railroads and mining companies had penetrated deep into central Mexico, spreading the word about the high wages being offered and even providing free transportation to the U.S.

They were soon followed by recruiters for Texas cotton growers, Colorado sugar beet growers, and even industrial employers in midwestern cities connected to Mexico by the railroads. Sometimes, rather than directly recruiting workers in the Mexican interior, hired agents working under contracts to a variety of U.S. companies would simply advertise the merits and location of their employment offices in the border cities and provide instructions on crossing the border.

The efforts of private U.S. firms to recruit large numbers of Mexican workers were facilitated by a series of legislative and administrative actions (or deliberate inactions), which themselves served as powerful inducements to migration to the U.S. Mexicans were specifically exempted from the $4 head tax imposed on each immigrant by the Immigration Act of 1907. In sharp contrast to their practice in East Coast ports of entry, U.S. immigration officials along the border with Mexico did not enforce the clause of the 1907 act which prohibited the entry of penniless aliens who would be "likely to become public charges."

The Contract Labor Law of 1885, which prohibited the entry of laborers who had been induced to come to the U.S. by specific job offers or promises of contracts, also went unenforced along the U.S.–Mexico border.

Passage by Congress of the Immigration Act of 1917 proved to be an indirect, but powerful, stimulant to Mexican migration to the U.S. By sharply restricting the entry of southern and eastern Europeans, the law automatically increased U.S. employer demand for Mexican labor. The 1917 law cut the supply of European laborers by almost 50 per cent, and the immigration laws enacted in 1921 and 1924 reduced it still further. Meanwhile, the U.S. was maintaining an open-door policy for refugees (both economic and political) from the Mexican Revolution, exempting them from most of the restrictions specified in the immigration laws. After the U.S. entry into World War I, the U.S. secretary of labor, acting under a proviso of the 1917 Immigration Act permitting him to suspend any parts of the law in the event of a labor shortage, specifically exempted Mexican agricultural workers from all restrictions imposed by the 1917 Act and the 1885 Contract Labor Law: the $8 head tax, the literacy test, and the prohibition on entry of contract laborers. Over 72,000 Mexican farm workers were formally admitted to the U.S. between 1917 and March 1921, under the terms of this waiver. In July 1918, the secretary of labor extended the waiver to include nonagricultural workers from Mexico (mostly contract laborers for the railroads, mines, and construction companies), a waiver which also remained in effect until March 1921. Direct recruitment of workers in the Mexican interior was stepped up.

After a brief interlude (the "repatriation" of 1920–1921), U.S. business and its allies in the Harding and Coolidge administrations resumed the courtship of the Mexican migrant. Seeking to promote U.S. economic growth through foreign investment and trade, Secretary of Commerce Herbert Hoover won approval of a new U.S. policy toward Mexico designed to create the best possible climate for expansion of U.S. trade and investments in Mexico. A central element of the "new relationship" with Mexico was nonenforcement of a racial exclusion clause of the 1924 Immigration Act, which prohibited the entry of persons having "more than 50 per cent Indian blood." Since enforcement of this clause would have had the effect of excluding a large proportion of Mexican workers—the vast majority of whom were mixed-blood *mestizos*—border officials were ordered to get around it by classifying all incoming Mexicans as "white."

Also, the provision of the 1924 Immigration Act requiring all entrants to obtain visas went unenforced along the U.S.–Mexico border until 1929. The newly established Border Patrol busied itself enforcing the customs and alcohol prohibition laws. Even on those rare occasions when Mexican illegals were apprehended by immigration officials, they were not deported. Instead, their U.S. employers were required to pay the visa and head tax charges for the worker (a total of $18); "then the worker was brought to the nearest border entry point and allowed to reenter the U.S."

With the coming of the Great Depression, it was no longer profitable or necessary to attract a large supply of Mexican workers. The door was slammed shut, and mass roundups and less obvious forms of coercion were employed to rid ourselves of "the intolerable burden" of Mexican workers who did not leave of their own volition. But 12 years later, with the labor shortages created by U.S. entry into World War II, the Mexican worker suddenly became a highly valuable commodity once again. In 1942, the *bracero* program was launched by passage of Public Law 45, which enabled U.S. employers to recruit Mexican contract laborers for short-term work in agriculture (the duration of the contracts ranged from 45 days to 6 months). Extended under a series of U.S. statutes and bi-national agreements from 1942 to December 1964, the *bracero* program brought more than 4 million Mexican workers (including many "repeaters") to the United States. Extensive publicity about the hiring centers established in Mexico City, Guadalajara, Irapuato, Aguascalientes, Monterrey, and other cities was beamed by radio into the smallest villages, many of which had not previously contributed many migrants to the U.S.-bound flow. In the village of Tzintzuntzan, Michoacán, for example, 53 per cent of all household heads and an additional unknown number of single men had been to the U.S. as *braceros* by the time the program was terminated in 1964. The *bracero* program was also a milestone in the history of several of the communities included in my study. Before 1942, the volume of emigration from these communities to the U.S. had been relatively low; but especially during the heyday of the *bracero* program in the late 1950s, "just about everyone went," as one informant recalls.[4] By the time the program ended in 1964, migration to the U.S., as a strategy of income maintenance or improvement, had been thoroughly institutionalized in thousands of Mexican villages and towns with the active encouragement of the U.S. government and U.S. agribusiness.

The interlocking of U.S. and Mexican economies has promoted Mexican migration in other ways. The U.S. has powerfully influenced the kind of economic development that has occurred in Mexico since the 1920s through direct private investment. In Mexico, as in other Latin American countries, the technologies introduced by U.S. firms and U.S.-based multinational corporations have tended to be highly capital-intensive—certainly more capital-intensive than the technologies used by most Mexican enterprises. Over the years, many local firms, increasingly unable to compete with the more efficient subsidiaries of U.S.-based multinationals, have been absorbed by them. The result has been a higher rate of labor displacement—or a lower rate of job creation—than would otherwise have occurred in some sectors of the Mexican economy.[5] This is also true of the agricultural sector, particularly in the irrigated farming areas of northwestern and central Mexico. There, the system of "contract farming" introduced by U.S.-based food-processing corporations, such as Del Monte, Campbell's, and General Foods, has served the interests of larger growers at the expense of smaller, more marginal farmers. The companies' preference for working with larger growers—and favoring them with credit, use of machinery, and advantageous marketing arrangements—has left the smaller producers in an increasingly uncompetitive position.

Eventually, many of the small landowners rent or sell their land to the larger growers, and then either work as wage-laborers for the large growers or migrate.

In more and more a general sense, the economies of the U.S. and Mexico are now so closely intertwined that we invariably export our recessions and inflationary spirals to Mexico, thus increasing the volume of illegal migration. This can hardly be avoided under a trade relationship in which 69 per cent of all Mexican exports go to the U.S. and about 61 per cent of the goods imported by Mexico come from the U.S. It should come as no surprise that the serious economic problems experienced by Mexico since 1969 have coincided, albeit with a time lag, with the U.S. recession-inflation cycles of the 1970s.

Finally, while the U.S. federal government continues to do battle against illegal migrants from Mexico and elsewhere, state and local government officials in many parts of the country either welcome their presence or acquiesce in it. Among other things, state and local governments issue licenses and permits for all sorts of economic activity—from retail commerce to roof repair—with no proof of U.S. citizenship or legal resident status required. Such practices enable the illegal migrant who manages to accumulate some capital to go into business for himself. Since it is virtually impossible to make the issuance of such permits "secure" (even if proof of legal resident status is required, the birth certificates or other credentials used to demonstrate such status can easily be purchased or fraudulently obtained), illegal migrants will continue to receive them. Many local school districts actively recruit Mexican migrants—regardless of legal status—into their adult education programs. Especially in border areas, there seems to be a plethora of groups and organizations—church groups, private social service agencies, legal defense organizations, and so on—which provide assistance to illegal migrants. The point is not that such assistance should be denied to the illegal migrant; it is simply to call attention to another facet of the U.S. role in initiating and perpetuating this migratory movement.

Through extensive labor recruiting, manipulations of the immigration laws, the investments and practices of U.S. firms within Mexico, the activities of a wide variety of public and private entities on our side of the border, and in many other ways, the U.S. has done much to "push" and "pull" Mexican migrants into this country.

The point of departure for "illegal alien" policy making should be a recognition that the U.S. bears a heavy share of responsibility for the present situation. Yet, while we continue to welcome with open arms the Indochinese "refugees from Communism," to whose condition we contributed, the refugees from poverty streaming across our border with Mexico—to whose condition and behavior we have also contributed—are shunned.

Does illegal migration "create unemployment" among the U.S. domestic work force? While restrictionists seem to feel that the drawing of "common sense" inferences is sufficient to prove their case and have not pursued the kind of research that might generate direct evidence bearing on the question, there are fragmentary data available which—if anything— demonstrate how tenuous is the purported relationship between illegal migration and the U.S. unemployment problem.

If illegal migration from Mexico were decreasing job opportunities for significant numbers of American workers—either directly or indirectly— it follows that unemployment rates should be higher in those parts of the country having large concentrations of Mexican illegals, and lower in areas with few illegals. Of course, this is not the case: some of the lowest unemployment rates in the U.S. are found in the "Sunbelt" areas having the largest concentrations of illegal Mexican migrants. The data presented in Table 1 show that during all but two of the last 10 years, the unemployment rate in eight of the labor markets most heavily affected by Mexican migration has been *lower* than the national unemployment rate—during a period in which the volume of illegal Mexican migration (as indicated by INS apprehensions) was increasing at an average annual rate of 25 per cent. Nationwide, there seems to be virtually no correlation between numbers of illegal Mexican migrants and levels of unemployment. Research at the local level has also failed to demonstrate the existence of significant job displacement resulting from Mexican migration. A detailed study of Mexican illegals' participation in the labor market of the San Antonio metropolitan area found that

Mexican illegal aliens in no way compete with or displace workers in the primary [skilled] labor market. In the secondary [low-skilled] labor market, where they work alongside blacks and Chicanos, illegals usually represent an additional supply of labor. . . . Blacks and Mexican-Americans worked in similar industries but in basically different jobs. . . . For example, in a typical small construction firm, the Mexican illegal aliens worked as laborers while the Mexican-Americans and blacks had jobs as craftsmen. In a manufacturing industry such as meatpacking, the illegals worked in occupations that Mexican-Americans and blacks shunned because of dirty working conditions." (Cardenas, 1976)

Table 1   Unemployment in the U.S.
and in Major Labor Areas
Highly Affected by Mexican
Migration, 1968–1977

| | Unemployment Rate° | |
Year	United States	"High Impact" Labor Areas†
1968	3.6%	3.0%
1969	3.5	3.1
1970	4.9	5.2
1971	5.9	6.1
1972	5.6	5.3
1973	4.9	4.8
1974	5.6	5.2
1975	8.5	7.5
1976	7.7	7.3
1977	7.0	6.7
1968–1977 (Avg.)	5.7	5.4

°Unemployed as percent of total labor force. Sources: U.S. Dept. of Labor and U.S. Dept. of Health, Education and Welfare, *Employment and Training Report of the President, 1977*, Table D-8, pp. 246–248; U.S. Dept. of Labor, *Manpower Report of the President, 1969*, Table D-8, pp. 284–286; *Monthly Labor Review*, March, 1978, Table 1, p. 63.

†Unemployment rate averaged across the following labor areas (as defined by the U.S. Dept. of Labor): Los Angeles–Long Beach, Calif.; Anaheim–Santa Ana–Garden Grove, Calif.; San Diego, Calif.; Dallas, Texas; Fort Worth, Texas (data combined for Dallas-Ft. Worth labor area since 1974); Houston, Texas; San Antonio, Texas; Oklahoma City, Okla.; and Chicago, Ill.

While systematic research on the labor market impacts of illegal migration is just beginning, the evidence available at present indicates that even in the most highly "impacted" areas, the effects of unemployment among domestic workers are not nearly as great as those agitating for a more restrictive immigration policy would have us believe. There is simply not enough credible evidence to establish the existence of a cause-and-effect relationship—even an *indirect* one—between illegal migration and domestic unemployment.

The point of departure for public policy making, with respect to both domestic unemployment and illegal immigration, should be a recognition that the two phenomena are not related to one another in a simple supply-and-demand situation. We must accept the fact that there are certain kinds of jobs—even in an advanced technological society—which most native-born Americans will not do, even at substantially higher wages, because of the nature of the work itself and/or the limited prospects for upward mobility which it offers. Moreover, it is not in the interests of many disadvantaged Americans to take these jobs, which would clearly limit their long-term income and growth potential.

For generations, the American public has been led to believe that a restrictive immigration policy is necessary to achieve full employment. . . . In fact, there is no evidence whatsoever that "tightening up low-wage labor markets" through a restrictive immigration policy would be highly beneficial to the "structurally unemployed" among the U.S. labor force. Today, no less than in the past, it is bad—as well as misleading—public policy to elevate a crackdown on illegal migrants to the status of a central element of the government's overall strategy for reducing unemployment.

IMPACT ON SOCIAL SERVICE COSTS AND TAX REVENUES

Since the onset of the Great Depression of the 1930s, Mexican migrants have often been accused, simultaneously, of (1) being a burden on the U.S. taxpayer by going on welfare, and (2) holding jobs at the expense of American workers. If my own mail and various public opinion polls are any guide, these perceptions of the negative consequences of Mexican migration remain fused in the minds of most Americans; the obvious contradiction ("they're all on welfare and they're taking our jobs away") never occurs to most people. The use of illegal migrants as scapegoats for rising social service costs and higher taxes is particularly common in the Southwest; witness, for example, the explicit invocation of the "illegal alien" issue by groups promoting the "taxpayer revolt" in California during the first six months of 1978. Such appeals feed upon racism and the traditional U.S. stereotype of the Mexican as being lazy, indolent, and thieving.

The reality of the situation is quite different. At least six different field studies of Mexican illegals have found extremely low rates of utilization of such tax-supported programs as unemployment compensation, welfare assistance, food stamps, and public education—usually in the 1 to 3 per cent range. A comprehensive study of welfare assistance in Los Angeles County—which undoubtedly contains more Mexicans than any other county in the United States—found that the total cost of aiding illegal migrants in the county during 1976 represented about two-tenths of 1 per cent of the county's total welfare (AFDC) budget, and the costs for 1977 were expected to be even lower. Similarly, when some 80,000 persons receiving welfare payments in San Diego County were screened during 1976–1977, it was discovered that only about 800 individuals—about 1 per cent of the case load—were illegal migrants. Again, San Diego County is one of the most highly "impacted" counties in the United States: in 1975 it accounted for 43 per cent of all apprehensions of illegal migrants along the southern U.S. border and 25 per cent of all apprehensions throughout the nation.

It should come as little surprise that relatively few illegal migrants from Mexico make use of tax-supported social services. In the first place, popular stereotypes notwithstanding, the work ethic is very strong among Mexican migrants. They come from a culture in which acceptance of "welfare" or other kinds of public handouts is strongly frowned upon. Second, their illegal status militates against social service usage: making application for welfare, unemployment compensation, and other kinds of benefits forces the migrant to identify himself to a government agency, thereby increasing his risk of apprehension and deportation—a powerful deterrent to service utilization. In many places, applicants for welfare and other service programs are routinely "referred" to the Immigration and Naturalization Service for a check of immigration status. In fact, such "referrals" to the INS from public service agencies constitute one of the most important sources of information leading to apprehensions of illegal migrants in the interior of the United States. Those who do apply for welfare or food stamps are usually denied such benefits, even it they escape deportation. Finally, most Mexican migrants have what they consider to be a superior alternative to public assistance programs in times of need: informal support networks of relatives and friends who have preceded them in migration to the United States. When unemployed, they rely on these kinship-friendship networks for temporary support, or else return to their community of origin in Mexico.

All of the studies completed thus far show that illegal Mexican migrants are more likely to make use of health care than any other type of public service. However, the available data do not provide a useful measure of the "taxpayer burden" imposed by medical care for illegal migrants, because of the way in which most survey questions about medical care have been worded. The data undoubtedly overstate the extent of medical assistance received by Mexican illegals *at taxpayers' expense,* for two reasons: (1) It is not known whether the U.S. hospitals or clinics mentioned by survey respondents were, in fact, tax-supported institutions; and (2) in many cases, even though the migrant himself did not pay the full cost of the medical care received, the costs were covered by the migrant's employer, or through hospitalization insurance paid for by the migrant and his employer. Forty-four per cent of the illegal migrants in North & Houstoun's (1976) survey had hospitalization insurance deducted from their wages, and 34 per cent of the respondents in the Orange County Task Force (1978) survey reported such deductions.

The longer the migrant stays in the U.S., the more likely he is to have dependents living here who require social services. But the Orange County Task Force study (1978) demonstrated that even among the more-or-less "permanent" population of Mexican illegals, there is very little utilization of tax-supported programs (2.8 per cent had collected welfare payments, 1.6 per cent had received food stamps, 9.0 per cent had received medical care). Because of the procedure used to locate respondents, the sample in this study was biased toward long-term residents, whose presence in a given neighborhood would be better known to the interviewers than more recent arrivals. Ninety per cent of the Orange County respondents had been in the U.S. for more than one year; the average duration of stay was more than 2.5 years. . . .

Ironically, the presence of Mexican illegals in a community may *increase* the level of public services available to legal residents needing them, at no cost to the locality. The in-migration of low-income Mexicans has the effect of lowering the median income of a community, which qualifies it for more federal housing rehabilitation money, more federal aid to public schools, and more money from a variety of other federal programs which dispense funds to local communities on the basis of per capita income. Not surprisingly, many financially pressed local governments in the U.S. Southwest tend to view Mexican migrants as something of a godsend. More generally, Mexican migrants represent a windfall for the United States, in the sense that they are young, highly productive workers, whose health care, education, and other costs of rearing have been borne by Mexico, and whose maintenance during periods of unemployment and retirement is also usually provided by their relatives in Mexico. The significance of this windfall becomes apparent when we consider that as of 1977 the cost of preparing a U.S.-born man or woman for integration into the U.S. labor force was about $44,000.

There is another sense in which Mexican migration actually subsidizes, rather than burdens, U.S. society. In most cases, illegal Mexican migrants pay for social services that they rarely, if ever, use. And the cost of the services they do use is greatly exceeded by their contributions to tax revenues: state and federal income taxes, Social Security, local property taxes, sales taxes, and so forth. Again, there are abundant data from studies using widely varying methodologies, showing that income and Social Security taxes are withheld from the wages of about two-thirds to three-quarters or more of Mexican illegals. In addition, the majority of Mexican illegals do not file for an income tax refund even if it is due them, either because of lack of knowledge or fear of being apprehended if they apply for a refund. And Mexican migrants are clearly subsidizing the U.S. Social Security system—to the tune of hundreds of millions of dollars per year—since those who work in the U.S. for only brief periods, never settling here permanently, will never draw pension benefits from the Social Security fund; and even those who do remain here permanently cannot qualify for benefits unless they somehow legalize their status. Without this "subsidy," the Social Security trust fund would be depleted even earlier than current financing schedules indicate.

Conclusion

The reassessment of U.S. immigration policy which is currently underway in Congress and the executive branch must eventually confront one basic question. Three years or so from now, the INS will no doubt possess sufficient manpower and hardware to sharply reduce the influx of illegal migrants from Mexico, though certainly not to halt it. But at what *cost* to the economies and societies of the U.S. and Mexico? While our knowledge of the impacts of illegal migration on the two countries is still limited, the available evidence does point to one general conclusion: that stopping or severely reducing the migration would *not* be a cost-free decision for the United States itself.

The probable costs would include:

• Loss of jobs for American workers in firms that mechanize, relocate in a foreign country, or shut down entirely in response to a sharp reduction in the supply of migrant labor.

• Loss of jobs for American workers due to reduced consumer spending, both in those areas of the U.S. where the migrants have been concentrated and in Mexico, where the demand for U.S.-made imports would fall off.

• A higher rate of inflation in the United States because of the higher prices that consumers would pay for goods currently produced with migrant labor, and because of upward pressure on the overall wage structure.

• A lower rate of future economic growth and more limited mobility opportunities for disadvantaged Americans as the U.S. population declines and ages.

• Increased public hostility and discrimination in hiring against all Spanish-speaking people in the U.S., regardless of immigration status.

• A sharp deterioration in our bilateral relations with Mexico and, if the migration is reduced too rapidly, the possibility of economic and political disruptions within Mexico that would eventually threaten U.S. interests.

After assessing the probable costs of a much more restrictive immigration policy, another question remains: Who will *benefit* from such a policy, aside from the politicians who can take electoral credit for it, and the army of bureaucrats who are hired to administer it? The benefits of a restrictive immigration policy to its alleged main beneficiaries—"The already disadvantaged workers—blacks, Hispanics, women, teenagers, the handicapped, low-skilled legal immigrants"—seem to have been vastly overestimated. Do the conceivable benefits of a restrictive policy to the United States outweigh the probable costs? The answer is very likely to be no. The long-term interests of Mexico would probably be best served by a reduction of the flow, but *only* if that reduction is gradual, and if alternative income-earning opportunities can be created at a commensurate rate within Mexico.

Unfortunately, given a domestic political climate favoring draconian "solutions" to the "illegal alien problem," gradualist approaches have little appeal to U.S. political leaders and their constituents. In fact, some restrictionists argue that only by adopting drastic measures to reduce the flow of migrants by whatever means necessary—up to and including closure of the U.S.-Mexican border—can the U.S. compel the kinds of policy changes by the Mexican government that would be needed to cut the migration off at its source.

In fact, a policy of "benign neglect" would be more consistent with the existing evidence than most of the restrictive measures currently under consideration. But inaction may no longer be politically feasible, due to the large increases in the flow of illegal migrants in recent years and the arousal of public concern about the phenomenon by government officials and the mass media since 1973. Polls show that public tolerance in the U.S. for immigration in general—legal and illegal—has declined during the past decade, while public approval for draconian "solutions" has increased. A majority of the American people now opposes any form of amnesty for illegal immigrants, while 62 to 80 per cent support employer sanctions legislation to deny them jobs, and 57 per cent would approve "operation wetback"-style roundups and mass deportations. Such attitudes will only harden during the next U.S. recession, which is not too far away according to most economists.

Under the circumstances, there is serious doubt that the U.S. will be able to rise above scapegoating, political expedience, and racial prejudice to pursue an immigration policy that will serve its own long-term national interests as well as those of Mexico and other sending countries. Like some West European nations, the U.S. may well have lost the capacity to respond rationally, constructively, and humanely to large-scale migration from less developed countries. The implications of this are profoundly disturbing, but Mexico and other sending countries would be well advised to ponder them.

NOTES

1. Ray Marshall, testimony before the Senate Judiciary Subcommittee on Immigration, U.S. Senate, Washington, D.C., May 11, 1978.

2. Testimony before a subcommittee of the House Committee on Appropriations (*Hearing on Undocumented Aliens*, 1978: 20).

3. The real number of entrants is, of course, considerably larger than the apprehension statistics indicate, since many of those entering illegally manage to evade the INS and eventually return to Mexico undetected. However, a downward correction must also be applied to INS apprehension statistics, because of multiple apprehensions of some illegals within the same year. The apprehension statistics represent events, not people per se. It is not uncommon for a single illegal migrant to be apprehended twice (or more) in a given year; INS Commissioner Castillo recently reported apprehending one man five times in a single day.

4. The data from the family migration histories in these communities bear him out. Not until 1974 did emigration to the U.S. once again reach the level attained in 1959, when virtually all of the migrants went as *braceros*.

5. By 1968, at least 625 subsidiaries of U.S.-based corporations were operating in Mexico. Fifty-eight per cent of these enterprises were in the manufacturing sector, and of these 365 subsidiaries, 43 per cent had been established by acquisition of Mexican-owned firms.

BIBLIOGRAPHY

Cardenas, Gilbert (1976) "Illegal Aliens in the Southwest: A Case Study," pp. 66–69 in National Council on Employment Policy, *Illegal Aliens: An Assessment of the Issues.* Washington, D.C.

Lesko Associates (1975) "Final Report: Basic Data and Guidance Required to Implement a Major Illegal Alien Study During Fiscal Year 1976." Report for U.S. Immigration and Naturalization Service, Washington, D.C.

North, David S., and Marion F. Houstoun (1976) *The Characteristics and Role of Illegal Aliens in the U.S. Labor Market: An Exploratory Study.* Washington, D.C., Linton and Co.

Orange County, California, Task Force on Medical Care for Illegal Aliens (1978) *The Economic Impact of Undocumented Immigrants on Public Health Services in Orange County, California.*

12

AMERICAN INDIANS: STRUGGLING FOR POWER AND IDENTITY

Howell Raines

American Indians gave up beads-and-blanket capitalism on Jan. 31, 1975, in Billings, Mont. That day, at a meeting in a small college planted on a frigid escarpment of the Rockies, a group of tribal leaders got a look at the generous contracts under which American energy companies now do business with oil-rich third-world nations. For the Indians, it was an instant education in the real value of their "worthless" reservations. They learned that, unlike the canny oil merchants of the Middle East, their tribes were still being ripped off with Colonial-era prices for the vast mineral wealth that lies under the feet of this nation's most impoverished minority. Prophetically, the meeting in Billings was entitled "Indian Tribes as Emerging Nations."

In the ensuing years, more and more Indians have come to think of their reservations as tiny sovereign nations within the United States. If a new generation of Indian leaders has its way, they are going to be rich little nations, too. For the 50 million acres of despised and for the most part barren lands pawned off on the Indians in the last century contain about one-third of the American West's strippable coal and half of the nation's uranium, not to mention enough oil to bedazzle the eyes of Texas. At today's prices, the 70 billion tons of coal under Indian land is worth over $1,000 billion, or $1 trillion.

Swiftly, the drive for economic power has become the main thrust of Indian activism throughout the nation—in the Rocky Mountain coal fields, along the salmon rivers of the Northwest and on vast Eastern tracts where, after almost 200 years of silence, Indians stunned and infuriated whites by claiming "aboriginal title." "We are trying to prove," said LaDonna Harris, the Comanche activist whose Americans for Indian Opportunity organized the Billings conference, "that you don't have to be poor to be an Indian."

But development-minded Indians face formidable obstacles, including proposals to take over their energy reserves by abolishing the reservations. Indeed, white sympathy and guilt over the treatment of Indians seem to be fading before a new mood of fiscal austerity. The first Americans are facing a white backlash that, spreading east from Seattle in ever-widening circles of outrage, may be felt all the way from oil-company board rooms to the United States Supreme Court. Last summer's 3,000 mile, cross-country trek to the nation's capital, the Longest Walk, was an attempt to combat this problem, but because of deep and historic divisions in their own ranks, Indians have so far been unable to meet the backlash with an effective, united front.

There is, for instance, the cultural gap between the 650,000 Indians living on or near reservations and the 350,000 urban Indians in the red ghettos of Minneapolis, Chicago, Los Angeles and other cities. Also, the tribal tradition means that many native Americans think of themselves as, say, Kiowas first and Indians second. Within most major tribes, government is so radically democratic that it is virtually impossible to find a native American who expects to see the emergence of a red Martin Luther King, Jr. who can speak for Indian America. Beyond that, conservative Indians view with suspicion those tribal leaders who want to rip open Mother Earth. To them, the cancer outbreak among Navajo uranium miners symbolizes the deady dangers of bringing white commerce to Indian Country.

The term Indian Country first came into the language as a name for the seemingly limitless territories beyond the westernmost white settlements. As used by today's Indians, it refers to both their scattered pockets of land and to a state of mind. What should white Americans think about both the territory and the mentality that is Indian Country? Can even a rough justice be now imposed on the despair-filled history of the nation's oldest social conflict? Does history, in fact, demand a justice that penalizes 220 million people for the good of a minority that has willfully resisted the assimilative process that has brought prosperity to other impoverished minorities? The answers, such as they are, are as diverse as the terrain and people of an Indian Country that stretches from the beige corridors of the Bureau of Indian Affairs in Washington, D.C., to the red grit hills of Arizona and New Mexico.

COAL-SMOKE SIGNAL

In her tarpaper shack on a windy hilltop in Fruitland, N.M., Emma Yazzie dreams of an enchanted ancestral past. But she is living, literally and quite unwillingly, on the ramparts of the Indian future. "I want it to be as though I was living a long time ago," said the 72-year-old Navajo sheepherder, speaking carefully in English, her second language. "It used to be such a beautiful place. We had all kinds of colored grass."

Today, the grass that feeds Emma Yazzie's 19 sheep is uniformly brown.

For this, she blames pollution from the nearby Four Corners Power Plant, the huge, coal-fired electrical generator whose plume of smoke is visible for miles across the desert.

That plant towers over Emma Yazzie's tiny farmstead on the northern rim of the 14-million-acre Navajo Reservation. To the west, where the one-room hogans of her relatives once dotted the mesas, lies the 31,000-acre strip mine leased from her tribe to provide the Four Corners plant with cheap Navajo coal. To the south, along the San Juan River where the Yazzie clan once held idyllic summer encampments, the pumps of the generating plant suck at the stream beside which Miss Yazzie was born.

Emma Yazzie has lost much and gained nothing. Gone are the landscapes and pellucid skies she loved. Yet, the pumps bring her no water, and the humming power lines bypass her lightless shack. So, of course, does the money. Utah International Mining Company, a subsidiary of General Electric, pays a royalty of only 15 cents per ton to the Navajo tribe for the coal used at Four Corners. Yet, on today's market, a white landowner would receive a royalty of $1.50 per ton. Utah International and General Electric owe this windfall to the Bureau of Indian Affairs: For years, the B.I.A. negotiated all reservation coal leases for the Indians to assure that the tribal leaders wouldn't make any naïve or stupid deals.

But Emma Yazzie and the other American Indians who own 4 percent of the nation's land want to make their own decisions about how their lands are used. "Self-determination" and "sovereignty" are the Indians new catchwords. Like the black movement that started in the South in the 50's, the Indian movement gained its momentum from Federal court decisions that have upset many whites. In 1975, for example, the courts upheld tribal claims to the northern two-thirds of Maine, and that case signaled Easterners that the "Indian problem" was not restricted to the Far West. Last October, the Maine case was finally settled when the Passamaquoddy and Penobscot tribes gave up their claim to 12.5 million acres in return for a relatively modest payment of $37 million and the right to expand their reservations by 100,000 acres. But the settlement left standing the ruling that Indians have an aboriginal title to lands occupied by whites who never obtained the Congressional approval required by the long-ignored Indian Non-Intercourse Act of 1790.

Comparisons between the black movement and the Indian movement can be pushed too far. Indians lack the numbers and unity of the black minority, and, while blacks sought assimilation into the American mainstream, Indians face the far more complicated question of whether to preserve separate Indian culture. Moreover, the key issue to the blacks was social justice, and, to many Indian leaders, at least, it is economic power. They want to take advantage of the world's new competition for scarce land and dwindling resources. So, Emma Yazzie notwithstanding, the leaders want to use the new leverage gained from the mineral wealth of their reservations as a substitute for the marching feet that carried black demands to national attention.

Emma Yazzie has been educated by history to view all developers, white and Indian alike, with contempt and despair. "They want to stick their noses in the ground like a pig," she says. Clasping rough hands around her chipped turquoise brooch, the old woman gazes toward the plant. "They kill the grass," she continues. "They kill a lot of Navajo, too. That smoke smells bad and it goes into our hearts. The horse is not strong anymore. It's weak. And the sheep come up blind."

INDIAN OPEC

Eighty miles from Emma Yazzie and her dreams of the past, lives the man who has offered himself as the hope of the Indian future. He drives a Lincoln Continental, favors pin-striped suits and when indicted for embezzlement in 1977 hired F. Lee Bailey to plead his case, which ended in a hung jury. The most important icon in his office in Window Rock, Ariz., is not a tribal artifact, but a softball-sized lump of coal on a brass stand.

Peter MacDonald, the 50-year-old chairman of the Navajo Nation, is organizer and chairman of the Council of Energy Resources Tribes (CERT), which he described in a letter to President Carter as "the native American OPEC." Mr. MacDonald intends for CERT to serve much the same function for the Indian tribes, whose reservations he views as "dependent, yet sovereign," nations within the United States.

"We used the same trick that John Wayne would use," Mr. MacDonald said of the impulse that led to the founding of CERT. "We circled the wagons. We circled the tribes and said, 'By golly, if you're going to get the coal, you're not going to deal just with the Crow or just with the Navajo or just with the Cheyenne. You've got to deal with the rest of us.' "

The CERT wagons are circled over the richest unexploited fossil fuel and mineral deposits on the continent. Mr. MacDonald created a public-relations crisis for the organization in 1977 when, snubbed in his request for a White House meeting, he announced he had contacted OPEC's Arab oil experts for advice on how to develop the reservations most profitably. Rather quickly, $200,000 and then $2 million in Federal grants showered on CERT—presumably to divert the Indians from striking an alliance with the Arab organization. Despite this Federal largesse, Mr. MacDonald, a Marine veteran of World War II, is still furious about accusations that he was unpatriotic to consult OPEC. "It sounded like I'm a traitor, that CERT tribes are enemies of the United States," he said. "It's all because I'm trying to cling to what little is left to us."

It is simply a matter, noted Mr. MacDonald, an electrical engineer who once worked in missile development for Hughes Aircraft, of Indians learning to play by the white man's rules. After all, the reservation system was structured to confine Indians to land that the Government experts of 100 years ago believed forever worthless. "We have now decided," he said with obvious delight at the irony, "to use the very structure devised by whites for their protection to assert what we describe as Indian self-determination, meaning that this is our reservation, that we have a certain sovereignty and we're going to exercise it."

As defined by CERT, self-determination and sovereignty mean, for one thing, that tribal governments rather than the Bureau of Indian Affairs ought to negotiate energy contracts. The argument heard all over Indian Country is that Indians couldn't possibly do any worse than the B.I.A. The bureau, for instance, neglected to put escalation or termination clauses in leases negotiated when coal was selling for $6 a ton. As a result, the Navajos are saddled with the 15-cents- to 37.5-cents-per-ton royalties even though the retail price of coal has soared to $15 to $20 per ton and standard royalties are up to $1.50 and more. The CERT tribes are, indeed, doing better. For one thing, the tribes are insisting on joint-venture contracts rather than the B.I.A.-approved leases under which the Indians signed over most of their powers as landowners to the mining companies. The Navajo tribal council recently received $6 million in front money in a proposed joint venture with Exxon to develop the uranium deposits on the nation's largest reservation. (Its 14 million acres in Utah, New Mexico and Arizona make the Navajo Nation the equal in size of West Virginia.) Unhappy with the 17.5-cents-per-ton royalty negotiated for them by the B.I.A., the Crow tribe of Montana is suing to overturn strip-mining contracts with Shell and AMAX, and is now shopping for a better deal. Mr. MacDonald and his tribe's Wall Street-trained attorney, George Vlassis of Phoenix, plan to challenge every company that enjoys a cheap lease, including the coal suppliers at the Four Corners Power Plant. "The next one on the hit list," Mr. Vlassis says bluntly, "is Utah International."

Mr. MacDonald's critics question whether his government can, and will, use the increased income to give the reservation the self-sufficient, business economy he envisions. With its $200 million a year in Federal subsidies, the reservation has, by tradition, a welfare-state economy in which the tribal government, with 7,000 workers, is the largest employer. Also, in the past few years, a number of other tribal officials have been charged with embezzlement, sparking demonstrations in which dissidents accused the "MacDollar" government of ripping off tribal income. (Mr. MacDonald said his own indictment, in which he was accused of getting about $7,900 by submitting false travel vouchers to an Arizona utility, was part of a conspiracy to discredit him as an Indian spokesman. The tribal chairman has also publicly accused Arizona Senator Barry Goldwater of involvement in a plot to foment violence on the reservation to bring about martial law, and, in an interview, Mr. MacDonald said he believed that part of the plan was to kill him. The alleged plot surfaced in court testimony of John Harvey Adamson, the confessed killer of Don Bolles, a muckraking reporter for The Arizona Republic. Mr. Adamson said he and a reservation "spy" for Mr. Goldwater discussed planting a bomb in Mr. MacDonald's car or office. Mr. Goldwater has publicly denied the accusations of both Mr. Adamson and Mr. MacDonald and voluntarily appeared before a grand jury. Federal investigators discounted Mr. Adamson's story of a plot involving Mr. Goldwater. But the informant's testimony led to two conspiracy convictions in the attempted bombing of an Indian health center in Phoenix.)

Such controversies aside, Mr. MacDonald and leaders of other tribes may face political obstacles to their plans to use mining income for economic development. So far, only a handful of Indians have benefited personally from the coal boom. For example, the 160 Navajos at a Gulf Oil subsidiary's strip mine near Window Rock make $9 to $12 per hour. But per capita income on the reservation remains only about $1,000 per year—one-seventh of the national average. In many cases, grandparents, parents and children live on dirt floors of one-room hogans with no plumbing and no privacy. And there is always the possibility that these impoverished reservation residents might vote against investment programs for their energy income and demand "per caps"—lump-sum, per capita payments that have a disastrous history of winding up in the pockets of a few white merchants and Indian hustlers.

"In a generation, the resource will be played out and you'll have a few native American sheiks and an impoverished mass," predicted John Redhouse, a Navajo activist who has organized traditionalist Indians to fight a coal-gasification plant proposed for Burnham, N.M., in the Four Corners area of the reservation. The Government and energy companies are simply using CERT, he says, to legitimize their plans to turn the Western reservations into "national-sacrifice areas." He called the plans "spiritual and physical genocide." Even Indians sympathetic to Mr. MacDonald's general goal of economic development fear that his tactics will contribute to the backlash. "My notion is that it's harmful to Indians," says Sam Deloria, the Standing Rock Sioux who heads the American Indian Law Center at the University of New Mexico, "to communicate the idea that Indians are going to get rich off other Americans' heating bills."

On one point, however, there is something approaching general agreement: As the Navajo Nation goes, so goes much of Indian Country. With a membership of more than 150,000, the tribe accounts for almost 20 percent of the nation's Indian population, and the Navajo chairman is often looked to by whites as the de facto leader of all Indians. In what can only be regarded as a mandate for his energy-development policies, Mr. MacDonald demolished 12 opponents in the 1978 tribal elections to win his third term as chairman.

As recently as Feb. 1, Mr. MacDonald and other CERT leaders were in New York to discuss the next step beyond joint ventures—Indian-owned energy companies that, with money from Eastern financial institutions, would extract and process coal, uranium and oil on the reservations. That would certainly mean more smoke in the skies over Emma Yazzie's place.

THE RED AND THE WHITE

If the prospect of unaccustomed prosperity looms before the Western reservations, a familiar despair still lurks in the bars of the red ghetto along East Franklin Avenue in Minneapolis. "The State Alcohol and Drug Commission says 43 to 45 percent of the Indian population are directly involved in alcoholism," says Dennis Hisgun, a 35-year-old Sioux. "And 80 to 85 percent are indirectly involved; that is, they belong to the family of a drinker. I can't prove those figures, but I think they're pretty accurate. We're now seeing our chronic age dropping to the late 20's and early 30's. It used to be in the 40's. So that means alcoholism is epidemic. We have three counselors. We're hardly making a dent."

Mr. Hisgun is social-services director of the Minneapolis Native American Center, and a former alcoholic who has discovered the Catch-22 of many Government programs for Indians. "Indian alcoholism is getting worse. Traditional treatment modalities don't work. Yet we're forced to use them to get funding. For instance, when I sobered up, I did it by turning to a group of Indian people attempting to stay sober. All we had was a house—a place to help one another get up off the ground. They were very unorthodox and that's not acceptable to funding agencies."

The nation's red ghettos are, like the alcohol therapies described by Mr. Hisgun, showcases for Federal policies and programs that don't work. The Eisenhower Administration's termination policy—so named because it sought to end the Government's legal relationship with the tribes—encouraged the relocation of Indians to the cities. Today, an estimated 8,000 to 15,000 Chippewas, Sioux and Oneidas live in what Mr. Hisgun describes as a chronically frustrated community that combines the worst of the reservation and urban worlds.

"One of the detrimental things of reservation life is it's a welfare state—homes, everything, on a hand-out basis—and they bring a lot of that to the city," Mr. Hisgun says. "But I think everybody who comes to the city has a dream—a dream of making it, a dream about improving their lives. But then prejudice slaps them right in the face and they're worse off. Call it culture shock. When your bubble is burst, there's nothing left but to go back home and start dreaming again. They get into that cycle. There's a high mobility between reservations and cities."

In the cities, Indians are not moving in any substantial way into the middle class, and they suffer disproportionately from the social, economic and health problems that go along with urban poverty. Half the Indian families in Minneapolis are on welfare; in more than half there is only one parent. At the American Indian Health Center, one of several agencies funded in response to the burst of activism that spawned the American Indian Movement (AIM) in 1968, the staff considers a patient over 50 "an old Indian." Infant mortality is three times the rate for whites, and doctors see a disproportionately high rate of mental-health problems.

One response to that panoply of problems has been a rebirth of faith in apocalyptic Indian prophecies about the doom of the white world. Clyde Bellecourt, the militant founder and president of AIM, has turned from confrontation politics to running the Heart of the Earth Survival School. It is one of several "bilingual, bicultural" schools around the country that, according to Mr. Bellecourt, are the only institutions that can save Indians from sharing the white man's fate.

"For our children to survive," he says, "they have to be able to hunt, fish, put up a tepee and go into a sacred sweat to purify themselves." A tall man who wears his hair in long braids, he fiddles with a butane cigarette lighter. "When the energy crisis closes the Safeway store, our children will be able to survive."

Such doomsday prophecies have been a powerful force in Indian Country since 1889, when the Ghost Dance cult sprang from a medicine man's vision that predicted the disappearance of the white man and the return of the buffalo. Last July's Longest Walk to Washington was inspired by the vision of a Sioux holy man, Eagle Feather. The protest, which was intended to remind Congress to respect Indian treaty rights, had little impact, and perhaps one reason is that many of its participants, including Mr. Bellecourt, now have less faith in the political process than in the Old Prophecy that the end for the white man must be near.

The Indians' Washington, D.C.

The Federal Government in Washington—or, more precisely, the Bureau of Indian Affairs—is in the eye of the storm over Indian Country. "We're probably under the most intense political pressure we've ever faced in this field," says Forrest J. Gerard, the Assistant Secretary of the Interior in charge of the B.I.A. Indian tribes have won significant legal victories, he says, but adds that those very victories have touched off white resistance that has "manifested itself through political channels, both in the Congress and in the executive branch." He estimates that at least 80 members of the House of Representatives would vote for laws to roll back treaty rights, to strip tribal governments of their powers, to sell off the reservations. Moreover, Mr. Gerard hints, he is among those who suspect Attorney General Griffin Bell of wanting the Government to abandon, or at least de-emphasize, the exercise of its historic "trust responsibility" for Indian resources.

Mr. Gerard, a 53-year-old Blackfoot, has been at B.I.A. since 1977. He is the fifth Indian to head the agency, which is widely despised in Indian Country even though almost 70 percent of its 13,000 employees are Indians. With his preppie blazer and well-trimmed hair, Mr. Gerard is the kind of Indian sometimes dismissed by militants as an "apple"—red on the outside, white on the inside. But what one Indian group calls "the year of the backlash" has afforded Mr. Gerard little opportunity to forget that he is the ranking guardian of Indian property in an Administration with an uncertain commitment to his people.

Early in 1978, Representative John Cunningham, Washington Republican, introduced a bill that would revive the dreaded "termination" policies of the Eisenhower Administration. The termination suggested by Mr. Cunningham was similar to that first used in the General Allotment Act of 1887. That act chopped the reservations into small farmsteads, which soon passed into white hands. Tribal land holdings fell from 138 million acres in 1887 to 48 million acres in 1935. The bitter memory of that experience caused Indians to scoff when Mr. Cunningham called his private-ownership bill the native American Equal Opportunity Act. "Whenever one hears the statement, 'Why don't we just sell off the reservations and break them up?' " said Mr. Gerard, "I think it's a thinly veiled effort to get at Indian resources."

The Indians believe that Attorney General Bell responded with undue sympathy when Senators Warren Magnuson and Henry Jackson wrote him to complain about Federal Judge George Boldt's "infamous 1974 fishing-rights decision." The judge affirmed the economic rights of 25 Puget Sound tribes under treaties enacted in the 1850's to secure their lands for white settlers; the judge ruled that those long-ignored treaties guarantee modern Indians the opportunity to take half the harvestable catch of valuable Pacific salmon. Like Southern Senators of the 60's, Messrs. Magnuson and Jackson complained that the Government was contributing to racial "tension" by having Justice Department lawyers push minority claims in the Federal courts.

Mr. Bell replied that "the problem lies in the trust relationship itself. Any alteration of that would be a most complex and controversial undertaking, involving not only the executive branch, but also the Congress." The equivocal tone of his comments about the trust relationship evoked deep alarm in Indian political circles and prompted demands for Mr. Carter to end what Indian lawyer Sam Deloria called the Indian "policy vacuum." It is not now enough, given the suspicion about Mr. Bell, that the Democratic Party platform of 1976 pledged to "implement our treaty obligations to the first Americans" and to protect for them "their lands, their water and their civil rights." Nor does it suffice that Vice President

Walter Mondale, in a meeting with Indian leaders in Albuquerque, has pledged that the Administration will, indeed, support Indian treaty claims. The pressure is on in Indian Country for a statement from Mr. Carter himself.

Yet Mr. Gerard himself is warning that now is not the time to ask Mr. Carter for a pledge of support. "The secret is not to push for anything too radical right now," Mr. Gerard is counseling those who want to hear from the President. "Just sit back and operate with what we have." Few people in Indian Country know that Mr. Gerard and his supporters at the Department of Interior have gone beyond counseling caution. The fact is, according to a White House source, that the President's domestic staff was drafting an Indian policy statement earlier this year. Then, in mid-summer, the Interior Department suddenly withdrew its recommendation that a statement was needed.

In explaining his caution, Mr. Gerard speaks of "the drift to the right" in the country and the Congress. Friends of the Indians can't afford to "get out front," he says. It is also to be remembered that Mr. Carter fared badly in the Western states in 1976, and the 500,000 Indians living on or near the reservations west of the Mississippi represent a mere sprinkling of votes. What the President must have is the votes of conservative whites in the very states that have already produced the best-organized opposition to the Indian movement. Those states are also to become the scene of the great legal battle over water rights that belong to the Indian reservations by law and the white cities by appropriation—what Mr. Gerard calls "the last big shoot-out in the West."

TAOS TUG-OF-WAR

"The Taos have never been a craft people. They were an agricultural people. Just in the last five years they've started making crafts. There's no reason not to accommodate the tourist traffic." As he speaks, the proprietor of Tony Reyna's Indian Shop in Taos, N.M., leans on a showcase full of turquoise jewelry and contemplates the paradox of his "traditionalist" tribe adapting itself to the marketplace. "It's a money age we live in," he concludes rather sadly. "Now we don't have time to raise our own crops. It's a deterioration of our heritage and culture. But let's face it. We're not pure."

The cultural tug-of-war he describes has been going on for almost 500 years, and remains the most heated debate in Indian Country. Even in the cities, Indian leaders give lip service to the slogan of the Red Power activists who proclaimed during the 1969 occupation of Alcatraz Island that "we must keep the old ways." But as the Pueblos of Taos and the Reyna family have learned, keeping the old ways is not so easy.

Mr. Reyna's shop—"Indian-owned since 1950"—is halfway between the Anglo town of Taos, where D. H. Lawrence and Mabel Dodge Luhan established a famed artists' colony, and the Pueblo village of Taos, where 1,700 Indians still live in the adobe high-rises that have stood on this red earth for more than 900 years. With one eye on the past and one on the future, Mr. Reyna built his shop in the old way, shaping the adobe bricks by hand. He stocked only genuine Indian goods made in the traditional patterns. As a member of the tribal council, he worked for return to tribal ownership of the sacred Blue Lake, from which, according to the tribe's religion, the Taos people first emerged. Mr. Reyna supported the ordinance passed by the council that prohibited electric lights and modern plumbing within 50 yards of the village walls.

Thus, every morning, as in centuries past, the Taos women fill water buckets at the clear creek that tumbles down to the village from the Blue Lake in the Sangre de Cristo Mountains. Alas, many mornings bring angry exchanges, too, between the villagers and the camera-toting tourists who are at once the village's curse and its indispensable economic resource. At Mrs. Luhan's suggestion, the Taos tribe long ago began charging admission at the village gate. Today, "photographers fees" and "artists fees" range from $2 for a still camera to $25 for the right to make a finished painting. The daily flow of out-of-state cars into the Taos Pueblo parking lot—at a $1.50 each—aggravates that deep sense of anger that Indians feel at being regarded as tourist attractions for the master race. Yet, as J. Vince Lujan, the tribal secretary explains, "a bulk of the tribal government is financed from tourist fees."

Equally paradoxical, is the village rule against electricity. The ambiance it creates attracts tourists but the inconvenience works against the goal of cultural preservation by creating a village of the elderly. "Most of our young people are giving way to Western culture," says Mr. Lujan. "They're moving out and finding dwellings in the countryside."

The same shift that is taking place in the Taos Pueblo is taking place in Tony Reyna's gift shop. Philip Reyna, 19, helps his father in the shop and is extremely knowledgeable about Indian jewelry and art. Philip does not credit the talk that the Indian economic movement will spark a Pan-Indian cultural renaissance among people his age. "It would be nice, but it's not going to happen," he says. "Indians have always been fighting among themselves—the Navajos were always attacking the Pueblos—and it hasn't changed. Then you have urbanized Indians in Los Angeles and elsewhere, and they have a completely different point of view. Their only contact with their culture is the powwows, and that's not real. Look at the costumes—polyester and artificial dyes. No uprising will ever occur because, as times go by, the culture will go down."

Philip himself is studying to become a sound engineer in a rock-and-roll recording studio.

FISHING RIGHTS, CIVIL RIGHTS

"We've been called the niggers of Washington," says Ramona Bennett, a small woman with a fine-boned face and a fierce manner. Her outrage fairly fills her office in the Puyallup headquarters at Tacoma, Wash., as she speaks of the court's guaranteeing "our rights that we can't get enforced because our skins are the wrong color.

"I was shot at last November when I was seven months pregnant," says Mrs. Bennett, former chairman of the tribal council, to which she still belongs as an elected member. She suspects it was white fishermen who "tried to blow my head off—our fishermen have been facing this harassment for 90 years."

And as so often happened with the black movement in the South, a gritty and lonely Federal judge stands at the epicenter of this controversy. George H. Boldt, now 74 and in frail health, was nearing the end of his career in 1974 when the fishing-rights case came before him. Then, like his fellow Eisenhower appointees to the Federal bench—Judges Frank Johnson and Richard Rives in Montgomery, Ala., and Elbert Tuttle in Atlanta—Judge Boldt found himself compelled by his reading of the law to render a civil-rights decision that made him a social and political outcast in the eyes of many whites who expected conservative rulings from a judge appointed by a conservative President.

In a rare interview, Judge Boldt recalls how he summoned his law clerk to his office in the Tacoma Post Office building and instructed him "to put on that table every single case from the beginning of the country that pertains in any way to the rights of Indians. The two of us went through every single one—an enormous task. We came down on Sundays."

Treaties enacted with Washington's Indians more than 100 years ago guaranteed the Indians the right to fish "at all usual and accustomed grounds . . . in common with all citizens of the territory." After studying 19th-century legal dictionaries, Judge Boldt decided that the term "in common with" meant, at the time the treaties were drafted, that the Indians had a right to the opportunity to take 50 percent of the fish in an annual salmon catch now worth $200 million a year.

White reaction was intense. When state fishery officials refused to enforce the judge's ruling, he took over regulation of the fishery, Washington's fifth-largest industry, in much the same way that other Federal judges have taken over school districts that refused to desegregate. His critics claimed to have raised $100,000 to finance an impeachment campaign. He was accused of having an Indian mistress. The Interstate Congress for Equal Rights and Responsibilities, which was formed to combat the decision and is now a political presence in 23 states, investigated the "background" of the judge and his wife. Bumper stickers read: "Let's

Give 50 Percent of Judge Boldt to the Indians." A bomb was exploded in the Federal building at Tacoma. When Judge Boldt had heart surgery in February, he was confined to an isolated, heavily guarded wing of the hospital.

"I was burned in effigy and they still do that," Judge Boldt says. "The [non-Indian] fishermen have a champion and he maligns me continually and steadily, and he's spurred on by the Attorney General here. He's got to be with the fishermen, don't you see? You can't just be honest in this state and get anywhere because of the enormous amount of condemnation heaped on me since I wrote that decision that day.

"Sometimes I get bales and bales of mail," the judge adds. "Loathsome material. Somtimes they say, and put it in the paper, that my wife is an Indian. Well, she wouldn't mind that at all, but she happens to be a Scotch Presbyterian." He ponders a question about whether such out-pourings bothered him. "Really, it doesn't," he says. "I took an oath of office. It's right up there on the wall, and I look at it every day, have for 25 years." After looking at the oath yet again, the old man walks into his darkened courtroom. He demonstrates his routine for opening the sessions that now meet under heavy security. "I address the flag and bow to it, the flag of our country," he says, "and then I sit down and face the court."

Judge Boldt's ruling must itself face the U.S. Supreme Court as a result of a maneuver that has further aroused deep suspicions of Attorney General Griffin Bell throughout Indian Country. The decision was upheld in April by the Ninth Circuit Court of Appeals and the Supreme Court refused to hear the case, thereby affirming it. But as the political protest mounted in Washington, the Solicitor General of the United States joined white fishermen and state officials in asking the Supreme Court to reconsider. The B.I.A. and Forrest Gerard opposed the Justice Department's effort to get the landmark case back before the court, but Mr. Gerard was overruled.

Yet down at Billy's Landing, where in 1968 the Indian "fishins" first brought the salmon wars to national attention, the view is that the outcome will make little real difference in the destiny of the Indians. Sid Mills, 30, lives near the spot on the Nisqually River where Marlon Brando, Jane Fonda and Dick Gregory once hauled nets to demonstrate their support of Mr. Mills and other Indians in this fishing village. That was about the time that Mr. Mills, a wounded combat veteran of Vietnam, served three months in an Army stockade as a result of his protest against the arrest of Indian fishermen. Now he views the future with a cynicism as profound as Emma Yazzie's.

"No court decision has ever changed Government policy, and the Government policy is genocide," says the long-haired young fisherman. "They've got the public believing it's a pro-Indian decision, but they're just using words instead of guns. The Government is not going to turn around. They haven't for 500 years, and anybody who thinks they're going to change now is crazy."

Sid Mills, with the music of the Nisqually roaring in his ears, sings the heart song of Indian Country. Two Seattle writers, Roberto Maestas and Bruce Johansen, have discovered that faith in white greed is so deeply ingrained in Indian culture that when the first white miners swept into the Black Hills gold fields, the Lakota didn't even bother to identify the invaders by skin color. They simply called them *Wasi-chu*—a campfire term that means "greedy person" or "he who takes the fat."

Who is to take the fat of the Indians' land is, of course, the issue to be decided. On some reservations, the militant young and old Indians who weep with nostalgia at the sight of a buffalo are banding together to stop the bulldozers. Others like LaDonna Harris, the wife of former Senator Fred Harris of Oklahoma, believe that, in an energy-hungry nation grumpily facing leaner times, development is inevitable. The only choice before the Indians, she said, is whether they get a good price or simply more beads and blankets.

The Indians who are ready to do business believe money from the earth can provide a defense against a threat to Indian survival that could prove as devastating as the Indian wars that ended in 1890 with the slaying of 200 Sioux at Wounded Knee, S.D. This new threat is the toughening mood of an American majority disenchanted with the doctrine of white guilt. As expressed in lawsuits challenging special treatment for minorities and in the spread of organizations such as the Interstate Congress for Equal Rights and Responsibilities, this view holds that there are no due bills to be collected from history. "I get sick and tired of these tribal leaders saying you took our land away," says Howard Gray, the dapper, 72-year-old Seattle public-relations man who founded the I.C.E.R.R. "There's not a soul living today that had anything to do with the injustice done to the Indians. I say discount the past. We're living in the present."

To Indians who cannot so easily forget the past, those words are as frightening as the rattle and thunder of approaching cavalry.

V

SEXISM

The 1960s were known as a decade of civil-rights struggles, black militancy, antiwar protests, and campus disturbances. It seemed unlikely that yet another social movement could take hold and grow; but the consciousness of feminine oppression could and did, with enormous impact over remarkably few years.

Black militancy, the student movement, the antiwar movement, youth militancy, and radicalism all affirmed freedom, equality, and liberation, but none of these was thought to be particularly necessary or applicable to women, especially by radical men. Ironically, it was political experience with radical men that led radical women to the consciousness of women as a distinctly oppressed group, and, therefore, a group with distinctive interests.

The feminism that emerged in the 1970s was in fact both novel and part of a long and often painful series of movements for the liberation of women. Women's rights proposals were first heard over a century ago. According to Peter Gabriel Filene, the movement for the equality of women ground to a halt around 1932, the darkest year of the depression, beginning a period he calls "The Long Amnesia," when the emergencies of the depression and World War II pushed aside feminist concerns. With victory, both sexes gratefully resumed the middle-class dream of family, security, and upward mobility. These years of the late 1940s and early 1950s were the years of "The Feminine Mystique," when the *domestic* role of women dominated American culture.

When women began, in the 1970s, once again to reassert themselves and claimed to be able to be doctors and lawyers and bankers and pilots, they were met with derision. The

183

"Long Amnesia" had taken hold and stereotyped woman's roles into those of the 1940s and 1950s. People, perhaps especially men, had come to regard female domesticity almost as a natural phenomenon. Nevertheless, women persisted; and in what was historically a brief period, it became inconceivable to see no female faces broadcasting the news, granting loans, and training to be jet pilots at the U.S. Air Force Academy.

The idea of sexual equality has surely made progress since the 1950s, but the struggle is hard, for reasons suggested by the readings. Although the idea of male supremacy may be on the way out in industrialized nations, female equality is not necessarily a social reality—in part, because, as Tavris and Offir suggest, conceptions of equality vary, depending upon a country's history and its definitions of political, economic, and social needs; and, in part, because no matter what the ideology, traditional roles with respect to women's work and relations to family seem to persist.

Joanna Bunker Rohrbaugh's article "Women in the Workplace" shows the pervasive influence of traditional sex roles even for professional women who work in high-level jobs. Women often have to be more talented and capable than men to attain such positions in the first place; once in them, they face substantial, if often subtle, forms of discrimination that keep them from advancing according to their abilities.

If serious problems of discrimination still afflict the most "successful" women, the situation is even more serious for women at the other end of the scale of income and status. As the selection from the National Advisory Council on Economic Opportunity documents, women—and children in families maintained by women—are a sharply increasing proportion of America's poverty population.

Perhaps the most disturbing recent trend has been the increasing popularity of violent pornography depicting women not only as sex objects but also as violence objects. Sarah McCarthy makes a compelling case linking the rise in rape to the increasing distribution and cultural acceptability of female victimization materials, epitomized by the "snuff" movie. Pornography has long presented a dilemma between the principles of freedom of expression and the dignity of women. Those who are committed to freedom of speech and expression might want to consider whether it should extend to

materials like these. If not, where should the lines be drawn
against various forms of pornography? Should it be legally
prohibited, or should it be combated politically, by organization and persuasion?

13
THE LONGEST WAR

Carol Tavris and Carole Offir

"Male supremacy is on the way out in all industrialized nations," says
Marvin Harris. "Male supremacy was just a phase in the evolution of
culture." Harris, an anthropologist, makes his matter-of-fact assertion by
taking the long view with an evolutionist's eye. In the twentieth century,
for the first time in human history, conditions have permitted societies to
experiment with equality. Birth control means that women can decide
when and even whether to have babies. Overpopulation means that families must get smaller. Industrialization has brought affluence to millions
and provided them with the leisure time to consider less traditional life
styles. Warfare is largely mechanized, and males have no particular edge
over females at pushing buttons to launch a deadly battle. The radically
and rapidly altered conditions of life in this century suggest, says Harris,
that male supremacy is just a long first act in a show that is not yet over.

Attempts at egalitarianism in this century have crossed national and
ideological boundaries. In some countries, such as Sweden, a more equal
division of labor between the sexes simply evolved, and political philosophy followed. Other efforts, such as the Israeli kibbutz, started from
scratch as attempts to put theory and dreams into practice. Some nations,
such as the Soviet Union and the People's Republic of China, went
through complete revolutionary overhauls that brought millions of feudal
peasants into the twentieth century in the flicker of an eyelid. By taking a

From *The Longest War: Sex Differences in Perspective* by Carol Tavris and Carole
Offir, copyright © 1977 by Harcourt Brace Jovanovich, Inc. Reprinted by permission of
the publishers. References appearing in the original have been deleted.

look at how these experiments are turning out, and at how ideology and reality differ, we can get an idea of the barriers to equality and of the prospects for overcoming them.

We can also see what the idea of "equality" means in different countries, and how it relates to a country's particular needs, history, and economic and political system. Equality can mean getting women out of the home and into the work force, or assuring women of political power, or breaking down all personality and task differences based on sex, or getting rid of archaic laws designed to keep women barefoot and pregnant. Some cultures are so far from equality by any definition that it is remarkable if women are allowed to show their faces or choose their husbands. In others, the term implies equal opportunity at all levels. As New York's State Education Commissioner put it, "Equality is not when a female Einstein gets promoted to assistant professor; equality is when a female schlemiel moves ahead as fast as a male schlemiel." Your evaluation of a country's efforts at equality will depend on your definition and your values.

CASE 1: THE SOVIET UNION

In every society, wrote Marx and Engels, "the degree of emancipation of women is a natural standard of the general emancipation." The Soviet Union was the first country to try to put this belief into practice; one of the first orders of business after the 1917 revolution was to change the laws affecting women. Women quickly got the right to work alongside men, to have abortions on demand for unwanted pregnancies, and to end unhappy, arranged marriages with easy divorces. During the first heady years after the revolution, reformers were optimistic that socialism, having destroyed the economic basis of inequality, would automatically bring the demise of the patriarchal bourgeois family and liberate women. Women would take their rightful place as "productive" members of society, doing work that benefited the nation as a whole and not just the individual or the family. The state would take over the service work, childcare, and household chores. As Engels wrote, "The modern individual family is based on the open or disguised domestic enslavement of the woman; private housekeeping should become a social industry." Communal dining rooms, government-run nursery schools, and professional laundries would solve the age-old problem of who does the dirty work.

In terms of the "productive work" part of this blueprint, the country's economic needs coincided with ideology. For most of this century the Soviet Union has suffered an acute shortage of men, because so many died during the revolution, a civil war, two world wars, periods of famine, and political upheavals. Before the revolution the ratio of women to men was about equal, but by 1938 it was 103.7 women for every 100 men. And the country Rumania outlawed most abortions and stopped importing contraceptives the same year.[1]

The course of liberation, like love, never runs smooth. The clearest rumple in the socialist blueprint concerns ideology about the family. Somehow, no one in the Soviet Union ever got around to solving the logistical problems of providing millions of families with professional laundry service, food delivery, and childcare; doing so would have required shifting funds and energies away from more pressing problems. As a result, guess who does the housework and childcare?

The domestic side of life is still regarded by both sexes as the woman's responsibility. Although many children go to state-run nursery schools, the nurseries are not free and not yet available to every child. So most mothers rely on friends or relatives to help them with childcare, and in a crisis it is usually the mother, not the father, who compromises the job for the family. It is usually the mother, not the father, who interrupts a career for a few years in an effort to juggle the needs of children, household, and job. And it is usually the mother, not the father, who stands in long lines at the market, prepares meals without benefit of fancy appliances, and cleans the house. The men "help out"—evoking a few sarcastic reactions from women:

No one who has followed the painful efforts to modernize socialist housework over the past three decades can fail to be struck by the way this is inevitably presented as "the debt we owe our women," as though women were responsible for all the wash that is dirtied and were the sole beneficiaries of clean windows and floors and ate all the potatoes that are lugged home.

There's a bachelor I knew in three periods of his life. First when he was married and, by his own words, didn't know how to put a teapot on to boil, never mind eggs. . . . Then he got divorced. A miracle followed. He could have been a professor of homemaking. His room wasn't simply clean, it was downright sterile, and the dinners he made for friends were beyond praise. . . . Then he remarried. And immediately stopped cooking dinners, making pickles, and it took an argument for his wife to get him to go down for bread.

Lenin had berated men for shirking their domestic duties. "Very few husbands, not even the proletarians, think of how much they could lighten the burdens and worries of their wives, or relieve them entirely, if they lent a hand in this 'woman's work.' But no, that would go against the privilege and dignity of the husband. He demands that he have his rest and comfort." That he does. Soviet writers have considered many ways to lighten woman's burden: giving women less strenuous jobs, arranging part-time work for women or shorter working days, distributing better household appliances, building more childcare facilities, and so on. But they seem to be overlooking Lenin's observation that the handiest labor-saving device is a husband.

CASE 2: THE PEOPLE'S REPUBLIC OF CHINA

Before the revolution of 1949, the Chinese say, all people carried three mountains on their backs—feudalism, capitalism, and imperialism—but women had a fourth burden, male supremacy. A proverb sums up the treatment of women in prerevolutionary China: "A woman married is like a pony bought—to be ridden or whipped at the master's pleasure." Women had no rights—not over their property, their bodies, or their marriages. Fathers sometimes drowned their infant daughters and sold their surviving daughters as concubines and prostitutes. Husbands could beat or even kill their wives with impunity, and landlords could rape them. When a women married she became subject to the wishes of her husband's family forever; divorce was almost impossible, and widows were forbidden to remarry.

The emancipation of Chinese women started in the nineteenth century, when capitalism began to break up the feudal system that had existed for thousands of years. Industrialization provided women with jobs in the port cities, and although both sexes labored from dawn to dusk for slave wages, women's small incomes did give them a measure of power in the family. Educational and professional opportunities for women increased slightly and feminist movements were organized, though these developments affected only a tiny minority of women. During the first half of this century the official policy of the government (the Kuomintang) was inconsistent. At times it reacted with cruel repression; in 1927, for instance, the Kuomintang executed several hundred women for wearing short haircuts, a symbol of liberation. At other times it became more liberal, at least on paper; in 1931 the Kuomintang gave women the rights to marry freely and to inherit property—though this change was never publicized, much less put into practice.

Long before it came to power, the Communist Party showed concern for the low status of women.[2] Party workers (cadres) discovered an effective way to rally women to their cause, to make women understand that their pains and burdens were shared and were not an inevitable part of being female. The cadres would go into a village and get the women to sit together and talk about their lives—nothing political at first, just their lives. Slowly, painfully, then bitterly, the stories came out: the beatings, the humiliations, the defeats. These sessions, which became known as Speak-Bitterness meetings, taught the Chinese women that they were not alone, that their experiences were the experiences of all women. And like consciousness-raising groups in the United States, the Chinese groups taught that in unity there is strength.

Then came 1949, Communist victory, and a series of sweeping reforms intended to clear away all the lingering feudal cobwebs. The new government quickly gave women property rights, a free choice in marriage, the right to vote, the right to divorce. It abolished polygamy, prostitution, wife-buying, and female infanticide. It declared that women were economically equal to men and would get the same pay for the same work. It wasn't easy to enforce all of these measures because of deep resistance from peasant males and even from loyal Communist males. Husbands did not want their wives going to Speak-Bitterness meetings before the revolution, and they were not happy about female equality after it. Some female activists who were sent to rural villages to explain the new rights of women were murdered by men who felt that their authority in the family and the community was under attack (as indeed it was). But gradually the measures gained acceptance, and attention turned to mobilizing women for productive work.

China today has had even less time than the Soviet Union to overturn centuries of feudalism and female subordination. Yet in twenty-eight years, scarcely a generation, extraordinary changes have taken place in the status of Chinese women. Ninety percent of them work outside the home, and there is a fairly extensive network of nurseries and daycare centers attached to the factories, hospitals, housing projects, and businesses where the parents work. As in Russia, women have entered jobs formerly reserved for men. They drive trucks, fly planes, and wield picks. (In 1957, China had a squadron of jet fighters run entirely by women.) They are doctors, teachers, engineers.

Of course, the entrance of women into the work force has not been steady and uncomplicated. Work for women has depended on the country's economic growth and on its shifting economic policies, as in Russia. Katie Curtin believes that an industrial slump in the mid-1950s was behind propaganda praising home life and the contributions of the housewife. (Similarly, a postwar slump in the United States evoked the "feminine mystique" that glorified large families and the joys of homemaking.) But when China developed an acute need for labor in 1958, and subsequently launched the "Great Leap Forward," the government proclaimed the liberating, patriotic effects of being a working woman. It set up daycare centers to make it possible for women to enter the work force in large numbers. The program was so successful that today a Chinese "housewife" is virtually an anachronism. In many places wives have gotten together to organize what they call "housewife factories," local enterprises that produce everything from embroidered pillows to insulation materials.

The Chinese Communists never were as concerned as the Russians about changing the basic nature of the family and sexual relations. The Chinese see no incompatibility between the family and female liberation; indeed, they believe the family is bedrock. Although a wave of divorces followed the revolution, ending thousands of brutal marriages, today divorce is more difficult to get, and a Chinese couple goes through considerable discussion and persuasion from colleagues and family before they make it to the divorce court. Further, the Chinese see no link between female liberation and sexual liberation. On the contrary. The Chinese are quite Victorian in their views: before marriage, the sexual rule is "all for none and none for all," and they will tell you seriously that their young people are too busy working for a socialist society to think of sex. Sex, the adolescents learn, saps your strength. Abortion and birth control are available to all women. The purpose, though, is not to make them sexually free but to keep the population down and the females working.

Although the Chinese have tried to strengthen, not eliminate, the family, they do believe it is unfair and uncommunist to expect women to handle all the domestic work as well as a job. How to right this common wrong, however, has not been figured out. When C. T. visited China in 1973, most of the people she talked to claimed to have egalitarian marriages, the political ideal. Whichever spouse came home first got the groceries (an easy task, since markets are attached to most housing clusters) and prepared the dinner. Both did the cleaning and cared for the children, when they were not in school or daycare or with grandparents (everyone's favorite babysitters, even in modern China). Women explained to her, with smiles and lots of stories, that a husband can't get away with male-chauvinist attitudes any more. If he persists in his "feudal" ways, the local Women's Association may decide to reeducate him, and so will his comrades at work, his in-laws, his neighbors, and his union. On the other hand, members of the Committee of Concerned Asian Scholars got other answers to the same question. When they asked who does the cooking, cleaning, shopping, washing and childcare, the usual reply was, "The wife, of course."

The discrepancy is probably a result of the size of the country and the size of the gap between policy and practice. Policy says that women will be equal and men will do housework, that families should have only two children and that girls are as good as boys, that women get equal pay for equal work. But in practice the old ways haven't changed overnight or for everyone. In much of the countryside, families still prefer sons.[3] On communes, which are huge agricultural collectives of up to 50,000 people, a system of work points determines a person's share of the collective income. The more physically strenuous the job, the more points one gets. Women earn fewer work points than men because they don't do the hardest work, because they tend to work shorter days in order to do housework (which is not regarded as productive labor), and because they don't get points for maternity leave or for days off during the menstrual period if they take them. In the cities, men still seem to wind up doing different work from women, even in the same factory, and getting more money—although wage differences by sex are nowhere near as great as they are in this country.

Some occupations are still regarded as "women's work" in China; almost all teachers in primary school, nurses, daycare attendants, and flight attendants are women. All visitors observe that fathers and grandfathers have a warm and tender relationship with their young relatives and spend much time with them, but there have been no efforts to get men to work professionally with children. "Women have more patience, after all," C. T. was told. "They are more gentle." Conversely, women are still a tiny minority in top political circles, even though the number of women accepted into the Communist Party is increasing steadily (20 percent of the delegates to the Tenth Party Congress in 1973 were women). In the prestigious People's Liberation Army (PLA), which produces the top political leaders, women work in separate battalions at service tasks such as running canteens, staffing offices, and giving medical aid. When C. T. asked why the PLA was segregated she was told, "Men are stronger, after all." This explanation was not convincing, because women get rigorous military training alongside men in the local militia units, where they have no apparent trouble learning to handle rifles, grenades, and machine guns.

To the Chinese, whatever remnants of male chauvinism still exist are mere trifles compared to what has been accomplished in the liberation of women. Because the majority of the population remembers the starvation, illness, and social problems that were so widespread before the revolution, the Chinese convey a spirit of optimism and strength. They believe they can solve whatever minor problems remain, and they are desperately determined to avoid the pitfalls that they believe entrapped the Soviet Union; a regression to capitalist competitiveness, renewed inequality between the sexes, and a premature complacency about the success of the revolution. Under Mao Tse-tung, who was unwavering in his fight against complacency, the Chinese believed that constant "revolutions" were necessary to keep a country from backsliding. Whether they will hold to that belief under the new leadership, and what priorities will be assigned to sexual equality in the future, is anybody's guess.

CASE 3: THE SCANDINAVIAN COUNTRIES, ESPECIALLY SWEDEN

Sweden and her sister countries are good examples of nations that are reaching sex-role equality through evolution, rather than revolution. In Sweden, industrialization began much sooner than it did in the U.S.S.R., and it brought a decrease in the proportion of children and an increase in the proportion of city dwellers. Twenty years ago, Sweden faced certain issues and economic problems that are only now coming to the fore in the United States. In the mid-fifties two sociologists, Alva Myrdal and Viola Klein, wrote *Women's Two Roles: Home and Work*, a book that explored the difficulties of combining those roles and suggested some solutions. The ideology of sex-role equality that is still struggling for acceptance in the United States came to Sweden years ago.

But in Scandinavia, as in China and elsewhere, ideology is one thing and daily life is another. Today in the Scandinavian countries only about one third of all married women work (in Russia, Finland, Poland, and Hungary, the figure is 50 percent; in the United States it is 43 percent). Scandinavian women are less likely to enter "masculine" professions than women in Eastern European nations, although they make up one-fifth to one-third of the physicians and lawyers and have taken over the fields of pharmacy and, especially in Denmark, dentistry. There are numerous government-sponsored nursery schools, though not enough for the children of all working women.

Because taxes and some legislation favor the two-income family, husbands and wives are redefining the division of labor in the household. Both partners are expected to share housework and childcare when both work, and—most radical innovation of all—husbands as well as wives have the option to stay home or work part-time. Sweden may be one of the few countries in the world in which a househusband is socially accepted. He may not be universally admired, but at least he need endure no snickers, and his masculinity is not questioned.

The role of Swedish women in the work force, like that of women elsewhere, has fluctuated with economic conditions. Between 1930 and 1946 droves of women left the labor force in what has been called a "mass flight" into marriage. "Aha," observers said. "See? Women are happier as housewives." However, their flight coincided with what a Swedish sociologist called an "enormously woman-hostile labor market during the Depression." After the Depression the economic standard was high enough for many women to afford to stay home, which has not been the case in the Soviet Union and Finland, for example. In the 1960s, a shortage of labor meant that Sweden needed its women in the work force. Accordingly, official policy shifted, childcare facilities were improved, and a national educational campaign for sex-role equality began. The defeat of the social-democrat system in 1976, and the apparent return to capitalism after forty-four years of socialist programs, make it hard to predict whether Sweden's need for working women, or its efforts toward equality, will continue.

Elina Haavio-Mannila compared the efforts of three neighboring nations—Sweden, Finland, and the Soviet Union—to liberate women from housework. The three countries have different ideologies about sex roles and different industrial histories, to say nothing of political philosophies.

Haavio-Mannila's study was based on interviews with 430 Soviet families in three cities (Leningrad, Moscow, and Pensa); 271 families in Helsinki, Finland; and 442 families in Uppsala, Sweden. She found no differences among these countries in the families' division of labor. It didn't matter whether the women had outside jobs or not, or how actively the government encouraged them to join the labor force or stay at home. In 70 percent of the households, only the wife bought food, made breakfast, fed the children, and washed the dishes; in 80 percent she cooked dinner. As shown in Table 1, the men were more likely to fix things around the house—and that's all. Househusbandry may be an approved way of life in Sweden, but it is far from a popular practice.[4]

As these case studies illustrate, most modern nations have made great strides in their efforts to unravel the work and family knot. To get women into the labor force, they have used a variety of approaches to enable women to combine "their" responsibilities of home and job. In one summary review, Constantina Safilios-Rothschild studied the male-female division of labor in twenty-three countries at all levels of economic development and noted four patterns.

1. *The Soviet Union, Poland, Hungary, Finland:* Women work, many in formerly male occupations, but men do not do women's work. State-supported nursery schools and daycare and a national ideology that favors communal child-rearing help women work but require no changes on the part of husbands.

2. *Scandinavian countries:* Fewer women work, though the ideology favors complete equality. Men are encouraged to split housework and childcare equally, though there are many fewer househusbands than housewives.

3. *Argentina, Austria, Japan, Greece, Turkey:* About one-third of the women work, and an even smaller proportion of wives. None of these countries provides daycare centers or nursery schools, except a few understaffed ones for working-class women. Wealthy wives can combine work and family because maid service is cheap and available and the extended family still thrives. Grandmothers often do housework and babysit for their working daughters.

4. *The United States, Canada, and to some extent England, France, West Germany, and Australia:* In these countries the cultural values are at odds with the realities. While many women work (at least one-third of all women, ranging to half), the reigning ideology is that childcare is a full-time occupation and that children need their mothers. These nations provide no system-wide professional help or daycare for working mothers, who are left to work out a solution on an individual basis. Partly because so many women in these countries must wait until their children are in school before they can work full-time, women have not entered traditionally male occupations in significant numbers.

*Table 1   Division of Household Tasks in Russian, Finnish,
and Swedish Cities, 1966*[a]

Household Task		Wife	Both Spouses	Husband
Feeding the family				
Buying the food	Three Soviet cities	70%	18%	4%
	Helsinki	74	20	2
	Uppsala	71	17	5
Preparing breakfast	Three Soviet cities	72	10	3
	Helsinki	72	16	8
	Uppsala	76	9	8
Preparing dinner	Three Soviet cities	80	5	1
	Helsinki	85	9	2
	Uppsala	86	5	2
Washing the dishes	Three Soviet cities	64	20	1
	Helsinki	70	20	4
Cleaning and washing				
Daily cleaning	Three Soviet cities	67	14	4
	Helsinki	73	18	1
	Uppsala	80	12	2
Washing the	Helsinki	51	32	6
windows	Uppsala	76	9	5
Washing clothes	Three Soviet cities	90	2	0
(Helsinki: men's	Helsinki	80	4	11
shirts and stockings)				
Family finances				
Paying regular bills	Three Soviet cities	47	13	28
	Helsinki	32	19	48
	Uppsala	29	18	49
Repairing				
Fixing things	Three Soviet cities	50	6	27
around the house	Helsinki	6	7	82
	Uppsala	10	13	70
Childcare				
Feeding the children	Helsinki	74	20	0
(if small children in	Uppsala	70	17	0
the family)				

[a]Horizontal percentages do not add to 100 because in some cases a third person does
the task.

In most of these countries women are steadily (though in some, slowly) being absorbed into the work force, doing a great number of jobs. Some countries make it harder, but none has succeeded in getting men to share domestic work equally. And in no nation are women 50 percent of the key politicians and leaders.

Perhaps it seems that equality on a national level would be more difficult and complicated to achieve than equality in a small, manageable unit. For this reason the example of the Israeli kibbutz is an important story.

CASE 4: THE ISRAELI KIBBUTZ

Perhaps no experiment in equality has been scrutinized as minutely as the kibbutz (plural: kibbutzim). Scarcely had the idea been planted before researchers began pulling it out by the roots to see how it was doing. The kibbutz is especially fascinating today because it seems to provide clear evidence that equality is doomed, that left to their druthers men and women will lapse into the traditional division of roles, power, and labor.

Kibbutzim are rural communities in which members collectively own all property. The first kibbutzim were founded early in this century by young socialist emigrants from Russia and Europe, who wanted to escape what they considered the stifling atmosphere of traditional urban Jewish life. They had read Marx and Freud and were determined to set up an alternative community that would represent the best of both. The founders therefore rejected the nuclear family, which they regarded as patriarchal and antifemale, a breeding ground for the Oedipus complex and sexual hostilities. They rejected the values associated with capitalism, especially competitiveness and financial ambition, and sought instead a community based on physical labor, austerity, equality, and group loyalty. There would be no salaries and no status distinctions based on wealth. Each member of the group would get the goods and services she or he needed, regardless of the work assigned.

The decision to break up the nuclear family came about for several reasons. The founders feared that family loyalties would compete with allegiance to the larger community, and in the face of harsh external conditions for survival the kibbutz could not afford much internal dissension, family squabbling, or personal ambition. Ideologically, the founders also believed that if parents dealt with their children as friendly comrades instead of as stern disciplinarians, a more democratic bond between adults and children would result. The children would be more secure as well, because they would be children of the kibbutz, nourished and loved by everyone. Finally, the founders believed that when women were free for "productive" work like plowing fields and building roads, when they didn't have to worry about cooking meals and ironing shirts, they would become equal partners with men once and for all—politically, economically, and sexually.

The kibbutz made almost all housekeeping a collective enterprise. Kibbutz members eat together in a communal dining room; they get their clothes, toothbrushes, and soap at a communal commissary; and they send their dirty linen to a communal laundry. Though they live in private apartments, the rooms are small and do not require much care. Child-rearing too is a collective procedure. Within a few days or weeks after birth, babies are brought to a special children's house, where they are cared for by a specially trained professional called a *metapelet* (nurse). Children visit with their parents in the late afternoons and on weekends, but they eat and sleep in their own quarters. A child's friends, not parents, are the primary contacts, and as a result the kibbutz child develops a strong allegiance to the peer group.

Today there are about 250 kibbutzim, with some 100,000 residents, a small, but influential proportion of the total Israeli population. They range in size from several dozen members to over 2,000; but most have a few hundred. The kibbutzniks have been remarkably successful at surviving in the face of extraordinary odds. Though life was hard and work seemed unending in the early days, today kibbutz members enjoy a standard of living that is higher than that of most Israelis. The collective principle still holds; residents together own all property and means of production.

In 1960–61 C. O. lived on a kibbutz for six months. Instead of working at a permanent job assignment she landed the job of pinch hitter, which gave her an opportunity to observe many kibbutzniks at work. Guess who was doing the cooking meals, cleaning toilets, scrubbing floors, ironing shirts, teaching children, and caring for infants. Not for their own families, to be sure, but for the several hundred souls on the commune. A few young women labored in the fields, but none drove tractors or worked in construction. C. O. never observed a man working in the children's houses or ironing. Though both sexes were required to do a month of kitchen duty every year (washing dishes, setting and waiting tables), few men held permanent jobs in the kitchen. Some old men helped out regularly in preparing meals, doing chores like plucking chickens.

Recent studies confirm these informal observations about the sexual division of labor on the kibbutz. Lionel Tiger and Joseph Shepher studied some 16,000 women in two communes, and Martha Mednick interviewed a random sample of kibbutzniks from fifty-five settlements, 400 original settlers and 918 adults of the second generation. The women are in fact back at the service jobs in the kitchen, laundry, and schools, and those who do work in agriculture are concentrated in poultry-raising and plant nurseries. Fewer occupations are open to women than to men, and the dream of a fifty-fifty share in the work of production has vanished. As the kibbutzim prospered and the population grew, the need for support services and the desire for physical amenities increased, and the women left the fields for the household.

It might seem that a sexual division of labor could still be equitable. After all, feeding an entire community and raising loyal members of the kibbutz are as important as driving a tractor or picking apples. But that is not how it is on the kibbutz. The jobs that produce income for the community, the jobs that men do, are held in higher esteem than the jobs women do. And when members rate their own status in the community, women rate themselves lower than men.

Work is the central value of the kibbutz. Moreover, productive work, that which results in economic gain, is valued most highly. On the other hand, services, which include the kitchen, the laundry, the clothing factory, and the dining room, are regarded as necessary, but nonproductive and therefore less valued.

Men have the political power, too, although there are no official barriers in the women's way. The kibbutz is a true participatory democracy. A general assembly of all members meets regularly to make major decisions, and each member has one vote. Yet women are not equal participants in this system. They rarely run for political office, although these positions rotate every few years; they show up in fewer numbers at the meetings; when they do attend, they are less vocal than the men. Although almost half of all kibbutz members serve on community committees, women work on those connected with education, social welfare, and cultural activities, while men dominate on the economic committee— which determines economic goals and policies, controls the budget, and wields the real power. The second-generation women, says Mednick, seem quite content to leave political matters to men. So although there are no status differences based on class and wealth, the bane of Marxist theory, there are status differences based on work and political participation. And men have the prestige.

As the kibbutzim became more successful, the "intrinsic antagonism" between the family and the community shifted in favor of the family. Most (though not all) women are enthusiastic about the trend toward traditionalism and are actively promoting it. They want larger families, and they don't want to delay having children until they have finished vocational training. Cosmetics, dresses, and beauty shops—once regarded as signs of decadent bourgeois values—are gaining acceptance. On some kibbutzim, parents are trying to reverse one of the founders' basic principles and have their children live with them, though this is permitted on fewer than 10 percent of the kibbutzim so far.

The kibbutz, then, presents us with a puzzle. Kibbutz women are even more economically independent than women in socialist countries. They do not get status from their husbands' incomes or jobs. They have total job security no matter how many children they choose to have, and they are guaranteed high-quality care and education for their children. They do not have complicated housework to contend with and they do not have to feed their families or clean up after them. Yet kibbutz women lack political power, and they don't seem to want it. They do not work in the high-prestige occupations, and they don't seem to want to. The feminine mystique has returned with a vengeance.

NOTES

1. Most of us are so concerned with the long-term consequences of over-population that it seems surprising that a government would want to increase its population. But a sudden drop in births can have serious short-term results—shortages of workers in critical occupations, reduced demand for consumer goods, a relative increase in the proportion of old people. Is the drop in the U.S. birth rate associated with efforts to strike down liberal abortion laws?

2. One critic argues, however, that the Communists' concern fluctuated, depending on whether they were trying to fight the Kuomintang or form an alliance with it. During efforts at accommodation, the Communists held some reforms in check, including women's rights. When Kuomintang leader Chiang Kai-Shek turned them down, they returned to a more radical line.

3. The Anshan Experiment, a new Chinese method of identifying the sex of a fetus, came up with this eerie, unintended finding. Of thirty fetuses that had been intentionally aborted after the mother knew its sex, twenty-nine were female.

4. For example, Sweden has a paid paternity-leave program: fathers can take up to seven months off after the birth of a child at 95 percent of full salary. (If the mother works too, the parents can share the leave period as they wish.) Though the number of participating fathers has more than quadrupled since 1974 and is still rising, only 7 percent of fathers took paternity leaves in 1976.

14

WOMEN IN THE WORKPLACE

Joanna Bunker Rohrbaugh

American women live their lives in a variety of different ways. Some are married, some are not; some have children, some do not; some are straight, others are gay. Ye[t] they all have one thing in common: at some point in their lives, most of them work outside the home. What kind of experience do they have on the job? What kind of work do they do, and how do they choose it? How do they handle the competition and other pressures in the workplace? Does being female influence their experience in a consistent way? Or have things changed so that gender is no longer crucial in employment?

Psychologists have looked at these questions in terms of women's motivation to succeed, their pattern of career choices, and their experiences as females in male-oriented surroundings. This research has focused on women in the professions—once again, psychologists study their own kind. Yet many of the basic issues apply to all women, as demonstrating the pervasive influence that sex roles have on yet another area of our lives.

DO WOMEN FEAR SUCCESS?

The bulk of the research on careers has focused on the achievement motive or the desire to do well in accordance with a standard of excellence. Some psychologists maintain that men have a stronger motive to achieve than do women. Others argue that women are actually afraid of success and actively avoid it. The controversy about this alleged fear of success in women has come to stand for many of the controversial issues surrounding women and careers. Do women have the personal characteristics required for the successful pursuit of a career? Is there an inherent contradiction between being feminine and having a career? Have achievement and success been defined in male terms, so that women are left in a no-win position?

Women's "Motive to Avoid Success"

Psychologists John Atkinson and David McClelland have developed a whole theory about achievement motivation. Motivation is usually measured by asking people to write a few paragraphs about a sentence or a picture that subtly suggests a work or an achievement situation. The stories are then scored for achievement themes or expressions of a desire to do well, for definite actions that lead to success, and for positive feelings about succeeding. Thus, in response to a picture of two men working on a machine, an achievement-oriented person might write: "He wants to be an inventor," "He's designing a new part," and "He feels great when it wins a prize for originality."

Innumerable studies of the achievement motive have shown that achievement imagery increases when the stories are written in a situation stressing leadership and competition. And the achievement imagery predicts a number of different behavior patterns. People with a high "need for achievement" (nAch) are more likely to get good grades in school, to do better in competitive than in noncompetitive situations, to engage in money-making activities, and to prefer tasks involving moderate difficulty and risk where one can expect to succeed and can assume that one's own efforts (not chance) were responsible for that success. The extent to which the theory can predict such behavior is impressive. There is just one problem: the theory only works for men. The results for women do not fit the theory, do not match the results for men, and are not even consistent with each other. This discrepancy did not bother the male psychologists who developed the theory; for in the book of almost nine-hundred pages outlining their research methodology, they discuss the theory as if it applied to everyone. Only a single footnote concerned with women tells a careful reader that the female data do not make sense.

While a graduate student at the University of Michigan, Matina Horner became intrigued with this problem. Why, she wondered, do women receive higher nAch scores than men do under neutral conditions but fail to show the predicted increase of achievement imagery in response to leadership and competition? And what interferes with the expression of the achievement motive in women's behavior? Horner reasoned that since successful achievement is viewed as the result of aggressively competitive behavior, it is also perceived as incompatible with femininity. Women may therefore be afraid that others will respond to their success by rejecting them as pushy and unfeminine. This fear may lead to a "motive to avoid success," or a permanent predisposition to feel anxious about the anticipated social rejection and loss of femininity that follows success. Since the anxiety is based on the incompatibility between femininity and competitive achievement, it should be more characteristic of women than of men. And since only those who want and expect to succeed are concerned about the consequences of that success, the motive to avoid success should be aroused more easily in achievement-oriented, high-ability women.

Horner tested her hypothesis in 1965 by having 178 undergraduates at the University of Michigan write stories to four standard achievement cues about characters of their own sex, such as "David (Carol) is looking into his (her) microscope." She added a fifth cue emphasizing the competitive aspect of achievement: "At the top of first term finals, Anne (John) finds herself (himself) at the end of her (his) medical school class." She scored the medical school stories for the presence or absence of "fear of success imagery" (FOS), defined as the expression of negative consequences or emotions about the success, of specific actions leading away from success, or of emotional conflict about the success. The FOS imagery was then interpreted as a reflection of an aroused "motive to avoid success."

Three main types of story were scored for FOS. The most common ones expressed fears of social rejection: Anne lost her friends or her eligibility as a date or a marriage partner, or became isolated, lonely, and unhappy. The second group expressed internal emotions independent of the response of others: regardless of whether anyone else knew about Anne's success, she doubted her femininity, felt guilty or in depair about her success, and wondered about her own normalcy. A third group actually denied the information given in the original sentence. For example:

Anne is a *code* name for a non-existent person created by a group of med students. They take turns taking exams and writing papers for Anne. . . . Anne is really happy she's on top, though Tom is higher than she—though that's as it should be. . . . Anne doesn't mind Tom winning.

Some FOS stories were quite bizarre, like the one that included these comments: "She starts proclaiming her surprise and joy. Her fellow classmates are so disgusted with her behavior that they jump on her in a body and beat her. She is maimed for life." Horner commented that "the intensity, hostility and symbolic quality of the language used by the subjects in writing their stories is very clear."

The sex differences in the medical school stories were startling: almost two-thirds (65 percent) of the women expressed FOS imagery, while less than one-tenth (8 percent) of the men did so. When Horner compared the FOS scores with the nAch scores, she found that the two went together: women with higher achievement motivation also tended to be scored for FOS. And the expression of FOS imagery was related to the student's achievement behavior. After they wrote their stories in the first session, Horner had them complete verbal and arithmetic tasks in a second session conducted under noncompetitive (solo) or competitive conditions. Achievement-oriented women displaying fear of success imagery did best in the noncompetitive condition. Achievement-oriented women without FOS, on the other hand, behaved just like the men with high nAch scores: they did best in the competitive situation.

These results supported Horner's hypothesis and led her to conclude that "Unfortunately, in American society, even today, femininity and competitive achievement continue to be viewed as two desirable but mutually exclusive ends." We may not need a social scientist to point this out. Horner reports that her own children were a source of inspiration for her research, as for example, "on the day when Tia, not yet 3, learned that a female friend of the family was a physician and after a lengthy silence inquired 'Is ――― still a girl?' 'Well then is she still Eric's mommy?' and before going on to other things concluded, 'She must be all mixed up.' "

Women's "Will to Fail"

Horner's work was greeted with great enthusiasm by the media. Many commentators implied, "Now we know why women aren't in leadership positions in industry, in finance, in government, or any of the professions. It has nothing to do with discrimination or antifemale bias. It's because women just aren't cut out to succeed. In fact, they don't even *want* to. They want to fail. Look, one of them has said it herself. Women's failure to achieve equal status and success is their own fault."

In their enthusiasm for an idea that blames the victim and lets male institutions off the hook, few people have noticed that Horner's concept has been distorted. She suggested that women simultaneously want to succeed and are afraid to for fear they will be punished. This is quite different from not wanting to succeed in the first place, and from having an active desire to fail. As Horner herself said in a later article:

I have suggested that women have a latent personality disposition or a "motive to avoid success"; i.e., that they become anxious because of success. This is not at all the same as saying that they have a "will to fail," i.e., a "motive to approach failure." This would imply that women actively seek out failure because they anticipate or expect positive consequences from failing. The [motive to avoid success], on the other hand, implies that women inhibit their positive achievement directed tendencies because of the arousal of anxiety about the negative consequences they expect will follow success.

The ludicrous nature of the "will to fail" idea is obvious when we recall that it was precisely those women with the strongest desire to achieve, as measured by nAch scores, who were most likely to show fear of success imagery in their stories.

The Fear-of-Success Controversy

Not only journalists, but also professors, students, and researchers, have been fascinated by the idea of fear of success. In the past ten years over 150 studies have appeared attempting to repeat or extend Horner's findings. Many people have hailed fear of success as the ultimate answer to the complex problems of female achievement. Others have rushed to refute a concept that they see as reinforcing the media image of women driven by some inner compulsion to fail. Let us take a look at some of the major issues in this *cause célèbre*.

One of the most common challenges is that fear of success is not a uniquely female phenomenon: males also show this imagery in their stories. The male rates of FOS imagery have increased over the years and are sometimes found to be as high as or higher than the female rates. The FOS imagery in male and female stories tends to be different, however. While women fear social rejection for being unfeminine, men express negative feelings about achievement per se—two very different emotional issues.

Another problem is that most of the studies continue to use the cue about Anne's and John's excelling in medical school—a traditionally masculine occupation. When the sex-typed nature of the occupation is varied in the cues, we find (1) that men, too, express fear of sanctions for sex-role nonconformity if they write about males in traditionally feminine occupations; (2) that both men *and* women express more FOS when writing about characters' succeeding in cross-sex-typed; and (3) that, in writing about female success in masculine occupations, men sometimes express *more* FOS imagery than women do.

If setting and gender of the successful character make so much difference, perhaps FOS actually taps realistic social expectations rather than deep-seated motives. The students may simply be describing the social sanctions that they expect to accompany sex-role deviance.

Another possibility is that the negative feelings expressed in FOS imagery reflect a natural envy of outstanding people, which may have nothing to do with competitive actions or academic and occupational aspirations. Thus, Shaver suggests that if Horner had used the cue, "Anne is by all accounts the most beautiful coed at the University of Michigan," she might have obtained the following results:

Sixty-five percent of the subjects mentioned negative consequences of Anne's exceptional beauty; some saw her as "probably stupid and immature," others suspected that her friends were secretly hostile and jealous. Several mentioned that Anne found it difficult to establish normal relationships with males because "the guys are frightened by her incredible good looks; at any time she may drop them in favor of someone better." A few said that Anne wasn't really all that beautiful; she just happened to have a father in the clothing business who gave her anything she wanted.

Would this have indicated a fear of beauty? Of course not. It would merely have indicated the subjects' expectation that some people would be envious and hostile of anyone who excelled in the area of physical appearance.

Other writers have objected that fear of success does not necessarily affect behavior—an objection that is usually substantiated by the fact that FOS is more typical of honors students and those at outstanding, competitive colleges. If they fear success, why are they so successful? This objection is spurious, however, for Horner suggested that the motive to avoid success is more easily *aroused* in high-ability women with a strong motive to achieve; she did not say that it was more *debilitating* in those women. Many anxious people are successful despite their anxiety. Their simultaneous anxiety and striving for achievement may, however, be costly. They may pay a high price in terms of various psychosomatic ailments such as headaches, ulcers, colitis, and insomnia. Or they may suffer greater feelings of ambivalance about themselves, their relations with others, and their professional goals.

On the other hand, repressing or inhibiting a strong desire to achieve may cause feelings of frustration, hostility, and aggression. In one study, for instance, Horner found that women who expressed a great deal of fear of success imagery in writing about achievement also tended to express much hostility and manipulative imagery in writing about personal relationships.

In spite of the personal anguish that may be caused by "fear of success," psychologists cannot agree on what it is. Unfortunately much of the research in this area seems to be done by people who are intensely interested in the issue of sex roles and femininity but who have only a vague understanding of the technical theory and methodology from which Horner derived her formulation of the "motive to avoid success." In order to assess individual differences in an internal motive, for instance, one has to use neutral cues. Cues that describe specific situations with conflicting demands (as for femininity and achievement) are more likely to evoke social expectations than to be expressions of more stable, internalized feelings and motives. The scoring for the stories needs to allow for a continuum of responses, not just for presence versus absence of motive. And in order to predict achievement behavior, one has to control for basic ability and motive to achieve. Horner is well aware of these issues and has developed a new scoring system that reflects them. Her original study was intended to be exploratory; it pointed to an important issue that may interfere with achievement behavior in women and hence may explain why the achievement research makes sense only for men. To examine this problem further, researchers have to do more than run around giving various groups the original medical school cue.

Not that nothing has been learned from this research. Regardless of whether FOS imagery reflects internal motivation or external social expectations, the underlying issues are crucial for many women today. No matter what life choices a woman makes, she tends to worry about her femininity. For one woman this may be a mild concern that emerges only fleetingly when a new wrinkle appears or when others disparage her womanhood. For another woman, however, it may be a constant source of anxiety that can make her hide her abilities and minimize her accomplishments in the male-dominated world of work.

PLANNING A CAREER

How does a woman decide whether to have a career and then what career to pursue? Is her choice based on personal ability, desire to achieve, and the opportunities provided by her economic background? Or do other things influence her decision?

In spite of the dramatic increase in female employment since World War II, most women still work at low-paying, low-status jobs, and many are "ghettoized" in a small number of fields that are seen as feminine, such as nursing, teaching, and secretarial work. Obviously job opportunities and pay scales have a tremendous amount to do with this pattern. But other factors may also be important. Psychologists have looked at this problem in terms of how women make decisions about their education and employment. Do particular personality factors and social pressures lead women to seek only certain kinds of work or careers?

Maximizing Femininity

The research on fear of success clearly suggests that being feminine is a major concern for most women. The unspoken questions are thus, How feminine am I? Is it possible to be feminine and still have a career? Are some types of career more suitable for a woman?

Not that being feminine is something that just happens automatically. Some writers have suggested that the social skills and activities central to the stereotype of female nurturance and femininity are an important area of achievement for women. While men direct their achievement motive into worldly, task-oriented accomplishments, women direct theirs into social interactions. Thus, concentrating on marriage and children can constitute a career in and of itself. Women who choose this option are not necessarily nonachievers; they are simply directing their energies in a traditional direction.

Women who do have a strong desire for worldly achievement, on the other hand, often feel that success threatens their femininity. They handle the conflict in a variety of ways. Some choose not to work outside the home (and are economically able to do so), satisfying their need for achievement vicariously through their husbands' careers. Some choose fields whose content is seen as feminine, avoiding such traditionally masculine fields as science and engineering. Some keep a low profile by playing down their accomplishments and staying in the lower echelons of their field, fearing that more successful participation might be seen as unfeminine. And many choose a career, such as teaching, that has a flexible schedule that can be meshed with child-rearing tasks.

Other women do not commit themselves to serious involvement in a career until their children are grown, when their family responsibilities will be fewer and they will have proved their femininity. And then there is the style of the "superwoman" who "may 'compensate' for her achievement striving by being superfeminine in appearance and personality": physically attractive, nonassertive, submissive, and emotionally expressive. Such a woman avoids some of the negative sanctions associated with the stereotype of a "career woman," who is perceived as "loud, aggressive, and domineering." This tactic of exaggerating traditional female characteristics has also been referred to as assuming a "mask of inferiority."

Following Mother's Example

What makes a woman career-oriented in the first place? Many researchers report that family background is crucial. They have found that women whose own mothers worked are likely to have higher educational and career aspirations during high school and college. The idea is that the mother provides a role model, showing the daughter that women can manage successfully to combine family responsibilities with a career or paid employment. This positive example, combined with the supportive attitudes of the father and the other family members, encourages a daughter to consider a broader range of options in her own life. In other words, childhood experience fosters a less rigid or traditional view of sex-role norms which does not limit a daughter to homemaking aspirations.

But parents are not always consistent in encouraging a daughter's career. When she gets to college, a daughter often finds that her parents will not spend as much money on her as they will on their son. Parents may feel that "a career may be okay for some women but not for our daughter." In fact, as a woman nears the end of her education, she may find that her parents reverse themselves and begin to stress the importance of marriage. Thus, many women today still share the experience reported by this college senior in 1942–43:

I get a letter from my mother at least three times a week. One week her letters will say, "Remember that this is your last year at college. Subordinate everything to your studies. You must have a good record to secure a job." The next week her letters are full of wedding news. This friend of mine got married; that one is engaged; my young cousin's wedding is only a week off. When, my mother wonders, will I make up my mind? Surely, I wouldn't want to be the only unmarried one in my group. It is high time, she feels, that I give some thought to it.

Other women are given a mixed message all along:

All through high school my family urged me to work hard because they wished me to enter a first-rate college. At the same time they were always raving about a girl schoolmate who lived next door to us. How pretty and sweet she was, how popular, and what taste in clothes! Couldn't I also pay more attention to my appearance and to social life? They were overlooking the fact that this carefree friend of mine had little time left for school work and had failed several subjects. It seemed that my family had expected me to become Eve Curie and Hedy Lamarr wrapped up in one.

When parents suddenly urge their daughter to marry, however, they do not necessarily get the response they expect. As one daughter put it: "There is a lot of pressure from my mother to get married and not have a career. *This is one reason I am going to have a career* and wait to get married. . . . There is also some pressure from my father to get married, too." Some women even say that they want to have careers precisely because their mothers did not. Listen to these college juniors:

My mother is now working as a secretary, but she didn't work until now. I don't want to end up like that.

Another reason (I am going to have a career and wait to get married) is a reaction to my mother's empty life.

By the time women are in college, then, parental attitudes and life styles may have become less important. The attitudes of other students are important, however—especially those of men. Women whose boyfriends encourage them are less likely to experience fear of success in college and tend to apply to graduate school in less traditional areas. Some women may even attribute their own ambitions to the important men in their lives:

He wants me to be intelligent. It is a source of pride to *him* that I do so well.

I would have to explain myself if I got a C. I want him to think I'm as bright as he is.

He thinks it would be a good idea for me to go to law school.

He feels very strongly that I should go to graduate school to get a Master's degree. He does not want to feel that he has denied me a complete education.

A woman's orientation toward the man in her life is not necessarily due to weakness or immaturity. As we saw in the section on working wives and mothers, a husband's attitude is so important to his wife's employment that Jesse Bernard has coined the phrase the "law of husband cooperation." College women are anticipating the realities of married life by applying the "law of boyfriend cooperation."

But what happens to a woman once she has finished her education? Are her aspirations translated into actual employment, or do they fade away along with the other dreams of youth? And is the outcome still influenced by parents and peers as much as it was while she was in school? Unfortunately we cannot really answer these questions, because the research, like most of that in psychology, has been done with (white, middle-class) college students.

The one study that did examine career involvement in older women suggests that parents become less important. By the seventh year after college graduation it does not matter whether mother worked, although a relatively modest financial background does seem to encourage a daughter to seek out a career. The crucial factor, however, is the daughter's own sex-role attitudes. Once a daughter is out on her own, then, she seems to make her career decisions independently of parental influences.

WOMEN ON THE JOB

Once a woman has decided to have a career, what is work like for her? First of all, it is not as lucrative as it should be. After a decade of equal opportunity laws, most women still bring home paychecks only 60 percent as large as those of their husbands, brothers, and lovers. After summarizing research on the "missing" 40 percent, Elizabeth Almquist concludes that this gap is due not to the characteristics of employed women—neither to their education, occupation, work experience, or marital status nor to the number of children at home—but apparently to employer discrimination against women.

If a woman is single, an employer expects her to marry. If she is married, an employer expects her to have children and drop out. Yet even if a woman does not drop out (women are doing so less and less these days), she is not paid or promoted as much as her male counterpart. When a man and a woman with identical skills and competencies apply for work, they are given different sorts of jobs, even within the same company. He enters an executive training program; she enters the secretarial pool. And the initial differences increase as, once on the job, men are urged upward and women are not. He becomes regional sales manager; she becomes his private secretary. Although there are now a number of legal remedies which women are using for these blatantly discriminatory practices, there are other, more subtle ways of keeping a woman in her place on the job. Even when a woman holds the same job title as a man, she inhabits a different social world. The fact of being female influences her daily interactions in a variety of ways that can not only be upsetting and discouraging but can also interfere with her job performance and advancement.

The Token Woman

Many women who enter predominantly male fields find that they are treated as outsiders whose very presence is suspect. They are constantly reminded that they do not belong to the exclusive male club of serious professionals and certainly cannot share in its camaraderie. Hazing from men often takes the form of "the putdown"—small but significant insults that range from making sexist jokes to accusing female colleagues of being "women's lib freaks."

The pressure often starts in graduate school and continues after the woman has completed her training. Young female attorneys, for example, report that when they enter the court house the bailiff may comment, "What are you doing here? Oh, you're a lawyer! Are you a women's lib?" And some arrogant male attorneys may say things like "that ... Public Defender is madly in love with you."

If sexist remarks were the only problem, a woman might be able to shrug them off; but they are combined with a pervasive social isolation that Bernard calls "the stag effect." Here again the difficulty begins in graduate school, when women are much less likely to have the benefit of a close working relationship with professors. Even a professor who does agree to be the mentor or sponsor for a female student is likely to treat her differently than he would a male student, expecting her to supply clerical help and other services. But the woman cannot really refuse, since the work done under the guidance of such an advisor or mentor usually forms the basis for her doctoral dissertation and the publications she needs to get a job.

Once she is on the job, the isolation continues. Many business and professional decisions are made over coffee, lunch, or cocktails. Important contacts are established and maintained on the golf course, on the squash court, and in other traditionally male settings. Being excluded from these informal social occasions does not just make the female professional feel lonely; it can seriously interfere with her ability to do her job. A female attorney who is excluded from the camaraderie of the officers of the court, for instance, may have more difficulty obtaining continuances, deals, and favors for her clients. Promotions, job openings, and professional referrals are also discussed informally; by the time the female professional finds out about them they have often been filled by that promising young man who plays squash so well. In an academic setting a woman is often excluded from the exchange of ideas and the joint projects that are essential to research—and hence to career advancement. One female assistant professor comments on this problem:

Although my research interests are clearly in line with one of the older males in my department, he has never asked me to share my ideas with him or even to read some of his research proposals. I wouldn't feel so badly but I have a male colleague who is my age and whose dissertation was much further removed from this senior professor's area of interest. My young friend has just been asked to help formulate a new research proposal with our older colleague. . . . My main contact with my older colleague is that his oldest daughter attends the same university I graduated from and that remains our main topic of conversation.

Why do men exclude their female colleagues from the "old boys' network" of shop talk and informal social interaction? Some men are used to relating to women only in a sexual manner and may be uncomfortable with them in any other situation. Kaufman suggests that this is a particular problem for single women and leads them to make comments like "I couldn't wait until my hair turned grey. . . . I felt people could no longer accuse me of 'hunting' for a husband, least of all someone else's."

Other researchers argue that men naturally tend to band together in all-male groups because of a genetic "male bond" or because they see other males as more powerful and stimulating because they control more resources than women do. Whatever the reason, men seem to feel that the presence of women interferes with the natural flow of things. A male school administrator expressed this in terms of the need for an emotional release possible only in a relaxed, all-male group:

When things get tough and uptight and we don't seem to be making any headway we lapse into other areas of common interest—football and basketball and the like. A woman would stop that very important process from occurring because apart from the job we wouldn't have any common areas of interest. I couldn't relax if a woman were an intergral part of the management team.

Not all men feel this way. When the same researcher asked other male school administrators about this "locker room" attitude, two of them said,

I've heard it. I've seen it, but I feel sorry for districts where administrators must operate on such levels of emotional catharsis.

I've heard that. There is truth in it. I just have confidence in human beings that it would change [if a woman were hired]. It's a matter of proving her skills and she would be accepted.

When faced with these subtle forms of discrimination, some women become discouraged and question their own competence. Although they resent being treated differently from men in the same position, they may still tolerate or even encourage the more benevolent forms of discrimination. Thus a woman may occasionally let her male colleagues protect her from controversy and pressure, which is initially reassuring but ultimately prevents her from obtaining valuable experience.

Other women are lucky enough to find individual men who perceive their abilities and encourage them in their work. Thus, a number of female school administrators report that they had not even considered management positions at first, because they knew no women who held such jobs; then each woman, after being encouraged by a man, took one on and was able to overcome her initial feelings of inadequacy.

A woman who receives no encouragement from male colleagues may try to make it on her own. But this is extremely difficult, as one female professor explained to Kaufman:

Although we don't like to admit it, it's not what you know but who you know in academe. My peers who have "made it" have done so on the coattails of some prominent man. This is true for both men and women. I'm not one of those older women who's going to tell you that it's easier now than it was some twenty years ago. In some ways I think it's harder for young women today than it was then. Discrimination has simply become more subtle. Women have the illusion that they can survive professionally on their own. I watch the young women enter our department out to prove they can make it. They don't form contacts with the older women, they are not accepted by the older men, and they compete directly among themselves and with the younger men. I watch them come and go.

Although they are often isolated from their male colleagues, women do have a source of support—each other. A feeling of solidarity often develops among them even if they do not see each other often. As one woman principal describes it:

It used to be when I walked into a room full of men and only one other woman I would tend to ignore her. Now when I walk into a similar situation the woman and I at least have eye-contact. I don't necessarily sit by her and I may not even talk to her, but we have a feeling of sisterhood and we support each other. There's too damn few of us (women); we found out we need to support each other. If there were more of us we would be free to act just as folks, but because there are so few of us, there is a common bond of being women.

This sisterhood may take more concrete forms. In academia, for instance, women are beginning to form "old girls' networks." The women in a department or a school often look to each other for emotional support and professional collaboration. Many of them feel that the men simply cannot be counted on. One unmarried woman who is a full professor stated this view firmly:

I have been in academia a long time and no matter how many changes occur it is still evident to me that the only colleagues one can really feel comfortable with are other women. We may start out believing differently but experience teaches us something else. You can count on your male colleagues to tell you about their personal problems and even share some ideas about departmental politics but when it really counts, when it's time to write the research proposal, when it's time to allocate the merit increases, you can count yourself out if you are a woman. . . . I've seen it happen so many times. University living is male living on male terms . . . when we try to break barriers we seem to fail. The two younger men with whom I've done research are no longer in this department, they were both denied tenure, need I say more?

As part of the attempt to build a support network, women academics seem to combine work and social lives more than men do: their close friends are more likely to be professional colleagues. But compared with the colleague-friends of men, those of women are less likely to share their specific research interests, to be older and more established, and to be helpful to the women's career advancement. There is a loose cluster of lower-ranking women in a variety of professional specialties. Although they are able to provide crucial emotional support for each other, these women cannot provide the avenues to career advancement that are available to their male counterparts through the guidance, cooperation, and friendship of powerful older males.

Acknowledging Female Achievements

Of course most woman do not enter predominantly male fields and hence do not suffer putdowns and social isolation. But many women find that their accomplishments, even in traditionally female occupations, are not acknowledged as readily as are those of men, for sex-role stereotypes tend to cloud the perception of women and their work.

Researchers have approached this problem by presenting the same piece of work to different college undergraduates and telling some that the work is by a woman and some that it is by a man; the subjects then rate the work's value and the creator's competence. In this classic study Goldberg found that college women rated male authors as better than female authors even though the male and female articles were identical. He concluded that prejudice against women is so pervasive that women themselves have internalized it.

This prejudice does not mean that people think that "no woman's achievement or work is as good as a man's." When Goldberg's study was repeated on other campuses, the results were confusing. Sometimes male students showed this bias while females did not, while at other times neither sex was influenced by a professional author's gender, yet women rated more positively student essays that they thought were written by other women. And when uneducated, middle-aged women were asked to evaluate professional articles on marriage, child discipline, and special education, they viewed the work of females more positively than that of males. This may have been due to the greater maturity of the raters or to the nature of the topics, since Mischel later found that males writing in predominantly masculine fields and females writing in predominantly feminine ones received higher ratings from college students.

In trying to account for these contradictory results, researchers have focused on different aspects of achievement. Some have looked at the characteristics that observers attribute to successful men and women. When a man and a woman are both presented as successful at a masculine task, for instance, students may think that the man must be skilled whereas the woman merely worked hard or was lucky. But with a less sex-typed job such as college teaching the professor's gender may be less important. Now the important thing may be subject matter: humanities professors may be seen as more friendly, attractive, and interested in teaching, while science professors may be seen as more logical, self-assured, and conscientious and as better scholars.

The sex-role stereotypes an individual associates with a particular task or occupation do not always affect his or her perception of the successful person performing it. One study asked college students to watch one woman succeed and one fail in assembling a carburetor. Here the successful woman was perceived as not only having more mechanical aptitude and interest in math and science than the unsuccessful woman, but also as being more worldly, warm, emotional, and creative. Thus, the woman succeeding at this masculine task was seen not as masculinized but, on the contrary, as having more of the positive characteristics associated with both the female and the male stereotypes.

Some researchers have argued that the contradictory results are largely due to the way the studies have been done. Not only are different colleges used each time, but also the students are given little information about the actual behavior of the supposedly successful men and women. The student raters may resort to sex-role stereotypes simply because they do not have much else to go on. Ellyn Kaschak tried to remedy this difficulty by describing the teaching methods of a man and a woman in traditionally masculine fields (business administration and chemistry), traditionally feminine fields (home economics and elementary education), and relatively nonsex-linked areas (psychology and history). She found that the academic field was not important, but the gender of the professor was. Male students rated male professors as more effective, powerful, concerned, likable, and excellent and indicated that they would be more likely to take a course from a male than from a female professor. Female students, on the other hand, did not rate male and female professors differently except in the area of power. In spite of their perception of the female faculty as less powerful, however, the female students still preferred to take courses with women. Since the relative powerlessness of female faculty members may be a reality, this study suggests that while males are still biased, some females are not and may even be starting to band together in response to male attitudes.

Even in Kaschak's study, however, the students were responding to written descriptions of people rather than to live individuals. Faced with a real person, they may pay more attention to actual behavior rather than to abstract stereotypes. In one study, for instance, undergraduates were interviewed by male and female counselors with or without diplomas prominently displayed in their offices: while the credentials increased the ratings of expertness, the sex of the counselor made no difference in them. Thus, even though male bias continues, it may be tempered by face-to-face contact with successful women. To feel that women in general are somehow less competent than men is one thing; to refuse to acknowledge the competence of a female one is actually dealing with is quite different.

All this research is recent and confusing. One major theme has appeared, however: nothing succeeds like success, especially for women. Once the quality of an individual's work is established, sexual bias seems to disappear. Thus, some researchers found that when paintings were presented as entries in a contest, the ones supposedly done by males were rated as better. When they were presented as winners, on the other hand, paintings done by males and females were valued equally. The same effect has been found in evaluations of professors. Undergraduates are more impressed by articles supposedly written by male as opposed to female graduate students, but they show no gender bias if they think the same articles were written by associate professors.

In fact, if a woman can get past the initial gender bias to become established in her field, she may actually be perceived *more* positively than a man in the same position. The researchers found this in studying the perception of lawyers and called it "the talking platypus phenomenon:" "that is, when an individual achieves a level of success not anticipated, his/her achievement tends to be magnified rather than diminished. After all, it matters little what the platypus says, the wonder is that it can say anything at all."

But is it unrealistic to perceive a successful professional woman as more competent than her male counterparts? After all, the barriers to female success are often so formidable that in order to succeed a woman has to be much more determined and talented than the men around her. Other professionals know this. Thus, in one study of school administrators almost everyone interviewed, man or woman, readily agreed that a woman must be "smarter, more competent and more capable" than a man to obtain an administrative position. This perception may even lead some men to expect their female colleagues to be "superwomen." One male principal, for instance, said he would leave his present position only if he were promoted—with one exception. He would accept a job transfer and even a cut in pay in order to go to a school district that had a female superintendent. He explained, "She'd be a wave-breaker. It would be an exciting district to work in because she would have been used to making waves. She would really be a super-stud!"

Although it may be flattering to be viewed as a superwoman, it can also make a woman feel pressured to prove her worth. Thus, when asked whether women had to be more qualified in order to get an administrative job, one woman retorted, "Of course, women are smarter and more competent. We'll have full equality in this field when we have as many mediocre women as we have mediocre men."

15
WOMEN AND POVERTY

National Advisory Council on Economic Opportunity

To the extent that there have been "winners" in the War on Poverty during the 1970's, they have been male—and mainly white. What one writer has called the "feminization of poverty"[1] has become one of the most compelling social facts of the decade. . . .

The shift toward an increasing proportion of women (and children in families with a female householder) among the poor has been disturbingly rapid. In 1976, they passed men (and children in male-householder families) in absolute numbers, and this trend has continued. Almost one female householder family in three is poor; about one in 19 families with a male householder is poor. The decline in poverty during the past decade has been almost entirely in male-householder families. In 1979, there were over 1 million fewer poor children in families with a male householder than a decade earlier. But there were more than 1.2 million *more* poor children in families with a female householder.[2]

From National Advisory Council on Economic Opportunity, *13th Annual Report*, Washington, D.C. 1981.

The main source of this startling shift has been the rising frequency of marital disruption, coupled with women's continuingly poor opportunities for decent earnings and inadequate benefits and supportive services for single women with children. In 1978, one in five families in the U.S. had a single parent, compared to one in nine in 1970. Most of those single parents are women, and their risks of poverty are almost three times that of single fathers—whose poverty rate, in turn, is more than twice that of married householders with children.

As in the case of the aged, the broad statistics mask two key facts about the state of single mothers: even those who are not poor by official measures are often not far from poverty; and those who also face the burdens of youth and/or minority status are much worse off than others. Two-thirds of under-25 female-householder families were poor in 1978—almost three out of four for similarly situated Blacks.

The crippling poverty of single mothers reflects both their exclusion from steady work and the rock-bottom earnings they often receive when working regularly. The majority of female householders with children work in the paid labor force at some point during the year, and they fare much better than those who are entirely dependent on income transfers for a living. Nine out of ten single mothers with children under 6 who did not work (in the paid labor force) during 1978 were below the poverty line—another comment on the limits of our supposedly "over-generous" welfare system. But women's earnings are often so low that even full-time work is no security against poverty: one-third of female householders with children under 6 who worked *full-time* at some point in 1978 were poor—including one in every ten working full-time and year-round.[3]

The much more rapid decline in poverty for men has meant that the inequality in life-chances between men and women has grown considerably over the past few years. At the end of the 1960's, women faced a much greater risk of poverty than men; in the 1970's, that disparity became even greater. In 1967, a female householder was about 3.8 times more likely to be poor than a male householder. By 1979, after more than a decade of anti-discrimination efforts, she was about 5.5 times more likely to be poor.[4] If anything, the evidence suggests that this trend will continue to worsen. One indication is that the income gap between the sexes, widest among the young, has grown still wider in recent years. A young (under 25) female householder in 1967 was about 5 times more likely than a young man to be poor; by 1978, 8 times.[5] It is among the rising generations of young women, then, that the poverty of the 1970's has been most devastating, and that the outlook for the 1980's is most bleak.

We have already noted that poverty has become increasingly concentrated in central cities. A closer look at the figures reveals that the increase in central-city poverty rates has been entirely among female-householder families: poverty among families with a male householder declined in the inner cities during the 1970's (by almost 23% from 1969 to 1978). But the poverty rate among families with a female householder rose by 14% in central cities in the same years.[6]

The deepening inequality between men and women is compounded, predictably, when joined with the division between minority and white: the poverty population is becoming more minority as it becomes more female. The pace of change is not as fast for minorities as it is for women, but the rate of change is significant. In 1969, the rate of poverty among Black householders was roughly 3.6 times that of whites. By 1979, it was 4 times the white rate.

That increase may seem fairly small, but its significance becomes clearer when we consider that it is only a relatively sharp drop in poverty rates for Black male-householder families that has kept Black poverty rates from leaping still faster ahead of the rates for whites. The relative situation of Black women has deteriorated sharply in the past decade. This is particularly apparent if we compare their poverty rates with those of white males. In 1967, a Black female householder had 7½ times the chance of being poor as did a white male; by 1979 she had more than 10 times the chance.[7]

The growth of the welfare state since the late 1960's, therefore, has had a critical impact on the shape of poverty in America. But that impact has had less to do with reducing the size of the poverty population, than with shifting the sex (and, to a lesser degree, the color) of the people within the poverty population. All other things being equal, if the proportion of the poor in female-householder families were to continue to increase at the same rate as it did from 1967 to 1978, the poverty population would be composed solely of women and their children before the year 2000.[8]

REFERENCES

1. Cf. Diana Pearce, *The Feminization of Poverty—Women, Work, and Welfare* (Unpublished manuscript, Department of Sociology, University of Illinois, Chicago Circle) 1978.

2. U.S. Bureau of the Census, Current Population Reports, Consumer Income Series P-60, #125. (Hereafter, CPR) Table 18, pp. 30–31. Beginning in 1979, the Census Bureau no longer uses the terms "male-headed" or "female-headed" families. To avoid the bias implicit in the concept of "heading" families, the Census Bureau now uses the terms "families with a male (or with a female) house-holder." In most cases, this usage has no effect, or only a slight effect, on the calculation of poverty rates. In this Report, we use the new "householder" terminology, except when referring to certain earlier studies or data where use of the newer terms might be confusing. For a detailed discussion of terminology changes, see *CPR* 124, Introduction.

3. *CPR* 124, p. 126. Comparable poverty rates for male householders with children under six were 5.7% for some full-time work, 3.5% for year-round full-time work. *Ibid.*, p. 123. The number of single parents in poverty would be much higher if the cost of day care had been considered in determining actual income.

4. Calculated from *CPR* 125, pp. 30–31.

5. Calculated from U.S. Bureau of the Census, *Current Population Reports*, Series P-60, No. 119, p. 30; and *CPR* 124, p. 33.

6. *CPR* 124, p. 7.

7. *CPR* 125, pp. 29–31. Between 1967 and 1979, the poverty rate for Black female householders dropped by only 13% (from 56% to 49%) while that for Black male householders was cut almost in half (from 25% to 13%). Hispanic female householders have the same poverty ratio to white males as do Black females—roughly half of Hispanic female householders are below the poverty level, compared to about one in twenty white male householders.

8. Based on *CPR* 124, pp. 16–18. Persons in female households were about 38% of the total poor in 1967, and 53% in 1978; or an increase by about 39% over their 1967 proportion. To reduce confusion, we should stress that this is not a prediction of what the poverty population will actually look like in the year 2000—but rather an illustration of the magnitude and speed of the "feminization of poverty" in recent years.

16
PORNOGRAPHY, RAPE, AND THE CULT OF MACHO

Sarah J. McCarthy

According to the California Department of Justice, pornography in this nation is a $4 billion a year business, outselling the combined sales of the movie and record industry. No mere whisper in the corner of our culture, the combined circulation of the porn magazines is 16 million monthly

This article first appeared in *The Humanist*, September/October 1980, pp. 11–20, 56, and is reprinted by permission.

Excerpts: From Philip Zimbardo et al., "A Pirandellian Prison," *The New York Times Magazine*, April 8, 1973. © 1973 by The New York Times Company. Reprinted by permission.

copies, and in an era of what Robin Morgan has named "Brutality Chic," the violence in these magazines is increasing. Snuff films, in which there is a simulated, or sometimes actual, murder of a woman, are selling for $1500, and at least one feminist with radical credentials has come close to defending them. Deidre English writes in the April 1980 *Mother Jones:* "The fact remains that, no matter how disturbing violent fantasies are, as long as they stay within the world of pornography they are still only fantasies. The man masturbating in a theater showing a snuff film is still only watching a movie, not actually raping and murdering." Referring to feminist groups who are organizing against violent pornography, English continues: "There is something wrong with attacking people not because of their actions but because of their fantasies—or their particular commercial style of having them."

But oppressed groups have never just concentrated their efforts on actions. The attitudes and prejudices that underlie racist acts, such as job discrimination, have always been dealt with, and yet, English asks that women dispassionately separate reality from fantasy. Are we to assume, then, that fantasy has no roots in attitudes? She asks us to consider the possibility that sexual violence is not just a result of "sex-role brainwashing" induced by pornography and other cultural conditioning, but that the violence may be the "expression of something profoundly real in the male psychology."

And what about the psychology of this man who is masturbating to a snuff film, how did he get this way, and what should women have to say about him? How and where did he acquire this penchant, or particular commercial style, of masturbating to women's deaths? And what sort of man reads *Hustler*? Is his psyche a boiling cauldron of male rage of mythic proportions brought on by centuries of mothering? Are his hormones raging out of w[h]ack, or has he simply evolved this way like an elephant seal?

Studies such as those done by the President's Commission on Obscenity and Pornography are not really germane to today's questions because they did not study the effects of the violent pornography that has since become commonplace. According to F.B.I. Uniform Crime Statistics, a twelve-year-old girl in the United States has a one in three chance of being raped in her lifetime, and if the research in social psychology and behaviorism in the past twenty years is valid, we can expect not a catharsis effect from the increase in violent porn, but a skyrocketing of rape statistics. For if psychologists have learned anything at all in the past twenty years, it is that societal "brainwashing" is very real and very deep, and that the power of the socialization process in shaping our behavior should not be underestimated.

In 1961, Stanford psychologist Albert Bandura concocted a series of experiments to study how children were affected by the observation of adult aggression. He invited a group of preschool children to observe adults playing with a Bobo doll (a five-foot inflated plastic doll). [T]he adults punched the doll, sat on it, hit it with a mallet, tossed it in the air yelling things such as "Sock him in the mouth." Another group of children were asked to watch an adult who sat quietly playing with some tinker toys, ignoring the presence of the doll. When the children who had not witnessed the adult aggression were left alone in the room with the Bobo doll, they exhibited little or no aggression. Those who had watched the violent display were twelve times as likely to be physically aggressive, and twenty-four times as likely to verbally aggress against the doll. Reporting on this study, [the] authors of the textbook *Social Psychology*, Freedman et al., concluded:

The children in this situation learned to attack a certain type of doll. They might also attack the same type of doll in a different situation, and perhaps a different kind of doll, as well. Just how far this would extend—whether or not they would also punch their brothers and sisters—is not clear; but it is clear that they would be somewhat more likely to attack some things than they were before. Through the process of imitation, these children showed more aggressive behavior.

Another study that illustrates the power of the socialization process and the impact of social role on behavior is the Stanford Prison Experiment. Stanford psychologist Philip G. Zimbardo, interested in the psychological effects of imprisonment, set up a mock prison complete with cells in the basement of Stanford's psychology building. He advertised in the local newspapers for volunteers who would live as guard and prisoner for $15 per day, selecting only those who were judged to be emotionally stable, physically healthy, mature law-abiding citizens. The sample of white, middle-class, college-aged males was divided by a flip of a coin into guards and prisoners. At the start there were no measurable differences between them. To duplicate a real prison, the prisoners were de-individualized by having to identify themselves by numbers rather than their names, to dress in knee-length smocks, to wear stocking caps that mimicked the shaved heads often found in real jails, and to obtain permission from the guards to engage in routine activities such as letter writing, cigarette smoking, or even going to the toilet.

The guards were likewise cast into their roles with all of the necessary paraphernalia and trimmings such as identical khaki uniforms, silver mirror sunglasses, billy clubs, whistles, handcuffs, and keys. "Although they received no formal training from us in how to be guards," says Zimbardo, "for the most part they moved with apparent ease into their roles. The media had already provided them with ample models of prison guards to emulate."

Since Zimbardo was as interested in the guard's behavior as he was in the prisoner's, "They were given considerable latitude to improvise and to develop strategies and tactics of prisoner management." Within hours the guards and prisoners were involved in a grimly serious power struggle:

Guard K:
During the inspection, I went to cell 2 to mess up a bed that the prisoner had made, and he grabbed me screaming. He grabbed my throat, and although I was really scared, I lashed out with my stick and hit him in the chin.

Guard M:
I was surprised at myself. . . . I made them call each other some names and clean the toilets with their hands. I practically considered the prisoners cattle, and I kept thinking: I have to watch out for them in case they try something.

Guard A (From his diary) Prior to the experiment:
As I am a pacifist and nonaggressive individual, I cannot foresee a time when I might maltreat other living things.

First day:
Feel sure that the prisoners will make fun of my appearance and I evolve my first basic strategy—mainly not to smile at anything they say or do which would be admitting this is only a game. . . . After we had our lights out Guard D and I held a loud conversation about going home to our girlfriends and *what we were going to do to them.* (Italics, mine)

Third day:
This was my first chance to exercise the kind of manipulative power that I really like—being a very noticed figure with almost complete control over what is said. When the parents talked to the prisoners, I sat on the edge of the table dangling my feet and contradicting anything I felt like. . . . This was the first part of the experiment I was really enjoying. . . . 817 is being obnoxious and bears watching.

Fourth day:
The psychologist rebuked me for handcuffing and blindfolding a prisoner. . . . and I resentfully replied that it is both necessary security and my business anyway.

Fifth day:
I harass Sarge who continues to stubbornly overrespond to commands. I have singled him out for special abuse both because he begs for it and because I simply don't like him. The real trouble is that 416 refuses to eat his sausage . . . we throw him into the hole (a small dark closet) ordering him to hold sausages in each hand. We have a crisis of authority; this rebellion potentially undermines the complete control we have over the others. I am very angry with this prisoner. I decided to force-feed him, but he wouldn't eat. I let the food slide down his face. I didn't believe it was me doing it. I hated myself for making him eat, but I hated him more for not eating.

Guard A was not the only one to become so swept away with all of this. The other guards, the prisoners, and Zimbardo, too, as he candidly admits, got carried away. Zimbardo was caught up in a very serious role of warden. When rumors of an impending prison break organized by prisoner 819 spread like wildfire through the basement prison, Zimbardo made a frantic call to the real jail in Palo Alto to see if they would house his prisoners. In the midst of this flurry, a fellow psychologist passed through to see how things were going. "What's your independent variable?" he asked. "Who has time to worry about independent variables," Zimbardo lashed out, "Can't you see I've got a prison break on my hands?"

Zimbardo concludes: "We had to end this experiment. We were caught up in the passion of the present, the suffering, the need to control people instead of variables, the escalation of power and all of the unexpected things that were erupting around and within us. So our planned two weeks simulation ended after only six (was it only six?) days and nights."

The frightening lesson of this experiment is the ease with which people who have no particular aggressive or authoritarian characteristics can, in a matter of hours, act in pathological ways when such behavior is viewed as appropriate to one's immediate environment or social role. For those who are suspicious of sex-role theory as it relates to female-male behavior, it is noteworthy that the guard-prisoner roles enacted in this experiment took only hours, rather than centuries, to develop. And these two studies are by no means isolated examples. There is a large body of research which indicates that people are a lot more malleable than previously thought; that we are like chameleons changing our colors from yellow to green to brown in response to our immediate background. Few people or chameleons will risk clashing with their environment. This does not mean, however, that we are blank slates. Behaviorist B. F. Skinner has written that all reinforcers (rewards and punishments) ultimately derive their power from evolutionary selection. We, just like chameleons, have probably inherited this fine-tuned responsiveness, this flexibility to the environment, because it has had survival value. Humans and other animals who were not highly responsive to the rewards and punishments meted out by the physical and social environment are presumably extinct (except, of course, for those intrepid few who are to be found on endangered species or socially ostracized lists).

That is the bad news, but there is a core of good news at the heart of all of this, and it is that people are educable, that consciousness can be raised as well as lowered, and that people are as responsive to a healthy world as they are to a bad one. In a very real sense, humans are the self-creating species, for so much of our behavior depends upon the environment that we create. Or, as Skinner writes in the last line of *Beyond Freedom and Dignity*: "We have not yet seen what man can make of man." With all of this in mind, it seems very reasonable to assume that this violence that lurks deep in the male psyche has been taught, and that if it has been learned, it can be unlearned.

Nazi Germany and the Jonestown suicides powerfully demonstrate the pliability of people to their cultural ideologies. Nazi Germany offered proof that people will kill millions of their fellow citizens in response to the demands of their culture, and Jonestown took things one step further. People are capable of killing themselves and their children in response to such demands.

Contrary to previous theories that the instinct for self-preservation was the most basic and powerful of human drives, the Guyana suicides demonstrate that the socialization process is even more powerful. In a 1972 *Esquire* article, "If Hitler Asked You to Electrocute a Stranger, Would You? . . . Probably," by Philip Meyer, Yale psychologist Stanley Milgram tells of his quest to understand how and why an entire nation would be mobilized to mass-murder under Hitler. At first, Milgram subscribed to the Germans-are-different theory as the most likely explanation for the Holocaust. This theory had been advanced by William Shirer in *The Rise and Fall of the Third Reich*, " . . . the Nazi regime has expressed something very deep in the German nature," a theory much like the men-are-different or violence-deep-in-the-male psyche hypotheses.

Milgram first set out to devise a test that would document his assumption that Germans were more obedient, and then he planned to test for factors in their culture that had caused such behavior. He devised an obedience test, but he never took it to Germany. His first unexpected findings were that Americans were highly obedient. "I found so much obedience," says Milgram softly, a little sadly, "I hardly saw the need for taking the experiment to Germany."

Milgram's test consisted of having subjects "shock" people who made mistakes on a learning task. (Unknown to the subjects, the machine was not really connected.) Two-thirds of those tested among thousands of subjects, shocked to the end of the scale when the experimenter requested that they do so, even though the machine read "lethal voltage" and the victims were screaming in mock pain.

"Many subjects will obey the experimenter no matter how vehement the pleading of the person being shocked," says Milgram in his book *Obedience to Authority*. He continues:

A commonly offered explanation is that those who shocked the victim at the most severe level were monsters, the sadistic fringe of society. But if one considers that almost two-thirds of the participants fall into the category of "obedient" subjects, and that they represented ordinary people from all walks of life, the argument becomes very shaky. Indeed, it is highly reminiscent of the issue that arose in connection with Hannah Arendt's book, *Eichmann in Jerusalem* (1963). Her conception of the banality of evil comes closer to the truth than one might dare imagine. The ordinary person who shocked the victim did so out of a sense of obligation—a conception of his duties as a subject. . . .

The force exerted by the moral sense of the individual is less effective than social myth would have us believe. Though such prescriptions as "Thou shall not kill" . . . occupy a preeminent place in the moral order, they do not occupy a correspondingly intractable position in the human psychic structure. A few changes in newspaper headlines, a call from the draftboard, orders from a man with epaulets, and men are led to kill with little difficulty. Even the forces mustered in a psychology experiment will go a long way toward removing the individual from moral controls. Moral factors can be shunted aside with relative ease by a calculated restructuring of the informational and social field.

What comprises the informational and social field of the young American male? Increasingly, a primary source of sex education for teenaged boys is pornography. It would be wise to learn what it is that Larry Flynt and others are telling our children.

"There's still something to be said for bashing a woman over the head, dragging her off behind a rock, and having her," said one of the guys in the February 1980 *Penthouse*, which has a monthly circulation hovering around five million, equal to or surpassing *Playboy*. Larry Flynt's *Hustler* ranks third with an approximate circulation of two million monthly copies. "Women Who Flirt With Pain" was the cover hype for a *Penthouse* interview with an assortment of resident Neanderthals (a name that would swell them with pride).

"We're basically rapists, because we're created that way," proclaims Dale. "We're irrational, sexually completely crazy. Our sexuality is more promiscuous, more immediate, and more fleeting, possibly less deep. We're like stud bulls that want to mount everything in sight."

Some of this information is not pleasant reading, but one of the primary purposes of feminists against pornography is to educate women and men who do not usually read porn, to show them how far from cheesecake things have come. When women talk about porn, it is important that we show it for what it is, how really raunchy things are, because men and boys are reading it, and we think that it is an incitement to rape. Much of pornography, and indeed our objections to it, hinges on violence and degradation, rather than sexuality.

The letters-to-the-editor in the February *Penthouse* contains an ugly letter from someone who claims to be a sophomore at a large midwestern university, and who is "into throat-fucking." He writes of Kathy and how he was "ramming his huge eleven-inch tool down her throat." Kathy "was nearly unconscious from coming." Gloria Steinem writes in the May 1980 *Ms.*: "Since *Deep Throat*, a whole new genre of pornography has developed. Added to the familiar varieties of rape, there is now an ambition to rape the throat. Porn novels treat this theme endlessly. Real-life victims of suffocation may be on the increase, so some emergency room doctors believe."

Another issue of *Penthouse* contains an article about what they have cleverly called "tossing." A college student from Albuquerque, who drives a 1974 Cadillac and who is "attracted to anything in a skirt," tells how it's done. "How did you get into tossing?" the *Penthouse* interviewer asks. "It just happened," says Daryl. "I was doing it in high school two years ago and didn't know I was. I'd date a chick once, fuck her in my car, and just dump her out. Literally."

Women against porn groups have come under fire for their difficulty in making clear the dividing line between pornography and erotica, but since we are generally opposed to censorhip, this blurry grey area need not be our major concern. Feminist analysis and education around pornography has mushroomed far beyond the traditional pro- or anticensorship dichotomy. Just as an EPA report of air pollution need not imply closing down the factory, or a diagnosis of alcoholism does not imply prohibition, a diagnosis of cultural pollution due to pornography does not imply censorship.

Women have generated a lot of powerful and profound thoughts about pornography; the lack of legalistic precision makes them no less profound. One of the more succinct thoughts was presented by Robin Morgan in *Going Too Far*. "Pornography is the theory," she said, "and rape is the practice." Gloria Steinem, writing in the November 1978 *Ms.*, in the article, "Erotica and Pornography, A Clear and Present Difference," says that "Erotica is about sexuality, but pornography is about power and sex-as-weapon—in the same way we have come to understand that rape is about violence, and not really about sex at all. Erotica is sexual expression between people who have enough power to be there by positive choice."

The slide shows put together by Women Against Violence in Pornography and Media and Women Against Pornography in New York make it clear that these groups are not antisex but antiviolence, particularly sexual violence. The slide show includes a *Hustler* cover picture of a nude woman being pushed head first into a meat grinder, coming out at the bottom as ground meat. I write these graphic descriptions hesitantly because they are so offensive, and then I remind myself that the picture was plastered on newstands from coast to coast in gas stations and drug stores, bought by fifteen-year-olds and their fathers. This issue sold two million copies, maybe more since it was promoted as *Hustler*'s last all-meat issue following Larry Flynt's rebirth at the hands of Ruth Carter Stapleton. Women should know about this. Inside this last all-meat issue is a nude woman lying on a plate looking like a piece of chicken covered with ketchup, and another who is laid out on a hamburger bun, also covered with ketchup. Another issue of *Hustler* displaying the pits of cynicism chic has a drawing of a man's scrotum pushed up against the ear of a retarded girl, his penis presumably filling up her empty head and semen squirting out the other ear. The text reads, "Good Sex with Retarded Girls—you can do anything you want cause who would believe a scrunched face retarded girl?" Will anyone print this, I wonder as I type? I was bleeped once for telling this story on a radio talk show, but Larry Flynt and Hugh Hefner are not censored.

The rest of the slide show is more of the same: women hanging on crosses, their nipples being pulled with pliers, and a kiddie porn section that assures anyone with child abuse on his mind that it's okay, the kids will love it. "I never dreamed it would be this wonderful," said one nude little girl in saddle shoes; and a little girl in a *Playboy* cartoon, getting dressed as she leaves the apartment of a sixty-year-old man, says, "And you call *that* being molested?" *Hustler* used to run a regular kiddie corner called "Chester the Molester." And, of course, there are men out there who believe this stuff. Such propaganda to rape will cause rape to become as common as smoking in the boys room or "kicking ass" after football games.

There is a long macho tradition in this culture that pronounces certain kinds of violence as perfectly appropriate, even expected, just as Nazis were expected to gas Jews, Klansmen to lynch blacks, and hunters to harvest deer. It did not require rage for an Eichmann to kill a Jew, or for a subject in a psychology experiment to electrocute a stranger, and it probably does not usually require rage for men to rape women. Because it would require a state of raging hatred for women to rape and murder men, women assume that it must be the motive behind male violence toward women, but I think such an assumption is a mistake. To assume this is to ignore or deny male cultural learning, the things they have been taught about women and themselves. Though I'm sure male rage exists, just as female rage exists, it is probably not the primary cause of rape. What we may be dealing with is the banality of rape, the sheer ordinariness of it as the logical end of macho, the ultimate caricature of our sexual arrangements. Some men may think that rape is just the thing to do. Its source could, in large part, be due to something as mundane as faulty sex education, rather than a wellspring of rage of mythic proportions. In many subcultures within the United States, violence against women has become acceptable, expected, and even trendy. In *Against Our Will*, Susan Brownmiller says it well:

Does one need scientific methodology in order to conclude that the antifemale propaganda that permeates our nation's cultural output promotes a climate where sexual hostility directed against women is not only tolerated, but ideologically encouraged? . . . Yet when it comes to the treatment of women, the liberal consciousness remains fiercely obdurate, refusing to be budged, for the sin of appearing prissy in the age of the so-called sexual revolution has become the worst offense of all.

In a chapter on rape and war, Brownmiller writes of some Americans in Vietnam. John Smail, a squad leader in the Third Platoon, said that rape was an everyday affair. "You can nail just about everybody on that— at least once. The guys are human, man." "Rape was," in the words of another Vietnam veteran, "pretty SOP—standard operating procedure, and it was a rare G.I. who possessed the individual courage or morality to go against his buddies and report, let alone stop, the offense."

Also in *Against Our Will*, Veteran George Phillips tells writer Lucy Komisar:

"They only do it when there are a lot of guys around. You know, it makes them feel good. They show each other what they can do. They won't do it by themselves."

"Did you rape too?"

"Nope."

"Why not?"

"I don't know, I just got a thing. I don't—of course, it got around the company, you know, well, 'the medic didn't do it.' "

"Did anybody report these incidents?"

"No. No one did. You don't dare. Next time you're out in the field you won't come back—you'll come back in a body bag."

Feminist thinkers like Brownmiller and Morgan and many others have generated most of the creative thoughts about pornography, and Brownmiller is right about them not needing scientific methodology to legitimize the plain common sense that is at the heart of the argument. However, occasionally science, too, exhibits a certain amount of common sense, and in this case the methodology of behaviorism and social psychology do buttress feminist arguments about porn in particular, and sex-role development in general.

Most psychologists, biologists, and even sociobiologists today see the heredity-environment arguments as a false dichotomy, preferring instead an interactionist position. For example, the human capacity for language is innate, but the actual use of language, down to the last vowel and consonant, depends upon our immediate environment. Even the precise dialect with which we speak, unless we make a conscious effort to the contrary, is determined by whether we live in Boston or Alabama or Brooklyn. The capacity for aggression is also thought to be innate, as best demonstrated by the rage of a newborn infant; but the expression of that anger, in childhood and adulthood, in its intensity and its focus, depends upon one's social environment. Attitude and interpretation are crucial to the expression of anger. A hitchhiker will feel natural anger if he is trying to get a ride on a cold, rainy night if large cars with one occupant keep passing him. If the car passing him is an occupied ambulance, his reaction will be different.

Another avenue of psychological research has been sex hormone research, both in regard to rape and to sex differences in general. As far as I know, sex hormones results have been very ambiguous, with some researchers indicating that they have found links between aggression and the male hormone, testosterone, and others challenging those findings. It seems that nothing definitive can be said at this point about the effects of sex hormones on human behavior. It does not seem illogical, though, given the evolutionary history of our species, that males could conceivably have a somewhat greater tendency toward aggression. A greater tendency, if in fact that is the case, does not translate into an irresistible compulsion to rape.

There is a principle highly thought of in the sciences called the Principle of Parsimony. It states that one should never employ a more complex explanation for an event when a less complex one will suffice, a principle that surely seems to apply to current discussion about the roots of male violence against women. In a culture that promotes the cult of macho, rapes should be expected.

Sociobiologists may argue that there is a link between sex and violence in the male brain, but recent research has unearthed a similar linkage in the female brain and nervous system. The September 16, 1978 issue of *Science News* has an article "Sex and Angry Women":

Numerous studies over the years have shown that certain types of erotic literature, pictures, and films can increase aggression in males. Generally more explicit sexual depictions tend to make men—already angered by experimenters—more angry and aggressive. At the same time, softer-core erotica materials seem to soothe the hostility in angry males.

In one of the first such experiments involving women, Robert A. Baron of Purdue University tested forty-five undergraduate women. The subjects were either angered by unflattering personal evaluations by another student or not angered and then exposed to varying degrees of erotic pictures of men and women, as well as to nonerotic pictures. Baron reported at the American Psychological Association meeting that heightened sexual arousal does increase aggression in women, as well as men; and there is indication that it may take less to make women more angry than it does for men.

This is an interesting line of research, especially in view of the fact that, when women are questioned about their "rape fantasies," it is always assumed that they are fantasizing about themselves as the victims of a rape rather than as the aggressor. There are, of course, perfectly understandable reasons for some women to have had fantasies in which they were raped. Women have almost always needed a pretext to have sex, and force is the most guiltless pretext of all. Women's rape fantasies, however, are nothing like real rapes. In a fantasy the woman controls the rapist, even chooses him. A real rape has nothing to do with choice or control, and the result of it is violence and degradation, not sexual pleasure.

Researchers Feshbach of UCLA and Malamuth of Manitoba reported that 51 percent of the men they interviewed after watching violent pornography said there was at least some possibility they would commit rape if assured they would not be caught. "There seems to be within the general population a high proportion of men who are similar to rapists," Malamuth says. "It's only a matter of degree." Professor Ed Donnerstein of the University of Wisconsin found that rapists were aroused by films that showed violence against women, even if they had no sexual content at all. Donnerstein is fast emerging as the primary aggression researcher in the area of social psychology, primarily aggression against women as incited by violent porn. In a paper titled "Pornography Commission Revisited: Aggressive-Erotica and Violence Against Women," Donnerstein reports that:

> There is good evidence to suggest that the observation of such aggressive acts could reduce restraints against subsequent aggressive behavior. Furthermore, as noted in the work of Berkowitz, one important determinant of whether an aggressive response is made is the presence of aggressive cues. Not only objects, but individuals can take on aggressive-cue value if they have been associated with observed violence. This increase in aggression should be especially true for previously angered individuals who are already predisposed to aggress. . . . The present results show that exposure to an aggressive-erotic film was able to increase aggression to a higher level than that of the erotic film.

Donnerstein also reports that angered males who had watched the aggressive-erotica displayed aggression selectively to females but not to males. This study further demonstrates the point that interpretation and attitude as well as imitation cause aggression to be selectively exhibited. Once a particular person is seen as a scapegoat, he or she will be the target for aggression. Donnerstein asks, "Why would the aggression against the female be increased after exposure to the aggressive-erotic film? One potential explanation is that the female's association with the victim in the film made her an aggressive stimulus which could elicit aggressive responses."

These research results, of course, directly contradict Freud's theory of catharsis, as does much of the psychological research. In fact, in *Social Psychology* (Freedman et al.) it is said that: "The vast majority of laboratory experiments have shown that observing aggression provokes greater aggressive behavior, not less. The catharsis effect simply does not occur in these experiments, except in rare instances."

There are probably as many reasons for rape as there are for murder. As well as the condoned red-blooded-American-boy rapes, there are those that can be quietly placed on the doorstep of patriarchal religion. Dread of women grows easily in men who have been taught by puritanical religions that sex is sinful, who must be forever on guard against modern-day temptresses, the daughters of Eve and Salome, Bathsheba and Delilah, who are about to rob them of their morality, their strength, their garden. For they are all there in the Bible—Sarah, Anne, and Mary—divided like the sheep and the goats into good and bad women, forever categorized as Madonnas or whores. The lucky whores who were forgiven were permitted to wash their master's feet with their hair.

Mary Daly, in *Beyond God the Father*, writes of the scapegoat syndrome and how society as we know it has a perverse need to create the "other" as an object of condemnation so that those who condemn can judge themselves as good. She quotes St. Augustine:

What can be more sordid, more devoid of modesty, more full of shame than prostitutes, brothels, and every other evil of this kind? Yet remove prostitutes from human affairs and you will pollute all things with lust; set them among honest matrons, and you will dishonor all things with disgrace and turpitude.

She then quotes St. Thomas Aquinas:

Prostitution in the world is like filth in the sewer. Take away the sewer and you will fill the place with pollution; take away prostitutes from the world and you will fill it with sodomy.

And, of course, there was St. Paul who proclaimed that it was better to marry than to burn. (I have a special fondness for this one because a religious uncle passed it along to my husband in the reception line at our wedding.)

In view of all this, it is not surprising that men like the Hillside Strangler and Jack the Ripper, and the son of Jack the Ripper now operating in Britain, have vented their rage against prostitutes, temptresses whom they would resist even if they had to kill them.

Given the antiwomen and antisex attitudes that flourish in many religious and right-wing groups, it is understandable that many women and liberals are somewhat suspicious of the new feminist antiporn groups. Most women would have to be dragged kicking and screaming before they would again be hoisted upon the pedestal, placed there like "Christmas card virgins with glued hands" as Marge Piercy has written.

The President's Commission on Obscenity and Pornography reported that a "recent survey showed that 41 percent of American males and 46 percent of American females believe that sexual materials lead people to lose respect for women." In the book *Philosophy and Women*, Ann Garry writes:

If a person makes two traditional assumptions—that sex is dirty and that women fall into two classes, good and bad—it is easy to see how that person might think that pornography could lead people to lose respect for women or that pornography itself is disrespectful to women. If one sees these women as symbolic representations of all women, then all women fall from grace with these women. . . . Can we imagine 41 percent of men and 46 percent of women answering "yes" to the question, "Do movies showing men engaging in violent acts lead people to lose respect for men?" Think of the following: women are temptresses, blacks cheat the welfare system, Italians are gangsters, but the white males in the Nixon administration were an exception—white males as a group did not lose respect because of Watergate and related scandals.

And what of women, what of their role in this, for surely we have a role in this, for surely we have a role, just as the prisoners in Zimbardo's prison had their part to play? Sally Kempton has written, "It is hard to fight an enemy that has outposts in your head." There can be no doubt that both the father-confessors of patriarchal religion and the sugar daddies like Hugh Hefner, who pass out goodies for women who take off their clothes, have outposts in our heads. There are none of us who has not been caught in their cross-fires, and they are both our enemy.

Society, religion, and biology (for example, unwanted pregnancies) have insisted that women say no to sex when they meant yes. This is the mustard seed of truth that lies at the heart of the rumor that women want to be raped. The female side of rape is the sexual credibility gap: women who said "No" because they had no other choice, when they meant "Yes." The lies of these women were not lost on men who latched onto this wonderfully self-serving nugget, and the message spread like wildfire that women want to be forced. Myths die hard, even after sexual revolutions, especially when one's ego and sexual gratification are at stake.

There is another women's problem. It is one to be seen in women's literature over the centuries—some have called it the Compassion Trap, some have personified it as Lady Bountiful; Robin Morgan has named it the Pity the Poor Rapist mentality—it is the problem of self-abnegation, the denial of one's self. Black feminist poet and author Alice Walker has written of it in *Meridian*. Lynne is a white woman who has gone South in the sixties to work for civil rights, where she marries a black man, Truman. Lynne and Truman have a friend named Tommy Odds who one day has his lower arm shot off in a demonstration. Because he was angry, and because Lynne was white, he wanted to make love to her.

For of course it was Tommy Odds who raped her. As he said, it wasn't really rape. She had not screamed once, or even struggled very much. To her, it was worse than rape because she felt that circumstances had not permitted her to scream. As Tommy Odds said, he was just a lonely one-arm nigger down on his luck that nobody had time for anymore. But she would have time—wouldn't she? Because she was not like those rough black women who refused to be sympathetic and sleep with him—was she? She would be kind and not like those women who turned him down because they were repulsed and prejudiced and the maroon stump of his arm made them sick. She would be a true woman and save him—wouldn't she?

"But Tommy Odds," she pleaded, pushing against his chest, "I'm married to your friend. You can't do this."

Water stung in her eyes as she felt her hair being tugged out at the roots.

"Please don't do this," she whimpered softly.

"You knows I cain't hep myself," he said in loose-lipped mockery.

His hand came out of her hair and was quickly inside her blouse. He pinched her nipples until they stung.

"Please," she begged.

There was a moment when she knew she could force him from her. But it was a flash. She lay instead thinking of his feelings, his hardships, of the way he was black and belonged to people who lived without hope; she thought about the loss of his arm. She felt her own guilt. And he entered her and she did not any longer resist but tried instead to think of Tommy Odds as he was when he was her friend—and near the end her arms stole around his neck, and before he left she told him she forgave him and she kissed his round slick stump that was the color of baked liver, and he smiled at her from far away, and she did not know him. "Be seein' you," he said.

The next day Tommy Odds appeared with Raymond, Altuna, and Hedge.[°]

Women are beginning to fight back, speak out against rape images wherever they are to be found. Women Against Pornography in New York is conducting tours of the Times Square porn district for other women who have been too intimidated to go alone, and organized a "Take Back the Night" march in which ten thousand people marched. Women Against Violence Against Women in Los Angeles and NOW organized a boycott of all Warner Communications products, beginning with the "Some Girls" album by the Rolling Stones, and its corresponding billboard that read "I'm Black and Blue from the Rolling Stones and I Love It." A group of women spray painted the billboard during the night, and the next day it was removed. At a press conference in Los Angeles, the President of Warner Communications recently announced that WCI "opposes the depiction of violence against women or men on album covers or in related promotional materials." Women Against Violence in Pornography and Media in San Francisco put together a slide show of pornographic images of women to raise public consciousness about this issue, to show that we have come a long way from cheesecake to the meat-grinder. Women Against Sexist Violence in Pittsburgh recently held a conference on pornography as an incitement to rape, and held workshops at which they discussed the possibility of legislation that would outlaw only violent pornography.

There are women walking around New York and Los Angeles, Chicago and Pittsburgh with big black and gold buttons that announce: "Women Against Pornography: It's About Time."

INSTITUTIONS
IN CRISIS

VI
THE FAMILY

Is there a crisis in the American family? Certainly it is a time of change for the family, and many believe it is also a time of trouble. The divorce rate has risen—in some places precipitously—and the birth rate has decreased. The "traditional" family, with the husband as the sole source of financial support and the wife as a full-time homebody, still exists, of course, but it is now a statistical minority. Increasingly large numbers of women, married or not, have entered the labor force. Others live in unconventional intimate arrangements and contribute to the increasing diversity of American family lifestyles. All of this diversity, this permissiveness, if you will, seems to many to be menacing the integrity and stability of the American family.

Still, the American family will doubtless remain with us for a long time. It may look less and less like the conventional family of suburbia—with its traditional male and female roles—but the family will nevertheless continue, with accompanying transformations, readjustments, and problems.

These changes do not, however, necessarily signal decline or decay—just difference. To conclude that the family is declining, one must point to a historical era when things were rosier. Certainly the ideal of home, motherhood, and apple pie is part of our romantic mythology, but the myth did not always match the experience. As one historian concludes, "There is no Golden Age of the Family gleaming at us from far back in the historical past."

Still, because of change, many Americans—men and women, husbands and wives, parents and children—are experiencing marked uncertainties and anxieties. We have known deep changes in family life and in society. But our understanding of how to interpret these changes—and to deal with them—has been impaired in large part "because," as Kenneth Keniston observes, "our reactions are shaped by an outmoded set of views about how families work." More specifically, these views derive from misunderstandings about the relationship between family life and society, particularly about the impact of societal imperatives, structures, and constraints upon the everyday workings of family life.

The social realities of family life are made vivid in Lillian Breslow Rubin's study of working-class and middle-class families. Rubin had two central concerns in writing her book. One was to show the complexity of the family as an institution. It is, she writes, "both oppressive and protective and, depending on the issue, is experienced sometimes one way, sometimes the other—often as some mix of the two—by most people who live in families."

Rubin's second concern is to show how other social factors—especially the relation between gender role and social class—influence the family institution. For example, as Rubin points out in her introductory chapter (not reprinted here), working-class men often hold uninteresting jobs requiring little, too little, commitment of self, while middle-class professionals hold jobs demanding too much. Each reality impinges differently on family life. The chapter we have reprinted explores aspects of such sources of strain. In it Rubin explores how working-class values and upbringing impede marital communication. Marital partners have emotional needs that are frequently undermined by the role segregation and widely differing socialization patterns of men and women, especially in the working class.

Family strain can, and often does, erupt into violence. Husbands beat wives, wives beat husbands more frequently than is commonly supposed, and both hit children. Most of what passes for child abuse is, however, culturally permitted, even encouraged. Parents who discipline their children—raising welts and sometimes breaking bones—often believe they are training their children's character. "Spare the rod, and spoil the child," the saying goes.

Spouse beating is also as American as apple pie, but it is far more covert. It is not unusual to see a parent "spanking" a child in a public place—a restaurant, park or street—but spouses rarely, if ever, beat each other in public. Spouse beating is something about which people are ashamed, but which occurs with such frequency as to be a serious social problem and a somewhat reluctantly accepted method for dealing with family strain. "The marriage license," as Straus, Gelles, and Steinmetz conclude, "is a hitting license." It may not be good or necessary, but it often happens because, as they comment, ". . . violence is built into the very structure of the society and the family system itself." Why, one might ask, should that be?

17
THE TRANSFORMATION OF THE FAMILY

Kenneth Keniston

When we Americans perceive unsettling changes in social patterns, such as the tremendous shifts in family life, we commonly blame them on the individuals involved. One current reaction to changes in families, for example, is the proposal for more "education for parenthood," on the theory that this training will not only teach specific skills such as how to change diapers or how to play responsively with toddlers, but will raise parents' self-confidence at the same time. The proposed cure, in short, is to reform and educate the people with the problem. One kind of education for parenthood takes the form of programs, such as high school courses on "parenting" or lectures and demonstrations in hospitals for expectant mothers and fathers. In addition, a growing number of agencies and companies offer workshops, often at high fees, on "effective" parenting, or on how to stimulate children's development, or on how to increase their IQ's. A parallel for families defined as "disadvantaged" are federally funded "Home Start" courses that try to teach parents to play, "interact," and talk "more responsively" with their children. And, of course, by far the largest movement in parent education is the informal instruction American parents seek from newspapers, books, and magazines. No newspaper or family magazine is complete without one or more

From *All Our Children: The American Family Under Pressure* by Kenneth Keniston and The Carnegie Council on Children, © 1977 by Carnegie Corporation of New York. Reprinted by permission of Harcourt Brace Jovanovich, Inc.

regular columns of advice on child rearing; drugstores have volumes of paperback counsel about every aspect of raising children.

Not that experts agree. Burton White, a psychologist at Harvard, argues in a recent book[1] that the first three years are crucial in determining the rest of a child's life. His Harvard colleague, psychologist Jerome Kagan, says that the importance of the first three years has been overrated[2]—that late starts are not lost starts. Traditional child psychoanalysts advise parents to attend to their children's inner fantasies, fears, and dreams, while behaviorists counsel ignoring these and simply rewarding desired behavior.

Although the experts differ, they share one basic assumption: that parents alone are responsible for what becomes of their children. Of course, many parents can use information, advice, and counseling on everything from how to deal with illness to what can be expected of a moody teenager. But the columns and courses rarely mention the external pressures on parents' and children's lives—for example, the possibility that a harassed working parent who does not "interact responsively" with a child may not have much time or energy to do so after a long and exhausting day. It is not surprising that research on parent education in past decades[3] does not provide grounds for much optimism about the power of this approach to make significant changes in the family life of large numbers of people.

Naturally, if parents are considered solely responsible for what becomes of their children, they must be held at fault if things go awry. It is easy to leap from here to the conclusion that children's problems are caused entirely by the irresponsibility, selfishness, and hedonism of their parents. "Parents today are selfish and self-centered," one angry parent wrote us. "They aren't willing to make sacrifices for their children. But that's what being a parent is all about, so is it any wonder that the children grow up on drugs?" By this logic, everything from working mothers to the rising divorce rate can be blamed on the moral failings of those involved. Families on welfare are lazy, sponging chiselers. Parents who divorce are indulging themselves at the expense of their children. Working mothers neglect their children for a few dollars a day which they waste on clothes and vacations. If children get the outlandish idea from television advertising that there is a box or bottle with a cure for every problem, their parents must not be talking enough, guiding them enough, or supervising them enough. *Parents* are to blame; and if there is a solution, it must lie in reforming them.

Blaming parents and giving them advice both spring from the assumption that the problems of individuals can be solved by changing the individuals who have the problems. This implies a second assumption as well: that families are free-standing, independent, and autonomous units, relatively free from social pressures. If a family proves less than independent, if it is visibly needy, if its members ask for help, then it is by definition not an "adequate" family. Adequate families, the assumption runs, are self-sufficient and insulated from outside pressures.

These two assumptions form the core of the American myth of personal self-sufficiency. This myth has deep roots in American history, although it did not emerge in its full form until the early 1800's.

The notion of society as a voluntary assembly of independent and self-sufficient individuals who freely contract with each other to form a community or nation was at the heart of the Enlightenment-Age thinking that flourished in the American colonies 200 years ago. The revolution that freed Americans from British rule had a psychological impact that was particularly important in establishing the myth of family independence and self-sufficiency. The American colonies had never provided fertile soil for feudal ideas of hierarchy, interdependence, and mutual obligation—ideas that bound peasants, vassals, and serfs to lords, squires, and landowners in return for benevolent protection and support in times of crisis. After the Revolution, free from British rule and isolated from Europe by an ocean that took weeks to traverse, Americans felt truly independent. The expulsion of the Indians to the area west of the Mississippi under Jackson opened vast tracts of forests and prairie for farming and land speculation and helped confirm the view that any American possessed of a minimum of ingenuity and industriousness could become self-sufficient in short order.

There were moral, political, and economic lessons in the ideal of the self-made man who knew no master, depended on no one, and lived by his wits. First, this ideal assigned special virtue to personal independence. To depend on others was not merely a misfortune but virtually a sin. Being independent attested to the possession of *moral* qualities: industriousness, enterprise, self-control, ingenuity, and rectitude. The dependent were suspected above all of idleness (the cause, most Americans came to think, of "pauperism") and sensuality (manifest in such sins as intemperance with alcohol, sexual immorality, and general self-indulgence).

Politically, the ideal of self-sufficiency helped define the qualities of the new democratic man in America. He would be free to make up his own mind and beholden to no man and no superstition—above all, to no foreign allegiance, Pope, or prince. He was not to rely on the state, nor was the state to interfere in civil society except when absolutely necessary to protect his basic rights. In the triumph of democratic ideas in the early 1800's, the active exercise of state power came to be seen not only as tyrannical, but, perhaps even worse, as potentially weakening American independence and free spirit. Americans contrasted their democracy of free men to the allegedly decadent societies of Europe, where the political freedom, independence, and initiative or ordinary citizens supposedly

was sapped by an overactive and authoritarian state. The ideal society—
and most Americans believed that it was being realized in America—was
like an assembly of free atoms: men who came together occasionally to
vote and who expected the state to protect their freedoms, but who were
otherwise on their own.

As an economic doctrine, the myth of self-sufficiency was built on images of the independent farmer and entrepreneur. The economic facts of
life in seventeenth- and eighteenth-century America encouraged Americans to think of themselves as especially self-sufficient. The nation's economy was primarily agricultural. Before the development of large
agricultural markets and specialized farm production, most farmers in
the northern states were indeed largely able to provide for themselves,
raising their own food and bartering their surplus or their labor for the
necessities (few by today's standards) that they could not produce themselves. The myth was, in turn, closely connected to the work ethic, with
its glorification of work not as a means to an end but as a good in itself.
For children in particular, "industry"—industriousness—was a moral
quality as well as a useful one. It showed good character; it established a
presumption that the child was neither idle nor sensual, the two great
vices to be avoided. But children's industriousness, in addition to establishing their virtue, was a prerequisite to adult economic self-sufficiency,
which was thought possible for all those willing to work hard. The emerging capitalism of the early nineteenth century provided enough examples
of success apparently achieved through industriousness to make this aspect of the myth believable.

In the early nineteenth century, the doctrine of self-sufficiency came to
apply to families as well as individuals. Until then, families had been seen
as fundamentally similar to the wider society, as "little commonwealths,"
in the Puritan phrase, governed by the same principles of piety and respect as the community at large. In the early 1800's, however, the more
prosperous, urban classes pioneered a redefinition of the family. In their
thinking—soon widely accepted as the ideal—the family became a special protected place, the repository of tender, pure, and generous feelings
(embodied by the mother) and a bulwark and bastion against the raw,
competitive, aggressive, and selfish world of commerce (embodied by the
father) that was then beginning to emerge as the nation industrialized. A
contemporary essay titled was typical: "The Wife, Source of Comfort and
Spring of Joy."[4] The family's task—and especially the mother's—was to
protect the children's innocence against the temptations and moral cor-
ruptions of the threatening outside world. No longer simply a microcosm
of the rest of society, the ideal family became a womblike "inside" to be
defended against a corrupting "outside."

In performing this protective task, the good family was to be as self-
sufficient as the good man. Ideally, it needed no outside help to armor its

inhabitants against the vices of the streets. To be sure, an urban father had to venture into those streets to earn the family's living, and at times had to dirty his hands. But the pure wife-and-mother stayed at home, in part as a sign of the father's success, but also to protect her children from sin and temptation.

As the nineteenth century passed, Americans came to define the ideal family as one that was not only independent and self-sustaining, but almost barricaded, as if the only way to guard against incursions from the outside was to reduce all contact with the rest of the world to a minimum.

If anything, this pristine portrait represented upper middle-class life in the cities, but only a privileged few American families could afford the insulation of women and children that the myth decreed. Most families lived a very different kind of life. Indians, slaves, Mexicans, poor people, immigrants, and growing numbers of factory workers were rarely as self-sufficient and independent as the myth said they should be. The ideal merely defined them as groups to be changed, pitied, condemned, educated, uplifted, reformed, or Americanized.

Nonetheless this ideal, like many other ideals, became a myth—the myth of the self-sufficient individual and of the self-sufficient, protected, and protective family. And the myth prevailed. Even those who could not make it real in their own lives often subscribed to it and felt guilty about not meeting its standards. The myth determined who was seen as virtuous and who as wanting; it provided, and still provides, the rationale for defining familial adequacy and morality. This moralizing quality is one of its most important features. For this myth tells us that those who need help are ultimately inadequate. And it tells us that for a family to need help—or at least to admit it publicly—is to confess failure. Similarly, to give help, however generously, is to acknowledge the inadequacy of the recipients and indirectly to condemn them, to stigmatize them, and even to weaken what impulse they have toward self-sufficiency.

The myth of self-sufficiency blinds us to the workings of other forces in family life. For families are not now, nor were they ever, the self-sufficient building blocks of society, exclusively responsible, praiseworthy, and blamable for their own destiny. They are deeply influenced by broad social and economic forces over which they have little control.

THE NEW ROLE OF PARENTS

If parents' decisions are not wholly responsible for the changes, what is putting such a strain on families in America? Over the last centuries, families have not only been reduced in size but changed in function as well; expectations of what families do for their children have also been reduced. Mothers are no longer automatically expected to spend the whole day with their four year olds; fathers are no longer expected to train them in skills for a job. No one imagines that parents will try to manage a child's raging fever without help or teach a ten year old set theory in mathematics. As the forms of life have changed, institutions with a great deal of technical expertise have grown up to take over these functions, while parents have gone out to jobs that are less and less comprehensible to their young children. Conversely, children need training and experience to prepare them for a world already strikingly different from that of a generation earlier when their parents were growing up. As a result, families today have drastically changed in their functions and powers, especially in their power to raise children unaided.

Few people would dispute that we live in a society where parents must increasingly rely on others for help and support in raising their children. In a sense, parents have had to take on something like an executive, rather than a direct, function in regard to their children, choosing communities, schools, doctors, and special programs that will leave their children in the best possible hands. The lives parents are leading, and the lives for which they are preparing their children, are so demanding and complex that the parents cannot have—and often do not want—traditional kinds of direct supervision of their children. And although most of these changes have come about because of changes in our social and economic system, not because of the selfishness or immorality or negligence of individual parents, the extraordinary thing is that the myth of the self-sufficient family persists.

Changing Family Functions

All generalizations about "the family" have numerous exceptions. There are and always have been many kinds of families in America, different for reasons of class, region, ethnicity, and individual inclination. Moreover, scholars know less than they would like about the actual experience of family members in earlier times and often disagree about how to interpret what they do know. Finally, changes in family life have come unevenly and erratically.

Nevertheless, the major developments of the last two centuries seem clear enough, and the most important is a shift in the functions of families. Three centuries ago, almost all families resembled one part of the myth: they were largely self-sufficient agricultural units. They owned and occupied the farms and plantations of seventeenth- and eighteenth-century America. Apart from nails, salt, and a handful of other goods, these family farms produced, sometimes with the help of neighbors, most of what they needed to live: their own houses, their food, bedding, furniture, clothing, and fuel. Barter was more common than purchase for acquiring the goods the family could not produce (except in those regions of the South where cash crops such as tobacco and indigo were introduced early), and working for wages was rare in North and South alike. Family members were "paid" in room and board; most of the extra manpower that family members could not provide was supplied by indentured servants, bound apprentices, trading work between families or, in the South, by slaves.

The most important difference between these early American families and our own is that early families constituted economic units in which all members, from young children on up, played important productive roles within the household. The prosperity of the whole family depended on how well husband, wife, and children could manage and cultivate the land. Children were essential to this family enterprise from age six or so until their twenties, when they left home. (Indeed, in most seventeenth-century American paintings, they are portrayed in the same kind of clothes adults wore—a sign of how much they participated in the world of adult responsibilities.)[5] Families not blessed with children usually faced economic hardship as a result, for boys were necessary to the hard work of cultivating the land and harvesting the crops, while girls were essential to the "homework" of storing and cooking food, caring for domestic animals, spinning, weaving, and sewing.

Children were, in short, economic assets. Early in life, most children began to pay their own way by working with and for their families. Many years later, when the parents were elderly, children paid another economic dividend: in a time when there was no government old-age assistance or social security, grown children were often the chief source of their parents' support.

In the course of the nineteenth century all this began to change. Farm families began to find that raising one crop for sale and using the proceeds of that sale to buy goods produced by others could give them a higher standard of living than could self-sufficient agriculture. The production of cash crops such as grain and cotton replaced agriculture intended chiefly to provide for the family; money became the medium for obtaining necessities the family no longer produced; and families became less self-sufficient. In addition, an influential minority of families ceased entirely to be productive units in which parents and children worked together. Instead, family members (especially fathers) went out to work for wages in factories and businesses. As commerce and factory work became more common, family life and work were sundered: what a worker produced and what he or she consumed were increasingly not the same thing. Money—in the form of wages, salaries, or, for the wealthy, returns on speculation and investments—provided a new and more tenuous link between work and family.

This shift was gradual and uneven. Even in the late 1880's most American families lived on farms, while in cities, family-run stores and shops were far more common than today. And on farms, children remained part of the family productive unit until mechanization made agriculture a business of adults. One reason the nation's schools have long summer vacations is that their schedules were established in a time when children were needed to help in the peak farm season.

In our time, the family economy has disappeared almost completely. While once almost all American family members worked together at a common economic enterprise on whose success they collectively depended, today most American adult family members work for pay, while children rarely work at all. No common economic task remains. Work and family life are separate enterprises; families consume as a unit, but do not produce as a unit.

The economic "value" of children to families has changed as a result. If weighed in crass economic terms, children were once a boon to the family economy; now they have become an enormous economic liability. The total costs of housing, feeding, and clothing one child as well as educating him or her through high school now add up to more than $35,000 by very conservative estimates for a family living at a very modest level.[6] Moreover, as schooling has lengthened, the financial drain of having children is prolonged to an average of twenty years. Nor can children today be counted on for an economic return in the form of informal old-age assistance.

In the past then, the intrinsic pleasures of parenthood for most American families were increased by the extrinsic economic return that children brought. Today, parents have children *despite* their economic cost. This is a major, indeed a revolutionary, change.

Furthermore, as children more and more have come to be regarded in the economic hierarchy as "dependents" rather than contributors, child rearing itself has come to be seen as a nonproductive job. It yields no wages, and ever since the industrial revolution, people have come to value their work more and more for the cash income it produces.

A second major change in family functions is the removal of education from the family. To be sure, there were schools in colonial America, and a large proportion of boys, at least, especially in New England, attended them for at least a few years, giving the colonies an unprecedented literacy rate as compared to Europe. But over the course of a year children spent less time in schools than they do now, and most of them left school as soon as they learned to read, write, and cipher. And like everything else, most education went on at home, organized either around reading the Scriptures or around learning a trade. In both cases, and whether they were teaching their own children or apprentices, the major responsibility for education fell on parents, with schools playing a distinctly secondary role.

With the creation of the public "common school" in the middle of the nineteenth century under the leadership of Horace Mann, formal education began to replace family education rather than assist it. Compulsory, free public education was given many justifications, but among the most common was the argument that families—especially immigrant families—simply could not educate their children for a productive role in the growing, increasingly complicated American economy. Schools, it was claimed, could do what families were failing or unable to do: teach good work habits, pass on essential skills, form good character, and, in short, Americanize.

We will discuss more fully in the chapter on education the hopes and myths that have animated our American commitment to schooling. For now, the point is that acceptance of the doctrine of common public schooling marked another inroad on traditional family functions. A public institution, armed with the power of legal coercion, was taking over and expanding traditional family prerogatives. This shift was, again, gradual and uneven. We feel its full force only today, with nearly universal institutional attendance now often starting at age four or five and continuing after high school for at least a year or two of college, that is, until age nineteen or twenty. For a total of fourteen to sixteen years, the average American child spends the better part of most weekdays not in the presence of his or her family, but in the presence of day-care workers or teachers and other children the same age. It is hard to imagine a more crucial change in the role of the family.

In addition to economic production and schooling, a long list of other "traditional" family functions has been largely taken over by people and institutions outside the family. Sociologists and historians have pointed to the family's shrinking role in the care of the aged, the "relief" of the poor, the imparting of basic religious attitudes and values, and the care of the mentally ill. We will consider only one of these, the care of the sick, because it illustrates another, broader change: the way rising expectations accompany changing family functions.

Even one century ago, most care of the sick was a family matter. Doctors were rare and their ministrations of dubious benefit; many children survived despite the leeching of their blood by doctors, not because of it. Except for smallpox, preventive inoculations were unavailable; bacterial infections either cured themselves or led to more serious illness and often death. Hospitals did not exist in most localities; where they did, their staffs could do little more than make patients comfortable and wait for an illness to run its course. There were no specialties like pediatrics.

When children fell ill, their families nursed them and, if the children survived, watched over their convalescence. Except for information dispensed in popular magazines, preventive medicine was formally unknown, its informal precursors consisting of little more than keeping a special family watch on children considered frail or sickly. When children died, as they did far more often than today, they died in bed, at home, with their families beside them.

Today the family plays a diminished role in health care. Parents still make the crucial first decision about whether to call the doctor, and in most cases they still give simple care. But for anything complex, the diagnosis is in the hands of experts, not parents, and one crucial role for parents in the complicated business of nursing a sick child is to see that the child "follows the doctor's orders." In part, therefore, it is accurate to speak of health-care specialists assuming yet another traditional family function, but to stop there misses a central point: today we expect far more of health care for children than our forebears could. Most of what we expect of specialists did not exist a century ago: immunization against most life-threatening diseases, effective and accurate diagnosis of even obscure and rare illnesses, safe and hygienic surgery when needed, prompt treatment of bacterial infections, and medical correction of many handicaps. All of these are now considered among the basic rights of children. We are rightly shocked when children suffer or die from any of the host of childhood illnesses or conditions that today can be prevented or cured.

Rising expectations for what we want to give our children are crucial for understanding the transformation of families. Much of what we today consider the birthright of all American children and parents was simply unknown to our forebears. They did not need to rely on social workers to guide them, however tortuously, through welfare bureaucracies, because there were no welfare bureaucracies. They did not complain about inferior school facilities or poor vocational programs or inadequate compensatory education because few of these existed in any form, good or bad.

The point is obvious: at the same time that families have been shorn of many traditional roles with children, new expectations about children's needs have arisen and, along with them, new specialists and institutions to meet the expectations. Part of the change of family functions, which carries with it a new dependence on people and institutions outside the family, rests on the family's needs for forms of help and expert assistance that are the creations of the last century.

Not all the family functions that seem to have been transferred outside the family—or that romantics sometimes yearn to bring back—were there in the first place. It is often claimed that "extended families" (with three generations at home, aunts and uncles included) were the rule, and that they have now been replaced by "nuclear" families. But actually most Americans have always lived in families consisting only of parents and children, and in colonial days, just as today, most children moved away from their parents' homes to set up households of their own. Nor is the mobility that scatters kinfolk to widely separated regions a new thing;

historical studies indicate that frequent moves to new places have always been the rule in American life.[7]

A New Job for Parents:
The Weakened Executive

The genuine shifts in traditional family functions do not leave families with nothing to do. On the contrary, some needs and tasks appear even more concentrated in families than in the past. Among these is fulfilling the emotional needs of parents and children. With work life highly impersonal, ties with neighbors tenuous, and truly intimate out-of-family friendships rare, husbands and wives tend to put all their emotional hopes for fulfillment into their family life. Expectations of sharing, sexual compatibility, and temperamental harmony in marriage have risen as other family functions have diminished.

Most important, parents today have a demanding new role choosing, meeting, talking with, and coordinating the experts, the technology, and the institutions that help bring up their children. The specific work involved is familiar to any parent: consultations with teachers, finding good health care, trying to monitor television watching, and so on. No longer able to do it all themselves, parents today are in some ways like the executives in a large firm—responsible for the smooth coordination of the many people and processes that must work together to produce the final product.

This job is crucial for parents because they are usually the world's outstanding experts on the needs and reactions of their own particular children. Teachers, doctors, TV producers, all deal with a piece of the child, and are often more beholden to the interests of educational bureaucracies, medical societies, and the needs of advertisers and networks than to the child as a particular person with unique needs. Only parents are in a position to consider each influence in terms of a particular child and to judge how these outside influences should interact.

But, as an executive, the parent labors under enormous restricions. Ideally, an executive has firm authority and power to influence or determine the decisions of those whose work needs coordination. Today's parents have little authority over those others with whom they share the task of raising their children. On the contrary, most parents deal with those others from a position of inferiority or helplessness. Teachers, doctors, social workers, or television producers possess more status than most parents. Armed with special credentials and a jargon most parents cannot understand, the experts are usually entrenched in their professions and have far more power in their institutions than do the parents who are their clients. To be sure, professionals would often *like* to treat each child in accordance with his or her unique needs, and professional codes of conduct urge that they do so, but professionals who really listen to parents or who are really able to model their behavior in response to what parents tell them are still few and far between.

As a result, the parent today is usually a coordinator without voice or authority, a maestro trying to conduct an orchestra of players who have never met and who play from a multitude of different scores, each in a notation the conductor cannot read. If parents are frustrated, it is no wonder: for although they have the responsibility for their children's lives, they hardly ever have the voice, the authority, or the power to make others listen to them. What light does this analysis of changing families shed on the parental worries with which we began this chapter? Recall the "problem" of working mothers. Their entry into the labor force is not a product of selfish eagerness to earn pin money but is related to the disappearance of the family as an economically productive unit. Mothers on traditional farms played too vital a role in keeping the farm afloat to work for wages anywhere else. Stay-at-home mothers with wage-earning husbands, in contrast, are important to their families and indeed work hard at housekeeping and child rearing, but many find it hard to maintain the sense of self-worth that can come from doing work society values and pays for, and they do not contribute directly to the family cash flow.

The economic drain children now represent adds to the new economic pressures on families. Since most children now use family income for seventeen to twenty-five years and few yield significant income in return, the years of child rearing are the years of greatest financial stress on families; that stress helps push women out into paid jobs to maintain the family standard of living. This is particularly true of single-parent families headed by a woman; her work is a necessity if the family is to avoid welfare and the stigmas that accompany it. In 1974, the median family income was $16,928 if the wife also worked, $12,028 when she did not.[8] Many families are above the poverty line not because wages have kept abreast of needs and inflation, but because wives have gone to work to make up the difference. Mothers work outside the home for many reasons, but one of them is almost always because their families need their income to live up to their standards for their children.

At the same time, rising expectations have inflated most Americans' definition of a reasonable standard of living. A private home, labor-saving appliances, time and money for entertainment and vacations have all become part of normal expectations. Some of these components of a good life in turn make work outside the home more possible for those who can afford them: freezers can reduce shopping to once a week; automatic washers and dryers have eliminated long, hard hours at the washboard and clothesline, store-bought bread eliminates the need to bake. All of these add up to a greater opportunity to work yet in a circular fashion make the income from work more necessary.

We see the same circle connecting mothers' empolyment to schools. If a mother must work, having children in school for 200 days a year leaves her many childless hours during which she can work without neglecting them. School thus permits mothers to enter the paid labor force by indirectly providing the equivalent of "free" baby-sitting, making working possible without expensive child-care arrangements.

Finally, the changing nature of the job market has opened up millions of jobs to women. What sociologists call the "service sector"—jobs that consist primarily in providing personal services, help, and assistance such as nursing, social work, waiting on tables in restaurants, teaching, and secretarial work—is growing more rapidly than any other sector of the American economy.[9] Many jobs in this sector have traditionally been held by women. In a number of service jobs, qualities such as physical strength that favor men are irrelevant, and stereotypically "female" qualities such as helpfulness, nurturance, or interpersonal sensitivity are thought necessary and therefore employable. These jobs pay less than those usually taken by men—one reason for the poverty of female-headed households—but they are all that is available to most women, who have taken them for lack of anything else.

Most mothers work because they need the money. To be sure, other factors are important as well: for example, greater cultural acceptance of women being gainfully employed, and the new insistence on women's right to independence, security, and fulfillment in work. Birth control and increased longevity also play a role that is often overlooked. Whereas formerly many women kept on having children as long as they were fertile, women now have fewer children and space them closer together, so that on the average their last child is in school by the time they are in their late twenties or early thirties. Faced with the prospect of living to seventy-five instead of, say, sixty-five, a woman in her twenties today knows that the days are gone when her role as mother would occupy most of her adult years. A job, even when children are at home, is, among other things, a way of preparing for the decades when the nest is empty.

Over time, however, economic pressures and the way we define economic well-being have had the most pervasive—and most often ignored—influence on mothers working for wages. It follows that it is addressing the wrong issue to point to ignorance, selfishness, or immorality in explaining it.

Or consider the "problem" of the rising divorce rate against the backdrop of the changes in the family. The one crucial factor behind the increase in divorce rates is the reduction in the number of bonds that tie husband, wife, and children together. When family members had more tasks to perform together—and especially when they were united around work as a family—lack of emotional satisfaction with the marriage partner still left family members with much to do in common. Furthermore, parents by and large had less elevated expectations about finding complete emotional, sexual, and interpersonal fulfillment in marriage. Men and women alike were more willing to accept sexual dissatisfactions or frustrations in marriage; temperamental incompatibilities may have caused equal misery but less often led to divorce. A happy, long marriage was, then as now, a blessing and a joy; but an unhappy marriage was more likely to be accepted as simply a part of life.

Finally, in earlier times, the collapse of a marriage was far more likely to deprive both spouses of a great deal more than the pleasure of each other's company. Since family members performed so many functions for one another, divorce in the past meant a farmer without a wife to churn the cream into butter or care for him when he was sick, and a mother without a husband to plow the fields and bring her the food to feed their children. Today, when emotional satisfaction is the main bond that holds marriages together, the waning of love or the emergence of real incompatibilities and conflicts between husband and wife leave fewer reasons for a marriage to continue. Schools and doctors and counselors and social workers provide their supports whether the family is intact or not. One loses less by divorce today than in earlier times, because marriage provides fewer kinds of sustenance and satisfaction.

Even the presence of children in a family is less of a deterrent to divorce than in the past. One reason, as we have said, is that other people and institutions provide more continuity in children's lives when a marriage breaks up. Furthermore, many parents today believe what research usually confirms,[10] namely that preserving an unhappy marriage "for the sake of the children" may be doing the children more harm than good. And finally, the financial effects of divorce on children, though still very bad, are by no means as disastrous as they once were. The greater availability of jobs for women means that more middle-class children today survive their parents' divorce without a catastrophic plunge into poverty.[11]

The entry of women into the paid work force, moreover, has its own effects on divorce rates. A positive by-product of women's economic independence is that a woman who can earn a decent living herself does not have to remain trapped in an impossible marriage because of money alone. And a husband who knows that his wife can earn a good salary is less likely to be deterred from divorce by the fear that he will have to support his ex-wife financially for the rest of her life. Moreover, wives' employment subtly alters relationships of power and submission within marriage. A wife's new independence can strengthen the husband-wife relationship, but increased equality also can produce new stresses or cause old stresses and resentments to surface. Women who are less submissive by and large will put up with less and expect more. One consequence may be the realization that a marriage has not lived up to the high hopes of husband or wife and a decision to end it, particularly when cultural attutides toward divorce make it far less socially shameful than it once was.

At the same time, however, most American parents are competing on unequal terms with institutions on which they must depend or which have taken over their traditional functions. To be effective coordinators of the people and forces that are shaping their children, parents must have a voice in how they proceed, and a wide choice so they do not have to rely on people or programs they do not respect. Parents who are secure, supported, valued, and in control of their lives are more effective parents than those who feel unsure and who are not in control. Parents still have primary responsibility for raising children, but they must have the power to do so in ways consistent with their children's needs and their own values.

If parents are to function in this role with confidence, we must address ourselves less to the criticism and reform of parents themselves than to the criticism and reform of the institutions that sap their self-esteem and power. Recognizing that family self-sufficiency is a false myth, we also need to acknowledge that all today's families need help in raising children. The problem is not so much to reeducate parents but to make available the help they need and to give them enough power so that they can be effective advocates with and coordinators of the other forces that are bringing up their children.

As we have said, none of these changes is the result of an increase in selfishness, ignorance, or weakness in parents. This is not to say that parents are perfect. But few of these changes are within the power of individual parents to influence. Nor do these changes equal the "breakdown" or the "death" of families, as some claim. Most Americans marry and most marriages produce children. Most divorced people remarry in time, as if to demonstrate that their discontent was with their former partner and not with marriage itself.

What has changed is the content and nature of family life. Families were never as self-sufficient or as self-contained as the myth made them out to be, but today they are even less so than they used to be. They are extraordinarily *dependent* on "outside" forces and influences, ranging from the nature of the parents' work to the content of television programming, from the structure of local schools to the organization of health care. All families today need and use support in raising children; to define the "needy" family as the exception is to deny the simplest facts of contemporary family life.

There is nothing to be gained by blaming ourselves and other individuals for family changes. We need to look instead to the broader economic and social forces that shape the experience of children and parents. Parents are not abdicating—they are being dethroned, by forces they cannot influence, much less control. Behind today's uncertainty among parents lies a trend of several centuries toward the transformation and redefinition of family life. We see no possibility—or desirability—of reversing this trend and turning the clock back to the "good old days," for the price then was high in terms of poverty and drudgery, of no education in today's sense at all, and of community interference in what we today consider private life.

REFERENCES

1. Burton L. White, *The First Three Years of Life*, Englewood Cliffs, N.J.: Prentice-Hall, 1975.

2. Jerome Kagan and R. E. Klein, "Cross-Cultural Perspectives on Human Development," *American Psychologist*, Vol. 28, 1973, pp. 947–961.

3. Orville G. Brim, Jr., *Education for Child Rearing*, New York: Russell Sage Foundation, 1959.

4. John P. Demos, "The American Family in Past Time," *Contemporary Marriage: Structure, Dynamics and Therapy*, Henry Grunebaum and Jacob Christ, eds. Boston: Little, Brown & Co., 1976, p. 434.

5. *Ibid.*

6. This is a rough and conservative estimate based on the U.S. Department of Agriculture's standard estimations of raising children from under 1 year of life to age 18 in 1971, reported in Ritchie H. Reed and Susan McIntosh, "Costs of Children," *Economic Aspects of Population Change*, Vol. 2, Elliott R. Morse and Ritchie H. Reed, eds., Commission on Population Growth and the American Future. Washington, D.C.: Government Printing Office, 1972.

Based on the U.S. Department of Agriculture's data derived from the 1960–61 Consumer Expenditure Survey, the costs were estimated for families with from 2 to 5 children who have disposable family incomes which fall between $10,500 and $12,500, depending upon region and type of residence. The cost for 1 child ranged from $29,470 for a farm family to $32,830 for an urban family. Suburban costs were slightly higher at $32,990. These latter 3 figures do not take into account the initial cost of childbirth, which was estimated to be between $853 and $1,500, including hospital and medical care, basic nursery supplies, and maternity clothes.

For a family with from 2 to 5 children who had disposable family incomes of $7,000 to $8,000 (which characterized about one-third of the families in 1971), costs of raising a child ranged from $20,000 to $21,630, not including the cost of childbirth.

Edith Taittonen, chief of the Budget Standard Service for the Community Council of Greater New York, reported that 2 decades ago, it would have cost a New York City worker's family of 4, on a moderate income, $27,578 to raise a child born in 1958 up to 18 years of age. (This is a slightly lower figure than that estimated by the USDA.) Her projections show, however, that for the same family, a child born in 1976 and reared to age 18 would now cost a whopping $84,777. Excluded in this estimate are such costs as extraordinary medical or dental expenses, i.e., orthodontics; educational opportunities for a talented child; and music or art lessons (Research Note No. 22, Sept. 15, 1976, Community Council of Greater New York, New York City).

7. Demos, *op. cit.* See also testimony of Vincent P. Barabba, Director, Bureau of the Census, before the Senate Subcommittee on Children and Youth of the Committee on Labor and Public Welfare, the Ninety-third Congress, First Session, Sept. 24, 1973. Subject: "American Families, Trends and Pressures, 1973."

8. Between 1950 and 1974, the median annual income of families more than doubled when the wife was in the paid labor force and rose by only about four-fifths when she was not (figures adjusted for inflation) (*Monthly Labor Review*, May, 1976, U.S. Department of Labor, Bureau of Labor Statistics, p. 15).

9. Since 1950, the number of persons employed in the service sector has more than doubled, while the number working in the goods-producing sector rose by only about a fifth. By 1975, 82 percent of all women working in non-agricultural industries were employed in the service sector, where they held about 45 percent of all jobs. The proportion of wives who work even though their husbands are employed full time has increased from 36 out of 100 families in 1950 to 49 out of 100 in 1975. The contribution of their earnings to the family income, however, is proportionately the same as in 1920, 26 percent (*Monthly Labor Review*, May, 1976, U.S. Department of Labor, Bureau of Labor Statistics, pp. 13–15.).

10. Theodore Lidz, *The Person: His Development Throughout the Life Cycle*. New York: Basic Books, 1968.

11. Alimony and support payments help very little, however. In a recent study of alimony and support payments for mothers (of children under 18) who were divorced or separated, Isabel Sawhill and her co-researchers found that, on the average, only 3 percent received enough alimony and support payments to bring them up to or above the official U.S. poverty line without their going to work. Sixty-one percent did not receive anything, 24 percent received less than half the amount of the official poverty figure, and 12 percent received something over half but below the full poverty amount. Hence, the financial effects of divorce on children are particularly hard on those women who cannot work—because they lack skills demanded in today's economy—or who should not work—because they prefer to continue housekeeping and child rearing in their homes. (Carol Adair Jones, Nancy M. Gordon, and Isabel V. Sawhill, "Child Support Payments in the United States," Working Paper 992–03, October 1, 1976. Washington, D.C.: The Urban Institute, p. 74, Table IV.)

18
WORLDS OF PAIN

Lillian Breslow Rubin

*I give her a nice home, a nice car, all those fancy appliances. I
don't cheat on her. We got three nice kids—nobody could ask for
better kids. And with all that, she's not happy. I worry about it,
but I can't figure out what's the matter, so how can I know what
to do? I just don't know what she wants.*—TWENTY-NINE-YEAR-OLD
TRUCK DRIVER, MARRIED NINE YEARS

"I just don't know what she wants"—that's the plaintive and uncom-
prehending cry of most working-class men, the cry that bedevils most
marriages. Sadly, she often also doesn't know what she wants. She knows
only that the dream is not being fulfilled—that she's married, but feels
lonely:

It sounds silly, I know, but here I am in a house with three kids and my husband, and lots of times I feel like I might just as well be living alone.

. . . that life feels curiously empty:

You wake up one day and you say to yourself, "My God, is this all there is? Is it
really possible that this is what life is all about?"

. . . that she's often filled with an incomprehensible anger:

I feel like I go crazy-angry sometimes. It makes me say and do things to Randy
or the kids that I hate myself for. I keep wondering what makes me do those
things when one part of me knows I don't really mean it.

. . . and that guilt and anxiety are her steady companions:

I don't know what's the matter with me that I don't appreciate what I've got. I
feel guilty all the time, and I worry about it a lot. Other women, they seem to
be happy with being married and having a house and kids. What's the matter
with me?

"What's the matter" with her is that, even apart from the financial burdens incurred in buying all those goods, they add little to the emotional
satisfactions of life. The advertisers' promises of instant happiness prove

Chapter 7 from *Worlds of Pain: Life in the Working-Class Family* by Lillian Breslow
Rubin, © 1976 by Lillian Breslow Rubin. Reprinted by permission of Basic Books, Inc.,
Publishers, New York.

to be a lie—good for the gross national product but not for the human soul.

Sure, it's great to show those goodies off to friends and neighbors. After all those years of poverty, it makes you feel good finally to have something and to let people see it. Besides, they make life easier, more comfortable. Now there's time for things other than household drudgery. But what things? Companionship? Intimacy? Sharing? What are those things? And how does one find them?

She has a vague idea. Television shows, the women's magazines—they all talk about something called communication. Marriage partners have to communicate, they say; they have to talk, to tell each other how they feel. So she talks. And he tries to listen. But somehow, it doesn't work. He listens, but he cannot hear. Sometimes sooner, sometimes later, he withdraws in silence, feeling attacked:

When she comes after me like that, yapping like that, she might as well be hitting me with a bat.

. . . vulnerable:

It makes me feel like I'm doing something wrong, like I'm not a very good husband or something.

. . . and helpless:

No matter what I say, it's no good. If I try to tell her she's excited over nothing, that only makes it worse. I try to keep my cool and be logical, but nothing works.

This is the dilemma of modern marriage—experienced at all class levels, but with particular acuteness among the working-class families I met. For once marriage is conceived of as more than an economic arrangement—that is, as one in which the emotional needs of the individual are attended to and met—the role segregation and the consequent widely divergent socialization patterns for women and men become clearly dysfunctional.[1] And it is among the working class that such segregation has been most profound, where there has been least incentive to change.

Thus, they talk at each other, past each other, or through each other—rarely with or to each other. He blames her: "She's too emotional." She blames him: "He's always so rational." In truth, neither is blameworthy. The problem lies in the fact that they do not have a language with which to communicate, with which to understand each other. They are products of a process that trains them to relate to only one side of themselves—she, to the passive, tender, intuitive, verbal, emotional side; he, to the active, tough, logical, nonverbal, unemotional one.[2] From infancy, each has been programmed to be split off from the other side; by adulthood, it is distant from consciousness, indeed.[3]

They are products of a disjunction between thought and feeling, between emotionality and rationality that lies deep in Western culture. Even though she complains, both honestly believe what the culture has taught them. To be rational is the more desired state; it is good, sane, strong, adult. To be emotional is the less desired state; it is bad, weak, childlike. She:

I know I'm too emotional and I can't really be trusted to be sensible a lot of the time. I need him; he's the one in the family you can always count on to think about things right, not mixed up, like me.

He:

She's like a kid sometimes, so emotional. I'm always having to reason with her, to explain things to her. If it weren't for me, nothing would happen very rational around here.

This equation of emotional with nonrational, this inability to apprehend the logic of emotions, lies at the root of much of the discontent between the sexes, and helps to make marriage the most difficult of all relationships.

Her lifetime training prepares her to handle the affective, expressive side in human affairs; his, to handle the nonaffective, instrumental side. Tears, he has been taught, are for sissies; feelings, for women. A *real* man is the strong, silent type of the folklore—a guy who needs nothing from anyone, who ignores feelings and pain, who can take it on the chin without a whimper. For a lifetime, much of his energy has gone into molding himself in that image—into denying his feelings, refusing to admit they exist. Without warning or preparation, he finds himself facing a wife who pleads, "Tell me your feelings." He responds with bewilderment. "What is there to tell?"[4]

When they try to talk, she relies on the only tools she has, the mode with which she is most familiar; she becomes progressively more emotional and expressive. He falls back on the only tools he has; he gets progressively more rational—determinedly reasonable. She cries for him to attend to her feelings, her pain. He tells her it's silly to feel that way; she's just being emotional. That clenched-teeth reasonableness invalidates her feelings, leaving her sometimes frightened:

I get scared that maybe I'm crazy. He's always so logical and reasonable that I begin to feel, "What's the matter with me that I'm so emotional?"

. . . sometimes angry:

When he just sits there telling me I'm too emotional, I get so mad, I go up the wall. Sometimes I get so mad I wish I could hit him. I did once, but he hit me back, and he can hurt me more than I can hurt him.

. . . almost always tearful and despairing:

I wind up crying and feeling terrible. I get so sad because we can't really talk to each other a lot of times. He looks at me like I'm crazy, like he just doesn't understand a word I'm saying.

Repeatedly, the experience is the same, the outcome of the interaction, predictable. Yet, each has such a limited repertoire that they are consigned to playing out the same theme over and over again—he, the rational man; she, the hysterical woman.

But these almost wholly sociological notions—notions which speak to socialization patterns—tell only one part of the story of human development. The other part is told in the language of psychology—a language that is given its fullest and most complex expression in psychoanalytic theory. From that theory, Nancy Chodorow has presented us with a brilliant and provocative reformulation of Oedipal theory which successfully crosses the sociological with the psychological as it accounts for the dynamics of both the inner and outer world as they affect sex-role development.[5]

Her argument starts from the premise that the differences in male and female personality are rooted in the structure of the family—in particular, in the fact that women are the primary childrearers. As a result, the mother becomes the first object with which an infant—male or female—identifies, the first attachment formed. Coincident with the forming of these identifications and attachments, other developmental tasks emerge in the period between infancy and childhood—a primary one being the development of an appropriate gender identity. For a girl, that task is a relatively straightforward one—a continuous and gradual process of internalization of a feminine identity with mother as model. For a boy, however, role learning is discontinuous involving, as it must, the rejection of his early identification with his mother as he seeks an appropriate masculine identity.

Since a girl need not reject that early identification in order to negotiate the Oedipal phase successfully, feminine personality is based on less repression of inner objects, less fixed and firm ego-splitting, and greater continuity of external relationships. With no need to repress or deny their earliest attachment, girls can define and experience themselves as part of and continuous with others. Consequently, women tend to have more complex inner lives, more ability to engage in a variety of interpersonal relationships, and more concern with ongoing relational issues.

On the other hand, boys must repress these same attachments as they shift their identification from mother to father. That means that they must distinguish and differentiate themselves in a way that girls need not. In doing so, they come to define and experience themselves as more separate from others and with more rigid ego boundaries; and adult masculine personality comes to be defined more in terms of denial of connection and relations.

Such ideas present profound implications for the marriage relationship. For if it is true that their earliest experiences in the family mean that men must deny relations and connection while women must be preoccupied with them, we are faced anew with the realization—this time from the psychoanalytic perspective—that the existing structure of family relations, especially in its delegation of the parenting function solely or dominantly to the mother, makes the attainment of compatible relations between women and men extraordinarily difficult.

It hardly need be said that such relationships between men and women are not given to the working-class alone. Without doubt, the description I have been rendering represents the most common interactional pattern in American marriage. These are the behavioral consequences of the dominant sex-role socialization patterns in the culture and of the existing structure of family relations within which boys and girls internalize an appropriate identity—patterns which generate the role stereotypes that women and men bring to marriage and which effectively circumscribe their emotional negotiations.

Still, it is also true that the norms of middle-class marriage for much longer have called for more companionate relationships—for more sharing, for more exploration of feelings, and for more exchange of them. Thus, middle-class women and men have more practice and experience in trying to overcome the stereotypes. And, perhaps more important, they have more models around them for how to do so. This is not to suggest that they have done it so well, as a casual glance at the divorce rate will show; only that the demands on the marriage partners for different behaviors have been around for much longer, that there is a language that gives those demands legitimacy, and that there has been more experimentation in modifying the stereotypes.

Among working-class couples, the demand for communication, for sharing, is newer. Earlier descriptions of working-class family life present a portrait of wives and husbands whose lives were distinctly separate, both inside and outside the home—the wife attending to her household role, the husband to his provider role. He came home at night tired and taciturn; she kept herself and the children out of his way. For generations, it was enough that each did their job adequately—he, to bring home the bacon; she, to cook it. Intimacy, companionship, sharing—these were not part of the dream.[6]

But dreams change—sometimes before the people who must live them are ready. Suddenly, new dreams are stirring, *Intimacy, companionship, sharing*—these are now the words working-class women speak to their men, words that turn *both* their worlds upside down. For while it is the women who are the discontented, who are pushing for change, they, no less than their men, are confused about what they are asking:

I'm not sure what I want. I keep talking to him about communication, and he says, "Okay, so we're talking; now what do you want?" And I don't know what to say then, but I know it's not what I mean.

. . . and frightened and unsure about the consequences:

I sometimes get worried because I think maybe I want too much. He's a good husband; he works hard; he takes care of me and the kids. He could go out and find another woman who would be very happy to have a man like that, and who wouldn't be all the time complaining at him because he doesn't feel things and get close.

The men are even worse off. Since it's not *their* dream, they are less likely still to have any notion of what is being asked of them. They only know that, without notice, the rules of the game have been changed; what worked for their fathers, no longer works for them. They only know that there are a whole new set of expectations—in the kitchen, in the parlor, in the bedroom—that leave them feeling bewildered and threatened.[7] She says:

I keep telling him that the reason people get divorced isn't *only* financial but because they can't communicate. But I can't make him understand.

He says:

I swear, I don't know what she wants. She keeps saying we have to talk, and then when we do, it always turns out I'm saying the wrong thing.

I get scared sometimes. I always thought I had to think things to myself; you know, not tell her about it. Now she says that's not good. But it's hard. You know, I think it comes down to that I like things the way they are, and I'm afraid I'll say or do something that'll really shake things up. So I get worried about it, and I don't say anything.

For both women and men, the fears and uncertainties are compounded by the fact that there are no models in their lives for the newly required and desired behaviors. Television shows them people whose lives seem unreal—outside the realm of personal experience or knowledge. The daytime soap operas, watched almost exclusively by women, *do* picture men who may be more open and more available for intimacy. But the men on the soaps don't work at ordinary jobs, doing ordinary things, for eight, ten, twelve hours a day. They're engaged either in some heroic, life-saving, glamour job to which working-class viewers can't relate or, worse yet, work seems to be one long coffee break during which they talk about their problems. Nighttime fare, when the men are home, is different, but no less unreal, featuring the stoic private eye, the brave cop, the [t]ight-lipped cowboy.

The argument about the impact of the mass media on blue-collar workers is complex, contradictory, and largely unsatisfactory. Some observers insist that the mass media represent the most powerful current by which blue-collar workers are swept into conformity with middle-class values and aspirations;[8] others that blue-collar men especially resist exposure to middle-class manners and mores as they are presented on television—minimizing that exposure by exercising great discrimination in program choices;[9] still others that the idealized and romanticized figures on television are so unreal to the average blue-collar viewer that they have little impact on their lives and little effect on their behavior.[10]

Perhaps all three of these seemingly irreconcilable perspectives are true. The issue may not be *whether* television or other mass media affect people's lives and perceptions. Of course they do. The question we must ask more precisely is: In what ways are Americans of any class touched and affected by their exposure to television? For the professional middle class, it may well be an affirming experience; for the working class, a disconfirming one since there are no programs that deal with their problems, their prospects, and their values in sympathetic and respectful ways.[11]

If their own lives in the present provide no models and the media offer little that seems relevant, what about the past? Unfortunately for young working-class couples, family backgrounds provide few examples of openness, companionship, or communication between husbands and wives:

I don't think we ever had a good concept of what marriage was about. His family was the opposite of mine. They didn't drink like mine did, and they were more stable. Yet he feels they didn't give him a good concept either. There wasn't any drinking and fighting and carrying on, but there wasn't any caring either.

Even those few who recall their parents' marriages as good ones don't remember them talking much to one another and have no sense at all that they might have shared their inner lives:

Would you describe a typical evening in the family when you were growing up?

A twenty-five-year-old manicurist, mother of two, married seven years, replies:

Let me think. I don't really know what happened; nothing much, I guess. My father came home at four-thirty, and we ate right away. Nobody talked much at the table; it was kind of a quiet affair.

What about your parents' relationship? Do you remember how they behaved with each other; whether they talked to each other?

Gee, I don't know. It's hard to think about them as being *with* each other. I don't think they talked a lot; at least, I never saw them talking. I can't imagine them sitting down to talk over problems or something like that, if that's what you mean.

Yes, that *is* what I mean. But that was the last generation; what about this one? *Would you describe a typical evening in your own family now?*

For some, less than half, it's better—a level of companionship, caring, and sharing that, while not all they dream of, is surely better than they knew in their past. Fathers attend more to children; husbands at least try to "hear" their wives; couples struggle around some of the emotional issues I have identified in these pages. For most, however, nothing much has changed since the last generation. Despite the yearning for more, relations between husband and wife are benumbed, filled with silence; life seems empty and meaningless; laughter, humor, fun is not a part of the daily ration. Listen to this couple married seven years. The wife:

Frank comes home from work; now it's about five because he's been working overtime every night. We eat right away, right after he comes home. Then, I don't know. The kids play a while before bed, watch TV, you know, stuff like that. Then, I don't know; we don't do anything except maybe watch more TV or something like that. I don't know what else—nothing, I guess. We just sit, that's all.

That's it? Nothing else?

Yeah, that's right, that's all. *A short silence, then angrily.* Oh yeah, I forgot. Sometimes he's got one of his projects he works on. Like now, he's putting that new door in the kitchen. It's still nothing. When he finishes doing it, we just sit.

Her husband describes the same scene:

I come home at five and we eat supper right away. Then, I sit down with coffee and a beer and watch TV. After that, if I'm working on a project, I do that for a little while. If not, I just watch.

Life is very predictable. Nothing much happens; we don't do much. Everyone sits in the same place all the time and does the same thing every night. It's satisfying to me, but maybe it's not for her, I don't know. Maybe she wants to go to a show or something once in a while, I don't know. She doesn't tell me.

Don't you ask her?

No. I suppose I should, but it's really hard to think about getting out. We'd need someone to stay with the kids and all that. Besides, I'm tired. I've been out all day, seeing different people and stuff. I don't feel like going out after supper again.

Is there some time that you two have for yourselves, to talk things over and find out how you feel about things?

The wife:

There's plenty of time; we just don't do it. He doesn't ever think there's anything to talk about. I'm the one who has to nag him to talk always, and then I
get disgusted.

He'd be content just living, you know, just nothing but living for the rest of his
life. It don't make no difference to him where he lives or how people around
him are feeling. I don't know how anybody can be like that.

A lot of times I get frustrated. I just wish I could talk to him about things and
he could understand. If he had more feelings himself, maybe he'd understand
more. Don't you think so?

Her husband agrees that he has problems handling both his feelings
and hers:

I'm pretty tight-lipped about most things most of the time, especially personal
things. I don't express what I think or feel. She keeps trying to get me to, but,
you know, it's hard. Sometimes I'm not even sure what she wants me to be
telling her. And when she gets all upset and emotional, I don't know what to say
or what to do.

Sometimes she gets to nagging me about what I'm thinking or feeling, and I tell
her, "Nothing," and she gets mad. But I swear, it's true; I'm not thinking about
anything.

Difficult for her to believe, perhaps, but it *is* true. After a lifetime of
repressing his feelings, he often *is* a blank, unaware that he's thinking or
feeling anything. Moreover, when emotions have been stored for that
long, they tend to be feared as especially threatening or explosive. He
continues:

Maybe it sounds a little crazy, but I'm afraid once I let go, I might get past the
point where I know what I'm doing. If I let myself go, I'm afraid I could be
dangerous. She keeps telling me that if you keep things pent up inside you like
that, something's going to bust one day.

I think a lot of the problem is that our personalities are just very different. I'm
the quiet type. If I have something I have to think about, I have to get by
myself and do it. Elly, she just wants to talk about it, always talking about her
feelings.

Yakketty-yakkers, that's what girls are. Well, I don't know; guys talk, too. But,
you know, there's a difference, isn't there? Guys talk about things and girls talk
about feelings.

Indeed that *is* the difference, precisely the difference I have been
pointing to—"Guys talk about things and girls talk about feelings"—a
difference that plagues marriage partners as they struggle to find ways to
live with each other.

Again, the question presents itself: Is this just a phenomenon of working-class life? Clearly, it is not, for the social and psychological processes that account for the discrepant and often incompatible development of women and men apply across class and throughout the culture. Still, there are important class differences in the way these broad socio-cultural mandates are interpreted and translated into behavior differences that are rooted in class situation and experience. Thus, there are differences in the early childhood and family experiences of children who grow up in working-class homes and those who live in professional middle-class homes, differences in the range of experiences through their adolescence and young adulthood, and differences in the kinds of problems and preoccupations they face in their adult lives—on the job and in the family.

Whether boys or girls, children in the homes of the professional middle class have more training in exploring the socio-emotional realm and more avenues for such exploration. It's true that for the girls, this usually is the *focus* of their lives, while for the boys, it is not. Nevertheless, compared to childrearing patterns in working-class families, professional middle-class families make fewer and less rigid sex-role distinctions in early childhood.[12] As small children, therefore, boys in such middle-class homes more often get the message that it's all right to cry, to be nurturant as well as nurtured, to be reflective and introspective, even at times to be passive—in essence, in some small measure, to relate to their expressive side.

Not once in a professional middle-class home did I see a young boy shake his father's hand in a well-taught "manly" gesture as he bid him good night. Nor once did I hear a middle-class parent scornfully—or even sympathetically—call a crying boy a sissy or in any way reprimand him for his tears. Yet, these were not uncommon observations in the working-class homes I visited. Indeed, I was impressed with the fact that, even as young as six or seven, the working-class boys seemed more emotionally controlled—more like miniature men—than those in the middle-class families.

These differences in childrearing practices are expressed as well in the different demands the parents of each class make upon the schools—differences that reflect the fact that working-class boys are expected to be even less emotional, more controlled than their middle-class counterparts.[13] For the working-class parent, school is a place where teachers are expected to be tough disciplinarians; where children are expected to behave respectfully and to be punished if they do not; and where one mark of that respect is that they are sent to school neatly dressed in their "good" clothes and expected to stay that way through the day. None of these values is highly prized in the professional middle class. For them, schools are expected to be relatively loose, free, and fun; to encourage initiative, innovativeness, creativity, and spontaneity; and to provide a place where children—boys as well as girls—will learn social and interpersonal skills. The children of these middle-class families are sent to nursery school early—often as young as two and a half—not just because their mothers want the free time, but because the social-skill training provided there is considered a crucial part of their education.

These differences come as no surprise if we understand both the past experience and the future expectations of both sets of parents. Most highly educated parents have little fear that their children won't learn to read, write, and do their sums. Why should they? They learned them, and learned them well. Their children have every advantage that they had and plenty more: books, games, toys—all designed to excite curiosity and to stimulate imagination—and parents who are skillful in aiding in their use.

Working-class parents, however, have no such easy assurances about their children's educational prospects. Few can look back on their own school years without discomfort—discomfort born of painful reminders of all they didn't learn, of the many times they felt deficient and inadequate. Further, when they look at the schools their children attend now, they see the same pattern repeating itself. For, in truth, the socio-economic status of the children in a school is the best indicator of schoolwide achievement test scores—that is, the lower the socio-economic status, the lower the scores.[14]

Observing this phenomenon, many analysts and educators argue that these low achievement records in poor and working-class schools are a consequence of the family background—the lack of culture and educational motivation in the home—an explanation that tends to blame the victim for the failure of our social institutions. Elsewhere, I have entered the debate about *who* is to blame for these failures on the side of the victims.[15] Here, the major point is simply that, regardless of where we think responsibility lies, working-class parents quite rightly fear that their children may not learn to read very well; that they may not be able to do even the simple arithmetic required to be an intelligent consumer. Feeling inadequate and lacking confidence that they can pass on their slim skills to their children, such parents demand that the schools enforce discipline in the belief that only then will their children learn all that they themselves did not.

This, however, is only one part of the explanation of why the sons of the professional middle class are brought up in a less rigidly stereotypic mode than are the sons of the working class—the part that is rooted in past experience. But past experience combines with present reality to create future expectations, because parents, after all, do not raise their children in a vacuum—without some idea of what the future holds for them, some sense of what they will need to survive the adult world for which they are destined. In fact, it is out of just such understandings that parental attitudes and values about childraising are born.[16] Thus, professional middle-class parents, assuming that their children are destined to do work like theirs—work that calls for innovation, initiative, flexibility, creativity, sensitivity to others, and a well-developed set of interpersonal skills—call for an educational system that fosters those qualities. Working-class parents also assume that their children will work at jobs roughly similar to their own. But in contrast to the requirements of professional or executive work, in most working-class jobs, creativity, innovation, initiative, flexibility are considered by superiors a hindrance. ("You're not getting paid to think!" is an oft-heard remonstrance.) Those who must work at such jobs may need nothing so much as a kind of iron-willed discipline to get them to work every day and to keep them going back year after year. No surprise, then, that such parents look suspiciously at spontaneity whether at home or at school. No surprise, either, that early childhood training tends to focus on respect, orderliness, cleanliness—in a word, discipline—especially for the boys who will hold these jobs, and that schools are called upon to reinforce these qualities.

Finally, men in the professional middle class presently live in an environment that gives some legitimacy to their stirrings and strivings toward connection with their emotional and expressive side. The extraordinary proliferation of the "growth-movement" therapies, which thrive on their appeal to both men and women of the upper middle class, is an important manifestiation of that development. Another is the nascent men's movement—a response to the women's movement—with its men's groups, its male authors who write to a male audience encouraging their search for expressiveness. While it may be true that numerically all these developments account for only a small fraction of American men, it is also true that whatever the number, they are almost wholly drawn from the professional middle class.

For working-class men, these movements might as well not exist. Most don't know of them. The few who do, look at their adherents as if they were "kooks," "queers," or otherwise deficient, claiming to see no relevance in them to their own lives. Yet if one listens carefully to what lies beneath the surface of their words, the same stirrings for more connection with other parts of themselves, for more intimate relations with their wives are heard from working-class men as well. Often inchoate and inarticulately expressed, sometimes barely acknowledged, these yearnings, nevertheless, exist. But the struggle for their realization is a much more lonely and isolated one—removed not only from the public movements of our time but from the lives of those immediately around them—a private struggle in which there is no one to talk to, no examples to learn from. They look around them and see neighbors, friends, brothers, and sisters who are no better—sometimes far worse off—than they:

We're the only ones in the two families who have any kind of a marriage. One of my brothers ran out on his wife, the other one got divorced. Her sister and her husband are separated because he kept beating her up; her brother is still

married, but he's a drunk. It makes it hard. If you never saw it in your family
when you were growing up, then all the kids in both families mess up like that,
it's hard to know what a good marriage is like. I guess you could say there
hasn't been much of a model of one around us.

Without models, it is indeed hard—hard to know what to expect, hard
to know how to act. You can't ask friends because they don't seem to have
the same problems, not even the same feelings. One twenty-nine-year old
husband lamented:

I sometimes think I'm selfish. She's the support—the moral support—in the
family. But when she needs support, I just don't give it to her. Maybe it's not just
selfishness, it's that I don't know what she wants and I don't know how.

The worst thing is, I've got nobody to talk to about how a guy can be different.
The guys at work, all they ever talk about is their cars or their trucks. Oh, they
talk about women, but it's only to brag about how they're making it with this
chick or that one. And my brother, it's no use talking to him; he don't know
where anything's at. He runs around every night, comes home drunk, beats up
his wife.

I know Joanie's not so happy, and I worry about what to do about it. But the
guys I know, they don't worry about things like that.

Don't they? He doesn't really know because he dare not ask.

How do you know they don't worry about such things? Have you asked them?

He looks up, puzzled, as if wondering how anybody could even think
of such a thing, and answers quickly:

Ask them? No! Why would I do that? They'd think I was nuts or something.
People don't talk about those things; you just *know* where those guys are; you
don't have to ask them.

In fact, many of those men are suffering the same conflicts and concerns—wondering, as he does, what happened to the old familiar world;
fearful, as he is, that their masculine image will be impaired if they talk
about the things that trouble them. But if they can't talk to brothers,
friends, work mates, where do they turn?

*Maybe you could talk to Joan about what you could do to make things better
in your marriage?*

Dejectedly, he replies:

What good would that do? She's only a girl. How would she know how a guy is
supposed to act?

The women generally also suffer alone. Despite all the publicity generated by the women's movement about the dissatisfactions women experience in marriage, most working-class women continue to believe that

their feelings are uniquely theirs. Few have any contact with the movement or the people in it; few feel any support for their struggle from that quarter:

They put you down if you want to be married and raise kids, like there's something the matter with you.

Nor do they want it. For the movement is still a fearsome thing among working-class wives, and their responses to it are largely ambivalent, largely dominated by the negative stereotypes of the media. "Braburners," "man-haters"—these labels still are often heard.

Most believe in equal pay for equal work, but even that generally is not unequivocal:

Yes, I believe women should be paid the same as men if they're doing the same job. I mean, most of the time, I believe it. But if a man has a family to support and she doesn't, then it's different.

Few believe that women should compete equally in the job market with men:

If a man with a wife and kids needs a job, no woman ought to be able to take it away from him.

Neither response [is] a surprise, given their history of economic deprivation and concern. Neither response [is] to be heard among the wives of professional men. Also no surprise, given their lifetime of greater financial security and the fact that they "take for granted" that their husbands will provide adequately for the family.

Beyond these two issues, one after the other the working-class women responded impatiently and with almost identical words to questions about what they know about the movement:

I don't know anything about it, and I don't care to know either.

You sound angry at the women's movement.

That's right, I am. I don't like women who want to be men. Those libbers, they want men and women to be just alike, and I don't want that to happen. I think men should be men and women should be women. They're crazy not to appreciate what men do for women. I like my husband to open the car door for me and to light my cigarettes. It makes me feel like a lady.

As if reciting a litany, several women spoke the same words over and over—"I like a man to open the car door and light my cigarettes." Perplexed at the repetition, at the assertion of value of these two particular behaviors, I finally asked:

When was the last time your husband opened a car door for you or lit your cigarette?

Startled, the open face of the woman who sat before me became suffused with color; she threw her head back and laughed. Finally recovering, she said:

I've gotta admit, I don't know why I said that. I don't even smoke.

Of course, she doesn't know why. To know would mean she'd have to face her fears and anxieties more squarely, to recognize that in some important ways the movement speaks to the issues that plague and pain her in her marriage. If, instead, she can reach for the stereotypes, she need not deal with the reality that these issues have become a part of her own life and aspirations, that their questions are also hers, that her own discontent is an example of what so many women out there are talking about.

For her, a major problem is that it remains "out there." Unlike the experience of the women in professional families, it is not *her* sisters, *her* friends, *her* neighbors who talk of these things, but women she doesn't know, has never met; women who aren't her "kind." So she hides her pain and internalizes her guilt.

Do you talk to your friends about some of the things we've been discussing—I mean about your conflicts about your life and your marriage, and about some of the things you dream about and wish for?

No, we don't talk about those kinds of things. It's kind of embarrassing, too personal, you know. Besides, the people I know don't feel like I do, so it's no point in talking to them about those things.

How do you know how they feel if you don't talk about it?

You just know, that's all. I know. It's why I worry sometimes that maybe there's something the matter with me that I'm not satisfied with what I've got. I get depressed, and then I wonder if I'm normal. I *know* none of my friends feels like that, like maybe they need a psychiatrist or something.

It's all right to complain about money, about a husband who drinks or stays out late, even about one who doesn't help around the house. But to tell someone you're unhappy because your husband doesn't talk to you— who would understand that?

You don't talk about things like that to friends like I've got. They'd think I was another one of those crazy women's libbers.

Yes, there is concern among these working-class women and men about the quality of life, about its meaning. Yes, there is a deep wish for life to be more than a constant struggle with necessity. The drinking, the violence, the withdrawn silences—these are responses of despair, giving evidence that hope is hard to hold on to. How can it be otherwise when so often life seems like such an ungiving, uncharitable affair—a struggle without end? In the early years, it's unemployment, poverty, crying babies, violent fights. That phase passes, but a whole new set of problems emerge—problems that often seem harder to handle because they have less shape, less definition; harder, too, because they are less understandable, farther outside the realm of anything before experienced. But if there is one remarkable characteristic about life among the working class, it is the ability to engage the struggle and to survive it—a quality highly valued in a world where life has been and often remains so difficult and problematic. With a certain grim satisfaction, a twenty-six-year-old housewife, mother of two, summed it up:

I guess in order to live, you have to have a very great ability to endure. And I have that—an ability to endure and survive.

NOTES

1. Historian Barbara Easton (1975, 1976) presents a compelling account of the change in family ideology in America. In her fascinating work, she demonstrates the link between the technological developments that made obsolete the relationship between the household and the productive forces and the emergence of the ideology which holds women responsible for the social-emotional content of the marriage relationship and men for the economic-instrumental side. For other historical perspectives on the relationship between the family and the economy—its evolution from the public to the private sphere— and the consequent changes in the roles and responsibilities that were defined as women's, see Ariès (1962); Lasch (1974); Lazerson (1975); Shorter (1975); Zaretsky (1973).

See also Balswick and Peek (1974) who write about the tragic consequences to modern marriage of the "inexpressive male."

2. See Broverman, et al. (1972) for an intriguing study which shows that practicing psychotherapists (both male and female) hold a different standard of mental health for women and men and that, among others, they divide on these very traits to which I refer here. The study shows that for these clinicians, the definitions of a healthy adult and a healthy male are identical; the definition of a healthy female is exactly the opposite from the other two.

3. The recent literature on sex-role socialization, both scientific and journalistic, is rich and abundant. For an excellent review as well as a fine bibliography, see Hochschild (1973). In a particularly interesting study, Johnson, et al. (1975) reexamine the expressive-instrumental distinction and distinguish between a negative and positive pole on each attribute. After examining the self-ratings of four hundred female and male college students, the authors conclude that:

... men associate independence with negative expressiveness. While the women in our sample were able to incorporate positive expressiveness, positive instrumentalness, and independence in their self-pictures, the men in our sample could not include expressiveness with independence and instrumentalness. This supports the theory that development of masculinity involves the rejection of femininity. The young boy becomes a man not by accepting masculine traits but by rejecting feminine ones.

For further development of this theme, see Stockard (1975); also Balswick and Peek (1974); Broverman, et al. (1972); Chodorow (1971).

4. See Shostak (1971, 1973) for a moving description of the bewilderment with which blue-collar husbands face these new demands from their wives.

5. Chodorow (1977 forthcoming).

6. For rich descriptions of the earlier patterns of interaction and communication between working-class couples, see Komarovsky (1962); Rainwater, Coleman, and Handel (1959); Shostak (1969, 1971).

7. Cf., Shostak (1971).

8. Bogart (1964:417).

9. Shostak (1969:188–190) writes: "In a very important way TV is essentially a confirmatory exercise. By exercising discrimination at channel-switching, blue-collarites are able to expose themselves only, or especially, to a particular brand of TV fare (a phenomenon much in effect like visiting only with members of one's extended family or old neighborhood). . . . Undesired themes and values are screened out, the blue-collarite gaining only resonance of cultural commonplaces from a media that seems itself intent at times on deserting its own potential to challenge, stir, and inform."

10. Komarovsky (1962).

11. See U.S. Department of Health, Education, and Welfare (1973b:34–35) and Chapter 4, Note 4.

12. See Kohn (1959, 1963, 1969) for some of the most important work in the field on class differences in childrearing patterns. Also Bronfenbrenner (1966); Grey (1969); Pearlin and Kohn (1966).

13. See Joffe (1974) and Rubin (1972) for empirical studies showing the class differences in educational values.

14. From the famous Coleman (1966) study onward, analysts have documented this point and variations on the theme over and over again. To mention a few, Bowles (1972); Bowles and Gintis (1973); Jencks (1972, 1976); Rist (1970); Rosenthal (1973); Rosenthal and Jacobson (1968); Rubin (1972); Schafer, et al. (1970); Sexton (1964, 1967); Wilson and Portes (1975).

15. Rubin (1972).

16. Cf., Kohn (1969).

BIBLIOGRAPHY

Aries, Philippe. *Centuries of Childhood: A Social History of Family Life.* New York: Vintage Books, 1962.

Balswick, Jack, and Charles Peek. The Inexpressive Male: A Tragedy of American Society. In *Intimacy, Family, and Society,* edited by Arlene Skolnick and Jerome Skolnick. Boston: Little, Brown, 1974.

Bogard, Leo. The Mass Media and the Blue-Collar Workers. In *Blue-Collar World*, edited by Arthur Shostak and William Gomberg. Englewood Cliffs, N.J.: Prentice-Hall, 1964.

Bowles, Samuel. Getting Nowhere: Programmed Class Stagnation. *Society* 9 (1972):42–49.

———, and Herbert Gintis. I.Q. in the U.S. Class Structure. *Social Policy* 3 (1973):65–96.

Bronfenbrenner, Urie. Socialization and Social Class through Time and Space. In *Class, Status, and Power*, 2d ed., edited by Reinhard Bendix and Seymour M. Lipset. New York: Free Press, 1966.

Broverman, Inge K., et al. Sex-Role Stereotypes: A Current Appraisal. *Journal of Social Issues* 28 (1972):59–78.

Chodorow, Nancy. Being and Doing: A Cross-Cultural Examination of the Socialization of Males and Females. In *Woman in Sexist Society*, edited by Vivian Gornick and Barbara K. Moran. New York: Basic Books, 1971.

———. *The Reproduction of Mothering: Family Structure and Feminine Personality*. Berkeley: University of California Press, 1977.

Coleman, James, et al. *Equality of Educational Opportunity*. Washington, D.C.: U.S. Government Printing Office, 1966.

Easton, Barbara Leslie. Women, Religion, and the Family: Revivalism as an Indicator of Social Change in Early New England. Ph.D. dissertation, University of California, Berkeley, 1975.

———. Industrialization and Femininity: A Case Study of Nineteenth Century New England. *Social Problems* 23, 1976.

Grey, Alan L., ed. *Class and Personality in Society*. New York: Atherton Press, 1961.

Hochschild, Arlie Russell. A Review of Sex Role Research. *American Journal of Sociology* 78 (1973): 1011–1029.

Jencks, Christopher, et al. *Inequality: A Reassessment of the Effect of Family and Schooling in America*. New York: Basic Books, 1972.

Joffe, Carole E. Marginal Professions and Their Clients: The Case of Childcare. Ph.D. dissertation, University of California, Berkeley, 1974.

Johnson, Miriam, et al. Expressiveness Reevaluated. *School Review* 83 (1975): 617–644.

Kohn, Melvin. Social Class and Parental Values. *American Journal of Sociology* 64 (1959): 337–351.

———. Social Class and Parent-Child Relationships. *American Journal of Sociology* 68 (1963): 471–480.

———. *Class and Conformity*. Homewood, Ill.: Dorsey Press, 1969.

Komarovsky, Mirra. *Blue-Collar Marriage*. New York: Vintage Books, 1962.

Lasch, Christopher. Divorce and the Decline of the Family. In *The World of Nations*, edited by Christopher Lasch. New York: Vintage Books, 1974.

Lazerson, Marvin. Social Change and American Families: Some Historical Speculations. Xerox, 1975.

Pearlin, Leonard, and Melvin Kohn. Social Class, Occupation, and Parental Values: A Cross-National Study. *American Sociological Review* 31 (1966): 466–479.

Rainwater, Lee, Richard P. Coleman, and Gerald Handel. *Working-man's Wife*. New York: MacFadden Books, 1959.

Rist, Ray C. Student Social Class and Teacher Expectations: The Self-Fulfilling Prophecy in Ghetto Education. *Harvard Educational Review* 40 (1970): 411–451.

Rosenthal, Robert. The Pygmalion Effect Lives. *Psychology Today* 7 (1973): 56–63.

———, and Lenore Jacobson. *Pygmalion in the Classroom*. New York: Holt, Rinehart and Winston, 1968.

Rubin, Lillian B. Busing and Backlash: *White against White in an Urban School District*. Berkeley: University of California Press, 1972.

Schafer, Walter E., et al. Programmed for Social Class: Teaching in High School. *Trans-Action* 7 (1970): 39–46.

Sexton, Patricia Cayo. Wife of the "Happy Worker." In *Blue-Collar World*, edited by Arthur Shostak and William Gomberg. Englewood Cliffs, N.J.: Prentice-Hall, 1964.

Shorter, Edward. *The Making of the Modern Family*. New York: Basic Books, 1975.

Shostak, Arthur B. *Blue-Collar Life*. New York: Random House, 1969.

———. Working Class Americans at Home: Changing Expectations of Manhood. Delivered at the Conference on Problems, Programs, and Prospects of the American Working Class in the 1970s, Rutgers University, New Brunswick, N.J., September 1971.

———. Ethnic Revivalism, Blue-Collarities, and Bunder's Last Stand. In *Rediscovery of Ethnicity*, edited by Sallie Teselle. New York: Harper Colophon, 1973.

Stockard, Jean, et al. Sex Role Development and Sex Discrimination: A Theoretical Perspective. Delivered at the Seventieth Annual Meeting of the American Sociological Association, San Francisco, Calif., August 25–29, 1975.

U.S. Department of Health, Education and Welfare. *Work in America*. Cambridge, Mass.: MIT Press, 1973.

Wilson, Kenneth L., and Alejandro Portes. The Educational Attainment Process: Results from a National Sample. *American Journal of Sociology* 81 (1975): 343–363.

Zaretsky, Eli. Capitalism, the Family, and Personal Life: Parts I and II. *Socialist Revolution* 3 (1973): 69–126, 19–70.

19

THE MARRIAGE LICENSE AS A HITTING LICENSE

Murray A. Straus, Richard Gelles,
and Susan Steinmetz

Wife-beating is found in every class, at every income level. The wife of the president of a midwestern state university recently asked one of us what she could do about the beatings without putting her husband's career in danger. Japan's former Prime Minister Sato, a winner of the Nobel Peace Prize, was accused publicly by his wife of many beatings in their early married life. Ingeborg Dedichen, a former mistress of Aristotle Onassis, describes his beating her till he was forced to quit from exhaustion. "It is what every Greek husband does, it's good for the wife," he told her.

What is at the root of such violent attacks? Proverbs such as "A man's home is his castle," go a long way in giving insights into human nature and society. The home belongs to the man. It is the woman who finds herself homeless if she refuses further abuse.

The image of the "castle" implies freedom from interference from outsiders. What goes on within the walls of the castle is shielded from prying eyes. And a modern home, like a medieval castle, can contain its own brand of torture chamber. Take the case of Carol, a Boston woman who called the police to complain that her husband had beaten her and then pushed her down the stairs. The policeman on duty answered, "Listen, lady, he pays the bills, doesn't he? What he does inside of his own house is his business."

The evidence we documented . . . suggested that, aside from war and riots, physical violence occurs between family members more often than it occurs between any other individuals. At the same time we also pointed out the limitations of the data. In particular, no research up to now gives information on how often each of the different forms of family violence occurs in a representative sample of American families.

THE OVER-ALL LEVEL OF
HUSBAND-WIFE VIOLENCE

Violence Rates

A first approach to getting a picture of the amount of violence between the 2,143 husbands and wives in this study is to find out how many had engaged in any of the eight violent acts we asked about. For the year we studied this works out to be 16 per cent. In other words, every year about one out of every six couples in the United States commits at least one violent act against his or her partner.

If the period considered is the entire length of the marriage (rather than just the previous year), the result is 28 per cent, or between one out of four and one out of three American couples. In short, if you are married, the chances are almost one out of three that your husband or wife will hit you.

When we began our study of violence in the family, we would have considered such a rate of husbands and wives hitting each other very high. In terms of our values—and probably the values of most other Americans—it is still very high. But in terms of what we have come to expect on the basis of the pilot studies, this is a low figure. *It is very likely a substantial underestimate.*

Later in this chapter we will give the reasons for thinking it is an underestimate. But for now, let us examine the violent acts one by one. This is important if we are to get a realistic picture of the meaning of the over-all rates of 28 per cent. One needs to know how much of the violence was slaps and how much was kicking and beating up. This information is given in [Figure] 1.

Slaps, Beatings, and Guns

[Figure] 1 shows that in almost seven of every hundred couples either the husband or the wife had thrown something at the other in the previous year, and about one out of six (16 per cent) had done this at some point in their marriage.

The statistics for *slapping* a spouse are about the same: 7 per cent in the previous year and 18 per cent at some time.

The figures for pushing, shoving, or grabbing during an argument are the highest of any of the eight things we asked about: 13 per cent had done this during the year, and almost one out of four at some time in the marriage.

At the other extreme, "only" one or two out of every hundred couples (1.5 per cent) experienced a *beating-up* incident in the previous year. But a "beating up" had occurred at some time in the marriages of one out of every twenty of the couples we interviewed.

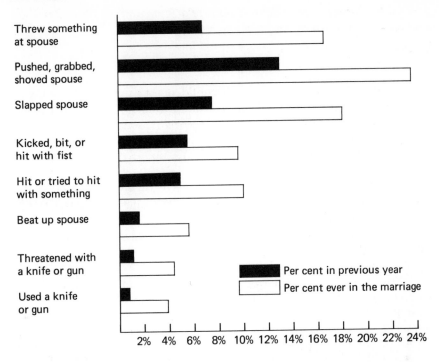

Threw something at spouse
Pushed, grabbed, shoved spouse
Slapped spouse
Kicked, bit, or hit with fist
Hit or tried to hit with something
Beat up spouse
Threatened with a knife or gun
Used a knife or gun

■ Per cent in previous year
□ Per cent ever in the marriage

2% 4% 6% 8% 10% 12% 14% 16% 18% 20% 22% 24%

Figure 1   Rate at Which Violent Acts Occurred in the Previous Year and Ever in the Marriage

The rates for actually *using a knife or gun* on one's spouse are one out of every two hundred couples in the previous year, and almost one out of twenty-seven couples at some point in the marriage.

We were surprised that there was not a bigger difference between the rate of occurrence for "mild" violent acts (such as pushing and slapping) and the severe acts of violence (such as beating up and using a knife or gun). This is partly because the rates for the more violent acts turned out to be greater than we expected, and partly because the rates for the "ordinary" acts of husband-wife violence were less than expected. Whatever the reasons, it seems that couples are using more than slaps and shoves when violence occurs.

Indeed, the statistics on the number of husbands and wives who had ever "beaten up" their spouses or actually used a knife or gun are astoundingly high. The human meaning of these most extreme forms of violence in the family can be understood better if we translate the percentages into the total number of marriages affected. Since there were about 47 million couples living together in the United States in 1975, the rates just given mean that *over 1.7 million Americans had at some time*

*faced a husband or wife wielding a knife or gun, and well over 2 million
had been beaten up* by his or her spouse.

How Accurate Are the Statistics?

It is difficult to know how much confidence to put in these statistics
because several different kinds of error are possible. First, these are estimates based on a sample. But the sample is reasonably large and was
chosen by methods which should make it quite representative of the U.S.
population. Comparisons with characteristics reported in the U.S. census
show that this in fact is the case.

Still, there is the possibility of sampling error. So we computed what is
known as the "standard error" for each of the rates in [Figure] 1. The
largest standard error is for the over-all violence index. Even that is low:
there is a 95 per cent chance that the true percentage of couples *admitting to* ever having physically assaulted one another is somewhere between 26.8 and 28.8 per cent of all couples.

"Admitting to" was italicized to highlight a much more serious and
more likely source of error, that of an underestimate. The 26.8 to 28.8 per
cent figure assumes that everyone "told all." But that is very unlikely.
Three of the reasons are:

(1) There is one group of people who are likely to "underreport" the
amount of violence. For this group a slap, push, or shove (and sometimes
even more severe violence) is so much a normal part of the family that it
is simply not a noteworthy or dramatic enough event always to be remembered. Such omissions are especially likely when we asked about
things which had happened during the entire length of the marriage.

(2) At the opposite end of the violence continuum, there is another
group who fail to admit or report such acts because of the shame involved
if one is the victim, or the guilt if one is the attacker. Such violent attacks
as being hit with objects, bitten, beaten up, or attacked with a knife or
gun go beyond the "normal violence" of family life and are often unreported.

(3) A final reason for thinking these figures are drastic underestimates
lies in the nature of the sample. We included only couples currently living
together. Divorced people were asked only about their present marriage.
Since "excessive" violence is often a cause of divorce, the sample probably omits many of the high violence cases.

The sample was selected in this way because a major purpose of the
study was to investigate the extent to which violence is related to other
aspects of husband-wife interaction. Questions were limited to current
marriages because of interview time limits and limits on what people
could be expected to remember.

The figures therefore could easily be twice as large as those revealed by the survey. In fact, based on the pilot studies and informal evidence (where some of the factors leading to underreporting were not present), it seems likely that *the true rate is closer to 50 or 60 per cent of all couples than it is to the 28 per cent who were willing to describe violent acts to our interviewers.*

MEN AND WOMEN

Traditionally, men have been considered more aggressive and violent than women. Like other stereotypes, there is no doubt a kernel of truth to this. But it is far from the clear-cut difference which exists in the thinking of most people. This is also the case with our survey. About one out of eight husbands had carried out at least one violent act during the course of a conflict in the year covered by the survey, *and* about the same number of wives had attacked their husbands (12.1 per cent of the husbands versus 11.6 per cent of the wives).

Mutual Violence

One way of looking at this issue is to ask what percentage of the sample are couples in which the husband was the only one to use violence? What per cent were couples in which the only violence was by the wife? And in what percentage did both use violence?

The most common situation was that in which both had used violence. One man who found himself in the middle of a family battle, reported it this way:

It started sort of slowly . . . so I couldn't tell for sure if they were even serious. . . . In the beginning they'd push at each other, or shove, like kids—little kids who want to fight but they don't know how. Then, this one time, while I'm standing there not sure whether to stay or go, and them treating me like I didn't even exist, she begins yelling at him like she did.

"You're a bust, you're a failure, I want you out of here, I can always get men who'll work, good men, not scum like you." And they're pushing and poking with their hands, like they were dancing. She pushes him, he pushes her, only she's doing all the talking. He isn't saying a word.

Then all of a sudden, she must have triggered off the right nerve because he lets fly with a right cross that I mean stuns. I mean she goes down like a rock! And he's swearing at her, calling her every name in the book. Jesus, I didn't know what the hell to do.

What I wanted to do was call the police. But I figured, how can I call the police and add to this guy's misery, because she was pushing him. . . . She was really pushing him. I'd have done something to her myself.

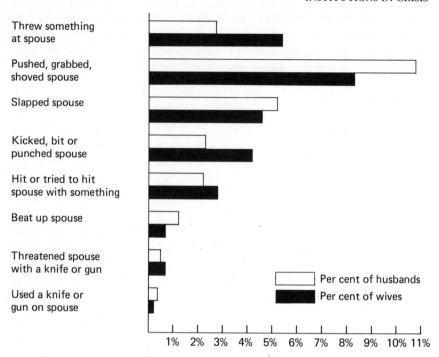

Figure 2   Comparison of Husband and Wife Violence in Previous Year

Of those couples reporting any violence, 49 per cent were of situations of this type, where both were violent. For the year previous to our study, a comparison of the number of couples in which only the husband was violent with those in which only the wife was violent shows the figures to be very close: 27 per cent violent husbands and 24 per cent violent wives. So, as in the case of the violence rates, there is little difference between the husbands and wives in this study.

Specific Violent Acts

[Figure] 2 compares the men and women in our study on each of the eight violent acts. Again, there is an over-all similarity. But there are also some interesting differences, somewhat along the lines of the stereotype of the pot- and pan-throwing wife.

I got him good the last time! He punched me in the face and I fell back on the stove. He was walking out of the kitchen and I grabbed the frying pan and landed it square on his head. Man, he didn't know what hit him.

The number of wives who threw things at their husbands is almost twice as large as the number of husbands who threw things at their wives. The rate for kicking and hitting with an object is also higher for wives than for husbands. The husbands on the other hand had higher rates for pushing, shoving, slapping, beating up, and actually using a knife or gun.

WIFE-BEATING—AND HUSBAND-BEATING

Wife-beating has become a focus of increasing public concern in the last few years. In part this reflects the national anguish over all aspects of violence, ranging from the Vietnam war to the upward surge of assault and murder. Another major element accounting for the recent public concern with wife-beating is the feminist movement. Behind that are the factors which have given rise to the rebirth of the feminist movement in the late 1960s and early 1970s.

What Is Wife-Beating?

To find out how much wife-beating there is, one must be able to define it in a way which can be objectively measured. When this is tried, it becomes clear that "wife-beating" is a political rather than a scientific term. For some people wife-beating refers only to those instances in which severe damage is inflicted. Less severe violence is not considered violence or it is laughed off. A joke one of us heard while driving across northern England in 1974 is no doubt familiar to many readers of this book. It goes like this in the BBC version: One woman asks another why she feels her husband doesn't love her any more. The answer: "He hasn't bashed me in a fortnight." Or take the following letter to Ann Landers:

Dear Ann Landers: Come out of the clouds, for Lord's sake, and get down here with us humans. I am sick to death of your holier-than-thou attitude toward women whose husbands give them a well deserved belt in the mouth.

Don't you know that a man can be pushed to the brink and something's got to give? A crack in the teeth can be a wonderful tension-breaker. It's also a lot healthier than keeping all that anger bottled up.

My husband hauls off and slugs me every few months and I don't mind. He feels better and so do I because he never hits me unless I deserve it. So why don't you come off it?—REAL HAPPY.

Dear Real Happy: If you don't mind a crack in the teeth every few months, it's all right with me. I hope you have a good dentist.

So a certain amount of violence in the family is "normal violence." In fact, most of the violent acts which occur in the family are so much a part of the way family members relate to each other that they are not even thought of as violence.

At what point does one exceed the bounds of "normal" family violence? When does it become "wife-beating"? To answer this question, we gathered data on a series of violent acts, ranging from a slap to using a knife or gun. This allows anyone reading this book to draw the line at whatever place seems most appropriate for his or her purpose.

Measuring Wife-Beating

This "solution," however, can also be a means of avoiding the issue. So in addition to data on each violent act, we also combined the most severe of these into what can be called a Severe Violence Index. If these are things done by the husband, then it is a "Wife-beating Index." The Wife-beating Index consists of the extent to which the husband went beyond throwing things, pushing or grabbing, and slapping and attacked his wife by kicking, biting, or punching; hitting with some object; beating her up; threatening her with a gun or knife; or using a knife or gun (the last five behaviors in [Figure] 1).

Why limit the Wife-beating Index to "only" the situations where the husband went beyond throwing things, pushing, grabbing, and slapping? Certainly we don't want to imply that this reflects our conception of what is permissible violence. None of these are acceptable for relationships between husband and wife—just as they are unacceptable between student and teacher, minister and parishioner, or colleagues in a department. In short, we follow the maxim coined by John Valusek: "People are not for hitting."

What then is the basis for choosing kicking, biting, or punching; hitting with an object; beating up; threatening with a knife or gun; and using a knife or gun for the Wife-beating Index? It is simply the fact that these are all acts which carry with them a high risk of serious physical injury.

What Percentage Are Beaten?

How many husbands and wives experience the kind of attack which is serious enough to be included in the Wife-beating and Husband-beating Indexes? A remarkably large number. In fact, since our survey produced a rate of 3.8 per cent, this means that about one out of twenty-six American wives get beaten by their husbands every year, or a total of almost 1.8 million per year.

Staggering as are these figures, the real surprise lies in the statistics on husband-beating. These rates are slightly higher than those for wife-beating! Although such cases rarely come to the attention of the police or the press, they exist at all social levels. Here is an example of one we came across:

A wealthy, elderly New York banker was finally granted a separation from his second wife, 31 years his junior, after 14 years of marriage and physical abuse. According to the presiding judge, the wife had bullied him with hysteria, screaming tantrums and vicious physical violence.

The husband wore constant scars and bruises. His ear had once been shredded by his wife with her teeth. She had blackened his eyes, and on one occasion injured one of his eyes so badly that doctors feared it might be lost.

Some 4.6 per cent of the wives in the sample admitted to or were reported by their husbands as having engaged in an act which is included in the Husband-beating Index. That works to be about one out of twenty-two wives who attacked their husbands severely enough to be included in this Husband-beating Index. That is over 2 million very violent wives. Since three other studies of this issue also found high rates of husband-beating, some revision of the traditional view about female violence seems to be needed.

How Often Do Beatings Happen?

Let us look at just the couples for which a violent incident occurred during the year previous to our study. Was it an isolated incident? If not, how often did attacks of this kind occur?

It was an isolated incident (in the sense that there was only one such attack during the year) for only about a third of the violent couples. This applies to both wife-beating and husband-beating. Almost one out of five of the violent husbands and one out of eight wives attacked their partner this severely twice during the year. Forty-seven per cent of the husbands who beat their wives did so three or more times during the year, and 53 per cent of the husband-beaters did so three or more times. So, for about half the couples the pattern is that if there is one beating, there are likely to be others—at least three per year! In short, violence between husbands and wives, when it occurs, tends to be a recurrent feature of the marriage.

Was There Ever a Beating?

A final question about how many beatings took place can be answered by looking at what happened over the entire length of the marriage. Did something that can be called a beating *ever* happen in the marriage?

There are several reasons why even a single beating is important. First, even one such event debases human life. Second, there is the physical danger involved. Third is the fact that many, if not most, such beatings are part of a struggle for power in the family. It often takes only one such event to fix the balance of power for many years—or perhaps for a lifetime.

Physical force is the ultimate resource which most of us learn as children to rely on if all else fails and the issue is crucial. As a husband in one of the families interviewed by LaRossa said when asked why he hit his wife during an argument:

. . . She more or less tried to run me and I said no, and she got hysterical and said, "I could kill you!" And I got rather angry and slapped her in the face three or four times and I said "Don't you ever say that to me again!" And we haven't had any problem since.

Later in the interview, the husband evaluated his use of physical force as follows:

You don't use it until you are forced to it. At that point I felt I had to do something physical to stop the bad progression of events. I took my chances with that and it worked. In those circumstances my judgement was correct and it worked.

Since greater size and strength give the advantage to men in such situations, the single beating may be an extremely important factor in maintaining male dominance in the family system.

We found that one out of eight couples (12.6 per cent) experienced at least one beating incident in the course of marriage. That is approximately a total of 6 million beatings. However, as high as that figure is, the actual statistics are probably higher. This is because things are forgotten over the years, and also because (as was pointed out earlier) the violent acts in question are only about the current marriage. They leave out the many marriages which ended in divorce, a large part of which were marked by beatings.

Wives and Husbands as Victims

This study shows a high rate of violence by *wives* as well as husbands. But it would be a great mistake if that fact distracted us from giving first attention to wives *as victims* as the focus of social policy. There are a number of reasons for this:

(1) The data in [Figure] 2 shows that husbands have higher rates of the most dangerous and injurious forms of violence (beating up and using a knife or gun).

(2) Steinmetz found that abuse by husbands does more damage. She suggests that the greater physical strength of men makes it more likely that a woman will be seriously injured when beaten up by her husband.

(3) When violent acts are committed by a husband, they are repeated more often than is the case for wives.

(4) The data do not tell us what proportion of the violent acts by wives were in self-defense or a response to blows initiated by husbands. Wolf-

gang's study of husband-wife homicides suggests that this is an important factor.

(5) A large number of attacks by husbands seem to occur when the wife is pregnant, thus posing a danger to the as yet unborn child. This isn't something that happens only on Tobacco Road:

The first time Hortense Barber's husband beat her was the day she told him she was pregnant with their first child. "He knocked out my two front teeth and split open my upper lip," the 32 year old honors graduate told a New York Senate Task Force on Women. Later Mrs. Barber's husband regularly blacked her eyes during her pregnancy and threw a knife at her "in jest," cutting her knee.

(6) Women are locked into marriage to a much greater extent than men. Women are bound by many economic and social constraints, and they often have no alternative to putting up with beatings by their husbands. The situation is similar to being married to an alcoholic. Nine out of ten men leave an alcoholic wife, but only one out of ten women leave an alcoholic husband.

Most people feel that social policy should be aimed at helping those who are in the weakest position. Even though wives are also violent, they are in the weaker, more vulnerable position in respect to violence in the family. This applies to both the physical, psychological, and economic aspects of things. That is the reason we give first priority to aiding wives who are the victims of beatings by their husbands.

At the same time, the violence *by* wives uncovered in this study suggests that a fundamental solution to the problem of wife-beating has to go beyond a concern with how to control assaulting husbands. It seems that violence is built into the very structure of the society and the family system itself. . . . Wife-beating . . . is only one aspect of the general pattern of family violence, which includes parent-child violence, child-to-child violence, and wife-to-husband violence. To eliminate the particularly brutal form of violence known as wife-beating will require changes in the cultural norms and in the organization of the family and society which underlie the system of violence on which so much of American society is based.

NORMS AND MEANINGS

Just as we need to know the extent to which violent *acts* occur between husbands and wives, parents and children, and brothers and sisters, it is also important to know how family members feel about intrafamily violence. Just how strongly do they approve or disapprove of a parent slapping a child or a husband slapping a wife? To what extent do people see violence in the family as one of those undesirable but necessary parts of life?

It is hard to find out about these aspects of the way people think about family violence. One difficulty is there are contradictory rules or "norms." At one level there are norms strongly opposed to husbands and wives hitting each other. But at the same time, there also seem to be implicit but powerful norms which permit and even encourage such acts. Sometimes people are thinking of one of these principles and sometimes of the other.

Another thing is that violence is often such a "taken for granted" part of life that most people don't even realize there are socially defined rules or norms about the use of violence in the family.

The existence of these implicit norms is illustrated by the case of a husband who hit his wife on several occasions. Each time he felt that it was wrong. He apologized—very genuinely. But still he did it again. The husband explained that he and his wife got so worked up in their arguments that he "lost control." In his mind, it was almost involuntary, and certainly not something he did according to a rule or norm which gives one the right to hit his wife.

But the marriage counselor in the case brought out the rules which permitted him to hit his wife. He asked the husband why, if he had "lost control," he didn't stab his wife! This possibility (and the fact that the husband did not stab the wife despite "losing control") shows that hitting the wife was not just a bubbling over of a primitive level of behavior. Although this husband did not realize it, he was following a behavioral rule or norm. It seems that the unrecognized but operating norm for this husband—and for millions of other husbands—is that it is okay to hit one's wife, but not to stab her.

There is other evidence which tends to support the idea that the marriage license is also a hitting license. For example, "Alice, you're going to the moon," was one of the standard punch lines on the old Jackie Gleason "Honeymooners" skits which delighted TV audiences during the 1950s, and which are currently enjoying a revival. Jokes, plays, such as those of George Bernard Shaw, and experiments which show that people take less severe actions if they think the man attacking a woman is her husband are other signs.

It has been suggested that one of the reasons neighbors who saw the attack didn't come to the aid of Kitty Genovese in the 1964 Queens murder case was because they thought it was a man beating his wife! Or take the following incident:

Roy Butler came over to help his bride-to-be in preparations for their wedding, which is why the wedding is off.

Roy, 24, made the mistake of going to a stag party first.

On the way to fiancée Anthea Higson's home, he dropped the wedding cake in the front garden.

In the shouting match that followed, he dropped Anthea's mother with a right cross to the jaw.

Anthea, 21, promptly dropped Roy. She said the wedding was off and she never wanted to see him again.

"If he had hit me instead of my mother, I probably would have married him all the same," [italics added] she said yesterday after a court fined Butler $135 for assaulting Mrs. Brenda Higson.

"But I'm not having any man hitting my mum," Anthea said.

Interesting as are these examples, none of them provide the kind of systematic and broadly representative evidence which is needed. That is what we attempted to get in this study.

Measuring the Meaning of Violence

To find out how our sample felt about violence in the family, we used the "semantic differential" method. For husband-wife violence, we asked subjects to rate the phrase "Couples slapping each other." They were asked to make three ratings: unnecessary . . . necessary; not normal . . . normal; and good . . . bad.

How many of the husbands and wives rated "Couples slapping each other" as "necessary," "normal," or "good"? Over all just under one out of four wives and one out of three husbands (31.3 and 24.6 per cent) saw this type of physical force between spouses as at least somewhat necessary, normal, or good.

These statistics are remarkably close to those from a national sample studied by the U.S. Violence Commission. The Violence Commission found that about one quarter of the persons interviewed said they could think of circumstances in which it would be all right for a husband to hit his wife or a wife to hit her husband. This is slightly lower than the percentages for our sample. But if the Violence Commission survey data had been analyzed in the way we examined our data, the results could well have been almost identical.

The separate ratings for violence being necessary, normal, or good are interesting in the contrast they provide with each other and in the way men and women think about violence. On the one hand, there are big differences in the percentage of husbands as compared to wives who could see some situations in which it is necessary for a husband or wife to slap the other (see [Figure] 3). There is also a larger percentage of husbands who could see some situations in which this would not be a bad thing to do. In fact, for both these ratings, twice as many husbands as wives felt this way.

On the other hand, the percentages for the not normal . . . normal rating are particularly interesting because they are larger and because there is little difference between the men and the women. The figures in the

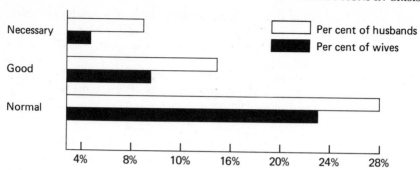

Figure 3   *Per Cent of Husbands and Wives Who Rated "A Couple*
Slapping Each Other" as at Least Somewhat Necessary,
Good, or Normal

chart show that a large proportion of American husbands and wives see
violence as a normal part of married life. It may not be good, and it may
not be necessary, but it is something which is going to happen under normal circumstances. The marriage license is a hitting license for a large
part of the population, and probably for a much greater part than could
bring themselves to rate it as "normal" in the context of this survey.

SUMMING UP

We are reasonably confident that the couples in the study are representative of American couples in general. But we suspect that not everyone
told us about all the violence in his or her family. In fact, the pilot studies
and informal evidence suggest that the true figures may be double those
based on what people were willing to admit in a mass survey such as this.
If this is the case, then about a third of all American couples experience a
violent incident every year, and about two thirds have experienced such
an incident at least once in the marriage.

Of course, a large part of these "violent incidents" are pushes and slaps,
but far from all of them. A large portion are also actions which could
cause serious injury or even death. We know from the fact that so many
murderers and their victims are husband and wife that this is not just
speculation. For the couples in this sample, in fact, almost one out of
every twenty-five had faced an angry partner with a knife or gun in
hand.

If the "dangerous violence" is not limited solely to use of a knife or
gun, and includes everything *more serious* than pushing, grabbing, shoving, slapping, and throwing things, the rate is three times as high. In

short, almost one out of every eight couples admitted that at some point in the marriage there had been an act of violence which could cause serious injury.

Another way of grasping this is to compare the rates for wife-beating and husband-beating in our survey with assaults which are reported in official statistics. The Uniform Crime Reports on "aggravated assault" are given in rate per 100,000. But the rates in this chapter are percentages, i.e., rates per 100, not per 100,000.

We can translate the rates for this survey into rates per 100,000 per year. They are 3,800 per 100,000 for assaults on wives, 4,600 for assaults on husbands, and a combined rate of 6,100 per 100,000 couples. Compare this with the roughly 190 per 100,000 aggravated assaults of all kinds known to the police each year.

Of course, many crimes are not reported to the police. So there have been surveys asking people if they were the victims of a crime. The rate of aggravated assault coming out of the National Crime Panel survey is very high: 2,597 per 100,000. But our rate for wife-beating and husband-beating of 6,100 per 100,000 is almost two and a half times higher. Also, since the Uniform Crime Reports, and especially the National Crime Panel data, include many within-family assaults, the amount by which husband-wife assault exceeds any other type of assault is much greater than these rates suggest.

Leaving aside the fact that our figures on husband-wife violence are probably underestimates, and even leaving aside the psychological damage that such violence can produce, just the danger to physical health implied by these rates is staggering. If any other crime or risk to physical well-being involved almost 2 million wives and 2 million husbands per year, plus a much larger number at some point in the marriage, a national emergency would probably be declared.

VII

THE ENVIRONMENT

The tragedy of environmental destruction is all around us, a part of our daily lives we can't ignore. We feel it—literally— with every breath we take. But there is little agreement on its causes or its cures.

Three different approaches to environmental problems have crystallized in the past few years. The first regards environmental destruction as a necessary "trade-off" for economic growth. In this view, we've already gone too far in our concern for the environment and have hobbled business and industry with too many cumbersome and silly environmental regulations. Lessening that concern and lifting some of those regulations would help "get the economy moving again."

The second approach takes environmental problems more seriously, arguing that they are the inevitable result of a high level of industrialization, expanding population, and our craving for more and more consumer goods and scarce supplies of energy. From this perspective, the basic problem is *people*— too many of them, consuming too much, and making extravagant demands on the earth's limited resources. And the remedy (if there is one) is seen in terms of self-renunciation; we must learn to do with less—less population, less energy consumption, fewer material goods, and reduced aspirations. Many people who share this perspective, in fact, see *no* likely solutions to the environmental crisis and urge us to withdraw into our own private worlds, stock up on food and other means of survival, and wait for the catastrophe.

A third approach focuses on the specific social, political, and economic forces that shape the crisis of the environment. It acknowledges that the sheer number of people, the growth of industry, and the limits of energy resources would lead to serious environmental problems in any socio-economic system. But it argues that the depth of the environmental crisis in the United States, as well as the resistance to developing effective means of dealing with it, are reflections of the drive for private profit at the heart of the American economy. The quest for profit is not responsible for *all* of our environmental problems, but it does aggravate those that already exist and creates new ones all its own.

How does the drive for profit result in destruction of the environment? The selections in this chapter illustrate several ways in which this happens. In the selection from his book *The Closing Circle*, Barry Commoner develops a general argument explaining the relation between pollution and profit in the capitalist economy. According to Commoner, the key problem is the profitability of introducing new technologies—technologies that may have a devastating impact on the natural environment and ultimately even on the functioning of the industry itself, but that provide a very high rate of profit for the corporations, at least in the short run. In Commoner's view, the dramatic destruction of the environment in the years since World War II has been primarily the result of the explosion of these new technologies, which enriched the large corporations while impoverishing everyone else.

One of the most important sources of those new technologies has been the chemical industry. After World War II, particularly, this industry developed thousands of new products that have changed the way we live in countless ways. But no one gave much thought to the unanticipated human and environmental impact of many of those products until the dimensions of the problem of "toxic wastes" began to be revealed in the 1970s. Michael H. Brown's account of the tragedy of the chemical waste dump at Love Canal in Niagara Falls, New York, is a compelling illustration of the costs of technological development when it is not controlled by larger social priorities.

Finally, in his study of the history of American ground transport, Bradford Snell provides a shocking story of corporate complicity in the destruction of the environment. It is well known that the automobile has been the source of much of our air pollution problem—not to mention the more general distortion of the urban and rural landscape produced by freeways, parking lots, and the other artifacts of automotive civilization. Snell shows that the rise of the private automobile and the decline of other, more efficient and less polluting means of transportation was, in large part, the result of a conscious policy by the auto and oil corporations—especially General Motors—to destroy other forms of ground transportation in order to create dependency on the automobile. His study speaks volumes about the relation between corporate profit and the deepening destruction of the natural and social environment in the twentieth century.

20
THE ECONOMIC MEANING OF ECOLOGY

Barry Commoner

What is the connection between pollution and profit in a private enterprise economic system such as the United States? Let us recall that in the United States, intense environmental pollution is closely associated with the technological transformation of the productive system since World War II. Much of our pollution problem can be traced to a series of large scale technological displacements in industry and agriculture since 1946. A number of the new, rapidly growing productive activities are much more prone to pollute than the older ones they have displaced.

Thus, since World War II, in the United States, private business has chosen to invest its capital preferentially in a series of new productive enterprises that are closely related to the intensification of environmental pollution. What has motivated this pattern of investment? According to Heilbroner:

Whether the investment is for the replacement of old capital or for the installation of new capital, the ruling consideration is virtually never the personal use or satisfaction that the investment yields to the owners of the firm. Instead, the touchstone of investment decisions is profit.

The introduction of new technology has clearly played an important role in the profitability of postwar business enterprise. The economic factor that links profit to technology is *productivity*, which is usually defined as the output of product per unit input of labor. Productivity has grown rapidly since World War II and, according to Heilbroner, this is largely due to the introduction of new technologies in that period of time. The following relationship seems to be at work: new investment in the postwar economy, as expected, has moved in directions that appeared to promise, and in fact yielded, increased profit; these investments have been heavily based on the introduction of new technology, which is a major factor in the notable increase in productivity, the major source of profit.

If these relationships have been operative in the technological displacements that, as we have seen, have played such an important role in generating the environmental crisis in the United States, then we would expect to find, in the appropriate statistics, that production based on the new technology has been more profitable than production based on the old technology it has replaced. That is, the new, more polluting technologies should yield higher profits than the older, less polluting technologies they have displaced.

The available data seem to bear out this expectation. A good example is the pervasive displacement of soap by synthetic detergents. As it happens, United States government statistics report economic data on the combined soap and detergent industry. In 1947, when the industry produced essentially no detergents, the profit was 30 per cent of sales. In 1967, when the industry produced about one-third per cent soap and two-thirds per cent detergents, the profit from sales was 42 per cent. From the data for intervening years it can be computed that the profit on pure detergent sales is about 52 per cent, considerably higher than that of pure soap sales. Significantly, the industry has experienced a considerable increase in productivity, labor input relative to output in sales having declined by about 25 per cent. Clearly, if profitability is a powerful motivation, the rapid displacement of soap by detergents—and the resultant environmental pollution—has a rational explanation. This helps to explain why, despite its continued usefulness for most cleaning purposes, soap has been driven off the market by detergents. It has benefitted the investor, if not society.

The synthetic chemical industry is another example that illustrates some of the reasons for the profitability of such technological innovations. This is readily documented from an informative volume on the economics of the chemical industry published by the Manufacturing Chemists' Association. The chemical industry, particularly the manufacturers of synthetic organic chemicals, during the 1946–66 period recorded an unusually high rate of profit. During that period, while the average return on net worth for all manufacturing industries was 13.1 per cent, the chemical industry averaged 14.7 per cent. The MCA volume offers an explanation for this exceptionally high rate of profit. This is largely based on the introduction of newly developed materials, especially synthetic ones. For about from four to five years after a new, innovative chemical product reaches the market, profits are well above the average (innovative firms enjoy about twice the rate of profit of noninnovative firms). This is due to the effective monopoly enjoyed by the firm that developed the material, that permits the establishment of a high sales price. After four to five years, smaller competitors are able to develop their own methods of manufacture; as they enter the market, the supply increases, competition intensifies, the price drops, and profits decline. At this point the large innovative firm, through its extensive research and development effort, is ready to introduce a new synthetic substance and can recover a high rate of profit. And so on. As the MCA volume points out: "The maintenance of above average profit margins requires the continuous discovery of new products and specialities on which high profit margins may be earned while the former products in that category evolve into commodity chemicals with lower margins." It is therefore no accident that the synthetic organic chemical industry has one of the highest rates of investment in research and development (in 1967, 3.7 per cent of sales, as compared with an average of 2.1 per cent for all manufacturing industries).

Thus, the extraordinarily high rate of profit of this industry appears to be a direct result of the development and production at rapid intervals of new, usually unnatural, synthetic materials—which, entering the environment, for reasons already given, often pollute it. This situation is an ecologist's nightmare, for in the four to five year period in which a new synthetic substance, such as a detergent or pesticide, is massively moved into the market—and into the environment—there is literally not enough time to work out its ecological effects. Inevitably, by the time the effects are known, the damage is done and the inertia of the heavy investment in a new productive technology makes a retreat extraordinarily difficult. The very system of enhancing profit in this industry is precisely the cause of its intense, detrimental impact on the environment.

It is significant that since 1966, the profit position of the chemical industry has declined sharply. Industry spokesmen have themselves described environmental concern as an important reason for this decline. For example, at recent congressional hearings, an industry official pointed out that a number of chemical companies had found pesticide manufacturing decreasingly profitable because of the need to meet new environmental demands. Because of these demands, costs of developing new pesticides and of testing their environmental effects have risen sharply. At the same time, cancellation or suspension of official pesticide registrations increased from 25 in 1967 to 123 in 1970. As a result, a number of companies have abandoned production of pesticides, although over-all production continues to increase. One company reported that it had dropped pesticide production "because investments in other areas promised better business."

Another explicit example of the impact of environmental concern on the profitability of new chemicals is NTA, a supposedly nonpolluting substitute for phosphate in detergents. Under the pressure of intense public concern over water pollution due to detergent phosphates, the industry developed NTA as a replacement. Two large firms then proceeded to construct plans for the manufacture of NTA—at a cost of about $100 million each. When the plants were partially built, the United States Public Health Service advised against the use of NTA, because of evidence that birth defects occur in laboratory animals exposed to NTA. The new plants had to be abandoned, at considerable cost to these firms. As a result of such hazards, research and development expenditures in the chemical industry have recently declined—a process which is likely to reduce the industry's profit position even more.

Nitrogen fertilizer provides another informative example of the link between pollution and profits. In a typical United States Corn Belt farm, a yield that is more than from 25 to 30 bushels per acre below present averages may mean no profit for the farmer. . . . [P]resent corn yields depend on a high rate of nitrogen applications. Under these conditions, the uptake of nitrogen by the crop is approaching saturation, so that an appreciable fraction of the fertilizer drains from the land and pollutes surface waters. In other words, under present conditions, it appears that the farmer *must* use sufficient fertilizer to pollute the water if he is to make a profit. Perhaps the simplest way to exemplify this tragic connection between economic survival and environmental pollution is in the words of one thoughtful farmer in recent testimony before the Illinois State Pollution Control Board:

Money spent on fertilizer year in and year out is the best investment a farmer can make. It is one of our production tools that hasn't nearly priced itself out of all realm of possibility as is the case with machinery and other farm inputs. Fertilizer expense in my case exceeds $20 per acre, but I feel I get back one to three dollars for every dollar spent on fertilizer. . . . I doubt that I could operate if I lost the use of fertilizers and chemicals as I know them today. I hope adequate substitutes are developed and researched if the government decides our production tools are a danger to society.

National statistics support this farmer's view of the economic importance of fertilizers or pesticides. These statistics show that, whereas such chemicals yield three or four dollars per dollar spent, other inputs—labor and machinery, for example—yield much lower returns.

This is evidence that a high rate of profit is associated with practices that are particularly stressful toward the environment and that when these practices are restricted, profits decline.

Another important example is provided by the auto industry where the displacement of small, low-powered cars by large, high-powered ones is a major cause of environmental pollution. Although specific data on the relationship between profitability and crucial engineering factors such as horsepower do not appear to be available, some more general evidence is at hand. According to a recent article in *Fortune* magazine:

As the size and selling price of a car are reduced, then, the profit margin tends to drop even faster. A standard United States sedan with a basic price of $3,000, for example, yields something like $250 to $300 in profit to its manufacturer. But when the price falls by a third, to $2,000, the factory profit drops by about half. Below $2,000, the decline grows even more precipitous.

Clearly, the introduction of a car of reduced environmental impact, which would necessarily have a relatively low-powered, low-compression engine and a low over-all weight, would sell at a relatively low price. It would therefore yield a smaller profit relative to sales price than the standard heavy, high-powered, high-polluting vehicle. This may explain the recent remark by Henry Ford II, that "minicars make miniprofits."

. . . [P]rominent among the large-scale technological displacements that have increased environmental impacts are certain construction materials: steel, aluminum, lumber, cement, and plastics. In construction and other uses, steel and lumber have been increasingly displaced by aluminum, cement (in the form of concrete), and plastics. In 1969 the profits (in terms of profit as per cent of total sales) from steel production (by blast furnaces) and lumber production were 12.5 per cent and 15.4 per cent, respectively. In contrast, the products that have displaced steel and lumber yielded significantly higher profits: aluminum, 25.7 per cent; cement, 37.4 per cent; plastics and resins, 21.4 per cent. Again, displacement of technologies with relatively weak environmental impacts by technologies with more intensive impacts is accompanied by a significant increase in profitability.

A similar situation is evident in the displacement of railroad freight haulage (relatively weak environmental impact) and truck freight haulage (intense environmental impact). In this case, economic data are somewhat equivocal because of the relatively large capital investment in railroads as compared to trucks (the trucks' right-of-way being provided by government-supported roads). Nevertheless, truck freight appears to yield significantly more profit than railroad freight; the ratio of net income to shareholders' and proprietors' equity in the case of railroads is 2.61 per cent, and for trucks, 8.84 per cent (in 1969).

In connection with the foregoing examples, in which profitability appears to increase when a new, more environmentally intense technology displaces an older one, it should be noted that not all new technologies share this characteristic. For example, the displacement of coal-burning locomotives by diesel engines *improved* the environmental impact of railroads between 1946 and 1950, for diesel engines burn considerably less fuel per ton-mile of freight than do coal-burning engines. Unfortunately, this improvement has been vitiated by the subsequent displacement of railroad freight haulage by truck freight, and at the same time made no lasting improvement in the railroads' economic position. It is also evident that certain new technologies, which are wholly novel, rather than displacing older ones—for example, television sets and other consumer electronics—may well be highly profitable without incurring an unusually intense environmental impact. The point of the foregoing observations is not that they establish the rule that increased profitability inevitably means increased pollution, but only that many of the heavily polluting new technologies have brought with them a higher rate of profit than the less polluting technologies they have displaced.

Nor is this to say that the relationship is intentional on the part of the entrepreneur. Indeed, there is considerable evidence, some of which has been cited earlier, that the producers are typically unaware of the potential environmental effects of their operation until the effects become manifest, after the limits of biological accommodation have been exceeded, in ecological collapse or human illness. Nevertheless, despite these limitations, these examples of the relationship between pollution and profit-taking in a private enterprise economic system need to be taken seriously, I believe, because they relate to important segments of the economic system of the world's largest capitalist power.

In response to such evidence, some will argue that such a connection between pollution and profit-taking is irrational because pollution degrades the quality of the environment on which the future success of even the most voracious capitalist enterprise depends. In general, this argument has a considerable force, for it is certainly true that industrial pollution tends to destroy the very "biological capital" that the ecosystem provides and on which production depends. A good example is the potential effect of mercury pollution from chloralkali plants on the successful operation of these plants. Every ton of chlorine produced by such a plant requires about 15,000 gallons of water, which must meet rigorous standards of purity. This water is obtained from nearby rivers or lakes, in which purity is achieved by ecological cycles, driven by the metabolic activities of a number of microorganisms. Since mercury compounds are highly toxic to most living organisms, the release of mercury by chloralkali plants must be regarded as a serious threat to the source of pure water on which these plants depend. Nevertheless, it is a fact that in this and other instances, the industrial operation—until constrained by outside forces—has proceeded on the seemingly irrational, self-destructive course of polluting the environment on which it depends.

A statistician, Daniel Fife, has recently made an interesting observation that helps to explain this paradoxical relationship between the profitability of a business and its tendency to destroy its own environmental base. His example is the whaling industry, which has been driving itself out of business by killing whales so fast as to ensure that they will soon become extinct. Fife refers to this kind of buisness operation as "irresponsible," in contrast with a "responsible" operation, which would only kill whales as fast as they can reproduce. He points out that even though the irresponsible business will eventually wipe itself out, it *may be profitable to do so*—at least for the entrepreneur, if not for society—if the extra profit derived from the irresponsible operation is high enough to yield a return on investment elsewhere that outweighs the ultimate effect of killing off the whaling business. To paraphrase Fife, the "irresponsible" entrepreneur finds it profitable to kill the goose that lays the golden eggs, so long as the goose lives long enough to provide him with sufficient eggs to pay for the purchase of a new goose. Ecological irresponsibility can pay—for the entrepreneur, but not for society as a whole.

The crucial link between pollution and profits appears to be modern technology, which is both the main source of recent increases in productivity—and therefore of profits—and of recent assaults on the environment. Driven by an inherent tendency to maximize profits, modern private enterprise has seized upon those massive technological innovations that promise to gratify this need, usually unaware that these same innovations are often also instruments of environmental destruction. Nor is this surprising, for . . . technologies tend to be designed at present as single-purpose instruments. Apparently, this purpose is, unfortunately, too often dominated by the desire to enhance productivity—and therefore profit.

Obviously, we need to know a great deal more about the connection between pollution and profits in private enterprise economies. Meanwhile, it would be prudent to give some thought to the meaning of the functional connection between pollution and profits, which is at least suggested by the present information.

The general proposition that emerges from these considerations is that environmental pollution is connected to the economics of the private enterprise system in two ways. First, pollution tends to become intensified by the displacement of older productive techniques by new, ecologically faulty, but more profitable technologies. Thus, in these cases, pollution is an unintended concomitant of the natural drive of the economic system to introduce new technologies that increase productivity. Second, the cost[s] of environmental degradation are chiefly borne not by the producer, but by society as a whole, in the form of "externalities." A business enterprise that pollutes the environment is therefore being subsidized by society; to this extent, the enterprise, though free, is not wholly private.

21

LOVE CANAL AND THE POISONING
OF AMERICA

Michael H. Brown

Niagara Falls is a city of unmatched natural beauty; it is also a tired industrial workhorse, beaten often and with a hard hand. A magnificent river—a strait, really—connecting Lake Erie to Lake Ontario flows hurriedly north, at a pace of a half-million tons a minute, widening into a smooth expanse near the city before breaking into whitecaps and taking its famous 186-foot plunge. Then it cascades through a gorge of overhung shale and limestone to rapids higher and swifter than anywhere else on the continent.

The falls attract long lines of newlyweds and other tourists. At the same time, the river provides cheap electricity for industry; a good stretch of its shore is now filled with the spiraled pipes of distilleries, and the odors of chlorine and sulfides hang in the air.

Many who live in the city of Niagara Falls work in chemical plants, the largest of which is owned by the Hooker Chemical Company, a subsidiary of Occidental Petroleum since the 1960s. Timothy Schroeder did not. He was a cement technician by trade, dealing with the factories only if they needed a pathway poured, or a small foundation set. Tim and his wife, Karen, lived in a ranch-style home with a brick and wood exterior at 460 99th Street. They saved all the money they could to redecorate the inside and to make such additions as a cement patio, covered with an extended roof. One of the Schroeders' most cherished purchases was a Fiberglas pool, built into the ground and enclosed by a redwood fence.

Karen looked from a back window one morning in October 1974, noting with distress that the pool had suddenly risen two feet above the ground. She called Tim to tell him about it. Karen then had no way of knowing that this was the first sign of what would prove to be a punishing family and economic tragedy.

Mrs. Schroeder believed that the cause of the uplift was the unusual groundwater flow of the area. Twenty-one years before, an abandoned hydroelectric canal directly behind their house had been backfilled with industrial rubble. The underground breaches created by this disturbance, aided by the marshland nature of the region's surficial layer, collected large volumes of rainfall and undermined the back yard. The Schroeders allowed the pool to remain in its precarious position until the following summer and then pulled it from the ground, intending to pour a new pool, cast in cement. This they were unable to do, for the gaping excavation immediately filled with what Karen called "chemical water," rancid liquids of yellow and orchid and blue. These same chemicals had mixed with the groundwater and flooded the entire yard, attacking the redwood posts with such a caustic bite that one day the fence simply collapsed. When the chemicals receded in the dry weather, they left the gardens and shrubs withered and scorched, as if by a brush fire.

How the chemicals got there was no mystery. In the late 1930s, or perhaps early 1940s, the Hooker Company, whose many processes included the manufacture of pesticides, plasticizers, and caustic soda, began using the abandoned canal as a dump for at least 20,000 tons of waste residues—"still-bottoms," in the language of the trade.

Karen Schroeder's parents had been the first to experience problems with the canal's seepage. In 1959, her mother, Aileen Voorhees, encountered a strange black sludge bleeding through the basement walls. For the next twenty years, she and her husband, Edwin, tried various methods of halting the irritating intrusion, pasting the cinder-block wall with sealants and even constructing a gutter along the walls to intercept the inflow. Nothing could stop the chemical smell from permeating the entire household, and neighborhood calls to the city for help were fruitless. One day, when Edwin punched a hole in the wall to see what was happening, quantities of black liquid poured from the block. The cinder blocks were full of the stuff.

Although they later learned they were in imminent danger, Aileen and Edwin Voorhees had treated the problem as a mere nuisance. That it involved chemicals, industrial chemicals, was not particularly significant to them. All their lives, all of everyone's life in the city, malodorous fumes had been a normal ingredient of the ambient air.

More ominous than the Voorhees' basement was an event that occurred at 11:12 P.M. on November 21, 1968, when Karen Schroeder gave birth to her third child, a seven-pound girl named Sheri. No sense of elation filled the delivery room. The child was born with a heart that beat irregularly and had a hole in it, bone blockages of the nose, partial deafness, deformed ear exteriors, and a cleft palate. Within two years, the Schroeders realized Sheri was also mentally retarded. When her teeth came in, a double row of them appeared on her lower jaw. And she developed an enlarged liver.

The Schroeders considered these health problems, as well as illnesses among their other children, as acts of capricious genes—a vicious quirk of nature. Like Mrs. Schroeder's parents, they were concerned that the chemicals were devaluing their property. The crab apple tree and evergreens in the back were dead, and even the oak in front of the home was sick; one year, the leaves had fallen off on Father's Day.

The canal had been dug with much fanfare in the late nineteenth century by a flamboyant entrepreneur named William T. Love, who wanted to construct an industrial city with ready access to water power and major markets. The setting for Love's dream was to be a navigable power channel that would extend seven miles from the Upper Niagara before falling two hundred feet, circumventing the treacherous falls and at the same time providing cheap power. A city would be constructed near the point where the canal fed back into the river, and he promised it would accommodate half a million people.

So taken with his imagination were the state's leaders that they gave Love a free hand to condemn as much property as he liked, and to divert whatever amounts of water. Love's dream, however, proved grander than his resources, and he was eventually forced to abandon the project after a mile-long trench, ten to forty feet deep and generally twenty yards wide, had been scoured perpendicular to the Niagara River. Eventually, the trench was purchased by Hooker.

Few of those who, in 1977, lived in the numerous houses that had sprung up by the site were aware that the large and barren field behind them was a burial ground for toxic waste. That year, while working as a reporter for a local newspaper, the Niagara *Gazette*, I began to inquire regularly about the strange conditions reported by the Schroeders and other families in the Love Canal area. Both the Niagara County Health Department and the city said it was a nuisance condition, but no serious danger to the people. Officials of the Hooker Company refused comment, claiming only that they had no records of the chemical burials and that the problem was not their responsibility. Indeed, Hooker had deeded the land to the Niagara Falls Board of Education in 1953, for a token $1. With it the company issued no detailed warnings of the chemicals, only a brief paragraph in the quitclaim document that disclaimed company liability for any injuries or deaths which might occur at the site.

The board's attorney, Ralph Boniello, says he received no phone calls or letters specifically relating the exact nature of the refuse and what it could do, nor did the board, as the company was later to claim, threaten condemnation of the property in order to secure the land. "We had no idea what was in there," Boniello said.

Though Hooker was undoubtedly relieved to rid itself of the contaminated land, the company was so vague about the hazards involved that one might have thought the wastes would cause harm only if touched, because they irritated the skin; otherwise, they were not of great concern. In reality, as the company must have known, the dangers of these wastes far exceeded those of acids or alkalines or inert salts. We now know that the drums Hooker had dumped in the canal contained a veritable witch's brew—compounds of truly remarkable toxicity. There were solvents that attacked the heart and liver, and residues from pesticides so dangerous that their commercial sale was shortly thereafter restricted outright by the government; some of them were already suspected of causing cancer.

Yet Hooker gave no hint of that. When the board of education, which wanted the parcel for a new school, approached Hooker, B. Klaussen, at the time Hooker's executive vice president, said in a letter to the board, "Our officers have carefully considered your request. We are very conscious of the need for new elementary schools and realize that the sites must be carefully selected so that they will best serve the area involved. We feel that the board of education has done a fine job in meeting the expanding demand for additional facilities and we are anxious to cooperate in any proper way. We have, therefore, come to the conclusion that since this location is the most desirable one for this purpose, we will be willing to donate the entire strip of property which we own between Colvin Boulevard and Frontier Avenue to be used for the erection of a school at a location to be determined. . . ."

The board built the school and playground at the canal's midsection. Construction progressed despite the contractor's hitting a drainage trench that gave off a strong chemical odor and the discovery of a waste pit nearby. Instead of halting the work, the authorities simply moved the school eighty feet away. Young families began to settle in increasing numbers alongside the dump, many of them having been told that the field was to be a park and recreation area for their children.

Children found the "playground" interesting, but at times painful. They sneezed, and their eyes teared. In the days when the dumping was still in progress, they swam at the opposite end of the canal, occasionally arriving home with hard pimples all over their bodies. Hooker knew children were playing on its spoils. In 1958, three children were burned by exposed residues on the canal's surface, much of which, according to residents, had been covered with nothing more than fly ash and loose dirt. Because it wished to avoid legal repercussions, the company chose not to issue a public warning of the dangers it knew were there, nor to have its chemists explain to the people that their homes would have been better placed elsewhere.

The Love Canal was simply unfit as a container for hazardous substances, poor even by the standards of the day, and now, in 1977, local authorities were belatedly finding that out. Several years of heavy snowfall and rain had filled the sparingly covered channel like a bathtub. The contents were overflowing at a frightening rate, sopping readily into the clay, silt, and sandy loam and finding their exit through old creekbeds and swales and into the neighborhood.

The city of Niagara Falls, I was assured, was planning a remedial drainage program to halt in some measure the chemical migration off the site. But no sense of urgency had been attached to the plan, and it was stalled in red tape. No one could agree on who should pay the bill—the city, Hooker, or the board of education—and engineers seemed confused over what exactly needed to be done.

Niagara Falls City Manager Donald O'Hara persisted in his view that, however displeasing to the eyes and nose, the Love Canal was not a crisis matter, mainly a question of aesthetics. O'Hara reminded me that Dr. Francis Clifford, county health commissioner, supported that opinion.

With the city, the board, and Hooker unwilling to commit themselves to a remedy, conditions degenerated in the area between 97th and 99th streets, until, by early 1978, the land was a quagmire of sludge that oozed from the canal's every pore. Melting snow drained the surface soot onto the private yards, while on the dump itself the ground had softened to the point of collapse, exposing the crushed tops of barrels. Beneath the surface, masses of sludge were finding their way out at a quickening rate, constantly forming springs of contaminated liquid. The Schroeder back yard, once featured in a local newspaper for its beauty, had reached the point where it was unfit even to walk upon. Of course, the Schroeders could not leave. No one would think of buying the property. They still owed on their mortgage and, with Tim's salary, could not afford to maintain the house while they moved into a safer setting. They and their four children were stuck.

Apprehension about large costs was not the only reason the city was reluctant to help the Schroeders and the one hundred or so other families whose properties abutted the covered trench. The city may also have feared distressing Hooker. To an economically depressed area, the company provided desperately needed employment—as many as 3000 blue-collar jobs in the general vicinity, at certain periods—and a substantial number of tax dollars. Perhaps more to the point, Hooker was speaking of building a $17 million headquarters in downtown Niagara Falls. So anxious were city officials to receive the new building that they and the state granted the company highly lucrative tax and loan incentives, and made available to the firm a prime parcel of property near the most popular tourist park on the American side, forcing a hotel owner to vacate the premises in the process.

City Manager O'Hara and other authorities were aware of the nature of Hooker's chemicals. In fact, in the privacy of his office, O'Hara, after receiving a report on the chemical tests at the canal, had informed the people at Hooker that it was an extremely serious problem. Even earlier, in 1976, the New York State Department of Environmental Conservation had been made aware that dangerous compounds were present in the basement sump pump of at least one 97th Street home, and soon after, its own testing had revealed that highly injurious halogenated hydrocarbons were flowing from the canal into adjoining sewers. Among them were the notorious PCBs; quantities as low as one part PCBs to a million parts normal water were enough to create serious environmental concerns; in the sewers of Niagara Falls, the quantities of halogenated compounds were thousands of times higher. The other materials tracked, in sump pumps or sewers, were just as toxic as PCBs, or more so. Prime among the more hazardous ones was residue from hexachlorocyclopentadiene, or C-56, which was deployed as an intermediate in the manufacture of several pesticides. In certain dosages, the chemical could damage every organ in the body.

While the mere presence of C-56 should have been cause for alarm, government remained inactive. Not until early 1978—a full eighteen months after C-56 was first detected—was testing conducted in basements along 97th and 99th streets to see if the chemicals had vaporized off the sump pumps and walls and were present in the household air. The U.S. Environmental Protection Agency conducted these tests at the urging of local Congressman John LaFalce, the only politician willing to approach the problem with the seriousness it deserved.

While the basement tests were in progress, the rains of spring arrived at the canal, further worsening the situation. Heavier fumes rose above the barrels. More than before, the residents were suffering from headaches, respiratory discomforts, and skin ailments. Many of them felt constantly fatigued and irritable, and the children had reddened eyes. In the Schroeder home, Tim developed a rash along the backs of his legs. Karen could not rid herself of throbbing pains in her head. Their daughter, Laurie, seemed to be losing some of her hair.

Three months passed before I was able to learn what the EPA testing had shown. When I did, the gravity of the situation became clear: benzene, a known cause of cancer in humans, had been readily detected in the household air up and down the streets. A widely used solvent, benzene was known in chronic-exposure cases to cause headaches, fatigue, loss of weight, and dizziness followed by pallor, nosebleeds, and damage to the bone marrow.

No public announcement was made of the benzene hazard. Instead, officials appeared to shield the finding until they could agree among themselves on how to present it. Indeed, as early as October 18, 1977, Lawrence R. Moriarty, an EPA regional official in Rochester, had sent to the agency's toxic substances coordinator a lengthy memorandum stating that "serious thought should be given to the purchase of some or all of the homes affected. . . . This would minimize complaints and prevent further exposure to people." Concern was raised, he said, "for the safety of some 40 or 50 homeowners and their families. . . ."

Dr. Clifford, the county health commissioner, seemed unconcerned by the detection of benzene in the air. "We have no reason to believe the people are imperiled," he said. "For all we know, the federal limits could be six times too high. . . . I look at EPA's track record and notice they have to err on the right side." O'Hara, who spoke to me in his office about the situation, told me I was overreacting to the various findings. The chemicals in the air, he said, posed no more risk than smoking a couple of cigarettes a day.

Dr. Clifford's health department refused to conduct a formal study of the people's health, despite the air-monitoring results. A worker from the department made a perfunctory call to the school, 99th Street Elementary, and when it was discovered that classroom attendance was normal, apparently the department ceased to worry about the situation. For this reason and because of the resistance growing among the local authorities, I went to the southern end of 99th Street to take an informal health survey of my own. I arranged a meeting with six neighbors, all of them instructed beforehand to list the illnesses they were aware of on their block, with names and ages specified for presentation at the session.

The residents' list was startling. Though unafflicted before they moved there, many people were now plagued with ear infections, nervous disorders, rashes, and headaches. One young man, James Gizzarelli, said he had missed four months of work owing to breathing troubles. His wife was suffering epileptic-like seizures which her doctor was unable to explain. Meanwhile, freshly applied paint was inexplicably peeling from the exterior of their house. Pets too were suffering, most seriously if they had been penned in the back yards nearest to the canal, constantly breathing air that smelled like mothballs and weedkiller. They lost their fur, exhibited skin lesions, and, while still quite young, developed internal tumors. A great many cases of cancer were reported among the women, along with much deafness. On both 97th and 99th streets, traffic signs warned passing motorists to watch for deaf children playing near the road.

Evidence continued to mount that a large group of people, perhaps all of the one hundred families immediately by the canal, perhaps many more, were in imminent danger. While watching television, while gardening or doing a wash, in their sleeping hours, they were inhaling a mixture of damaging chemicals. Their hours of exposure were far longer than those of a chemical factory worker, and they wore no respirators or goggles. Nor could they simply open a door and escape. Helplessness and despair were the main responses to the blackened craters and scattered cinders behind their back yards.

But public officials often characterized the residents as hypochondriacs. Timothy Schroeder would wander to his back land and shake his head. "They're not going to help us one damn bit," he said, throwing a rock into a puddle coated with a film of oily blue. "No way." His wife's calls to the city remained unanswered while his shrubs continued to die. Sheri needed expensive medical care and he was afraid the time would come when he could no longer afford to provide it. A heavy man with a round stomach and gentle voice, he had struck me as easygoing and calm, ready with a joke and a smile. That was disappearing now. His face—in the staring eyes, in the tightness of the lips and cheeks—candidly revealed his utter disgust. Every agent of the government had been called on the phone or sent pleas for help, but none offered aid.

Commissioner Clifford expressed irritation at my printed reports of illness, and disagreement began to surface in the newsroom on how the stories should be printed. "There's a high rate of cancer among my friends," Dr. Clifford argued. "It doesn't mean anything." Mrs. Schroeder said that Dr. Clifford had not visited the homes at the canal, nor had he seen the black liquids collecting in the basements. Nor had the County Health Commissioner properly followed an order from the state commissioner to cover exposed chemicals, erect a fence around the site, and ventilate the contaminated basements. Instead, Dr. Clifford arranged for the installation of two $15 window fans in the two most polluted basements and a thin wood snow fence that was broken within days of its erection and did not cover the entire canal.

Partly as a result of the county's inadequate response, the state finally announced in May 1978 that it intended to conduct a health study at the dump site's southern end. Blood samples would be drawn to test for unusual enzyme levels showing liver destruction, and extensive medical questionnaires were to be answered by each of the families.

As interest in the small community increased, further revelations shook the neighborhood. In addition to the benzene, eighty or more other compounds were found in the makeshift dump, ten of them potential carcinogens. The physiological effects they could cause were profound and diverse. At least fourteen of them could impact on the brain and central nervous system. Two of them, carbon tetrachloride and chlorobenzene, could readily cause narcotic or anesthetic consequences. Many others were known to cause headaches, seizures, loss of hair, anemia, or skin rashes. Together, the compounds were capable of inflicting innumerable illnesses, and no one knew what new concoctions were being formulated by their mixture underground.

Edwin and Aileen Voorhees had the most to be concerned about. When a state biophysicist analyzed the air content of their basement, he determined that the safe exposure time there was less than 2.4 minutes—the toxicity in the basement was thousands of times the acceptable limit for twenty-four-hour breathing. This did not mean they would necessarily become permanently ill, but their chances of contracting cancer, for example, had been measurably increased. In July, I visited Mrs. Voorhees for further discussion of her problems, and as we sat in the kitchen, drinking coffee, the industrial odors were apparent. Aileen, usually chipper and feisty, was visibly anxious. She stared down at the table, talking only in a lowered voice. Everything now looked different to her. The home she and Edwin had built had become their jail cell. Their yard was but a pathway through which toxicants entered the cellar walls. The field out back, that proposed "park," seemed destined to be the ruin of their lives. I reached for her phone and called Robert Matthews, a city engineer who had been given the job of overseeing the situation. Was the remedial program, now in the talking stage for more than a year, ready to begin soon? No. Could he report any progress in deciding who would pay for it? No. Could Mr. and Mrs. Voorhees be evacuated? Probably not, he said—that would open up a can of worms, create a panic.

SOME OTHER POISON PITS

The Love Canal is not the only chemical dump site that has caused problems in the past or that can be expected to in the future. During 1979, the United States Environmental Protection Agency listed 103 sites known to pose certain hazards, a figure widely acknowledged as much too small. The first EPA survey identified 32,254 sites where hazardous waste was stored or buried, but a subsequent study suggested the number may be as large as 51,000, with potentially "significant problems" at anywhere between 1200 and 34,000 of them. Approximately 35 million tons of hazardous wastes are generated each year, according to federal figures, 90 percent or more of it improperly disposed of.

Most of the "problem" dump sites are poisoning watercourses and drinking wells as well as infiltrating basement walls. Drinking wells have been closed in New Jersey, Long Island, Maine, Connecticut, Tennessee, Texas, Michigan, and California, among other states. In some instances, illnesses similar to those in the Love Canal area have been reported. An entire neighborhood near Medon, Tennessee, was recently placed on an emergency water supply after its wells were discovered to have been severely poisoned by a large dump site owned by the Velsicol Chemical Corporation of Chicago. Several people living by that dump reported ailments ranging from dizziness to paralysis.

Particularly serious ground contamination problems remain in Montague, Michigan, where approximately 2 billion gallons of groundwater have been fouled; in Baton Rouge, Louisiana, where 540 acres of farmland have been inundated by a waste pit; in Jackson Township, New Jersey, where a landfill once owned by the town has led to the closing of 140 drinking wells and produced numerous complaints of illness; in an area near Charles City, Iowa, where a dump site may have infiltrated an aquifer supplying water to 300,000 people in the state; and on the outskirts of Riverside, California, where abandoned acid pits have overflowed during heavy rains onto streets near a school.

Meanwhile, authorities have been tracking "midnight dumpers," who collect industry's toxic trash and then turn a quick profit by illegally discharging it at the most convenient settings. Last year 210 miles of highway shoulder in North Carolina were contaminated by PCBs intentionally allowed to leak from a truck that made its runs in the dark of night. Similarly, federal officials learned that a Kentucky man had collected at least 15,000 waste drums on a twenty-acre plot soon to be known as the "Valley of the Drums." Among the chemicals were about ten suspected carcinogens. Some of the wastes were seeping into a tributary of the Ohio River—a drinking source for thousands downstream.

No solution is yet in sight. Federal legislation is being implemented to force an upgrading of landfills, and President Carter has urged Congress to raise a $1.6 billion fund over the next four years to clean up hazardous spills, but no one can be sure a landfill will maintain its integrity for the life of the chemicals, and neither the technology nor the money exists to render the waste innocuous.

—M.H.B.

On July 14 I received a call from the state health department with some shocking news. The preliminary review of the health questionnaires was complete. And it showed that women living at the southern end had suffered a high rate of miscarriages and had given birth to an abnormally high number of children with birth defects. In one age group, 35.3 percent had records of spontaneous abortions. That was far in excess of the norm. The odds against it happening by chance were 250 to one. These tallies, it was stressed, were "conservative" figures. Four children in one small section of the neighborhood had documentable birth defects, club feet, retardation, and deafness. Those who lived there the longest suffered the highest rates.

The data on miscarriages and birth defects, coupled with the other accounts of illness, finally pushed the state's bureaucracy into motion. A meeting was scheduled for August 2, at which time the state health commissioner, Dr. Robert Whalen, would formally address the issue. The day before the meeting, Dr. Nicholas Vianna, a state epidemiologist, told me that residents were also incurring some degree of liver damage. Blood analyses had shown hepatitis-like symptoms in enzyme levels. Dozens if not hundreds of people, apparently, had been adversely affected.

In Albany, on August 2, Dr. Whalen read a lengthy statement in which he urged that pregnant women and children under two years of age leave the southern end of the dump site immediately. He declared the Love Canal an official emergency, citing it as a "great and imminent peril to the health of the general public."

When Commissioner Whalen's words hit 97th and 99th streets, by way of one of the largest banner headlines in the Niagara *Gazette's* 125-year history, dozens of people massed on the streets, shouting into bullhorns and microphones to voice frustrations that had been accumulating for months. Many of them vowed a tax strike because their homes were rendered unmarketable and unsafe. They attacked their government for ignoring their welfare. A man of high authority, a physician with a title, had confirmed that their lives were in danger. Most wanted to leave the neighborhood immediately.

Terror and anger roiled together, exacerbated by Dr. Whalen's failure to provide a government-funded evacuation plan. His words were only a recommendation: individual families had to choose whether to risk their health and remain, or abandon their houses and, in so doing, write off a lifetime of work and savings.

On August 3, Dr. Whalen decided he should speak to the people. He arrived with Dr. David Axelrod, a deputy who had directed the state's investigation, and Thomas Frey, a key aide to Governor Hugh Carey.

At a public meeting, held in the 99th Street School auditorium, Frey was given the grueling task of controlling the crowd of 500 angry and frightened people. In an attempt to calm them, he announced that a meeting between the state and the White House had been scheduled for the following week. The state would propose that the Love Canal be classified a national disaster, thereby freeing federal funds. For now, however, he could promise no more. Neither could Dr. Whalen and his staff of experts. All they could say was what was already known: twenty-five organic compounds, some of them capable of causing cancer, were in their homes, and because young children were especially prone to toxic effects, they should be moved to another area.

Dr. Whalen's order had applied only to those living at the canal's southern end, on its immediate periphery. But families living across the street from the dump site, or at the northern portion, where the chemicals were not so visible at the surface, reported afflictions remarkably similar to those suffered by families whose yards abutted the southern end. Serious respiratory problems, nervous disorders, and rectal bleeding were reported by many who were not covered by the order.

Throughout the following day, residents posted signs of protest on their front fences or porch posts. "Love Canal Kills," they said, or "Give Me Liberty, I've Got Death." Emotionally exhausted and uncertain about their future, men stayed home from work, congregating on the streets or comforting their wives. By this time the board of education had announced it was closing the 99th Street School for the following year, because of its proximity to the exposed toxicants. Still, no public relief was provided for the residents.

Another meeting was held that evening, at a firehall on 102nd Street. It was unruly, but the people, who had called the session in an effort to organize themselves, managed to form an alliance, the Love Canal Homeowners Association, and to elect as president Lois Gibbs, a pretty, twenty-seven-year-old woman with jet-black hair who proved remarkably adept at dealing with experienced politicians and at keeping the matter in the news. After Mrs. Gibbs's election, Congressman John LaFalce entered the hall and announced, to wild applause, that the Federal Disaster Assistance Administration would be represented the next morning, and that the state's two senators, Daniel Patrick Moynihan and Jacob Javits, were working with him in an attempt to get funds from Congress.

More disturbing facts continued to accumulate. From the slopes of the terrain, and the low points where creekbeds and swales had been filled, investigators found indications that chemicals had long ago traveled outside of the channel's banks, farther even than the first two "rings" of homes alongside the dump. Nearly a mile from the Schroeder home, to the north, I noticed one such downgrade of land near a small, neat house with a nameplate saying "Moshers" hung on a post in the front yard. I knocked on the door and a thin, pale man reluctantly received me. We went into the kitchen to meet his wife, Velma, a fifty-four-year-old woman confined to a wheelchair and barely able to speak. She too was pale and fragile. "I'm just so tired all the time," she explained. "I'm just so tired, and I don't think they know what's really wrong with me." She said her great fatigue had set in more than a dozen years before, when she was operating a beauty shop in her basement. "It didn't smell right down there," she added. "Not at all. I'd get headaches all the time. I would go out back at night, to play croquet, and my legs would give way, just collapse." She closed the salon when she could no longer navigate the stairs.

Mr. Mosher was not as candid as his wife. He stepped back from me when I asked about his health, as if I had spoken a blasphemy. The reaction, I soon learned, was out of fear that any publicity would affect his standing at a local carbon plant, where he held a managerial position.

I walked toward the back door leading to the basement. "Do you have a flashlight?" I asked.

Mr. Mosher nodded his head and returned with one promptly. As we descended the stairs, he explained that no one had checked his home for contamination, so he had not worried about it. I stirred the sump pump sediment with a piece of wood and switched on the flashlight; there it was, a red, rubbery substance like that described by another person I had interviewed and which, upon testing, had been found to contain cancer-producing chemicals.

I grew impatient with Mr. Mosher's reticence about his health, warning him that he could be endangered. Having seen, in the sludge of the sump pump, that chemicals might have found a path into his cellar, he said, "Well, I've got some heart problems. And I had an enlarged spleen removed. It was twelve and a half pounds."

Velma heard the conversation and began to speak of the summer nights when strong fumes from the canal rendered their bedroom a trap for pungent air in which they could not properly breathe. As she recounted those many unpleasant nights, the woman weakly cocked her head to one side and stared up at her husband. "Tell him about your problem," she insisted.

Mr. Mosher stood where the hallway met the kitchen and stared at the floor. After a minute's silence, he looked up at me. In a low tone he said, "I've got cancer, in the bone marrow. They're treating me for it now."

Upon returning to the office, I searched through a book on toxicology, *Dangerous Properties of Industrial Materials,* for the symptoms of benzene poisoning. The lengthy list included fatigue, edema, narcosis, anemia, and hypoplastic or hyperplastic damage to the bone marrow. It was nearly midnight and a Sunday, but I felt compelled to call Dr. Axelrod of the state health department to inform him of the Moshers' condition. Dr. Axelrod was concerned and told me that, not far from the Moshers' home, researchers from his unit had detected benzene in the air.

With the Love Canal story now attracting attention from the national media, the Governor's office announced that Hugh Carey would be at the 99th Street School on August 7 to address the people. Decisions were being made in Albany and Washington. Hours before the Governor's arrival, a sudden burst of "urgent" reports from Washington came across the newswires. President Jimmy Carter had officially declared the Hooker dump site a national emergency.

Hugh Carey was applauded on his arrival. The Governor announced that the state, through its Urban Development Corporation, planned to purchase, at fair market value, those homes rendered uninhabitable by the marauding chemicals. He spared no promises. "You will not have to make mortgage payments on homes you don't want or cannot occupy. Don't worry about the banks. The state will take care of them." By the standards of Niagara Falls, where the real estate market was depressed, the houses were in the middle-class range, worth from $20,000 to $40,000 apiece. The state would assess each house and purchase it, and also pay the costs of moving, temporary housing during the transition period, and special items not covered by the usual real estate assessment, such as installation of telephones.

Soon the state, coordinating management of the crisis through its health and transportation departments, began the awesome task of mass evacuation. Ironically, their offices were put into the endangered 99th Street School while the students transferred to classrooms elsewhere in the city. Houses were appraised individually and, one by one, the homeowners were brought in by appointment to negotiate a settlement. Some residents, more worried about their bank accounts than their health, refused to leave, causing an endless cycle of renegotiations until compromises were reached.

First in a trickle and then, by September, in droves, the families gathered their belongings and carted them away. Moving vans crowded 97th and 99th streets. Linesmen went from house to house disconnecting the telephones and electrical wires, while carpenters pounded plywood over the windows to keep vandals away. By the following spring, 237 families were gone; 170 of them had moved into new houses. In time the state erected around a six-block residential area a green chain-link fence, eight feet in height, clearly demarcating the contamination zone.

In October 1978, the long-awaited remedial drainage program began at the south end. Trees were uprooted, fences and garages torn down, and swimming pools removed from the area. So great were residents' apprehensions that dangerous fumes would be released over the surrounding area that the state, at a cost of $500,000, placed seventy-five buses at emergency evacuation pickup spots during the months of work, in the event that outlying homes had to be vacated quickly because of an explosion. The plan was to construct drain tiles around the channel's periphery, where the back yards had been located, in order to divert leakage to seventeen-foot-deep wet wells from which contaminated groundwater could be drawn and treated by filtration through activated carbon. (Removing the chemicals themselves would have been financially prohibitive, perhaps costing as much as $100 million—and even then the materials would have to be buried elsewhere.) After the trenching was complete, and the sewers installed, the canal was to be covered by a sloping mound of clay and planted with grass. One day, city officials hoped, the wasteland would become a park.

In spite of the corrective measures and the enormous effort by the state health department, which took thousands of blood samples from past and current residents and made uncounted analyses of soil, water, and air, the full range of the effects remained unknown. In neighborhoods immediately outside the offical "zone of contamination," more than 500 families were left near the desolate setting, their health still in jeopardy. The state announced it would buy no more homes.

The first public indication that chemical contamination had probably reached streets to the east and west of 97th and 99th streets, and to the north and south as well, came on August 11, 1978, when sump-pump samples I had taken from 100th and 101st streets, analyzed in a laboratory, showed the trace presence of a number of chemicals found in the canal itself, including lindane, a restricted pesticide that had been suspected of causing cancer in laboratory animals. While probing 100th Street, I had knocked on the door of Patricia Pino, thirty-four, a blond divorcee with a young son and daughter. I had noticed that some of the leaves on a large tree in front of her house exhibited a black oiliness much like that on the trees and shrubs of 99th Street; she was located near what had been a drainage swale.

After I had extracted a jar of sediment from her sump pump for the analysis, we conversed about her family situation and what the trauma now unfolding meant to them. Ms. Pino was extremely depressed and embittered. Both of her children had what appeared to be slight liver abnormalities, and her son had been plagued with "non-specific" allergies, teary eyes, sinus trouble, which improved markedly when he was sent away from home. Patricia told of times, during the heat of summer, when fumes were readily noticeable in her basement and sometimes even upstairs. She herself had been treated for a possibly cancerous condition on her cervix. But, like others, her family was now trapped.

On September 24, 1978, I obtained a state memorandum that said chemical infiltration of the outer regions was significant indeed. The letter, sent from the state laboratories to the U.S. Environmental Protection Agency, said, "Preliminary analysis of soil samples demonstrates extensive migration of potentially toxic materials outside the immediate canal area." There it was, in the state's own words. Not long afterward, the state medical investigator, Dr. Nicholas Vianna, reported indications that residents from 93rd to 103rd streets might also have incurred liver damage.

On October 4, a young boy, John Allen Kenny, who lived quite a distance north of the evacuation zone, died. The fatality was due to the failure of another organ that can be readily affected by toxicants, the kidney. Naturally, suspicions were raised that his death was in some way related to a creek that still flowed behind his house and carried, near an outfall, the odor of chlorinated compounds. Because the creek served as a catch basin for a portion of the Love Canal, the state studied an autopsy of the boy. No conclusions were reached. John Allen's parents, Norman, a chemist, and Luella, a medical research assistant, were unsatisfied with the state's investigation, which they felt was "superficial." Luella said, "He played in the creek all the time. There had been restrictions on the older boys, but he was the youngest and played with them when they were old enough to go to the creek. We let him do what the other boys did. He died of nephrosis. Proteins were passing through his urine. Well, in reading the literature, we discovered that chemicals can trigger this. There was no evidence of infection, which there should have been, and there was damage to his thymus and brain. He also had nosebleeds and headaches, and dry heaves. So our feeling is that chemicals probably triggered it."

The likelihood that water-carried chemicals had escaped from the canal's deteriorating bounds and were causing problems quite a distance from the site was not lost upon the Love Canal Homeowners Association and its president, Lois Gibbs, who was attempting to have additional families relocated. Because she lived on 101st Street, she was one of those left behind, with no means of moving despite persistent medical difficulties in her six-year-old son, Michael, who had been operated on twice for urethral strictures. Mrs. Gibbs's husband, a worker at a chemical plant, brought home only $150 a week, she told me, and when they subtracted from that the $90 a week for food and other necessities, clothing costs for their two children, $125 a month for mortgage payments and taxes, utility and phone expenses, and medical bills, they had hardly enough cash to buy gas and cigarettes, let alone vacate their house.

Assisted by two other stranded residents, Marie Pozniak and Grace McCoulf, and with the professional analysis of a Buffalo scientist named Beverly Paigen, Lois Gibbs mapped out the swale and creekbed areas, many of them long ago filled, and set about interviewing the numerous people who lived on or near formerly wet ground. The survey indicated that these people were suffering from an abnormal number of kidney and bladder aggravations and problems of the reproductive system. In a report to the state, Dr. Paigen claimed to have found, in 245 homes outside the evacuation zone, thirty-four miscarriages, eighteen birth defects, nineteen nervous breakdowns, ten cases of epilepsy, and high rates of hyperactivity and suicide.

In their roundabout way, the state health experts, after an elaborate investigation, confirmed some of the homeowners' worst fears. On February 8, 1979, Dr. David Axelrod, who by then had been appointed health commissioner, and whose excellence as a scientist was widely acknowledged, issued a new order that officially extended the health emergency of the previous August, citing high incidences of birth deformities and miscarriages in the areas where creeks and swales had once flowed, or where swamps had been. With that, the state offered to evacuate temporarily those families with pregnant women or children under the age of two from the outer areas of contamination, up to 103rd Street. But no additional homes would be purchased; nor was another large-scale evacuation, temporary or otherwise, under consideration. Those who left under the new plan would have to return when their children passed the age limit.

Twenty-three families accepted the state's offer. Another seven families, ineligible under the plan but of adequate financial means to do so, simply left their homes and took the huge loss of investment. Soon boarded windows speckled the outlying neighborhoods.

The previous November and December, not long after the evacuation of 97th and 99th streets, I became interested in the possibility that Hooker might have buried in the Love Canal waste residues from the manufacture of what is known as 2,4,5-trichlorophenol. My curiosity was keen because I knew that this substance, which Hooker produced for the manufacture of the antibacterial agent hexachlorophene, and which was also used to make defoliants such as Agent Orange, the herbicide employed in Vietnam, carries with it an unwanted by-product technically called 2,3, 7,8-tetrachlorodibenzo-para-dioxin, or tetra dioxin. The potency of dioxin of this isomer is nearly beyond imagination. Although its toxicological effects are not fully known, the few experts on the subject estimate that if three ounces were evenly distributed and subsequently ingested among a million people, or perhaps more than that, all of them would die. It compares in toxicity to the botulinum toxin. On skin contact, dioxin causes a disfiguration called "chloracne," which begins as pimples, lesions, and cysts, but can lead to calamitous internal damage. Some scientists suspect that dioxin causes cancer, perhaps even malignancies that occur, in galloping fashion, within a short time of contact. At least two (some estimates went as high as eleven) pounds of dioxin were dispersed over Seveso, Italy, in 1976, after an explosion at a trichlorophenol plant: dead animals littered the streets, and more than 300 acres of land were immediately evacuated. In Vietnam, the spraying of Agent Orange, because of the dioxin contaminant, was banned in 1970, when the first effects on human beings began to surface, including dioxin's powerful teratogenic, or fetus-deforming, effects.

The ban on herbicidal warfare that involved Agent Orange was sparked by articles in *The New Yorker* under the byline of Thomas Whiteside. I called him for an informed viewpoint. "It's an extremely serious situation if they find dioxin there," he said. "This is most serious. If they buried trichlorophenol, there are heavy odds, heavy odds, that dioxin, in whatever quantities, will be there too."

After our conversation, I called Hooker. Its sole spokesman, Bruce

Davis, executive vice president, was by now speaking to the media, but obtaining information from the firm was not the easiest, nor the most pleasant, of tasks. Often, questions had to be submitted days before they were answered; they would be circulated through the legal hands and sometimes sent on to Hooker's parent company, Occidental Petroleum in Los Angeles. I posed two questions concerning trichlorophenol: Were wastes from the process buried in the canal? If so, what were the quantities?

On November 8, before Hooker answered my queries, I learned that, indeed, trichlorophenol had been found in liquids pumped from the remedial drain ditches. No dioxin had been found yet, and some officials, ever wary of more emotionalism among the people, argued that, because the compound was not soluble in water, there was little chance it had migrated off-site. Officials at Newco Chemical Waste Systems, a local waste disposal firm, at the same time claimed that if dioxin had been there, it had probably been photolytically destroyed. Its half-life, they contended, was just a few short years.

I knew from Whiteside, however, that in every known case, waste from 2,4,5-trichlorophenol carried dioxin with it. I also knew that dioxin *could* become soluble in groundwater and migrate into the neighborhood upon mixing with solvents such as benzene. Moreover, because it had been buried, sunlight would not break it down.

On Friday, November 10, I called Hooker again to urge that they answer my questions. Davis came to the phone and, in a controlled tone, gave me the answer: His firm had indeed buried trichlorophenol in the canal—200 tons of it.

Immediately I called Whiteside. His voice took on an urgent tone. According to his calculations, if 200 tons of trichlorophenol were there, in all likelihood they were accompanied by 130 pounds of tetra dioxin, an amount equaling the estimated total content of dioxin in the thousands of tons of Agent Orange rained upon Vietnamese jungles. The seriousness of the crisis had deepened, for now the Love Canal was not only a dump for highly dangerous solvents and pesticides; it was also the broken container for the most toxic substance ever synthesized by man.

I reckoned that the main danger was to those working on the remedial project, digging in the trenches. The literature on dioxin indicated that, even in quantities at times too small to detect, the substance possessed vicious characteristics. In one case, workers in a trichlorophenol plant had developed chloracne, although the substance could not be traced on the equipment with which they worked. The mere tracking of minuscule amounts of dioxin on a pedestrian's shoes in Seveso led to major concerns, and, according to Whiteside, a plant in Amsterdam, upon being found contaminated with dioxin, had been "dismantled, brick by brick, and the material embedded in concrete, loaded at a specially constructed dock, on ships, and dumped at sea, in deep water near the Azores." Workers in trichlorophenol plants had died of cancer or severe liver damage, or had suffered emotional and sexual disturbances.

Less than a month after the first suspicions arose, on the evening of December 9, I received a call from Dr. Axelrod. He asked what my schedule was like.

"I'm going on vacation," I informed him. "Starting today."

"You might want to delay that a little while," he replied. "We're going to have something big next week."

That confused me. "What do you mean by that?"

He paused, then said, "We found it. The dioxin. In a drainage trench behind 97th Street. It was in the part-per-trillion range."

The state remained firm in its plans to continue the construction, and, despite the ominous new findings, no further evacuations were announced. During the next several weeks, small incidents of vandalism occurred along 97th and 99th streets. Tacks were spread on the road, causing numerous flat tires on the trucks. Signs of protest were hung in the school. Meetings of the Love Canal Homeowners Association became more vociferous. Christmas was near, and in the association's office at the 99th Street School, a holiday tree was decorated with bulbs arranged to spell "DIOXIN."

The Love Canal people chanted and cursed at meetings with state officials, cried on the telephone, burned an effigy of the health commissioner, traveled to Albany with a makeshift child's coffin, threatened to hold officials hostage, sent letters and telegrams to the White House, held days of mourning and nights of prayer. On Mother's Day [that] year, they marched down the industrial corridor and waved signs denouncing Hooker, which had issued not so much as a statement of remorse. But no happy ending was in store for them. The federal government was clearly not planning to come to their rescue, and the state felt it had already done more than its share. City Hall was silent and remains silent today. Some residents still hoped that, miraculously, an agency of government would move them. All of them watched with anxiety as each newborn came to the neighborhood, and they looked at their bodies for signs of cancer.

One hundred and thirty families from the Love Canal area began leaving their homes last August and September, seeking temporary refuge in local hotel rooms under a relocation plan funded by the state which had been implemented after fumes became so strong, during remedial trenching operations, that the United Way abandoned a care center it had opened in the neighborhood.

As soon as remedial construction is complete, the people will probably be forced to return home, as the state will no longer pay for their lodging. Some have threatened to barricade themselves in the hotels. Some have mentioned violence. Anne Hillis of 102nd Street, who told reporters her first child had been born so badly decomposed that doctors could not determine its sex, was so bitter that she threw table knives and a soda can at the state's on-site coordinator.

In October, Governor Carey announced that the state probably would buy an additional 200 to 240 homes, at an expense of some $5 million. In the meantime, lawyers have prepared lawsuits totaling about $2.65 billion and have sought court action for permanent relocation. Even if the latter action is successful, and they are allowed to move, the residents' plight will not necessarily have ended. The psychological scars are bound to remain among them and their children, along with the knowledge that, because they have already been exposed, they may never fully escape the Love Canal's insidious grasp.

22
AMERICAN GROUND TRANSPORT

Bradford Snell

The manufacture of ground transportation equipment is one of this Nation's least competitive industrial activities. . . .

Ground transport is dominated by a single, diversified firm to an extent possibly without parallel in the American economy. General Motors, the world's largest producer of cars and trucks, has also achieved monopoly control of buses and locomotives which compete with motor vehicles for passengers and freight. Its dominance of the bus and locomotive industries, moreover, would seem to constitute a classic monopoly. Although GM technically accounts for 75 percent of current city bus production, its only remaining competitor, the Flxible Co., relies on it for diesel propulsion systems, major engine components, technical assistance, and financing. In short, Flxible is more a distributor for GM than a viable competitor; virtually its sole function is the assembly of General Motors' bus parts for sale under the Flxible trade name. Likewise, in the production of intercity buses, its only remaining competitor, Motor Coach Industries, is wholly dependent upon GM for diesel propulsion systems and major mechanical components. In addition, General Motors accounts for 100 percent of all passenger and 80 percent of all freight locomotives manufactured in the United States. Such concentration in a single firm of control over three rival transportation equipment industries all but precludes the existence of competitive conduct and performance.

The distribution of economic power in this sector is remarkably asymmetrical. . . . [E]conomic power is fundamentally a function of concentration and size. In terms of concentration, the ground transport sector is virtually controlled by the Big Three auto companies. General Motors, Ford, and Chrysler account for 97 percent of automobile and 84 percent of truck production: GM alone dominates the bus and rail locomotive industries. Accordingly, the automakers have the power to impose a tax, in the form of a price increase, on purchasers of new cars to underwrite political campaigns against bus and rail systems.

In terms of size, there is an enormous divergence between the competing automotive and nonautomotive industries. Moreover, General Motors' diversification program has left only a small portion of the bus and rail industries in the hands of independent producers. As measured by aggregate sales, employment, and financial resources, therefore, the independent bus and rail firms are no match for the automakers. The Big Three's aggregate sales of motor vehicles and parts amount to about $52 billion each year, or more than 25 times the combined sales of trains, buses, subway and rapid transit cars by the four largest firms other than GM which produce bus and rail vehicles: Pullman and Budd (railway freight and passenger cars, subway and rapid transit cars); Rohr (buses and rapid transit cars); General Electric (commuter railcars and locomotives). The Big Three automakers employ nearly 1½ million workers, or more than three times as many as their four principal rivals: General Motors alone maintains plants in 19 different states. The Big Three also excel in their ability to finance lobbying and related political activities. GM, Ford, and Chrysler annually contribute more than an estimated $14 million to trade associations which lobby for the promotion of automotive transportation. By contrast, their four leading rivals contribute not more than $1 million, or less than one-tenth this amount, to rail transit lobbies. The magnitude of their sales, employment, and financial resources, therefore, affords the automakers overwhelming political influence.

It may be argued, moreover, that due to their conflicting interlocks with the motor vehicle manufacturers, these bus and rail firms would be reluctant to set their economic and political resources against them. Eighty percent of Budd's sales, for example, consist of automotive components purchased by the Big Three; Rohr, which also owns the Flxible Co., is wholly dependent upon GM for major bus components; Pullman derives more income from manufacturing trailers for highway trucks than from selling freight cars to the railroads; and General Electric manufactures a vast range of automotive electrical equipment, including about 80 percent of all automotive lamps. In sum, the independent bus and rail equipment manufacturers are probably unable and possibly unwilling to oppose the Big Three automakers effectively in political struggles over transportation policy.

Lacking a competitive structure, the group of industries responsible for providing us with ground transportation equipment fail to behave competitively. Diversification by General Motors into bus and rail production may have contributed to the displacement of these alternatives by automobiles and trucks. In addition, the asymmetrical distribution of economic and political power may have enabled the automakers to divert Government funds from rail transit to highways.

The Big Three automakers' efforts to restrain nonautomotive forms of passenger and freight transport have been perfectly consistent with profit maximization. One trolley coach or bus can eliminate 35 automobiles; 1 streetcar, subway, or rapid transit vehicle can supplant 50 passenger cars; an interurban railway or railroad train can displace 1,000 cars or a fleet of 150 cargo-laden trucks. Given the Big Three automakers' shared monopoly control of motor vehicle production and GM's diversified control of nonautomotive transport, it was inevitable that cars and trucks would eventually displace every other competing form of ground transportation.

The demise of nonautomotive transport is a matter of historical record. By 1973 viable alternatives to cars and trucks had all but ceased to exist. No producers of electric streetcars, trolley coaches, or interurban electric trains remained; only two established railcar builders (Pullman and Rohr) were definitely planning to continue production; a single firm (General Electric) still manufactured a handful of electric locomotives; and General Motors accounted for virtually all of an evershrinking number of diesel buses and locomotives.

There were, of course, a number of factors involved in this decline. For example, the popularity of motor vehicles, due in large part to their initial flexibility, most certainly affected public demand for competing methods of travel. On the other hand, the demise of bus and rail forms of transport cannot, as some have suggested, be attributed to the public's desire to travel exclusively by automobile. Rather, much of the growth in autos as well as trucks may have proceeded from the decline of rail and bus systems. In short, as alternatives ceased to be viable, automobiles and trucks became indispensable.

The sections which immediately follow relate in considerable detail how General Motors' diversification into bus and rail production generated conflicts of interest which necessarily contributed to the displacement of alternatives to motor vehicle transportation. A subsequent section will consider how asymmetry in the ground transport sector led to the political restraint of urban rail transit.

Before considering the displacement of bus and rail transportation, however, a distinction between intent and effect should be carefully drawn. This study contends that certain adverse effects flow inevitably from concentrated multi-industry structures regardless of whether these effects were actually intended. Specifically, it argues that structural concentration of auto, truck, bus, and rail production in one firm necessarily resulted in the promotion of motor vehicles and the displacement of competing alternatives. Whether that firm's executives in the 1920's actually intended to construct a society wholly dependent on automobiles and trucks is unlikely and, in any case, irrelvant. That such a society developed in part as the result of General Motors' common control of competing ground transport industries is both relevant and demonstrable.

1. THE SUBSTITUTION OF BUS FOR RAIL PASSENGER TRANSPORTATION

By the mid-1920's, the automobile market had become saturated. Those who desired to own automobiles had already purchased them; most new car sales had to be to old car owners. Largely as a result, General Motors diversified into alternative modes of transportation. It undertook the production of city and intercity motor buses. It also became involved in the operation of bus and rail passenger services. As a necessary consequence, it was confronted with fundamental conflicts of interest regarding which of these several competing methods of transport it might promote most profitably and effectively. Its natural economic incentives and prior business experience strongly favored the manufacture and sale of cars and trucks rather than bus, and particularly rail, vehicles. In the course of events, it became committed to the displacement of rail transportation by diesel buses and, ultimately, to their displacement by automobiles.

In 1925, General Motors entered bus production by acquiring Yellow Coach, which at that time was the Nation's largest manufacturer of city and intercity buses. One year later, it integrated forward into intercity bus operation by assisting in the formation of the Greyhound Corp., and soon became involved in that company's attempt to convert passenger rail operations to intercity bus service. Beginning in 1932, it undertook the direct operation and conversion of interurban electric railways and local electric streetcar and trolleybus systems to city bus operations. By the mid-1950's, it could lay claim to having played a prominent role in the complete replacement of electric street transportation with diesel buses. Due to their high cost of operation and slow speed on congested streets, however, these buses ultimately contributed to the collapse of several hundred public transit systems and to the diversion of hundreds of thousands of patrons to automobiles. In sum, the effect of General Motors' diversification program was threefold: substitution of buses for passenger trains, streetcars and trolleybuses; monopolization of bus production; and diversion of riders to automobiles.

Immediately after acquiring Yellow Coach, General Motors integrated forward into intercity bus operation. In 1926, interests allied with GM organized and then combined with the Greyhound Corp. for the purpose of replacing rail passenger service with a GM-equipped and Greyhound-operated nationwide system of intercity bus transportation. By mutual arrangement, Greyhound agreed to purchase virtually all of its buses from GM, which agreed in turn to refrain from selling intercity buses to any of Greyhound's bus operating competitors. In 1928, Greyhound announced its intention of converting commuter rail operations to intercity bus service. By 1939, six major railroads had agreed under pressure from Greyhound to replace substantial portions of their commuter rail service with Greyhound bus systems: Pennsylvania RR (Pennsylvania Greyhound Lines), New York Central RR (Central Greyhound Lines), Southern Pacific RR. (Pacific Greyhound Lines), New York, New Haven & Harford RR. (New England Greyhound Lines), Great Northern RR. (Northland Greyhound Lines), and St. Louis Southwestern Railway (Southwestern Greyhound Lines). By 1950, Greyhound carried roughly half as many intercity passengers as all the Nation's railroads combined.

During this period, General Motors played a prominent role in Greyhound management. In 1929, for example, it was responsible for the formation, direct operation, and financing of Atlantic Greyhound, which later became Greyhound's southeastern affiliate. Three years later, in 1932, when Greyhound was in serious financial trouble, it arranged for a million dollar cash loan. In addition, I. B. Babcock, the president of GM's bus division, served on Greyhound's board of directors until 1938, when he was replaced by his successor at GM, John A. Ritchie. Until 1948, GM was also the largest single shareholder in the Greyhound Corp. In short, through its interlocking interests in and promotion of Greyhound, General Motors acquired a not insignificant amount of influence over the shape of this Nation's intercity passenger transportation. As the largest manufacturer of buses, it inevitably pursued a policy which would divert intercity traffic from rails to the intercity buses which it produced and Greyhound operated. Although this policy was perfectly compatible with GM's legitimate interest in maximizing returns on its stockholders' investments, it was not necessarily in the best interest of the riding public. In effect, the public was substantially deprived of access to an alternative form of intercity travel which, regardless of its merits, was apparently curtailed as a result of corporate rather than public determination.

After its successful experience with intercity buses, General Motors diversified into city bus and rail operations. At first, its procedure consisted of directly acquiring and scrapping local electric transit systems in favor of GM buses. In this fashion, it created a market for its city buses. As GM general Counsel Henry Hogan would observe later, the corporation "decided that the only way this new market for (city) buses could be created was for it to finance the conversion from streetcars to buses in some small cities." On June 29, 1932, the GM-bus executive committee formally resolved that "to develop motorized transportation, our company should initiate a program of this nature and authorize the incorporation of a holding company with a capital of $300,000." Thus was formed United Cities Motor Transit (UCMT) as a subsidiary of GM's bus division. Its sole function was to acquire electric streetcar companies, convert them to GM motorbus operation, and then resell the properties to local concerns which agreed to purchase GM bus replacements. The electric streetcar lines of Kalamazoo and Saginaw, Mich., and Springfield, Ohio, were UCMT's first targets. "In each case," Hogan stated, GM "successfully motorized the city, turned the management over to other interests and liquidated its investment." The program ceased, however, in 1935 when GM was censured by the American Transit Association (ATA) for its self-serving role, as a bus manufacturer, in apparently attempting to motorize Portland's electric streetcar system.

As a result of the ATA censure, GM dissolved UCMT and embarked upon a nationwide plan to accomplish the same result indirectly. In 1936 it combined with the Omnibus Corp. in engineering the tremendous conversion of New York City's electric streetcar system to GM buses. At that time, as a result of stock and management interlocks, GM was able to exert substantial influence over Omnibus. John A. Ritchie, for example, served simultaneously as chairman of GM's bus division and president of Omnibus from 1926 until well after the motorization was completed. The massive conversion within a period of only 18 months of the New York system, then the world's largest streetcar network, has been recognized subsequently as the turning point in the electric railway industry.

Meanwhile, General Motors had organized another holding company to convert the remainder of the Nation's electric transportation system to GM buses. In 1936, it caused its officers and employees, I. B. Babcock, E. J. Stone, E. P. Crenshaw, and several Greyhound executives to form National City Lines, Inc. (NCL). During the following 14 years General Motors, together with Standard Oil of California, Firestone Tire, and two other suppliers of bus-related products, contributed more than $9 million to this holding company for the purpose of converting electric transit systems in 16 states to GM bus operations. The method of operation was basically the same as that which GM employed successfully in its United Cities Motor Transit program: acquisition, motorization, resale. By having NCL resell the properties after conversion was completed, GM and its allied companies were assured that their capital was continually reinvested in the motorization of additional systems. There was, moreover,

little possibility of reconversion. To preclude the return of electric vehicles to the dozens of cities it motorized, GM extracted from the local
transit companies contracts which prohibited their purchase of "... any
new equipment using any fuel or means of propulsion other than gas."

The National City Lines campaign had a devastating impact on the
quality of urban transportation and urban living in America. Nowhere
was the ruin more apparent than in the Greater Los Angeles metropolitan
area. Thirty-five years ago it was a beautiful region of lush palm trees,
fragrant orange groves, and clean, ocean-enriched air. It was served then
by the world's largest interurban electric railway system. The Pacific
Electric system branched out from Los Angeles for a radius of more than
75 miles, reaching north to San Fernando, east to San Bernardino, and
south to Santa Ana. Its 3,000 quiet, pollution-free, electric trains annually
transported 80 million people throughout the sprawling region's 56 separately incorporated cities. Contrary to popular belief, the Pacific Electric,
not the automobile, was responsible for the area's geographical development. First constructed in 1911, it established traditions of suburban living long before the automobile had arrived.

In 1938, General Motors and Standard Oil of California organized Pacific City Lines (PCL) as an affiliate of NCL to motorize west coast electric railways. The following year PCL acquired, scrapped, and substituted bus lines for three northern California electric rail systems in Fresno,
San Jose, and Stockton. In 1940 GM, Standard Oil, and Firestone "assumed the active management of Pacific (City Lines)" in order to super-
vise its California operations more directly. That year, PCL began to
acquire and scrap portions of the $100 million Pacific Electric system
including rail lines from Los Angeles to Glendale, Burbank, Pasadena,
and San Bernardino. Subsequently, in December 1944, another NCL affiliate (American City Lines) was financed by GM and Standard Oil to
motorize downtown Los Angeles. At the time, the Pacific Electric shared
downtown Los Angeles trackage with a local electric streetcar company,
the Los Angeles Railway. American City Lines puchased the local system,
scrapped its electric transit cars, tore down its power transmission lines,
ripped up the tracks, and placed GM diesel buses fueled by Standard Oil
on Los Angeles' crowded streets. In sum, GM and its auto-industrial allies
severed Los Angeles' rail links and then motorized its downtown heart.

Motorization drastically altered the quality of life in southern California. Today, Los Angeles is an ecological wasteland: The palm trees are
dying from petrochemical smog; the orange groves have been paved over
by 300 miles of freeways; the air is a septic tank into which 4 million cars,
half of them built by General Motors, pump 13,000 tons of pollutants
daily. With the destruction of the efficient Pacific Electric rail system, Los
Angeles may have lost its best hope for rapid rail transit and a smog-free
metropolitan area. "The Pacific Electric," wrote UCLA Professor Hilton,

"could have comprised the nucleus of a highly efficient rapid transit system, which would have contributed greatly to lessening the tremendous traffic and smog problems that developed from population growth." The substitution of GM diesel buses, which were forced to compete with automobiles for space on congested freeways, apparently benefited GM, Standard Oil, and Firestone considerably more than the riding public. Hilton added: "the (Pacific Electric) system, with its extensive private right of way, was far superior to a system consisting solely of buses on the crowded streets." As early as 1963, the city already was seeking ways of raising $500 million to rebuild a rail system "to supersede its present inadequate network of bus lines." A decade later, the estimated cost of constructing a 116-mile rail system, less than one-sixth the size of the earlier Pacific Electric, had escalated to more than $6.6 billion.

By 1949, General Motors had been involved in this replacement of more than 100 electric transit systems with GM buses in 45 cities including New York, Philadelphia, Baltimore, St. Louis, Oakland, Salt Lake City, and Los Angeles. In April of that year, a Chicago Federal jury convicted GM of having criminally conspired with Standard Oil of California, Firestone Tire and others to replace electric transportation with gas- or diesel-powered buses and to monopolize the sale of buses and related products to local transportation companies throughout the country. The court imposed a sanction of $5,000 on GM. In addition, the jury convicted H. C. Grossman, who was then treasurer of General Motors. Grossman had played a key role in the motorization campaigns and had served as a director of PCL when that company undertook the dismantlement of the $100 million Pacific Electric system. The court fined Grossman the magnanimous sum of $1.

Despite its criminal conviction, General Motors continued to acquire and dieselize electric transit properties through September of 1955. By then, approximately 88 percent of the nation's electric streetcar network had been eliminated. In 1936, when GM organized National City Lines, 40,000 streetcars were operating in the United States; at the end of 1955, only 5,000 remained. In December of that year, GM bus chief Roger M. Kyes correctly observed: "The motor coach has supplanted the interurban systems and has for all practical purposes eliminated the trolley (streetcar)."

The effect of General Motors' diversification into city transportation systems was substantially to curtail yet another alternative to motor vehicle transportation. Electric street railways and electric trolley buses were eliminated without regard to their relative merit as a mode of transport. Their displacement by oil-powered buses maximized the earnings of GM stockholders; but it deprived the riding public of a competing method of travel. Moreover, there is some evidence that in terms of air pollution and energy consumption these electric systems were superior to diesel buses.

In any event, GM and its oil and tire co-conspirators used National City Lines as a device to force the sale of their products regardless of the public interest. As Professor Smerk, an authority on urban transportation, has written, "Street railways and trolley bus operations, even if better suited to traffic needs and the public interest, were doomed in favor of the vehicles and material produced by the conspirators."

General Motors' substitution of buses for city streetcar lines may also have contributed in an indirect manner to the abandonment of electric railway freight service. During the 1930's merchants relied extensively on interurban electric railways to deliver local goods and to interchange distant freight shipments with mainline railroads. The Pacific Electric, for example, was once the third largest freight railroad in California; it interchanged freight with the Southern Pacific, the Union Pacific and the Santa Fe. In urban areas, these railways often ran on local streetcar trackage. The conversion of city streetcars to buses, therefore, deprived them of city trackage and hastened their replacement by motor trucks, many of which, incidentally, were produced by GM.

General Motors also stood to profit from its interests in highway freight transport. Until the early 1950's, it maintained sizable stock interests in two of the Nation's largest trucking firms, Associated Transport and Consolidated Freightways, which enjoyed the freight traffic diverted for the electric railways. By 1951, these two companies had established more than 100 freight terminals in 29 states coast-to-coast and, more than likely, had invested in a substantial number of GM diesel-powered trucks.

GM's diversification into bus and rail operations would appear not only to have had the effect of foreclosing transport alternatives regardless of their comparative advantages but also to have contributed at least in part to urban air pollution problems. There were in fact some early warnings that GM's replacement of electric-driven vehicles with diesel-powered buses and trucks was increasing air pollution. On January 26, 1954, for instance, E. P. Crenshaw, GM bus general sales manager, sent the following memorandum to F. J. Limback, another GM executive:

There has developed in a number of cities "smog" conditions which has resulted in Anti-Air Pollution committees, who immediately take issue with bus and truck operations, and especially Diesel engine exhaust. In many cases, efforts are being made to stop further substitution of Diesel buses for electric-driven vehicles. . . .

Three months later, in April 1954, the American Conference of Governmental Industrial Hygienists adopted a limit of 5 parts per million for human exposure to nitrogen oxides. Diesel buses, according to another report by two GM engineers, emitted "oxides of nitrogen concentrations over 200 times the recommended" exposure limit. Nevertheless, the dieselization program continued. Crenshaw reported to Limback in 1954:

The elimination of street-cars and trolley-buses and their replacement by our large GM 51-passenger Diesel Hydraulic coaches continues steadily . . . in Denver, Omaha, Kansas City, San Francisco, Los Angeles, New Orleans, Honolulu, Baltimore, Milwaukee, Akron, Youngstown, Columbus, etc.

2. THE DISPLACEMENT OF BUS TRANSIT BY AUTOMOBILES

Diversification into bus production and, subsequently, into bus and rail operation inevitably encouraged General Motors to supplant trains, street-cars and trolleybuses with first gasoline and then diesel buses. It also contributed to this firm's monopolization of city and intercity bus production. The effect of GM's mutually exclusive dealing arrangement with Greyhound, for example, was to foreclose all other bus manufacturers and bus operating concerns from a substantial segment of the intercity market. At least by 1952, both companies had achieved their respective monopolies: GM dominated intercity bus production and Greyhound dominated intercity bus operation. By 1973, GM's only competitor, Motor Coach Industries (established in 1962 by Greyhound as the result of a Government anti-trust decree) was wholly dependent on it for major components; and Greyhound's only operating competitor, Trailways, had been forced to purchase its buses from overseas. In the process, a number of innovative bus builders and potential manufacturers, including General Dynamics' predecessor (Consolidated Vultee) and the Douglas Aircraft Co., had been driven from the industry.

Likewise, in the city bus market, GM's exclusive bus replacement contracts with National City Lines, American City Lines, Pacific City Lines, the Omnibus Corporation, Public Transport of New Jersey and practically every other major bus operating company foreclosed competing city bus manufacturers from all but a handful of cities in the country and assured GM monopoly control of this market as well. Since 1925 more than 50 firms have withdrawn from city bus manufacturing including Ford, ACF-Brill, Marmon-Herrington, Mack Trucks, White Motor, International Harvester, Studebaker Twin Coach, Fifth Avenue Coach, Chrysler (Dodge), and Reo Motors. By 1973, only the Flxible Company, which had been established and controlled until 1958 by C. F. Kettering, a GM vice-president, remained as effectively a competitor-assembler of GM city buses. One other firm, AM General (American Motors), had announced its intention to assemble GM-powered city buses for delivery in late 1973. The ability of this firm, or for that matter Flxible and Motor Coach Industries, to survive beyond 1975, however, was seriously doubted by industry observers. That year a Government antitrust decree compelling GM to supply bus assemblers with diesel engines, transmissions and other major components will expire.

Monopolization of bus production and the elimination of electric street transportation has brought an end to price and technological competition in these industries. In this regard, several cities led by New York have filed a lawsuit charging that General Motors sets higher-than-competitive prices for its diesel buses and receives millions of dollars annually in monopoly profits. The suit also alleges that GM may be disregarding technological innovations in propulsion, pollution control and coach design, which would help attract patrons out of their automobiles.

In light of our swindling petroleum supplies and mounting concerns about air pollution, the decline of technological competition in bus manufacturing is particularly unfortunate. ACF-Brill, Marmon-Herrington, Pullman-Standard, Twin Coach, and St. Louis Car once built electric buses and electric streetcars. Other firms manufactured steam-driven buses. According to a number of studies, these alternative forms of motive power would be preferable in terms of energy consumption, efficiency, pollution, noise, and durability to the diesel engine. Exclusion of these innovative firms, however, and GM's apparent disinterest in steam- or electric-powered vehicles (whose longer life, fewer parts, and easier repair would drastically reduce her placement sales), have precluded the availability of these technological alternatives today. Moreover, domination of domestic bus manufacturing by the world's largest industrial concern tends to deter entry by smaller, innovative firms. Lear Motors, for example, has developed quiet, low-pollution steam turbine buses; Mercedes-Benz, which sells buses in 160 countries, has produced low-pollution electric buses. Neither these nor any other firms, however, have been able to break into the GM-dominated American bus market. Furthermore, GM's conversion of much of this country's streetcar and interurban trackage to bus routes has precluded the survival of domestic streetcar builders and deterred entry by foreign railcar manufacturers. As a result, there remain few transit alternatives to GM diesel buses. None of the early White or Doble steam buses are still in operation. The last electric streetcars were built in 1953; only one electric bus (built in Canada) has been delivered since 1955. In 1973, only five American cities continued to operate electric buses, and eight ran a handful of ancient streetcars.

General Motors' gross revenues are 10 times greater if it sells cars rather than buses. In theory, therefore, GM has every economic incentive to discourage that effect. Engineering studies strongly suggest that conversion from electric transit to diesel buses results in higher operating costs, loss of patronage, and eventual backruptcy. They demonstrate, for example, that diesel buses have 28 percent shorter economic lives, 40 percent higher operating costs, and 9 percent lower productivity than electric buses. They also conclude that the diesel's foul smoke, ear-splitting noise, and slow acceleration may discourage ridership. In short, by increasing the costs, reducing the revenues, and contributing to the collapse of hundreds of transit systems, GM's dieselization program may have had the long-term effect of selling GM cars.

Today, automobiles have completely replaced bus transportation in many areas of the country. Since 1952, the year GM achieved monopoly control of bus production, ridership has declined by 3 billion passengers and bus sales have fallen by about 60 percent. During that same period, GM automobile sales have risen from 1.7 million to more than 4.8 million units per year. By 1972, in a move which possibly signified the passing of bus transportation in this country, General Motors had begun converting its bus plants to motor home production.

3. THE DISPLACEMENT OF RAILROAD TRANSPORTATION BY AUTOMOBILES AND TRUCKS

As described in the preceding section, General Motors' diversification into bus transportation contributed to two developments: The displacement of passengers from rail to bus and eventually to automobile travel, and the shift in freight from rail to trucks. GM's integration into locomotive production was arguably an additional factor in the diversion of rail passengers to automobiles and rail freight to trucks. In 1930, it entered the locomotive industry by acquiring Winton Engine and Electro-Motive. At that time, Winton was the largest manufacturer of heavy diesel engines. Electro-Motive, a principal customer of Winton, was the leading firm in the application of diesel engines to railroad motive power. By combining these firms, GM became the Nation's largest manufacturer of train locomotives.

As the world's largest manufacturer of cars and trucks, General Motors was inherently ill suited to promote train transportation. Indeed, it had every economic incentive to repress this method of travel. A single GM-powered passenger train could displace as many as 1,000 GM cars; a GM-powered freight train could supplant a fleet of 150 GM trucks. From the standpoint of economies, however, GM's gross revenues were from 25 to 35 times larger if it sold cars and trucks rather than train locomotives.

In fact, General Motors' diversification into railroads probably weakened this industry's ability to compete with motor vehicles. More specifically, GM eliminated technological alternatives in train motive power which were arguably more efficient than the diesel combustion system it promoted. Its production of diesels rather than electric- or steam-driven locomotives, however, was entirely rational in terms of profit maximization. First, dieselization would vastly increase locomotive sales. A diesel locomotive, for example, lasted one-half as long, did one-third the work, and cost three times more than an electric locomotive. Second, as compared with railroad electrification, dieselization was substantially less of a threat to car and truck transportation. Diesel trains were sluggish, noisy, and generally less attractive to passengers than rapid, quiet, pollution-free electric trains. In addition, they were less powerful and therefore not as efficient in hauling freight. As the Nation's largest shipper of freight, GM was able to exert considerable influence over the locomotive purchasing policies of the Nation's railroads. It used this powerful form of leverage to sell its diesel locomotives. Before long, it had dieselized the entire American railroad industry, and simultaneously had obtained a monopoly in the production of locomotives. As a consequence, alternative forms of motive power, such as electricity which might have enabled the railroads to compete more effectively with cars and trucks, were disregarded.

General Motors dieselized the Nation's railroads by using its freight business to coerce them to purchase its diesel locomotives. In 1935, with barely 2.4 percent of industry sales, it embarked upon a dual plan to monopolize locomotive production and to dieselize the American railroad industry. At that time, electric locomotives outnumbered diesel units 7 to 1, and several firms were developing a steam turbine engine to replace the conventional steam locomotive. In November, GM ordered its traffic division to begin routing freight over railroads which agreed reciprocally to scrap their electric and steam equipment for GM diesels. For the next 35 years it used its formidable leverage as the largest commercial shipper to exclude locomotive competitors and to force the railroads to convert to all-diesel operation. By 1970, it had effectively dieselized the entire industry: steam units were virtually extinct; and diesels, 80 percent of which were manufactured by GM, outnumbered electric locomotives 100 to 1.

The dieselization of America's railroads did not require blatant acts of coercion. Rail executives were fully aware of GM's formidable freight leverage. As an interoffice legal memorandum drafted by GM's antitrust attorneys stated, "GM could, in all probability, have successfully capitalized upon the railroad's sensitivity to reciprocity by frequently reminding them of GM's considerable traffic, and could have done so without ever interfering substantially with the economical routing of traffic." Nevertheless, on occasion, GM may have resorted to blatant pressure.

In November 1948, for instance, Roy B. White, President of the Baltimore & Ohio Railroad, was apparently contacted by Alfred P. Sloan, Jr., Chairman of General Motors, regarding GM's offer to locate one of its warehouses on B. & O.'s tracks in return for B. & O.'s agreement to convert to GM diesels. Later that month, White replied by letter to Sloan to the effect: "Here is your Christmas present . . . we will purchase 300 diesel locomotives . . . we now expect to receive a New Year's gift from you . . . locate your warehouse near our tracks." Likewise, in the fall of 1958 a General Motors official informed Gulf, Mobile & Ohio Railroad that certain GM traffic would not be routed over its lines because other railroads had purchased more GM diesel locomotives than Gulf.

Through its shrewd use of freight leverage, GM eliminated all but one of its competitors by 1970. Westinghouse, a pioneer in railway electrification, announced its departure from the history in 1954. Baldwin-Lima-Hamilton, one of the Nation's oldest railroad builders, built its last locomotive in 1956. Fairbanks-Morse, which attempted to enter in 1944, was forced out by 1958. In 1969, American Locomotive, an aggressive manufacturer of gas turbine, electric, steam turbine as well as diesel locomotives, and the leading exporter of rail equipment, was purchased by one of GM's automotive parts suppliers (Studebaker-Worthington) and immediately withdrawn from locomotive production. By 1973, 99 percent of the locomotive fleet was dieselized and GM's only competitor, General Electric, accounted for less than 17 percent of total production.

The immediate effect of dieselization was suppression of an alternative system of train propulsion: namely, electrification. In 1935, when GM initiated its dieselization program, two of the country's major railroads had electrified their systems and several others contemplated similar action. The New York, New Haven & Hartford had constructed the world's first 11,000-volt, 25-cycle alternating current system along 500 miles of New England track. The Pennsylvania had inaugurated electric passenger and freight train operations between New York and Washington. By dieselizing these and other roads, GM may have curbed in its incipiency a trend toward electrification. By 1960, when virtually every other industrialized Nation in the world was electrifying their trains, America was locked-in to GM diesel locomotives.

The long-term effect of dieselization was impairment of the railroads' ability to compete effectively with cars and trucks. By vastly increasing operating, maintenance and depreciation costs, dieselization contributed to the curtailment of maintenance and service, and eventual bankruptcy of many American railroads. This process was arguably apparent in General Motors' conversion of the New Haven system from electric to diesel power. In 1956, GM reportedly used its freight leverage to coerce the railroad into scrapping all of its electric passenger and freight locomotives in favor of GM diesel passenger units. The conversion was followed by loss of a substantial portion of the New Haven's passenger and freight traffic to cars and trucks. Dieselization may have been the responsible factor. The slower GM diesels were less attractive to New Haven passengers accustomed to rapid electric trains. They were also less powerful and, consequently, less suitable for moving freight than the electric locomotives they replaced. Within a short time the company began to experience serious operating deficits. These deficits coupled with the diesel's higher operating and depreciation costs compelled, in turn, cutbacks in maintenance and service, which generated another round of traffic diversion to cars and trucks.

A subsequent investigation by the Interstate Commerce Commission in 1960 confirmed that in fact dieselization had contributed to the New

Haven's severe financial crisis and eventual bankruptcy. Observing that "without an intelligent locomotive policy, no efficient railroad operation can possibly be conducted," the ICC hearing officers stressed the significant economic advantages which the New Haven had derived from the durability, efficiency and extraordinary power of electric locomotives. They noted that the life of an electric locomotive was about twice that of a diesel (30 years versus 15 years, respectively) and being a less complicated, more efficient and less delicate piece of machinery, was substantially cheaper to operate and maintain. In addition, they emphasized that a single electric locomotive could do the work of three diesels and that new electric locomotives cost only one-third as much as the diesel locomotives sold to the New Haven by General Motors. The examiners found, however, that despite the numerous advantages of electric operation as compared with diesel and contrary to the advice of its own independent engineering consultants, the New Haven had relied instead on General Motors' "ridiculous" representations as to the savings to be derived from dieselization.

According to the ICC officials, GM's claims of anticipated savings proved to be "a mirage." The New Haven's replacement of its electric locomotive with GM diesels generated higher operating, maintenance and depreciation expenses and substantial losses in passenger and freight revenues. During 50 years of electrical operation, it had never failed to show an operating profit. In 1955, the year before dieselization, it earned $5.7 million carrying 45 million passengers and 814 thousand carloads of freight. By 1959, 7 years after GM dieselization began, it lost $9.2 million hauling 10 million fewer passengers and 130 thousand fewer carloads of freight. In 1961, it was declared bankrupt; by 1968, when it was acquired by the Penn Central, it had accumulated a capital deficit of nearly $300 million.

In 1961, the ICC upheld the hearings officers' recommended report on the bankrupt New Haven and censured General Motors for contributing to the railroad's financial ruin. Of the several factors it listed as responsible for the New Haven's downfall, it placed special emphasis on the elimination of electric locomotives. Although it refrained from suggesting that GM was guilty of fraudulent misrepresentation, the Commission found the automakers' estimates of savings from conversion to diesels "erroneous," "inflated," and "manifestly absurd." Referring to the "great advances in railway electrification made in Europe and in the Soviet Union," it concluded with a recommendation that the trustees undertake a study of the economic feasibility of complete reelectrification of the New Haven's main line.

The New Haven was probably not the only casualty of GM's dieselization program. All six of the major railroads serving the Northeast corridor are today bankrupt, and those in the rest of the country are earning an average of less than 2 percent on investment. Had these roads electrified, they might have fared better financially and might have been better able to compete effectively with motor vehicles. That technological option, however, was foreclosed to them as a result, in part, of GM's diversification into railroad locomotives.

Since GM began its dieselization campaign in 1935, the railroads have progressively lost traffic first to buses and then to cars and trucks, most of which are manufactured by GM. In 1939 they carried half a million passengers and accounted for 75 percent of all freight revenues; by 1972 they had lost 50 percent of their passengers to cars, and nearly 75 percent of all freight revenue to trucks. Whether this result was actually intended by GM is irrelevant. Nonetheless, it is difficult to believe that a firm fundamentally interested in marketing cars and trucks would develop an efficient high-speed train system that might diminish their sales.

The impact of dieselization on this Nation's railroads has been the subject of expert scrutiny. H. F. Brown, an international authority on railroad motive power, has concluded that dieselization "was the single most important factor responsible for the demise of America's railroads." Significantly, his studies of America's experience with GM diesels helped persuade Parliament to electrify rather than dieselize the British railway system.

4. THE POLITICAL RESTRAINT OF RAIL TRANSIT

General Motors' diversification into streetcar, bus and railroad transportation was very likely a significant factor in their eventual displacement by automobiles and trucks. A second structural feature, the asymmetrical distribution of economic power in the ground transport sector, may also have generated the political restraint of a third alternative to automobile transportation: rail rapid transit (subways).

. . . [S]mall deconcentrated industries are less able to influence government policymaking as effectively as their concentrated rivals. This may explain, in part, the political disregard until quite recently of rail transit as an alternative in congested urban areas to automotive transportation. Due to its high concentration and gigantic sales volume, the auto industry has accumulated hundreds of millions of dollars in revenues from higher-than-competitively-priced motor vehicles. It has used some of these revenues to finance political activities which, in the absence of effective countervailing activities by competing ground transport industries, induced government bodies to promote their product (automobiles) over other alternatives, particularly rail rapid transit.

Every industry, of course, has the constitutionally protected right to petition Government bodies and to mobilize public opinion as a means of shaping Government policies to its own private corporate advantage. This study does not take exception with that privilege. It does, however, suggest that the presence of a relatively large and highly concentrated automotive industry in the important multi-industry ground transportation sector may have resulted in the distortion of political processes to the advantage of this industry and to the disadvantage of the riding public. The effect, in short, may have been to deprive the public of the opportunity of choosing among competing transportation alternatives. More specifically, an imbalanced distribution of political power in favor of the automakers may have encouraged the Government to allocate overwhelmingly disproportionate sums of money to highways rather than to rail systems.

Generally, the automakers' political activities have been twofold in nature: establishment of a powerful lobbying organization to promote the public financing of highways, and participation in competing associations which favored the construction of subways.

On June 28, 1932, Alfred P. Sloan, Jr., president of General Motors, organized the National Highway Users Conference to combine representatives of the Nation's auto, oil, and tire industries in a common front against competing transportation interests. Sloan became its permanent chairman and served in that capacity until 1948, when he was succeeded by the new chairman of GM, Albert Bradley, who continued as its chairman through 1956. Its announced objectives were dedication of highway taxes solely to highway purposes, and development of a continuing program of highway construction.

In a statement issued the following January, NHUC formally proclaimed its political commitment to automotive transportation: "Until now those interested in automotive transportation have fought their battles independently. Participating in the National Highway Users Conference are a large majority of the interested groups. The manufacturers of motorcars and accessories have joined with the users of their equipment in the common cause of defense." The "interested groups" included the Motor Vehicle Manufacturers Association (representing automobile and truck companies), the American Petroleum Institute (spokesman for the oil industry), the American Trucking Association (representing the trucking interests), the Rubber Manufacturers Association (comprising the tire companies) and the American Automobile Association (purporting to speak for the Nation's millions of motorists). Although it disclaimed any intention of lobbying on behalf of these highway interests, it proposed to serve as "an agency for the coordination of activities of interested groups" and to cooperate with "such State organizations as are set up along the same lines as the national body." Implicitly, therefore, its function was to influence Congress and the state legislators where it claimed "the membership may be badly informed or where a considerable part of it may yield to the influence of selfish interests."

During the succeeding 40 years, the National Highway Users Conference has compiled an impressive record of accomplishments. Its effect, if not purpose, has been to direct public funds away from rail construction and into highway building. At the state level, its 2,800 lobbying groups have been instrumental in persuading 44 of the Nation's 50 legislatures to adopt and preserve measures which dedicated State and local gasoline tax revenues exclusively to highway construction. By promoting these highway "trust funds," it has discouraged governors and mayors from attempting to build anything other than highways for urban transportation. Subways and rail transit proposals have had to compete with hospitals, schools and other governmental responsibilities for funding. By contrast, highways have been automatically financed from a self-perpetuating fund which was legally unavailable for any other purpose. Largely as a result, highways, not subways, have been built. From 1945 through 1970, states and localities spent more than $156 billion constructing hundreds of thousands of miles of roads. During that same period, only 16 miles of subway were constructed in the entire country.

Likewise, at the Federal level this organization has been very successful in promoting highways over rail transportation. For example, under the early and exceptionally capable leadership of GM's Sloan and Bradley, it became a principal architect of the world's largest roadbuilding effort, the 42,500-mile $70-billion Interstate Highway System. During the years prior to passage in 1956 of the Interstate Highway Act, NHUC and allied highway groups had worked assiduously building support among Congressmen, Federal administrators, academicians and engineers. They contributed to congressional campaigns, placed their members in important administrative posts, and granted millions of dollars to highway research.

At the time, few opposed the idea of building a system of interstate highways. Only one witness during more than 2 years of congressional hearings even raised the issue of what effect it might have on the Nation's railroads. In retrospect, the national highway program was unquestionably needed. Whether its tremendous scope and budgetary commitment, however, might preclude Federal financing of alternative rail transport systems was a point which should have been debated at that time. The uneven distribution of political resources between automakers and rail manufacturers may explain why this important question received virtually no political attention.

When Congress finally began hearings on the Interstate Highway Act in 1956, the outcome was a foregone conclusion. Only the manner of financing the program was at issue. In the end, the National Highway Users Conference managed to persuade Congress to adopt the same trust fund arrangement which it had successfully promoted earlier to the state legislatures. The impact of the Federal Highway Trust Fund on transportation spending was similar to that which occurred at the state level. While urban rail proposals were forced to compete for funds with dozens of Federal priorities including national defense, health, and social security, thousands of miles of highways were built automatically with gasoline tax revenues, unavailable for any other purpose. From 1956 through 1970, the Federal Government spent approximately $70 billion for highways; and only $795 million, or 1 percent, for rail transit.

Today, the National Highway Users Conference, now known as Highway Users Federation for Safety and Mobility (HUFSAM), works effectively with highway-related groups such as the Motor Vehicle Manufacturers Association (MVMA) to promote the automakers' interest in more highways and less rail transit. With combined annual budgets of nearly $16 million, most of which comes from the Big Three auto companies, HUFSAM and MVMA fight State and Federal attempts to "divert" highway funds for rail transit purposes. In this regard they are aided by a score of allied highway interests which collectively spend an estimated $500 million a year lobbying to preserve highway trust funds. They are also active in financing research groups which invariably conclude that automobiles, trucks, and, if necessary, "bus transit" complete with underground diesel "busways" can satisfy every ground transportation need.

By comparison, the three leading transit lobby groups are financially weak and torn by the conflicting interest of their membership. The American Transit Association, the largest element of the transit lobby, operates on an annual budget of about $700,000 which must be apportioned between the conflicting political needs of its bus and rail transit manufacturing members. The Railway Institute spends an estimated $600,000 a year. The third and smallest element of the transit body, the Institute for Rapid Transit, operates on a meager budget of about $200,000 a year. In short, HUFSAM and MVMA alone outspend the three principal transit organizations by more than 10 to 1. Furthermore, General Motors, whose personnel organized and continue to direct the highway lobby, has secured the power to influence the policies of two of these three transit groups. Due to its position as the Nation's largest producer of bus and rail vehicles, it is a major financial contributor to both the American Transit Association and the Railway Progress Institute. It is also an influential member of the Institute for Rapid Transit.

Absent a powerful and unequivocal rail transit lobby, those interested in balanced transportation are no match for the organized highway interests. Legislators including Senators Kennedy, Muskie, and Weicker, citizen and municipal groups such as the Highway Action Coalition and the League of Cities, Mayors Alioto (San Francisco), White (Boston), Daley (Chicago), and numerous others have failed repeatedly to shift anything other than token amounts of state and Federal gas tax revenues from highways to rail transit. As an apparent consequence, national transportation policy principally reflects the legislative objective of the auto[makers]: Building more highways which sell more cars and trucks.

Publicly, the automakers proclaim their support for mass transit. They cultivate this seemingly paradoxical image for two reasons. First, a pro-transit posture at a time of petroleum shortages and environmental concerns is good for public relations. Second, and perhaps more importantly, they seek to control and direct the development of nonautomotive transport technology in a manner least threatening to their fundamental interest: selling cars. In this regard, Ford is developing "horizontal elevators" and PRT (personal rapid transit) vehicles capable of moving people short distances within strictly downtown areas. Ford's transit vehicles would compete, therefore, not with automobiles but with pedestrians. Likewise, General Motors is engaged in a continuing effort to divert Government funds from rapid rail transit, which seriously threatens the use of cars in metropolitan areas, to GM buses, which fail consistently to persuade people to abandon their autos. In place of regional electric rail systems, for instance, it promotes diesel-powered "bus trains" of as many as 1,400 units, each spaced 80 feet apart. Instead of urban electric rail, it advocates the use of dual-mode gas/electric vehicles which would be adapted from GM's minimotor homes. In sum, the automakers embrace transit in order to prevent it from competing effectively with their sales of automobiles.

General Motors' diversification into the bus and rail industries and the asymmetrical distribution of power between automakers and rail builders would appear to have contributed at least in part, therefore, to the decline of competing alternatives to motor vehicles. By 1973 five different forms of nonautomotive transportation had either disappeared or been seriously impaired: electric streetcars, trolley coaches, interurban electric railways, buses, and trains. In short, diversification and asymmetry in ground transport manufacturing may have retarded the development of mass transportation and, as a consequence, may have generated a reliance on motor vehicles incompatible with metropolitan needs.

5. CURRENT PERFORMANCE OF THE GROUND TRANSPORTATION SECTOR

Due to its anticompetitive structure and behavior, this country's ground transport sector can no longer perform satisfactorily. It has become seriously imbalanced in favor of the unlimited production of motor vehicles. Unlike every other industrialized country in the world, America has come to rely almost exclusively on cars and trucks for the land transportation of its people and goods. Cars are used for 90 percent of city and intercity travel; trucks are the only method of intracity freight delivery and account for 78 percent of all freight revenues. This substitution of more than 100 million petroleum-consuming cars and trucks for competing forms of alternately powered ground transportation is a significant factor in this sector's unacceptable level of inefficient and nonprogressive performance.

Efficiency in terms of market performance may be defined as a comparison of actual prices or costs with those that would [be obtained] in a competitively structured market. Currently, Americans pay $181 billion per year for motor vehicle transportation. In terms of high energy consumption, accident rates, contribution to pollution, and displacement of urban amenities, however, motor vehicle travel is possibly the most inefficient method of transportation devised by modern man.

More specifically, the diversion of traffic from energy-efficient electric rails to fuel-guzzling highway transport has resulted in an enormous consumption of energy. Rails can move passengers and freight for less than one-fifth the amount of energy required by cars and trucks. The displacement of rails by highways, therefore, has seriously depleted our scarce supplies of energy and has increased by several billion dollars a year the amount consumers must pay for ground transportation. It has been estimated, for example, that the diversion of passengers in urban areas from energy-efficient electric rail to gasoline automobiles results in their paying $18 billion a year more in energy cost alone. In addition, economists have found that the inefficient diversion of intercity freight from rail to trucks costs consumers $5 billion per year in higher prices for goods.

The substitution of highways for rails has also reduced efficiency by imposing higher indirect costs on the public in the form of accidents, pollution, and land consumption. Rail travel is 23 times as safe as travel by motor vehicles. The diversion to highways has cost the public an estimated $17 billion each year in economic damages attributable to motor vehicle accidents. This figure, however, cannot reflect the incalculable human costs of motor vehicle accidents: The violent deaths each year by car and truck of 55,000 Americans, more than all who died in the entire 12 years of our involvement in Vietnam, and the serious injuries to an additional 5 million of our citizens.

Likewise, the costs of urban air pollution have been greatly accentuated by the imbalance in favor of cars and trucks. Motor vehicles annually consume 42 billion gallons of petroleum within the densely populated 2 percent of the U.S. geographic area classified as urban. The consumption of this enormous quantity of fuel in urban areas produces in excess of 60 million tons of toxic pollutants, which in turn cost urban residents more than $4 billion in economic damages.

The presence of high concentrations of these motor vehicle pollutants, particularly oxides of nitrogen, in densely populated areas has also generated smog. The hazards of carbon monoxide and hydrocarbon emissions from automobiles have been widely acknowledged. Less well known are the potentially more serious effects of oxides of nitrogen produced primarily by diesel trucks and buses in high concentrations on congested city streets. When inhaled, these oxides combine with moisture in the lungs to form corrosive nitric acid which permanently damages lung tissues and accelerates death by slowly destroying the body's ability to resist heart and lung diseases. By contrast, if electric rail transportation were substituted in cities for motor vehicles, urban air pollution might be reduced substantially. Although the burning of fuels to generate this increased electrical energy would produce some pollution, it would pose a substantially less serious hazard to public health. Electric powerplants can often be located in areas remote from population centers. Moreover, the increased pollution by generating facilities would be offset by a reduction in pollution due to oil refinery operations. Furthermore, the abatement of air pollution at a relatively small number of stationary powerplants would represent a far easier task than attempting to install and monitor devices on 100 million transient motor vehicles.

The diversion of traffic from rail to highways has imposed a third cost on consumers—the consumption of vast amounts of taxable urban landscapes from 60 to 65 percent of our cities' land area is devoted to highways, parking facilities, and other auto- and truck-related uses. In downtown Los Angeles, the figure approaches 85 percent. This has led to an erosion in the cities' tax base and, concomitantly, to a decline in their ability to finance the delivery of vital municipal services. Electric rail transportation, by comparison, requires less than one-thirteenth as much space as highways to move a comparable amount of passengers or goods, and in many cases can be located underground.

Progressiveness in terms of market performance is generally understood as a comparison of the number and importance of actual innovations with those which optimally could have been developed and introduced. The substitution of highways for rails has resulted in the decrease in mobility and has precluded important innovations in high-speed urban and intercity ground transportation. The decrease in mobility is most acute in urban areas. The average speed of rush hour traffic in cities dependent on motor vehicles, for example, is 12 miles per hour. Studies indicate that city traffic moved more quickly in 1890. Moreover, 20 percent of our urban population (the aged, youth, disabled, and poor) lack access to automobiles and, due to the nonexistence of adequate public transportation, are effectively isolated from employment or educational opportunities and other urban amenities. Substitution of highways for rails has also retarded innovations in high-speed urban and intercity transport. Technologically advanced rail transit systems, which currently operate in the major cities of Europe and Japan, would relieve congestion and contribute to urban mobility. High-speed intercity rail systems, such as Japan's 150-mile-per-hour electric Tokaido Express, would help to relieve mounting air traffic congestion and offer a practical alternative to slower and more tedious travel by car or truck. But the political predilections of the automakers have become the guidelines for American transportation policy. In contrast to the advanced rail transport emphasis of Europe and Japan, this country has persisted in the expansion of highway transport. As a result, America has become a second-rate nation in transportation.

There are strong indications, moreover, that due to mounting concerns about air pollution and a worldwide shortage of petroleum, our motor-vehicle-dominated transportation system will perform even worse in the future. The Environmental Protection Agency has warned that by 1977 motor vehicle emissions in major urban areas may compel a cutback in automobile, truck, and diesel bus use of as much as 60 percent. In addition, the Department of the Interior has forecast that the current petroleum crisis might cripple transportation and cause "serious economic and social disruptions." More precisely, an excessive reliance in the past on fuel-guzzling motor vehicles for transport has contributed to a crisis in energy which now threatens to shut down industries, curb air and ground travel, and deprive our home of heating oil for winter.

Despite these adverse trends, the automakers appear bent on further motorization. Henry Ford II, for instance, has noted that notwithstanding "the energy crisis, the environmental crisis, and the urban crisis" new car sales in the United States "have increased by more than a million during the past 2 model years." General Motors' chief operating executive has predicted that soon each American will own a "family of cars" for every conceivable travel activity including small cars for trips, recreational vehicles for leisure, and motor homes for mobile living. GM is also engaged in the displacement of what little remains of this Nation's rail systems. To that end, it is developing 750-horsepower diesel engines to haul multiple trailers at speeds of 70 miles per hour along the nearly completed Interstate Highway System. These "truck trains" are slated to replace rail freight service. As substitutes for regional subway systems, GM is also advocating 1,400-unit diesel "bus trains," which would operate on exclusive busways outside cities and in bus tunnels under downtown areas. Both diesel truck trains and underground bus trains, however, would seem grossly incompatible with public concerns about petroleum shortages and suffocating air pollution.

The automakers' motorization program, moreover, is worldwide in scope. The superior bus and rail systems which flourish in the rest of the industrialized world interfere with the sale of cars and trucks by the Big Three's foreign subsidiaries. "The automobile industry put America on wheels," said GM Chairman Gerstenberg in September of 1972. "Today," he added, "expanding markets all around the world give us the historic opportunity to put the whole world on wheels."

VIII
THE WORKPLACE

During the past 200 years, work has held a central position in the ideas of philosophers and social scientists. Of these, the most influential and enduring commentator was Karl Marx. His analysis of the workplace during the industrial revolution was distinguished by its sympathy for the plight of the industrial worker, its analytical power, and its empirical grounding (derived from observations of the industrial workplace by British Commissions of Inquiry).

Marx wrote during the mid-nineteenth century, when manufacturing had evolved from the family cottage to the "factory"—an appropriately speeded-up word invented to describe the new industrial form. In analyzing the human effects of capitalist industry, Marx emphasized the subordination of the worker's own needs to the requirements of production for profit:

What constitutes the alienation of labour? First, that the work is *external* to the worker, that it is not part of his nature; and that, consequently, he does not fulfill himself in his work but denies himself, has a feeling of misery rather than well-being, does not develop freely his mental and physical energies but is physically exhausted and mentally debased. The worker, therefore, feels himself at home only during his leisure time, whereas at work he feels homeless. His work is not voluntary but imposed, *forced labour*. It is not satisfaction of a need, but only a *means* for satisfying other needs. Its alien character is clearly shown by the fact that as soon as there is no physical or other compulsion it is avoided like the plague.[1]

Should work be interesting and significant, or is work simply an unpleasant task that must be done to live and to provide resources for spending on leisure activities away from the workplace? Is it possible to reform work, that is, to make it less dull, less dangerous, less exhausting?

339

All recent evidence suggests that work continues to mean a great deal to people. Despite the managerial ideology of a decline of initiative, stability, and interest in work, survey after survey shows that actual hours of work time have not declined. People want, perhaps above all, to be employed, but they are also deeply concerned about the kind of work they do. Thus, after reviewing a wide variety of studies of work and its meaning, Rosabeth Moss Kanter concludes:

Work, then, may still be important to Americans for self-respect and meaning in life—but not just any work, and not under just any conditions. For a sizable segment of the population, work is expected to provide more than merely material rewards, and the cost of material rewards themselves should not be too high. At the very least, work should be a source of pride, and it should contribute to the realization of cherished personal values.[2]

In particular, workers do not enjoy being automatons. But, as Harry Braverman's "Final Note on Skill" suggests, the whole thrust of managerial ideology has been (1) to make work more automatic while (2) pretending, perhaps even believing, that the requisite level of skill for factory work has risen, whereas while in fact the thrust of the automated factory has been to decrease skill requirements. When the worker is construed as part of the machine, as merely part of a system of production to be managed for profit, observes Braverman, "the very concept of skill becomes degraded. . . ."

Braverman's thesis is illustrated in the two articles that follow. Robert Howard's "Brave New Workplace" describes the problems of degradation of work in the telecommunications industry. As that industry's technology has become increasingly sophisticated, so has control over workers by (1) upgrading technician's tasks to a management level and (2) developing the technical ability for advanced computerized surveillance of the work-product of the lowliest clerical worker. Hence, "The Brave New Workplace" of the title.

If the telecommunications industry represents the emergent workplace problems of relatively affluent American labor, Ehrenreich and Fuentes' "Global Assembly Line" describes the far more harsh and dismal working conditions prevailing in the factories run by American corporations in Third World countries. Here, workers will accept $5 a day for work that Americans wouldn't do for $5 an hour. As a result, "first world" industry is increasingly moving its factories to Third World countries and paying as little as the local ununionized traffic will bear. Most of the hardworking locals on the global assembly line are young women, and they bear a great deal indeed. For them, the workplace is not only psychically degrading—it is physically harmful.

REFERENCES

1. Quoted in Shlomo Avineri, *The Social and Political Thought of Karl Marx*, Cambridge University Press, 1971, p. 106.

2. Rosabeth Moss Kanter, "Work in a New America," *Daedelus*, Winter 1978, pp. 47–78.

23
A FINAL NOTE ON SKILL

Harry Braverman

In a study of the mechanization of industry, conducted for the National Bureau of Economic Research in the 1930s, Harry Jerome concluded: "As to the effect on skill of further mechanization in the future . . . there is considerable reason to believe that the effect of further changes will be to raise the average skill required."[1] Forty years later there are few who would disagree with this judgment. The idea that the changing conditions of industrial and office work require an increasingly "better-trained," "better-educated," and thus "upgraded" working population is an almost universally accepted proposition in popular and academic discourse. Since the argument that has been thus far made in this work appears to clash directly with this popular idea, it is now necessary to confront the conventional view. The concepts of "skill," "training," and "education" are themselves sufficiently vague, and a precise investigation of the arguments which are used to support the thesis of "upgrading" is further hampered by the fact that they have never been made the subject of a

From Harry Braverman, *Labor and Monopoly Capital: The Degradation of Work in the Twentieth Century.* Copyright © 1974 by Harry Braverman. Reprinted by permission of Monthly Review Press.

coherent and systematic presentation. We can grapple with the issue only by attempting to give coherence to what is essentially an impressionistic theory, one which is obviously considered so self-evident as to stand above the need for demonstration.

In the form given to it by Jerome in the sentence cited above, the phrase upon which the issue turns is "average skill." Since, with the development of technology, and the application to it of the fundamental sciences, the labor processes of society have come to embody a greater amount of scientific knowledge, clearly the "average" scientific, technical, and in that sense "skill" content of these labor processes is much greater now than in the past. But this is nothing but a tautology. The question is precisely whether the scientific and "educated" content of labor tends toward *averaging*, or, on the contrary, toward *polarization*. If the latter is the case, to then say that the "average" skill has been raised is to adopt the logic of the statistician who, with one foot in the fire and the other in ice water, will tell you that "on the average," he is perfectly comfortable. The mass of workers gain nothing from the fact that the decline in their command over the labor process is more than compensated for by the increasing command on the part of managers and engineers. On the contrary, not only does their skill fall in an absolute sense (in that they lose craft and traditional abilities without gaining new abilities adequate to compensate the loss), but it falls even more in a *relative* sense.

The same ambiguity is to be seen in another common formulation of the "upgrading" thesis, one which points to the proliferation of trained and educated specialties. Omar Pancoast, for instance, says: "It is an historical fact that an increasing number of positions require special skills. The evidence for this is well summarized by J. K. Norton with the comment: 'No extensive study of occupational trends arrives at an opposite conclusion.' "[2] In this form the claim is probably unexceptionable, but it may *not* be taken, as it often is, to mean that an *increasing portion of the working population* occupies positions that require special skills, if the word "skill" is given an interpretation of substance.

For most of those who hold it, the "upgrading" thesis seems to rest upon two marked trends. The first is the shift of workers from some major occupational groups into others; the second is the prolongation of the average period of education. It will repay our efforts to consider both of these matters in some detail, not only because such a consideration is necessary to establish a realistic picture of the historical trends of skill, but also because in this consideration we shall see a splendid example of the manner in which conventional social science accepts carefully tailored appearances as a substitute for reality.

Let us begin first with the shifts that have taken place within the occupational categories used by statisticians to identify the various portions

Table 1

	1900	1970
Craftsmen, foremen, and kindred	10.5	13.9
Operatives and kindred	12.8	17.9
Nonfarm laborers	12.5	4.7
Total	35.8	36.5

of the "manual" working class. At the turn of the century the three classifications of workers today known as *craftsmen, foremen, and kindred, operatives and kindred,* and *nonfarm laborers* together made up slightly less than 36 percent of employed persons. Seventy years later these three categories made up just over 36 percent (although in the intervening decades their total had risen to around 40 percent—in the 1920 to 1950 censuses—and then fallen back again). But during these seventy years the distribution of this group among its three statistical components had changed sharply. In terms of percentages of the entire employed population, the changes [are given in Table 1].[3]

The most marked feature of this tabulation is the decline in laborers. A large part of this classification had become operatives (we are still speaking in terms of percentages, since in terms of absolute numbers the total of the three groups was about 2⅔ times as many people) and the rest had become craftsmen and foremen. This shift is taken, on its face, to represent a massive "upgrading" of workers to higher categories of skill.*

Classifications of workers, however, are neither "natural" nor self-evident, nor is the degree of skill a self-evident quality which can simply be read from the labels given to various such classifications. The first socioeconomic occupational classifications used in the United States were

---

*It would be wrong to try to derive any comforting conclusions from the rise in the category of craftsmen and foremen between 1900 and 1970. We have already discussed the dispersal and deterioration of craft skills in the machine shop, for example, and many of the possessors of partial skills continue to carry the label of craftsmanship. In a discussion of traditional apprenticeships in British industry, for example, one British authority points out that "although apprentices theoretically emerge as skilled craftsmen much of the work they are put to would be regarded as semi-skilled, because of the fragmentation of many industrial processes." Because, this writer says, the need is for "semi-skilled" workers, "the apprenticeship system encourages unrealistic and rigid job definitions."[4] In the United States such attacks against the apprenticeship system are no longer necessary, since there is little left of it. And it should also be noted that much of the growth of the craftsmen classification is due to the rapid increase of the "mechanics and repairmen" category (the largest grouping of which is that of automobile mechanics) which does not conform to traditional standards of craftsmanship and represents an ever slighter level of technical capacity and training.

those of William C. Hunt, an employee of the Bureau of the Census who, in 1897, grouped all gainful workers into four categories: proprietors, clerical employees, skilled workers, and laborers. The group we now call "operatives" did not exist in this classification, and the division of manual workers into two classes was a clear and unambiguous one: There were the craftsmen—the mechanics in various trades, whose admission into this category of skilled workers was thus dependent upon satisfying the traditional requirements of craft mastery. Laborers were all others; they were thus a residual category.

In the 1930s a revision of these classifications was carried out by Dr. Alba Edwards, for many years an official of the Bureau of the Census, who reconstructed the conceptual basis of occupational statistics in a fundamental fashion. The change which he made that is of concern to this discussion is his division of the former group of laborers into two parts. Those who tended or operated machines, or attended mechanized processes, he called operatives. Laborers, still a residual category, now consisted of those nonfarm workers who were neither craftsmen nor machine operatives. These classifications were first applied in the census of 1930. Edwards, however, did the massive work of reconstructing the census data back to the turn of the century, and even earlier, in accord with his new classification scheme. The class of workers known as "operatives," therefore, insofar as we find it in the census statistics earlier than those of 1930, is a backward projection of a category that did not exist in these earlier censuses. Edwards' work has been the chief basis for all similar reconstructions since done by others.[5]

The three Edwards classifications were taken to correspond, both in official terminology and in common parlance, to levels of skill. Craftsmen continued to be called skilled workers and laborers "unskilled"; operatives were now called "semi-skilled." But it must be noted that the distinction between the skills of the two latter categories was based not upon a study of the occupational tasks involved, as is generally assumed by the users of the categories, but upon a simple *mechanical* criterion, in the fullest sense of the word. The creation of "semi-skill" by Edwards thus brought into existence, retroactively to the turn of the century and with a mere stroke of the pen, a massive "upgrading" of the skills of the working population. By making a connection with machinery—such as machine tending or watching, machine feeding, machine operating—a criterion of skill, it guaranteed that with the increasing mechanization of industry the category of the "unskilled" would register a precipitous decline, while that of the "semi-skilled" would show an equally striking rise. This statistical process has been automatic ever since, without reference to the actual exercise or distribution of "skills."

Let us take as an example the categories of teamster on the one side, and the operators of motor vehicles (such as truckdrivers, chauffeurs and taxi drivers, routemen and deliverymen, etc.) on the other. These categories are important because that of teamster was, before World War I, one of the largest of occupational groups, while the drivers of various sorts are, taken together, one of the largest today. The former are classified, retroactively, among the "unskilled" laborers, while the latter, because of their connection with machinery, are classed as operatives and hence "semi-skilled." When the Edwards scale is applied in this fashion, a skill upgrading takes place as a consequence of the displacement of horse-drawn transport by motorized. Yet it is impossible to see this as a true comparison of human work skills. In the circumstances of an earlier day, when a largely rural population learned the arts of managing horses as part of the process of growing up, while few as yet knew how to operate motorized vehicles, it might have made sense to characterize the former as part of the common heritage and thus no skill at all, while driving, as a learned ability, would have been thought of as a "skill." Today, it would be more proper to regard those who are able to drive vehicles as unskilled in that respect at least, while those who can care for, harness, and manage a team of horses are certainly the possessors of a marked and uncommon ability. In reality, this way of comparing occupational skill leaves much to be desired, depending as it does on relativistic or contemporary notions. But there is certainly little reason to suppose that the ability to drive a motor vehicle is more demanding, requires longer training or habituation time, and thus represents a higher or intrinsically more rewarding skill than the ability to manage a team of horses.

It is only in the world of census statistics, and not in terms of direct assessment, that an assembly line worker is presumed to have greater skill than a fisherman or oysterman, the forklift operator greater skill than the gardener or groundskeeper, the machine feeder greater skill than the longshoreman, the parking lot attendant greater skill than the lumberman or raftsman. And with the routinization of machine operation, there is less and less reason to rate the operative above many other classifications of laborers, such as craftsmen's helpers. The entire concept of "semi-skill," as applied to operatives, is an increasingly delusory one. The prefix *semi* means "half" or "partly." When this prefix is attached to the noun *skill*, the resulting compound word leaves the impression of a level of training and ability that lies somewhere—perhaps about halfway—between skill and the total lack of it. But for the category of operatives, training requirements and the demands of the job upon the abilities of the worker are now so low that one can hardly imagine jobs that lie significantly below them on any scale of skill.

Even pick and shovel work takes more learning before it can be done to required standards than many assembly or machine-feeding jobs. "Studies of final assembly line work in a major automobile company by the Technology Project of Yale University found the average time cycle for jobs to be 3 minutes. As to learning time, a few hours to a week sufficed. Learning time for 65 percent of the work force was less than a month."[6] And yet assembly jobs are the most representative type of operative jobs into which there has been so great an influx in the past three-quarters of a century, and which, by a marvel of definition, have produced a striking upgrading of the skills of the working population.*

The imaginary creation of higher categories of skill by nomenclatural exercises does not end with the transformation of most urban labor into "semi-skilled" work. We have yet to consider the phenomenon of the decline of farm laborers. Here the statistical category involved was especially large and the transformation especially illusory. At the turn of the century, 17.7 percent of the working population was classified as "farm laborers and foremen" (almost all of them "laborers," few of them foremen). But here there is not even a hint in the census classification of an attempt to sort workers by skill. For the population employed on farms, the census has no differentiated categories at all, no class of "skilled farmers," or "farming craftsmen." *All* farm labor employed by farm owners is classified in the "farm laborers and foremen" category. The only distinction drawn by the census is a purely proprietary one, between owners on the one side (with a very small group of managers included with owners), and "laborers and foremen" on the other. Among the 17.7 percent of the working population of the United States which, at the time of the 1900 census, was employed by farm proprietors, a great many—perhaps most—were fully qualified farmers who had themselves owned and operated farms and lost them, or who had grown up in farm families and learned the entire broad craft. The farm hired hand was able to be of assistance to the farmer because he was the product of years of farm life and had a mastery of a great many skills involving a knowledge of land, fertilizer, animals, tools, farm machinery, construction skills, etc., and the traditional abilities and dexterities in the handling of farm tasks. Only in this way could he be set to work by the farmer in plowing, milking, caring for animals, mending fence, harvesting, etc. To be sure, there was unquestionably a distribution of skills, and many farmworkers, such as those employed in cotton or fruit picking and other such "plantation"

---

*It must not be imagined that these training times—so short as to mock the very term "training"—are characteristic only of assembly line and other factory work. Charles Silberman, a *Fortune* editor, reports: "A detailed manpower survey by the New York State Department of Labor, for example, revealed that approximately two-thirds of all the jobs in existence in that state involve such simple skills that they can be—and are— learned in a few days, weeks, or at most months of on-the-job training."[7] "Two-thirds of all the jobs in existence" would have to include all operatives, clerical workers, service workers, sales workers on the retail level, laborers—and some portions of other occupational categories as well.

tasks, did not possess the all-around skills of the working farmer. But to disregard, as is now customary, the broad range of abilities required of so many farmworkers and to be deceived by the use of the catch-all designation of "laborer" is to deal not in social science but in promotional labeling. Of all categories of labor, this one has suffered the most complete decimation, having plunged to 1.7 percent by 1970. In the world of the sociologists, this represents a triumphant ascent of an enormous mass of workers to higher levels, since *every* classification of labor is rated by them above farm labor in "skill."

On the other side, the labor classification whose names conceal a woeful lack of skill or training have, like the "semi-skilled," grown rapidly. For example, beginning with the 1950 census another change was introduced into the classification schema. The Alba Edwards system was modified, for that and subsequent censuses, by the introduction of the new category of nonhousehold "service" workers, and again this classification was used to reinterpret the figures of earlier censuses. At one stroke this reclassification significantly reduced the major occupational groups usually included in the so-called blue-collar categories. The new service category was composed of approximately one-fourth of workers who had previously been classified as "semi-skilled," and three-fourths of workers previously classed as "unskilled." Since, by the common consent of social scientists, "service workers" are at least several cuts above "laborers," and since some even think that because they produce "services" instead of working in factories and wearing "blue collars" while producing goods, they should be rated above operatives, another substantial "upgrading" was brought about. There is no need to add here to what is known about the jobs of the mass of service workers as shown in the listing of the occupations in this category, or the relative pay of these workers compared not only to operatives but even to laborers.

We must finally mention the strength drawn by the illusory upgrading of skills from the statistics which show the very rapid growth of clerical and sales occupations. The reflex response which causes governmental and academic social scientists automatically to accord a higher grade of skill, training, prestige, and class position to any form of office work as against any and all forms of manual work is a tradition of long standing in American sociology which few have ventured to challenge. Caplow has pointed out that the "superiority of white-collar work" is "undoubtedly the most important" of the assumptions underlying not only the census scale but a number of other socioeconomic occupational scales used by American sociology.[8] (Those scales which break with this tradition go no further than to put skilled craftsmen on approximately the same level as clerical workers!) The weight of the prejudice which rates all "white-collar" above all "blue-collar" work is such that the growth of the former at the expense of the latter is again taken as evidence of an increase in skill and training for which no real factual backing is required, so self-evident is this conclusion for the conventional wisdom.*

The lengthening of the average period spent in school before entry into the "labor force," which is the other common ground for assuming that a better-educated working population is needed by modern industry and trade, must also be analyzed and separated into its component parts. Time spent in school has been increasing: the median years of school completed by the employed civilian working population rose from 10.6 in 1948 to 12.4 by the end of the 1960s;[10] and this was merely the culmination of a secular trend which had been going on for a century. In this we see first of all the fact that the requirements of literacy and familiarity with the numbers system have become generalized throughout the society. The ability to read, write, and perform simple arithmetical operations is demanded by the urban environment, not just in jobs but also for consumption, for conformity to the rules of society and obedience to the law. Reading and figuring are, apart from all their other meanings, the elementary attributes of a manageable population, which could no more be sold, cajoled, and controlled without them than can symbols be handled by a computer if they lack the elementary characteristics of identity and position. Beyond this need for basic literacy there is also the function of the schools in providing an attempted socialization to city life, which now replaces the socialization through farm, family, community, and church which once took place in a predominantly rural setting. Thus the average length of schooling is generally higher for urban populations, and the shift of a population from farm to city brings with it, almost as an automatic function, an increase in the term of education.

During the past century, moreover, the vastly increased practice of the scientific and technical specialties in production, research, management, administration, medicine, and in education itself have called into being a greatly expanded apparatus of higher education for the provision of professional specialists in all these areas. This, of course, has also had a marked effect upon the average length of school attendance.

These two factors, which tend to define educational requirements from an occupational standpoint, obviously explain some of the increase in mass schooling, but just as clearly they do not explain all of it. A complete picture of the functions and functioning of education in the United States and other capitalist countries would require a thorough historical study of

---

*That self-evident, conventional wisdom can vary with time, place, and social circumstances was strikingly displayed by Jerome Davis in a study he made of the social attitudes of Soviet schoolchildren in the mid-twenties. In rating a list of occupations adapted from one of the common U.S. "prestige" scales, these children reversed the order of rank found in the use of the scale in the United States, putting farmers first and bankers last.[9]

the manner in which the present standards came into being, and how they were related, at each step of their formation, to the social forces of the society at large. But even a sketch of the recent period suffices to show that many causes, most of them bearing no direct relationship to the educational requirements of the job structure, have been at work.

The Depression was responsible for the enactment, late in the 1930s, of legislation restricting the labor-force participation of youths, the object of which was to reduce unemployment by eliminating a segment of the population from the job market. The anticipated consequence of this was the postponement of the school-leaving age. World War II temporarily solved this problem with its immense mobilization of the population for production and service in the armed forces, but as the war drew to an end fears revived that the return of the demobilized soldiers and sailors, together with the cutback of war orders, would renew the Great Depression. Among the measures enacted to ward this off was the veterans' educational subsidy, which, after both World War II and the Korean War, swelled school enrollment, subsidized educational institutions, and contributed further to the prolongation of the average schooling period. Throughout the postwar period the rapid pace of capital accumulation stimulated the demand for specialized managerial and semi-managerial employees and other professionals, and this demand, in the situation of governmental subsidy to education, brought forth, not unexpectedly, so great a supply of college-trained people that by the end of the 1960s it began to manifest itself as an oversupply. The encouragement to an entire generation to train itself for "careers," when all that would be available for at least three-quarters of that generation were working-class jobs requiring minimal education and offering working-class pay, began to backfire.

In the meanwhile, as a result of the generalized secondary education, employers tended to raise their screening requirements for job applicants, not because of educational needs but simply because of the mass availability of high school graduates. Herbert Bienstock, New York regional director of the Bureau of Labor Statistics, described this trend in these words: "The completion of a high school education has become an important requirement for entry into the labor market of today. Employers, finding persons with high school diplomas becoming more available in a period of rising educational attainment, have come to use the diploma as a screening device, often seeking people with higher levels of education even when job content is not necessarily becoming more complex or requiring higher levels of skill. This has been true in many of the rapidly growing job categories in the clerical, sales, and service fields."[11] This spreading policy reinforced the other pressures tending to postpone the school-leaving age by making the "diploma" a ticket of admission to almost any kind of job. It was used in factory as well as office: "Most factory type jobs require only *6th grade competency* in arithmetic, spelling, reading, and writing, and speaking," we are told by the personnel director of the Inorganic Chemicals Division of the Monsanto Chemical Company. "Too often," he continues, "business has used the requirement of a high school diploma or certificate as an easy means of screening out job applicants."[12]

Thus the continuing extension of mass education for the nonprofessional categories of labor increasingly lost its connection with occupational requirements. At the same time, its place in the social and economic structure became ever more firmly guaranteed by functions which have little or nothing to do with either job training or any other strictly educational needs. The postponement of school leaving to an average age of eighteen has become indispensable for keeping unemployment within reasonable bounds. In the interest of working parents (the two-parent-job-holding family having become ever more common during this period), and in the interest of social stability and the orderly management of an increasingly rootless urban population, the schools have developed into immense teen-sitting organizations, their functions having less and less to do with imparting to the young those things that society thinks they must learn. In this situation the content of education deteriorated as its duration lengthened. The knowledge imparted in the course of an elementary education was more or less expanded to fill the prevalent twelve-year educational sojourn, and in a great many cases school systems have difficulty in instilling in twelve years the basic skills of literacy and numbers that, several generations ago, occupied eight. This in turn gave a greater impetus to employers to demand of job applicants a high school diploma, as a guarantee—not always valid—of getting workers who can read.

We cannot neglect the direct economic impact of the enlarged school system. Not only does the postponement of the school-leaving age limit the growth of recognized unemployment, but it also furnishes employment for a considerable mass of teachers, administrators, construction and service workers, etc. Moreover, education has become an immensely profitable area of capital accumulation for the construction industry, for suppliers of all sorts, and for a host of subsidiary enterprises. For all these reasons—which have nothing to do with either education or occupational training—it is difficult to imagine United States society without its immense "educational" structure, and in fact, as has been seen in recent years, the closing of even a single segment of the schools for a period of weeks is enough to create a social crisis in the city in which this happens. The schools, as caretakers of children and young people, are indispensable for family functioning, community stability, and social order in general (although they fulfill even these functions badly). In a word, there is no longer any place for the young in this society other than school. Serving to fill a vacuum, schools have themselves become that vacuum, increasingly emptied of content and reduced to little more than their own form. Just as in the labor process, where the more there is to know the less the worker need know, in the schools the mass of future workers attend the more there is to learn, the less reason there is for teachers to teach and students to learn. In this more than in any other single factor—the purposelessness, futility, and empty forms of the educational system—we have the source of the growing antagonism between the young and their schools which threatens to tear the schools apart.

It follows that the growing recognition among corporate managers and educational researchers that the commonly made connection between education and job content is, for the mass of jobs, a false one, will not necessarily result in a reversal of the educational trend and bring about an earlier school-leaving age. Capitalist society in the United States has little choice but to maintain this educational establishment as a social institution with transcendent functions. Yet the recognition of how little is accomplished in the years of elementary and high school attendance in the way of job preparation, and how little in the way of educational preparation these jobs require, is spreading.

Ivar Berg, for example, in one of the more detailed examinations of this subject carried out in recent years, arrives at the conclusion that educational "achievements" have already "exceeded requirements in most job categories," and that the demand for "better-educated" labor cannot therefore be explained by "technological and related changes attending most jobs."[13] His most startling finding is that investigations show that education may in fact be a *liability* for the employer. His study of productivity, turnover, and absenteeism in a group of textile workers found that "educational achievement was *inversely* related to performance thus conceived."[14] A sample study in the clerical field yielded the same conclusion: "Performance in 125 branch offices of a major New York bank, measured by turnover data and by the number of lost accounts per teller, was inversely associated with the educational achievements of these 500 workers. The branches with the worst performance records were those in which a disproportionately (and significantly) high number of employees were attending educational programs after working hours! There was also evidence that performance was worst in precisely those branches in which, besides the educational achievements being higher, the managers stressed education in consultation with tellers concerning their futures with the bank."[15] Berg was able to report instances in which managers automatically assumed that their most competent workers had more education, when the opposite was true, "as in one company in which managers reported that the better-educated technicians in their employ were the 'best' technicians." The data from this company showed that "the less-educated technicians received higher evaluations from supervisors and had longer service than technicians with higher educational achievements in comparable jobs; the managers, however, assumed that these 'better' employees had completed more years of schooling!"[16] In part, the explanation for this may lie in the finding, also reported by Berg, that "education is more often than not an important factor accounting for dissatisfaction among workers in many occupational categories. . . ."[17]

As one consequence of the recognition by managers of these facts, the emphasis on more years of education has begun to disappear from the hiring policies of many firms. During the period when high school education had not yet become so general as it is now, unemployment tended to settle more heavily among those with less formal schooling. This was of course given enormous publicity during the 1950s and early 1960s, both as evidence for the educational requirements of modern scientific industry and also in the simpleminded hope that giving everyone a high school education would eliminate unemployment. The latter conclusion, of course, rested upon the assumption that unemployment was a consequence of the functional inadequacy of the unemployed in an economy that demanded higher educational attainments. This notion, as Stanley Lebergott pointed out, "misapprehends at least one fundamental characteristic of the unemployed," which is that they "are marginal in the existing state of offer and demand in the labor market. If all workers in the labor force had their education improved, some would still be marginal," but "their marginality would then appear to be associated with some other simple single characteristic."[18]

This is in fact what has happened, although the change has not received the same publicity as the earlier disparity between educational levels of employed and unemployed. A study by the Bureau of Labor Statistics in 1971 reaches this unequivocal conclusion: "In the past, jobholders had more education than did jobseekers—in 1959, for example, the median education of the employed was 12.0 years, while that of the unemployed was only 9.9 years. Since then, the average education of unemployed workers has risen so that by 1971 the difference between the median education of employed and unemployed workers, 12.4 and 12.2 years respectively, is no longer statistically significant."[19] This convergence between the schooling of employed and unemployed has been more rapid for women than for men, so that by the mid-1960s there was no longer any significant difference between the median educational attainments of employed and unemployed women. In the case of men, the difference in the late 1950s was much greater than it was for women, but by the start of the 1970s that gap has also been closed. Thus a chart on educational attainments by sex and employment status begins as a broad fan in 1957, with unemployed men averaging below 9 years of school, unemployed women 10½ years, employed men above 11 years, and employed women just above 11 years. By the date of the above-cited study, March 1971, the fan had closed completely and all were bunched together in the same narrow range between 12 and 12½ years: men and women, employed and unemployed.

For the worker, the concept of skill is traditionally bound up with craft mastery—that is to say, the combination of knowledge of materials and processes with the practice of manual dexterities required to carry on a specific branch of production. The breakup of craft skills and the reconstruction of production as a collective or social process have destroyed the traditional concept of skill and opened up only one way for mastery over labor processes to develop: in and through scientific, technical, and engineering knowledge. But the extreme concentration of this knowledge in the hands of management and its closely associated staff organizations has closed this avenue to the working population. What is left to workers is a reinterpreted and woefully inadequate concept of skill: a specific dexterity, a limited and repetitious operation, "speed as skill," etc.° With the development of the capitalist mode of production, the very concept of skill becomes degraded along with the degradation of labor and the yardstick by which it is measured shrinks to such a point that today the worker is considered to possess a "skill" if his or her job requires a few days' or weeks' training, several months of training is regarded as unusually demanding, and the job that calls for a learning period of six months or a year—such as computer programming—inspired a paroxysm of awe. (We may compare this with the traditional craft apprenticeship which rarely lasted less than four years and which was not uncommonly seven years long.)

In the early 1920s, Georges Sorel wrote that "the modern factory is a field of experiment constantly enlisting the worker in scientific research," and Albert Thierry said in the same vein: "Our entire civilization is a system of physics, the simplest worker is a physicist."[21] Georges Friedmann quoted these two remarks with his customary ambiguity, not knowing whether to applaud them for their optimism or deprecate them as pious but unfounded hopes. The past half-century has removed all doubt, if there ever was any, about the falsity of these views.

° "With reference to Marshall and Smith on the subject of 'dexterity,' " says M. C. Kennedy in his unpublished Ph.D. dissertation on the division of labor, "one thing should be made clear. Both men confuse increased dexterity with skill or talent. When a cabinet maker is skilled in his craft, skill covers his ability to imagine how things would appear in final form if such and such tools and materials were used. When he can estimate accurately both aesthetic appeal and functional utility, organize his tools, his power and his materials in a way which accomplishes his task and gives him livelihood and recognition—then, we are speaking of his skill. But if the man should be able rapidly and with facility to do nothing but snap his fingers over and over again for livelihood, then we would be speaking of dexterity. It is the latter that Marshall calls skill. Yet, in large industry today, increased dexterity means decreased skill."[20]

REFERENCES

1. Harry Jerome, *Mechanization in Industry* (New York, 1934), p. 402.
2. Omar Pancoast, Jr., *Occupational Mobility* (New York, 1941), p. 14.
3. For 1900, see David L. Kaplan and M. Claire Casey, *Occupational Trends in the United States: 1900 to 1950*, Bureau of the Census Working Paper No. 5 (Washington, 1958), Table 2. For 1970, see U.S. Bureau of the Census, *Census of Population: 1970, Final Report PC(2)-7A* (Washington, D.C., 1973), Table 1.
4. S. R. Parker, "Industry and Education," in S. R. Parker, R. K. Brown, J. Child, and M. A. Smith, *The Sociology of Industry* (rev. ed.; London, 1972), p. 36.
5. Theodore Caplow, *The Sociology of Work* (Minneapolis, 1954), Chapter 2, esp. pp. 31–36; Joseph A. Kahl, *The American Class Structure* (New York, 1957), pp. 64–65; J. E. Morton, *On the Evolution of Manpower Statistics* (Kalamazoo, Mich., 1969), p. 46.
6. Charles R. Walker, "Changing Character of Human Work Under the Impact of Technological Change," in National Commission on Technology, Automation, and Economic Progress, *The Employment Impact of Technological Change*, Appendix Volume II, *Technology and the American Economy* (Washington, D.C., 1966), p. 299.
7. Charles Silberman, *The Myths of Automation* (New York, 1966), p. 52.
8. Caplow, *The Sociology of Work*, pp. 42–43.
9. Jerome Davis, "Testing the Social Attitudes of Children in the Government Schools in Russia," *American Journal of Sociology* (May 1927); cited in ibid., p. 40.
10. *Manpower Report of the President* (Washington, 1972), p. 207.
11. *Collective Bargaining Today*, Proceedings of the Collective Bargaining Forum (1969), p. 334.
12. K. B. Bernhardt, speaking to the Community Relations Division (Justice Department) Conference on Job Opportunities for Minorities, Chicago, June 1967; quoted in R. A. Nixon, *The Labor Market Framework of Job Development: Some Problems and Prospects* (New York, 1967), p. 41.
13. Ivar Berg, *Education and Jobs: The Great Training Robbery* (Boston, 1971), pp. 14–15.
14. Ibid., p. 87.
15. Ibid., pp. 93–94.
16. Ibid., pp. 16–17.
17. Ibid., p. 17.
18. Stanley Lebergott, *Men Without Work: The Economics of Unemployment* (Englewood Cliffs, N.J., 1964), p. 11.
19. William V. Deutermann, "Educational Attainment of Workers, March 1971," *Monthly Labor Review* (November 1971), p. 31.
20. M. C. Kennedy, *The Division of Labor and the Culture of Capitalism: A Critique* (Ann Arbor, Mich., 1968), p. 172n.
21. Georges Sorel, *Les illusions du progrès* (Paris, 1921), p. 282; Albert Thierry, *Réflexions sur l'education* (Paris, 1923), pp. 99–100; quoted by Friedmann in *Industrial Society* (Glencoe, Ill., 1955), p. 240.

24

BRAVE NEW WORKPLACE

Robert Howard

In December 1979, some 500 local union officials and staff members of the Communications Workers of America (CWA) met in Dearborn, Michigan, to hold the first conference on workplace technology ever sponsored by an American labor union. Not far from the former home of Henry Ford, patron saint of the assembly line, conference participants examined a very different kind of workplace, one shaped by the widespread computerization of work in the telecommunications industry.

The terminology they used was new, but the experiences that telephone workers described would have been familiar to the early mechanics and craftsmen in the American automobile industry: traditional skills made obsolete by new technology; jobs fragmented and downgraded to lower pay; work reorganized and rigidly centralized; workers subject to automatic pacing and monitoring, oversupervision, and job-induced psychological stress. Like the shift from craft to mass production in the auto industry, new technology in telecommunications has eroded workers' sense of control over their work lives. "Members feel that they have lost the challenge of the job, the authority to make decisions," said a local union president at the conference. "Also, they have lost their sense of accomplishment, freedom, and overall prestige."

The CWA technology conference reflects growing concern in the labor movement about the implications of new workplace technology. "The widespread application of computers, silicon chips, and industrial robots, and the speed with which these and similar technological advances are being developed, portend vast changes in all segments of the workplace," writes Dennis Chamot of the AFL-CIO's Professional Employees Department. "In essence, our society is involved in a rapid and massive redesign of work."

For industry and government, this redesign promises to boost lagging productivity and stimulate the revitalization of American industry. Robert Noyce, of the Intel Corporation, calls high technology sectors like telecommunications, computers, and semiconductors the "jewels of American innovation." They are to play the same role in the American economy of the future that the automobile industry and its assembly lines

Reprinted with permission from *Working Papers for a New Society*, November/December 1980. © The Trusteeship Institute, 1980.

played in the past. The only obstacle to this scenario—"the potential fly in the ointment," according to *Business Week* magazine—is opposition from organized labor.

Whatever the fears of the business community, most unions have addressed the technology issue in the narrowest of terms—whether technology will reduce jobs. What the CWA conference suggests, however, is that the new technology also threatens to radically transform those jobs that remain. In fact, like the assembly line before it, the computerization of work is ushering in a whole new economic era, one that will disrupt past customs and compromises established over decades of labor relations—to challenge labor's hard-won gains of the past fifty years.

To consider new technology, therefore, is to consider not only jobs, but power. "If labor does not find a way to control technology," writes Harley Shaiken, a technology consultant to the United Auto Workers, "then management will use technology to control labor." This struggle for control of workplace technology promises to be one of the most important arenas of conflict between corporations and unions in the decades ahead. And no industry offers a clearer example of what is at stake for American workers than that jewel of American innovation, the telecommunications industry.

Technological change is certainly no stranger to telecommunications. But the current wave of new technology is revolutionizing both the character of telephone service and the economic structure of the industry itself. Rapid advances in computer technology during the past ten to twenty years are blurring the boundaries between heretofore distinct industries. Telecommunications, data processing, and business machines are all beginning to merge into an undifferentiated mass of information processing services and equipment, supplied interchangeably by telephone or computer firms. And under the impact of this change, the commercial structure of telecommunications is being transformed.

In 1968, the Federal Communications Commission inaugurated the long range deregulation of key sectors in the telephone industry. The FCC's "Carter-fone" decision gave outside firms the right to manufacture and supply telecommunications equipment for connection to Bell System lines, and to provide "specialized communications services" to businesses. Over the last ten years, a score of corporations including IBM, TRW, MCI, and Rockwell International have entered the so-called "interconnect" market, which in 1979 totalled $730 million. Last April, the deregulation pendulum swung in Bell's direction. The FCC's "Computer Inquiry Two" opened the lucrative "enhanced services" market—computer and data transmission equipment at each end of the telephone line—to AT&T. The corporation recently announced what the *New York Times* termed "the most sweeping reorganization in its 103-year history," establishing an independent subsidiary as required by the FCC ruling in order to compete in the unregulated computer business.

In effect, telecommunications is rapidly turning into data communications. "What is at hand," according to *Bell Telephone Magazine*, in-house publication of AT&T, is nothing less than "the realization, at long last, of something that has been imagined for decades, if not centuries: The Information Society. And telecommunications will form much of the technical basis of that 'age of the mind.' " What the new age will also bring is a competitive battle of corporate giants with AT&T and IBM taking the lead in a fight for mastery of what has been estimated as a $400 billion integrated information industry.

The effects of such a struggle on work are predictable. AT&T has redoubled its efforts to reduce labor costs, increase productivity, and tighten its control over the Bell System workforce. The computerization of work makes these goals easier to achieve. A memorandum from an AT&T vice-president to Bell System managers describing a new computer system called MLT gives a taste of prevailing corporate policy. "A word of caution," the executive warned. "The savings available from MLT implementation will only occur if you plan for them to occur and then actually get the people off the payroll. Too often, we are intrigued with the capabilities of new mechanized systems and forget the real reasons for their existence. . . ."

According to AT&T, the changes in telecommunications will *not* reduce the total number of Bell System jobs. Overall employment is expected to grow during the next decade much as it has over the last twenty years, when the rapid expansion of telephone business more than made up for the 100,000 operators' jobs lost to new technology. But unlike earlier technological changes, the widespread computerization of work will entirely transform the occupational structure of the Bell System—with serious implications for the Communications Workers' union.

"Because of the growing need for 'knowledge' workers and the lessening need for 'tool' workers," says *Bell Telephone Magazine*, most of the growth in employment will be confined to the ranks of management. Bell's 260,000 managers could expand by as much as one-third—a rate of increase three times that estimated for nonmanagement personnel. Not surprisingly, the majority of these new jobs will be in two areas: mid-level management categories associated with the increasing computerization of work—electronic data processors, data systems designers, "the people who draw on the skills of the computer, who define and set up mechanized systems," in the words of one AT&T official—and sales and marketing personnel as AT&T gears up for the new era of competition ahead.

The few new nonmanagement jobs (Bell's nonmanagement workforce of 780,000 is expected to grow by one-tenth) will be limited to unskilled, primarily clerical, work. And this growth in unskilled jobs will be matched by a precipitous decline in the skilled crafts. From 1974 to 1978, craft employment dropped by almost 22,000 jobs, a trend that is certain to continue.

These developments prefigure a serious weakening of the CWA's power base. Unlike computers or semiconductors, telecommunications is the one high technology industry with a unionized workforce. The skilled crafts have traditionally been the backbone of the union's bargaining power. But current trends in industry employment not only shift most of the new jobs out of the union's bargaining unit; they effectively cut off unionized workers from the considerable new skills that computerization of work brings in its wake.

"Certainly, technological wonders . . . may exact some cost in human attitudes," says *Bell Telephone Magazine*: "the way employees feel about themselves, their work and their business." But, "the key to helping human and machine get along in the 1980s would seem to be to get them to know each other." This peculiar version of computer dating is already well under way in the plants and offices of the Bell System. Though they never use it themselves, the phrase that best describes what telephone workers express is Harry Braverman's "the degradation of work." What follows, then, is a close look at what workers in one industry have come to know about the new technology. It is a tour of the degradation of work in the Information Society.

The din of a cross-bar switching system sounds like a roomful of teletype machines amplified over a loudspeaker. Thousands of metal switches, stacked in long library-like rows, click and clatter in irregular rhythms as they make and unmake the connections that route telephone signals from one phone to another. When traffic is heavy, the noise is intense, a mad chorus of chattering metal. You have to raise your voice to be heard.

In contrast, the only sound produced by the new electronic switching system (ESS) is a faint, hypnotic hum. As its name implies, ESS transfers calls electronically. It has no moving parts, it operates by stored-program computer control. ESS can handle 550,000 calls in an hour, four times the amount of its electromechanical predecessor. The "1A" central processor, the most advanced computer brain of the electronic switching system, can direct traffic, silently and efficiently, at the rate of 150 calls per second.

For about fifty years, electromechanical cross-bar switching has been the work-horse of the American telephone system. But since ESS was first introduced in 1965, it has grown to serve over 30 percent of the telephone central offices in the nation. By 1985, 50 percent of central offices will carry electronic switching. By the year 2000, the din of the cross-bar will be heard no more.

Electronic switching systems are at the heart of the current wave of technological change in telecommunications. According to the final report of the CWA technology conference, "the impact of the introduction of ESS has apparently affected employees in all job categories. . . ." But the job that has borne the weight of this change is that of the switching technician.

Switching technicians are responsible for the maintenance of central office equipment. They locate malfunctions, figure out what is wrong, and make the necessary repairs or direct other craft personnel to do so. Traditionally, the job has required a high degree of skill, and switchmen have enjoyed substantial autonomy. In a typical central office, there might be anywhere from twenty to thirty switching technicians and other skilled craft workers under the direction of a single foreman who rarely interferes in their work

Electronic switching, however, radically changes this work environment. First, ESS cuts down on the need for switching technicians in some fairly simple and obvious ways. For example, the system monitors its own performance and diagnoses circuitry problems by itself; computers do much of the analysis and trouble-shooting that technicians used to do. Also, the system has no moving parts, thus eliminating the need for mechanical repair skills. Technicians simply replace one malfunctioning circuit-pack with another. The installation of ESS in the typical central office would probably cut the workforce in half.

But the effects of ESS on switchmen do not stop there. Despite all the rhetoric about computers enabling decentralization, the Bell System has used computer control of the switching process to centralize the monitoring and repair functions of the switching technician. "Automatic Switching Control Centers" now observe a number of central offices at once by remote telemetry. With the Control Center, the number of technicians at the central switching office itself can be reduced to one or two; some switching offices have none at all.

It is this move to the Control Center that has made the most difference in the way the switching technician does his job. Centralization replaces the autonomy of the central office with rows of video display terminals (VDTs) where anywhere from forty to sixty technicians keep watch on the system's performance. The foreman of the central office gives way to an extended management team. Dave Newman, a switchman in New York City, describes the Control Center as "a large room like a mass-production office, a clerical type of thing. Right away, that's culture shock, especially for the guys. You are just about literally chained to a desk."

Centralization also fragments the switching technician's job into isolated segments. For example, one traditional task of the switchman has been to identify and repair malfunctioning trunk lines. In the central switching office, a trunk line "trouble report" would arrive on a teletype; the technician would locate the trunk and put it out of service. Later, when he had the time to analyze the problem and devise a way to repair it, he would return.

Now that trunk line trouble reports are fed into the Control Center, however, they can all be assigned to two or three technicians. They spend their day in front of their VDT screens keying messages to the computer to put faulty trunks on busy. They do not fix the malfunctioning lines themselves; other technicians are sent out from the Control Center to do the necessary repairs on site.

"People *hate* the Control Center," says Ilene Winkler, shop steward at the mid-town Manhattan Control Center. "No one wants to work there. You sit there like an idiot in front of your terminal. We can't even figure out what our jobs are supposed to be anymore." According to Winkler and other technicians, the most momentous change associated with the shift from central office to Control Center is the enormous expansion of management supervision. Not only are there a lot more managers at the Control Center than at the old central office; increased supervision also means tighter control over the assignment and direction of work. Gone is the rarely interfering foreman.

Expanding management control of work has even been designed into the computer itself. By a new procedure known as "pricing and loading," clerks type each switching technician's schedule for the day into the computer. The schedule lists a series of jobs along with the estimated amount of time each should take. Technicians receive their assignments by accessing the computer at their own VDT. As each assigned task is completed, they also enter the amount of time it took into the computer. Pricing and loading takes away the last remnants of autonomy from a job that, according to Ilene Winkler, "just a few years ago was totally craft-controlled."

In theory, there is nothing inherent in the new technology of electronic switching that requires the systematic deterioration of the switching technician's job. True, ESS has made certain electromechanical repair skills obsolete, but it demands far more complicated technical skills and educational training—for example, knowledge of electronics-based systems and programming concepts. The problem is that access to these skills is restricted to Bell System management.

First, new maintenance tasks associated with electronic switching—the editing of computer programs, for example—are the sole responsibility of management engineers. According to Ilene Winkler, serious breakdowns at the mid-town Manhattan Control Center—what are known as "central processing troubles"—are immediately "escalated" up to management (unless they happen in the middle of the night; then, technicians are allowed to work on them). "There is no opportunity to learn on the technology," adds Dave Newman. "They don't train you to do that. They don't want you to do that."

Management also expands its own control at the expense of craft workers by a procedure best described as "phony upgrading." As switching control functions have been computerized, tasks that used to belong to technicians have been redefined as management responsibility. The steady encroachment of management on switching technicians' work has led to an ongoing conflict between union and company over who has the right to operate certain computer systems.

One such conflict that the union won involved the "Computerized Maintenance Administrative System." COMAS stores information on past malfunctions in switching equipment and is used by technicians as a handy reference system to help identify the sources and causes of new problems. By comparing present difficulties with past performance, the job of tracking down breakdowns is simplified. Before COMAS, foremen were never directly involved in the work of tracing and repairing switching equipment malfunctions. But when the system was introduced in 1971, management personnel began using it to do what had always been the work of switching technicians.

The union fought management operation of COMAS through the grievance procedure, claiming it was an unwarranted intrusion into the work of the switching technician. The arbitrator agreed. But the struggle for control of COMAS and other computerized data systems continues. It is a common policy among Bell operating companies to systematically force questions of access to each new workplace computer system into arbitration.

In effect, the job of the switching technician is being split in two. The most interesting and skilled tasks are disappearing into management, leaving behind tasks shorn of skill and reduced to clerical work. This division is occurring throughout the "dual labor market": on one side of the divide, highly skilled work controlled by non-union management personnel; on the other, degraded computerized work relegated to the unionized workers of the CWA bargaining unit.

The skilled crafts are bearing the brunt of the degradation of work made possible by new technology in telecommunications, but no job category is immune. Clerical workers have been deeply affected by the dozen new computer-based administration systems introduced in the past decade. In one sense, computerization has made clerical work easier. Customer records are now at the tip of one's fingers instead of buried in mammoth files. But, as in the case of the switching technician, computerization also brings centralization and a thorough reorganization of work that isolates clerical workers and subjects them to more rigid supervision and control.

THE UAW AND NEW TECHNOLOGY

The American union that has gone farthest in attempting to protect its members from the negative impacts of new technology is the United Auto Workers. During automobile industry negotiations last year, the UAW's Ford department put the most comprehensive list of technology demands to date on the bargaining table. Besides traditional provisions for advance notice and new training programs, the UAW Ford plan included:

• full union access to all information created by any computerized system;
• company assurances that computers would not be used to monitor, time study, or discipline workers;
• creation of a "data committeeman" position in each union local to monitor the projected introduction of new systems and determine their potential impact on workers;
• establishment of new technology committees at both the local and company-wide levels;
• the right to strike, upon approval of the UAW Ford department, over technology conflicts that cannot be resolved by the company-wide joint committee.

In the face of company opposition, and in the absence of rank-and-file mobilization, the union had to back down from the most ambitious of these demands. Nevertheless, it won the establishment of a National Committee on Technological Progress, programs to train workers in computer-controlled machinery, and an assurance from Ford that the corporation "fully respects the integrity of the contract unit" and would not use new technology to take work away from unionized employees.

Similar technology committees have been set up at GM and at Chrysler's salaried departments, and last year's contract gains have already made local-level technology agreements easier to reach. UAW tradesmen at the GM Technical Center in Warren, Michigan, now load computer programs, and operate, service, and maintain terminals. Workers at GM's Guide Lamp plant in Anderson, Indiana, have won the right to install, maintain, and program industrial robots used in spray painting. And skilled electricians at GM's New Departure-Hyatt Bearing plant in Sandusky, Ohio, are now "reprogramming" computer chips—erasing the old programs and burning in new ones—while other skilled workers at Sandusky are programming numerically controlled metal-cutting machines. All these jobs were previously done by nonbargaining unit personnel.

So far, most of the concern about new technology—and most of the benefits resulting from the new contract—have been limited to UAW skilled tradesmen. But the hope is that, as new technology spreads, workers at all levels will come to see what it will take to meet the challenge. "Employers like Ford tell you only what they want you to know about a new piece of technology," says Rene Jacques, a UAW lab technician at a Ford testing facility in Windsor, Ontario. "Since the companies won't tell us, we've got to become computer-wise ourselves—and I mean from the bottom to the top of the union."

LMOS stands for "Line Maintenance Operating System"; it is, essentially, a computerized file. When a repair service attendant answers a 611 customer report of malfunctioning equipment, she types the customer's phone number into the computer and receives on her VDT screen a complete record of past problems, known as the "line card." The clerk adds the information provided by the customer to the line card and gives the customer a "commitment time" provided by the computer indicating when a repair crew will visit the customer's home. Then she transfers the line card, complaint, and commitment time to the repair garage via computer print-out.

Michelle Brooking is a shop steward for repair service attendants in Washington, D.C. She says LMOS may soumd efficient but isn't. "It's easier in getting information, but as far as getting your phone fixed, it takes a lot longer now than it ever did before." Before LMOS, repair service attendants worked in local repair bureaus linked to the central offices. They were in frequent telephone contact with repair and installation crews. Often, they would relay messages between the customers and the crews—changes in commitment time, last minute repair jobs, etc. "You knew how many men you had on the street," says Brooking, "how many troubles you could handle." With LMOS, all the attendants are in centralized bureaus. Their only contact with the repair crews is one way, via the computer. They do not know if the crew actually makes it to the customer's house at the appointed time (though, often, they have to listen to the customer's complaints if it does not). "Now, you're doing it blindly," says Brooking. "You're not able to give it the little personal touch you did before."

Michelle Brooking thinks it would have made more sense to have installed LMOS directly into the local repair centers. That way, clerks would have the convenience and efficiency of computerization along with the flexibility of the local work unit. But to use the new computer technology in this fashion would not accomplish the goals the Bell System management has set for it. Thus, computerization is used to facilitate the close supervision of work but at the price of fragmentation, less efficient service, and more customer inconvenience. Telephone workers are aware of the deterioration of service that has, ironically, accompanied the vast reorganization of work inspired by the new technology. Often, it seems illogical to them. But the logic behind these changes is found elsewhere—in management's effort to perfect its control of the labor process.

The computerized control of work has become so pervasive in Bell's clerical sector that management now has the capacity to measure how many times a phone rings before it is answered, how long a customer is put on hold, how long it takes a clerk to complete a call. Charles Sangmeister, district representative of the CWA in Washington, D.C., claims that management has the technical ability to maintain a complete print-out of a clerical worker's output for the day. "They haven't done it yet," he says, "but I can see that this is the next step coming down the road."

In some Bell operating companies, it is here already. FADS (for "Force Administration Data System") is a computer system which, by measuring the pattern of traffic into a particular office each day, can anticipate employment needs for the next. Each morning, workers receive computer print-outs listing their break and lunch times based on the anticipated traffic pattern for the day.

The FADS procedure has been in existence for a long time, but recently it has been computerized. Like other administrative systems, computer control squeezes out what little flexibility workers had before. Before computerization, a worker's morning break normally came about two hours after the beginning of the shift; now, it can come as early as fifteen minutes into the work day. Workers cannot go to the bathroom unless they find someone to take their place. "If you close your terminal," says Jean Miller, a service representative in Washington, "right away the computer starts clacking away and starts ringing a bell." In some offices, where FADS has been computerized, the computer even gives the supervisor a print-out of how many calls each clerk takes per day and how many times she leaves her position. One repair service attendant calls it "being put on the hot seat."

Oversupervision in the telephone company is, of course, nothing new. But just as computerization can build skills into the technology, it can build in supervision as well. "The computer watches you for the supervisor," says Jean Miller. "It is constantly alert to the atmosphere of the office. It's the same idea they've been using in Traffic for years."

The L'Enfant TSPS office is one of three long distance operator offices in Washington, D.C. TSPS stands for "Traffic Service Position System," the computerized successor to the phone company's old "cord-board." The L'Enfant office is about the size of a gradeschool classroom with the atmosphere to match. Magic marker posters with hortatory slogans adorn the walls; the supervisors' desks at the front of the room face about fifty battleship gray TSPS terminals lined up in rows of two.

Operators do not have their own work stations; instead they simply plug their head-sets (kept in lockers in an adjoining room) into any available position at the start of the work day. On the TSPS console, there are rows of square buttons that operators push to connect collect or credit card calls or to calculate time and charges. A small screen on the top of the console gives a digital read-out of this information much like the computerized cash register in a grocery store.

Gloria Newsome, one of seven group supervisors at L'Enfant, demonstrates the TSPS. Calls "drop in" to the console with an electronic beep. Gloria answers them in her professional, slightly sing-song, Bell System voice. Her fingers flash over the console pushing a bewildering array of buttons. In a matter of seconds, the call is completed only to be followed by another beep and another call. The longest time between two calls is about five seconds. Gloria admits that the job can get rough sometimes, "but it also can be very rewarding, if you like to talk with people."

Working a TSPS terminal is easier than the old cord-board. Pushing buttons is faster and less physically demanding than manipulating the plugs of the traditional switchboard. The TSPS also times calls and makes certain computations that previously operators had to do themselves. Not surprisingly, TSPS has sent productivity soaring. Whereas an operator could handle about twenty calls per hour on the old switchboard, now she can average around one hundred.

This does not mean that operators have more control over their work; in fact, they have considerably less. With the cord-board, operators could regulate somewhat the pace at which they responded to calls. And when all the positions on an operator's terminal were occupied, she was free to wait until one opened again. With TSPS, calls drop in one after another, routed by an "automatic call distributor," the moment one's line is free. And ESS means an operator can handle an unending succession of calls. There is no such thing as a full terminal.

Each TSPS office has a "call-waiting box" which indicates any calls that are waiting to be routed to an individual terminal. If a call is kept waiting for more than ten seconds—what is known as a "high answer"—a light on the box begins flashing. Supervisors can also determine from the call-waiting box whether any of the terminals in the office have been disconnected or put on busy. TSPS groups are evaluated on the number of high answers they have per day.

One of the slogans in neat magic marker attached to the wall of the L'Enfant office reads: "There will be *no* talking until we achieve our 98 Index." A 98 Index is the "outstanding" rating in the Bell System evaluation procedure for TSPS performance. Operators are monitored for courtesy, accuracy, and performance—thus, the evaluation program's acronym, "CAP."

For half an hour, two times each week, every operator is timed by computer to determine her "average working time" or AWT. According to Gloria Newsome, the AWT at L'Enfant is 37 seconds per call, but in some offices it is as low as 30. Operators are also evaluated on their "speed of answer." After the electronic beep, they have three seconds to respond to a call. While most operators admit that working the TSPS is easier and more efficient than the cord-board, many still complain that the pace of their work has increased. "You'd think you were at the Indianapolis Speedway," says a Washington operator. "If you don't keep your AWT down, they start riding you." Willy Leggett, shop steward at CWA Local 2300, the operators' local in Washington, considers AWT a quota to force down the average time spent on calls. When an operator consistently beats the office average, other members of the group are pushed to match her time.

In addition to the twice weekly AWT productivity studies, each operator is monitored by a supervisor for thirty calls per month to evaluate courtesy and accuracy, the other two elements of the CAP program. These tests are called "official evaluatives" or "remote performance observations." Like the AWT studies, operators do not know when they are being observed. "Faults" and "irregularities" are recorded and figured into the individual's Index.

There are still other observations that an operator does know about— "diagnostics," "parallels" (so called because the supervisor sits directly next to the operator), or "performance improvements." There is no limit to the number an operator may receive. Officially, these tests are for training purposes only, but according to Willy Leggett, they are used in employee evaluations. Gloria Newsome confirms this: "If I hear one of my girls doing something she shouldn't do, she *will* be disciplined." In the recent contract signed between the CWA and AT&T last August, language was included expressly forbidding the use of diagnostics for disciplinary purposes. But Willy Leggett claims that it is virtually impossible to prove whether a fault occurred during a diagnostic or an official evaluation.

AWT studies, official evaluatives, and diagnostics are not the only observation that TSPS operators are subject to. There are entirely separate offices which listen in on TSPS groups. evaluate their work, and inform their supervisors. When Elinor Langer wrote about her experiences working at the New York Telephone Company ten years ago, she described similar layers of supervision. "One result of the constant observation (the technology being unbounded)," Langer wrote, "is that one can never be certain where the observation stops. It is company policy to stress its finite character, but no one ever knows for sure." The computerization of work has intensified this sense of powerlessness and spread it throughout the telecommunications workforce.

The "rapid and massive redesign of work" that the AFL-CIO's Dennis Chamot describes also threatens the institutional power of American unions. It is not only that the computerization of work undermines union wages, thins the ranks of union membership, attacks the integrity of the bargaining unit, and provides the techniques for the creation of a strike-proof workplace. By feeding workers' sense of their inability to shape their work lives, new technology is a potent weapon of division and de-mobilization.

Unfortunately, there is little in the history of the American labor movement to help unions meet this challenge. While union resistance to new technology has always been well-publicized, it has been the rare, and universally unsuccessful, practice of only a few craft unions. For a few years in the mid-sixties, Local 6 of the International Typographers Union won veto power over new automation at New York City newspapers. But the agreement only hurried the slide into bankruptcy of a number of already financially ailing papers and the elimination of typographers' jobs. ". . . A strong and effective union stance in some plants," writes sociologist Andrew Zimbalist, "resulted in failure for New York City typographers as a whole."

In contrast, most American unions have unhesitatingly ceded to management the right to develop and use technology as it sees fit—usually in exchange for generous productivity wage gains, job security provisions, and buy-out clauses. The classic example is the "mechanization and modernization" agreements of the International Longshoremen's Union in the 1960s. In effect, longshoremen gave up their considerable control over working conditions for a $25 million fund providing for early retirement, no lay-offs, and a guaranteed minimum work week. But the plan only protected the most senior workers at the expense of the rest. And like most American union technology agreements, it came "after the fact" when any attempt to influence the actual direction of change was too late. "When it comes to technological change," Harley Shaiken says of America's labor movement, "there has been no more cooperative sector in society."

The new wave of computer-based innovation has inspired some criticism of the defensive practices of the past. Some unionists have begun to call for a more offensive labor strategy, one that would confront the implications of new technology *before* it becomes a fait accompli on the shop floor. This demand for some kind of union influence over technological change is often expressed in the language of "workers' control"; it could be the starting point for the redefinition of labor's approach to new technology. For the present, however, the call for worker control of technology does not so much provide a solution as define an immense problem. The gap between ideas and practical blueprints for union action is extremely wide.

The Communications Workers' union provides a striking example of the dilemmas surrounding the technology issue. Like most unions, the CWA has historically supported management-directed technological change as long as the fruits of increased productivity have been shared with its members. When new technology displaced workers—as it has over 100,000 operators since World War II—the union has negotiated a variety of programs to cushion the blow: attrition plans, transfers, termination payments. This primary emphasis on job security has continued into the present. In the new Bell System contract signed last August, the union won an expanded early retirement plan and a guarantee that workers with fifteen years seniority or more would be exempt from technological downgrading.

However, the widespread effects of computerization have elicited a call from within the union for "reshaping and rethinking" its response to technological change. Union leaders, often under the pressure of the rank-and-file, have begun to perceive the connections between technology issues and deteriorating working conditions like over-supervision and job pressures. There is much talk about "worker participation," "quality of work life," a shortened work week, and more extensive training programs. "Those kinds of things can't be solved in the traditional union sense," says Patsy Fryman, an assistant to CWA president Glenn Watts. "We ought to be willing to experiment, to try some innovative things." The most recent Bell System contract is full of first steps in this direction—six months advance notice of all technological changes, a joint management-labor technology committee to examine the implications of new technology, an industry-wide quality of work life committee, and most important, a special joint committee to establish the criteria for a comprehensive redefinition of industry job categories.

One central feature of the new direction in union thinking is the idea of "comparable worth." It is an attempt to redefine the standards by which wages are set. "Technology potentially simplifies jobs," reads the pre-negotiation resolution of the CWA Bell System Bargaining Council. "Yet at the very same time, it complicates and adds greater responsibilities to some employees' positions." According to comparable worth, workers should be paid not so much for the skills they possess as for the responsibility their jobs entail. The clerical employee who operates a computer that does the job a skilled craftsman used to do may not have the skills or training of the craftsman; nevertheless, he or she has inherited the respon-sibility. Likewise the worker who uses new technology to do the same amount of work as three workers did before. In both cases, the job is worth more to the company and the wages of the workers should reflect that increase in worth.

Comparable worth can prevent the use of technology to downgrade jobs. Under a wage system based on comparable worth, skills may be-come obsolete, jobs may even disappear, but the wages of the workers who remain behind will reflect their corresponding increase in responsi-bility for operating technology-intensive equipment. In a modified ver-sion of this principle, the union won a wage raise in the last contract for the clerical workers who operate the new MLT computer system. De-signed to "get the people off the payroll," MLT has caused major reduc-tions in the skilled category of test-desk technician. But the new contract gives the MLT operator a wage rate that is 80 percent of the test-desk technician's pay.

New ideas like comparable worth or the other technology provisions in the Bell System contract are a first step. But they do not move very far beyond the constraints of traditional defensive protectionism. While they may protect workers' wages, they are incapable of addressing the more intractable problems of the deterioration of skill and the expansion of management control over work. For this reason, Harley Shaiken describes the CWA technology policy as "essentially, to manage an orderly retreat."

Some CWA members have also criticized what one worker calls the union's "band-aid approach" to technology issues. "The bottom line for the union is pay and a job," says Dave Newman. "That's changing. That has to change." Newman and a small group of New York Telephone em-ployees publish an independent newsletter for telephone workers called *The Bell Wringer*. They have urged a more aggressive stance that would protect the job responsibilities of the skilled crafts. "It should be a basic trade union principle," writes Newman in *The Bell Wringer*, "that no matter how the technology of a job changes, the job title and pay rate remain the same (if not get better!). . . . The introduction of new technol-ogy cannot be stopped, but it does not have to lead to boring, routinized, less-skilled and low-paying jobs."

The difficulty of protecting skills, however, can be seen in the case of the MLT computer system, the most important struggle to date over new technology in telecommunications and one that the union lost. First intro-duced in 1976, the MLT system automatically runs tests on certain tele-phone equipment—tests previously performed by the highly skilled test-desk technician. Management assigned the operation of MLT to a clerical category in order to reduce the labor costs of equipment maintenance. In New York City, CWA Local 1101 disputed this assignment through the industry's grievance procedure.

The union argued that the computer is a tool, just like any other. MLT might be faster and more efficient but it is essentially no different from the meters used by the test-desk technician in his work. Therefore, to assign to a clerk a job traditionally done by a skilled worker was to violate the integrity of industrial occupational categories.

The arbitrator disagreed. Siding with the company, he found that computerization transfers the skill from the worker to the machine. While the output of the two jobs "is generally similar," there is "no basic skill parity." Moreover, even if what the union claimed were true, said the arbitrator, the union contract gave management an "absolute right" to assign work to whomever it chose.

The lesson of the MLT case is that to confront the problem of skill, a union must go far beyond protecting traditional occupational categories. Even if the test-desk technician won the right to operate the MLT as Local 1101 had argued (or even if the new MLT operator won 100 percent parity with the test-desk technician's pay, which amounts to the same thing), the problem of deskilling remains. For the idea of protecting workers' skills to have any meaning, it must include the demand for workers' access to new skills. But before unions will be able to do this, they will have to take a giant step: to directly challenge traditional management prerogatives to exclusive control of both technology and the organization of work itself.

At this point, control of workplace technology becomes a political issue. New ideas, experiments in workers' participation, joint management-labor committees will be meaningless unless they are linked to the mobilization of a broad cross-section of workers, skilled and unskilled alike, around technology issues. Harley Shaiken has formulated the outlines of an agenda for such a political movement—explicit union rights concerning the alteration of skill and the organization of work (how computers are used to monitor workers, for example); effective union input in design of new technology; recognition of the "social costs" of technological change, and guarantees protecting workers from these costs; and effective procedures to police any labor-management agreement concerning technology issues. But in the absence of rank-and-file mobilization and participation, even the most comprehensive programs are bound to fall short.

There are some countries where such a movement for worker control of technology is being built. In Scandinavia, workers have won extensive rights through both collective bargaining and legislation that guarantees them a say in the design and implementation of new technology. In Norway, unions have negotiated "data agreements" with management on both local and national levels outlining union rights to participate in all technology decisions. A new union position has been created in the workplace called the "data shop steward" who is responsible for analyzing all new systems from the workers' perspective and making sure they contain no features used to restrict workers' freedom and control. The specific provisions of these agreements vary from country to country, but the central feature of the Scandinavian experience has been the rapid expansion in recent years of innovative union education programs that bring pro-union computer technicians and local union members together to learn from each other about the dangers and the opportunities of the new technology. These experiments make clear that any serious worker control of technology requires not only independent union expertise but also an informed, "technologically literate," and politically active workforce (see box).

WORKER CONTROL OF TECHNOLOGY IN SCANDINAVIA

". . . Technology bargaining has become the new thing in Western Europe," Herman Rebhan, general secretary of the International Metalworkers' Association, told a conference of UAW technical, office, and professional employees last February. "The theme is change—but only by consent" of workers and their unions. Nowhere is this more true than in Norway and Sweden. In both countries, a budding movement for worker control of technology is being built on the foundation of nearly ten years of innovative workplace experiments.

From 1971 to 1973, the Norwegian Iron and Metal Workers' Union ran a pilot project that brought workers from local union "clubs" together with pro-union technicians from the state-run Norwegian Computer Center to study specific cases of workplace technological change and formulate worker alternatives to management plans. "As a result of this unprecedented effort," writes MIT's David Noble, "computer technology was demystified for the union, and the union—and labor in general—was demystified for the computer scientists. . . ; the union became more sophisticated about the technology and the technical people became more attuned to the needs and disciplines of trade unionists."

This project led to the precedent-setting "Data Agreement" between the Norwegian Federation of Trade Unions and that country's employer association in 1975 and subsequently was written into law in the 1977 Working Environment Act. The agreement established the position of "data shop steward" and gave workers the right of pre-notification of all proposed technological changes, access to company data banks, and participation in all decisions that affect the form and content of their jobs. Experiments similar to the metal workers' project have involved Norwegian office and chemical workers.

From 1977 to 1979, the government-funded Swedish Center for Working Life initiated the first Swedish workplace technology experiments in cooperation with the Swedish Trade Union Confederation. Known as the "Demos Project" (for "democratic planning and control of working life"), unionists and researchers worked together in a variety of workplaces to formulate the "negotiation model" for workplace planning in which unions, armed with independent expertise, present their demands to management *before* new computer systems are designed and put in place. The Center has continued its work in other pilot projects with workers in the insurance industry, state civil service, and commerce. In 1978, the Swedish Labor Ministry set up a special commission on computerization and its effects on work, the first step toward enactment of new legislation.

What distinguishes these workplace technology experiments from the "humanization of work" projects of the sixties is their rejection of both union-management collaboration and dependence on "neutral" experts. "This is not a situation in which union and management cooperate harmoniously," writes Noble, describing one of the sites of the Norwegian Iron and Metal Workers' project, "nor is it a management-devised job-enlargement scheme. The task of the data shop steward, and the union in general, is to engage as effectively as possible in a struggle over information and control, a struggle engaged in, with equal sophistication and earnestness, by the other side."

In this context, the role of the computer technician is unapologetically partisan—to be not only a union expert but to impart to workers the technical tools that allow them to confront the problems they face on the shop floor. In this way, participants say, workers become able to criticize the new technology in terms of their own work experience. It loses its "inevitable" character to become another facet of working life, open to social action and control.

In the present context of American labor relations and with American unions on the political defensive, it is hard to imagine a major campaign of worker education and rank-and-file mobilization over technology issues taking place in the near future. But there is, perhaps, a historical parallel between the shift from craft production to mass production in the American automobile industry and what is happening in the telephone industry today. During that earlier period of massive technological change, new ways of organizing work were also used to fragment jobs and isolate workers. Traditional forms of worker resistance and traditional structures of trade unionism proved inadequate. At the same time, divisions among workers were worn down by the centralization of mass industry. And the large unskilled workforce of the assembly line—long considered incapable of organizing—began to cohere. Out of the new conditions came a new unity and new forms of political action—industrial unionism and the sit-down strike.

There are similar trends in telecommunications today. The same technology that fragments jobs and destroys skills brings workers from a wide variety of occupational categories together in a way they have not been before. Computerization is also creating whole new categories of workers who are defined as "management" and usually considered unsympathetic to unionism—computer programmers, sales personnel, middle level technicians—who will inevitably face problems and pressures similar to what unionized telephone workers are experiencing today. Most important of all, the computerized workplace, with its concentration of expensive and highly complex technology, is especially vulnerable to disruption by small numbers of centrally located individuals. With increased responsibility come new forms of leverage and potential power.

Of course, what form worker militancy in the Information Society will take—whether sit-down strikes in TSPS offices or worker occupations of Automatic Switching Control Centers—is impossible to predict. But the greatest failure of imagination would be to assume there will be none.

25
LIFE ON THE GLOBAL ASSEMBLY LINE

Barbara Ehrenreich and Annette Fuentes

In Ciudad Juárez, Mexico, Anna M. rises at 5 A.M. to feed her son before starting on the two-hour bus trip to the maquiladora (factory). He will spend the day along with four other children in a neighbor's one-room home. Anna's husband, frustrated by being unable to find work for himself, left for the United States six months ago. She wonders, as she carefully applies her new lip gloss, whether she ought to consider

Reprinted from *Ms.* magazine, January 1981, by permission of the authors.

*herself still married. It might be good to take a night course, become a
secretary. But she seldom gets home before eight at night, and the factory, where she stitches brassieres that will be sold in the United States
through J.C. Penney, pays only $48 a week.*

*In Penang, Malaysia, Julie K. is up before the three other young
women with whom she shares a room, and starts heating the leftover
rice from last night's supper. She looks good in the company's green-
trimmed uniform, and she's proud to work in a modern, American-
owned factory. Only not quite so proud as when she started working
three years ago—she thinks as she squints out the door at a passing group
of women. Her job involves peering all day through a microscope, bond-
ing hair-thin gold wires to a silicon chip destined to end up inside a
pocket calculator, and at 21, she is afraid she can no longer see very
clearly.*

Every morning, between four and seven, thousands of women like Anna
and Julie head out for the day shift. In Ciudad Juárez, they crowd into
ruteras (run-down vans) for the trip from the slum neighborhoods to the
industrial parks on the outskirts of the city. In Penang they squeeze, 60 or
more at a time, into buses for the trip from the village to the low, modern
factory buildings of the Bayan Lepas free trade zone. In Taiwan, they
walk from the dormitories—where the night shift is already asleep in the
still-warm beds—through the checkpoints in the high fence surrounding
the factory zone.

This is the world's new industrial proletariat: young, female, Third
World. Viewed from the "first world," they are still faceless, genderless
"cheap labor," signaling their existence only through a label or tiny im-
print—"made in Hong Kong," or Taiwan, Korea, the Dominican Republic, Mexico, the Philippines. But they may be one of the most
strategic blocs of womanpower in the world of the 1980s. Conservatively,
there are 2 million Third World female industrial workers employed now,
millions more looking for work, and their numbers are rising every year.
Anyone whose image of Third World women features picturesque peasants with babies slung on their backs should be prepared to update it. Just
in the last decade, Third World women have become a critical element in
the global economy and a key "resource" for expanding multinational
corporations.

It doesn't take more than second-grade arithmetic to understand what's
happening. In the United States, an assembly-line worker is likely to earn,
depending on her length of employment, between $3.10 and $5 an hour.
In many Third World countries, a woman doing the same work will earn
$3 to $5 a *day.* Acording to the magazine *Business Asia,* in 1976 the
average hourly wage for unskilled work (male or female) was 55 cents in
Hong Kong, 52 cents in South Korea, 32 cents in the Philippines, and 17

cents in Indonesia. The logic of the situation is compelling: why pay someone in Massachusetts $5 an hour to do what someone in Manila will do for $2.50 a day? Or, as a corollary, why pay a male worker anywhere to do what a female worker will do for 40 to 60 percent less?

And so, almost everything that can be packed up is being moved out to the Third World; not heavy industry, but just about anything light enough to travel—garment manufacture, textiles, toys, footwear, pharmaceuticals, wigs, appliance parts, tape decks, computer components, plastic goods. In some industries, like garment and textile, American jobs are lost in the process, and the biggest losers are women, often black and Hispanic. But what's going on is much more than a matter of runaway shops. Economists are talking about a "new international division of labor," in which the process of production is broken down and the fragments are dispersed to different parts of the world. In general, the low-skilled jobs are farmed out to the Third World, where labor costs are minuscule, while control over the overall process and technology remains safely at company headquarters in "first world" countries like the United States and Japan.

The American electronics industry provides a classic example: circuits are printed on silicon wafers and tested in California; then the wafers are shipped to Asia for the labor-intensive process by which they are cut into tiny chips and bonded to circuit boards; final assembly into products such as calculators or military equipment usually takes place in the United States. Garment manufacture too is often broken into geographically separated steps, with the most repetitive, labor-intensive jobs going to the poor countries of the southern hemisphere. Most Third World countries welcome whatever jobs come their way in the new division of labor, and the major international development agencies—like the World Bank and the United States Agency for International Development (AID)—encourage them to take what they can get.

So much any economist could tell you. What is less often noted is the *gender* breakdown of the emerging international division of labor. Eighty to 90 percent of the low-skilled assembly jobs that go to the Third World are performed by women—in a remarkable switch from earlier patterns of foreign-dominated industrialization. Until now, "development" under the aegis of foreign corporations has usually meant more jobs for men and—compared to traditional agricultural society—a diminished economic status for women. But multinational corporations and Third World governments alike consider assembly-line work—whether the product is Barbie dolls or missile parts—to be "women's work."

One reason is that women can, in many countries, still be legally paid less than men. But the sheer tedium of the jobs adds to the multinationals' preference for women workers—a preference made clear, for example, by this ad from a Mexican newspaper: We *need female workers; older*

than 17, younger than 30; single and without children: minimum edu-
cation primary school, maximum education one year of preparatory
school [high school]: available for all shifts.

It's an article of faith with management that only women can do, or
will do, the monotonous, painstaking work that American business is ex-
porting to the Third World. Bill Mitchell, whose job is to attract United
States businesses to the Bermudez Industrial Park in Ciudad Juárez told us
with a certain macho pride: "A man just won't stay in this tedious kind of
work. He'd walk out in a couple of hours." The personnel manager of a
light assembly plant in Taiwan told anthropologist Linda Gail Arrigo:
"Young male workers are too restless and impatient to do monotonous
work with no career value. If displeased, they sabotage the machines and
even threaten the foreman. But girls? At most, they cry a little."

In fact, the American businessmen we talked to claimed that Third
World women genuinely enjoy doing the very things that would drive a
man to assault and sabotage. "You should watch these kids going into
work," Bill Mitchell told us. "You don't have any sullenness here. They
smile." A top-level management consultant who specializes in advising
American companies on where to relocate their factories gave us this
global generalization: "The [factory] girls genuinely enjoy themselves.
They're away from their families. They have spending money. They can
buy motorbikes, whatever. Of course it's a regulated experience too—
with dormitories to live in—so it's a healthful experience."

What is the real experience of the women in the emerging Third
World industrial work force? The conventional Western stereotypes leap
to mind: You can't really compare, the standards are so different. . . .
Everything's easier in warm countries. . . . They really don't have any
alternatives. . . . Commenting on the low wages his company pays its
women workers in Singapore, a Hewlett-Packard vice-president said,
"They live much differently here than we do. . . ." But the differences
are ultimately very simple. To start with, they have less money.

The great majority of the women in the new Third World work force
live at or near the subsistence level for one person, whether they work for
a multinational corporation or a locally owned factory. In the Philippines,
for example, starting wages in U.S.-owned electronics plants are between
$34 to $46 a month, compared to a cost of living of $37 a month; in
Indonesia the starting wages are actually about $7 a month less than the
cost of living. "Living," in these cases, should be interpreted minimally: a
diet of rice, dried fish, and water—a Coke might cost a half-day's
wages—lodging in a room occupied by four or more other people.
Rachael Grossman, a researcher with the Southeast Asia Resource Center,
found women employees of U.S. multinational firms in Malaysia and the
Philippines living four to eight in a room in boardinghouses, or squeezing
into tiny extensions built onto squatter huts near the factory. Where com-

panies do provide dormitories for their employees, they are not of the "healthful," collegiate variety implied by our corporate informant. Staff from the American Friends Service Committee report that dormitory space is "likely to be crowded, with bed rotation paralleling shift rotation—while one shift works, another sleeps, as many as twenty to a room." In one case in Thailand, they found the dormitory "filthy," with workers forced to find their own place to sleep among "splintered floorboards, rusting sheets of metal, and scraps of dirty cloth."

"Mass Hysteria" as Job Action?

Hysteria was supposed to have gone out with the 19th century, but it's making a comeback in today's ultramodern, high-tech electronics industry. For Malaysian women employed in the painstaking work of assembling microcircuits, mass hysteria has become a form of resistance. It starts when one young woman sees a *hantu* or *jin*, which are particularly hideous varieties of ghosts. She falls to the floor in convulsions, screaming, and within minutes the hysteria spreads up and down the assembly line. Sometimes the plant has to be closed for a week or more to exorcise the spirits.

Western managers have tried Valium, smelling salts, and traditional healers to combat hysteria before it paralyzes production. But Malaysian academics who have studied the phenomenon point out that attacks are likely to be preceded by a speedup or a tightening of plant discipline. Since the Malaysian government does not permit labor unions, more conventional forms of protest are hard to organize. Besides, eight or ten hours a day spent peering through a microscope at tiny wires—for about $2 a day pay—is enough to make anyone hysterical.

Wages do increase with seniority, but the money does not go to pay for studio apartments or, very likely, motorbikes. A 1970 study of young women factory workers in Hong Kong found that 88 percent of them were turning more than half their earnings over to their parents. In areas that are still largely agricultural (such as parts of the Philippines and Malaysia), or places where male unemployment runs high (such as northern Mexico), a woman factory worker may be the sole source of cash income for an entire extended family.

But wages on a par with what an 11-year-old American could earn on a paper route, and living conditions resembling what Engels found in 19th-century Manchester are only part of the story. The rest begins at the factory gate. The work that multinational corporations export to the Third World is not only the most tedious, but often the most hazardous part of the production process. The countries they go to are, for the most part, those that will guarantee no interference from health and safety inspectors, trade unions, or even free-lance reformers. As a result, most Third World factory women work under conditions that already have broken or will break their health—or their nerves—within a few years, and often before they've worked long enough to earn any more than a subsistence wage.

Consider first the electronics industry, which is generally thought to be the safest and cleanest of the exported industries. The factory buildings are low and modern, like those one might find in a suburban American industrial park. Inside, rows of young women, neatly dressed in the company uniform or T-shirt, work quietly at their stations. There is air conditioning (not for the women's comfort, but to protect the delicate semiconductor parts they work with), and high-volume piped-in Bee Gees hits (not so much for entertainment, as to prevent talking).

For many Third World women, electronics is a prestige occupation, at least compared to other kinds of factory work. They are unlikely to know that in the United States the National Institute on Occupational Safety and Health (NIOSH) has placed electronics on its select list of "high health-risk industries using the greatest number of toxic substances." If electronics assembly work is risky here, it is doubly so in countries where there is no equivalent of NIOSH to even issue warnings. In many plants toxic chemicals and solvents sit in open containers, filling the work area with fumes that can literally knock you out. "We have been told of cases where ten to twelve women passed out at once," an AFSC field worker in northern Mexico told us, "and the newspapers report this as 'mass hysteria.'"

In one stage of the electronics assembly process, the workers have to dip the circuits into open vats of acid. According to Irene Johnson and Carol Bragg, who toured the National Semiconductor plant in Penang, Malaysia, the women who do the dipping "wear rubber gloves and boots, but these sometimes leak, and burns are common." Occasionally, whole fingers are lost. More commonly, what electronics workers lose is the 20/20 vision they are required to have when they are hired. Most electronics workers spend seven to nine hours a day peering through microscopes, straining to meet their quotas.

One study in South Korea found that most electronics assembly workers developed severe eye problems after only one year of employment: 88 percent had chronic conjunctivitis; 44 percent became nearsighted; and 19 percent developed astigmatism. A manager for Hewlett-Packard's Malaysia plant, in an interview with Rachael Grossman, denied that there were any eye problems: "These girls are used to working with 'scopes.'"

We've found no eye problems. But it sure makes me dizzy to look through those things."

Electronics, recall, is the "cleanest" of the exported industries. Conditions in the garment and textile industry rival those of any 19th-century (or 20th—see below) sweatshop. The firms, generally local subcontractors to large American chains such as J.C. Penney and Sears, as well as smaller manufacturers, are usually even more indifferent to the health of their employees than the multinationals. Some of the worst conditions have been documented in South Korea, where the garment and textile industries have helped spark that country's "economic miracle." Workers are packed into poorly lit rooms, where summer temperatures rise above 100 degrees. Textile dust, which can cause permanent lung damage, fills the air. When there are rush orders, management may require forced overtime of as much as 48 hours at a stretch, and if that seems to go beyond the limits of human endurance, pep pills and amphetamine injections are thoughtfully provided. In her diary (originally published in a magazine now banned by the South Korean government) Min Chong Suk, 30, a sewing-machine operator, wrote of working from 7 A.M. to 11:30 P.M. in a garment factory: "When [the apprentices] shake the waste threads from the clothes, the whole room fills with dust, and it is hard to breathe. Since we've been working in such dusty air, there have been increasing numbers of people getting tuberculosis, bronchitis, and eye diseases. Since we are women, it makes us so sad when we have pale, unhealthy, wrinkled faces like dried-up spinach. . . . It seems to me that no one knows our blood dissolves into the threads and seams, with sighs and sorrow."

SWEATSHOPS—MADE IN USA

Not every manufacturer has the resources to run away to the cheap labor reservoirs of the Southern Hemisphere. An alternative is to try to duplicate in the United States the conditions that give the Third World its business appeal—substandard wages, controlled unions (if any), and the kind of no-frills work conditions that you might expect to find in Seoul or Taiwan. In the fiercely competitive light-manufacturing industries (toys, garments, artificial flowers), companies are turning to the sweatshop.

In Los Angeles, Chicago, Boston, New York, cities in New Jersey—anyplace where garment production has roots, sweatshops are springing up by the hundreds. Exact numbers are hard to come by since the shops are, by and large, unlicensed and illegal. Anyone with a few thousand dollars can start up a garment shop. All you need is a dozen sewing machines, a low-rent building, and people,

usually immigrants, desperate for work. Manufacturers ("jobbers")
ship out bundles of precut clothes to the shop owners ("contractors")
who hire workers to stitch the pieces together. A contractor in New
York's South Bronx blames the jobbers for exploitation: "Do they
pay enough? You got to be kidding. I pay the girls $1.25 a dress. All
I get is $2.60, and I've got to run the shop, rent machines, pay for
electricity."

Women are 90 percent of the sweatshop work force in this country. Here or in the Third World, women are industry's best bargain.
A union organizer in Los Angeles says: "One woman I talked to this
year put in a sixty-hour week and made fifty dollars." A year ago,
the Department of Labor cited 85 garment shops in New York's
Chinatown for violations of minimum-wage, child-labor, and overtime regulations. In many cases, a boss would punch time cards in
and out for employees.

Sweatshop workers are heads of households, needing a steady, if
meager, income to support their families. They are mothers without
access to day-care centers who can bring their children with them to
the "informal" setting of the sweatshop. Some are women who need
an extra, but unreported, income to survive on welfare. And others
are older women supplementing inadequate pensions.

Jobs in these garment shops are easy to get, and require little or
no experience. Walk down 149th Street in the South Bronx and see
one sign after another—*se necesita operadoras* (operators wanted),
many with the dubious promise of *Buena Paga* (good pay). A visit
to Damak Sportswear in the Bronx revealed a typical neighborhood
garment operation. Thirteen Puerto Rican women were bent over
sewing machines in a poorly lit room. The shop, on the third floor of
an old tenement building with wooden stairs and floors, lacked fire
alarms and a sprinkler system. But that's par for the course, according to Louis Berthold at the South Bronx Working Center, an
ILGWU community outreach program. "One building on 161st
Street had more than forty health and fire violations, and housed
four shops. It wouldn't surprise me if there was another Triangle
fire," he remarked.

"Homework" is another abuse spawned by the demands of industry. Women carry bundles of precut garments from the shops to
stitch them at home, using their own sewing machines, paying for
their own electricity, and often enlisting the help of their children to
meet deadlines.

Undocumented workers, known as illegal aliens in the media, are
especially vulnerable, because of their fear of discovery and deportation. Ironically, unions, industry, and the government concur in
blaming "illegals" for the existence and spread of sweatshops—as if

the immigrants bring the miserable conditions into this country along with their family photographs. Kurt Barnard of the Federation of Apparel Manufacturers claims that "the illegals are the cause of sweatshops and the government helps by failing to enforce immigration laws."

A study of undocumented workers in New York done by the North American Congress on Latin America (NACLA . . .) found that labor abuse was not restricted to the undocumented, but that "these are the conditions of labor that now prevail in the sectors of industry where new immigrant workers, legal or not, come to dwell." The study confirms the connection between runaway industry in the Third World and the deterioration of labor conditions at home. Charles Wang, director of New York's Chinatown Planning Council, calls on unions to become "watchdogs and take a militant stand against these conditions."

Despite their vulnerable position, women in sweatshops are beginning to organize. In 1975, 125 Chinese women at the Jung Sai garment shop in San Francisco began the longest strike in Chinese-American history; it ended nearly a year later with an ILGWU contract. In 1977, 250 workers struck the W and W Knitting Mill in Brooklyn for six months; 75 were undocumented and risked deportation to march on the picket lines. From Taiwan to New York, female labor may still be cheap, but it can't be counted on to be docile.   —A.F.

In all the exported industries, the most invidious, inescapable health hazard is stress. On their home ground United States corporations are not likely to sacrifice productivity for human comfort. On someone else's home ground, however, anything goes. Lunch breaks may be barely long enough for a woman to stand in line at the canteen or hawkers' stalls. Visits to the bathroom are treated as privilege; in some cases, workers must raise their hands for permission to use the toilet, and waits up to a half hour are common. Rotating shifts—the day shift one week, the night shift the next—wreak havoc with sleep patterns. Because inaccuracies or failure to meet production quotas can mean substantial pay losses, the pressures are quickly internalized; stomach ailments and nervous problems are not unusual in the multinationals' Third World female work force. In some situations, good work is as likely to be punished as slow or shoddy work. Correspondent Michael Flannery, writing for the AFL-CIO's *American Federationist*, tells the story of 23-year-old Basilia Altagracia, a seamstress who stitched collars onto ladies' blouses in the La Romana (Dominican Republic) free trade zone (a heavily guarded industrial zone owned by Gulf & Western Industries, Inc.):

"A nimble veteran seamstress, Miss Altagracia eventually began to earn as much as $5.75 a day. . . . 'I was exceeding my piecework quota by a lot.' . . . But then, Altagracia said, her plant supervisor, a Cuban emigré, called her into his office. 'He said I was doing a fine job, but that I and some other of the women were making too much money, and he was being forced to lower what we earned for each piece we sewed.' On the best days, she now can clear barely $3, she said. 'I was earning less, so I started working six and seven days a week. But I was tired and I could not work as fast as before.' " Within a few months, she was too ill to work at all.

As if poor health and the stress of factory life weren't enough to drive women into early retirement, management actually encourages a high turnover in many industries. "As you know, when seniority rises, wages rise," the management consultant to U.S. multinationals told us. He explained that it's cheaper to train a fresh supply of teenagers than to pay experienced women higher wages. "Older" women, aged 23 or 24, are likely to be laid off and not rehired.

We estimate, based on fragmentary data from several sources, that the multinational corporations may already have used up (cast off) as many as 6 million Third World workers—women who are too ill, too old (30 is over the hill in most industries), or too exhausted to be useful any more. Few "retire" with any transferable skills or savings. The lucky ones find husbands.

The unlucky ones find themselves at the margins of society—as bar girls, "hostesses," or prostitutes.

At 21, Julie's greatest fear is that she will never be able to find a husband. She knows that just being a "factory girl" is enough to give anyone a bad reputation. When she first started working at the electronics company, her father refused to speak to her for three months. Now every time she leaves Penang to go back to visit her home village she has to put up with a lecture on morality from her older brother—not to mention a barrage of lewd remarks from men outside her family. If they knew that she had actually gone out on a few dates, that she had been to a discotheque, that she had once kissed a young man who said he was a student . . . Julie's stomach tightens as she imagines her family's reaction. She tries to concentrate on the kind of man she would like to marry: an engineer or technician of some sort, someone who had been to California, where the company headquarters are located and where even the grandmothers wear tight pants and lipstick—someone who had a good attitude about women. But if she ends up having to wear glasses, like her cousin who worked three years at the "scopes," she might as well forget about finding anyone to marry her.

One of the most serious occupational hazards that Julie and millions of women like her may face is the lifelong stigma of having been a "factory girl." Most of the cultures favored by multinational corporations in their search for cheap labor are patriarchal in the grand old style: any young woman who is not under the wing of a father, husband, or older brother must be "loose." High levels of unemployment among men, as in Mexico, contribute to male resentment of working women. (Ironically, in some places the multinationals have increased male unemployment—for example, by paving over fishing and farming villages to make way for industrial parks.) Add to all this the fact that certain companies—American electronics firms are in the lead—actively promote Western-style sexual objectification as a means of insuring employee loyalty: there are company-sponsored cosmetics classes, "guess whose legs these are" contests, and swim-suit-style beauty contests where the prize might be a free night *for two* in a fancy hotel. Corporate-promoted Westernization only heightens the hostility many men feel toward any independent working women—having a job is bad enough, wearing jeans and mascara to work is going too far.

Anthropologist Patricia Fernandez, who has worked in a *maquiladora* herself, believes that the stigmatization of working women serves, indirectly, to keep them in line. "You have to think of the kind of socialization that girls experience in a very Catholic—or, for that matter, Muslim—society. The fear of having a 'reputation' is enough to make a lot of women bend over backward to be 'respectable' and ladylike, which is just what management wants." She points out that in northern Mexico, the tabloids delight in playing up stories of alleged vice in the *maquiladoras*—indiscriminate sex on the job, epidemics of venereal disease, fetuses found in factory rest rooms. "I worry about this because there are those who treat you differently as soon as they know you have a job at a *maquiladora*," one woman told Fernandez. "Maybe they think that if you have to work, there is a chance you're a whore."

And there is always a chance you'll wind up as one. Probably only a small minority of Third World factory workers turn to prostitution when their working days come to an end. But it is, as for women everywhere, the employment of last resort, the only thing to do when the factories don't need you and traditional society won't—or, for economic reasons, can't—take you back. In the Philippines, the brothel business is expanding as fast as the factory system. If they can't use you one way, they can use you another.

There has been no international protest about the exploitation of Third World women by multinational corporations—no thundering denunciations from the floor of the United Nations' general assembly, no angry resolutions from the Conference of the Non-Aligned Countries. Sociologist Robert Snow, who has been tracing the multinationals on their way south and eastward for years, explained why: "The Third World governments *want* the multinationals to move in. There's cutthroat competition to attract the corporations."

The governments themselves gain little revenue from this kind of investment, though—especially since most offer tax holidays and freedom from export duties in order to attract the multinationals in the first place. Nor do the people as a whole benefit, according to a highly placed Third World woman within the UN. "The multinationals like to say they're contributing to development," she told us, "but they come into our countries for one thing—cheap labor. If the labor stops being so cheap, they can move on. So how can you call that development? It depends on the people being poor and staying poor." But there are important groups that do stand to gain when the multinationals set up shop in their countries: local entrepreneurs who subcontract to the multinationals; Harvard- or Berkeley-educated "technocrats" who become local management; and government officials who specialize in cutting red tape for an "agent's fee" or an outright bribe.

In the competition for multinational investment, local governments advertise their women shamelessly, and an investment brochure issued by the Malaysian government informs multinational executives that: "The manual dexterity of the Oriental female is famous the world over. Her hands are small, and she works fast with extreme care. . . . Who, therefore, could be better qualified by nature and inheritance, to contribute to the efficiency of a bench-assembly production line than the Oriental girl?"

RECKLESS, EASILY EXCITED, RIPE FOR LABOR AGITATORS?

If you're a Korean factory worker, you wouldn't expect to get a free lunch, but you are likely to get a free book. Written by a man who is a former member of the Korean Central Intelligence Agency, the book explains why "Communists" and labor-reform religious groups "are very much more interested in getting women workers than men workers":

First, women are more susceptible than men. They are emotional and less logical. They cannot differentiate between true and false or good and bad. . . . They are easily excited and are very reckless and do things hastily. . . . Third, most women workers are sentimental young girls. Fourth, women workers are so caught by vanity that they spend much more

> money than men workers. . . . Sixth, management, union leaders, and city
> administrators find it very difficult to deal with women workers when
> they cause trouble. The women weep and cry and behave exaggeratedly
> . . . and for men this kind of behavior is very troubling.

The Royal Thai Embassy sends American businesses a brochure guaranteeing that in Thailand, "the relationship between the employer and
employee is like that of a guardian and ward. It is easy to win and maintain the loyalty of workers as long as they are treated with kindness and
courtesy." The facing page offers a highly selective photo-study of Thai
womanhood: giggling shyly, bowing submissively, and working cheerfully
on an assembly line.

Many "host" governments are willing to back up their advertising with
whatever amount of brutality it takes to keep "their girls" just as docile as
they look in the brochures. Even the most polite and orderly attempts to
organize are likely to bring down overkill doses of police repression:

• In Guatemala in 1975 women workers in a North American-owned
factory producing jeans and jackets drew up a list of complaints that included insults by management, piecework wages that turned out to be
less than the legal minimum, no overtime pay, and "threats of death." In
response, the American boss made a quick call to the local authorities to
report that he was being harassed by "Communists." When the women
reported for work the next day they found the factory surrounded by two
fully armed contingents of military police. The "Communist" ringleaders
were picked out and fired.

• In the Dominican Republic, in 1978, workers who attempted to organize at the La Romana industrial zone were first fired, then obligingly
arrested by the local police. Officials from the AFL-CIO have described
the zone as a "modern slave-labor camp," where workers who do not
meet their production quotas during their regular shift must stay and put
in unpaid overtime until they do meet them, and many women workers
are routinely strip-searched at the end of the day. During the 1978 organizing attempt, the government sent in national police in full combat
gear and armed with automatic weapons. Gulf & Western supplements
the local law with its own company-sponsored motorcycle club, which
specializes in terrorizing suspected union sympathizers.

• In Inchon, South Korea, women at the Dong-II Textile Company
(which produces fabrics and yarn for export to the United States) had
succeeded in gaining leadership in their union in 1972. But in 1978 the
government-controlled, male-dominated Federation of Korean Trade
Unions sent special "action squads" to destroy the women's union. Armed
with steel bars and buckets of human excrement, the goons broke into the

union office, smashed the office equipment, and smeared the excrement over the women's bodies and in their hair, ears, eyes, and mouths.

Crudely put (and incidents like this do not inspire verbal delicacy), the relationship between many Third World governments and the multinational corporations is not very different from the relationship between a pimp and his customers. The governments advertise their women, sell them, and keep them in line for the multinational "johns." But there are other parties to the growing international traffic in women—such as the United Nations' Industrial Development Organization (UNIDO), the World Bank, and the United States government itself.

UNIDO, for example, has been a major promotor of "free trade zones." These are enclaves within nations that offer multinational corporations a range of creature comforts, including: freedom from paying taxes and export duties; low-cost water, power, and buildings; exemption from whatever labor laws may apply in the country as a whole; and, in some cases, such security features as barbed-wire, guarded checkpoints, and government-paid police.

Then there is the World Bank, which over the past decade has lent several billion dollars to finance the roads, airports, power plants, and even the first-class hotels that multinational corporations need in order to set up business in Third World countries. The Sri Lankan garment industry, which like other Third World garment industries survives by subcontracting to major Western firms, was set up on the advice of the World Bank and with a $20 million World Bank loan. This particular experiment in "development" offers young women jobs at a global low of $5 for a six-day week. Gloria Scott, the head of the World Bank's Women and Development Program, sounded distinctly uncomfortable when we asked her about the bank's role in promoting the exploitation of Third World women. "Our job is to help eliminate poverty. It is not our responsibility if the multinationals come in and offer such low wages. It's the responsibility of the governments." However, the Bank's 1979 World Development Report speaks strongly of the need for "wage restraint" in poor countries.

But the most powerful promoter of exploitative conditions for Third World women workers is the United States government itself. For example, the notoriously repressive Korean textile industry was developed with the help of $400 million in aid from the U.S. State Department. Malaysia became a low-wage haven for the electronics industry, thanks to technical assistance financed by AID and to U.S. money (funneled through the Asian Development Bank) to set up free trade zones. Taiwan's status as a "showcase for the free world" and a comfortable berth for multinationals is the result of three decades of financial transfusions from the United States. On a less savory note, the U.S. funds an outfit called the Asian-American Free Labor Institute, whose ostensible purpose is to encourage "free" (*i.e.*, non-Communist) trade unions in Asia, but whose actual mission is to discourage any truly militant union activity. AAFLI works closely with the Federation of Korean Trade Unions, which was responsible for the excrement-smearing incident described above.

But the most obvious form of United States involvement, according to Lenny Siegel, the director of the Pacific Studies Center, is through "our consistent record of military aid to Third World governments that are capitalist, politically repressive, and are not striving for economic independence." Ironically, says Siegel, there are "cases where the United States made a big investment—through groups like AAFLI or other kinds of political pressure—to make sure that any unions that formed would be pretty tame. Then we put in even more money to support some dictator who doesn't allow unions at all." And if that doesn't seem like a sufficient case of duplicate spending, the U.S. government also insures (through the Overseas Private Investment Corporation) outward-bound multinationals against any lingering possibility of insurrection or expropriation.

What does our government have to say for itself? It's hard to get a straight answer—the few parts of the bureaucracy that deal with women and development seem to have little connection with those that are concerned with larger foreign policy issues. A spokesman for the Department of State told us that if multinationals offer poor working conditions (which he questioned), this was not their fault: "There are just different standards in different countries." Offering further evidence of a sheltered life, he told us that "corporations today are generally more socially responsible than even ten years ago. . . . We can expect them to treat their employees in the best way they can." But he conceded in response to a barrage of unpleasant examples, "Of course, you're going to have problems wherever you have human beings doing things." Our next stop was the Women's Division within AID. Staffer Emmy Simmons was aware of the criticisms of the quality of employment multinationals offer, but cautioned that "we can get hung up in the idea that it's exploitation without really looking at the alternatives for women." AID's concern, she said, was with the fact that population is outgrowing the agricultural capacity of many Third World countries, dislocating millions of people. From her point of view, multinationals at least provide some sort of alternative: "These people have to go somewhere."

Anna, for one, has nowhere to go but the maquiladora. Her family left the farm when she was only six, and the land has long since been bought up by a large commercial agribusiness company. After her father left to find work north of the border, money was scarce in the household for years. So when the factory where she now works opened in the early 1970s, Anna felt it was "the best thing that had ever happened" to her. As a wage-earner, her status rose compared to her broth-

ers with their on-again, off-again jobs. Partly out of her new sense of confidence, she agreed to meet with a few other women one day after work to talk about wages and health conditions. That was the way she became what management called a "labor agitator" when, six months later, 90 percent of the day shift walked out in the company's first south-of-the-border strike.

Women like Anna—or Julie K. in Malaysia—need their jobs desperately. They know the risks of organizing. Beyond that, there's the larger risk that—if they do succeed in organizing—the company can always move on in search of a still-docile, job-hungry work force. Yet thousands of women in the Third World's industrial work force have chosen to fight for better wages and working conditions. Few of these struggles reach the North American media. We know of them from reports, often fragmentary, from church and support groups:

• Nuevo Laredo, Mexico, 1973: 2,000 workers at Transitron Electronics walked out in solidarity with a small number of workers who had been unjustly fired. Two days later, 8,000 striking workers met and elected a more militant union leadership.

• Mexicali, Mexico, 1974: 3,000 workers, locked out by Mextel (a Mattel subsidiary), set up a 24-hour guard to prevent the company from moving in search of cheaper labor. After two months of confrontations, the company moved away.

• Bangkok, Thailand, 1976: 70 young women locked their Japanese bosses out and took control of the factory. They continued to make and sell jeans and floppy hats for export, paying themselves 150 percent more than their bosses had.

• South Korea, 1977: 3,000 women at the American-owned Signetics plant went on a hunger strike for a 46.8 percent wage hike above the 39 cents an hour they were receiving. Since an actual walkout would have been illegal, they remained in the plant and held a sit-in in the cafeteria. They won a 23 percent increase.

• South Korea, 1978: 1,000 workers at the Mattel toy company in Seoul, which makes Barbie dolls and Marie Osmond dolls, staged a work slowdown to protest their 25 cents-an-hour wages and 12-hour shifts.

• South Korea, 1979: 200 young women employees of the YH textile-and-wig factory staged a peaceful vigil and fast to protest the company's threatened closing of the plant. On August 11, the fifth day of the vigil, more than 1,000 riot police, armed with clubs and steel shields, broke into the building where the women were staying and forcibly dragged the women out. Twenty-one-year-old Kim Kyong-suk was killed during the melee. It was her death that touched off widespread rioting throughout Korea that many thought led to the overthrow of President Park Chung Hee.

• Ciudad Juárez, Mexico: September, 1980: 1,000 women workers occupied an American Hospital Supply Corporation factory. They demanded better working conditions, paid vacations, and recognition of the union of their choice. The women, who are mostly in their teens and early twenties, began the occupation when 180 thugs, which the company claims were paid by a rival union, entered the factory and beat up the women's leaders. The occupation is over, but the struggle goes on.

Regarding the 1979 vigil in South Korea, Robert Snow points out: "Very few people realize that an action which began with 200 very young women factory workers led to the downfall of a government. In the 1980s Third World factory women like this are going to be a political force to reckon with." So far, feminism, first-world style, has barely begun to acknowledge the Third World's new industrial womanpower. Jeb Mays and Kathleen Connell, co-founders of the San Francisco-based Women's Network on Global Corporations ... are two women who would like to change that. "There's still this idea of the Third World woman as 'the other'—someone exotic and totally unlike us," Mays and Connell told us. "But now we're talking about women who wear the same styles in clothes, listen to the same music, and may even work for the same corporation. That's an irony the multinationals have created. In a way, they're drawing us together as women."

Saralee Hamilton, an AFSC staff organizer of a 1978 conference on "Women and Global Corporations" (held in Des Moines, Iowa) says: "The multinational corporations have deliberately targeted women for exploitation. If feminism is going to mean anything to women all over the world, it's going to have to find new ways to resist corporate power internationally." She envisions a global network of grass-roots women capable of sharing experiences, transmitting information, and—eventually—providing direct support for each other's struggles. It's a long way off; few women anywhere have the money for intercontinental plane flights or even long-distance calls, but at least we are beginning to see the way. "We all have the same hard life," wrote Korean garment worker Min Chong Suk. "We are bound together with one string."

IX

HEALTH AND WELFARE

One of the most devastating inequalities in American society is the social stratification of health and illness—the absence of decent medical care for many people and the subjection of many groups, including minorities, women, and blue-collar workers, to living and working conditions that systematically undermine their health.

Similar inequalities in medical care exist in many societies, but the health record of the United States is worse than that of any other developed country. In fact, as a National Advisory Commission on Health Manpower put it in 1967, the health statistics of certain groups—the rural poor, urban ghetto-dwellers, migrant workers, and others—"occasionally resemble the health statistics of a developing country."[1] Moreover, the quality of health care available to the middle classes is erratic and in some ways diminishing.

The inequality of American health care has several sources: Industries more concerned with profit than with the well-being of workers; professional groups jealously guarding their control over the distribution of medical services; and deeply rooted ideologies stressing the beneficial role of competition and private enterprise, even in the area of human health. The dimensions of the crisis in health care are surveyed in Barbara and John Ehrenreich's, article, "The American Health Empire." Medical care in the United States is expensive, fragmented, and clothed in frightening mystification. Its practitioners are increasingly unaccountable to the people they serve. Contrary to those who believe that the crisis in medical care results from the fact that our health care system is an unorganized "nonsystem," the Ehrenreichs argue that medical care in the United States is, in fact, a very organized enterprise—but organized toward generating profit, rather than providing decent health care.

"Getting Cancer on the Job" illustrates this point more specifically. Larry Agran shows how the epidemic of cancer among blue-collar workers is fed by the systematic unconcern of American industries, which have been known to cover up evidence produced by their own staff physicians of unsafe levels of cancer-causing chemicals. Government response to the growth of industrial cancer has been minimal at best; the regulatory agencies are either too timid to take on the industries or are so understaffed and poorly funded that they can barely begin to seek solutions to the massive problem of industrial disease.

The problems of health care reflect a larger theme that affects most social services in America. Human welfare is seen as dependent on individual effort. The more traditional idea that society as a whole should have responsibility for the welfare of its members is generally rejected. There are exceptions to this, of course: Large corporations that run into financial trouble are not hesitant to ask for support from the rest of us in the form of government subsidies. But for most people, such basic human needs as health care, shelter, and the care of children are things that we have to acquire on our own, if we can. For those who can't, government programs do exist to provide basic social services—but all too often, they are provided skimpily and inhumanely. And as we've seen so sharply in the 1980s, our social services are among the first casualties of governmental "budget balancing" in the name of economic "renewal."

A central theme of the welfare system, since its beginnings in the repressive and puritanical mentality of seventeenth-century England, has been the division of the poor into the categories of "deserving" and "undeserving"—the former including the aged and disabled, the latter comprising those who are presumably physically able to work. Most of our current programs for the poor, as well as recent government proposals for welfare reform, tend to treat them as undeserving. Benefits are contingent on "good" behavior and are accompanied by a host of special restrictions applying only to those "on welfare." In return for providing support, the welfare system assumes the authority to demand of the poor behavior that is not demanded of anyone else. In this way, a "dual system of law" has developed—one for the poor, another for everyone else.

If, as many people have argued, this system is cruel and unjust, why has it persisted? In "The Relief of Welfare," Frances Fox Piven and Richard A. Cloward argue that the welfare system serves to regulate the labor force in capitalist societies. The puny and demeaning levels of assistance and the tendency to throw people off the welfare rolls for "immoral" behavior are means of enforcing low-wage work during times when labor is needed; but under conditions of massive unemployment, the welfare rolls are expanded in order to forestall disorder. Thus, the persistence of a degrading welfare apparatus, for Piven and Cloward, is linked to the most fundamental requirements of an essentially unstable economic system. As long as we are unwilling to provide ample and decently paid work, there must be a system to enforce work by making nonwork degrading and painful.

The attitude that we are each individually responsible for our own welfare also shapes our treatment of the aged, for whom, as Robert N. Butler shows, growing old has become an increasingly painful and demeaning process in America. There is no public commitment to providing an adequate standard of living for the aged. Those with sufficient means may be able to afford good housing and medical care; but for many, aging means poverty, uselessness, and, often, segregation into custodial institutions on the grounds of "senility." Job programs ignore the old; inflation eats away at pensions and other resources. Adding insult to injury, America's neglect of the aged is justified through shopworn myths about their incompetence.

REFERENCE

1. Report of the National Advisory Commission on Health Manpower, quoted in R. M. Titmuss, "Ethics and Economics of Medical Care," in *Commitment to Welfare* (New York: Pantheon, 1968), p. 268.

26

THE AMERICAN HEALTH EMPIRE:
THE SYSTEM BEHIND THE CHAOS

Barbara and John Ehrenreich

The American health crisis became official in 1969. President Nixon announced it in a special message in July. Liberal academic observers of the health scene, from Harvard's John Knowles to Einstein College of Medicine's Martin Cherkasky, hastened to verify the existence of the crisis. Now the media is rushing in with details and documentation. *Time, Fortune, Business Week*, CBS, and NBC are on the medical scene, and finding it "chaotic, "archaic," and "unmanageable."

For the great majority of Americans, the "health care crisis" is not a TV show or a presidential address; it is an on-going crisis of survival. Every day three million Americans go out in search of medical care. Some find it; others do not. Some are helped by it; others are not. Another twenty million Americans probably ought to enter the daily search for medical help, but are not healthy enough, rich enough, or enterprising enough to try. The obstacles are enormous. Health care is scarce and expensive to begin with. It is dangerously fragmented, and usually offered in an atmosphere of mystery and unaccountability. For many, it is obtained only at the price of humiliation, dependence, or bodily insult. The stakes are high—health, life, beauty, sanity—and getting higher all the time. But the odds of winning are low and getting lower.

For the person in search of medical help, the illness or possibility of illness which prompted the search is quickly overshadowed by the difficulties of the medical experience itself.

PROBLEM ONE: FINDING A PLACE
WHERE THE APPROPRIATE CARE IS OFFERED
AT A REASONABLE PRICE

For the poor and for many working-class people, this can be all but impossible. Not long ago it was commonly believed that sheer distance from doctors or hospitals was a problem only in rural areas. But today's resident of slums, like Brooklyn's Bedford-Stuyvesant, or Chicago's south

side, is as effectively removed from health services as his relatives who
stayed behind in Mississippi. One region of Bedford-Stuyvesant contains
only one practicing physician for a population of one hundred thousand.
Milwaukee County Hospital, the sole source of medical care for tens of
thousands of poor and working-class people, is sixteen miles outside the
city, an hour and a half bus ride for many. A few years ago, a social
science graduate student was able to carry out her thesis work on rural
health problems in a densely populated Chicago slum.

After getting to the building or office where medical care is offered,
the next problem which affects both poor and middle-class people is paying for the care. Except at a diminishing number of charitable facilities,
health care is not free; it is a commodity which consumers purchase from
providers at unregulated, steadily increasing prices. Insurance plans like
Medicaid, Medicare, and Blue Cross help soften the blow for many, but
many other people are too rich for Medicaid, too poor for Blue Cross, and
too young for Medicare. A total of twenty-four million Americans have
no health insurance of any variety. Even for those who are insured, costs
remain a major problem: first there is the cost of the insurance itself, then
there is the cost of all those services which are not covered by insurance.
102 million Americans have no insurance coverage for visits to the doctor,
as opposed to hospital stays. They spend about ten dollars just to see a
doctor; more, if laboratory tests or specialists are needed. Otherwise, they
wait for an illness to become serious enough to warrant hospitalization.
Hardly anyone, of course, has insurance for such everyday needs as dental care or prenatal care.

Supposing that one can afford the cost of the care itself, there remains
the problem of paying for the time spent getting it. Working people must
plan on losing a full work-day for a simple doctor's appointment, whether
with a private physician or at a hospital clinic. First, there is a long wait
to see the doctor. Middle-class people may enjoy comfortable chairs, magazines, and even coffee, while waiting in their doctor's anteroom, but
they wait just the same. As busy private doctors try to squeeze more and
more customers into their day, their patients are finding that upwards of
an hour's wait is part of the price for a five- or ten-minute face-to-face
encounter with a harried physician.

Not all kinds of care are as available, or unavailable, as others. In a city
studded with many major hospitals the person with multiple bullet
wounds or a rare and fatal blood disease stands a far better chance of
making a successful medical "connection," than the person with stomach
pains, or the parents of a feverish child. Hospitals, at all times, and physicians, after 7:00 P.M. (if they can be located) are geared to handling the
dramatic and exotic cases which excite professional interest. The more
mundane, or less obviously catastrophic, case can wait—and wait. For
psychiatric problems, which are probably the nation's single greatest

source of disability, there are almost no outpatient facilities, much less sympathetic attention when one finds them. Those of the mentally ill who venture forth in search of help are usually rewarded with imprisonment in a state institution, except for the few who are able to make the investment required for private psychiatric care. Even for the wealthy, borderline problems, like alcoholism and addiction, may as well be lived with—there are vanishingly few facilities of any kind to deal with them.

PROBLEM TWO: FINDING ONE'S WAY AMIDST THE MANY AVAILABLE TYPES OF MEDICAL CARE

Most of us know what buildings or other locations are possible sources of medical help. Many of us can even arrange to get to these buildings in a reasonable amount of time. But, having arrived at the right spot, the patient finds that his safari has just begun. He must now chop through the tangled morass of medical specialization. The only system to American health services, the patient discovers, is the system used in preparing the tables of contents of medical textbooks. Everything is arranged according to the various specialties and subspecialties doctors study, not according to the symptoms and problems which patients perceive.

The middle-class patient is relatively lucky. He has a private doctor who can serve as a kind of guide. After an initial examination, which may cost as little as five dollars or as much as fifty dollars, the patient's personal doctor sends him to visit a long list of his specialist colleagues—a hematologist, allergist, cardiologist, endocrinologist, and maybe a urologist. Each of these examines his organ of interest, collects twenty dollars and up, and passes the patient along to the next specialist in line. If the patient is lucky, his illness will be claimed by one of the specialists fairly early in the process. If he is not so lucky, none of them will claim it, or—worse yet—several of them will. Only the very wealthy patient can afford the expense of visiting and retaining two medical specialists.

The hospital clinic patient wanders about in the same jungle, but without a guide. The hospital may screen him for his ills and point him in the right direction, but, from then on, he's on his own. There's nobody to take overall responsibility for his illness. He can only hope that at some point in time and space, one of the many specialty clinics to which he has been sent (each at the cost of a day off from work) will coincide with his disease of the moment.

Just as exasperating as the fragmentation of medical care is the fragmentation of medical care financing. Seymour Thaler, a New York state senator from Queens, likes to tell the story of one of his constituents who came to Thaler's office, pulled out his wallet, and emptied out a stack of cards. "Here's my Medicaid card, my Medicare card, my Blue Cross sup-

plementary card, my workmen's compensation card, and my union retirement health plan card." "So what are you complaining about?"
Thaler asked. "I've got a stomach ache," the old man answered, "so what
do I do?"

A family makes matters even more complicated and confusing. Grandparents have Medicare, children have Medicaid, the parents may have
one or several union hospitalization insurance plans. No one is covered for
everything, and no mother is sure just who is covered for what. If three
members of the family came down with the same illness, they would
more than likely end up seeing three different doctors, paying for it in
three (or more) different ways, and staying in separate hospitals. In 1968,
a New York father of six quit his job and applied for welfare, claiming he
couldn't work and see to his children's health care. One child, diagnosed
as retarded, had to be taken to and from a special school each day. All
required dental care, which was free at a Health Department clinic on
Manhattan's lower east side. For dental surgery, however, they went to a
clinic a bus ride away, at Bellevue. The youngest children went to a
neighborhood pediatrician who accepted Medicaid patients. An older
child, with a rare metabolic defect, required weekly visits to a private
hospital clinic a half hour's trip uptown. The father himself, the victim of
a chronic back problem, qualified for care at a union health center on the
west side. For him, family health maintenance was a full-time job, not, as
it is for most parents, just a busy sideline.

Doctors like to tell us that fragmentation is the price of quality. We
should be happy to be seeing a specialist, twice as happy to be seeing two
of them, and fully gratified to have everyone in the family seeing a special one of his own. In many difficult cases, specialization does pay off.
But evidence is accumulating that care which is targeted at a particular
organ often completely misses the mark. Take the case of the Cleveland
woman who had both a neurological disease and a damaged kidney. Since
the neurologist had no time to chat, and since she assumed that doctors
know a good deal more than their patients, she never mentioned her
kidney to her neurologist. Over a period of time, her urologist noted a
steady deterioration of her kidney problem. Only after the kidney had
been removed did the urologist discover that his colleague, the neurologist, has been prescribing a drug which is known to put an extra strain on
the kidney.

The patient may have only one problem—as far as his doctors are concerned—and still succumb to medical fragmentation. Recently, an elderly
man with a heart condition was discharged from a prestigious private
medical center, assured he was good for another decade or two. Four
weeks later he died of heart failure. Cause? Overexertion. He lived on the
fifth floor of a walk-up apartment—a detail which was obviously out of
the purview of his team of hospital physicians, for all the time and tech-

nology they had brought to bear on his heart. Until human physiology adapts itself to the fragmentation of modern medical practice, it is up to the patient himself to integrate his medical problems, and to integrate them with the rest of his life.

Problem Three: Figuring Out
What They Are Doing To You

Many people are not satisfied to have found the correct doctor or clinic. They also want to know what is being done to their bodies, and why. For most, this is not just idle curiosity. If the patient has to pay all or some of the bill, he wants to know whether a cheaper treatment would be just as efficacious, or whether he should really be paying for something much fancier. The doctors' magazine *Medical Economics* tells the story of the family whose infant developed bronchopneumonia. The physician who visited the home judged from the furnishings that the family could not afford hospitalization. With little or no explanation, he prescribed an antibiotic and left. The baby died six hours later. The parents were enraged when they learned the diagnosis and realized that hospitalization might have helped. They wanted to know the risks, and make the decision themselves.

More commonly, the patients fear they will be overtreated, hence overbilled, for a medical problem. A twenty-five-year-old graduate student, a victim of hayfever, was told by an allergist at prestigious New York Hospital that his case would require several years of multiple, weekly, antiallergy injections. When he asked to know the probability that this treatment would actually cure his hayfever, the allergist told him, "I'm the doctor, not you, and if you don't want to trust my judgement you can find another doctor—or be sick forever for all I care!" Following this advice, the patient did, indeed, find a new doctor. And when the limitations of the treatment were explained to him, he decided the treatment was probably worth the trouble after all. The important thing is that *he* decided.

Some people, perhaps more trusting of doctors, never ask for an explanation until they have to in sheer self-defense. Residents of Manhattan's lower east side tell the story of the woman who was admitted to a ward at Bellevue for a stomach operation. The operation was scheduled for Thursday. On Wednesday a nurse told her she was to be operated on that day. The patient asked why the change. "Never mind," said the nurse, "give me your glasses." The patient could not see why she should give up her glasses, but finally handed them over at the nurse's insistence. Inside the operating room, the patient was surprised when she was not given general anesthesia. Although her English was poor, she noticed that the doctors were talking about eye cancer, and looking at her eyes. She sat up and said there was nothing wrong with her eyes—her stomach was the problem. She was pushed back on the operating table. With the strength of panic, she leapt up and ran into the hall. A security guard caught her, running sobbing down the hall in an operating gown. She was summarily placed in the psychiatric ward for a week's observation.

Even when confronted with what seems to be irrational therapy, most patients feel helpless to question or complain. A new folklore of medicine has emerged, rivaling that of the old witch doctors. Medical technology, from all that the patient has read in the newspapers, is as complex and mystifying as space technology. Physicians, from all he has seen on TV serials or heard thirdhand from other patients, are steely-nerved, omniscient, medical astronauts. The patient himself is usually sick-feeling, often undressed, a nameless observer in a process which he can never hope to understand. He has been schooled by all the news of medical "space shots"—heart transplants, renal dialysis, wonder drugs, nuclear therapy, etc.—to expect some small miracle in his own case—a magical new prescription drug or an operation. And miracles, by their very nature, are not explainable or understandable. Whether it's a "miracle detergent," a "miracle mouth wash," or a "miracle medical treatment," the customer can only pay the price and hope the product works.

PROBLEM FOUR: GETTING A HEARING IF THINGS DON'T GO RIGHT

Everything about the American medical system seems calculated to maintain the childlike, dependent, and depersonalized condition of the patient. It is bad enough that modern medical technology has been infused by its practitioners with all the mystery and unaccountability of primitive shamanism. What is worse is that the patient is given absolutely no means of judging what care he should get or evaluating what he has gotten. As one Washington, D.C. taxi driver put it, "When I buy a used car, I know it might be a gyp. But I go over it, test it, try to figure out if it's O.K. for the price. Then take last year when I got started getting some stomach problem. The doctor says I need an operation. How do I know I need an operation? But what can I do—I have an operation. Later I get the bill—$1700—and Blue Cross left over $850 for me to pay. How should I know whether the operation should cost $50 or $1700? Now I think my stomach problem is coming back! Do I get my money back?"

Doctors and hospitals have turned patients into "consumers," but patients have none of the rights or protections which consumers of other goods and services expect. People in search of medical care cannot very easily do comparative shopping. When they're sick, they take help wherever they can get it. Besides, patients who switch doctors more than once are viewed by other doctors as possible neurotics. Health consumers know what they'd like—good health—but they have no way of knowing what this should entail in terms of services—a new diet, a prescription, or a thousand-dollar operation. Once they've received the service, the doctor, not their own perception, tells them whether it did any good. And if they suspect that the price was unduly high, the treatment unnecessarily complicated or drastic, there is no one to turn to—no Better Business Bureau or Department of Consumer Protection.

When something goes really wrong—a person is killed or maimed in the course of medical treatment—there is still no formal avenue of recourse for the patient or his survivors. Middle-class people, who know the ropes and have some money to spend, can embark on a long and costly malpractice suit, and win, at best, a cash compensation for the damage done. But this process, like everything else in a person's encounter with doctors and hospitals, is highly individualistic, and has no pay-off in terms of the general health and safety of the community. For the poor, there is usually no resource at all short of open resistance. A Manhattan man, infuriated by his wife's treatment in the emergency room of New York's Beth Israel Medical Center, beat up the intern on duty. Another man, whose child died inexplicably at a big city public hospital, solitarily pickets City Hall summer after summer.

PROBLEM FIVE: OVERCOMING THE BUILT-IN RACISM AND MALE CHAUVINISM OF DOCTORS AND HOSPITALS

In the ways that it irritates, exhausts, and occasionally injures patients, the American medical system is not egalitarian. Everything that is bad about American medicine is especially so for Americans who are not male or white. Blacks, and in some areas Indians, Puerto Ricans, or Mexicans, face unique problems of access to medical care, and not just because they are poor. Many hospitals in the south are still unofficially segregated, or at least highly selective. For instance, in towns outside of Orangeburg, South Carolina, blacks claim they are admitted to the hospital only on the recommendation of a (white) employer or other white "reference."

In the big cities of the north, health facilities are available on a more equal footing to blacks, browns, and poor whites. But for the nonwhite patient, the medical experience is more likely to be something he will not look forward to repeating. The first thing he notices about the large hospital—he is more likely to be at a hospital clinic than at a private doctor's office—is that the doctors are almost uniformly white; the nonskilled workers are almost entirely brown or black. Thus the nonwhite patient enters the hospital at the bottom end of its social scale, quite aside from any personal racial prejudices the staff may harbor. And, in medicine, these prejudices take a particularly insulting form. Black and Puerto Rican patients complain again and again of literally being "treated like animals" by everyone from the clerks to the M.D.'s. Since blacks are assumed to be less sensitive than white patients, they get less privacy. Since blacks are assumed to be more ignorant than whites, they get less by way of explanation of what is happening to them. And since they are assumed to be irresponsible and forgetful, they are more likely to be given a drastic, one-shot treatment, instead of a prolonged regimen of drugs, or a restricted diet.

Only a part of this medical racism is due to the racist attitudes of individual medical personnel. The rest is "institutional racism," a built-in feature of the way medicine is learned and practiced in the United States. As interns and residents, young doctors get their training by practicing on the hospital ward and clinic patients—generally nonwhite. Later they make their money by practicing for a paying clientele—generally white. White patients are "customers"; black patients are "teaching material." White patients pay for care with their money; black patients pay with their dignity and their comfort. Clinic patients at the hospital affiliated with Columbia University's medical school recently learned this distinction in a particularly painful way. They had complained that anesthesia was never available in the dental clinic. Finally, a leak from one of the dental interns showed that this was an official policy: the patient's pain is a good guide to the dentist-in-training—it teaches him not to drill too deep. Anesthesia would deaden the pain and dull the intern's learning experience.

Hospitals' institutional racism clearly serves the needs of the medical system, but it is also an instrument of the racist, repressive impulses of the society at large. Black community organizations in New York have charged hospitals with "genocidal" policies towards the black community. Harlem residents tell of medical atrocities—cases where patients have unwittingly given their lives or their organs in the cause of medical research. A more common charge is that, to public hospital doctors, "the birth control method of choice for black women is the hysterectomy." Even some doctors admit that hysterectomies are often performed with pretty slim justification in ghetto hospitals. (After all, they can't be expected to take a pill every day, can they? And one less black baby is one less baby on welfare, isn't it?) If deaths from sloppy abortions run highest in the ghetto, it is partly because black women are afraid to go to the hospital for an abortion or for treatment following a sloppy abortion, fearing that an involuntary sterilization—all for "medical" reasons—will be the likely result. Aside from their medical policies, ghetto hospitals have a reputation as racist because they serve as police strongholds in the community. In the emergency room, cops often outnumber doctors. They interrogate the wounded—often before the doctor does, and pick up any vagrants, police brutality victims, drunks or addicts who have mistakenly come in for help. In fact, during the 1964 riots in New York, the police used Harlem Hospital as a launching pad for their pacification measures.

Women are the other major group of Americans singled out for special treatment by the medical system. Just as blacks face a medical hierarchy dominated by whites, women entering a hospital or doctor's office encounter a hierarchy headed by men, with women as nurses and aides playing subservient, hand-maid roles. And in the medical system, women face all the male supremacist attitudes and superstitions that characterize American society in general—they are the victims of sexism, as blacks are of racism. Women are assumed to be incapable of understanding complex technological explanations, so they are not given any. Women are assumed to be emotional and "difficult," so they are often classified as neurotic well before physical illness has been ruled out. (Note how many tranquilizer ads in medical journals depict women, rather than men, as likely customers.) And women are assumed to be vain, so they are the special prey of the paramedical dieting, cosmetics, and plastic surgery businesses.

Everyone who enters the medical system in search of care quickly finds himself transformed into an object, a mass of organs and pathology. Women have a special handicap—they start out as "objects." Physicians, despite their supposed objectivity and clinical impersonality, share all the sexual hangups of other American men. The sick person who enters the gynecology clinic is the same sex as the sexual "object" who sells cars in the magazine ads. What makes matters worse is that a high proportion of routine medical care for women centers on the most superstitious and fantasy-ridden aspect of female physiology—the reproductive system. Women of all classes almost uniformly hate or fear their gynecologists. The gynecologist plays a controlling role in that aspect of their lives society values most, the sexual aspect—and he knows it. Middle-class women find a man who is either patronizingly jolly, or cold and condescending. Poorer women using clinics, are more likely to encounter outright brutality and sadism. Of course, black women have it worst of all. A shy teenager from a New York ghetto reports going to the clinic for her first prenatal check-up, and being used as teaching material for an entire class of young, male medical students learning to give pelvic examinations.

Doctors and hospitals treat pregnancy and childbirth, which are probably among the healthier things that women experience, as disease—to be supervised by doctors and confined to hospitals. Women in other economically advanced countries, such as Holland, receive their prenatal care at home, from nurses, and, if all goes well, are delivered at home by trained midwives. (The Netherlands rank third lowest in infant mortality rate; the U.S. ranks fourteenth!) But for American women, pregnancy and childbirth are just another harrowing, expensive medical procedure. The doctor does it; the woman is essentially passive. Even in large cities, women often have to go from one obstetrician to another before they find one who approves of natural childbirth. Otherwise, childbirth is handled as if it were a surgical operation, even to the point of "scheduling" the event to suit the obstetrician's convenience through the use of possibly dangerous labor-inducing drugs.

Most people who have set out to look for medical care eventually have to conclude that there is no American medical system—at least there is no systematic way in America of getting medical help when you need it, without being financially ruined, humiliated, or injured in the process. What system there is—the three hundred thousand doctors, seven thousand hospitals and supporting insurance plans—was clearly not designed to deal with the sick. In fact the one thing you need most in order to qualify for care financially and to survive the process of obtaining it is *health*, plus, of course, a good deal of cunning and resourcefulness. The trouble is that it's almost impossible to stay healthy and strong enough to be able to tackle the medical system. Preventive health care (regular check-ups, chest X-rays, pap tests, etc.) is not a specialty or even an interest of the American medical system.

The price of this double bind—having to be healthy just to stay healthy—is not just consumer frustration and discomfort. The price is lives. The United States ranks fourteenth among the nations of the world in infant mortality, which means that approximately 33,000 American babies under one year old die unnecessarily every year. (Our infant mortality statistics are not, as often asserted, so high because they are "spoiled" by the death rates for blacks. The statistics for white America alone compare unfavorably to those for countries such as Sweden, the Netherlands, Norway, etc.) Mothers also stand a better chance of dying in the United States, where the maternal mortality rate ranks twelfth among the world's nations. The average American man lives five years less than the Swedish man, and his life expectancy is shorter than for males in seventeen other nations. Many American men never live out their already relatively short lifetime, since the chance of dying between ages forty and fifty is twice as high for an American as it is for a Scandinavian. What is perhaps most alarming about these statistics is that they are, in a relative sense, getting worse. The statistics improve a little each year, but at a rate far slower than that for other advanced countries. Gradually, the United States is slipping behind most of the European nations, and even some non-European nations, in its ability to keep its citizens alive. These are the symptoms; unhealthy statistics, soaring costs and mounting consumer frustration over the quality and even the quantity of medical care. Practically everyone but the A.M.A. agrees that something is drastically wrong. The roster of public figures actively concerned about the health care crisis is beginning to read like *Who's Who in America:* Labor leaders Walter Reuther of the Auto Workers and Harold Gibbons of the Teamsters, businessmen like General James Gavin of Arthur D. Little, Inc., politicians like New York's Mayor John Lindsay and Cleveland's Mayor Carl Stokes, doctors like Michael DeBakey of Baylor College of Medicine, and civil rights leaders like Mrs. Martin Luther King, Jr. and Whitney Young, Jr. With the help of eminent medical economists like Harvard's Rashi Fein and Princeton's Ann Somers, these liberal leaders have come up with a common diagnosis of the problem: the medical care system is in a state of near-chaos. There is no one to blame—medical care is simply adrift, with the winds rising in all directions. In the words of the official pamphlet of the committee for National Health Insurance (a coalition of one hundred well-known liberals): "The fact is that we do not have a health care system at all. We have a 'nonsystem.' " According to this diagnosis, the health care industry is, in the words of the January, 1970, *Fortune* magazine, a "cottage industry." It is dominated by small, inefficient and uncoordinated enterprises (private doctors, small hospitals, and nursing homes), which add up to a fragmented and wasteful whole—a nonsystem.

Proponents of the nonsystem theory trace the problem to the fact that health care, as a commodity, does not obey the orderly, businesslike laws of economics. With a commodity like bacon, demand reflects people's desire to eat bacon and ability to pay for bacon. Since the supply gracefully adjusts itself to demand, things never get out of hand—there is a *system* of bacon production and sales. No such invisible hand of economic law operates in the health market. First, people buy medical care when they have to, not when they want to or can afford to. Then, when he does go to purchase care, the consumer is not the one who decides what and how much to buy—the doctor or hospital does. In other words, in the medical market place, it is the supplier who controls the demand. Finally, medical care suppliers have none of the usual economic incentives to lower prices or rationalize their services. Most hospitals receive a large part of their income on a cost-plus basis from insurance organizations, and couldn't care less about cost or efficiency. Doctors do not compete on the basis of price. In fact, given the shortage of doctors (which is maintained by the doctors themselves through the A.M.A.'s prevention of medical school expansion), they don't have to compete at all.

Solutions offered by the liberal viewers of the medical nonsystem are all along the lines of putting the health industry on a more "rational," i.e., businesslike basis. First, the consumer should not have to fish in his pocket each time the need for care arises; he should have some sort of all-purpose medical credit card. With some form of National Health Insurance, all consumers, rich or poor, would have the same amount of medical credit, paid for by the government, by the consumer, or both through payroll taxes. . . . Second, the delivery of health services must be made more efficient. Just as supermarkets are more efficient than corner groceries, and shopping centers are more efficient than isolated supermarkets, the medical system ought to be more efficient if it were bigger and more integrated at all levels. Doctors should be encouraged to come together into group practices, and group practices, hospitals and medical schools should be gradually knitted together into coordinated regional medical care systems. Since they are the centers of medical technology, the medical schools should be the centers and leaders of these regional systems—regulating quality in the "outposts," training professional and paraprofessional personnel, and planning to meet changing needs. . . .

There is only one thing wrong with this analysis of the health care crisis: it's based on a false assumption. The medical reformers have assumed, understandably enough, that the function of the American health industry is to provide adequate health care to the American people. From this it is easy enough to conclude that there is no American health *system*. But this is like assuming that the function of the TV networks is to give comprehensive, penetrating, and meaningful information to the viewers—a premise which would quickly lead us to believe that the networks have fallen into wild disorganization and confusion. Like the mass media, the American medical industry has many items on its agenda other than service to the consumers. Analyzed in terms of all of its functions, the medical industry emerges as a coherent, highly organized system. One particular function—patient care—may be getting slighted, and there may be some problems in other areas as well, but it remains a *system*, and can only be analyzed as such.

The most obvious function of the American medical system, other than patient care, is profit-making. When it comes to making money, the health industry is an extraordinarily well-organized and efficient machine. The most profitable small business around is the private practice of medicine, with aggregate profits running into the billions. The most profitable big business in America is the manufacture and sale of drugs. Rivaling the drug industry for Wall Street attention is the burgeoning hospital supply and equipment industry, with products ranging from chicken soup to catheters and heart-lung machines. The fledgling nursing home (for profit) industry was a speculator's dream in 1968 and 1969, and even the stolid insurance companies gross over ten billion dollars a year in health insurance premiums. In fact, the health business is so profitable that even the "nonprofit" hospitals make profits. All that "nonprofit" means is that the hospital's profit, i.e., the difference between its income and its expenditures, is not distributed to shareholders. These nonprofits are used to finance the expansion of medical empires—to buy real estate, stocks, plush new buildings, and expensively salaried professional employees. The medical system may not be doing too well at fighting disease, but, as any broker will testify, it's one of the healthiest businesses around.

Next in the medical system's list of priorities is research. Again, if this undertaking is measured in terms of its dividends for patient care, it comes out looking pretty unsystematic and disorganized. Although the vast federal appropriations for biomedical research are primarily motivated by the hope of improving health care, only a small fraction (much smaller than need be) of the work done in the name of medical research leaks out to the general public as improved medical care. But medical research has a *raison d'être* wholly independent of the delivery of health services, as an indispensable part of the nation's giant research and development enterprise. Since the Second World War, the United States has developed a vast machinery for R.&D. in all areas—physics, electronics, aerospace as well as biomedical sciences—financed largely by the government and carried out in universities and private industry. It has generated military and aerospace technology, and all the many little innovations which fuel the expansion of private industry.

For the purposes of this growing R.&D. effort, the medical system is important because it happens to be the place where R.&D. in general comes into contact with human material. Medical research is the link. The nation's major biomedical research institutes are affiliated to hospitals to a significant extent because they require human material to carry out their own, usually abstract, investigations. For instance, a sophisticated (and possibly patentable) technique for investigating protein structure was recently developed through the use of the blood of several dozen victims of a rare and fatal bone marrow disease. Even the research carried out inside hospitals has implications for the entire R.&D. enterprise. Investigations of the pulmonary disorders of patients in Harlem Hospital may provide insights for designing space units, or it may contribute to the technology of aerosol dissemination of nerve gas. Or, of course, it may simply lead to yet another investigation.

Human bodies are not all that the medical care system offers up to R.&D. The sociological and psychological research carried out in hospitals and ghetto health centers may have pay-offs in the form of new counterinsurgency techniques for use at home and abroad. And who knows what sinister—or benignly academic—ends are met by the routine neurological and drug research carried out on the nation's millions of mental hospital inmates?

Finally, an important function of the medical care system is the production of its key personnel—physicians. Here, again, there seems to be no system if patient care is the ultimate goal. The medical schools graduate each year just a few more doctors than are needed to replace the ones who retire, and far too few doctors to keep up with the growth of population. Of those who graduate, a growing proportion go straight into academic government, or industrial biomedical research, and never see a patient. The rest, according to some dissatisfied medical students, aren't trained to take care of patients anyway—having been educated chiefly in academic medicine (a mixture of basic sciences and "interesting" pathology). But all this is not as irrational as it seems. The limited size of medical school classes has been maintained through the diligent, and entirely systematic, efforts of the A.M.A. Too many—or even enough—doctors would mean lower profits for those already in practice. And the research orientation of medical education simply reflects the medical schools' own consuming preoccupation with research.

Profits, research and teaching, then, are independent functions of the medical system, not just adjuncts to patient care. But they do not go on along separate tracks, removed from patient care. Patients are the indispensable ingredient of medical profit-making, research, and education. In order that the medical industry serve these functions, patient care must be twisted to meet the needs of these other "medical" enterprises.

Different groups of patients serve the ends of profit-making, research and education in different ways. The rich, of course, do much to keep medical care profitable. They can afford luxury, so, for them, the medical system produces a luxury commodity—the most painstaking, super-technological treatment possible; special cosmetic care to preserve youth, or to add or subtract fatty tissue; even sumptuous private hospital rooms with carpeting and a selection of wines at meals. The poor, on the other hand, serve chiefly to subsidize medical research and education—with their bodies. City and county hospitals and the wards and clinics of private hospitals provide free care for the poor, who, in turn, provide their bodies for young doctors to practice on and for researchers to experiment with. The lucky poor patient with a rare or interesting disease may qualify for someone's research project, and end up receiving the technically most advanced care. But most of the poor are no more interesting than they are profitable, and receive minimal, low-quality care from bored young interns.

The majority of Americans have enough money to buy their way out of being used for research, but not enough to buy luxury care. Medical care for the middle class is, like any commodity, aimed at a mass market: the profits are based on volume, not on high quality. The rich man may have his steak dinners catered to him individually; the middle-class consumer waits for his hamburger in the check-out line at the A&P. Similarly, the middle-class patient waits in crowded waiting rooms, receives five minutes of brusque, impersonal attention from a doctor who is quicker to farm him out to a specialist than to take the time to treat him himself, and finally is charged all that the market will bear. Preventive care is out of the question: it is neither very profitable nor interesting to the modern, science-oriented M.D.

The crisis experienced by the poor and middle-class consumer of health care can be traced directly to the fact that patient care is not the only, or even the primary, aim of the medical care system. But what has turned the consumer's private nightmare into a great public debate about the health care crisis is that the other functions of the system are also in trouble. Profit-making, research, and education are all increasingly suffering from financial shortage on the one hand and institutional inadequacies on the other. The solutions offered by the growing chorus of medical reformers are, in large measure, aimed at salvaging profits, research, and education as much as they are aimed at improving patient care. They are simple survival measures, aimed at preserving and strengthening the medical system as it now operates.

No one, so far, has seen through the proposed reforms. Union and management groups, who have moved into the forefront of the medical reform movement, seem happy to go along with the prescription that the medical system is writing for itself. The alternative—to marshall all the force of public power to take medical care out of the arena of private enterprise and recreate it as a public system, a community service, is rarely mentioned, and never considered seriously. To do this would be to challenge some of the underlying tenets of the American free enterprise system. If physicians were to become community employees, if the drug companies were to be nationalized—then why not expropriate the oil and coal industries, or the automobile industry? There is an even more direct antipathy to nationalizing the health industry: a host of industries, including the aerospace industry, the electronic industry, the chemical industry, and the insurance industry, all have a direct stake in the profitability of the medical care system. (And a much larger sector of American industry stands to profit from the human technology spun off by the medical research enterprise.) Of course, the argument never takes this form. Both business and unions assert, in their public pronouncements, that only a private enterprise system is capable of managing medical services in an efficient, nonbureaucratic, and flexible manner. (The obvious extrapolation, that all medical services, including voluntary and city hospitals, would be in better shape if run as profit-making enterprises, is already being advanced by a few of the more visionary medical reformers.)

For all these reasons, business and unions (and, as a result, government) are not interested in restructuring the medical care system in ways contrary to those already put forth by the doctors, hospitals, and medical industry companies. Their only remaining choice is to go along with the reforms which have been proposed, in the hope that lower costs, and possibly even more effective care, will somehow fall out as by-products.

For the health care consumer, this is a slim hope. What he is up against now, what he will be up against even after the best-intentioned reform measures, is a system in which health care is itself only a byproduct, secondary to the priorities of profits, research, and training. The danger is that, when all the current reforms are said and done, the system as a whole will be tighter, more efficient, and harder to crack, while health services, from the consumer's point of view, will be no less chaotic and inadequate. Health care will remain a commodity, to be purchased at great effort and expense, and not a right to be freely exercised.

But there are already the beginnings of a consumer rebellion against the reformer-managers of the medical care system. . . . The demand is to turn the medical system upside down, putting human care on top, placing research and education at its service, and putting profit-making aside. Ultimately, the growing movement of health care consumers does not want to "consume" health care at all, on any terms. They want to take it—because they have to have it—even if this means creating a wholly new American health care system.

27
GETTING CANCER ON THE JOB

Larry Agran

In April 1973, Joseph Fitman's doctor told him he had lung cancer. A few days later, he underwent a radical left pneumonectomy—the removal of his left lung. Recovery from the surgery was very slow, difficult and imperfect. At 63, after more than four decades of industrial labor, Joe Fitman was finished as a productive worker.

Now, two years after his cancer operation, Fitman is alive but not well. He sees his life in narrowly measured terms:

I can't do too much. Mostly I just watch TV or walk to the patio and sit down. I tried to work, but I just can't, 'cause I'm fightin' so many things. If I do too much, I wind up goin' to the hospital, an emergency. I get the feelin' like if you ran around the block, stopped, sat down—you'd be takin' deep breaths. Well that's my problem. I get spells where my air was bein' shut off and I feel I'm not gettin' oxygen, and I found myself strugglin' for some air.

Statistically, Joe Fitman's case is one of more than 600,000 new cancer cases in the United States in 1973. But upon analysis, it becomes evident that his cancer was not an inexplicable, unpredictable occurrence. His

Larry Agran, "Getting Cancer on the Job," *The Nation*, April 12, 1975. Copyright 1975, The Nation Associates. Reprinted by permission.

work history suggests a classic case of job-caused cancer. Fitman toiled for a quarter-century as a hot metalworker, first in a Pennsylvania tin mill and after that as a blacksmith in a steel mill. Long-time metalworkers who are exposed to iron oxides and a host of metallic dusts and fumes develop lung cancer at rates significantly higher than the general population. Later on, in 1958, Fitman went to work for Douglas Aircraft in Long Beach, Calif. His job was to operate a bench saw, cutting fiberglass. While he wore goggles to shield his eyes, he did not wear a respirator; unwittingly, he was inhaling millions of tiny fiberglass particles, now suspected to be a cancer-causing agent. After he was laid off at Douglas in 1961, Fitman took a job, his last one, with a Southern California plastics firm. There, daily for twelve years he handled and breathed a variety of recognized carcinogens, including asbestos, carbon black and vinyl chloride. It is impossible to say which of these agents was chiefly responsible for his malignancy, but it is reasonable to conclude that it originated with one or more of them.[1]

In 1973, more than 353,000 Americans died from cancer, up by almost 7,000 from the 1972 death toll. More than a decade ago, a World Health Organization committee of cancer experts concluded that a majority of human cancers could well be attributed to known environmental carcinogens. Since then, U.S. and international authorities have estimated that 80 per cent of human cancers, perhaps even 90 per cent, are environmentally induced: that is, they result from exposures to certain cancer-causing substances in the air, water and soil—at work, in the community, or in the home. To those who study such things, it is apparent that the vast majority of these environmentally induced cancers derive from direct and indirect exposure to industrial carcinogens.

In 1942, Dr. Wilhelm C. Hueper, then a research pathologist, wrote a monumental text, *Occupational Tumors and Allied Diseases*. Drawing upon studies of selected worker populations both here and abroad, Hueper convincingly established the relationship between occupational contact with certain chemicals, metals and minerals and a subsequent high incidence of cancer. In the book, he urged adoption of comprehensive preventive measures to minimize the cancer hazards faced by the industrial workforce. His words had little effect.

From the late 1940s through the 1950s, evidence mounted to support Hueper's theory. Still, despite the persuasive body of evidence, public health authorities remained, for the most part, unmoved. By this time, Hueper had become chief of the National Cancer Institute's Environmental Cancer Section and an embattled pioneer in the field of occupational cancer. In 1964, at the age of 70, he was co-author of a second massive text, *Chemical Carcinogenesis and Cancers*. There, Hueper wrote ominously of an impending "epidemic in slow motion." He noted that human cancer ordinarily does not appear until ten, twenty, or even thirty years after exposure to a carcinogen. With this long latent period in mind, he warned that the unbridled proliferation of cancer-causing substances which accompanied the frenetic industrialization after 1940 would, in time, produce a terrible cancer epidemic in the United States. It now appears that a continuing policy of national neglect is, with the passage of time, proving Hueper right.

Rubber workers, routinely exposed to multiple cancer-causing substances, are dying of cancer of the stomach, cancer of the prostate and of leukemia and other cancers of the blood- and lymph-forming tissues at rates ranging from 50 to 300 per cent greater than in the general population.

Steelworkers, particularly the thousands who handle coal as it is transferred to coke ovens for combustion and distillation, fall victim of lung cancer at excessive rates. Those who labor atop the hot coke ovens are most vulnerable to the carcinogenic coal-tar emissions and experience a lung cancer rate seven times as great as would normally be expected.

Asbestos workers, including those who mill the mineral and those who must use it regularly in construction work and elsewhere, die from lung cancer at a rate more than seven times that of comparable control groups. Mesothelioma, a fatal malignancy which attacks the lining of the lungs and abdominal organs, used to be an extremely rare form of cancer. But it has become relatively commonplace among asbestos workers, even those with short-term occupational exposures.

Workers who produce dyestuffs, using benzidine and other so-called aromatic amines, have evidenced notoriously high rates of bladder cancer.

Miners of uranium, iron ore, nickel, chromium and other industrial metals succumb to a wide range of occupationally related cancers. In the case of uranium miners, the lung cancer rate is extraordinary, accounting for upward of 50 per cent of all deaths among these workers.

An estimated 2 million workers, among them dry cleaners, painters, printers and rubber and petroleum workers, are exposed to the solvent benzene, a known leukemia-producing agent.

Another 1.5 million laborers, among them insecticide workers, farm workers and copper and lead smelter workers, are exposed to inorganic arsenic, a carcinogen which causes high rates of lung cancer and lymphatic cancer.

Machinists, chemical workers, woodworkers, roofers—and many more—join an ever expanding list of workers who hold jobs posing special cancer risks of one kind or another.

These developments, and others, indicate that we are in the grip of an emerging national epidemic of blue-collar cancer. Yet for decades, federal and state health agencies have treated occupational cancer as a relatively inconsequential issue. A partial explanation for this neglect might be attributed to the widely held but thoroughly misguided expectation of a universal cancer "cure," a dramatic breakthrough which would obviate the need for expensive preventive policies. But a more probable explanation is the tendency of key public health officials, frequently acting with industry spokesmen, to play down the question of occupational cancer, lest it "frighten" workers and possibly impair production.

Even today, federal policy in the area of occupational cancer is only a notch or two above the do-nothing policies of the 1940s, 1950s and 1960s. In 1970, hope rose temporarily among health-conscious reformers when Congress passed the Occupational Safety and Health Act, an ambitious measure establishing a federal framework for the adoption and enforcement of nationwide occupational health standards to assure that "no employee will suffer diminished health, functional capacity, or life expectancy as a result of his work experience." Sponsors of the legislation had reason to believe that the Department of Labor's Occupational Safety and Health Administration (OSHA), an agency created to administer the act, would give top priority to setting the toughest possible standards for protection against job-caused cancer.

No such luck. Throughout 1971, OSHA adopted no new federal standards. This was no ordinary case of bureaucratic sloth. As we now know, in June of 1972 George C. Guenther, then head of OSHA, sent a confidential memo to higher-ups in the Department of Labor, assuring these administration loyalists that, prior to Election Day, "no highly controversial standards will be proposed by OSHA." Eager to enlist the agency in the Nixon re-election drive, he stressed the attractiveness of a management-oriented OSHA as a "sales point for fund raising."

True to his word, Guenther did not offend management when OSHA finally adopted its first cancer-related work standard, a standard for asbestos exposure. Studies dating back to the 1930s had established airborne asbestos fibers to be a dangerous carcinogen, but the recent work of Dr. Irving Selikoff at the Mount Sinai Medical Center in New York brought out the shocking extent of the damage. About 18 per cent of Americans die of cancer; among asbestos insulation workers, Selikoff found, the toll approaches 50 per cent. Twenty per cent of all long-term asbestos workers die of lung cancer. Another 5 per cent die from the previously rare cancer, mesothelioma. Stomach and colon cancer accounts for still more of the excess cancer deaths.

Armed with this data, Selikoff and labor officials urged upon OSHA the only prudent course when dealing with a carcinogen of such demonstrated potency: adoption of a standard which allows "no detectable level" of exposure. For its part, the industry proposed a standard which would permit the prevailing death-dealing asbestos exposure levels to continue. In the end, OSHA adopted a standard which fell between the

two proposals, cutting maximum exposure levels in half. OSHA thus ignored a fundamental principle of cancer prevention policy: there is no
"safe level" for exposure to a cancer-causing agent. While lowering the
level of exposure can ordinarily be expected to lower the incidence, anything short of a "zero tolerance level" carries the strong likelihood of excessive cancer deaths.

Quite obviously OSHA officials were attempting to balance competing
interests by striking a compromise with their new asbestos standard, but
the compromise is so weak in content that it will have only marginal
effect on cancer rates among asbestos workers. Accordingly, it will certainly lead to still thousands more of needless cancer deaths among the
several hundred thousand asbestos workers in the United States.

In early 1974, the Occupational Safety and Health Administration passed
up an extraordinary opportunity to get a firm hold on the entire problem
of workplace carcinogens. The Oil, Chemical, and Atomic Workers
Union and the Washington-based Health Research Group filed a petition
with OSHA requesting that exposure levels for ten recognized workplace
carcinogens be set at "zero tolerance." Even more important, the petition
included a request that OSHA adopt a precedent-setting permit system
whereby carcinogens would be barred in industrial processes unless a
firm had sought and received a government-issued use permit. In that
way, a manufacturer could not legally use specified carcinogens until
OSHA had surveyed the work environment and certified it to be ex-
posure-proof.

OSHA did adopt fairly rigorous standards for the ten cancer-causing
substances, and for another four substances. But it rejected the all-important permit proposal, on the dubious ground that initiation of such a system was beyond the scope of its statutory authority. For the first time, an
industry producing or using certain carcinogens would have been required to make a convincing showing that: (1) the substance was essential
to its operations; (2) there were no appropriate substitutes of lesser danger; and (3) all necessary steps were being taken to safeguard employees
against any exposure whatever. OSHA determined this was too much to
ask.

Without a permit system, OSHA will need a veritable army to enforce
even the limited number of carcinogen standards adopted to date. No
such army exists. There are at present 800 federal occupational health
and safety compliance officers. And, of these, fewer than 100 are technically qualified industrial hygienists. Charged with monitoring all of the
abuses of the workplace—among them, noise, heat and the use of toxic
but non-carcinogenic chemicals—this staff cannot pretend to police effectively the country's plants and factories.

Joe Fitman was a helpless victim of this kind of lax enforcement effort, particularly during his last twelve years as a worker when he was employed by a Southern California plastics outfit. It was with some bitterness that he described the squalid conditions of his labor:

In a way I knew the materials I was workin' with was dangerous, but when you're up in age like me—your age is against you. You've got a house payment. You've got five kids around the table.

I feel sorry for the fellas that are tryin' to hold their jobs in that place because only I know, due to my experience, how dangerous that place is to work. From my point of view, that place is filthy up there. And I just wonder, throughout this country, if the rest of the places are like that.

The Occupational Safety and Health Act took effect on April 28, 1971. But Joe Fitman couldn't remember any inspections ever taking place, either before or after that date.

A second federal agency intimately involved with the occupational cancer issue is the National Institute for Occupational Safety and Health (NIOSH). It is the research agency responsible for conducting studies and recommending workplace standards to OSHA. But while OSHA is part of the Department of Labor, NIOSH is within the Department of Health, Education, and Welfare. It was set up as a worker-oriented health protection agency and the caliber of its work has been in keeping with that purpose. Thanks to a staff of aggressive young technicians, there has never been any real problem with the quality of NIOSH's work, but there has always been a problem with the quantity. The institute is starved for funds and for personnel. Its entire 1974–75 budget for occupational cancer was a puny $1.8 million. To conduct a single study on the effects that a suspect carcinogen has had on the death rates of a defined population of workers costs $250,000 and occupies six people for at least a year. Since the equivalent of only twenty-eight full-time staff positions are devoted to these occupational cancer studies, it is obvious that only a handful of studies can be completed each year. As a result, the backlog of both recognized and suspect carcinogens not yet studied by NIOSH grows ever larger: commercial talc, mineral wool, antimony, wood dust, phosphoric acid, benzidine—there are scores of urgent studies left undone for lack of resources.

Though a relatively small proportion of chemicals induce cancers, nevertheless hundreds of commercially important compounds are known to be cancer-causing, or at least are highly suspect. And the industrial process feeds hundreds of new substances into industrial and commercial channels each year. Only the foolhardy would assume them all to be noncarcinogenic.

In years past, the cancer-causing properties of new compounds were generally not discovered until at least two or three decades after their adoption by industry. The method of discovery was a crude kind of human experimentation: counting the number of cancer victims among the dead workers to see if any abnormal trends could be detected. That was how vinyl chloride was spotted.

Vinyl choloride was first produced commercially in this country in 1939. It is an organic chemical, a gas at normal air temperature and pressure. Chemical plants convert this gas into a hard granular resin, called polyvinyl chloride, which has become the base for a cornucopia of solid and flexible plastics: food wrappings, bottles, vinyl tiles, phonograph records, water pipes, toys, car upholstery, tubing and thousands of other commonly used plastic products. The country now produces more than 7 *billion* pounds of polyvinyl chloride a year. Some 300,000 workers are involved in the chain of production—from the synthesis of the gas to the manufacture of the resin to the fabrication of the plastics. They work with vinyl chloride in its principal cancer-causing forms, and they have borne the brunt of this latest occupational peril.

Raymond P. Gettelfinger, Jr. began to work with vinyl chloride in 1954, when at the age of 22 he hired on at the B.F. Goodrich plant in Louisville. His job included operating the giant vat-like reactors used to transform the gas into resin. Gettelfinger recalls that the sweet smell of vinyl chloride was always thick in the air, but that it was worst when he and his colleagues had to climb down into the reactors and spend as many as four hours at a time cleaning and scraping the residue of the resin off the walls.

You have a residue build-up on the wall of your reactor and in some cases you have a water residue in the bottom. When I went to work there, that was the job of the helper—to get in and take the residue off the wall, which we done with scrapers. And if there was any left on the bottom . . . you'd pick it out with your hands—bare hands or leather gloves and your hands were wet. . . . When I began we wore nothing for protection. All we done was took an exhaust hose and stuck it in there and sucked the vinyl chloride out and we got in. . . .

Now, vinyl chloride has a characteristic that if there should be a mixture near the bottom of the vessel or reactor you were in, your feet would start feeling cold if there was much in there. Then you would know it was time to get out and see what is wrong. That, in the early years when I worked there, that was the first warning sign. . . . We didn't even—it wasn't in the safety regulations when I began working there to keep your exhaust hose in the reactor with you all the time.

It was in the mid-1960s, more than ten years after Gettelfinger joined Goodrich, that some of the workers there began to worry about the effect of vinyl chloride on their health. According to Gettelfinger:

We just got to noticing that there was just a few too many of us young men—the men working in the company, we were young men—they were losing too many guys. As we sat and ate and had our breaks, we just got to thinking that maybe there might be a little too much—too many of us guys getting out of this world too young.

It wasn't until January 1974, that the company publicly acknowledged similar fears. Dr. John L. Creech, a Louisville surgeon who is also the plant physician at Goodrich, was alert enough to notice that three Goodrich workers had died of angiosarcoma of the liver, an extremely rare form of cancer that attacks the blood vessels of the liver. Some months earlier, industry representatives had received in secret the results of animal studies commissioned by European plastics manufacturers. They showed that rats breathing air with vinyl chloride concentrations as low as 250 ppm—250 parts per million—developed a variety of cancers, including angiosarcomas of the liver. Then, in June 1974, it was found that angiosarcomas could be induced in rats with exposures of only 50 ppm. Yet for years workers had been breathing air with vinyl chloride concentrations ranging as high as 8,000 ppm.

After what was apparently an industry attempt to withhold the animal cancer findings from NIOSH during the last six months of 1973, in January 1974, Goodrich announced the cause of the three deaths that Dr. Creech had noticed. Once the story was out, the body count began in earnest. From the beginning, interest centered primarily on victims of angiosarcoma. This type of liver tumor had previously been so rare that there were thought to be fewer than thirty cases a year in the United States. Yet, so far, at the Louisville plant alone nine workers are reported to have the disease. In other U.S. plants, another dozen victims have been found, with new cases turning up almost monthly. All but two are now dead. One of the victims was Raymond Gettelfinger; age 43, the father of six. He died on March 11.

Since a latent period of ten to thirty years is typical for this and other human cancers, it is apparent that we are now seeing just the onset of this particular outbreak of occupational cancer. Reduced exposure levels were adopted last fall by OSHA (exposures as high as 25 ppm are still permitted), but the malignant cells are already loose in the bodies of countless vinyl chloride workers, and it seems likely that during the next twenty years the liver cancer toll will climb into the hundreds. Moreover, while the victims of angiosarcoma have received the major share of public concern, the even more tragic fact is that vinyl chloride also produces less exotic cancers at alarmingly excessive rates: cancers of the lung and respiratory system at more than one and one-half times the normal expectancy, lymphoma and leukemia at nearly twice normal and brain cancer at five and one-half times normal.

Of course the industry could have done more than it did to prevent this suffering. But more important, public policy should have required more.

The animal studies of vinyl chloride which were completed in Europe in 1973 should have been done in 1939, before plastics became a multi-billion-dollar industry in which workers are the unwitting subjects of a vast on-the-job experiment in human carcinogenesis.

In response to the vinyl chloride disaster, and to similar but less publicized cancer episodes over the years, the new Congress will almost certainly adopt a proposed Toxic Substances Control Act. This legislation would establish machinery to require the animal testing of specified chemical compounds for their toxic and carcinogenic properties. But which compounds would be subject to testing is not all that clear. Apparently, the Congress intends to vest enormous discretionary authority with the director of the Environmental Protection Agency. Under pending proposals, the director could require the testing of any substance which he or she "has reason to believe may pose an unreasonable threat to human health or the environment."

If the Toxic Substances Control Act had been in effect ten years ago, would the government have ordered testing of vinyl chloride? Maybe yes, maybe no; at the time the evidence did not necessarily compel such a course. That is why it would be preferable if the Congress adopted a Toxic Substances Control Act which required—perhaps over a ten-year span—that *all* industrially and commercially significant substances be tested for their carcinogenicity and other destructive effects. It would be an enormous undertaking, but one more than matched by the need to gain firm control over the industrial environment. Are there other vinyl chlorides lurking out there? Certainly. Perhaps less dramatic in impact, but certainly. The tens of thousands of substances now in use make it certain that in the years ahead more workplace disasters will be uncovered.

There is yet another dimension to the menace of job-caused cancer: occupational carcinogens frequently do not remain within the factory gates. Certain of them, such as asbestos fibers, pose a distinct take-home risk. Family members are inadvertently exposed when work clothes covered with millions of tiny fibers are brought home to be hung or washed. This kind of incidental exposure has already produced a number of documented cases of the ever fatal mesothelioma. And X-rays of the families of asbestos workers have revealed excessive rates of the lung abnormalities common to the workers themselves.

Nor are the relatives of workers the only members of the community who face such hazards. Many plants producing or using carcinogens pose exceptional risks to those who live nearby. In this case of asbestos, both South African and U.S. studies have related a high incidence of "neighborhood cases" of mesothelioma to exposure to fibers airborne from nearby production sites. In the case of vinyl chloride, even at this early point victims of angiosarcoma of the liver have been reported among citizens who have never worked with the substance but who have lived for some time near a vinyl chloride plant. The neighborhood victims of vinyl chloride-induced lung cancer can never be identified with any measure of certainty. Statistically, they are lost in a national swamp of 80,000 annual lung cancer deaths. Last year, plastics producers discharged more than 200 million pounds of vinyl chloride into the air. Nevertheless, according to Environmental Protection Agency officials—the EPA monitors emissions beyond the factory gates—it will be another year before the agency adopts standards to limit community exposures to vinyl chloride.

Vinyl chloride and asbestos are only tiny aspects of the community cancer question. A study of Los Angeles County cancer rates recently reported a markedly higher incidence of lung cancer among residents in the heavily industrialized south-central area. The study attributed the excess lung cancers to particularly high levels of benzo(a)pyrene, a carcinogen that is probably formed of effluents from the petroleum and chemical industries concentrated in the area. Years earlier, a similar study on Staten Island, New York disclosed that unusually high lung cancer rates in certain areas were related to wind conditions and the resultant exposure to airborne industrial carcinogens.

The indirect effect of occupational carcinogens was brought home again recently when elevated cancer rates in New Orleans and several other cities were attributed to water supplies contaminated with industrial carcinogens. Biostatisticians are only now beginning to consider the question of miscarriages among the wives of male workers exposed to carcinogens. The phenomenon was first noted among the wives of anesthesiologists who were regularly exposed to the gases present in an operating room. Now, among the wives of vinyl chloride workers, early evidence indicates a striking increase in the rates of both miscarriages and stillbirths.

In a related and highly disturbing development, two Canadian investigators surveyed the records of several hundred children who died of malignant diseases. Upon checking the occupations of their fathers at their time of birth, the investigators found that a disproportionately high number held jobs that exposed them to recognized cancer-causing agents: for example, service-station attendants, painters, dyers and cleaners working with solvents. The possibility of take-home exposure in this study looms large, since the developing cells of the fetus are known to be particularly vulnerable to carcinogens that cross the placental barrier. A second possibility, more frightening still, is that the workplace carcinogens have damaged the father's sperm cells, initiating a "carcinogenetic defect" which is then transmitted at conception, producing a child who subsequently develops cancer as a youngster.

If this society is to come to terms with the multiple horrors of occupational cancer, it must begin by discarding the distracting notion of a universal and imminent cancer "cure." Despite the more than $500 million per year spent on cancer research, there is no reason to believe that a major breakthrough is at hand. There will be no quick fix for occupational cancers, or for any other environmentally induced cancers. It is equally important that we discard the fatalistic notion that "everything causes cancer." While many widely used industrial and commercial substances are carcinogenic, the vast majority—both at the workplace and elsewhere—are in this respect harmless. The real task is to identify the agents that are carcinogens and then enforce the strictest measures to prevent human exposure to them.

If this Congress were to adopt a tough Toxic Substances Control Act, requiring the prior testing of all commercially and industrially significant substances, it would be taking an important step toward isolating workplace carcinogens much earlier than is now the case. But, if it is to be more than a gesture, the Congress must back that kind of legislation with major appropriations to the Environmental Protection Agency which will administer its provisons. Furthermore, the Congress should see to it that the chemical testing program within the National Cancer Institute is accelerated with significantly larger appropriations. Currently, the Chemical Carcinogenesis Program receives only 6 per cent of the National Cancer Institute's funds, despite the evidence that cancers are largely the result of chemical exposures.

Beyond the animal testing programs, there is the question of on-site worker studies carried out by NIOSH. Its present $1.8 million budget for occupational cancer studies is disgracefully inadequate. Just to keep from being overwhelmed by a backlog of undone studies, NIOSH needs another $10 million earmarked for occupational cancer.

The situation is perhaps most discouraging with respect to the Occupational Safety and Health Administration, the Department of Labor's standards-setting and enforcement agency. In the area of occupational carcinogens, and in other areas as well, OSHA has been a bitter disappointment during its four-year history. Perhaps by way of Congressional mandate, the agency can be compelled to adopt a use-permit system to assure the most stringent and effective controls over occupational carcinogens. Its snail-paced operations indicate that OSHA lacks the money, manpower and single-minded determination to carry out its mission on behalf of American workers. Congress can remedy the first two problems; the third will probably have to await a new administration.

When he wrote *Occupational Tumors and Allied Diseases* in 1942, Dr.

Hueper began with a chapter dealing with what he called "the new artificial environment." He observed that the great medical advances of the late 19th century and the first half of the 20th century came with an understanding of the biologically destructive effects of bacteria, viruses and other microorganisms. Similarly, he argued, the great challenge for the second half of the 20th century was to recognize the cancer-causing effects of many chemicals and other substances which have been introduced at the workplace in burgeoning numbers as part of the industrial age. It was a vital message, one that has been largely ignored for thirty-three years.

NOTE

1. Joe Fitman died on March 30.

28
THE RELIEF OF WELFARE

Frances Fox Piven
and Richard A. Cloward

Aid to Families with Dependent Children (AFDC) is our major relief program. It has lately become the source of a major public controversy, owing to a large and precipitous expansion of the rolls. Between 1950 and 1960, only 110,000 families were added to the rolls, yielding a rise of 17 percent, In the 1960's, however, the rolls exploded, rising by more than 225 percent. At the beginning of the decade, 745,000 families were receiving aid; by 1970, some 2,500,000 families were on the rolls. Still, this is not the first, the largest, or the longest relief explosion. Since the inauguration of relief in Western Europe three centuries ago, the rolls have risen and fallen in response to economic and political forces. An examination of these forces should help to illuminate the meaning of the current explosion, as well as the meaning of current proposals for reform.

Relief arrangements, we will argue, are ancillary to economic arrangements. Their chief function is to regulate labor, and they do that in two general ways. First, when mass unemployment leads to outbreaks of turmoil, relief programs are ordinarily initiated or expanded to absorb and control enough of the unemployed to restore order; then, as turbulence subsides, the relief system contracts, expelling those who are needed to populate the labor market. Relief also performs a labor-regulating function in this shrunken state, however. Some of the aged, the disabled, and others who are of no use as workers are left on the relief rolls, and their treatment is so degrading and punitive as to instill in the laboring masses a fear of the fate that awaits them should they relax into beggary and pauperism. To demean and punish those who do not work is to exalt by contrast even the meanest labor at the meanest wages. These regulative functions of relief are made necessary by several strains toward instability inherent in capitalist economics.

LABOR AND MARKET INCENTIVES

All human societies compel most of their members to work, to produce the goods and services that sustain the community. All societies also define the work their members must do and the conditions under which they must do it. Sometimes the authority to compel and define is fixed in tradition, sometimes in the bureaucratic agencies of a central government. Capitalism, however, relies primarily upon the mechanisms of a market—the promise of financial rewards or penalties—to motivate men and women to work and to hold them to their occupational tasks

But the development of capitalism has been marked by periods of cataclysmic change in the market, the main sources being depression and rapid modernization. Depressions mean that the regulatory structure of the market simply collapses; with no demand for labor, there are no monetary rewards to guide and enforce work. By contrast, during periods of rapid modernization—whether the replacement of handicraft by machines, the relocation of factories in relation to new sources of power or new outlets for distribution, or the demise of family subsistence farming as large-scale commercial agriculture spreads—portions of the laboring population may be rendered obsolete or at least temporarily maladjusted. Market incentives do not collapse; they are simply not sufficient to compel people to abandon one way of working and living in favor of another.

In principle, of course, people dislocated by modernization become part of a labor supply to be drawn upon by a changing and expanding labor market. As history shows, however, people do not adapt so readily to drastically altered methods of work and to the new and alien patterns of social life dictated by that work. They may resist leaving their traditional communities and the only life they know. Bred to labor under the discipline of sun and season, however severe that discipline may be, they may resist that discipline of factory and machine, which, though it may be no more severe, may seem so because it is alien. The process of human adjustment to such economic changes has ordinarily entailed a generation of mass unemployment, distress, and disorganization.

Now, if human beings were invariably given to enduring these travails with equanimity, there would be no governmental relief systems at all. But often they do not, and for reasons that are not difficult to see. The regulation of civil behavior in all societies is intimately dependent on stable occupational arrangements. So long as people are fixed in their work roles, their activities and outlooks are also fixed; they do what they must and think what they must. Each behavior and attitude is shaped by the reward of a good harvest or the penalty of a bad one, by the factory paycheck or the danger of losing it. But mass unemployment breaks that bond, loosening people from the main institution by which they are regulated and controlled.

Moreover, mass unemployment that persists for any length of time diminishes the capacity of other institutions to bind and constrain people. Occupational behaviors and outlooks underpin a way of life and determine familial, communal, and cultural patterns. When large numbers of people are suddenly barred from their traditional occupations, the entire network of social control is weakened. There is no harvest or paycheck to enforce work and the sentiments that uphold work; without work, people cannot conform to familial and communal roles; and if the dislocation is widespread, the legitimacy of the social order itself may come to be questioned. The result is usually civil disorder—crime, mass protests, riots—a disorder that may even threaten to overturn existing social and economic arrangements. It is then that relief programs are initiated or expanded.

Western relief systems originated in the mass disturbances that erupted during the long transition from feudalism to capitalism beginning in the sixteenth century. As a result of the declining death rates in the previous century, the population of Europe grew rapidly; as the population grew, so did transiency and beggary. Moreover, distress resulting from population changes, agricultural and other natural disasters, which had characterized life throughout the Middle Ages, was now exacerbated by the vagaries of an evolving market economy, and outbreaks of turbulence among the poor were frequent. To deal with these threats to civil order, many localities legislated severe penalties against vagrancy. Even before the sixteenth century, the magistrates of Basel had defined twenty-five different categories of beggars, together with appropriate punishments for each. But penalties alone did not always deter begging, especially when economic distress was severe and the numbers affected were large. Consequently, some localities began to augment punishment with provisions for the relief of the vagrant poor.

CIVIL DISORDER AND RELIEF

A French town that initiated such an arrangement early in the sixteenth century was Lyons, which was troubled both by a rapidly growing population and by the economic instability associated with the transition to capitalism. By 1500 Lyons' population had already begun to increase. During the decades that followed, the town became a prosperous commercial and manufacturing center—the home of the European money market and of expanding new trades in textiles, printing, and metalworking. As it thrived it attracted people, not only from the surrounding countryside, but even from Italy, Flanders, and Germany. All told, the population of Lyons probably doubled between 1500 and 1540.

All this was very well as long as the newcomers could be absorbed by industry. But not all were, with the result that the town came to be plagued by beggars and vagrants. Moreover, prosperity was not continuous: some trades were seasonal and others were periodically troubled by foreign competition. With each economic downturn, large numbers of unemployed workers took to the streets to plead for charity, cluttering the very doorsteps of the better-off classes. Lyons was most vulnerable during periods of bad harvest, when famine not only drove up the cost of bread for urban artisans and journeymen but brought hordes of peasants into the city, where they sometimes paraded through the streets to exhibit their misfortune. In 1529 food riots erupted, with thousands of Lyonnais looting granaries and the homes of the wealthy; in 1530, artisans and journeymen armed themselves and marched through the streets; in 1531, mobs of starving peasants literally overran the town.

Such charity as had previously been given in Lyons was primarily the responsibility of the church or of those of the more prosperous who sought to purchase their salvation through almsgiving. But this method of caring for the needy obviously stimulated rather than discouraged begging and created a public nuisance to the better-off citizens (one account of the times describes famished peasants so gorging themselves as to die on the very doorsteps where they were fed). Moreover, to leave charity to church and citizen meant that few got aid, and those not necessarily according to their need. The result was that mass disorders periodically erupted.

The increase in disorder led the rulers of Lyons to conclude that the giving of charity should no longer be governed by private whim. In 1534, churchmen, notables, and merchants joined together to establish a centralized administration for disbursing aid. All charitable donations were consolidated under a central body, the "Aumone-Generale," whose responsibility was to "nourish the poor forever." A list of the needy was established by a house-to-house survey, and tickets for bread and money were issued according to fixed standards. Indeed, most of the features of modern welfare—from criteria to discriminate the worthy poor from the unworthy, to strict procedures for surveillance of recipients as well as measures for their rehabilitation—were present in Lyons' new relief administration. By the 1550's, about 10 percent of the town's population was receiving relief.

Within two years of the establishment of relief in Lyons, King Francis I ordered each parish in France to register its poor and to provide for the "impotent" out of a fund of contributions. Elsewhere in Europe, other townships began to devise similar systems to deal with the vagrants and mobs cast up by famine, rapid population growth, and the transition from feudalism to capitalism.

England also felt these disturbances, and just as it pioneered in developing an intensively capitalist economy, so it was at the forefront in developing nationwide, public relief arrangements. During the closing years of the fifteenth century, the emergence of the wool industry in England began to transform agricultural life. As sheep raising became more profitable, much land was converted from tillage to pasturage, and large numbers of peasants were displaced by an emerging entrepreneurial gentry which either bought their land or cheated them out of it. The result was great tumult among the peasantry, as the Webbs were to note:

When the sense of oppression became overwhelming, the popular feeling manifested itself in widespread organized tumults, disturbances, and insurrections, from Wat Tyler's rebellion of 1381, and Jack Cade's march on London of 1460, to the Pilgrimage of Grace in 1536, and Kett's Norfolk rising of 1549—all of them successfully put down, but sometimes not without great struggle, by the forces which the government could command.

Early in the sixteenth century, the national government moved to try to forestall such disorders. In 1528 the Privy Council, anticipating a fall in foreign sales as a result of the war in Flanders, tried to induce the cloth manufacturers of Suffolk to retain their employees. In 1534, a law passed under Henry VIII attempted to limit the number of sheep in any one holding in order to inhibit the displacement of farmers and agricultural laborers and thus forestall potential disorders. Beginning in the 1550's the Privy Council attempted to regulate the price of grain in poor harvests. But the entrepreneurs of the new market economy were not so readily curbed, so that during this period another method of dealing with labor disorders was evolved.

Early in the sixteenth century, the national government moved to replace parish arrangements for charity with a nationwide system of relief. In 1531, an act of Parliament decreed that local officials search out and register those of the destitute deemed to be impotent and give them a document authorizing begging. As for those who sought alms without authorization, the penalty was public whipping till the blood ran.

Thereafter, other arrangements for relief were rapidly instituted. An act passed in 1536, during the reign of Henry VIII, required local parishes to take care of their destitute and to establish a procedure for the collection and administration of donations for that purpose by local officials. (In the same year Henry VIII began to expropriate monasteries, helping to assure secular control of charity.) With these developments, the penalties for beggary were made more severe, including an elaborate schedule of branding, enslavement, and execution for repeated offenders. Even so, by 1572 beggary was said to have reached alarming proportions, and in that year local responsibility for relief was more fully spelled out by the famous Elizabethan Poor Laws, which established a local tax, known as the poor rate, as the means for financing the care of paupers and required that justices of the peace serve as the overseers of the poor.

After each period of activity, the parish relief machinery tended to lapse into disuse, until bad harvests or depression in manufacturing led again to widespread unemployment and misery, to new outbreaks of disorder, and then to a resuscitation and expansion of relief arrangements. The most illuminating of these episodes, because it bears so much similarity to the present-day relief explosion in the United States, was the expansion of relief during the massive agricultural dislocations of the late eighteenth century.

Most of the English agricultural population had lost its landholdings long before the eighteenth century. In place of the subsistence farming found elsewhere in Europe, a three-tier system of landowners, tenant farmers, and agricultural workers had evolved in England. The vast majority of the people were a landless proletariat, hiring out by the year to tenant farmers. The margin of their subsistence, however, was provided by common and waste lands, on which they gathered kindling, grazed animals, and hunted game to supplement their meager wages. Moreover, the use of the commons was part of the English villager's birthright, his sense of place and pride. It was the disruption of these arrangements and the ensuing disorder that led to the new expansion of relief.

By the middle of the eighteenth century, an increasing population, advancing urbanization, and the growth of manufacturing had greatly expanded markets for agricultural products, mainly for cereals to feed the urban population and for wool to supply the cloth manufacturers. These new markets, together with the introduction of new agricultural methods (such as cross-harrowing), led to large-scale changes in agriculture. To take advantage of rising prices and new techniques, big landowners moved to expand their holdings still further by buying up small farms and, armed with parliamentary Bills of Enclosure, by usurping the common and waste lands which had enabled many small cottagers to survive. Although this process began much earlier, it accelerated rapidly after 1750; by 1850, well over six million acres of common land—or about one-quarter of the total arable acreage—had been consolidated into private holdings and turned primarily to grain production. For great numbers of agricultural workers, enclosure meant no land on which to grow subsistence crops to feed their families, no grazing land to produce wool for home spinning and weaving, no fuel to heat their cottages, and new restrictions against hunting. It meant, in short, the loss of a major source of subsistence for the poor.

New markets also stimulated a more businesslike approach to farming. Landowners demanded the maximum rent from tenant farmers, and tenant farmers in turn began to deal with their laborers in terms of cash calculations. Specifically, this meant a shift from a master-servant relationship to an employer-employee relationship, but on the harshest terms. Where laborers had previously worked by the year and frequently lived with the farmer, they were now hired for only as long as they were needed and were then left to fend for themselves. Pressures toward short-term hiring also resulted from the large-scale cultivation of grain crops for market, which called for a seasonal labor force, as opposed to mixed subsistence farming, which required year-round laborers. The use of cash rather than produce as the medium of payment for work, a rapidly spreading practice, encouraged partly by the long-term inflation of grain prices, added to the laborer's hardships. Finally the rapid increase in rural population at a time when the growth of woolen manufacturing continued to provide an incentive to convert land from tillage to pasturage produced a large labor surplus, leaving agricultural workers with no leverage in bargaining for wages with their tenant-farmer employers. The result was widespread unemployment and terrible hardship.

None of these changes took place without resistance from small farmers and laborers who, while they had known hardship before, were now being forced out of a way of life and even out of their villages. Some rioted when Bills of Enclosure were posted; some petitioned the Parliament for their repeal. And when hardship was made more acute by a succession of poor harvests in the 1970's, there were widespread food riots.

Indeed, throughout the late eighteenth and early nineteenth centuries, the English countryside was periodically beseiged by turbulent masses of the displaced rural poor and the towns were racked by Luddism, radicalism, trade-unionism and Chartism, even while the ruling classes worried about what the French Revolution might augur for England. A solution to disorder was needed, and that solution turned out to be relief. The poor-relief system—first created in the sixteenth century to control the earlier disturbances caused by population growth and the commercialization of agriculture—now rapidly became a major institution of English life. Between 1760 and 1784 taxes for relief—the poor rate—rose by 60 percent; they doubled by 1801, and rose by 60 percent more in the next decade. By 1818, the poor rate was over six times as high as it had been in 1760. Hobsbaum estimates that up to the 1850's, upwards of 10 percent of the English population were paupers. The relief system, in short, was expanded in order to absorb and regulate the masses of discontented people uprooted from agriculture but not yet incorporated into industry.

Relief arrangements evolved more slowly in the United States, and the first major relief crisis did not occur until the Great Depression. The inauguration of massive relief-giving was not simply a response to widespread economic distress, for millions had remained unemployed for several years without obtaining aid. What finally led the national government to proffer aid was the great surge of political disorder that followed the economic catastrophe, a disorder which eventually led to the convulsive voting shifts of 1932. After the election, the federal government abandoned its posture of aloofness toward the unemployed. Within a matter of months, billions of dollars were flowing to localities, and the relief rolls skyrocketed. By 1935, upwards of 20 million people were on the dole.

The contemporary relief explosion, which began in the early 1960's, has its roots in agricultural modernization. No one would disagree that the rural economy of America, especially in the South, has undergone a profound transformation in recent decades. In 1945, there was one tractor per farm; in 1964 there were two. Mechanization and other technological developments, in turn, stimulated the enlargement of farm holdings. Between 1959 and 1961, one million farms disappeared; the three million remaining farms average 377 acres in size—30 percent larger than the average farm ten years earlier. The chief and most obvious effect of these changes was to lessen the need for agricultural labor. In the years between 1950 and 1965 alone, a Presidential Commission on Rural Poverty was to discover, "New machines and new methods increased farm output in the United States by 45 percent, and reduced farm employment by 45 percent." A mere 4 percent of the American labor force now works the land, signaling an extraordinary displacement of people, with accompanying upheaval and suffering. The best summary measure of this dislocation is probably the volume of migration to the cities; over 20 million people, more than four million of them black, left the land after 1940.

Nor were all these poor absorbed into the urban economic system. Blacks were especially vulnerable to unemployment. At the close of the Korean War, the national nonwhite unemployment rate leaped from 4.5 per cent in 1953 to 9.9 percent in 1954. By 1958, it had reached 12.6 percent, and it fluctuated between 10 and 13 percent until the escalation of the war in Vietnam after 1964.

These figures pertain only to people unemployed and looking for work. They do not include the sporadically unemployed or those employed at extremely low wages. Combining such additional measures with the official unemployment measure produces a subemployment index. This index was first used in 1966—well after the economic downturns that characterized the years between the end of the Korean War and the escalation of the war in Vietnam. Were subemployment data available for the "Eisenhower recession" years, especially in the slum ghettos of the larger central cities, they would surely show much higher rates than prevailed in 1966. In any event, the figures for 1966 revealed a nonwhite subemployment rate of 21.6 percent compared with a white rate of 7.6 percent.

However, despite the spread of economic deprivation, whether on the land or in the cities, the relief system did not respond. In the entire decade between 1950 and 1960, the national AFDC caseload rose by only 17 percent. Many of the main urban targets of migration showed equally little change: the rolls in New York City moved up by 16 percent and in Los Angeles by 14 percent. In the South, the rolls did not rise at all.

But in the 1960's, disorder among the black poor erupted on a wide scale, and the welfare rolls erupted as well. The welfare explosion occurred during several years of the greatest domestic disorder since the 1930's—perhaps the greatest in our history. It was concurrent with the turmoil produced by the civil-rights struggle, with widespread and destructive rioting in the cities, and with the formation of a militant grass-roots movement of the poor dedicated to combating welfare restrictions. Not least, the welfare rise was also concurrent with the enactment of a series of ghetto-placating federal programs (such as the antipoverty program) which, among other things, hired thousands of poor people, social workers, and lawyers who, it subsequently turned out, greatly stimulated people to apply for relief and helped them obtain it. And the welfare explosion, although an urban phenomenon generally, was greatest in just that handful of large metropolitan counties where the political turmoil of the mid- and late 1960's was the most acute.

The magnitude of the welfare rise is worth noting. The national AFDC caseload rose by more than 225 percent in the 1960's. In New York City, the rise was more than 300 percent; the same was so in Los Angeles. Even in the South, where there had been no rise at all in the 1950's, the bulk of the increase took place after 1965—that is, after disorder reached a crescendo. More than 80 percent of the national rise in the 1960's occurred in the last five years of the decade. In other words, the welfare rolls expanded, today as at earlier times, only in response to civil disorder.

While muting the more disruptive outbreaks of civil disorder (such as rioting), the mere giving of relief does nothing to reverse the disintegration of lower-class life produced by economic change, a disintegration which leads to rising disorder and rising relief rolls in the first place. In-

deed, greatly liberalized relief-giving can further weaken work and family norms. To restore order in a more fundamental sense the society must
create the means to reassert its authority. Because the market is unable to
control men's behavior, a surrogate system of social control must be
evolved, at least for a time. Moreover, if the surrogate system is to be
consistent with normally dominant patterns, it must restore people to
work roles. Thus even though obsolete or unneeded workers are temporarily given direct relief, they are eventually succored only on condition that they work. As these adjustments are made, the functions of relief
arrangements may be said to be shifting from regulating disorder to regulating labor.

Restoring Order by Restoring Work

The arrangements, both historical and contemporary, through which relief recipients have been made to work vary, but broadly speaking, there
are two main ways: work is provided under public auspices, whether in
the recipient's home, in a labor yard, in a workhouse, or on a public-
works project; or work is provided in the private market, whether by
contracting or indenturing the poor to private employers, or through subsidies designed to induce employers to hire paupers. And although a relief system may at any time use both of these methods of enforcing work,
one or the other usually becomes predominant, depending on the economic conditions that first gave rise to disorder.

Publicly subsidized work tends to be used during business depressions,
when the demand for labor in the private market collapses. Conversely,
arrangements to channel paupers into the labor market are more likely to
be used when rapid changes in markets or technology render a segment
of the labor supply temporarily maladapted. In the first case, the relief
system augments a shrunken labor market; in the other, its policies and
procedures are shaped to overcome the poor fit between labor demand
and supply.

Public work is as old as public relief. The municipal relief systems initiated on the Continent in the first quarter of the sixteenth century often
included some form of public works. In England, the same statute of
1572 that established taxation as the method for financing poor relief
charged the overseers of the poor with putting vagrants to work. Shortly
afterwards, in 1576, local officials were directed to acquire a supply of
raw goods—wool, hemp, iron—which was to be delivered to the needy
for processing in their homes, their dole to be fixed according to "the
desert of the work."

The favored method of enforcing work throughout most of the history
of relief was the workhouse. In 1723, an act of Parliament permitted the
local parishes to establish workhouses and to refuse aid to those poor who

would not enter; within ten years, there were said to be about fifty work-houses in the environs of London alone.

The destitute have also sometimes been paid to work in the general community or in their own homes. This method of enforcing work evolved in England during the bitter depression of 1840–1841. As unemployment mounted, the poor in some of the larger cities protested against having to leave their communities to enter workhouses in order to obtain relief, and in any case, in some places the workhouses were already full. As a result, various public spaces were designated as "labor yards" to which the unemployed could come by the day to pick oakum, cut wood, and break stone, for which they were paid in food and clothing. The method was used periodically throughout the second half of the nineteenth century; at times of severe distress, very large numbers of the able bodied were supported in this way.

The first massive use of public work under relief auspices in the United States occurred during the 1930's when millions of the unemployed were subsidized through the Works Progress Administration. The initial response of the Roosevelt administration was to appropriate billions for direct-relief payments. But no one liked direct relief—not the President who called for it, the Congress that legislated it, the adminstrators who operated it, the people who received it. Direct relief was viewed as a temporary expedient, a way of maintaining a person's body, but not his dignity; a way of keeping the populace from shattering in despair, discontent, and disorder, at least for a while, but not of renewing their pride, of bringing back a way of life. For their way of life had been anchored in the discipline of work, and so that discipline had to be restored. The remedy was to abolish direct relief and put the unemployed to work on subsidized projects. These reforms were soon instituted—and with dramatic results. For a brief time, the federal government became the employer of millions of people (although millions of others remained unemployed).

Quite different methods of enforcing work are used when the demand for labor is steady but maladaptions in the labor supply, caused by changes in methods of production, result in unemployment. In such circumstances, relief agencies ordinarily channel paupers directly into the private market. For example, the rapid expansion of English manufacturing during the late eighteenth and early nineteenth centuries produced a commensurately expanded need for factory operatives. But it was no easy matter to get them. Men who had been agricultural laborers, independent craftsmen, or workers in domestic industries (i.e., piecework manufacturing in the home) resisted the new discipline. Between 1778 and 1830, there were repeated revolts by laborers in which local tradesmen and farmers often participated. The revolts failed, of course; the new industry moved forward inexorably, taking the more dependent and tractable under its command, with the aid of the relief system.

The burgeoning English textile industry solved its labor problems during the latter part of the eighteenth century by using parish children, some only four or five years old, as factory operatives. Manufacturers negotiated regular bargains with the parish authorities, ordering lots of fifty or more children from the poorhouses. Parish children were an ideal labor source for new manufacturers. The young paupers could be shipped to remote factories, located to take advantage of the streams from which power could be drawn. (With the shift from water power to steam in the nineteenth century, factories began to locate in towns where they could employ local children; with that change, the system of child labor became a system of "free" child labor.) The children were also preferred for their docility and for their light touch at the looms. Moreover, pauper-children could be had for a bit of food and a bed, and they provided a very stable labor supply, for they were held fast at their labors by indentures, usually until they were twenty-one.

Sometimes the relief system subsidizes the employment of paupers—especially when their market value is very low—as when the magistrates of Lyons provided subsidies to manufacturers who employed pauper children. In rural England during the late eighteenth century, as more and more of the population was being displaced by the commercialization of agriculture, this method was used on a very large scale. To be sure, a demand for labor was developing in the new manufacturing establishments that would in time absorb many of the uprooted rural poor. But this did not happen all at once: rural displacement and industrial expansion did not proceed at the same pace or in the same areas, and in any case the drastic shift from rural village to factory system took time. During the long interval before people forced off the land were absorbed into manufacturing, many remained in the countryside as virtual vagrants; others migrated to the towns, where they crowded into hovels and cells, subject to the vicissitudes of rapidly rising and falling markets, their ranks continually enlarged by new rural refugees.

These conditions were not the result of a collapse in the market. Indeed, grain prices rose during the second half of the eighteenth century, and they rose spectacularly during the Revolutionary and Napoleonic wars. Rather, it was the expanding market for agricultural produce which, by stimulating enclosure and business-minded farming methods, led to unemployment and destitution. Meanwhile, population growth, which meant a surplus of laborers, left the workers little opportunity to resist the destruction of their traditional way of life—except by crime, riots, and incendiarism. To cope with these disturbances, relief expanded, but in such a way as to absorb and discipline laborers by supporting the faltering labor market with subsidies.

The subsidy system is widely credited to the sheriff and magistrates of Berkshire, who, in a meeting at Speenhamland in 1795, decided on a scheme by which the Poor Law authorities would supplement the wages of underpaid agricultural workers according to a published scale. It was a time when exceptional scarcity of food led to riots all over England, sometimes suppressed only by calling out the troops. With this "double panic of famine and revolution," the subsidy scheme spread, especially in counties where large amounts of acreage had been enclosed.

The local parishes implemented the work subsidy system in different ways. Under the "roundsman" arrangement, the parish overseers sent any man who applied for aid from house to house to get work. If he found work, the employer was obliged to feed him and pay a small sum (6 d) per day, with the parish adding another small sum (4 d). Elsewhere, the parish authorities contracted directly with farmers to have paupers work for a given price, with the parish paying the combined wage and relief subsidy directly to the pauper. In still other places, parish authorities parceled out the unemployed to farmers, who were obliged to pay a set rate or make up the difference in higher taxes. Everywhere, however, the main principle was the same: an underemployed and turbulent populace was being pacified with public allowances, but these allowances were used to restore order by enforcing work, at very low wage levels. Relief, in short, served as a support for a disturbed labor market and as a discipline for a disturbed rural society. As the historians J. L. Hammond and Barbara Hammond were to say, "The meshes of the Poor Law were spread over the entire labor system."

The English Speenhamland plan, while it enjoys a certain notoriety, is by no means unique. The most recent example of a scheme for subsidizing paupers in private employ is the reorganization of American public welfare proposed in the summer of 1969 by President Richard Nixon; the general parallel with the events surrounding Speenhamland is striking. The United States relief rolls expanded in the 1960's to absorb a laboring population made superfluous by agricultural modernization in the South, a population that became turbulent in the wake of forced migration to the cities. As the relief rolls grew to deal with these disturbances, pressure for "reforms" also mounted. Key features of the reform proposals included a national minimum allowance of $1,600 per year for a family of four, coupled with an elaborate system of penalties and incentives to force families to work. In effect, the proposal was intended to support and strengthen a disturbed low-wage labor market by providing what was called in nineteenth-century England a "rate in aid of wages."

ENFORCING LOW-WAGE WORK DURING PERIODS OF STABILITY

Even in the absence of cataclysmic change, market incentives may be insufficient to compel all people at all times to do the particular work required of them. Incentives may be too meager and erratic, or people may not be sufficiently socialized to respond to them properly. To be sure, the productivity of a fully developed capitalist economy would allow for wages and profits sufficient to entice most of the population to work; and in a fully developed capitalist society, most people would also be reared to want what the market holds out to them. They would expect, even sanctify, the rewards of the marketplace and acquiesce in its vagaries.

But no fully developed capitalist society exists. (Even today in the United States, the most advanced capitalist country, certain regions and population groups—such as southern tenant farmers—remain on the periphery of the wage market and are only partially socialized to the ethos of the market.) Capitalism evolved slowly and spread slowly. During most of this evolution, the market provided meager rewards for most workers, and none at all for some. There are still many for whom this is so. And during most of this evolution, large sectors of the laboring classes were not fully socialized to the market ethos. The relief system, we contend, has made an important contribution toward overcoming these persisting weaknesses in the capacity of the market to direct and control men.

Once an economic convulsion subsides and civil order is restored, relief systems are not ordinarily abandoned. The rolls are reduced, to be sure, but the shell of the system usually remains, ostensibly to provide aid to the aged, the disabled, and such other unfortunates who are of no use as workers. However, the manner in which these "impotents" have always been treated, in the United States and elsewhere, suggests a purpose quite different from the remediation of their destitution. These residual persons have ordinarily been degraded for lacking economic value, relegated to the foul quarters of the workhouse, with its strict penal regimen and its starvation diet. Once stability was restored, such institutions were typically proclaimed the sole source of aid, and for a reason bearing directly on enforcing work.

Conditions in the workhouse were intended to ensure that no one with any conceivable alternatives would seek public aid. Nor can there be any doubt of that intent. Consider this statement by the Poor Law Commissioners in 1834, for example:

Into such a house none will enter voluntarily; work, confinement, and discipline will deter the indolent and vicious; and nothing but extreme necessity will induce any to accept the comfort which must be obtained by the surrender of their free agency, and the sacrifice of their accustomed habits and gratifications. Thus the parish officer, being furnished an unerring test of the necessity of applicants, is relieved from his painful and difficult responsibility: while all have the gratification of knowing that while the necessitous are abundantly relieved, the funds of charity are not wasted by idleness and fraud.

The method worked. Periods of relief expansion were generally followed by "reform" campaigns to abolish all "outdoor" aid and restrict relief to those who entered the workhouse—as in England in 1722, 1834, and

1871 and in the United States in the 1880's and 1890's—and these campaigns usually resulted in a sharp reduction in the number of applicants seeking aid.

The harsh treatment of those who had no alternative except to fall back upon the parish and accept "the offer of the House" terrorized the impoverished masses in another way as well. It made pariahs of those who could not support themselves; they served as an object lesson, a means of celebrating the virtues of work by the terrible example of their agony. That, too, was a matter of deliberate intent. The workhouse was designed to spur men to contrive ways of supporting themselves by their own industry, to offer themselves to any employer on any terms, rather than suffer the degraded status of pauper.

All of this was evident in the contraction of relief which occurred in the United States at the close of the Great Depression. As political stability returned, emergency relief and work relief programs were reduced and eventually abolished, with many of those cut off being forced into a labor market still glutted with the unemployed. Meanwhile, the Social Security Act had been passed. Widely hailed as a major reform, this measure created our present-day welfare system, with its categorical provisions for the aged, the blind, and families with dependent children (as well as, in 1950, the disabled).

The enactment of this "reform" signaled a turn toward the work-enforcing function of relief arrangements. This became especially evident after World War II during the period of greatly accelerated agricultural modernization. Millions were unemployed in agriculture; millions of others migrated to the cities, where unemployment in the late 1950's reached extremely high levels. But few families were given assistance. By 1960, only 745,000 families had been admitted to the AFDC rolls. That was to change in the 1960's, as we have already noted, but only in response to the most unprecedented disorder in our history.

That families without jobs or income failed to secure relief during the late 1940's and the 1950's was in part a consequence of restrictive statutes and policies—the exclusion of able-bodied males and, in many places, of so-called employable mothers, together with residence laws, relative responsibility provisions, and the like. But it was also—perhaps mainly—a consequence of the persistence of age-old rituals of degradation. AFDC mothers were forced to answer questions about their sexual behavior ("When did you last menstruate?"), open their closets to inspection ("Whose pants are those?"), and permit their children to be interrogated ("Do any men visit your mother?"). Unannounced raids, usually after midnight and without benefit of warrant, in which a recipient's home is searched for signs of "immoral" activities, have also been part of life on AFDC. In Oakland, California, a public-welfare case-worker, Bennie Parish, refused to take part in a raid in January 1962 and was dismissed for insubordination. When he sued for reinstatement, the state argued successfully in the lower courts that people taking public assistance waive certain constitutional rights, among them the right to privacy. (The court's position had at least the weight of long tradition, for the withdrawal of civil rights is an old feature of public relief. In England, for example, relief recipients were denied the Franchise until 1918, and as late as 1934 the constitutions of fourteen American states deprived recipients of the right to vote or hold office.)

The main target of these rituals is not the recipient, who ordinarily is not of much use as a worker, but the able-bodied poor who remain in the labor market. It is for these people that the spectacle of the degraded pauper is intended. For example, scandals exposing "welfare-fraud" have diffuse effects, for they reach a wide public—including the people who might otherwise apply for aid but who are deterred because of the invidious connotations of being on welfare. Such a scandal occurred in the District of Columbia in 1961, with the result that half of all AFDC mothers were declared to be ineligible for relief, most of them for allegedly "consorting with men." In the several years immediately before the attack, about 6,500 District of Columbia families had applied for aid annually; during the attack, the figure dropped to 4,400 and it did not rise for more than five years—long after that particular scandal had itself subsided.

In sum, market values and market incentives are weakest at the bottom of the social order. To buttress weak market controls and ensure the availability of marginal labor, an outcast class—the dependent poor—is created by the relief system. This class, whose members are of no productive use, is not treated with indifference, but with contempt. Its degradation at the hands of relief officials serves to celebrate the virtue of all work and deters actual or potential workers from seeking aid.

THE CURRENT CALL FOR REFORM

From our perspective, a relief explosion is a reform just because a large number of unemployed or underemployed people obtain aid. But from the perspective of most people, a relief explosion is viewed as a "crisis." The contemporary relief explosion in the United States, following a period of unparalleled turbulence in the cities, has thus resulted in a clamor for reform. Similar episodes in the past suggest that pressure for reform signals a shift in emphasis between the major functions of relief arrangements—a shift from regulating disorder to regulating labor.

Pressure for reform stems in part from the fiscal burden imposed on localities when the relief rolls expand. An obvious remedy is for the federal government to simply assume a greater share of the costs, if not the entire cost (at this writing, Congress appears likely to enact such fiscal reform).

However, the much more fundamental problem with which relief reform seeks to cope is the erosion of the work role and the deterioration of the male-headed family. In principle, these problems could be dealt with by economic policies leading to full employment at decent wages, but there is little political support for that approach. Instead, the historic approach to relief explosions is being invoked, which is to restore work through the relief system. Various proposals have been advanced: some would force recipients to report regularly to employment offices; others would provide a system of wage subsidies conditional on the recipient's taking on a job at any wage (including those below the federal minimum wage); still others would inaugurate a straightforward program of public-works projects.

We are opposed to any type of reform intended to promote work through the relief system rather than through the reform of economic policies. When similar relief reforms were introduced in the past, they presaged the eventual expulsion of large numbers of people from the rolls, leaving them to fend for themselves in a labor market where there was too little work and thus subjecting them once again to severe economic exploitation. The reason that this happens is more than a little ironic.

The irony is this: when relief is used to enforce work, it tends to stabilize lower-class occupational, familial, and communal life (unlike direct relief, which merely mutes the worst outbreaks of discontent). By doing so, it diminishes the proclivities toward disruptive behavior which give rise to the expansion of relief in the first place. Once order is restored in this far more profound sense, relief-giving can be virtually abolished as it has been so often in the past. And there is always pressure to abolish large-scale work relief, for it strains against the market ethos and interferes with the untrammeled operation of the marketplace. The point is not just that when a relief concession is offered up, peace and order reign; it is, rather that when peace and order reign, the relief concession is withdrawn.

The restoration of work through the relief system, in other words, makes possible the eventual return to the most retrictive phase in the cycle of relief-giving. What begins as a great expansion of direct relief, and then turns into some form of work relief, ends finally with a sharp contraction of the rolls. Advocates of relief reform may argue that their reforms will be long-lasting, that the restrictive phase in the cycle will not be reached, but past experience suggests otherwise.

Therefore, in the absence of economic reforms leading to full employment at decent wages, we take the position that the explosion of the rolls is the true relief reform, that it should be defended, and that it should be expanded. Even now, hundreds of thousands of impoverished families remain who are eligible for assistance but who receive no aid at all.

29
THE TRAGEDY OF OLD AGE IN AMERICA

Robert N. Butler

What is it like to be old in the United States? What will our own lives be like when we are old? Americans find it difficult to think about old age until they are propelled into the midst of it by their own aging and that of relatives and friends. Aging is the neglected stepchild of the human life cycle. Though we have begun to examine the socially taboo subjects of dying and death, we have leaped over that long period of time preceding death known as old age. In truth, it is easier to manage the problem of death than the problem of living as an old person. Death is a dramatic, one-time crisis while old age is a day-by-day and year-by-year confrontation with powerful external and internal forces, a bittersweet coming to terms with one's own personality and one's life.

Those of us who are not old barricade ouselves from discussions of old age by declaring the subject morbid, boring or in poor taste. Optimism and euphemism are other common devices. People will speak of looking forward to their "retirement years." The elderly are described respectfully as "senior citizens," "golden agers," "our elders," and one hears of old people who are considered inspirations and examples of how to "age well" or "gracefully." There is the popularly accepted opinion that Social Security and pensions provide a comfortable and reliable flow of funds so the elderly have few financial worries. Medicare has lulled the population into reassuring itself that the once terrible financial burdens of late-life illnesses are now eradicated. Advertisements and travel folders show relaxed, happy, well-dressed older people enjoying recreation, travel and their grandchildren. If they are no longer living in the old family home, they are pictured as delighted residents of retirement communities with names like Leisure World and Sun City, with lots of grass, clean air and fun. This is the American ideal of the "golden years" toward which millions of citizens are expectantly toiling though their workdays.

But this is not the full story. A second theme runs through the popular view of old age. Our colloquialisms reveal a great deal: once you are old you are "fading fast," "over the hill," "out to pasture," "down the drain," "finished," "out of date," an "old crock," "fogy," "geezer" or "biddy." One hears children saying they are afraid to get old, middle-aged people declaring they want to die after they have passed their prime, and numbers of old people wishing they were dead.

What can we possibly conclude from these discrepant points of view? Our popular attitudes could be summed up as a combination of wishful thinking and stark terror. We base our feelings on primitive fears, prejudice and stereotypes rather than on knowledge and insight. In reality, the way one experiences old age is contingent upon physical health, personality, earlier-life experiences, the actual circumstances of late-life events (in what order they occur, how they occur, when they occur) and the social supports one receives: adequate finances, shelter, medical care, social roles, religious support, recreation. All of these are crucial and interconnected elements which together determine the quality of late life.

Old age is neither inherently miserable nor inherently sublime—like every stage of life it has problems, joys, fears and potentials. The process of aging and eventual death must ultimately be accepted as the natural progression of the life cycle, the old completing their prescribed life spans and making way for the young. Much that is unique in old age in fact derives from the reality of aging and the imminence of death. The old must clarify and find use for what they have attained in a lifetime of learning and adapting; they must conserve strength and resources where necessary and adjust creatively to those changes and losses that occur as part of the aging experience. The elderly have the potential for qualities of human reflection and observation which can only come from having lived an entire life span. There is a lifetime accumulation of personality and experience which is available to be used and enjoyed.

But what are an individual's chances for a "good" old age in America, with satisfying final years and a dignified death? Unfortunately, none too good. For many elderly Americans old age is a tragedy, a period of quiet despair, deprivation, desolation and muted rage. This can be a consequence of the kind of life a person has led in younger years and the problems in his or her relationships with others. There are also inevitable personal and physical losses to be sustained, some of which can become overwhelming and unbearable. All of this is the individual factor, the existential element. But old age is frequently a tragedy even when the early years have been fulfilling and people seemingly have everything going for them. Herein lies what I consider to be the genuine tragedy of old age in America—we have shaped a society which is extremely harsh to live in when one is old. The tragedy of old age is not the fact that each of us must grow old and die but that the process of doing so has been made unnecessarily and at times excruciatingly painful, humiliating, debilitating and isolating through insensitivity, ignorance and poverty. The potentials for satisfactions and even triumphs in late life are real and vastly underexplored. For the most part the elderly struggle to exist in an inhospitable world.

Are things *really* that bad? Let's begin by looking at the basic daily requirements for survival. Poverty or drastically lowered income and old age go hand in hand. People who are poor all their lives remain poor as they grow old. Most of us realize this. What we do not realize is that these poor are joined by multitudes of people who become poor only after growing older. When Social Security becomes the sole or primary income, it means subsistence-level life styles for many, and recent increases do not keep up with soaring costs of living. Private pension plans often do not pay off, and pension payments that do come in are not tied to inflationary decreases in buying power. Savings can be wiped out by a single unexpected catastrophe. In January, 1971, half of the elderly, or over 10 million people, lived on less than $75 a week, or $10 per day. Most lived on far less. Even the relatively well-off are not assured of an income that will support them:

Rose Anderson was 90 years old, wispy and frail. She lived in a room filled with yellowed newspapers, magazines and books; it was filthy. There were cockroaches. There was an ugly permeating stench. She was too weary to clean. She gave her energy to caring for her canary.

She had been the wife of a prominent physician but she had the "misfortune" of living to a ripe old age and outliving both the $300,000 her husband had carefully provided for her and her only child, a son, who died at the age of 57 when she was 76. She had given over some of her money to support her daughter-in-law and grandchildren. But most of it went for her own extensive medical expenses. She ended up living on welfare.

It has been estimated that at least 30 percent of the elderly live in substandard housing. Many more must deprive themselves of essentials to keep their homes in repair:

Seventy-three-year-old Emil Pines was picked up by the police wandering along Market Street in San Francisco. He was mentally confused and unable to remember his name and address. After a medical examination it was determined that he had not eaten for several days and was dehydrated. Food and liquids were immediately prescribed and shortly thereafter his mind cleared.

He remembered that he had used his pension check to pay for emergency house repairs and had not had enough left for food that month.

The American dream promised older people that if they worked hard enough all their lives, things would turn out well for them. Today's elderly were brought up to believe in pride, self-reliance and independence. Many are tough, determined individuals who manage to survive against adversity. But even the tough ones reach a point where help should be available to them:

Now 81, Joseph Bartlett could look back on a long and useful life. He was living in a dusty Oklahoma town where he had lived since leaving farming and becoming a barber. He had been present at the opening of Indian Territory to white settlers and during the later oil boom. He had lost his wife and his only son ten years before. Since he had been self-employed he had no Social Security and was forced to turn to welfare. He was without transportation in the rural village. There were no social services, and medical care was inaccessible. His close friends and family had died, and he was too proud to ask other townspeople for the help he needed. He admitted to living in pain for a number of years but declared he would never burden anyone—"I will make do for myself."

Age discrimination in employment is unrestrained, with arbitrary retirement practices and bias against hiring older people for available jobs. Social Security penalizes the old by reducing their income checks as soon as they earn more than $1,400 a year. Job-training programs don't want the elderly (or the middle-aged, for that matter), so there is no opportunity to learn new skills. Employers rarely make concessions for the possible physical limitations of otherwise valuable older employees, and instead they are fired, retired or forced to resign.

It is obvious that the old get sick more frequently and more severely than the young, and 86 percent have chronic health problems of varying degree. These health problems, while significant, are largely treatable and for the most part do not impair the capacity to work. Medicare pays for only 45 percent of older people's health expenses; the balance must come from their own incomes and savings, or from Medicaid, which requires a humiliating means test. A serious illness can mean instant poverty. Drugs prescribed outside of hospitals, hearing aids, glasses, dental care and podiatry are not covered at all under Medicare. There is prejudice against the old by doctors and other medical personnel who don't like to bother with them. Psychiatrists and mental-health personnel typically assume that the mental problems of the old are untreatable. Psychoanalysts, the elite of the psychiatric profession, rarely accept them as patients. Medical schools and other teaching institutions find them "uninteresting." Voluntary hospitals are well known for dumping the "Medicare patient" into municipal hospitals; municipal hospitals in turn funnel them into nursing homes, mental hospitals and chronic-disease institutions without the adequate diagnostic and treatment effort which might enable them to return home. Persons who do remain at home while in ill health have serious difficulties in getting social, medical and psychiatric services brought directly to them:

Professor Frank Minkoff, a 70-year-old Russian immigrant with a university degree in engineering, was still teaching mathematics at an evening school. He was unmarried, the only member of his family in the United States, and lived in an apartment crammed with books. Suddenly he became confused and disoriented. He was frightened and refused to leave his room. Concerned neighbors quickly called a doctor, who expressed his unwillingness to make a home visit, saying, "There is nothing I can do. He needs to be in a nursing home or a mental institution." The neighbors were unconvinced, remembering Mr. M.'s earlier good functioning. They pleaded with the doctor and, under pressure, he angrily complied and visited the home. While there he again repeated his conviction that Mr. M. needed "custodial" care. Mr. M. was coherent enough to refuse, saying he would never voluntarily go to a nursing home of mental hospital. He did agree to be admitted to a medical hospital. Admission took place and studies resulted in the diagnosis "reversible brain syndrome due to acute viral infection." Mr. M. was successfully treated and released to his home in good condition in less than a week.

Many others are not so fortunate. Afflicted with reversible conditions of all kinds, they are frequently labeled "senile" and sent to institutions for the rest of their lives.

Problems large and small confront the elderly. They are easy targets for crime in the streets and in their homes. Because of loneliness, confusion, hearing and visual difficulties they are prime victims of dishonest door-to-door salesmen and fraudulent advertising, and buy defective hearing aids, dance lessons, useless "Medicare insurance supplements," and quack health remedies. Persons crippled by arthritis or strokes are yelled at by impatient bus drivers for their slowness in climbing on and off buses. Traffic lights turn red before they can get across the street. Revolving doors move too quickly. Subways usually have no elevators or escalators.

Old women fare worse than old men. Women have an average life expectancy of seven years longer than men and tend to marry men older than themselves; so two-thirds (six million) of all older women are widows.° When widowed they do not have the same social prerogatives as older men to date and marry those who are younger. As a result, they are likely to end up alone—an ironic turn of events when one remembers that most of them were raised from childhood to consider marriage the only acceptable state. The income levels of older working women are generally lower than those of men; many never worked outside the home

---

°Twenty percent of American women are widows by 60, 50 percent by 65, 66⅔ percent by 75.

until their children were grown and then only at unskilled, low-paying jobs. Others who worked all their lives typically received low wages, with lower Social Security and private retirement benefits as a result. Until 1973, housewives who were widowed received only 82.5 percent of their husbands' Social Security benefits even though they were full-time home-makers.

Black, Mexican-American and American Indian elderly all have a lower life expectancy than whites, due to their socioeconomic disadvan-tages. Although the life expectancy of 67.5 years for white men remained the same from 1960 to 1968, the life expectancy for black men *declined* a full year during that time (from 61.1 to 60.0). Blacks of all ages make up 11 percent of the total United States population, but they constitute only 7.8 percent of the elderly. The life expectancy for Mexican-Americans is estimated as 57 years, and for American Indians at 44 years. Most do not live long enough to be eligible for the benefits of Social Security and Medicare. Poverty is the norm. Scant attention is paid to their particular cultural interests and heritage.

Asian-American elderly (Chinese, Japanese, Korean, Filipino and Sa-moan) are victims of a public impression that they are independently cared for by their families and therefore do not need help. However, patterns of immigration by Asian-Americans to this country, the cultural barriers, language problems and discrimination they have faced have all taken a toll of their elderly and their families.° This is particularly true of older Chinese men, who were not allowed to bring their wives and fami-lies with them to the United States or to intermarry.

MYTHS AND STEREOTYPES ABOUT THE OLD

In addition to dealing with the difficulties of physical and economic sur-vival, older people are affected by the multitude of myths and stereotypes surrounding old age:

An older person thinks and moves slowly. He does not think as he used to or as creatively. He is bound to himself and to his past and can no longer change or grow. He can learn neither well nor swiftly and, even if he could, he would not wish to. Tied to his personal traditions and growing conservatism, he dislikes innovations and is not disposed to new ideas. Not only can he not move for-ward, he often moves backward. He enters a second childhood, caught up in increasing egocentricity and demanding more from his environment than he is willing to give to it. Sometimes he becomes an intensification of himself, a car-icature of a lifelong personality. He becomes irritable and cantankerous, yet

---

°One recommendation of the 1971 White House Conference on Aging was for fully crediting toward Social Security and other benefits the accumulated time spent by Japanese-Americans in United States "relocation" camps during World War II.

shallow and enfeebled. He lives in his past; he is behind the times. He is aimless and wandering of mind, reminiscing and garrulous. Indeed, he is a study in decline, the picture of mental and physical failure. He has lost and cannot replace friends, spouse, job, status, power, influence, income. He is often stricken by diseases which, in turn, restrict his movement, his enjoyment of food, the pleasures of well-being. He has lost his desire and capacity for sex. His body shrinks, and so too does the flow of blood to his brain. His mind does not utilize oxygen and sugar at the same rate as formerly. Feeble, uninteresting, he awaits his death, a burden to society, to his family and to himself.

In its essentials, this view I have sketched approximates the picture of old age held by many Americans. As in all clichés, stereotypes and myths there are bits of truth. But many of the current views of old age represent confusions, misunderstandings or simply a lack of knowledge about old age. Others may be completely inaccurate or biased, reflecting prejudice or outright hostility. Certain prevalent myths need closer examination.

The Myth of "Aging"

The idea of chronological aging (measuring one's age by the number of years one has lived) is a kind of myth. It is clear that there are great differences in the rates of physiological, chronological, psychological and social aging within the person and from person to person. In fact, physiological indicators show a greater range from the mean in old age than in any other age group, and this is true of personality as well. Older people actually become more diverse rather than more similar with advancing years. There are extraordinarily "young" 80-year-olds as well as "old" 80-year-olds. Chronological age, therefore, is a convenient but imprecise indicator of physical, mental and emotional status. For the purposes of this book old age may be considered to commence at the conventionally accepted point of 65.

We do know that organic brain damage can create such extensive intellectual impairment that people of all types and personalities may become dull-eyed, blank-faced and unresponsive. Massive destruction of the brain and body has a "leveling" effect which can produce increasing homogeneity among the elderly. But most older people do not suffer impairment of this magnitude during the greater part of their later life.

The Myth of Unproductivity

Many believe the old to be unproductive. But in the absence of diseases and social adversities, old people tend to remain productive and actively involved in life. There are dazzling examples like octogenarians Georgia O'Keeffe continuing to paint and Pope John XXIII revitalizing his church, and septuagenarians Duke Ellington composing and working his hectic concert schedule and Golda Meir acting as her country's vigorous Prime Minister. Substantial numbers of people become unusually creative for the first time in old age, when exceptional and inborn talents may be discovered and expressed. What is more pertinent to our discussion here, however, is the fact that many old people continue to contribute usefully to their families and community in a variety of ways, including active employment. The 1971 Bureau of Labor Statistics figures show 1,780,000 people over 65 working full time and 1,257,000 part time. Since society and business practice do not encourage the continued employment of the elderly, it is obvious that many more would work if jobs were available.

When productive incapacity develops, it can be traced more directly to a variety of losses, diseases or circumstances than to that mysterious process called aging. Even then, in spite of the presence of severe handicaps, activity and involvement are often maintained.

The Myth of Disengagement

This is related to the previous myth and holds that older people prefer to disengage from life, to withdraw into themselves, choosing to live alone or perhaps only with their peers. Ironically, some gerontologists themselves hold these views. One study, *Growing Old: The Process of Disengagement,* presents the theory that mutual separation of the aged person from his society is a natural part of the aging experience. There is no evidence to support this generalization. Disengagement is only one of many patterns of reaction to old age.

The Myth of Inflexibility

The ability to change and adapt has little to do with one's age and more to do with one's lifelong character. But even this statement has to be qualified. One is not necessarily destined to maintain one's character in earlier life permanently. True, the endurance, the strength and the stability in human character structure are remarkable and protective. But most, if not all, people change and remain open to change throughout the course of life, right up to its termination. The old notion, whether ascribed to Pope Alexander VI or Sigmund Freud, that character is laid down in final form by the fifth year of life can be confidently refuted. Change is the hallmark of living. The notion that older people become less responsive to innovation and change because of age is not supported by scientific studies of healthy older people living in the community or by everyday observations and clinical psychiatric experience.

A related cliché is that political conservatism increases with age. If one's options are constricted by job discrimination, reduced or fixed income and runaway inflation, as older people's are, one may become conservative out of economic necessity rather than out of qualities innate in the psyche. Thus an older person may vote against the creation of better schools or an expansion of social services for tax reasons. His property—his home—may be his only equity, and his income is likely to be too low to weather increased taxes. A perfectly sensible self-interest rather than "conservatism" is at work here. Naturally, conservatives do exist among the elderly, but so do liberals, radicals and moderates. Once again diversity rather than homogeneity is the norm.

The Myth of "Senility"

The notion that old people are senile, showing forgetfulness, confusional episodes and reduced attention, is widely accepted. "Senility" is a popularized layman's term used by doctors and the public alike to categorize the behavior of the old. Some of what is called senile is the result of brain damage. But anxiety and depression are also frequently lumped within the same category of senility, even though they are treatable and often reversible. Old people, like young people, experience a full range of emotions, including anxiety, grief, depression and paranoid states. It is all too easy to blame age and brain damage when accounting for the mental problems and emotional concerns of later life.

Drug tranquilization is another frequent, misdiagnosed and potentially reversible cause of so-called senility. Malnutrition and unrecognized physical illnesses, such as congestive heart failure, may produce "senile behavior" by reducing the supply of blood, oxygen and food to the brain. Alcoholism, often associated with bereavement, is another cause. Because it has been so convenient to dimiss all these manifestations by lumping them together under an improper and inaccurate diagnostic label, the elderly often do not receive the benefits of decent diagnosis and treatment.

Actual irreversible brain damage,° of course, is not a myth, and two major conditions create mental disorders. One is cerebral arteriosclerosis (hardening of the arteries of the brain); the other, unfortunately referred to as senile brain disease, is due to a mysterious dissolution of brain cells. Such conditions account for some 50 percent of the cases of major mental disorders in old age, and the symptoms connected with these condi-

---

°Human beings react in varying ways to brain disease just as they do to other serious threats to their persons. They may become anxious, rigid, depressed and hypochondriacal. (Hypochondriasis comprises bodily symptoms or fear of diseases that are not due to physical changes but to emotional concerns. They are no less real simply because they do not have a physical origin.) These reactions can be ameliorated by sensitive, humane concern, talk and understanding even though the underlying physical process cannot be reversed. Therefore, even the irreversible brain syndromes require proper diagnosis and treatment of their emotional consequences.

tions are the ones that form the basis for what has come to be known as senility. But, as I wish to emphasize again, similar symptoms can be found in a number of other conditions which *are* reversible through proper treatment.

The Myth of Serenity

In contrast to the previous myths, which view the elderly in a negative light, the myth of serenity portrays old age as a kind of adult fairyland. Now at last comes a time of relative peace and serenity when people can relax and enjoy the fruits of their labors after the storms of active life are over. Advertising slogans, television and romantic fiction foster the myth. Visions of carefree, cookie-baking grandmothers and rocking-chair grandfathers are cherished by younger generations. But, in fact, older persons experience more stresses than any other age group, and these stresses are often devastating. The strength of the aged to endure crisis is remarkable, and tranquility is an unlikely as well as inappropriate response under these circumstances. Depression, anxiety, psychosomatic illnesses, paranoia, garrulousness and irritability are some of the internal reactions to external stresses.

Depressive reactions are particularly widespread in late life. To the more blatant psychotic depressions and the depressions associated with organic brain diseases must be added the everyday depressions that stem from long physical illness or chronic discomfort, from grief, despair and loneliness, and from an inevitably lowered self-esteem that comes from diminished social and personal status.

Grief is a frequent companion of old age—grief for one's own losses and for the ultimate loss of one's self. Apathy and emptiness are a common sequel to the initial shock and sadness that come with the deaths of close friends and relatives. Physical disease and social isolation can follow bereavement.

Anxiety is another common feature. There is much to be anxious about; poverty, loneliness and illness head the list. Anxiety may manifest itself in many forms: rigid patterns of thinking and behaving, helplessness, manipulative behavior, restlessness and suspiciousness, sometimes to the point of paranoid states.°

Anger and even rage may be seen:

° No less a thinker than Aristotle failed to distinguish between the intrinsic features of aging and the reaction of the elderly to their lives. He considered cowardice, resentment, vindictiveness and what he called "senile avarice" to be intrinsic to late life. Cicero took a warmer and more positive view of old age. He understood, for example, "If old men are morose, troubled, fretful and hard to please . . . these are faults of character and not of age." So he explained in his essay *"De Senectutue."*

Mary Mack, 73, left her doctor's office irritable, depressed and untreated. She was angry at the doctor's inattention. She charged that he simply regarded her as a complainer and did not take the necessary time to examine her carefully. She had received the same response from other doctors. Meanwhile her doctor entered the diagnosis in his file: hypochondriasis with chronic depression. No treatment was given. The prognosis was evidently considered hopeless.

John Barber, an elderly black man, spent all his life working hard at low wages for his employers. When he was retired he literally went on strike. He refused to do anything. He would sit all day on his front porch, using his family as the substitute victim of his years of pent-up anger. He had always been seen as mild mannered. Now he could afford to let himself go into rages and describe in vicious detail what he was going to do to people. A social worker viewing his behavior declared to his family that he was "psychotic." But Mr. Barber was not insane; he was angry.

AGEISM—THE PREJUDICE AGAINST THE ELDERLY

The stereotyping and myths surrounding old age can be explained in part by lack of knowledge and by insufficient contact with a wide variety of older people. But there is another powerful factor operating—a deep and profound prejudice against the elderly which is found to some degree in all of us. In thinking about how to describe this, I coined the word "ageism"° in 1968:

Ageism can be seen as a process of systematic stereotyping of and discrimination against people because they are old, just as racism and sexism accomplish this with skin color and gender. Old people are categorized as senile, rigid in thought and manner, old-fashioned in morality and skills. . . . Ageism allows the younger generations to see older people as different from themselves; thus they subtly cease to identify with their elders as human beings.[4]

Ageism makes it easier to ignore the frequently poor social and economic plight of older people. We can avoid dealing with the reality that our productivity-minded society has little use for nonproducers—in this case those who have reached an arbitrarily defined retirement age. We can also avoid, for a time at least, reminders of the personal reality of our own aging and death.

Ageism is manifested in a wide range of phenomena, both on individual and institutional levels—stereotypes and myths, outright disdain

---

°I first publicly described my notion of ageism at the time of stormy opposition to the purchase of a high-rise in northwest Washington for public housing for the elderly.[1] I also developed it in observing the social and economic impact of the extended life span.[2] Ageism is a broader concept than "gerontophobia," the classic fear of old age. Gerontophobia refers to a rarer "unreasonable fear and/or irrational hatred of older people whereas ageism is a much more comprehensive and useful concept."[3]

and dislike, or simply subtle avoidance of contact; discriminatory practices in housing, employment and services of all kinds; epithets, cartoons and jokes. At times ageism becomes an expedient method by which society promotes viewpoints about the aged in order to relieve itself of responsibility toward them. At other times ageism serves a highly personal objective, protecting younger (usually middle-aged) individuals—often at high emotional cost—from thinking about things they fear (aging, illness, death).

The media illustrate the extremes to which negative attitudes toward the old can lead:

August 29, 1970

Mr. Douglas J. Stewart in *The New Republic* (Vol. 163, No. 8–9) advocated that all persons lose their vote after retirement, or at the age of 70, or at 55 when moving to another state.

Mr. Stewart, 37 years old at the time, was an associate professor of classics at Brandeis University. Perhaps one should allow for the possibility that he was speaking tongue in cheek, implying that the old are already effectively disenfranchised. But there can be no doubt about the serious-mindedness of the following proposal.

From Livermore, California, in what was described as an imaginative Rand Corporation study, a report entitled "The Post Attack Population of the United States"[5] suggested methods the United States should initiate with regard to old people, chronic invalids, and the insane in the event of nuclear war. The famous think tank said survivors of a nuclear war "would be better off without . . . old and feeble members." The author, Ira S. Lowry, stated that after a nuclear war, policy makers would be presented with a difficult problem because "the working members of the society would insist on transferring some part of their personal advantages to members of their families who were not directly contributing to output." The report continues by saying,

Policy makers would presumably have to draw the line somewhere, however, in making such concessions and those most likely to suffer are people with little or no productive potential; old people, chronic invalids and the insane. Old people suffer the special disadvantage of being easily identified as a group and, therefore, subject to categorical treatment. . . . In a literate community, the elderly do not even serve their prehistoric function as repositories of traditional wisdoms . . . the amount of care and attention necessary to sustain life increases with age. . . . In this sense, at least, a community under stress would be better off without its old and feeble members . . . .[6]

The easiest way to implement a morally repugnant but socially beneficial policy is by inaction. Under stress, the managers of post-attack society would most likely resolve their problems by failing to make any special provision for the special needs of the elderly, the insane, and the chronically ill. Instead of Medicare for persons under 65, for example, we might have Medicare for persons under 15. Instead of pensions, we might have family allowances. To be sure, the government would not be able—nor would it be likely to try—to prevent the relatives and friends of old people from helping them; but overall the share of the elderly in the national product would certainly drop.[7]

Lowry, an economist and demographer, was quoted in a telephone conversation to Roger Rapaport of the Washington *Star* as follows: "The AEC (Atomic Energy Commission) told me that they were very satisfied with the final product." Extreme though this may sound, the abandonment of older people in time of crises is obviously not unthinkable.

Ageism, like all prejudices, influences the self view and behavior of its victims. The elderly tend to adopt negative definitions of themselves and to perpetuate the very stereotypes directed against them, thereby reinforcing society's beliefs. As one older woman describes it:

Part of the neglect [of old people] can be attributed to the attitudes of the senior citizen himself. Rather than face the fact that being old is just another stage in the external aging process and being thankful that he has been blessed to reach his pinnacle in life, he has chosen to contemplate his plight with resignation, and even in some instances with disgust and frustration. This defeatist attitude has been adopted by society in general. We are now trying to reverse this trend.[8]

The elderly's part in eliciting the kind of response which they receive from the young and from society at large is often a subtle but powerful factor in the public's generally disparaging views of them. They collaborate with their ostracizers. Some individuals act "senile"; others may deny their true feelings in an attempt to "age graciously" and obtain the approval which is otherwise denied them. Psychologist Margaret Thaler Singer observed similarities between the Rorschach test findings in members of a National Institute of Mental Health sample of aged volunteers who were resigned in the face of aging and those in American GI prisoners of war who collaborated with their captors in Korea.

Other self-sabotaging behavior can be a refusal to identify oneself as elderly at all. One sees older persons who affect the dress and behavior patterns of the young, pretending like Peter Pan that they have never grown up. Older women can be seen engaging in sad, frantic attempts to appear young, as if this would ensure appreciation and acceptance in the eyes of others.

A significant minority of older people conceal their age from themselves as well as from others. In a study of 1,700 elderly persons, Taves and Hansen[9] found that one-sixth thought of themselves as old between the ages of 54 and 69, one-third between the ages of 70 and 79, and only 40 percent by age 80 and over. About one person in seven said they never thought of themselves as old.

In a study by Tuckman and Lorge [10] that queried over 1,000 persons from 20 to 80, those under 30 classified themselves as young, and of those between 30 and 60, most classified themselves as middle-aged. At age 60 only a small proportion classified themselves as old, and at age 80 slightly over half called themselves old. A small percentage of the 80-year-olds persisted in describing themselves as young.

Of course, considering oneself "young" is not simply a prejudice or a delusion.[11] Healthy older people do feel strong and vigorous, much as they did in their earlier days. The problem comes when this good feeling is called "youth" rather than "health," thus tying it to chronological age instead of to physical and mental well-being.

Lack of empathy is a further reaction by the elderly to their experiences in the larger culture. Out of emotional self-protection, many healthy, prosperous, well-educated old people feel no identification with or protectiveness toward the poor elderly. A lack of compassion is of course not unique to the aged, but it has a special irony here—with the advent of catastrophic illnesses or the exhaustion of resources that goes with a long life, they too run a high risk of finding themselves among the poor, facing similar indifference from their wealthier peers.

Older people are not always victims, passive and fated by their environment. They, too, initiate direct actions and stimulate responses. They may exploit their age and its accompanying challenges to gain something they want or need, perhaps to their own detriment (e.g., by demanding services from others and thus allowing their own skills to atrophy). Exploitation can backfire; excessive requests to others by an older person may be met at first, but as requests increase they are felt as demands—and may indeed be demands. Younger people who attempt to deal with a demanding older person may find themselves going through successive cycles of rage, guilt and overprotectiveness without realizing they are being manipulated. In addition to his "age," the older person may exploit his diseases and his impairments, capitalizing upon his alleged helplessness. Invalids of all ages do this, but older people can more easily take on the appearance of frailty when others would not be allowed this behavior. Manipulation by older people is best recognized for what it is—a valuable clue that there is energy available which should be redirected toward greater benefit for themselves and others.

It must also be remembered that the old can have many prejudices against the young. These may be a result of their attractiveness, vigor and sexual prowess. Older people may be troubled by the extraordinary changes that they see in the world around them and blame the younger generation. They may be angry at the brevity of life and begrudge someone the fresh chance of living out a life span which they have already completed.

Angry and ambivalent feelings flow, too, between the old and the middle-aged, who are caught up in the problems unique to their age and position within the life cycle. The middle-aged bear the heaviest personal and social responsibilities since they are called upon to help support—individually and collectively—both ends of the life cycle: the nurture and education of their young and the financial, emotional and physical care of the old. Many have not been prepared for their heavy responsibilities and are surprised and overwhelmed by them. Frequently these responsibilities trap them in their careers or life styles until the children grow up or their parents die. A common reaction is anger at both the young and the old. The effects of financial pressures are seen primarily in the middle and lower economic classes. But the middle-aged of all classes are inclined to be ambivalent toward the young and old since both age groups remind them of their own waning youth. In addition—with reason—they fear technological or professional obsolescence as they see what has happened to their elders and feel the pressure of youth pushing its way toward their position in society. Furthermore, their responsibilities are likely to increase in the future as more and more of their parents and grandparents live longer life spans.

The Elderly Population Explosion

There are now well over twenty million people over 65 years of age in the United States, comprising 10 percent of the population.° A population of older people has been under way for a number of decades, and the elderly are now the fastest-growing group in the United States. Between 1960 and 1970 the aging increased by 21 percent, compared with an 18 percent increase among those under 65.

Older people have become a highly visible phenomenon only since the nineteenth century; before then relatively few people were long lived. In 1900 only three million, or 4 percent of the population, were 65 and older. Influenza, pneumonia, tuberculosis, typhoid and paratyphoid fever, diphtheria and scarlet fever were major killers, causing high death rates all along the life cycle. Increased life expectancy followed medical advances in the prevention and treatment of these diseases, as well as generally improved public-health measures, particularly in sanitation. Lowered rates of infant and maternal mortality enabled larger numbers of people to reach old age, and once there, new drugs and medical techniques allowed many old people to survive once-fatal illnesses.

The average life expectancy at the turn of the century was 47 years; now it is 70.4 years. A boy born today can expect to live to 66.8 years; a girl to age 74.3. Half of all older people (ten million) are over 73;

°Two of every ten Americans are now between 45 and 65. This is 20 percent of the population, or 42 million people.

1,000,000 elderly are 85 and over; and the 1970 census reports 106,441 centenarians (over 100 years old).

Every day 1,000 people reach 65; each year 365,000. More than 70 percent of the 65-and-over age group in 1970 entered that category after 1959. With new medical discoveries, an improved health-care delivery system and the presently declining birth rate, it is possible that the elderly will make up 15 percent of the total population by the year 2000. Major medical advances in the control of cancer or heart and vascular diseases could increase the average life expectancy by ten or even fifteen years. Discovery of deterrents to the basic causes of aging would cause even more profound repercussions. The presence of so many elderly, and the potential of so many more, has been a puzzlement to gerontologists, public-health experts and demographers, who don't know whether to regard it as "the aging problem" or a human triumph over disease. What is clear is that it will result in enormous changes in every part of society.

Changes will therefore occur in our definition of the aging process itself. Much of what we think of as aging today is actually disease and illness, and not a part of fundamental physical aging. This includes many of the physical, mental and emotional conditions seen in older people. The major diseases of late life may become preventable or at least treatable. The mental depressions of late life and the acute brain syndromes are already treatable and reversible. The removal of pathogenic elements—excessive sun exposure and cigarette smoking (both are causes of skin wrinkles), air pollution and others—may slow down the physical appearances of deterioration. Even genetic traits responsible for such changes as graying and loss of hair may eventually be controllable. What is in the future if acute and chronic disease states are identified and largely eliminated, undesirable genetic traits mainly nullified and pathogenic environmental conditions alleviated? We should see for the first time that flow of human life from birth through death truly called aging. Aging refers to patterns of late-life changes which are eventually seen in all persons but which vary in rate and degree. Although human beings will never be able to live indefinitely, they can live much longer and more comfortably, mostly free from the violent ravages of disease, with perhaps a gradual and fairly predictable decline toward eventual death.

The physical health of the majority of the elderly is already better than is generally believed. Eighty-one percent of those over 65 are fully ambulatory and move about independently on their own. Ninety-five percent live in the community; at any one time only 5 percent are in nursing homes, chronic-disease hospitals and other institutions—a startling fact when one thinks of the popular image of the old "dumped" en masse into institutions by their families because they have become enfeebled.

Our view of who is old and when aging happens will also change. It is becoming more common to find retired people in their sixties and seventies who have living parents in the eighties and nineties. Sometimes it is the 80-year-old who is taking care of the 60-year-old! Chronological age is an inaccurate measure of how old one is because aging as we presently experience it occurs unevenly—one may be at very different "ages" at one and the same time in terms of mental capacity, physical health, endurance, creativity and emotions. Society has arbitrarily chosen ages 60–65 as the beginning of late life (borrowing the idea from Bismarck's social legislation in Germany in the 1880s) primarily for the purpose of determining a point for retirement and eligibility for services and financial entitlements for the elderly. This social definition has had its legitimate uses but also its abuses. Not everyone is ready to retire at 60 or 65. Older people do not appreciate the "social" definition of old age encroaching into every corner of their lives, rigidly stamping them with a uniform label regardless of condition or functioning. Gerontologists divide old age into early old age, 65 to 74 years, and advanced old age, 75 and above. A much more flexible view, which took actual capacities into account, would be more realistic.

STUDYING THE OLD

We have put precious little work and research into examining the last phase of life. What research has been done has concentrated primarily on studies of the 5 percent of elderly who are in institutions. The few research studies on the healthy aged living in the community have produced exciting new looks at the possibilities and problems of this age group.[12] But on the whole medicine and the behavioral sciences seem to have shared society's negative views of old age and have quite consistently presented *decline* as the key concept of late life, with *neglect* forming the major treatment technique and research response.

Why study the elderly? Why spend research money on old people when there are compelling priorities for other age groups, particularly the young? In the first place, life cannot be carved up into bits and pieces—what affects one age group affects another. To illustrate this on the biological level, it is well known that carcinoma in the breast of a woman has a much more fulminating malignant course if it occurs in young women than in old. Leukemia, another form of cancer, tends to be more chronic in the old and more acute in the young. Diabetes is much more severe in childhood than in the aged. Why? Is there something we can learn about disease processes in the old that may help both them and those who are younger? Many of the diseases occurring in old age do not begin there. Arteriosclerosis, a major cause of much morbidity and mortality (affecting such major organs as the kidney, the heart and the brain), begins early in life. If we are to stop it, it must be studied, prevented and treated in its earliest phases. Stroke, typically thought of as occurring in late life, also kills the young in significant numbers.

In the psychological sphere, too, our understanding of emotions like grief can gain enormously from the study of the old, in whom grief occurs with such frequency and profundity. This is true of a whole variety of human reactions to stress, as well as to the normal events in late life. The natural history of human character and its disorders can only really be studied in the old. The degree to which change and improvement in mental diseases and emotional illnesses occur, the nature of survival characteristics, and successful modes of adaptation, among other matters, are natural subjects for study in those who have lived an entire life span.

Ultimately interest must focus on clarifying the complex, interwoven elements necessary to produce and support physical and mental health up to the very end of life rather than our present preoccupation with "curing" ills after they develop. Understanding what interferes with healthy development throughout the life cycle gives us a chance to prevent problems, instead of rushing frantically and often futilely to solve them after they occur. Life is a continuing process from birth until death and it seems strange that it so seldom occurs to us to study life as a whole.

Finally, from a philosophic view, a greater understanding and control over the diseases and difficulties of later life would hopefully make old age less frightening and more acceptable as a truly valuable last phase of life. The relief of human suffering has merit in itself, but it also releases human beings from the fears and defenses they build up around it.

Whose Responsibility Are They?

Are older Americans entitled to decent income, health, housing, transportation and opportunities for employment as well as to social status and participation in society? Who should see to it that they get them? Why can't they manage their lives themselves? The struggle to decide on the place of the old in a culture has been familiar throughout history. Cultural attitudes have ranged from veneration, protectiveness, and sentimentality to derogation, rejection, pity and abandonment. William Graham Summer, in his *Folkways*, published in 1907, wrote in a section, "Mores of Respect or Contempt for the Aged":

[There are] two sets of mores as to the aged: (1) in one set of mores the teaching, and usages, inculcate conventional respect for the aged who are therefore arbitrarily preserved for their wisdom and counsel, perhaps also sometimes out of affection and sympathy; (2) in the other set of mores the aged are regarded as societal burdens which waste the strength of the society, already inadequate for its tasks. Therefore, they are forced to die, either by their own hands or those of their relatives. It is very far from being true that the first of these policies is practiced higher up in civilization than those who practice the second. The people in lower civilizations profit more by the counsel from the aged than those in higher civilizations and are educated by this experience to respect and value the aged.

Older Americans of today—indeed the old people in any society—contributed to the growth of the society in which younger people live. One might assume that they would have a justifiable expectation of sharing in what is referred to as America's affluence. All of us, whatever our age, are now contributing taxes and services to our nation and are collectively preparing for our own old age. What will the future bring for us? Will anyone help us if we cannot adequately help ourselves?

There are people who believe that the responsibility for one's old age can and should be assumed by the individual alone. They hold that improvidence is the major cause of an impoverished old age and agree with the nineteenth-century Social Darwinist, Herbert Spencer:

Pervading all nature we may see at work a stern discipline, which is a little cruel that it may be very kind. . . . The poverty of the incapable, the distresses that come upon the imprudent, the starvation of the idle, and the shouldering aside of the weak by the strong . . . are the decrees of a large, far-seeing benevolence. . . . Similarly, we must call spurious philanthropists who, to prevent a present misery, would entail greater misery upon future generations. All defenders of a poor-law must be classed among them. . . . Blind to the fact that under the natural order of things society is constantly excreting its unhealthy, imbecile, slow, vacillating, faithless members, those unthinking, though well-meaning, men advocate an interference which not only stops the purifying process but even increases the vitiation.[13]

Such a harsh view fails to take into account the life circumstances and historical conditions of today's older Americans. Americans born in the 1900s found themselves, in the prime of their earning years, trapped in the massive Depression of the 1930s. Many lost jobs, homes, savings and their morale.

By the 1960s, when they were retiring, inflation eroded their fixed incomes to an alarming degree. Economic forces, not improvidence, have placed today's elderly in their predicament.

The Depression of the 1930s convinced many rugged individualists that forces beyond the control of the individual could bring widespread devastation and poverty. A legislative landmark of Roosevelt's New Deal was the inauguration of Social Security in 1935, a consequence of many pressures that included the Townsend movement;* perhaps the final impetus came from the need to have the old retire in order to provide employment for the young. Thus, years after most Western European

---

*A movement representing older persons and led by Dr. Francis Townsend, a retired physician.

industrial nations had introduced it, the United States made its decision for the collective insurance-policy form of income maintenance for the disable and retired. Eighty-five cents ($0.85) of every federal dollar now expended annually for programs for the elderly derive from Social Security trusts funds to which we all contribute—as did the majority of the present elderly themselves in their working days.

Social Security, Medicare and federal housing programs have helped to gain for the elderly *some* income security, *some* health care and *some* housing. But the task has not been finished and the efforts do not match the needs.

REFERENCES

1. Carl Bernstein, "Age and Race Fears Seen in Housing Opposition," Washington *Post*, March 7, 1969.

2. Robert N. Butler, "The Effects of Medical and Health Progress on the Social and Economic Aspects of the Life Cycle," *Industrial Gerontology*, 2 (1969), pp. 1–9. Presented at National Institute of Industrial Gerontology, March 13, 1969.

3. See Erdman Palmore, "Gerontophobia Versus Ageism," *The Gerontologist*, 12 (1972), p. 213.

4. Robert N. Butler and Myra I. Lewis, *Aging and Mental Health: Positive Psychosocial Approaches* (St. Louis: C. V. Mosby, 1973).

5. Memorandum RM-5115-TAB, prepared for Technical Analysis Branch, United States Atomic Energy Commission, the Rand Corporation, Santa Monica, California, December, 1966.

6. *Ibid.*, p. 122.

7. *Ibid.*, p. 123.

8. Mrs. Mae B. Phillips, president, Senior Citizens Clearinghouse Committee, Washington, D.C. Hearings on Needs of Senior Citizens, D.C. City Council, October 15, 1968.

9. Marvin J. Taves and G. O. Hansen, "1,700 Elderly Citizens," in Arnold M. Rose (ed.), *Aging in Minnesota* (Minneapolis: University of Minnesota Press, 1963), pp. 73–181.

10. Jacob Tuckman and Irving Lorge, "Classification of the Self as Young, Middle-aged or Old," *Geriatrics*, 9 (1954), pp. 534–36.

11. See, for example, Talcott Parsons, "Age and Sex of the Social Structure of the United States," in *Essays in Sociological Theory* (Glencoe, Illinois: Free Press, 1954), especially pp. 89–103.

12. James E. Birren, Robert N. Butler, Samuel W. Greenhouse, Louis Sokoloff and Marion R. Yarrow, *Human Aging: A Biological and Behavioral Study*, U.S. Public Health Service Publication No. 986 (Washington, D.C.: U.S. Government Printing Office, 1963, reprinted 1971, 1974).

13. Herbert Spencer, *Social Statics, or The Conditions Essential to Human Happiness Specified*, 1851.

X

CRIME AND JUSTICE

In recent years, crime has come to be perceived by the public as America's number-one social problem. People seem to be more afraid of being robbed, raped, or murdered than of almost anything else. The point has often been made that, from an actuarial standpoint, people are about ten times more likely to be killed by riding in an automobile or three times more likely to die from a fall—slipping in the bathtub or tumbling from a ladder—than from being killed by street crime. Yet people are much more afraid of violence at the hand of a stranger.

The fear of street crime has been accompanied by a return to the "just desserts" philosophy of punishment and has resulted in longer sentences, mandated by the legislature. Such sentencing practices have led to severe prison overcrowding, so severe that James Lieber calls the American prison a "tinderbox." At the time of Lieber's article, the overcrowding issue had been placed before the U.S. Supreme Court in a case involving the constitutionality of putting two men in a cell built for one. The Court decided the question on June 15, 1981, ruling that "double-celling" was constitutionally permissible. The prison situation described by Lieber can therefore only be expected to worsen during the 1980s.

Things are not better on the streets. Whether crime has risen as much as fear is a matter of some dispute, but there can be no question that police use of deadly force has escalated. In Los Angeles, as Susan Stern and Richard Cohen report, police killings resulted in the creation of a special D.A.'s investigation squad, geared to "rollout" to every police shooting. Predictably, the LAPD has resisted such investigations and has been aided by the Los Angeles Police Protective League, the city's powerful police union. Unlike the LAPD, the LAPPL can bring direct political pressure to bear on candidates for municipal and statewide office. The question is, Does this sort of organized police power—a phenomenon of the late 1960s—render the police less accountable to the general public, especially those portions of the public having the most daily involvement with police? What might be the solution? Is the answer to get rid of police unions? Or find new sources of police recruitment? Are minority police less likely to use deadly force—especially against minority suspects—than white police are?

We are all too familiar with street crime, prisons, and police. Corporate crime is also coming to be widely recognized—even by *Fortune* magazine—as a major crisis point in a society presumably based on a free-enterprise system. In fact, corporate crime extracts far more from the public annually in money terms than do robberies and burglaries. Furthermore, business crime can be very dangerous, as, for example, when dangerously defective products are produced or when life-threatening pollution is the result. For example, might it not be fair to conclude that the original Pintos (see Selection 1) and the chemical wastes from the Love Canal (see Selection 21) are at least as perilous as crime in the streets?

One might ask, then, why corporate criminals tend to be treated more leniently by courts. Three reasons are worth considering: first, corporate crimes are subtle, so victims may be unaware they are being victimized until something dramatic happens. Second, it is often difficult to pin down who is responsible for corporate crime. Finally, business offenders are otherwise respectable and socially "attractive." Do these reasons seem compelling? If not, how can judges and prosecutors be made more responsive to the hazards inherent in the lawless corporation?

30
THE AMERICAN PRISON: A TINDERBOX

James Lieber

Like the Attica riot, the uprising at the New Mexico State Prison at Santa Fe earned a place in the nation's collective consciousness of terror. For 36 hours last year, gangs of convicts seized control of the maximum-security penitentiary on the outskirts of a city whose name, to much of the rest of the nation, had formerly meant sun on stucco, working ranches and Indian art. Now it became the focus of an intense hell: Prisoners, wielding knives, clubs, stolen riot gear and acetylene torches, took 12 guards hostage, stripped them and dragged them through the 24-year-old fortress, savagely beating, slashing and in some cases sexually assaulting them. But the worst was reserved for fellow prisoners, especially suspected informers and other outcasts of prison life, such as the mentally disturbed or retarded. Gangs raped them repeatedly, blow-torched their eyes and genitals, lynched men from tiers, decapitated them or fired tear-gas canisters point blank into their faces. When it was over, authorities counted 33 bodies. Physicians treated about 90 more for drug overdoses, stab wounds, fractures and traumatic amputations.

Just as disturbing as the fact that Santa Fe happened at all are the strong indications that similar horror could now erupt at any moment at any one of several major prisons in the United States because of severe overcrowding. These conditions have resulted in large part from a revolutionary wave of new legislative sentencing policies that have been aimed at curbing judicial inconsistency and leniency in American criminal courts. With the public fear about crime growing daily, with the Chief Justice expressing alarm about a criminal "reign of terror" hitting American cities, with state after state packing more and more criminal offenders into less and less space, the American state and Federal prison population has shot from 196,000 inmates in 1973 to more than 314,000 in 1981—the sharpest rise in history. As a result, says Anthony Travisono, executive director of the American Correctional Association, "conditions are ripe for another Santa Fe . . . all the elements are there."

John Moran, the respected Director of the Rhode Island Department of

Corrections who has previously headed systems in Delaware and Arizona, says the possibility exists for major uprisings in at least a half-dozen state prisons, which he declines to name lest he help incite the very riots he fears. It's not that all prisons are badly run or inhumane. The cause for alarm is the increasing overpopulation, and this issue has been placed before the United States Supreme Court. In *Rhodes v. Chapman*, the Court is being asked to rule on whether the doubling up of inmates in cells designed for one, the compressing of prisoners into too small a space, in Ohio's maximum-security prison amounts to cruel and unusual treatment under the United States Constitution. The decision, however it goes, will raise more difficult issues: If the states are not required to build new prison space, how will they deal with the worsening threat of violence? If they are, where will they put it and how will they afford it.?

No one can say, of course, how the Court will decide, but the Chief Justice himself stated in a recent speech before the American Bar Association convention in Houston that allocating money to attack the nation's crime rate—though there is serious disagreement about how great that rate increase really is—should be "as much a part of our national defense as the budget of the Pentagon," and he called for a "broad-scale physical rehabilitation of all prisons." Thirty-six states have joined Ohio—and the American Medical Association and the American Public Health Association have sided with the prisoners—in the suit now regarded by many as one of the most important in the history of American penal law.

When Ohio opened its maximum-security prison at Lucasville in 1972 with 1,600 single-occupancy cells, the institution was hailed as the very model of proper, efficient and secure confinement. But in the mid-70's, because of the growing concern about crime, the institution's population suddenly shot to 2,300. About 1,400 prisoners were double-celled, some for virtually every hour of the day. An inmate named Kelly Chapman, a wiry, blue-eyed Kentuckian, filed a court petition to halt the doubling up of prisoners in single cells. Chapman referred to an Ohio State veterinarian services specification of 43 square feet of space for a calf once it reaches 5 weeks old. "I went around measuring the cell—or my half of it," he said in a recent interview, "and I have 32 square feet. I couldn't accept that a calf is entitled to more living space than a man." Many Lucasville inmates also spoke about the dangers created by two men locked into a 6-by-10-foot area, because of the increased risks of sexual assault, violent arguments or simply the indignity of being present while another person is using the toilet.

Following a Federal District Court trial in 1977, a judge ordered the prison to cut its inmate count approximately to design capacity and not to double-bunk except on a temporary basis. Lucasville's population stands now at 1,645 with only a few double cells in use. Chapman, an armed robber serving an additional 16 to 60 years for his role in the 1968 break-out riot from the Ohio Penitentiary at Columbus where five inmates were killed, said: "There would be a blood bath in here in five to six months if they made us double up again. Some of us longtimers can't take it, especially in the summer roasting with two men in a cell. I'm either gonna take space to live in or I'm gonna take space to die in."

Generally, the guards agree with Chapman that double celling is dangerous. "It may be a necessary evil," confided one, "but when you put two men in a cell, tempers run kind of high—especially on a hot day." An end to double-celling at Santa Fe was one of five final rioters' demands. If the Supreme Court reverses the lower court ruling in Ohio, the results could be dramatic. "If they reverse," said attorney Ralph Knowles of the American Civil Liberties Union's National Prison Project, "it'll have a devastating effect. Legislators will read it as saying you can stack people on top of each other."

Not only have the male populations increased but the female as well. During the 70's the number of women in American prisons rose from 6,329 to 12,927. Most of the women are young, black, poor and the head of a family and are serving time for property offenses, such as passing worthless checks, credit-card fraud and forgery. Historically, members of minority groups have been imprisoned at a higher rate than others; currently, blacks are being placed in state prisons at a rate that is about nine times greater than whites, and Hispanics, about two times greater.

Why the sharp increase in prison populations? Certainly they reflect the public perception of rapidly increasing crime rates as well as anger and frustration over the whole issue. Polls conducted during the 70's indicate that most Americans believed that crime was increasing every year. One recent study reports that 41 percent of Americans were highly fearful of becoming the victims of violent crimes, another 29 percent are moderately fearful and that, as a result, more and more citizens were taking such measures as acquiring guns, dressing plainly and placing extra locks on the doors of their homes and apartments. Studies also indicate that 85 percent of Americans favor harsher sentences, and 67 percent advocate use of the death penalty.

Leaders, by and large, have mirrored these feelings. Citing "a crisis of violence," New York's Governor Carey asked the legislature on Jan. 7, 1980 for more prisons, prosecutors and tougher sentences. Recently, Mayor Koch said he represented "7.5 million people who are fed up with the criminal-justice system." Koch accused the judiciary of undue leniency because "judges fear that they might not be reappointed if they offend the defense bar," implying that the criminal-justice bar looks unfavorably on those considered too tough. Justice E. Leo Milonas, deputy chief administrative judge for the New York City courts, rejected the allegation as "an attempt to pressure and intimidate the judiciary."

Arrests do lead to indictment only about half as often in New York City as in outlying counties (probably because of limited prosecution resources). But after indictment, New York City judges have become the toughest in the state. More than 50 percent of local convicted defendants received at least a year of incarceration in 1979. Only 27.4 percent of cases resulted in such sentences in the metropolitan suburban counties of Westchester, Rockland, Nassau and Suffolk. The 53 upstate counties imposed equivalent punishment in only 26.5 percent of felony cases. Between 1971 and 1980, the percentage of defendants sentenced to more than three years rose in New York City from 26 to 85 percent.

Whether there is a national epidemic of crime as well as an epidemic of fear is a matter of dispute. Newspapers and broadcasters uncritically recount the figures of the F.B.I.'s Uniform Crime Reports, invariably referring to them as the "crime rate." Between 1973 and 1979 (the last year for which figures are available), the overall rate of reported crime went up by 33 percent, violent crime by 28 percent, and property crime by 33 percent. But it is important to realize that these figures represent offenses reported to police and then submitted to the F.B.I. rather than the actual amount of crime, so that the apparent increases may only reflect dramatically increased reporting.

As a result of a concern about this possible discrepancy, the Federal Government created the National Crime Survey, a collaborative effort of the Law Enforcement Assistance Administration and the U.S. Bureau of Census, which polls individuals in 60,000 households and 50,000 businesses on the numbers of crimes of which they have been the victims. Since respondents are questioned about offenses which they may have or may not have brought to police attention, the National Crime Survey is a better measure than merely reported crime. Between 1973, its first year, and 1979, the crime-victims survey has registered far more moderate gains in crime than the F.B.I. reports. The victims survey showed an overall crime-rate increase of 5.9 percent per 100,000 people, an increase in the rate of violence of 6.1 percent and an increase in the rate of property crime of 5.9 percent. But the survey actually shows decreases in some serious-crime areas where the F.B.I. showed increases. The survey reported a decrease of 7 percent in robbery, while the F.B.I. reported an increase of 16 percent; the survey, a decrease of 1.5 percent in aggravated assault, the F.B.I., an increase of 39 percent. The survey did show sharp rises in the rate of rape, up by 14 percent (the F.B.I. reports it up by 41 percent), and increases in simple assault of 17 percent and household larceny, 25 percent (the F.B.I. does not have strictly comparable figures for the latter two categories).

Experts believe that reporting has grown faster than actual crime because of greater victim access to telephones, growing willingness to report domestic offenses, increased police responsiveness to ghetto calls and, above all, because of continuous improvements in data-gathering methods.

There are other reasons—besides public pressure and the actual, if moderate, increase in crime rates—for the expanding prison populations. The steady emptying of mental hospitals, whose former patients often spill into criminal court, and joblessness (historically, a 1 percent rise in unemployment yields a 4 percent jump in imprisonment—the national unemployment rate climbed from 4.9 percent in 1973 to 7.1 percent last year) are important causes. Corrections administrators and analysts increasingly point to the principal factor, however, as the change being made in procedures for handing out criminal punishment. The change is coming about as a result of state legislatures' attempts to eliminate the discretionary powers of judges and parole boards by mandating minimum prison terms.

Legislative sentencing probably is best understood in terms of what it has replaced. Traditionally, legislators involved themselves marginally in the punishment of criminals, except murderers, for whom they wrote mandatory sentences—usually life or death. For the rest, they merely set nonbinding maximum terms. As long as a judge didn't exceed these, he had complete power to give an offender any sentence, including imprisonment, jail, probation, a fine, restitution or no punishment at all. The goal was to structure justice to rehabilitate the individual rather than to punish his crime. A decade ago, this system existed throughout America. Today, less than a dozen states fully retain it. The only large one is Pennsylvania, and its legislature is currently contemplating the change.

A better illustration even than Ohio's Lucasville of the difficult conditions that now exist at many state prisons in the United States may be the Indiana State Prison at Michigan City.

In 1976 and 1977, before the state's new sentencing code took effect, its prison population grew by only 1 percent per year. In 1979, it increased by 15 percent, and it jumped another 15 percent in 1980. The number of adults in the Indiana system rose from 4,200 in 1977 to about 6,000 today. About 40 percent of the new prison population is made up of persons convicted of minor crimes. For example, the new law requires at least a two-year prison sentence for second-time shoplifters. A recent Indiana study has shown burglars and rapists both serving 100 percent more time than in the past, armed robbers about 30 percent longer. By last fall, the state-prison population exceeded its own rated capacity figure by 30 percent.

From the road, in Michigan City, one sees the usual walls and towers of a state penitentiary. Inside, the turn-of-the-century housing blocks hold 390 cells on five tiers. Averaging about 57 square feet of floor space, each dimly lighted windowless unit contains a bed, toilet—some lidless—and a man's effects. Outside the cells, on catwalks enclosed with steel fencing, it is practically dark. The tiers are self-segregating, with blacks on top and whites below. As in all prisons, some men keep immaculate space and others live like pigs. But the overall condition is one of filth.

Garbage cans are not in evidence. Trash collects in loose heaps. Some as tall as men must have been left for days. Officials, unlike those at many American prisons, refused to admit photographers. The plumbing and ventilation are oppressive. Toilets are stuffed, showers flooded. The air in places is heavy with the sulfurous reek of leaking sewer gas. Recent inspections have disclosed that antiquated plumbing uses cross-connections between waste pipes and potable water lines, a substantial health hazard.

It is a fearful and, to a large extent, lawless prison. Only about 300 of the 1,792 inmates receive any vocational training. Another 300 work at prison industries, primarily in a license-plate shop. Others have maintenance or food-service jobs that take a few hours or less. Most of the men have little to do but lie about or get in trouble.

RETURN OF 'JUST DESSERTS'

The institution of the prison in the United States began as an institution of reform. After the American Revolution, the new nation rejected British justice, under which common penalties were branding, lashing, ear-cropping, expulsion to penal colonies, and, last but not least, execution. More than 200 crimes, many of them minor, were punishable by death.

The earliest reformers, Quakers, believed that repentence and Bible study in solitary confinement would lead inmates to see their errors and turn from evil. Instead, apparently many grew violent or became mad. As a result, during most of the 19th century, punishment rather than rehabilitation became the justification for prisons, which often packed killers, thieves, first offenders, vagrants, women and sometimes children together in filth.

Progressive leaders, including Zebulon Brockway of New York and Jane Addams of Illinois, began advocating special facilities for women and youths, and the first "reformatory" was opened in 1876 at Elmira, N.Y., with Brockway, a religious zealot and educator, as warden. Sentences were not fixed. Once an inmate received sufficiently high scores in education and religious instruction, he was regarded as reformed and released. The idea spread to prisons with male felons, and parole boards sprang up across the country to judge whether prisoners were rehabilitated and could be freed. By 1935, most states had adopted indeterminate sentences with parole, and by 1962, the writers of the influential Model Penal Code wrote individualized treatment and rehabilitation into their sentencing goals—without once mentioning punishment.

Reformers of the 1960's stressed a "medical model" of corrections. Karl Menninger, the forensic psychiatrist, declared: "I most certainly . . . believe the majority of [criminal offenders] would prove to be curable." During the early 70's, academic researchers studied rehabilitation. The late Robert Martinson, a sociologist at the City University of New York, analyzed 231 therapy, vocational and educational programs and concluded that "the rehabilitative efforts that have been reported so far have had no effect on recidivism." Others showed that parole boards, too, were ineffective, having no real basis for predicting which inmate, if released, would obey the law.

By and large, rehabilitation has again fallen out of favor and been replaced by the "just-desserts" theory of Prof. Andrew von Hirsch of Rutgers University: Imprisonment meets the community's need for retribution following a serious offense. A less-heeded part of the idea holds that prison should be used as a last resort and that term lengths should rarely exceed five years, as is the case in Western Europe.

Some authorities, however, continue to believe that certain inmates can be successfully returned to society. They cite recent successes with work-release programs, and they point out that a high proportion (estimates in some prison systems range up to 25 percent) of incarcerated men are veterans, primarily of the Vietnam War, who do not have destructive juvenile-delinquency backgrounds and who are often motivated and responsive. Conjugal privileges, now available to inmates in three states and the Federal system, also seem to have a positive effect. The New York Family Reunion Program, which allows a prisoner with a good institutional record to spend weekends with his spouse and other family members in a neatly appointed trailer, has a 5 percent recidivism rate contrasted with 30 percent for the whole system.

Now, for the most part, prison administrators hold little faith in rehabilitation.

—J.L.

With one voice, the inmates claim that the guards allow trouble and predation to occur. "I don't know what to do," says Ted Freshour, a 55-

year-old inmate who looks 85 and who is serving a four-year term for wheeling a cart full of food out of a supermarket without paying for it. "I've got heart trouble. I'm hypertensive. We've got close quarters here, but you don't know if you walk out of your cell if you're gonna get knifed and I spend my time hiding from guys who rip off old men." Lifer Chuck Adams, who was attacked by other inmates, says, "I sleep with my eyes open now. I don't even close my eyes when I shampoo my hair."

Clearly, however, the dangerous conditions cannot be blamed entirely on the guards' unwillingness to protect vulnerable prisoners. There are only about 200 guards who come in contact with the inmates, and these are spread across three shifts. The 1-to-30 guard-to-inmate ratio is about one-third of what most experts believe to be minimally necessary. The officers often appear to hang back in the sally ports and administrative desk areas. (Not only are they undermanned, but, as in most prisons, the guards are grossly underpaid, which makes it difficult to maintain a high-caliber staff.)

Back in the cells everything is for sale. While some inmates wash clothes in their cold-water sinks, others pay someone in the laundry not to "lose" items. Some prisoners have hot water because they hire inmate "plumbers" to connect their taps to the hot-water lines feeding the showers. Inmates permitted to own radios sell time on ear phones. Perhaps more significant is the administration's use of inmates as so-called range tenders. Cells are locked at night; during the day, an antiquated roll bar is passed through the cell doors to keep them closed, and the range tenders are in charge of this mechanism. If a prisoner has permission to go in or out of his cell, the range tender "rolls the bar" for him. While the prisoner is out, the tender can be bribed to open the cell to a burglar. "Cells get broken into all the time," says Robert Phillips, 34, a Bronx native doing four years for the theft of a $25 calculator. "Anything not nailed down will go."

Another side of custody is treatment. Indiana provides little of it. Only 10 counselors are on the staff. If they work eight hours a day interviewing inmates, they cannot even give each prisoner an hour per month to help straighten out conflicts or resolve personal and family problems that sometimes catalyze misbehavior. No staff psychiatrist is available to cope with 10 percent to 15 percent of the population believed to need psychological care. Under these circumstances, suicidal types and fire starters are generally not identified until too late.

Most hobby groups and social clubs (except one for lifers) have disintegrated. When this happened at Santa Fe, according to a report prepared for New Mexico's Gov. Bruce King, peaceful inmate leadership vanished. What emerged in its place were the hierarchies of violence and fear—gangs, which had the most brutal inmates at the top. One Indiana inmate,

Richard Owen, who is serving 27 years for attempted murder and is a "cell-block lawyer" respected by other prisoners and the administration, says this problem is beginning to develop.

By modern standards Michigan City is a deficient prison. Its warden, Jack Duckworth, a ramrod-straight former missionary, agrees that it could not possibly be accredited by the American Correctional Association— "though accreditation would be a very good thing for Indiana." The 110-year-old association is made up of wardens and other representatives of the nation's prison administrations and sets prison-operation guidelines. The warden concedes that plumbing and electrical systems need total overhaul and that too many of the inmates are not "meaningfully occupied." Michigan City has had a history of disturbances so that if an outbreak occurs there of the dimension of Santa Fe or Attica it will not come as a surprise. "I would not be shocked," Duckworth says, but "I would be very disappointed."

The biggest problems, he feels, have come from having to receive increasing numbers of less serious offenders, now about a quarter of the population, who had to be mixed with traditional heavy felony types. But another problem, according to Ed Jones, the prison's director of classification, is that the new Indiana law has made bad actors and the always difficult imprisonment conditions, such as racial tension or conflicting and explosive temperaments, much worse. Increasingly, the prison is receiving violent offenders with extraordinarily long terms. The law, like much of the new legislation enacted in other states, has abolished parole boards, so, in fact, they have little incentive to behave or conform to institutional rules. According to Stewart Miller, a counselor, a third of the men must serve at least 20 years. "To a young guy," says Miller, "that seems like forever." Jones adds that the original idea of determinate sentencing has been perverted. The originators of the concept, such as David Fogel of the University of Illinois, "didn't mean for sentences to get so long," Jones says. The idea was to make them equal, fair and certain. "But then it went to the legislature and got political. That's our real problem. If you could control the legislature, you could control the prison."

Because Michigan City has no real program for the young long-term offenders, it often resorts to locking them in solitary confinement for periods ranging from 15 days to three years. A guard notes that, when a prisoner finally emerges from such confinement, he may be totally disoriented. One prisoner, he says, forgot even how to turn a doorknob. The prison maintains that no one is locked away solitarily unless he has committed a rules infraction. Inmates say, however, that anyone may be put there with or without reason—that some stay for their entire term—and that this practice was one cause of an outbreak last year in which six guards were taken hostage for 16 hours. The other grievance issue was a healthcare system in which inmate "nurses" set bones and pulled teeth.

My requests to interview those offenders in the cell block where the riot started were refused, according to prison officials, because weapons recently were found there. The inmates have pulled pieces of metal out of the mesh facing the cells, sharpened and wrapped them in cloth to make multiple-pointed knives. Also, someone has fashioned a garrote with what appears to be piano wire. I can, however, visit another isolation wing. It is even darker than the rest of the prison. A constant, eerie moaning or occasional howling is heard. The cells themselves are stark, barren of personal effects. The inmates here must eat in their cells, and pieces of food (either thrown in by guards, or out by prisoners) are encrusted on the bars. At least one of the alleged riot leaders, all of them black, is confined there. Boyd McChristian, 23, sits half naked on a sheetless bed. He has now been indicted on kidnapping charges stemming from a previous prison incident, and, like others in the unit, is deeply bitter; he says he drew a life term for his first offense, a $30 armed robbery when he shot the victim in the knee, and was placed in the solitary wing three years ago just because "the guards felt like it." The administration would not comment on why McChristian was segregated.

Indiana's answer to the overcrowding problem is to build two unwalled large dormitories, slated to open in May. Each will hold bunks for 200 inmates judged not to require heavy security. But this was also supposed to be a solution to Santa Fe's overcrowding problem. "Anything can happen in dorms and does," says Anthony Travisono of the American Correctional Association, who adds that in many institutions guards will not even go into the buildings at night, a procedure that permits unbridled conduct among inmates. The basis of guards' fear is that would-be assailants crouching between bunks cannot be seen until they pounce. On Feb. 2, 1980, three guards at Santa Fe had the courage to "floor walk" dorm E-2. They were jumped, taken hostage and the riot began. "I get sick when I see dorms now," says Travisono. "They have no intrinsic value whatsoever." Indiana may be making matters worse rather than better.

"You've got to stop the intake," says Judge William Bontrager, in his Elkhart, Ind., chambers. "The flow is just going crazy." A tall, raw-boned outdoorsman with close-cut hair, Judge Bontrager, who comes from deeply religious and Republican roots, has been regarded as a conscientious judge and generally a tough sentencer. Recently, however, he set off legal shock waves throughout the state by disobeying the law. As one of two Superior Court criminal judges in his county, he hears hundreds of cases; in both a robbery case and a first-degree burglary, he refused to apply the code's mandatory minimum sentences of 10 years because he felt that both defendants had rehabilitated themselves during long periods on bond. The Supreme Court placed Bontrager on "disciplinary investigation" status and appointed a temporary judge, who imposed the sentences.

"We had Attica in 1971," says Judge Bontrager, "New Mexico nine years later, and next year, it could be Indiana. God knows, haven't we learned anything?"

Judges, as might be expected, have been cool to the new practice of legislative sentencing. "They have taken any human consideration out of the process," says Judge Richard Klein of Philadelphia. Critics maintain that the new system does not root out discretion from the justice system but merely monopolizes it in the offices of prosecutors who control sentence length through the charging and plea-bargaining processes.

Norman Carlson, the director of the Federal Bureau of Prisons, says, "While most would agree that our nation's criminal laws are in need of major revision, the 'knee-jerk' response of many legislatures in passing harsher sentencing statutes threatens to totally overwhelm our correctional systems. Unfortunately, in considering such legislation, few elected representatives realize the long-run consequences of their actions. They fail to recognize that in many instances, they are compounding an already serious problem."

He may be right. In California, a new determinate-sentencing code went into effect in 1977 and swelled inmate counts to unprecedented proportions. Late in 1979 the state system exploded in a series of gang riots that left several dead. Many other states—Washington, Arizona, Florida, Oregon, Maine, Illinois, New York—which have adopted legislative sentencing have also subsequently had overcrowding and violence. Thomas Coughlin, New York's Corrections Commissioner, says: "I'm convinced that it's true that the closeness of another human being and the inability to get away and just sit by yourself for a little bit has a lot to do with the way people react. It's like those classic studies about rats—10 in a cage and they're fine; 20 and they're at each other's throats."

Generally, prison administrators no longer hold out much hope for prison rehabilitation. When asked about his objectives for New York inmates, Commissioner Coughlin responded: "Not that we're going to improve anybody. . . . What we have to do is to take the mass of people, the 9,000 people that we get every year, and we have to say, 'Here are the range of options. If you don't speak English, we'll teach you English as a second language. If you don't have a fifth-grade education, we're going to try to give you a fifth-grade education. If you want to go to school—college, we'll provide a college program for you. If you want to learn a skill, we'll provide a skill for you.' Now that's what a prison system's supposed to do. You can't just lock 'em up 23 hours a day, because, when you do that, prisons blow up, and you have New Mexicos."

Nor do the prison administrators hold out much hope for tough legislative sentencing as affecting the crime rate, though it is too soon for valid statistical analysis. Imprisoning more defendants for longer terms hasn't affected the rate so far, says Coughlin, and he doesn't expect it will because it "doesn't go to the real root of crime," which he labels "unemployment, poor housing and a nonexistent family structure." Dr. Norman Hunt, an Indiana state corrections official, adds: "We may have the toughest sentencing code in the 50 states and the Communist countries, too," but, he says, it has not reduced crime. One connection he, too, sees, however, is between crime and unemployment: Indiana's crime problem, he says, seems to follow layoffs in the auto industry.

A traditional way to deal with growth in inmate population is to build new prisons, but this, too, has become unpopular, as well as expensive. It costs $70,000 per cell to build a prison in accordance with constitutional standards. Recently, citizens in Oregon, Michigan, Ohio and Rhode Island have refused to pay for prisons. But even when the money has been available, people in states around the country have fought the location of prisons in their communities. Community groups have successfully blocked at least 50 proposed sites in Florida, for example, most recently in South Dade where protestors carried signs proclaiming: "Save our community, our farms, our homes."

Clearly, other approaches in addition to building must be found. Edward Davis, former Los Angeles Police Chief and a law-and-order conservative, predicts in an interview with Corrections Magazine that eventually states will begin returning to an indeterminate system with judicial discretion and parole. He argues that "everyone is not the same; every criminal does not pose the same threat to society."

Bringing back such discretionary sentencing can help keep the lid on a prison population, but it would also bring back the old inequities. Minnesota seems to be making an intelligent compromise. Part of its 1980 criminal code requires a commission to draft sentences in a way that would not cause a rise in the state's prison population for at least five years. The commission gave slightly longer than previous sentences for violent crimes and shorter ones for property crimes. It refused to take low-grade property felons into the prison at all unless their records were extensive. Otherwise, judges could deal with them on a local level with jail, probation or fines. To date, the prison population has stabilized at about 90 percent of capacity, and the proportion of property criminals in the prison has begun to fall.

In several areas, sentencing alternatives have already begun to make something of a comeback. In Wilmington, Del., for example, a work program has been created to ease overcrowding; about 12 percent of convicted criminals—those whose acts are less serious than the others: some thieves, shoplifters, burglars and simple assaulters—receive fines. The defendants who cannot pay them due to indigency are assigned to state jobs, mostly in maintenance or at community agencies; their work is credited at $3.65 an hour. In Quincy, Mass., the Earn-It Program, in conjunction with the Chamber of Commerce, finds jobs for defendants sentenced to make restitution for theft, personal injury or property damage. In one recent case, Judge Albert Kramer sentenced a defendant to pay such restitution and also to work for 20 hours in a hospital emergency room. The Quincy program produces about $200,000 in restitution payments each year. Both Wilmington and Quincy use "tourniquet sentencing"; if a defendant fails to come to work without an excuse, he is jailed briefly; repeated failures lead to longer and longer terms. These courts claim that about 75 percent of defendants successfully complete their assignments.

Correctional administrators believe that crowding will grow much worse in American prisons unless more alternative work and treatment programs are adopted. One year after Santa Fe, it is worth noting that 14 of 33 men murdered there were nonviolent offenders, who arguably did not belong in a maximum-security setting in the first place. Dr. John Salazar, New Mexico's former Secretary of Corrections, criticizes the state's overreliance on imprisonment: "It's like a hospital. You get patients who have a broken toe, are pregnant or are suffering from cancer. And you give them all cobalt treatment. That's what we're doing in Santa Fe."

Increasingly, that's what they're doing in other states as well.

31
KILLER COPS

Susan Stern and Richard Cohen

Cornelius Tatum was edgy his first night on the job at the Power gas station. The station had been robbed recently. At forty-two, Tatum was still a vigorous, powerfully built black man, but he wasn't taking any chances. When he left his Lakewood home that evening, he packed a shotgun in his camper. It was a cold, slow January evening in south central Los Angeles. At about 8 P.M. there was a commotion at the liquor

Susan Stern and Richard Cohen, "Killer Cops" in *Inquiry*, November 10, 1980, pp. 10–17. Copyright 1980 by *Inquiry* magazine, 747 Front Street, San Francisco, California 94111. Reprinted by permission.

store across the street. Tatum had just sold a pack of Winstons to a man who continued to loiter near the station office. He didn't know that the man, Oscar Haney, was an aircraft mechanic who lived just behind the station.

When a black Pontiac Firebird with two young black women pulled into the station, Tatum carried his shotgun with him across the brightly lit lot. Johnnie and Eleanor McMurray had driven to the Power gas station because it sold the cheapest cigarettes in the neighborhood. When they saw Tatum walking toward them with his shotgun, they wished they'd gone elsewhere.

Johnnie McMurray was still nervous after Tatum explained the situation and stepped into the cashier's booth. She saw him put the shotgun down, but now she feared the station might be robbed at any moment. Johnnie remembers telling Tatum to hurry up and get the cigarettes, and he was, she says, reaching for a pack when she heard a funny noise and turned to see six men who looked like hippies running toward her with their guns drawn.

"Eleanor! Get down! They're going to shoot!" Johnnie screamed just before the bullets whizzed over the Firebird and shattered the glass near the cigarette rack. While the McMurrays crouched on the floor of their car, certain that their worst fears had come true, one of the white men ran up, leaned across the hood of their car, and pumped four more shots into the doorway of the cashier's booth.

Huddled near the wall of the service station office, Oscar Haney says he saw Tatum reaching for the cigarettes a split second before the first shot was fired. Then Tatum slumped down and disappeared into the booth. Haney was sure the station was being robbed.

When the shooting ceased, Haney walked over to the black Firebird. He was in the middle of assuring the shaken Johnnie McMurray that she didn't have to talk to the unidentified armed man standing at her window when the man flashed his badge and ordered Haney to move on.

The six men were Los Angeles undercover police officers working on the CRASH (Community Resources Against Street Hoodlums) unit. Seeing a black male with a shotgun walking across the lot, they thought he was a robber. Without taking the time to plan their move, they swung their unmarked cars into the station and charged. They say they shouted, "Police! Drop it!" as they surrounded the cashier's booth, but that Tatum had spun in the doorway of the booth and leveled his shotgun at Officer Norman Nelson. Officers Nelson, Cesario Reyes, and Harrell Compton immediately opened fire. They saw Tatum go down. Then Nelson dashed to the McMurrays' car and fired the four shots that permanently paralyzed Tatum from the waist down.

Cornelius Tatum was lucky. Fifty-eight other Angelenos were shot by the LAPD in 1979 and fourteen of them died. Few would have remem-

bered Tatum's story had it not been played out in a Los Angeles courtroom last summer, when the district attorney, for the first time in eight
years, brought LAPD officers to trial for a civilian shooting. The charge:
assault with a deadly weapon.

Los Angeles policemen answered District Attorney John Van de
Kamp's indictment last March with a picket line outside an expensive
Beverly Hills restaurant where the DA was enjoying a $250-a-plate fund-
raiser. Police Chief Daryl Gates angrily said the DA's staff had "acted
incorrectly and in an irresponsible manner." The sharpest attack, however, came from the Los Angeles Police Protective League, the city's
powerful police union. George Aliano, its president, denounced the indictment and charged that the DA was mixing politics with police work.

Mixing politics with police work is precisely what has been going on in
L.A., but not quite in the way the police describe it. For years certain Los
Angeles neighborhoods, notably the black and chicano districts to the
south and east, have been characterized as "war zones" by both police
and residents. Killings by police have become almost routine there during
the last decade, so much so that the House Subcommittee on Crime came
to Los Angeles for a series of public hearings on the use of "deadly force"
by police. As Gerald Caplan, former director of LEAA's National Institute of Criminal Justice and Law Enforcement, reported last year, there
have been shootings by police in L.A. which "would not have occurred in
many other communities or, if they did happen, would have resulted in
discipline or even criminal charges. . . . It is only a small hyperbole to
state that the view of the LAPD is that it is the community that has the
problem."

Plainly stated, the Los Angeles Police Department has stationed itself as
a virtual occupying army in a city where the order of the day is to shoot
first and, if pressed, ask questions later. The backbone of the force and the
fount of its war-zone mentality is not, however, the departmental hierarchy. It is instead the officers' union, the police protective league.

The league operates from a small gold stucco fortress in old downtown
L.A. Great heavy wooden doors and wrought iron window bars protect it
from the "war zones" outside. The league proclaims itself to be nothing
more than the dedicated champion of "the cop on the beat." In fact it is
one of the richest and most powerful political organizations in southern
California. Its members are required by the nature of their jobs to canvass
every block and alley of Los Angeles, its contributions to city council
elections are unsurpassed, and its professed objective is to breed a climate
of fear that no opponent will dare challenge.

Setting fear aside, a growing number of citizens have challenged the
league and the department. Foremost has been the Coalition Against Police Abuse (CAPA). "There's been a lot of bodies laid in the streets in
those years" since the last LAPD cop was indicted, says Charles Chapple,

CAPA chairman. And many of these deaths, he adds, were even more "questionable" than the Tatum shooting. One was Barry Evans, a seventeen-year-old black high-school student stopped in 1976 by two LAPD officers in the walkway of his family's apartment. An argument erupted that turned into a fight, and one of the officers fatally shot the unarmed Evans in the back, claiming that the teen-ager was going for his partner's gun.

Scores of black citizens demanded that the district attorney open an independent investigation. More than a hundred people banded together in an organization called People United. Nine months after the killing, Van de Kamp agreed to investigate. His conclusion, issued in language that would become routine over the next five years, was that there was insufficient evidence to prosecute. Calling the Evans shooting a murder, community activists plastered the streets with "Wanted" posters for the two officers.

The officers retaliated by suing People United for libel. Although the judge ultimately threw out the case, Chapple says the suit had a serious effect on the new organization. "I had no money so they could sue me all they wanted," Chapple laughed, "but we lost quite a few members who owned homes and other valuables. They were scared off."

It was in 1976 that the battle between the police and the community escalated to a new level. Over twenty community groups banded together to form CAPA, and in the same month the protective league legally incorporated.

The league, which represents virtually all of the LAPD's 6600 officers (including, oddly, Chief Gates), occasionally acknowledges its role as the "political arm of the police department."

"The LAPD cannot give an endorsement to help a candidate in an election, but your Los Angeles Police Protective League can," *Blue Line*, the league's monthly newspaper reported recently. "As an organization we can provide political muscle in Sacramento for the LAPD and we are currently doing just that on certain legislation." Come budget time, the LAPD benefits from the league's $1.2 million dues base, which allows it to make generous contributions to most city council members. Until this year, city funds paid the salaries of seven full-time league directors, whose lobbying activities are also an asset to the department. In 1976 the league won passage in the legislature of a police "Bill of Rights" that cut back the department's ability to investigate its officers for misconduct and freed officers from taking lie detector tests.

Even archconservative former police chief Ed Davis was appalled, and denounced the law as a "fatal blow." Davis charged that in Los Angeles, as in other cities, the police union has become preoccupied with fighting for the "rights" of officers charged with administrative and criminal offenses. He compared the trend in Los Angeles to that in Honolulu, where, he said, "police unions spend a great deal of their money, effort and energy not to get pay raises or better pensions, but to fight to keep on cops who are crooked, brutal. . . ."

When Ron Burkholder, a National Science Foundation fellow, was killed by the LAPD in August 1977, it was George Franscell, the league's flamboyant attorney, who represented the accused officer at the coroner's inquest. Naked and unarmed, Burkholder was cut down by six LAPD bullets as he walked down the street with his hands extended. After the Friends of Burkholder organization and CAPA protested their way onto the pages of *Newsweek* and the *Los Angeles Times*, the coroner convened the first inquest into a police shooting in six years. But the police department refused to turn over any records, and the officer who shot Burkholder refused to answer the coroner's questions.

Just three months before Burkholder was killed, KABC-TV reporter Wayne Satz broadcast a series of stinging reports on the lack of police accountability in Los Angeles. Satz criticized the district attorney for his failure to check police crime, and he attacked the internal investigations by the department's Officer Involved Shooting unit (OIS) as biased in its own interest. To underscore his charges Satz brought an active LAPD officer on the air to tell the inside story. Disguised in a frogman suit and a Lone Ranger mask, and with his voice electronically distorted, six-year LAPD veteran John Mitchell appeared anonymously on television at the dinner hour for five nights running.

"Policemen are eager to get into shootings," Mitchell declared. "It's supposed to look good in your package when you're up for promotion, the fellas are excited for an officer who has just been in a shooting. It's comparable to the excitement of a football team toward a player who has just scored a winning touchdown."

"I was never an aggressive officer myself," Mitchell said, summing up his six-year career with the LAPD in an interview for the documentary film *Deadly Force*, "but I never stood up to my partner and said, don't choke that person. I always backed up my partner, helped him make up stories [for police reports] to keep him out of trouble. . . . I perjured myself in court. . . . I wanted to fit into the system, I wanted to promote, I wanted to do well."

This spring, three police officers slapped KABC, Satz, and Mitchell with a multimillion dollar lawsuit for conspiracy to defame the LAPD. The suit was one of three recently filed by police against KABC, which has been the leading media critic of the police department.

The events of 1977 proved to be a turning point for both the public and the police. For decades the Los Angeles Police Commission had held little more than titular responsibility for the department. But in 1977, the mayor-appointed police commission rewrote LAPD gun policy, outlawing the shooting of nonviolent fleeing felons and mandating that "deadly force" could be used only to protect a police officer or citizen threatened with death or serious bodily injury. Ed Davis, Chief Gates, and the league fought the new shooting policy, claiming it would handcuff the police. But CAPA's Charles Chapple said it did nothing of the sort: "They announced their new shooting policy to the City Council and within two days they'd gunned down two more people."

Nevertheless, in 1977 CAPA succeeded in pressuring the city council to hold public hearings into the problem of police shootings. The city council took no action after the hearings, but CAPA's testimony struck to the heart of the police department's power. On the premise that public access to police records of citizens' complaints and OIS investigations would rein in what CAPA considered the department's unbridled power, the community group demanded that the police department disclose some OIS reports to the city council. Their request was denied. Meanwhile CAPA joined with the Greater Watts Justice Center in a lawsuit against the LAPD to gain public access to citizen complaint records. In retaliation, the police went to the state legislature. There, in 1978, they pushed a bill through that made police personnel "packages" privileged.

It's not just Los Angeles—it's Boston . . .

Since 1967 two Americans have been legally executed in the United States. Between 1967 and 1977, more than six thousand were shot dead in the streets by police, nearly two citizens each day. Last year a Department of Justice official warned that this use of "deadly force" is "one of the most serious and inflammatory community relations problems confronting the nation." Already, his words seem an understatement. This year police shootings have triggered riots and demonstrations in Miami, New Orleans, Philadelphia, and Michigan. In Baltimore, Chicago, Houston, and Boston police killings have brought out hundreds and sometimes thousands of demonstrators.

It was the shooting of fourteen-year-old Levi Hart that brought black Bostonians into the streets in July. "Police brutality" was a charge commonly heard in the black community, but it had been a secondary issue, overshadowed by the escalating violence between black and white citizens.

On July 15, Levi Hart and two friends went for a joyride in an allegedly stolen car. Officer Richard Bourque took up the chase. When the car finally screeched to a halt, the three fled on foot and Bourque pursued Hart. After a wrestling match between the six-foot-one, 220-pound police officer and the five-foot-four, 110-pound

Hart, the youth ended up with a bullet through his brain. Bourque claims Hart, who was unarmed, snatched the officer's police revolver from its holster and accidentally shot himself. But several witnesses say that Bourque ran after Hart with his gun drawn, and beat the fourteen-year-old over the head with the pistol several times before administering the *coup de grâce*.

Though Officer Bourque denies pistol whipping Hart, the youth suffered a massive skull fracture which the pathologists claim could have been caused only by a blunt object. None of Hart's fingerprints were found on Bourque's gun, nor did Hart's hands show the telltale traces of gunfire.

Blacks in Boston demanded that the inquest into Hart's death be open to the public, but to no avail.

Judge Richard Banks, who is black, ruled there was "criminal responsibility" in Hart's death. But, when the district attorney presented the case to the grand jury, it found there was insufficient evidence to indict Bourque. Hart's family has sued the city for $43 million, probably the largest police misconduct civil suit yet to hit the city of Boston.

No one in the Boston black community can even remember the last time the district attorney has prosecuted a cop for a shooting or a beating. Neither could David Rodman, executive assistant to the district attorney. "Boston just hasn't been out in the forefront in that area," he said.

"We have a public records act in this state that applies to other public officials so that we can see citizens' complaints against them," Bob Berke, a former Los Angeles public defender, notes, ". . . but if it's a police officer, armed with weapons, with the power to put a person in prison for life or the power to cripple someone like Tatum, we can't even see whether there have been complaints against him. We can't even see if the department is well managed."

SB 1436 not only hides police records from the public; it also restricts the information that may be obtained in the courtroom. The bill states, for example, that judges considering discovery motions may "make any order which justice requires to protect the officer or agency from unnecessary annoyance, embarrassment, or oppression." According to "Masked Policeman" John Mitchell, the police have pressed assault charges against citizens to cover their own brutality. After the California Supreme Court ruled in 1974 that records of citizens' complaints could be subpoenaed, defense attorneys throughout the state were able to demonstrate that their clients were actually the victims of cops who had long prior records of brutality.

Not surprisingly, the LAPD was incensed. And not surprisingly, it took little time for the department to find a pretext for destroying the incriminating personnel packages. In 1976 the police shredded four tons of citizens' complaints. Though the shredding was in violation of a state statute, a Los Angeles grand jury failed to press charges.

Interoffice memos that led to the shredding also revealed the city attorney's concern over the civil liability threat from citizens' complaints. In 1976 Los Angeles paid out $572,895 to victims of police brutality and false arrest. But by 1979 the bill for police misconduct civil suits had jumped to $1,970,278, and the total for 1970–79 was $7.4 million. Last January, a truck driver for the Los Angeles County school system won a $1.25 million judgment against the police, the largest misconduct award in the city's history. Roy Wyche had been stopped for having an allegedly loud muffler and a dimly lit license plate. When he protested, one of the officers bashed in his skull with a heavy police flashlight.

The LAPD's drive against citizen complaints went largely unnoticed until Eulia Mae Love was killed in 1979 and the city attorney advised that SB 1436 forbade the police commission to disclose any information on the case. The commission may have kept silent, but black Los Angeles was seething. Eulia Love, a widowed black mother of three, was gunned down by two policemen in her own home in a neat, middle-class section of south central L.A.

Delinquent in her Southern California Gas bill, Mrs. Love had struck a company employee who had come to turn off her gas. After the gas man left, the company called the police. Mrs. Love, meanwhile, had gone out to purchase a money order for her bill. It was in her purse when the two officers advanced on her with their guns drawn, and knocked a boning knife from her hand. As she picked up the knife and tossed it at them, the officers unloaded eight bullets into her body.

Virtually none of the people called to jury duty a year later, in the trial of Officers Nelson, Compton, and Reyes, remembered hearing about the shooting of Cornelius Tatum. Many of them had, however, heard of Love. After Love was shot, 200 women from black churches, including state assemblywoman Maxine Waters, mourned for her on the lawn of Parker Center, LAPD headquarters.

... AND HOUSTON ...

At least 50 percent of Americans killed by police officers are black, and in cities like Houston, chicanos are the main target of police bullets. Yet white citizens are also shot by police. It was the shooting of a white gay activist, Fred Paez, that brought thousands of candle-bearing marchers to the Houston city hall in June.

During Gay Pride Week, Officer K. M. McCoy was moonlighting as a security guard at a freight moving company. He and his buddy were sitting drinking beer at 2:30 A.M. when, they say, Fred Paez circled a couple of times around the block and then pulled up and "engaged them in conversation." McCoy and his friend say they went to the side of the building with Paez, at his suggestion. Then, in the language of the police report, Paez approached McCoy and "touched him between the legs."

McCoy, according to the police report, quickly flashed his badge and arrested Paez for public lewdness. Pistol in hand, McCoy had Paez bend over a parked car with his arms outstretched, in order to search him. But instead of getting searched, Paez got a bullet through the back of his skull. McCoy says Paez reached behind himself and tried to grab McCoy's gun, setting off the fatal bullet.

The Harris County medical examiner ruled the shooting accidental, but the Houston district attorney and the U.S. attorney's office are still investigating the case.

Fear of the police has become virtually a tradition in Houston. After twenty-three-year-old Joe Campos Torres was beaten and drowned by the Houston police in 1976, citizens of all races tended to agree with criminal lawyer Percy Forman when he called Houston a "police state."

Since 1976 Houston has been through three police chiefs and a series of police department reforms, including an expanded police misconduct investigation unit and a more restrictive policy on when cops can fire their guns.

But according to Jenifer Schaye of the Public Interest Advocacy Center, an LEAA-funded group that receives citizens' complaints of police abuse, the volume of police shootings and beatings in Houston has not declined.

Nor does the Houston DA seem to be prosecuting the police. Between 1974 and 1977 the Houston grand jury heard twenty-five police shooting cases and indicted only one officer. Since July 1979, the Houston DA has investigated sixty-eight police shooting cases; of those that have been presented to a grand jury, so far no indictments have been returned.

The district attorney did not indict the police officers in the Love case, but the police commission, for the first time in its history, conducted a major investigation into the shooting, and finally declared it in violation of the LAPD gun policy. The league was infuriated by the ruling. And it was even angrier when the commission later announced that in the future it would review every police shooting.

Using a tactic that would become its hallmark, the league immediately filed two lawsuits against the commission. In the words of *Blue Line*, "The League is at the forefront of the recent upswing in the number of lawsuits by police officers who are unwilling to suffer abuse and injury at the hands of the public." According to *Blue Line*, the league financed about fifty such lawsuits filed by members between 1973 and 1978.

Now, in its first suit against the police commission, the league seeks to prevent the panel from putting its report on the Love case into the involved officers' personnel files. The second suit seeks to prevent the commission from investigating police shootings. "If we have to go all the way to the supreme court, we're going," league attorney Franscell said. "You're going to see a major fight. We can't live with this."

The final blow to the police came last December, when Van de Kamp's Operation Rollout received funding from the federal Law Enforcement Assistance Administration (LEAA). Rollout is, by all accounts, the most vigorous effort launched by a district attorney to investigate police shootings. It puts teams of deputy district attorneys and investigators on twenty-four-hour alert to "roll out" immediately to the scene of police shootings and conduct investigations. On paper the project seemed to be a serious attempt to keep the police under control, but according to a report made by federal law enforcement authority Gerald Caplan in March, the LAPD has successfully impeded the effectiveness of Rollout.

"Not only has Chief Gates refused the D.A.'s personal request to promulgate guidelines . . . but the spirit of resistance has permeated the bottom ranks of the department," Caplan wrote. The police had handcuffed the Rollout team by withholding information from them and delaying them in interviewing witnesses. Even more troublesome, Caplan reported, are the "fact finding" procedures used by the LAPD in carrying out their internal investigations. "These suggest," he wrote, "that LAPD resistance to Rollout is rooted in something more significant than bureaucratic rivalry with the District Attorney, and that an impulse to conceal misconduct may be the motivating force." Plainly stated, police policy encourages cover-up.

When, right on the heels of the new Rollout program, Officers Nelson, Reyes, and Compton were indicted for shooting Cornelius Tatum, the league went directly to the city council. Its demand, supported by Chief Gates, was that the city pay for the officers' criminal defense.

After only forty-five minutes of discussion, the city council decided to comply with the league's wishes. Not that the league was especially surprised. In private individual meetings, league lobbyists had already reminded the elected council members of their responsibilities. Well before the meeting was gaveled to order, league president George Aliano could rest assured of the officials' unanimous support. As Councilman Marvin Braude explained, the police demand for funds put the council in an uncomfortable position. "It was like having a vote in the council: It is resolved that we support our police department. Who is going to vote against that? The police always gets what they want" from the council, he added.

When the trial of Officers Nelson, Compton, and Reyes finally got underway on July 28, the "war zone" between the police and the citizens of Los Angeles moved for thirteen days into an air-conditioned courtroom. Charles Chapple was there, and Maria Herbst, Ron Burkholder's widow. So was the league's City Hall lobbyist Sam Flores, along with a large phalanx of policemen in business suits. And when Cornelius Tatum was wheeled into the courtroom to face Norman Nelson, Cesario Reyes, and Harrell Compton, memory called to mind the names of the citizens and police officers who never made it to the witness stand.

It was, of course, only the shooting of Cornelius Tatum that was at issue—only the fragmented and conflicting story of what happened in five to seven seconds one night at the Power gas station. But in the politically polarized courtroom, where a nervous, frightened prosecutor faced off against the full power of the police protective league, many watched anxiously for an indication of who was winning the larger war.

Johnnie McMurray was nervous when she took the stand on the second day of the trial and recounted once again how she had driven her big black Firebird up to the gas station on that evening to buy cigarettes. Prosecutor Jay Lipman knew that McMurray, like all his witnesses, was terrified of testifying against the police. All of Lipman's eyewitnesses were black residents of south central Los Angeles. All the defense witnesses were police.

Keeping his questions brief and emotionless, Lipman brought out McMurray's story piece by piece. Yes, she had seen Tatum approaching with the shotgun and she had thought he was a robber. When he identified himself as the station attendant, she ordered Viceroys for herself and Marlboros for her sister-in-law Eleanor. "He put the shotgun down inside the booth," she testified, "and I asked him again to get the cigarettes and hurry up."

Like all Lipman's witnesses, Johnnie McMurray testified that the last thing she saw before the blast of police bullets was Tatum reaching for her cigarettes. "Did you ever see the person in that booth point a shotgun?" Lipman asked her.

"No, I did not," she answered.

Despite occasional tremors, Johnnie McMurray seemed sure of herself on the stand. Then defense counsel George Franscell took over. Armed with a tape recording of McMurray's statement to OIS investigators three hours after the shooting, Franscell began to batter away at the young woman's story. After a series of thunderous demands from Franscell and the introduction of the nearly unintelligible tape recording, she acknowledged that she had made contradictory statements to the police. "I was in a state of shock," she told the court. "They had me down there all night. How would you feel if you had just saw someone get killed?"

Set against the frightened young woman's testimony, the performance of the police officers was a model of seasoned decorum. And a performance is precisely what they gave. From the point of view of prosecutor Lipman, the entire police testimony about the shooting sounded "like a script."

Using phrases that would later be repeated almost verbatim in the testimony of Nelson and Reyes, Harrell Compton described how the three defendants, and the three other officers who charged but did not fire on Tatum, made a U-turn into the Power gas station after seeing the man they thought was a robber. Compton said he heard his partners yelling "Police officers, Halt! . . . Drop it! Drop it!" as they ran toward the cashier's booth with their guns drawn. But Tatum spun around, he said, got into a "semi-crouched" position, and leveled the shotgun at Nelson.

Lipman hammered away at Compton in his characteristic low-key style, but there was no way he could do to any of the officers what Franscell had done to McMurray. For the OIS investigators had chosen not to tape-record the police officers' statements on the night of the shooting. Though Lipman was unable to crack what he called the police "script," his examination did reveal the peculiar steps the OIS team had taken to create an almost impenetrable version of the shooting.

When Lipman asked Compton which of the police officers had yelled "Drop it! Police!" Compton hesitated and said, "I now know."

"You know that from later conversations?" shot Lipman.

"Yes," Compton admitted.

"Did you go back [to the scene that night] and reconstruct with the other officers?"

"Yes, I did."

"Is it because you went back that you now know?"

"Not entirely," said Compton.

Unlike Johnnie McMurray, Compton and the other officers not only had been escorted by the OIS team back to the police station after the shooting. They had all been interviewed together without the tape recorder running, escorted back to the gas station to reconstruct the shooting, and then returned to the police station for a second "group interview." (It was precisely this use of group interviews of officers that consultant Gerald Caplan cited as a critical flaw in OIS procedures. Without directly accusing the department of encouraging perjury among its men, Caplan pointed out that "Separating witnesses and taking their statements separately, without giving them opportunity to check with another and fashion a false narrative, is standard procedure elsewhere.")

OIS chief Charles Higbie admitted in an interview outside the court-room that the Los Angeles Police Commission had expressly ordered the OIS team to interview police officers separately, as it interviewed civilian witnesses, and to record the statements. Higbie acknowledged Caplan's criticism. However, when asked if he planned to comply with the com-mission's directive, Higbie had "no comment."

Throughout the case prosecutor Lipman accepted the fact that juries usually place more credence in police testimony than they do in the ac-counts of untrained civilian witnesses. All of that would change, he be-lieved, once the jury was taken to the scene of the shooting, the Power gas station. There, he reasoned, the jurors would see that a man of Tatum's height and girth could not possibly have contorted himself into the posi-tion the police described. They would have seen the five bullet holes in the glass next to the cigarette rack, several feet from where the police say Tatum was standing when they opened fire. And they would have seen, first hand, that the positions of Johnnie McMurray and Oscar Haney had provided them clear views of the assault. Common sense alone would have led them to the inescapable conclusion that the police had ruthlessly shot down an innocent gas station attendant who was doing nothing more than reaching for a pack of cigarettes. Beyond that "common sense" ap-proach, Lipman did very little other preparation.

And so it was that Jay Lipman suffered a devastating blow when, half-way through the trial, police attorney Franscell withdrew his motion to visit the gas station and the judge denied Lipman's own motion for the visit. The jury could not be taken to the scene, the judge ruled, because he feared demonstrators and reporters might cause a ruckus.

. . . AND CHICAGO . . .

Officer Howard Safford of Chicago's Afro American Police League claims that Chicago is "just as ripe as Miami or Philadelphia" for protests against police shootings and beatings.

This July, Richard Ramey, a fifty-one-year-old black man, was beaten to death by three young white Chicago cops after he al-legedly "resisted arrest" on the El train. His crime? Smoking a cig-arette.

It seems that the three plainclothes officers, assigned to watch for muggers on the subway, told Ramey to put his cigarette out. When Ramey refused, the officers arrested him for disorderly conduct.

About fifteen minutes later, when Officers Fred Christiano, Fred Eurallo, and Louis Klisz finally brought Ramey into the police sta-tion, he was semi-conscious and covered with blood. The officers charged Ramey with "resisting arrest" and "battery against a police officer." They were ordered to take him to a hospital.

Ramey died shortly after reaching the hospital. The police officers said they thought he'd suffered a heart attack. But the medical examiner found nine broken ribs, two broken legs, and a broken neck. He ruled that Ramey had died of "massive internal and external hemorrhaging" and called the beating a homicide.

The Cook County state's attorney indicted the three officers for murder. But according to Officer Saffold, the Cook County state's attorney's office has a history of refusing to prosecute the police, and of preparing "shoddy cases" against police officers on the rare occasion of indictments.

Officers Christiano, Eurallo, and Klisz were suspended from the Chicago police force, but the Teamsters' Union, vying to become the bargaining agent for the Chicago police, immediately stepped in and offered the officers janitorial jobs—above their police salary level. That brought black Chicagoans out to demonstrate in front of the McCormick Center, where the policemen are now working.

Said Saffold: "We don't need, we don't trust, and we'd rather not have the police. That's the way some people in Chicago feel."

Yet the constant, dominating presence of the police officers in the courtroom had begun to affect Lipman's performance. "I've been trying cases with policemen as my witnesses for years," he said after the trial. "Policemen are my friends. There were officers who walked in the courtroom who I've known for years, and they just turned their faces, they wouldn't even look at me. There was tremendous pressure." It was as though the police, by their constant presence and their barely submerged disgust toward the prosecution, had converted the trial into an attack on anyone who would dare question police authority. Lipman's best chance to break the spell and corroborate his witnesses' testimony was to take the jurors beyond the courtroom, to the site of Cornelius Tatum's tragedy, where they could be vividly reminded that the trial was about the shooting of a man who had been pointlessly paralyzed for life. Once he lost that critical motion, Lipman said only that he had no time to prepare any evidence that could bring the Power gas station into the courtroom.

Police attorney Franscell, meanwhile, with the aid of Lieutenant Higbie, managed quite ably to bring his version of the scene of the shooting to the jury. On the seventh morning of the trial Lieutenant Higbie walked toward the courtroom under the glare of news cameras, carrying a huge carton wrapped in brown paper. Other police officers followed carrying a video monitor. The LAPD has worked around Hollywood long enough to know how to set a scene.

That afternoon, Franscell played the jury a minute-long video tape in which Officers Nelson, Compton, and Reyes, one after another, walked into the cashier's booth of the Power gas station with a shotgun and turned as they say Tatum turned.

It was a rather convincing ballet, except for the fact that Tatum is much huskier than any of the defendants. And on the one night that Tatum stood in the booth, he had shared the cramped space with a stool. The stool, however, was not in the videotape version produced by the OIS.

Higbie then presented another distorted piece of defense evidence: a scale model of the cashier's booth with a "Tatum dummy" which even Franscell later admitted was too small. As the only three-dimensional representation of the Power gas station presented in the trial, the scale model was sadly misrepresentative of the way things were on the night Tatum was shot. Unaccountably, Lipman failed to lodge any objection. "There were so many missing things," one black juror complained after the trial. "Why didn't they have a scale model of the car? We [the jurors] asked if we could get a car, but were told we couldn't once the evidence was entered."

After all the eyewitnesses' stories had been told and retold and the miniature props examined, the only evidence left in the trial was the expert interpretation of bloodstains and the trajectories of the bullets the police had fired. The three experts were all members of the LAPD, and they supported their fellow officers' stories. When Lipman pressed the defendants on why almost all the bullet holes were near the cigarette rack and not at the door where they claimed Tatum was standing, the officers said merely that their marksmanship was poor. Lipman did not ask the police department for their marksmanship records.

Which led to the final anomaly. Why, if Cornelius Tatum had been holding a shotgun, were there no bullet marks on the gun from the four shots that had paralyzed him? Under cross-examination, one police expert did admit reluctantly that a bullet that had passed through Tatum's wrist might well have hit the shotgun Tatum was allegedly pointing, but it was an admission which Lipman failed to pursue through independent expert witnesses. Why also were there only two specks of blood on the shotgun when Tatum's jacket and the bills in his pocket were soaked with blood? The OIS investigators had no answer, and by the time they arrived at the scene, Officer Nelson had already removed the shotgun from the cashier's booth.

Thus the testimony in the trial of Cornelius Tatum ended. As police attorney George Franscell had presented the case, the only thought on the officers' minds that chilly January night was, "Oh my god, there's a robbery going on ... and a car with citizens in it." (In fact, the officers testified that they had not even seen the car before they swung into the gas station.) On the other hand, argued Lipman, "From the instant those officers saw Cornelius Tatum with the shotgun, his life was bought and sold. They had a free robber. They said to themselves, 'We'll shoot now and ask questions later.' "

The predominantly white jury deliberated almost four days before finding Reyes and Compton innocent. A mistrial was declared in the case of Nelson, however, when three of the four blacks on the jury held out for a guilty verdict after several ballots. But the whole jury was clearly shaken by the episode. In an impassioned, handwritten statement they declared their "concern and dismay with the actions of the officers."

"We do not believe that in the actions related to the shooting of Mr. Tatum, the police conducted themselves with due concern for the lives and welfare of the persons who could have been seriously injured," the jurors said. "Two women in a vehicle, almost in the line of fire, were disregarded by the officers."

"In short," the jury concluded, "We believe that the Los Angeles Police Dept. should view with grave concern the actions of these officers. If the actions of these experienced officers are examples of the training they receive, then all citizens should be concerned."

Jay Lipman, who claims to have won 98 percent of his cases against citizens before being transferred to the Rollout unit, appeared worn out by the trial and disappointed by the verdict. "People just don't want to convict the cops," he sighed. "My own next-door neighbor said to me 'Jay, I hope you lose, because I don't like to see policemen prosecuted.' "

George Franscell was jubilant: "This case had an awesome effect on the morale of the LAPD," Franscell declared. "There was more on trial here than three police officers. The integrity of the LAPD was at stake. And the jury upheld the integrity of our investigations."

But no cheer went up from the police officers in the courtroom when the verdict was announced. For the cops, league president Aliano explained, the trial itself was a major blow. The league had become convinced it was losing "clout" in Los Angeles politics largely as a result of being "beat up" in the media for everything it did. As Aliano sees it, now is the time for a new offensive. To regain that political clout and boost officers' morale, Aliano says the union must build public support and reinstill fear in the hearts of elected officials.

"I guess fear is what they believe in," Aliano said in an interview after the trial. "It's not being professional and all that; it's the clout that you have that makes them afraid. And what makes them afraid? Having the power to take somebody out of office and having a lot of public support, so they know if they mess with the police, the public is going to be down on them." To unseat its elected enemies, Aliano said the league intends to put police officers out in the streets walking precincts for and against public officials. The league's enemies, Aliano boasted, "will have to put volunteers out to walk districts for them . . . but we have our own army."

"If you start putting 500 police officers walking precincts in a council district," Aliano said, "and you're able to take somebody out, ears are going to be perked up and they're going to say 'these people know the combination now and we'd better start listening to them.' "

Aliano will not name politicians his group is planning to walk against in upcoming elections. So far the league has sent out its troops in only two races—to support Sid Trapp against Van de Kamp, and to support Stockton assemblyman Carmen Perino. In Perino's campaign the league bussed policemen to Stockton from all over the state. Both Trapp and Perino lost, however.

The league has also just launched a $1 million public relations campaign. The campaign will be directed by CAPS (Citizens Advocating Police Support). This new nonprofit organization established by the league will have a seventeen-member board made up of entertainers, business people, league directors, Chief Gates, a police commissioner, chamber of commerce representatives, and minority leaders. These board members, Aliano said, will be responsible for raising funds for the public relations campaign. Western Regional Banking and Union Oil, says Aliano, are among the major corporations that have already expressed interest in contributing. Aliano expects corporate gifts to be "in the six figures."

Meanwhile CAPA, the Coalition Against Police Abuse, is also going on the offensive, and has launched a voter initiative to establish a citizens review board. Immediately after the acquittals in the Tatum case, a newly formed coalition for a review board, of which CAPA is a member, handed out a ten-page indictment of prosecutor Lipman's handling of the trial; it criticized him as "careless, unconcerned, and unprepared." For CAPA and the hundred or so Los Angeles citizens groups united in the campaign, the trial of Nelson, Reyes, and Compton reinforced a growing feeling that such weak prosecutions are not enough to stem the tide of shootings by police in Los Angeles.

This summer marked the fifteenth anniversary of the riots in Watts, which were also triggered by a police shooting. Yet contrary to the fears of many observers, there was no explosion in Los Angeles ghettos when the LAPD officers were acquitted. Keith Wyatt, an attorney at the Greater Watts Justice Center, was not surprised. "There's about seven or eight people a year killed down here," Wyatt shrugged. "If people got upset about it the way they did in Miami, we'd be having a riot every other week."

Thirteen Los Angeles citizens have been shot by the police since Nelson, Reyes, and Compton were indicted last March. And at the Power gas station nearly all the traces of Tatum's tragedy have been removed. One week into the trial the gas station was sold, and Target Enterprises, the new owners, are remodeling. A new office building with bulletproof glass will be built. And most of the rest of the station is being slowly dismantled. The gas pumps were taken out midway through the trial, but the district attorney stopped Target Enterprises in the middle of sandblasting the jutting carport. All that remained was the cashier's booth, alone in the swirling sand, with its bullet holes and the sign that reads: "Warning, don't smoke. Turn off your car."

32
HOW LAWLESS ARE BIG COMPANIES?

Irwin Ross

Crime in the executive suites has come to command media attention of a sort formerly reserved for ax murders. An abundance of anecdotal evidence about corrupt practices—commercial bribery, price-rigging schemes, fraud against customers—has led critics of business to charge that far more crime exists than has come to light. Defenders of business, on the other hand, argue that the well-publicized episodes are aberrations, totally untypical of the way corporate America operates.

The big cases are often shockers. Bethlehem Steel, for example, was recently fined $325,000 in connection with an elaborate kickback scheme that involved the laundering in Europe of hundreds of thousands of dollars in phony commissions and the return of the cash by courier for distribution as bribes. Such sleazy goings-on by a company as prestigious as Bethlehem indicate that big-business crime hasn't been swept away in a tide of post-Watergate morality. . . .

Reprinted from Irwin Ross, "How Lawless are Big Companies?" in *Fortune*, December 1, 1980, pp. 57–64. © 1980 by Time Inc. All rights reserved. Portions of the original have been omitted.

THE GUIDELINES

There is, of course, no standard definition of corporate corruption. Our list is limited to five crimes about whose impropriety few will argue— bribery (including kickbacks and illegal rebates); criminal fraud; illegal political contributions; tax evasion; and criminal antitrust violations. The latter consist entirely of price-fixing and bid-rigging conspiracies and exclude the vaguer and more contentious area of monopolistic practices, which are the subject of civil antitrust suits. Also excluded are Federal Trade Commission complaints that have to do with the ways companies "signal" price changes to competitors.

No single case tells much about the extent of corporate delinquency in America. Of the 1,043 major corporations in the study, 117, or 11%, have been involved in at least one major delinquency in the period covered. . . . Some companies have been multiple offenders. In all, 188 citations are listed covering 163 separate offenses—98 antitrust violations; 28 cases of kickbacks, bribery, or illegal rebates; 21 instances of illegal political contributions; 11 cases of fraud; and five cases of tax evasion. This roll call of wrongdoing is limited to domestic cases; the list would have been longer had it included foreign bribes and kickbacks.

All the cases resulted either in conviction on federal criminal charges or in consent decrees (or similar administrative settlements), in which companies typically neither affirm nor deny past delinquencies but agree not to commit them in the future. Many of the defendants were convicted on pleas of nolo contendere (no contest)—tantamount to guilty pleas but often preferred by defendants for both psychological and practical reasons. To unsophisticated ears, a nolo plea does not have the ring of a confession of guilt. A practical benefit in an antitrust case is that the nolo plea cannot be used as automatic evidence of guilt in a civil suit for treble damages.

Eleven percent of major American corporations involved in corrupt practices is a pretty startling figure. It would hardly be as startling, of course, if it referred to businesses of modest size, for which data are lacking. The bribing of purchasing agents by small manufacturers and the skimming of receipts by cash-laden small retail businesses are a commonplace of commercial life.

Our compilation of cases covered a substantial slice of time, to be sure, and management changed in many of these large companies during the period; after a major scandal, the culprits were often sacked and the board of directors took sweeping measures to avoid a recurrence. On the other hand, it is axiomatic that there was more crime than was exposed in public proceedings.

A number of companies have been repeat offenders. Ashland Oil, for example, pleaded guilty to making a $100,000 illegal political contribution. It was also convicted, after a nolo plea, of fixing the price of resins. This year its construction subsidiary pleaded guilty in three cases of rigging bids for highway construction work in Virginia.

Gulf Oil has four entries on the list—two for illegal political contributions, one for bribing an IRS agent, one for fixing the price of uranium. International Paper was convicted three times, after nolo pleas, in major antitrust cases—involving paper labels, folding cartons, and corrugated containers. Eastex Packaging Inc., a subsidiary of Time Inc., the publisher of *Fortune*, was one of 22 other companies convicted in the folding-carton case.

BRIEFCASES FULL OF CASH

In the Bethlehem Steel case, the company pleaded guilty to criminal activity over five years, 1972–76, but the government contended that the kickbacks had been going on for a much longer time. The purpose of the scheme was to bribe representatives of ship lines to steer repair work to Bethlehem's seven shipyards or to speed up payment of bills.

Since 1961, according to the indictment, Bethlehem had been using a Swiss company called Office pour le Financement du Commerce et de l'Industrie to launder the kickback money. OFCI was a convenient conduit, for it had a worldwide network of agents who drummed up ship-repair business.

Clifford R. Wise, head of Bethlehem's ship-repair sales office in New York, would send payments to OFCI that ostensibly represented sales commissions but actually were levies fraudulently added to customers' bills. After the money was entered into OFCI's books (OFCI taking a cut for its cooperation), it was available for recycling back to the U.S. Typically, Wise or his secretary would fly to Switzerland, stuff a briefcase with cash, and return to New York. Over five years, according to the indictment, a million dollars was funneled into the U.S. and two South American countries; on just one day in August 1975, Wise flew $115,000 in cash over to New York. The government traced some $400,000 to kickbacks. What happened to the rest of the money is not altogether clear. Bethlehem is seeking the return of funds it claims Wise embezzled; he denies the charges.

In several celebrated cases, illegal corporate political contributions have also been part of an elaborate pattern of deception that went on for many years. For more than a decade, for example, Gulf Oil used a subsidiary in Nassau to launder funds sent from the U.S., ostensibly to be used to prospect for oil. At least $4.5 million returned to these shores to be distributed as political handouts.

Firestone Tire & Rubber Co., according to the findings of its audit committee, was in the business of doling out illegal political contributions from at least 1960 through 1973. But Firestone's audit committee discovered that the volume of funds "appropriated" for political purposes, as it put it, increased substantially after 1968, when Robert P. Beasley became chief financial officer and overseer of the political slush fund. In 1972, for example, Beasley got Raymond C. Firestone, then the chief executive, to initial a treasury voucher authorizing the transfer of $107,777 in Firestone funds to an outside bank account controlled by Beasley. Top officers of the corporation would make personal political contributions, all apparently quite legal, and be reimbursed in cash by Beasley.

Beasley was simultaneously "appropriating" Firestone funds for his own use—an indication of the sluice gates that are opened once accounting controls are relaxed. In the end, the U.S. Attorney for the Southern District of New York charged him with embezzling $1 million; he pleaded guilty to charges involving nearly half that sum and received a four-year sentence. Firestone was convicted on tax charges relating to $12.6 million in corporate income that Beasley had put in special reserve accounts and failed to report at the proper time.

From one point of view—say that of a librettist for a corporate version of *Guys and Dolls*—these shenanigans are pretty comic. A moralist, or even an amateur dabbler in corporate sociology, would find them hairraising. What indeed is going on here? Why do some of the largest, most prestigious corporations in America get involved in complex scenarios of illegality that rival the paranoid fantasies of their bitterest critics?

No single answer accounts for the variety of corporate misbehavior. One generalization often invoked plays on the distinction between *malum in se*—a crime in itself, like the immemorial offenses of the common law—and *malum prohibitum*—purely statutory crimes that vary with the society. As a celebrated corporate defense counsel recently put it, "These business crimes are perceived by individual actors as victimless. We all grew up in an environment in which we learned that thou shalt not murder, rape, rob, probably not pay off a public official—but not that it was a crime to fix prices."

Most of the economic crimes . . . do not bring the social obloquy that attaches to robbery or embezzlement. One chief executive recently boasted to *Fortune* about how he had once rid his company of some executives who had run afoul of the antitrust laws. "That sent the message to the organization," he said. Ten minutes later, however, he expressed dismay about how his statements would look in print. After all, some years had passed; the men were still living in the community; they had made their peace with the company. Would the same solicitude be accorded a bank robber?

THE "BOTTOM-LINE PHILOSOPHY"

Corrupt practices are certainly not endemic to business, but they do seem endemic to certain situations and certain industries. A persuasive explanation for many violations is economic pressure—the "bottom-line philosophy," as Stanley Sporkin, the SEC's enforcement chief, puts it. "In many instances where people are not lining their own pockets you can only explain corporate crime in terms of 'produce or perish.'"

The common practice of running a company through decentralized profit centers, giving each manager his head but holding him strictly accountable for the results, often provides a setting in which the rules can readily be bent. The temptation comes when heightened competition or a recession squeezes margins.

The pressures that led to criminal behavior in the folding-carton industry were exhaustively described in a 1978 article in the *Harvard Business Review* by Jeffrey Sonnenfeld and Paul L. Lawrence. Price fixing had long been common in the industry because profit margins were tight, competition was intense, and prices were set at a relatively low level in the corporate hierarchy—a consequence of the many kinds and shapes of boxes ordered. Top management had little control over the impulses of salesmen and junior managers to exchange price information, rig bids, and divvy up customers.

The authors quote the self-exculpatory statement of one executive: "We're not vicious enemies in this industry, but rather people in similar binds. I've always thought of myself as an honorable citizen. We didn't do these things for our own behalf . . . [but] for the betterment of the company."

In a similar vein, Irving S. Shapiro, Du Pont's chief executive, attributes antitrust violations to "weak companies" and "weak managements." For years, Shapiro had served as an antitrust lawyer at Du Pont, preaching the gospel of legal compliance to the managers down the line. But he had not long been installed as c.e.o. when the Justice Department, in 1974, hit the company with an indictment charging an antitrust conspiracy by Du Pont's dye group and several competitors.

The scheme began in 1970. Wanting to raise prices, Du Pont's dye people called on the competition and won agreement to a "follow the leader" scheme. The following January, Du Pont announced a 10% price increase; the competition followed suit in February and March. When brought to book, the nine companies involved all pleaded nolo and were fined between $35,000 and $50,000 each. Shapiro says he then laid down the law—he would countenance no further violations. Was the dye group a "weak"—that is, hardpressed—division? Indeed yes, said Shapiro; he got rid of most of it last year at a loss of $64 million. . . .

Rush to the Courthouse

Once the Justice Department starts looking into a suspicious pricing pattern, it often has no difficulty making a case. Most price fixers are anything but hardened criminals. It is also true that antitrust enforcement in the U.S. is in general tougher than abroad. By convening a grand jury and sending out subpoenas Justice can touch off what one official calls "a rush to the courthouse" by executives eager to trade testimony for immunity.

Competitive pressures can account for kickbacks and other forms of commercial bribery, but perhaps equally significant are industry custom and structure. In trucking, in construction, and on the docks, the pressure of time seems to be the key element. If goods are delayed in transit, or if construction is held up because of the inability to obtain materials or workers, great financial loss can result. Where bribes are not freely offered, they are often extorted.

Companies in regulated industries sometimes violate the law because of the simple fact of regulation. In the beer and liquor industries, for example, both the federal government and the states prohibit or curtail some normal techniques of salesmanship, such as discounts and rebates. The result: illegal rebates and gifts of merchandise to persuade liquor retailers to promote a company's products.

A Thumb on the Scales

The great grain-elevator scandal of the mid-Seventies clearly resulted from conditions that were pervasive in the industry in the New Orleans area. Thirteen grain-trading companies, together with several score employees, were convicted of shortchanging customers. Continental Grain, for one, was fined $500,000 on 50 counts of filing false export statements. Employees at Continental's elevator at Westwego, Louisiana, had set their scales to register one-twentieth of 1% more than the true weight. The company's lame excuse was that the employees thought they were within their rights because the law required scales to be accurate only within a tolerance of one-tenth of 1%. True enough, but not when they were systematically rigged to shortchange customers.

Simple economic incentives explain much illegal behavior: corruption seems to pay, at least in the near term. In industries like folding cartons or corrugated boxes, where antitrust cases were brought, executives perceived an advantage in maintaining price levels, sharing the market, and keeping marginal firms alive. In such a situation, of course, the customers pay and the whole economy suffers from a measure of inefficiency. When a corporation is caught, the shamefaced executives take a drastically different view of the cost-benefit ratio. Some companies might have been better off in the long run if they had followed the alternative, and legal, strategy of expanding their market share by driving their weaker brethren to the wall.

Except in cases hinging on illegal political contributions—once a way of life in many corporations and rarely investigated or prosecuted prior to Watergate—the chief executive is seldom personally implicated. Typically, even the executives running the guilty subsidiary or division disavow any knowledge of the wrongdoing below. Such was the situation at Bethlehem Steel, which in its public statement of contrition was careful to assert that top management—including the head of the shipbuilding division—had been ignorant of the kickback scheme.

CONSPIRACY OF SILENCE

Particularly when violations are persistent, however, it is hard to escape the cynical conclusion that if the line managers are ignorant, it is often because of an unspoken conspiracy of silence: the boss doesn't pry too vigorously, and his underlings get the impression that he would regard it as a betrayal if they volunteered too much.

A question that *Fortune*'s compilation inevitably leaves unanswered is whether corporate corruption was on the increase in the last decade. More wrongdoing was exposed because of the crackdown in the aftermath of Watergate. But there are no data to allow comparisons over time about the extent of corporate lawlessness.

The publicity accorded the business scandals of the Seventies has given some impetus to reform. If the chief executive of a multibillion-dollar corporation cannot police every corner of his organization, he can establish an appropriate policing program and do much to set the right tone. A number of companies, including some sued for treble damages, have mounted vigorous compliance programs to instruct employees about the dangers of getting too chummy with competitors. But hard-pressed managers will probably still be weighing the risks of detection against the benefits of sharing markets and bribing purchasing agents. It sometimes seems that the only true believers in unfettered competition are professors of economics and business journalists.

XI

NATIONAL SECURITY

There can be no doubt that the search for security is a legitimate and necessary concern of any nation. The U.S. Constitution authorizes Congress "to raise and support armies" and "to provide and maintain a navy." But to say that national security is a legitimate concern does not ensure that it will not also be a problematic one. Obviously, the technology of eighteenth-century armies and navies had little in common with the sophisticated and destructive weapons systems of contemporary military forces. Thus, the question for today is not whether the United States should have military forces—that seems settled—but rather, what policies should be followed in determining military growth and strategy? More directly, how are we to evaluate the evidence supporting or rejecting differing assumptions behind military—particularly nuclear—policy and projections?

This chapter examines the justifications behind the contemporary and emerging United States national security policy. On the whole, the writers are critical. They find the supporting reasoning and evidence weak and ill-considered, failing to take fully into account extraordinary political and technological changes occurring since World War II, and particularly, during the past fifteen to twenty years.

Richard J. Barnet, for example, points to four "revolutionary factors of contemporary life" that have transformed international politics and considerations of strategy—the power of the atom, the collapse of colonialism, the world-wide diffusion of nuclear technology, and the skyrocketing costs of advanced weapons systems. Taken together, he argues, these factors demand fundamental reconsideration of traditional national security assumptions, with special regard for their impact on the integrity of our human resources. To the extent that military spending undercuts support for schools, science, cities, cultural activities, we undermine our most fundamental sources of national strength. In sum, the search for national security should not be conceived narrowly, as a military problem, but more broadly, as a major social problem.

Given the costs of military weaponry, and the impact of such costs on other institutions, it becomes especially important to assess Soviet weakness and American strength accurately. There are costs to underestimating Soviet strength and intentions but, as the Center for Defense Information article we reprint here points out, there are also important costs to overestimating Soviet strength. The article offers a thoughtful assessment comparing the military and psychological assumptions of each nation.

Finally, we have reprinted a U.S. Congress-sponsored study of "The Effects of Nuclear War." The study is not comfortable to read, but it is nevertheless essential reading for the contemporary student of American social problems. Nuclear war, even "limited" nuclear war, would inflict calamitous death and destruction to the citizens of the United States, and of the whole world. Its genetic impact would affect the future of the entire human race. Nuclear war, upon which strategies for national security are increasingly based, is thus the ultimate, the most potentially catastrophic, social problem of our era.

33
THE SEARCH FOR
NATIONAL SECURITY

Richard J. Barnet

The real debate over national security in the United States is between those who believe that the nation has insufficient military power to create a world hospitable to American goods, American values, and the servicing of American needs and those who believe that the objective cannot be achieved with any quantity of military power but, if it is to be achieved, must be achieved in other ways. It is obvious that the world is dangerous, unsettled, violent, and maddeningly unpredictable. The taking of our people as hostages, the gratuitous insults to us in the United Nations, the monumental ingratitude of some of our petty clients, and the heavy-handed, often puzzling behavior of the Soviet Union all foster an impulse to reach for the gun. Yet when we do reach for the gun the threat does not seem to work the way it used to. Is this because something has happened to the American spirit, as the advocates of "get tough" policies insist, or is it because the world has changed?

When Albert Einstein observed, at the dawn of the nuclear age, that "the unleashed power of the atom has changed everything save our modes of thinking," he was identifying only one of the revolutionary factors of contemporary life which have transformed politics. At least three others have contributed to the change in the relationship between force and power. The first is the transformation over the last two generations of billions of people who were previously objects rather than subjects of international politics. With the collapse of the old colonial empires and the creation of scores of new nations, it is no longer possible for the fate of people in Asia, Africa, and Latin America to be settled in a few chancelleries of Europe. International politics, which was once a drawing-room drama, has become an extravaganza with a cast of thousands—not just the new nations but dissident groups and terrorist organizations that also have the power to make their presence felt. The rules for using violence have been changing—not the treaties regulating the use of force but the unspoken dictates that actually guide political leaders. On to center stage have come ancient religious and tribal rivalries that make it exceedingly difficult for the most powerful nations to organize global battle lines. Thus, arming Pakistan to fight the Russians in Afghanistan—a plausible, if dangerous, Cold War strategy—must be ruled out, because the Pakistanis and the Afghans cannot agree on their border in a region whose allegiance has long been a source of contention. In the Middle East, Saudi Arabia, like Iran, cannot be an effective surrogate wielder of military power, because of old scores in the region which have not yet been settled. When these ancient tensions and rivalries did not matter (because the people who cared passionately about them had no international visibility), it was fairly easy for the great powers, in their rivalries with one another, to ignore local conflicts—or, indeed, to exploit them.

In the early postwar years, when the decolonization process had just got under way, it was a relatively simple matter to organize the American security system on the principle of anti-Communism. Despite the precipitous decline in the appeal of Communism over the last twenty years—or perhaps because of it—an international security system based on anti-Communism is unrealizable. For most people in the world, the writings of Marx and Lenin, the virtues and deficiencies of the Soviet central-planning system, and the betrayed dreams of a classless society are not the issues that define reality. Hitlerism was an easy target, because there was only one Hitler and he gave every evidence of being a mad conqueror who had to be stopped. But in the past five years some of the bloodiest wars have been between nations calling themselves Communist—between Cambodia and Vietnam, between Vietnam and China—and some observers believe that the most likely spark for a world war is renewed fighting between the Soviet Union and China.

The enormous complexity of the contemporary world makes a simple security strategy obsolete. Violence, as Hannah Arendt put it in her extraordinary study "On Revolution," is politically effective only to the extent that its use is thought of as legitimate. Indeed, when it is seen as legitimate it does not need to be used much. And, as Britain found in India, once opposition grows to the point at which a colonial power must fight a war instead of conducting a low-level police operation, the use of violence becomes illegitimate and ultimately ineffective. Modern war achieves its political purpose through its psychological impact. *Schrecklichkeit*, as the early German theorists of modern warfare called it, creates the power to regulate the political behavior of masses of people by intimidating their leaders. For the strategy to work, there must be effective command and control; that is, the leaders who are to be intimidated must have the ability to surrender docile populations to the conqueror. The present situation in Iran is but an extreme case of a more general condition—the inability of political leaders, even under severe threat, to control popular passions or to pacify their own territory. In such a situation, the use of force from outside is ineffective for achieving political purposes. In international relations, it may still be legitimate to "punish" an adversary but not to "punish" leaderless crowds.

A second revolution has occurred in military technology. The spread of nuclear weapons is an accomplished fact. As early as 1975, the United States Arms Control and Disarmament Agency estimated that there would be enough weapons-grade nuclear material moving about the planet in 1985 to make twenty thousand nuclear weapons of the class that destroyed Hiroshima. South Africa and Israel—each a nation that will be involved in a potential life-and-death struggle over the next two decades—are presumed by many intelligence agencies to have nuclear weapons already. We now live in what the military historian Harvey A. DeWeerd calls a "Balkanized world"—a world of small, poor, but over-militarized states struggling for power. It is, he says, an "unmanageable" world, and a dangerous one for the United States, because a local conventional war can suck in the great powers. Emphasizing the familiar point that the generals are always preparing for the last war that was fought, DeWeerd notes that future wars are not likely to be either replays of the Second World War in Europe, to which most of our conventional forces are now addressed, or military expeditions in the desert. They will be small wars, and the belligerents will be exceedingly hard for outside powers to control. Modern weapons of all sorts are now readily available on the international market. Since the Second World War, the United States itself has sold, lent, or given away more than a hundred billion dollars' worth of armaments. Of the fifty largest American industrial companies, thirty-two make or export arms.

The purpose of arms shipments has been, as former Defense Secretary James Schlesinger put it in 1975, "to maintain influence." In defending huge arms shipments to the Shah of Iran and other Persian Gulf leaders, he declared, "The degree of influence of the supplier is potentially substantial, and, typically, those relationships are enduring." But the spread of military technology has had exactly the opposite effect. Instead of making the recipients dependent, it has turned out to be something of an equalizer. Poor, weak countries, though they may be hopelessly in debt and have populations that are starving, can and do conduct formidable military operations against their neighbors, and even against their own people. There is little that the great powers can do about this. Recent advances in military technology mean that bigger is not necessarily safer. The cruiser and the aircraft carrier—the modern vehicles for international swaggering—are vulnerable to shore-launched missiles of the sort that many Third World countries now have. The first thirty years of the postwar era were remarkably stable, largely because the United States had something approaching a monopoly of military power. It had most of the world's nuclear weapons, and it had the only fighting force that could be dispatched to distant corners of the globe. Today, in part because of the Soviet buildup, in part because of a worldwide arms buildup (to which the United States has been by far the largest contributor), the world is much less amenable to being managed by American military power. This reality is reflected in the schizophrenic reaction of certain Persian Gulf states, which privately urge the United States to take a tougher military role in their area but refuse to allow the United States to have a base on their territory. In Saudi Arabia, for example, the royal family knows that a base would arouse political opposition, domestic and foreign, and could not save their regime. The Reagan Administration, determined to have a presence in the Middle East, is proposing a string of military bases—in the Egyptian port of Ras Banas; on the island of Masirah, off Oman; at Mombasa, in Kenya; at Berbera, in Somalia; and on the island of Diego Gracia, in the Indian Ocean. How these bases would help stabilize this highly volatile area has not been explained.

The third transformation in the relationship between force and power has come about because of an upsurge in the cost of military might. As weapons have become more complex, they have become more expensive. They require esoteric metals and esoteric skills to produce. The nature of warfare itself and the development of democratic consciousness have combined to drive up manpower costs astronomically. In an all-out war to save their country from attack, men can be drafted and paid twenty-one dollars a month, as they were in 1940. In a war for more obscure goals, soldiers expect to be better paid—especially if the war appears to be a more or less permanent fixture. In a democratic society, the choice is either a draft that bows in the direction of universal service or a volunteer professional army. Since Vietnam, the United States has chosen the latter, and the taxpayer has been paying heavily for it, even though, with inflation, the pay is often inadequate. Ironically, the cost of maintaining politically effective military forces has gone up, even as the cost of mass destruction has gone down. In terms of cost effectiveness, atomic bombs are a bargain.

In the early nineteen-fifties, the United States tripled its military budget in about eighteen months to make the point urged so passionately in N.S.C. 68. The Korean War was the political occasion, but most of the buildup occurred in Europe, as a symbol of American global commitment. (No military leader at the time actually expected a Soviet attack.) As the French strategist Raymond Aron has pointed out, in the nineteen-eighties it would be impossible to repeat this feat. The Reagan budget calls for the United States to spend about a trillion and a half dollars in five years. The impact of military spending on the American economy has, oddly, never been subjected to a full-scale examination by the National Security Council or the Council of Economic Advisers. But there are increasing indications that the economic costs of military power weaken the economy in specific ways and, to that extent, damage national security.

In the nineteen-fifties, conservative Republicans, like Treasury Secre-

tary George Humphrey, believed that excessive military spending would
sap America's economic power, and in 1940 leading American industrial-
ists had opposed Roosevelt's rearmament plans, because they were convinced that a big military sector would distort production. It was the New
Dealers who believed that military spending, far from being harmful,
would actually stimulate the economy. After the war, Leon Keyserling,
the chairman of Harry Truman's Council of Economic Advisers, thought
that as much as twenty per cent of the gross national product could go for
defense with no ill effects. Pump-priming through military contracts became the economic underpinning of Cold War strategy. Curiously, fiscal
conservatives who today favor radical cuts in government spending in
every other area to combat inflation call for sharp increases in military
spending.

"The Johnson Administration was justly criticized for increasing defense spending without raising taxes," the economist Otto Eckstein notes.
The Reagan Administration is raising military expenditures at rates approaching those of the Vietnam buildup, but it is also proposing a large
tax cut. As Seymour Melman, a professor of industrial engineering at Columbia, has pointed out, there are compelling reasons that military spending is particularly inflationary. Cost-plus contracts drive prices up well
beyond what they would be in a competitive market. The beneficiaries of
military contracts are, for the most part, highly skilled engineers, scientists, technicians, and managers, whose services are removed from the
civilian economy. (As much as half the nation's scientists and engineers
work directly or indirectly for the Pentagon.) Personnel costs are bid up.
And, what is more serious, the civilian economy is starved of innovative
technical and managerial talent. The United States now lags behind every
other industrial nation in the percentage of its gross national product
which is devoted to research and development for the civilian economy.
A consequence of this neglect is the competitive advantage now enjoyed
by West Germany, Japan, and other smaller nations that can produce
important classes of sophisticated goods for export more cheaply and
more efficiently than the United States can.

The uncoupling of economic power and military power is a phenomenon of the past fifteen years. It used to be that the nations that could
afford the largest armies and navies—Britain under Queen Victoria, Germany under the Kaiser—were also the most dynamic industrial countries.
(Czarist Russia, with an enormous military machine and a relatively
primitive industrial economy, was always an anomaly.) In fact, a spectacu-
lar army and navy were intended to symbolize great economic power.
Only the richest could afford them. But in our time a nation with a modest military force, at least compared with that of either superpower, and a
nation with hardly any military force were ascendant economic powers.
West Germany and Japan are creating serious economic problems for the

United States by virtue of their competition in the export war to which all the industrial nations of the West are committed. Exactly because they have a modest defense burden, they are able to invest heavily in their civilian production. The Soviet Union, conversely, is becoming a more formidable military power, but at an increasing economic sacrifice. As Myron Rush, a professor of government at Cornell, has noted, the heavy military expenditures are at the expense of future growth. Like the United States, the Soviet Union has been shortchanging its civilian production machine. For the United States, the consequence has been a slow-growth economy. For a smaller and weaker economy, the consequence is stagnation.

The traditional debate over guns and butter somehow misses the point. The wish to spend scarce resources on schools, health care, the restoration of decayed cities, and clean air rather than on bombs and tanks is understandable—President Eisenhower once said that to spend resources on guns and warships when people were going hungry was "theft"—but those who advocate a shift of investment from military spending to spending for social services have been silenced by the notion that protection from enslavement is the most important social service a government can provide. Yet excessive military spending now produces some of the same consequences as military defeat; that is, it gives foreign governments greater control over the life of the country. Take the energy crisis. The decision to invest a trillion and a half dollars in the military rather than in a crash energy-development program to reduce America's dependence on foreign oil is a prime example of the way the nation's vulnerability is increased by the act of piling up hardware. The hardware cannot produce energy; it consumes energy. Nor can it assure access to energy; there is no military strategy that can effectively assure the flow of oil through a system vulnerable to sabotage. Useless military forces preëmpt investment funds, public and private, that could be spent on developing alternative national-security strategies appropriate to the new century that we are soon to enter.

National security cannot be achieved by a nation unwilling to invest in its own future. By abandoning our schools, our cities in the Northeast and the Middle West, our small farmers, even our police and firemen, by failing to find an appropriate industrial base, and by refusing to deal adequately with the overwhelming security threats—inflation and resource mismanagement—we are cutting deeply into the sources of national strength. Increasingly, national power comes out of innovative minds rather than out of the barrels of guns. The nation best able to confront the unprecedented problems of advanced industrial civilization, to recognize the limits of national power in an interdependent world, and to create a legitimate social order within the confines of a slow-growth economy is the one that is likely to emerge as No. 1.

34
AMERICAN STRENGTH, SOVIET WEAKNESS

Center for Defense Information

The view that the Soviet Union is the source of all the world's troubles is a traditional one in the United States. Even more than in the past, it is today widely believed that disparities in military strength between the U.S. and the Soviet Union are at the heart of America's foreign policy problems. . . .

But are huge increases in U.S. military spending necessary? Is the Soviet Union catching up with, or already ahead of the United States in military capacity? These are complex questions. Ultimately, however, the issues are neither so complicated nor so technical that the well-informed citizen cannot reach sound conclusions.

UNDERSTATING U.S. STRENGTH

There is an ingrained tendency in our government to overstate Soviet military power and understate U.S. and allied strengths. Although the best-known examples of this are in the past (the missile "gap," etc.), the problem is still much with us today. . . .

For example, American military officials regularly present comparisons of the U.S. and Soviet military budgets in which the U.S. is portrayed as spending less than the Soviets. But in the more relevant comparison of total military spending by the two alliances, NATO spends more than the Warsaw Pact—about $215 Billion for NATO in 1979 against the Pact's $175 Billion. Again, in comparing naval forces U.S. naval spokesmen focus their public comparisons on numbers of Soviet ships versus numbers of U.S. ships to show an apparent gap in favor of the Soviets. But the numbers include hundreds of very small Soviet ships. The official approach ignores the more relevant comparison of the two alliances. In numbers, NATO has some 400 major surface combatants compared with 235 for the U.S.S.R. and its allies; in tonnage, even counting all the very small Soviet ships, NATO has a more than two-to-one advantage.

Reprinted from David T. Johnson, CDI Director of Research, principal analyst, in *The Defense Monitor*, June 1980, Vol. IX, No. 5, pp. 1–8. Portions of the original have been omitted.

The tendency to exaggerate occurs for a number of reasons. Military officials, in order to get public and Congressional support for large budgets, believe their message must be dramatically conveyed. Our leaders tend to be much more acquainted and impressed with our own problems than with those of potential adversaries. We tend to focus primarily on those aspects of the competition in which we feel deficient, while ignoring aspects in which we may have an advantage. And there is an inevitable and perhaps understandable inclination on the part of military planners to err on the side of caution in the area of national defense. Military planning is conservative by nature, narrowly focused on dangers, and probably cannot be any other way.

It is very difficult for Americans to become reliably informed on these matters. Much of what goes on by way of public discussion of U.S.-Soviet military issues is a rhetorical game of oversimplification. The press is fond of portraying our relations with the Soviets in terms of drama, a soap opera of easily understood images, an athletic contest with winners and loosers.

VIEWS OF THE SOVIETS

While officials such as Secretary of Defense Harold Brown in their detailed reports to Congress often make available information that contradicts claims about U.S. military weakness, these same officials and many political leaders tend to make one-sided generalizations about our inadequacies and our opponent's successes in arguing for more military spending. Enough information is available from open sources to come to more reliable, independent appraisals of military issues, but it takes a lot of digging. And it is very difficult to compete with the vast apparatus of the Department of Defense in attempting to inform the American people.

Ignorance of the Soviet Union is a fundamental problem in the formation of U.S. policy. Our country suffers from a serious absence of expertise on Soviet affairs and foreign policy. Dr. Robert Legvold of the Council on Foreign Relations concludes that "the gaps in our knowledge are enormous. And they are growing." He believes that "our view of the Soviet Union is shaped increasingly by popular impressions, a priori analyses, built from superficial reflections on the Soviet actions that most catch the eye, and traditional habits of thought." Dr. Legvold is describing the situation *within* the U.S. government. Outside of government the problem is even worse.

There are American experts on the Soviet Union who do provide insights and sophisticated interpretations, including George Kennan, Marshall Shulman, Raymond Garthoff and Robert Legvold himself. But particularly in U.S. military planning, indifference to or distortions of Soviet perceptions are pervasive. It is remarkable how little informed attention is paid to these matters, especially when one recalls that U.S. military officials constantly reiterate that our military strategy is based on deterrence and that what is important about deterrence is what the other fellow thinks. A much higher priority should be given to understanding Soviet perceptions and intentions and integrating that into our military policy. Unfortunately, there is little serious effort of this nature in U.S. military planning.

The cliché in military circles is that military people have to be concerned only with capabilities, not with intentions. There is some truth in this slogan but not much. Military people *do* have ideas, often strenuously held, about Soviet intentions, and these ideas strongly influence U.S. military actions. U.S. military force structures would be much different today if they were based purely on the objective capabilities of potential adversaries. But any "real world" decisions about using scarce resources for military purposes rely on assumptions about the probability of war and the probability of particular contingencies.

The Soviet Union is a large power that, in important respects, has national interests that differ from those of the U.S. Russians look at things different from Americans for reasons that often have little to do with Marxism-Leninism or malignant Soviet intentions vis-a-vis the U.S. Even a modest knowledge of the history of Russia and the Soviet Union should be enough to alert Americans to why Russians and Americans have disagreements.

Russians and Americans have very different appraisals of each other's military situation. They disagree on what constitutes military forces adequate for the defense of the Soviet Union. How often have we heard U.S. officials proclaim the discovery that Soviet forces are in excess of defensive requirements and therefore alarming and illegitimate? The famous NSC-68 report of the U.S. National Security Council in 1950 reached the same conclusion uttered as an allegedly new insight today: "The Soviet Union actually possesses armed forces far in excess of those necessary to defend its territory."

Clearly, *both* the U.S. and the U.S.S.R. can be said to have forces far in excess of those required to defend their own territory. For the U.S. in particular, the bulk of our military spending does *not* go for the defense of the U.S. but to project our military power overseas to defend friends and allies. According to these simplistic ways of looking at the problem, probably a greater proportion of Soviet military spending goes strictly for purposes of national defense. But viewed from a different perspective, it can be argued that the military forces of both countries are completely inadequate to defend against nuclear war or to prevail over the other with any certainty in conventional war. This is the paradox of defense in the nuclear age. It is part of the reason why there can be such divergent views on what constitutes adequate forces for defense in both the U.S. and the Soviet Union.

MILITARY COMPARISONS

Official Defense Department sources make a strong case for the continuing military strength (if not superiority) of the U.S. and its military allies. In the areas of nuclear weapons, military spending, military technology, number of men under arms, naval forces, forces for intervention, forces in Europe, and the overall balance of world power the Soviet Union is inferior to the alliance of powers opposing it. Comparisons in these areas may be briefly outlined to demonstrate Defense Secretary Brown's conclusion that "By most relevant measures, we remain the military equal or superior to the Soviet Union."

U.S. NOT WEAK

By most relevant measures, we remain the military equal or superior to the Soviet Union.
> —Harold Brown, Secretary of Defense, February 1980

The Soviet Union is inferior to its antagonists in numbers of nuclear weapons. This is the crucial measure of nuclear strength and the U.S. and its allies will retain the advantage in the future as plans to produce more than 20,000 nuclear weapons over the next decade are implemented. In 1980 the U.S. has 9500 strategic nuclear weapons, the Soviets have 6000, and U.S. allies (including China) have about another 1000. Other measures of strategic forces also favor the U.S. side: long-range bombers, submarine-launched nuclear weapons, overall accuracy and higher alert rates and readiness. The U.S. is far ahead of the Soviet Union in submarine warfare and anti-submarine forces. The U.S. is in a much better position to exploit the emerging situation in which fixed, land-based systems are becoming vulnerable and obsolete.

Even utilizing the CIA's questionable methodology for comparing military budgets (which assumes that the Soviets pay as much as the U.S. does for soldiers and weapons), combined NATO military spending has exceeded that of the Warsaw Pact for many years. In 1979 NATO military spending was at least $215 Billion, compared to $175 Billion for the Warsaw Pact. Including Chinese military spending with the Western allies gives a combined anti-Soviet military expenditure of $265 Billion in 1979.

NATO's edge is accentuated by its superior industrial efficiency. Secretary Brown in an obvious reference to the less efficient Soviet industries recently said "the Soviets probably have to invest more defense resources than we do to achieve a comparable military result."

U.S. military leaders testify to the continuing U.S. edge in the quality and effectiveness of U.S. military technology. Secretary Brown says "our technology, on balance, continues to surpass theirs by a considerable margin." Edward R. Jayne, Assistant Director for National Security and International Affairs of the Office of Management and Budget, in April 1980 said: "I'm absolutely persuaded that not only do we have the technology edge, but that the edge is getting greater." Across the board from automated control and computers, to microelectronics and integrated circuits, and telecommunications and propulsion, the Defense Department has important advantages over the Soviets. In precision-guided weapons, which Dr. William Perry, head of Pentagon research, has called "the most significant application of technology to modern warfare since the development of radar," Perry states that the U.S. has a "substantial lead."

FOUR MAJOR MILITARY INDICATORS		
	Anti-Soviet (U.S., other NATO, China)	Soviet (Warsaw Pact)
Strategic Nuclear Weapons	10,500	6,000
Military Spending (1979)	$265 Billion	$175 Billion
Military Personnel	9.5 million	4.8 million
Major Surface Ships	445	235

The Soviet Union, which has traditionally maintained a huge standing Army, is nevertheless outnumbered in military personnel by its opponents. The Warsaw Pact has a total of about 4.8 million active duty military personnel. NATO has 5.1 million and China has 4.4 million, for a total of 9.5 million anti-Soviet military personnel. U.S. and NATO military manpower is better trained and man for man can operate with more initiative and resourcefulness. The U.S. has nearly 500,000 troops at many military bases around the world while the Soviet Union has very few bases outside its borders, except for Eastern Europe.

NATO naval superiority over the Warsaw Pact is striking. NATO has a substantial lead in major surface combatants (400 to 235) and a more than 2:1 advantage in total tonnage of naval forces. Large NATO naval vessels have superior military effectiveness and are much more capable of operating on distant patrols than Soviet ships. Most of the smaller Soviet ships lack large fuel reserves or nuclear power, adequate space for rations or ammunition storage, and have limited range. In a global role, the Soviet Navy would suffer greatly from a lack of air cover in operations away from the Soviet landmass. Of course, in an age of nuclear-armed missiles, all surface ships are quite vulnerable and both the U.S. and Soviet navies are struggling to cope with this unsolvable problem.

While the Soviets were able to invade neighboring Afghanistan, Soviet forces for more distant military intervention "are minimal at present," according to General David Jones, Chairman of the Joint Chiefs of Staff. The Soviet naval infantry (marines) number some 12,000 with minimal fire support compared to our 185,000-man Marine Corps. Our amphibious lift of 66 ships is far superior to the Soviet "blue water" ships. American airlift assets are also greatly superior. And, of course, the U.S. has its world wide base structure and alliance system. For these reasons, among others, General Jones recently emphasized U.S. ability to "devastate" a Soviet attack on the Persian Gulf.

With regard to forces in Europe, Secretary Brown recently stated that "in the Central Region of Europe, a rough numerical balance exists between the immediately available non-nuclear forces of NATO (including France) and those of the Warsaw Pact." This contradicts the widely held view that the Soviets could easily conquer Western Europe in a lightning blitzkreig. While in some cases the number of weapons favors the Warsaw Pact, NATO exceeds the Warsaw Pact in military personnel in Europe by about 1 million men. The quality of NATO weapons, including artillery, anti-tank weapons, surface-to-air missiles, military helicopters, tactical aircraft and air-launched missiles exceeds that of the Soviets. NATO's superiority in the quantity and quality of anti-tank weapons and advanced tactical aircraft perhaps more than compensates for the Pact's advantage in number of tanks.

A bottom line assessment of the balance of world power reveals a substantial inferiority on the part of the Soviet Union. An aggregation of important military and non-military factors demonstrates that the balance of world power is strikingly to the advantage of the West and its allies. The Center for Defense Information, utilizing indexes of power developed by former CIA official Ray Cline in his books on *World Power Trends*, has calculated this division of world power:

Pro-West and China: 70%
Soviet Union and its clients: 20%
Other: 10%

Any such calculation must be approximate but it is clear that the Soviets have not been successful in transforming their military power into dominant world influence.

The view from Moscow is far from euphoric as Soviet leaders examine the world around them and the kinds of military comparisons outlined here. The Soviets are far from having overwhelming military power and undoubtedly face more severe national security problems than does the U.S.

A MIRROR IMAGE

From all reliable reports, the Russians look at their armed forces primarily as reasonable defensive measures to protect the Soviet Union from pressing military threats. They also view their forces very much as [a] means of *deterring* military attacks on the Soviet Union (however remote those threats may appear to us). There are many Russians who worry about whether the Soviet Union is doing enough to protect itself, just as there are many Americans who question the adequacy of U.S. military forces. Military security is a serious business in the Soviet Union, but it is perceived as a painful burden thrust upon the Soviet people. The self-perceptions and rationalizations are very similar to those on the American side.

The more people know about the Soviet Union, the more they tend to be impressed with the limits of Soviet power. As Secretary of Defense Brown has commented, "we know our weaknesses and our limitations far better than we know those of the enemy."

These limits and problems are well-known to the Soviet leaders and there is no evidence of military hubris or geopolitical euphoria on the part of Soviet spokesmen. There are great political and economic challenges facing the Soviet Union, of which their leadership is aware. They have some awareness that military force provides no solution for these problems. Contrary to some Western analyses, the Soviets evidence awareness of security's growing subtlety and do not see military power as the principal tool of their foreign policy and [an] ingredient in the international correlation of forces.

The Soviet leaders do not appear to believe that the USSR is moving ahead of the U.S. (and NATO) in military power or is going to do so any time soon. Their dominant assessment today is that the West is poised to push for new military advantages over the Soviet Union. Secretary Brown has outlined the threatening NATO buildup: "The defense plans which have been adopted by the alliance—if they are fully implemented— promise to offset, and indeed to overshadow, the Warsaw Pact's gains." A CIA report outlines the strategic nuclear threat: "Today the U.S. is pursuing force modernization programs of which the Soviets are vocally and, we believe, genuinely fearful."

The irony for the Soviets is that because of increased foreign awareness of their military accomplishment, just when the Soviets might wish to consider slowing down the rate of growth of their military effort, they are faced with the consequences of this general reaction to their past activities.

For Soviet leaders, the issue of American intentions is as central as the issue of Soviet intentions is for the Americans. For them, the U.S. is on trial. A major debate has been going on within the Soviet Union for some years on whether the U.S. can be a reasonable partner or whether the U.S. will seize new developments to engage in a new round of positions-of-strength diplomacy. In the Soviet perception, the present situation is particularly dangerous. They fear that Western views of their economic and political weakness may lead the U.S. to attempt to pressure them. Their own sense of the difficulties they face stimulates their propensity to fear that others may try to exploit their weak points.

The potential emergence of an active anti-Soviet alliance of Japan, China, the U.S. and the rest of NATO is a major concern of the Soviets. The prospect of West Germany's becoming a base for launching deep nuclear attacks on the interior of the Soviet Union touches another very sensitive nerve. Traditional fears of encirclement and of Germany are aggravated.

Generally, the Soviets have been very insensitive to whether their military activities may be interpreted negatively abroad. Even their sophisticated and informed officials seem genuinely to believe that most if not all, Western complaints about their military programs are unwarranted— artificial issues fanned for ulterior motives. They reject the action/reaction phenomenon as does Secretary Brown. Whatever else one might say about it, President Brezhnev's recent actions to reduce Soviet forces in East Germany unilaterally could well be an indication of an increased sensitivity to foreign perceptions of Soviet programs and the desirability of their taking some independent action to diminish Western perceptions of Soviet threats.

THE ROLE OF THE MILITARY

A central issue in appraising the Soviet threat is the influence of their military. The conventional wisdom on this subject is to stress the very important role of the military, their dominance of military decision-making, the existence of a militarized civilian leadership and even a militarized society. This has gone so far that the traditional totalitarian image and model of the Soviet Union has been gradually replaced by the model of a militarized state.

Another interpretation of the influence of the Soviet military has been argued by Walter Clemens and Jerry Hough, among others. They conclude that the Soviet foreign policy community is *less* military in its orientation than its U.S. counterpart. This is a consequence in part of the fact that the military are more or less kept on the reservation, restricted to decision-making on issues directly within their professional competence. A recent article in the *Air University Review* by Donald Clark, who has served in the U.S. Embassy in Moscow and on the U.S. delegation to negotiate Mutual and Balanced Force Reductions (MBFR) with the Soviets in Vienna, also argues that "the U.S. military probably has better opportunities, consistently provided by formal mechanisms and procedures, to influence national decisions than do our Soviet counterparts. . . . The appearance of great influence by the Soviet military on national decisions is usually exaggerated."

FEAR OF SOVIETS

The bottom line on Soviet military power is fundamentally emotional. Nobody likes the Soviet Union. The images we receive in childhood are reinforced by more mature judgments on the quality of Soviet life. Among Western intellectuals on the left, in particular, their reputation is at an all-time low. President Carter's national security advisor, Zbigniew Brzezinski, has commented in another context: "There is not a single revolutionary party that would model its vision of the future on the Soviet Union."

The repellent quality of so many aspects of their domestic practice must inevitably create fear of the Soviet Union as a superpower acting to increase its international role and influence. No matter how conservative the Soviets may be in their foreign policy or how defensively oriented their military programs, it is simply unavoidable that there will be widespread suspicion in Western countries. This will be the case irrespective of artificial annd alarmist depictions of the Soviet military threat.

Trying to protect the Soviet Union from the kind of destruction that the U.S. has been capable of inflicting there has been the top priority in Soviet defense policy since World War II. The Russians *do* fear American military power and do believe it could be used against them, and would be but for their military might. They do not attribute to Americans the same good intentions we attribute to ourselves. It would be a miracle unprecedented in human history if they did have such selfless empathy with an opponent.

The lessons of Russian history and of war, as perceived by them, necessitates that the Soviet Union have large military forces that are viewed as threatening by others. These forces would not be an adequate deterrent if they were not perceived as threatening by those whom the Russians wish to deter. (It is a neglected truism that one person's deterrent is another person's threat.) The Soviet military, as the American military, believe it is their solemn duty to be prepared for war. In an age of nuclear weapons, when mass destruction could occur in 30 minutes, all military leaders believe that large forces must be maintained on a close-to-war status. There is really no important difference between the inclinations toward preparedness on the part of the American and Soviet military. Professionalism on both sides has its same fears and compulsions.

SOVIET OBJECTIVES

To capsulize a huge amount of evidence into a few summary remarks, Soviet objectives in the basic military areas may be outlined as follows.

In naval forces their seapower has developed in the years since World War II primarily as a force to attempt to protect the Soviet Union from U.S. naval power, particularly the nuclear forces based on our aircraft carriers and strategic submarines. The second priority has been the establishment of an invulnerable sea-based nuclear deterrent for the Soviet Union. Both of these objectives have been extremely demanding and have not yet really been achieved.

In strategic nuclear forces, they have been playing catch-up ball from the beginning and still firmly believe that is what they are doing today. The sense of being Number Two is somewhat modified by the view, which may not be shared by all Russians, that the Soviet Union has succeeded in some significant way in acquiring nuclear forces that balance those of the U.S. Many Russians, however, are very conscious that this may be a temporary achievement on their part and that new dangers to their country may open up if the U.S. spurts ahead in a new round of strategic weapons competition featuring mobile ICBMs (the MX), cruise missiles, revived ABM systems and military uses of space.

Some Russians do believe, as do some Americans, that it is worthwhile to think about what might happen if nuclear war came, and they believe in making certain preparations for such an event. Like some Americans, some Russians believe that deterrence is maximized by having forces that look as though they might in fact be used. There are dangers here, but the alleged distinction between a Soviet commitment to nuclear war versus an innocent American commitment to mutual assured destruction and deterrence has been tremendously overblown. Both Soviet and American *political* leaders, who must take broader considerations into account than their military advisors, share common insights about futile and dangerous aspects of the nuclear arms race and acknowledge the central reality of the enormous destructiveness of such a war. This does not mean that these leaders usually agree or can do anything they want to do. There are large constraints.

In the area of NATO–Warsaw Pact military confrontation in Europe, the Soviet Union has sought for many years to pose a substantial military threat to Western Europe. In earlier years, this was partially an attempt to compensate for an inability directly to threaten (and thus deter) the United States. In more recent years, as both NATO and the Warsaw Pact have acquired very substantial and very highly nuclearized military forces, the Soviets have perceived large military threats from Western Europe, particularly from nuclear forces there and the growth of West German capabilities. There have been numerous deficiencies in the ability of the Soviets to fight large-scale conventional warfare, and much of the most recent phase of military developments has been devoted to diversifying their capabilities.

Many analysts have discussed the blitzkrieg or offensive orientation of Soviet forces facing Western Europe. The Russians do place a high priority on being able to fight a future war to the maximum extent outside the Soviet Union. The devastating consequences of past wars fought on the soil of the Soviet Union inevitably pushes them toward their own version of a forward defense policy. "Never again" is a slogan embraced by all Russians with a fervor foreign to most Americans. The Soviets also believe that they maximize the deterrence of the outbreak of war in Europe by making it clear to possible opponents that they will suffer quick and massive destruction. This is traditional military thinking, shared by many Western officials.

MEANING OF AFGHANISTAN

The Soviet invasion of Afghanistan in December 1979 has been interpreted as a "watershed" event in international affairs. While there is nothing new in Soviet willingness to employ military power in adjacent territory when it feels its national security is at stake, the reappearance of Soviet tanks in a foreign country must be very troubling to Americans and others around the world. Pointing out that Afghanistan had already fallen within the Soviet sphere of influence is little consolation.

The long-term consequences of Soviet actions in Afghanistan and the nature of their future policy in the area are uncertain. Speculation is all that most analysts can offer. Three basic points seem to be worth making at this time. First, it appears that the Soviet move into Afghanistan was prompted primarily by the trend of events in that backward country and had little or nothing to do with alleged designs on neighboring countries and regions. Second, just as the U.S. could easily occupy adjacent Mexico militarily, the invasion of Afghanistan does not reflect any extraordinary military achievement on their part. They derive no particular military benefits from these operations (probably the truth is just the reverse).

Their capacity to carry out military activities in the Indian Ocean or the Persian Gulf is not significantly improved.

Thirdly, we should not neglect providing positive incentives for the Soviets to behave as we wish at the same time as we are preoccupied with attempts to punish them. The decline in the Soviet stake in good relations with the United States over the past five years helped to create a situation in which the Soviet leadership was willing to take steps contrary to American desires. The repudiation of détente, the failure to deliver on promises of expanded trade, the inability to ratify the SALT II treaty, the push toward large increases in military budgets and the plans to install new nuclear missiles in Europe have all been interpreted in Moscow as developments in the United States reflecting a fundamental rejection of cooperation. The Soviets have clearly reevaluated the priority they place on cultivating American interests. If they perceive nothing to be gained from good relations with the U.S., we should not be surprised at an acceleration of Soviet actions around the world that we do not approve of. It is not to our advantage to slam all doors in the Soviets' face.

Related to but distinct from the question of the relative military power of the Soviet Union is the question of its geopolitical success in recent times. A comprehensive study of trends of Soviet influence around the world from 1945 to 1980 published in *The Defense Monitor* (January, 1980) concludes that they have *not* been able to expand their influence consistently and that there is no evidence of any inexorable Soviet advances.

Particularly at this time of renewed cold war, it is important to stress the necessity of better understanding Soviet fears and objectives. It is damaging to American interests to ignore or dismiss Soviet attitudes. We cannot have a sensible military policy, invest our limited resources where they are really required, or reach achievable agreements with the Soviet Union that serve our interests, if we persist in self-imposed ignorance of the Russians.

35
THE EFFECTS OF NUCLEAR WAR

U.S. Office of Technology Assessment

At the request of the Senate Committee on Foreign Relations, the Office of Technology Assessment has undertaken to describe the effects of a nuclear war on the civilian populations, economies, and societies of the United States and the Soviet Union.

Nuclear war is not a comfortable subject. Throughout all the variations, possibilities, and uncertainties that this study describes, one theme is constant—a nuclear war would be a catastrophe. A militarily plausible nuclear attack, even "limited," could be expected to kill people and to inflict economic damage on a scale unprecedented in American experience; a large-scale nuclear exchange would be a calamity unprecedented in human history. The mind recoils from the effort to foresee the details of such a calamity, and from the careful explanation of the unavoidable uncertainties as to whether people would die from blast damage, from fallout radiation, or from starvation during the following winter. But the fact remains that nuclear war is possible, and the possibility of nuclear war has formed part of the foundation of international politics, and of U.S. policy, ever since nuclear weapons were used in 1945.

The premise of this study is that those who deal with the large issues of world politics should understand what is known, and perhaps more importantly what is not known, about the likely consequences if efforts to deter and avoid nuclear war should fail. Those who deal with policy issues regarding nuclear weapons should know what such weapons can do, and the extent of the uncertainties about what such weapons might do.

SECTION 1.—FINDINGS

1. The effects of a nuclear war that cannot be calculated are at least as important as those for which calculations are attempted. Moreover, even these limited calculations are subject to very large uncertainties.

Conservative military planners tend to base their calculations on factors that can be either controlled or predicted, and to make pessimistic assumptions where control or prediction are impossible. For example, planning for strategic nuclear warfare looks at the extent to which civilian

From U.S. Office of Technology Assessment, *The Effects of Nuclear War*, (Washington, D.C.: Government Printing Office, 1979), Publication # OTA–NS–89, pp. 1–12.

514

targets will be destroyed by blast, and discounts the additional damage which may be caused by fires that the blast could ignite. This is not because fires are unlikely to cause damage, but because the extent of fire damage depends on factors such as weather and details of building construction that make it much more difficult to predict than blast damage. While it is proper for a military plan to provide for the destruction of key targets by the surest means even in unfavorable circumstances, the non-military observer should remember that actual damage is likely to be greater than that reflected in the military calculations. This is particularly true for indirect effects such as deaths resulting from injuries and the unavailability of medical care, or for economic damage resulting from disruption and disorganization rather than from direct destruction.

For more than a decade, the declared policy of the United States has given prominence to a concept of "assured destruction": the capabilities of U.S. nuclear weapons have been described in terms of the level of damage they can surely inflict even in the most unfavorable circumstances. It should be understood that in the event of an actual nuclear war, the destruction resulting from an all-out nuclear attack would probably be far greater. In addition to the tens of millions of deaths during the days and weeks after the attack, there would probably be further millions (perhaps further tens of millions) of deaths in the ensuing months or years. In addition to the enormous economic destruction caused by the actual nuclear explosions, there would be some years during which the residual economy would decline further, as stocks were consumed and machines wore out faster than recovered production could replace them. Nobody knows how to estimate the likelihood that industrial civilization might collapse in the areas attacked; additionally, the possibility of significant long-term ecological damage cannot be excluded.

2. *The impact of even a "small" or "limited" nuclear attack would be enormous.* Although predictions of the effects of such an attack are subject to the same uncertainties as predictions of the effects of an all-out attack, the possibilities can be bounded. OTA examined the impact of a small attack on economic targets (an attack on oil refineries limited to 10 missiles), and found that while economic recovery would be possible, the economic damage and social dislocation could be immense. A review of calculations of the effects on civilian populations and economies of major counterforce attacks found that while the consequences might be endurable (since they would be on a scale with wars and epidemics that nations have endured in the past), the number of deaths might be as high as 20 million. Moreover, the uncertainties are such that no government could predict with any confidence what the results of a limited attack or counterattack would be even if there was no further escalation.

3. *It is therefore reasonable to suppose that the extreme uncertainties about the effects of a nuclear attack, as well as the certainty that the*

minimum consequences would be enormous, both play a role in the deterrent effect of nuclear weapons.

4. *There are major differences between the United States and the Soviet Union that affect the nature of their vulnerability to nuclear attacks, despite the fact that both are large and diversified industrial countries.* Differences between the two countries in terms of population distribution, closeness of population to other targets, vulnerability of agricultural systems, vulnerability of cities to fire, socioeconomic system, and political system create significant asymmetries in the potential effects of nuclear attacks. Differences in civil defense preparations and in the structure of the strategic arsenals compound these asymmetries. By and large, the Soviet Union is favored by having a bigger and better economy and (perhaps) a greater capacity for effective decentralization. The larger size of Soviet weapons also means that they are likely to kill more people while aiming at something else.

5. *Although it is true that effective sheltering and/or evacuation could save lives, it is not clear that a civil defense program based on providing shelters or planning evacuation would necessarily be effective.* To save lives, it is not only necessary to provide shelter in, or evacuation to, the right place (and only extreme measures of dispersion would overcome the problem that the location of safe places cannot be reliably predicted), it is also necessary to provide food, water, medical supplies, sanitation, security against other people, possibly filtered air, etc. After fallout diminishes, there must be enough supplies and enough organization to keep people alive while production is being restored. The effectiveness of civil defense measures depends, among other things, on the events leading up to the attack, the enemy's targeting policy, and sheer luck.

6. *The situation in which the survivors of a nuclear attack find themselves will be quite unprecedented.* The surviving nation would be weaker—economically, socially, and politically—than one would calculate by adding up the surviving economic assets and the numbers and skills of the surviving people. Natural resources would be destroyed; surviving equipment would be designed to use materials and skills that might no longer exist; and indeed some regions might be almost uninhabitable. Furthermore, prewar patterns of behavior would surely change, though in unpredictable ways. Finally, the entire society would suffer from the enormous psychological shock of having discovered the extent of its vulnerability.

7. *From an economic point of view, and possibly from a political and social viewpoint as well, conditions after an attack would get worse before they started to get better.* For a period of time, people could live off supplies (and, in a sense, off habits) left over from before the war. But shortages and uncertainties would get worse. The survivors would find themselves in a race to achieve viability (i.e., production at least equaling

consumption plus depreciation) before stocks ran out completely. A failure to achieve viability, or even a slow recovery, would result in many additional deaths, and much additional economic, political, and social deterioration. This postwar damage could be as devastating as the damage from the actual nuclear explosion.

SECTION 2.—APPROACH

The scope of this study is both broader and narrower than that of most other studies on this subject. It is broader in three respects:

1. it examines a full range of possible nuclear attacks, with attacking forces ranging in extent from a single weapon to the bulk of a superpower's arsenal;

2. it deals explicitly with both Soviet attacks on the United States and U.S. attacks on the Soviet Union; and

3. it addresses the multiple effects of nuclear war, indirect as well as direct, long term as well as short term, and social and economic as well as physical.

Those effects that cannot be satisfactorily calculated or estimated are described qualitatively. But this report's scope is narrower than most defense analyses because it avoids any consideration of military effects; although it hypothesizes (among other things) missile attacks against military targets, only the "collateral" damage such attacks would inflict on the civilian society are examined.

The approach used was to look at a series of attack "cases," and to describe the various effects and overall impact each of them might produce. By analyzing the impact of the same attack case for both a U.S. attack on the Soviet Union and a Soviet attack on the United States, the report examines the significance of the different kinds of vulnerabilities of the two countries, and offers some insights about the consequences of the differences between the two countries' nuclear weapon arsenals. The cases were chosen primarily to investigate the effects of variations in attack size and in the kinds of targets attacked. It is believed that the analysis is "realistic," in the sense that the hypothetical attacks are possible ones. Patterns of nuclear explosions were examined that are not very different from those that, OTA believes, the existing nuclear forces would produce if the military were ordered to make attacks of the specified size on the specified targets.

Case 1:

In order to provide a kind of tutorial on what happens when nuclear weapons are detonated, the study describes the effects of the explosion of a single weapon. Then it examines the effects of such an explosion over a single U.S. city (Detroit) and [a] single Soviet city (Leningrad) of comparable size. The base case was the detonation of a 1-megaton weapon (1 Mt = energy released by 1 million tons of TNT), since both the United States and the Soviet Union have weapons of roughly this size in their arsenals. Then, in order to look at the ways in which the specific effects and overall impact would vary if other weapons that might be available were used, the effects of a 25-Mt weapon over Detroit, the effects of a 9-Mt weapon over Leningrad, and the effects of 10 weapons of 40 kilotons (kt) each over Leningrad are described. An attempt was made to describe as well the effects of a small weapon in a large city (such as a terrorist group might set off) but was unsuccessful because the effects of such a weapon in a metropolitan setting cannot be inferred from the existing body of knowledge regarding military weapons.

The casualties from such attacks could range from 220,000 dead and 420,000 injured to 2,500,000 dead and 1,100,000 injured (many of the injured would wind up as fatalities), depending on the details of the attack and the assumptions made regarding conditions. The discussion in chapter II of the full report shows how the time of day, time of year, weather conditions, size of weapon, height of burst, and preparation of the population could all make a great difference in the number of casualties resulting from such an attack. The extent of fire damage is a further uncertainty. Even if only one city is attacked, and the remaining resources of a nation are available to help, medical facilities would be inadequate to care for the injured. A further imponderable is fallout (if the attack uses a surface burst), whose effects depend on the winds.

Case 2:

In order to examine the effects of a small attack on urban/industrial targets, the study examines a hypothetical attack limited to 10 SNDVs (strategic nuclear delivery vehicles, the term used in SALT to designate one missile or one bomber) on the other superpower's oil refineries. In "planning" this attack, which is not analogous to any described in recent U.S. literature, it was hypothesized that the political leadership instructed the military to inflict maximum damage on energy production using only 10 SNDVs without regard to the extent of civilian casualties or other damage. It was assumed that the Soviets would attack such targets with SS-18 missiles (each carrying 10 multiple independently targetable reentry vehicles, or MIRVs), and that the United States would use 7 MIRVed Poseidon missiles and 3 MIRVed Minute-man III missiles.

The calculations showed that the Soviet attack would destroy 64 percent of U.S. oil refining capacity [Table 1], while the U.S. attack would destroy 73 percent of Soviet refining capacity [Table 2]. Calculations were

Table 1 *Summary of U.S.S.R. Attack on the United States*

Footprint number	Geographic area	EMT[a]	Percent national refining capacity	Percent national storage capacity	Air burst prompt fatalities (× 1,000)
1	Texas	8	14.9	NA[b]	472
2	Indiana, Illinois, Ohio	8	8.1	NA	365
3	New Jersey, Pennsylvania, Delaware	8	7.9	NA	845
4	California	8	7.8	NA	1,252
5	Louisiana, Texas, Mississippi	8	7.5	NA	377
6	Texas	8	4.5	NA	377
7	Illinois, Indiana, Michigan	8	3.6	NA	484
8	Louisiana	8	3.6	NA	278
9	Oklahoma, Kansas	8	3.3	NA	365
10	California	8	2.5	NA	357
	Totals	80	63.7	NA	5,031

[a]EMT = Equivalent megatons.
[b]NA = Not applicable.

also made of "prompt fatalities," including those killed by blast and fall-out, assuming no special civil defense measures; they showed about 5 million U.S. deaths and about 1 million Soviet deaths. The results were different for the two countries for several reasons. Soviet oil refining capacity is more concentrated than U.S. oil refining capacity, so that a small attack can reach more of it. At the same time, Soviet oil refineries tend to be located away from residential areas (the available data on population location deals with where people live rather than with where they work) to a greater extent than U.S. refineries. A further difference is that a limitation on the number of delivery vehicles would lead each side to use weapons with many MIRVs, so the United States would attack most of the targets with Poseidon missiles which have small warheads, while the Soviets would use SS-18 intercontinental ballistic missiles (ICBMs) which carry much larger warheads, and large warheads cause more damage to things not directly targeted (in this case, people) than do small warheads.

One can only speculate about the consequences of such extensive destruction. There would have to be drastic changes in both the U.S. and

Table 2 Summary of U.S. Attack on U.S.S.R.

Footprint number	Geographic area (approx. center)	EMT[a]	Percent national refining capacity	Percent national storage capacity	Air burst prompt fatalities ($\times$ 1,000)	
					SS[b]	MS[c]
1	Moscow	1.20	10.5	2.1	62	41
2	Baku	0.96	9.8	1.5	224	152
3	Ishimbai	1.20	8.7	2.8	25	12
4	Polotsk	0.92	7.5	0.3	52	32
5	Kuibuyshev	1.20	7.4	3.1	127	83
6	Angarsk	0.92	6.9	0.4	130	54
7	Grozny	0.96	6.7	1.6	56	37
8	Kirishi	0.92	6.2	0.3	493	230
9	Gorki	1.20	5.6	1.5	228	153
10	Perm	0.96	3.6	2.1	61	42
	Totals	10.44	72.9	15.7	1,458	836

[a]EMT = Equivalanet megatons.
[b]SS = 100 percent of population in single-story buildings.
[c]MS = 100 percent of population in multistory buildings.

Soviet economies to cope with the sudden disappearance of the bulk of oil refining capacity. Productivity in virtually every industrial sector would decline, and some sectors would be largely wiped out. There would have to be strict allocation of the remaining available refined petroleum products. Some Soviet factory workers might end up working in the fields to replace tractors for which fuel was unavailable. The United States might have to ban commuting by automobile, forcing suburban residents to choose between moving and long walks to a bus stop. The aftermath of the war might lead to either an increase or a decrease in the amount of petroleum products required by the military. Changes in people's attitudes are impossible to predict. Calm determination might produce effective responses that would limit the damage; panic or a breakdown in civic spirit could compound the effects of the attack itself.

It is instructive to observe the asymmetries between the problems which the United States and the Soviets would face. Soviet agricultural production, which is barely adequate in peacetime, would probably decline sharply, and production rates would slow even in essential industries. However, the Soviet system is well adapted for allocating scarce resources to high-priority areas, and for keeping everybody employed even if efficient employment is unavailable. The relative wealth and freedom of the United States brings both advantages and disadvantages: while agriculture and essential industry would probably continue, there would be a staggering organizational problem in making use of resources that now depend on petroleum—one must ask what the employees of an automobile factory or a retail establishment on a highway would do if there were virtually no gasoline for cars.

A major question relating to these results is how much they could vary with changed assumptions. The figures for fatalities were based on air bursts, which would maximize destruction of the refineries. (As an excursion, U.S. fatalities were recalculated on the assumption of surface bursts, and use of the best fallout shelters within 2 miles of where each person lives. This reduced fatalities by one-third.) There was no data available on the types of Soviet residential construction in the vicinity of oil refineries: treating it parametrically gave casualty figures of about 1,500,000 if the construction is all houses, and about 800,000 if it is all apartment buildings. Perfect accuracy was assumed for missiles that are in fact somewhat inaccurate—some inaccuracy might reduce the extent of damage to the refineries, but it might well increase the number of deaths.

Case 3:

In order to examine the effects on civilian populations and economies of counterforce attacks, the study examined attacks on ICBM silos and attacks on silos, bomber bases, and missile submarine bases. Such attacks have received fairly extensive study in the executive branch in recent years, so OTA surveyed a number of these studies in order to determine the range of possible answers, and the variations in assumptions that produce such a range. An unclassified summary of this survey appears as appendix D of the full report. (The complete survey, classified secret, is available separately.)

A counterforce attack would produce relatively little direct blast damage to civilians and to economic assets; the main damage would come from radioactive fallout. The uncertainties in the effects of fallout are enormous, depending primarily on the weather and on the extent of fallout sheltering which the population makes use of. The calculations made by various agencies of the executive branch showed a range in "prompt fatalities" (almost entirely deaths from fallout within the first 30 days) from less than 1 to 11 percent of the U.S. population and from less than 1 to 5 percent of the Soviet population. This shows just how great a variation can be introduced by modifying assumptions regarding population distribution and shelter.

What can be concluded from this? First, if the attack involves surface bursts of many very large weapons, if weather conditions are unfavorable, and if no fallout shelters are created beyond those that presently exist, U.S. deaths could reach 20 million and Soviet deaths more than 10 million. (The difference is a result of geography; many Soviet strategic forces are so located that fallout from attacking them would drift mainly into sparsely populated areas or into China.) Second, effective fallout sheltering (which is not necessarily the same thing as a program—this assumes people are actually sheltered and actually remain there) could save many lives under favorable conditions, but even in the best imaginable case more than a million would die in either the United States or the U.S.S.R. from a counterforce attack. Third, the "limited nature" of counterforce attacks may not be as significant as the enormous uncertainty regarding their results.

There would be considerable economic damage and disruption as a result of such attacks. Almost all areas could, in principle, be decontaminated within a few months, but the loss of so many people and the interruption of economic life would be staggering blows. An imponderable, in thinking about the process of recovery, is the extent of any lasting psychological impacts.

Case 4:

In order to examine the kind of destruction that is generally thought of as the culmination of an escalatory process, the study looked at the consequences of a very large attack against a range of military and economic targets. Here too calculations that the executive branch has carried out in recent years were used. These calculations tend to assume that Soviet attacks on the United States would be a first strike, and hence use most of the Soviet arsenal, while U.S. attacks on the Soviet Union would be retaliatory strikes, and hence use only those weapons that might survive a Soviet counterforce attack. However, the difference in damage to civilian populations and economies between a "first strike" and a "second strike" seems to lie within the range of uncertainty created by other factors.

The resulting deaths would be far beyond any precedent. Executive branch calculations show a range of U.S. deaths from 35 to 77 percent (i.e., from 70 million to 160 million dead), and Soviet deaths from 20 to 40 percent of the population. Here again the range reflects the difference made by varying assumptions about population distribution and sheltering, and to a lesser extent differences in assumptions about the targeting policy of the attacker. Soviet casualties are smaller than U.S. casualties because a greater proportion of the Soviet population lives in rural areas, and because U.S. weapons (which have lower average yields) produce less fallout than Soviet weapons.

Some excursions have been run to test the effect of deliberately targeting population rather than killing people as a side effect of attacking economic and military targets. They show that such a change in targeting could kill somewhere between 20 million and 30 million additional people on each side, holding other assumptions constant.

These calculations reflect only deaths during the first 30 days. Additional millions would be injured, and many would eventually die from lack of adequate medical care. In addition, millions of people might starve or freeze during the following winter, but it is not possible to estimate how many. Attempts to calculate the further millions who might eventually die of latent radiation effects are shown in chapter V of the full report.

What is clear is that from the day the survivors emerged from their fallout shelters, a kind of race for survival would begin. One side of the race would be the restoration of production: production of food, of energy, of clothing, of the means to repair damaged machinery, of goods that might be used for trade with countries that had not fought in the war, and even of military weapons and supplies. The other side of the race would be consumption of goods that had survived the attack, and the wearing-out of surviving machines. If production rises to the rate of consumption before stocks are exhausted, then viability has been achieved and economic recovery has begun. If not, then each postwar year would see a lower level of economic activity than the year before, and the future of civilization itself in the nations attacked would be in doubt. This report cannot predict whether this race for economic viability would be won. The answer would lie in the effectiveness of postwar social and economic organization as much as in the amount of actual physical damage. There is a controversy in the literature on the subject as to whether a postattack economy would be based on centralized planning (in which case how would the necessary data and planning time be obtained?), or to individual initiative and decentralized decision-making (in which case who would feed the refugees, and what would serve for money and credit?).

An obviously critical question is the impact that a nuclear attack would have on the lives of those who survive it. The case descriptions in the full report discuss the possibilities of economic, political, social, and psychological disruption or collapse. However, the recital of possibilities and uncertainties may fail to convey the overall situation of the survivors, especially the survivors of a large attack that included urban-industrial targets. In an effort to provide a more concrete understanding of what a world after a nuclear war would be like, OTA commissioned a work of fiction that appears in appendix C of the full report. It presents some informed speculation about what life would be like in Charlottesville, Va., assuming that this city escaped direct damage from the attack. The kind of detail that such an imaginative account presents—detail that proved to be unavailable for a comparable Soviet city—adds a dimension to the more abstract analysis in the body of the full report.

Civil Defense:

Chapter III of the full report provides some basic information about civil defense measures, discusses the way in which they might mitigate the effects of nuclear attack, and discusses the uncertainties regarding their effectiveness. There is a lively controversy among experts as to the effectiveness of existing Soviet civil defense programs, and another controversy as to whether existing U.S. programs ought to be changed. The major points in dispute were identified, but no attempt was made to assess the merits of the arguments. For the purposes of this study, it was assumed that the existing civil defense programs, as described in the full report, would be in effect, and that a full-scale preattack evacuation of cities (sometimes called "crisis relocation") would not take place. This assumption was made because it appeared to be the only way to describe existing vulnerabilities while avoiding predictions about the course of events leading up to a nuclear war. While both the U.S. and the Soviet Governments profess to believe that urban evacuation prior to an attack on cities would save lives, ordering such an evacuation would be a crisis management move as well as a civil defense precaution.

Long-Term Effects:

While the immediate damage from the blasts would be long term in the sense that the damage could not be quickly repaired, there would be other effects which might not manifest themselves for some years after the attack. It is well established that levels of radiation too low (or too slowly absorbed) to cause immediate death or even illness will nevertheless have adverse effects on some fraction of a population receiving them. A nuclear attack would certainly produce both somatic effects (largely cancer) and genetic effects, although there is uncertainty about the number of victims. OTA calculated the ranges of such effects that might be produced by each of the attack cases analyzed. Cancer deaths and those suffering some form of genetic damage would run into the millions over the 40 years following the attack. For the comprehensive attack (Case 4), it appears that cancer deaths and genetic effects in a country attacked would be small relative to the numbers of immediate deaths, but that radiation effects elsewhere in the world would appear more significant. For counterforce attacks, the effects would be significant both locally and worldwide.

A 1975 study by the National Academy of Sciences (NAS)[1] addressed the question of the possibility of serious ecological damage, and concluded that while one cannot say just how such damage would occur, it cannot be ruled out. This conclusion still stands, although the NAS report may have been more alarmist about the possibility of damage to the ozone layer than recent research would support.

The results of the case studies are summarized in [Table 3].

SECTION 3.—UNCERTAINTIES

There are enormous uncertainties and imponderables involved in any effort to assess the effects of a nuclear war, and an effort to look at the entire range of effects compounds them. Many of these uncertainties are obvious ones: if the course of a snowstorm cannot be predicted 1 day ahead in peacetime, one must certainly be cautious about predictions of the pattern of radioactive fallout on some unknown future day. Similar complexities exist for human institutions: there is great difficulty in predicting the peacetime course of the U.S. economy, and predicting its course after a nuclear war is a good deal more difficult. The full report highlights the importance of three categories of uncertainties:

• Uncertainties in calculations of deaths and of direct economic damage resulting from the need to make assumptions about matters such as time of day, time of year, wind, weather, size of bombs, exact location of the detonations, location of people, availability and quality of sheltering, etc.
• Effects that would surely take place, but whose magnitude cannot be calculated. These include the effects of fires, the shortfalls in medical care and housing, the extent to which economic and social disruption would

Table 3 Summary of Effects

Case	Description	Main causes of civilian damage	Immediate deaths	Middle-term effects	Long-term effects
1	Attack on single city: Detroit and Leningrad; 1 weapon or 10 small weapons.	Blast, fire, & loss of infrastructure; fallout is elsewhere.	200,000–2,000,000	Many deaths from injuries; center of city difficult to rebuild.	Relatively minor.
2	Attack on oil refineries, limited to 10 missiles.	Blast, fire, secondary fires, fallout. Extensive economic problems from loss of refined petroleum.	1,000,000–5,000,000	Many deaths from injuries; great economic hardship for some years; particular problems for Soviet agriculture and for U.S. socioeconomic organization.	Cancer deaths in millions only if attack involves surface bursts.
3	Counterforce attack; includes attack only on ICBM silos as a variant.	Some blast damage if bomber and missile submarine bases attacked.	1,000,000–20,000,000	Economic impact of deaths; possible large psychological impact.	Cancer deaths and genetic effects in millions; further millions of effects outside attacked countries.

4	Attack on range of military and economic targets using large fraction of existing arsenal.	Blast and fallout; subsequent economic disruption; possible lack of resources to support surviving population or economic recovery. Possible breakdown of social order. Possible incapacitating psychological trauma.	20,000,000–160,000,000	Enormous economic destruction and disruption. If immediate deaths are in low range, more tens of millions may die subsequently because economy is unable to support them. Major question about whether economic viability can be restored—key variables may be those of political and economic organization. Unpredictable psychological effects.	Cancer deaths and genetic damage in the millions; relatively insignificant in attacked areas, but quite significant elsewhere in the world. Possibility of ecological damage.

For each case, the first section describes a Soviet attack on the United States, and the following section a U.S. attack on the Soviet Union.

magnify the effects of direct economic damage, the extent of bottlenecks and synergistic effects, the extent of disease, etc.

• Effects that are possible, but whose likelihood is as incalculable as their magnitude. These include the possibility of a long downward economic spiral before viability is attained, the possibility of political disintegration (anarchy or regionalization), the possibility of major epidemics, and the possibility of irreversible ecological changes.

One major problem in making calculations is to know where the people will be at the moment when the bombs explode. Calculations for the United States are generally based on the 1970 census, but it should be borne in mind that the census data describes where people's homes are, and there is never a moment when everybody in the United States is at home at the same time. If an attack took place during a working day, casualties might well be higher since people would be concentrated in factories and offices (which are more likely to be targets) rather than dispersed in suburbs. For the case of the Soviet population, the same assumption is made that people are at home, but the inaccuracies are compounded by the unavailability of detailed information about just where the Soviet rural population lives. The various calculations that were used made varying, though not unreasonable assumptions about population location.

A second uncertainty in calculations has to do with the degree of protection available. There is no good answer to the question: "Would people use the best available shelter against blast and fallout?" It seems unreasonable to suppose that shelters would not be used, and equally unreasonable to assume that at a moment of crisis all available resources would be put to rational use. (It has been pointed out that if plans worked, people behaved rationally, and machinery were adequately maintained, there would be no peacetime deaths from traffic accidents.) The Defense Civil Preparedness Agency has concluded from public opinion surveys that in a period of severe international crisis about 10 percent of all Americans would leave their homes and move to a "safer" place (spontaneous evacuation); more reliable estimates are probably impossible, but it could make a substantial difference to the casualty figures.

A third uncertainty is the weather at the time of the attack at the various places where bombs explode. The local wind conditions, and especially the amount of moisture in the air, may make an enormous difference in the number and spread of fires. Wind conditions over a wider area determine the extent and location of fallout contamination. The time of year has a decisive effect on the damage that fallout does to agriculture—while an attack in January might be expected to do only indirect damage (destroying farm machinery or the fuel to run it), fallout when plants are young can kill them, and fallout just before harvesttime would probably make it unsafe to get the harvest in. The time of year also has direct effects on population death—the attack in the dead of winter, which might not directly damage agriculture, may lead to greater deaths from fallout radiation (because of the difficulty of improvising fallout protection by moving frozen dirt) and from cold and exposure.

The question of how rapid and efficient economic recovery would be—or indeed whether a genuine recovery would be possible at all—raises questions that seem to be beyond calculation. It is possible to calculate direct economic damage by making assumptions about the size and exact location of bomb explosions, and the hardness of economic assets; however, such calculations cannot address the issues of bottlenecks and of synergy. Bottlenecks would occur if a key product that was essential for many other manufacturing processes could no longer be produced, or (for the case of a large attack) if an entire industrial sector were wiped out. In either case, the economic loss would greatly exceed the peacetime value of the factories that were actually destroyed. There does not appear to be any reliable way of calculating the likelihood or extent of bottlenecks because economic input/output models do not address the possibility or cost of substitutions across sectors. Apart from the creation of bottlenecks, there could be synergistic effects: for example, the fire that cannot be controlled because the blast destroyed fire stations, as actually happened at Hiroshima. Here, too, there is no reliable way to estimate the likelihood of such effects: would radiation deaths of birds and the destruction of insecticide factories have a synergistic effect? Another uncertainty is the possibility of organizational bottlenecks. In the most obvious instance, it would make an enormous difference whether the President of the United States survived. Housing, defined as a place where a productive worker lives as distinct from shelter for refugees, is another area of uncertainty. Minimal housing is essential if production is to be restored, and it takes time to rebuild it if the existing housing stock is destroyed or is beyond commuting range of the surviving (or repaired) workplaces. It should be noted that the United States has a much larger and more dispersed housing stock than does the Soviet Union, but that American workers have higher minimum standards.

There is a final area of uncertainty that this study does not even address, but which could be of very great importance. Actual nuclear attacks, unlike those described in the full report, would not take place in a vacuum. There would be a series of events that would lead up to the attack, and these events could markedly change both the physical and the psychological vulnerability of a population to a nuclear attack. Even more critical would be the events after the attack. Assuming that the war ends promptly, the terms on which it ends could greatly affect both the economic condition and the state of mind of the population. The way in which other countries are affected could determine whether the outside world is a source of help or of further danger. The postattack military situation (and nothing in this study addresses the effects of nuclear attacks on military power) could not only determine the attitude of other countries, but also whether limited surviving resources are put to military or to civilian use.

Moreover, the analyses in this study all assume that the war would end after the hypothetical attack. This assumption simplifies analysis, but it might not prove to be the case. How much worse would the situation of the survivors be if, just as they were attempting to restore some kind of economy following a massive attack, a few additional weapons destroyed the new centers of population and of government?

REFERENCE

1. *Long-Term Worldwide Effects of Multiple Nuclear-Weapons Detonations* (Washington, D.C.: National Academy of Sciences, 1975).

XII

EPILOGUE: OPTIONS AND STRATEGIES

For many years after the Second World War, the United States enjoyed a period that the late sociologist C. Wright Mills called the "American celebration"—a time when the stability of American institutions seemed assured, prosperity was taken for granted, and the American way of life was held up as a shining example for other countries to follow.

In the 1980s that period of serenity seems very distant. Dramatic changes have shaken the foundations of American institutions and values. Urban riots in the 1960s brought home the depth of racism in American society. The womens' movement forced a recognition of how deeply the American way of life has been rooted in the subordination of half the population. The war in Vietnam threw America's role in the larger world into question. And the economic crises of the 1970s and 1980s—inflation, unemployment, and shortages in housing and energy—shattered the myth of stable American affluence. All of this has brought a deep and continuing sense of crisis to American society and a wide variety of proposals for social, political, and economic change. The articles in this final chapter begin to explore some of the alternatives open to us in the 1980s and beyond.

One broad program for change is outlined in "Building a Democratic Economy," by Gar Alperovitz and Jeff Faux. They argue that the unresolved problems of American society will lead inexorably to some kind of intensified social and economic planning, aimed at bringing an increasingly unmanageable society under control. The question is, planning by whom, and for what ends? One direction, much favored by corporate interests, employs the rhetoric of free enterprise, but

531

actually uses the power of government to support and subsidize private profit while holding down wages and reducing social services. A second direction, already foreshadowed in some of our earlier articles (especially the selection by Currie, Dunn, and Fogarty, in Chapter 3), is toward greater public responsibility for economic life—toward "an economy that serves human priorities first."

Achieving that kind of economy once seemed like a utopian dream, fit only for romantic visionaries. But in the past few years, more and more talent and energy have been devoted to outlining tough-minded, practical social policies that could help bring a more humane economy and society into reality. Out of a wealth of possible articles, we have chosen Leonard Rodberg's careful, technical analysis of the way in which a serious commitment to solar power could help solve two pressing social problems—energy shortages and unemployment—at once.

The articles by Rodberg and Alperovitz and Faux point toward one set of options for confronting the crisis in American institutions. But, as Richard Barnet shows, a more democratic, humane society is by no means the only possible outcome of that crisis. A more ominous possibility is suggested by the rise of what Barnet calls the "lifeboat ethic"—the morality of an "age of scarcity," in which those who have, defend themselves against the needs of those who don't. At home, the "lifeboat ethic" means increasing neglect of the inner cities, the unemployed, and the poor; overseas, it means fortifying ourselves militarily and economically against the demands of the growing mass of hungry poor in the underdeveloped world. Barnet paints a bleak scenario of what may happen if the lifeboat ethic comes to dominate our public policies: a fortress society, continually threatened by terrorism and sinking steadily into authoritarianism and repression.

36
BUILDING A DEMOCRATIC ECONOMY

Gar Alperovitz and Jeff Faux

The energy crisis, and the unsolved problems of stagflation, urban decay, health care, and environmental degradation, are driving the final set of nails into the coffin of generalized Keynesian economics. The post-World War II era, in which the Federal Government's role was mostly limited to supplying dollars and credit to the corporate-dominated marketplace, is ending. In almost every major area of the economy the Federal Government will have to intervene much more directly or economic conditions will continue to deteriorate. This is not necessarily a matter of socialism. As Nobel Prize winning economist Wassily Leontief has said, planning will come, "not because some wild radicals demand it, but because businessmen will demand it to keep the system from sputtering to a halt."

The interest of the enlightened corporate community is not, of course, in planning for its own sake; it is in specific plans that will assure that Government intervention will serve their interests. These include tax and other subsidies to capital, sufficient unemployment and low social welfare programs to keep wages down, and elimination of consumer and environmental restraints on corporate operations. Financier [Felix] Rohatyn has even proposed the resurrection of the Reconstruction Finance Corporation of Depression days, which would formalize direct subsidies to ailing corporations so that firms like Lockheed would not have to go to the Congress every time they needed more Government money.

This is not a new plan for business. What is new is that the growing complexity of the economy, coupled with the deteriorating economic climate, is forcing businessmen—reluctantly but surely—to become more open and explicit in their demands for a strong Government authority to implement *their plans*.

The ideology of American business still opposes more Government planning, and at this stage sophisticated business leaders are still trying to convince their more conservative friends. This ideological opposition suits corporate interests well; it ensures that the initial forms of planning that survive the process of political compromise will be as accommodating as possible to their interests—just as the American Medical Association's long opposition to the initial planning of health delivery we call Medicare ensured that the program would fill the doctors' pockets.

This same political bind trapped efforts during the New Deal to establish economic planning accountable to public rather than private interests. As Professor George Lodge of the Harvard Business School points out, Franklin Roosevelt failed to gain public understanding of the role of government planning as a *substitute* for the market when he had the political opportunity. The innovations of the New Deal were rationalized instead in terms of free enterprise mythology; even the Tennessee Valley Authority (TVA) was sold as an "inspiration" to private initiative. Ducking the ideological issue did not change the fact of Government intervention in the economy, but it permitted the corporate sector to narrow that intervention to the support of corporate goals while maintaining an ideology of free market capitalism.

If planning is to work for a majority of Americans, this ideological veil must be pierced. This does not mean we must raise the red flag of socialism in a still conservative America. It does mean we must directly confront the need for public control over major economic decisions now in the hands of the private sector. It means we must develop a practical, sensible alternative that uses the power of Government to construct an economy that serves human priorities first. At the same time, we must take seriously the development of new democratic arrangements to avoid the dangers of centralized bureaucratic power.

Political reality and common sense suggest that we begin to build an alternative to corporate-dominated planning with those ideas that have already been developed and those trends—however modest—that are already in motion. As we look around, we find a variety of ideas, precedents, and even budding institutions that might fit together in a program for a planned American economic democracy.

A good place to begin is where the shoe is pinching the average American: scarce jobs and high prices.

Jobs

If planning is to be democratic and responsive to human priorities, it must be understood by the average citizen. Employment goals, therefore, must be simple and clear. Full employment should not be a statistical abstraction, but rather the condition in which every American willing and able to work has a job.

By now we know that our present system will not produce full employment; even such defenders of capitalism as Milton Friedman and Barry Goldwater concede the point, which once was argued only by the Left.

The only direct way to achieve jobs for all is through Government-supported employment. This was the answer of the *original* Humphrey-Hawkins Bill, the Full Employment and Equal Opportunity Act of 1975. The bill called on the Federal Government to act as the employer of last resort, providing a public service job to any American who applied. These jobs would not have to be "make-work"; there is plenty of real work to be done in America. At the beginning, jobs would be created in health, housing, environment, education, and other areas of need. Specific priorities would be set by local community boards which could decide how best to use the Federally funded jobs to fulfill local plans.

These key ideas—first, a job for every American who wants one, and second, local democratic planning—were deleted from the bill in the name of political "realism."

True political realism—and a strategy that can accomplish meaningful objectives—dictates going back to the principles of the original Humphrey-Hawkins Bill, particularly now that we are beginning to come to grips with the energy issue. One result of guaranteeing jobs will be to increase resources available to solve energy problems. For example, public employment can be used to rebuild rail beds to accommodate expanded traffic for an energy-conserving transportation system. Such a program would further stimulate new productive jobs in the manufacture, operation, and maintenance of railroads and mass transit vehicles and equipment.

It has been estimated that if one-fifth of ground traffic were shifted to public transport, 1 million new jobs would be created by 1985, including 450,000 in manufacturing. A significant proportion of these workers could be drawn from the ranks of those no longer needed in the auto industry. Transportation is one example. Government investment in such priority areas as energy, housing, solar development, medical care, and other sectors could also be programmed to *lead* rather than follow private allocation of resources to various sectors of the economy.

Guaranteed employment and the rational planning of jobs generated by public funds would have two important implications for other economic policies: First, it would reduce the fear of unemployment and economic ruin that is at the heart of most resistance to change. Defense workers would be less resistant to cuts in the military budget if they *knew* they would have decent immediate replacement jobs. White workers would feel less threatened by blacks, men less threatened by women. Workers in general would be less fearful of environmental restrictions on business and of the introduction of labor-saving equipment.

Second, such policies could stabilize employment conditions in specific localities, reducing the waste associated with unstable private investment. They would not end migration from place to place, but could certainly reduce a substantial portion of migration within and between cities that is forced upon people by the loss of jobs. Community economic stability would contribute to a more stable tax base, reducing pressure on the local taxpayer. And states and localities would not be forced into what is often ruinous competition for the location of industry.

INFLATION

The reimposition of wage-price controls seems certain over the next few years.

Without controls, any significant effort to reduce unemployment will be thwarted by rising prices. The major issue of controls is one of fairness; unions must be assured that controls will not be used once again, as one Nixon Administration official put it, to "zap" labor.

But price-wage-profit controls are not, in themselves, an adequate long-range solution to the problem of inflation. In the absence of a positive plan for allocating resources, controls will distort investment and lead to inefficiencies and inequities. Any anti-inflation program ought to be aimed at clear goals that make sense and can gather popular political support. One strategy is to stabilize directly the price of the basic necessities—food, housing, medical care, and a minimum level of energy—which alone make up almost 70 per cent of what the average family spends on goods and services.

Partial precedents for such an approach have already been set for those at the lower end of the income scale. For example, food stamps, Medicare, housing allowances, and the growing use of rent control are a direct attempt to stabilize the costs of necessities. So are state proposals for "lifeline" electricity rates which fix the price of a minimum amount of electric power for residential users and the new Carter proposals to hold down heating oil prices. Over the coming period of scarcities, the principle will gradually have to be extended to other Americans beyond the poor, for both political and economic reasons.

But programs which merely subsidize low-income or other consumers increase total demand. If there are no increases in supply, the result is more pressure on costs. Medicare, which increased demand for health services without increasing or rationalizing the supply, is a classic example. Responsible planning requires that the supply of necessities be secured. For example, stabilizing housing prices will require direct public action to allocate the two most costly items in building a new home—land and capital. This means more public control and ownership of land.

Direct public land development is common in Europe. But even in America, such communities as Milwaukee, Wisconsin; San Diego, California; St. George, Vermont; and Yellow Springs, Ohio, are beginning to experiment with land banking and other forms of public development.

The dependence of housing on capital markets is well documented.

When the general demand for capital increases, mortgage money dries up and housing is not built. Chairman Henry Reuss of the House Banking and Currency Committee has proposed what might be a first step toward the allocation of capital to major national priorities. Reuss has suggested that the Federal Reserve Board allocate capital to the nation's most pressing needs—such as low and moderate-income housing and mass transit.

Stabilizing consumer prices also requires a direct public food policy. Over the coming decade, food prices will continue to rise. As they do, the growing power of consumer and urban constituencies will put these groups in a position to rewrite old legislation once considered the private domain of the agribusiness "farm bloc." One model for achieving lower consumer food prices is the Canadian approach to wheat. In Canada, low consumer prices are established and farm production costs are supplemented by direct payments. The basic approach has been instituted in such nations as Sweden, Norway, and Japan, and was proposed for the United States as far back as 1949 by the Truman Administration.

A direct approach to inflation which aims to stabilize the price of necessities would not attempt to stabilize all prices. Prices for non-necessities—particularly those which use large amounts of energy—could be allowed to rise: We need to heat New England homes at fair prices, but *not* to run private jets or yachts at low cost. Profit controls and public allocation of capital would prevent high-price sectors from drawing investment from the necessity-oriented industries.

CONSERVATION

A serious commitment to job security and price stability would obviously make a planned reduction in energy consumption much more acceptable to the American people. But in order to achieve low energy growth we need to change our lifestyles and attitudes, and ultimately our social values. This too requires planning. But the implications of such changes are so awesome that politicians—from the President down—have stuck to platitudes and moralisms. The time has come for us to think seriously about how we will rid ourselves of institutions that make it difficult for us to shift our values to accommodate the new world we are entering.

For example, it is clear that we must begin to place limits on a major source of consumer stimulation—advertising. The incessant psychological pressure on American consumers to buy more and more is wasteful in its own terms and incompatible with the long-term need to conserve resources and to rebuild our lifestyle around new environmental realities. Polaroid is now spending twelve dollars each on advertising to promote a new camera which costs twenty dollars to make.

And we must push even further. Given its dynamic of unrestricted growth, the modern corporation is, over the long run, incompatible with a planned conserving economy. This is particularly true of corporations which control energy resources. It is not just the monopolistic practices that make these firms unfit to be in charge of our energy resources; it is their inherent need for growth—a need which requires them to push sales and competition. Thus, even if successful antitrust actions could be brought against the largest of the multinational energy companies (as it was 1911), the basic problem would not be solved.

Virtually every other Western industrailized nation has concluded that rational energy and conservation policies will require public ownership. The Stevenson-Magnuson Bill, which calls for a publicly owned oil and gas corporation on public lands (where the bulk of reserves lie), is a reasonable first step in this direction.

Despite the popular American assumption, the experience in Europe and Canada shows that when taken seriously, public corporations can be at least as efficient as private ones. This is also the evidence from more than 2,000 publicly owned electric utilities in the United States. Moreover, publicly owned firms tend to be more accountable to the public (their books are open), and more responsive to major economic policy needs. For example, it makes economic sense for a public enterprise to consider the social costs of its location decisions since its owner, the public, will have to pay them.

Public ownership does not necessarily guarantee sound resource use. The TVA, for example, is hardly less growth-oriented than most private electric companies. It will be necessary, therefore, to add a further dimension to the concept of ownership—whether public or private. The larger public itself must assume the responsibility of *trusteeship* over the land and natural resources needed for the next generation, and it must set limits to our exploitation policies. Trusteeship concepts have already been recognized in preliminary form in several states which now permit citizen suits against public officials for failing to fulfill their responsibilities as trustees for the common interest in our resources.

ECONOMIC DEMOCRACY

The logic of economic planning raises in many minds the specter of centralized bureaucracy. The socialist Soviet Union—to use the most frequently cited example—seems little less growth-oriented than the capitalist United States, and it offers no model for democratic planning. The need for new values, therefore, goes beyond the question of private or public control. To a large degree it is the alienation of the individual from his work and his community that has crowned wasteful, mindless consumerism as the king of American values. The feeling of powerlessness in senseless, often degrading work makes many of us eager for the latest overpriced fantasy the market produces in response to our "needs." We must begin to build an economy in which the individual can gain more satisfaction in the very processes of work and citizenship. The question of values is a practical political issue.

Over the next decade and beyond, Americans will be asked to make major adjustments and sacrifices. Only when there is a sense of community and a sense of participation will such plans have the confidence and trust of the population.

One important step on the path to restoring a sense of community in America will be the encouragement of employee ownership and participation in management. Public enterprises could lead the way. Portions of ownership could be sold to employees who could also take on larger responsibilities for management—a practice growing in Europe, and to a small degree, here. Although still few in number, worker-owned firms are springing up in a variety of places in the United States. The Department of Commerce has even financed the purchase of some companies by their workers—a lathe manufacturer in Indiana, for example, and an asbestos plant in Vermont. Beyond this, the community or communities where the plants are located could participate in new forms of ownership. Three-way "joint ventures"—involving governments, employees, and investors—have a number of partial precedents in Europe (for example, the ownership of Volkswagen) and could make for eminently sensible arrangements in industries that depend on Government contracts and—like transportation, defense, and energy—are crucial to long-range planning.

The experience in both Europe and the United States with "quality of work" projects in which workers are given more responsibility and control over the workplace has shown that worker participation often dramatically improves productivity. Generally, the resistance to such efforts has come from labor unions suspicious of management and unsure of their role *and* from those levels of management that become superfluous once workers begin to run their own shops. But there are signs of increasing interest in worker self-management among progressive labor unions, and guaranteed employment policies could reduce anxiety about being laid off because of increased efficiency. In any event, worker participation is crucial to the building of new values and should be systematically expanded and supported through research experimentation, financial incentives, and, above all, through a national moral commitment.

Second, as we move deeper into a planned economy, it is imperative that we begin to widen participation in the planning process itself. Fortunately, we do not have to start from scratch. We have behind us some ten years of experience with various attempts at citizen participation and community planning—from urban renewal to transportation to anti-poverty programs. Hundreds of thousands of ordinary citizens have had experience in organizing their neighbors, demonstrating in front of city hall, interpreting zoning maps, making community surveys, and the like. Many critical skills needed to build the capacity for democratic planning have been learned.

But the experience of the last decade took place in an environment where planning itself had little meaning. What good did it do to participate in the planning of one's community if key variables—like the location of jobs and housing—were out of the control of the community? In the context of a national commitment to secure jobs and fair capital allocation, community planning would be much more relevant. Ultimately, *community* plans for population growth, job development, housing, and transportation could and should be the basis upon which national resources are allocated.

A "second generation" of community planning, therefore, would provide assistance to citizens in neighborhoods and towns and states to engage in serious planning around the question of what they want their town or neighborhood or state to look like. Attempts at democratic planning are under way in such cities as New York, Minneapolis, and Washington, D.C., and at the regional and state level, in Hawaii, Washington, Iowa, and a dozen other states. Given the resources and time, communities could also begin to build *local* alternatives to the profit-seeking, growth-oriented corporation.

This brief survey suggests that a number of building blocks for economic democracy are already at hand. Without a party, without a common ideology, without much communication, Americans at local, state, and national levels of politics are already trying to put the blocks in place. It also suggests a political strategy: The experience of economic democracy—on the assembly line, in the local co-op, at the neighborhood block club—can create an appetite, and thus a constituency, for more.

But unless we begin to cement these pieces together as parts of a truly alternative strategy, they will not hold. Taken *alone*, these proposals, bills, and grass-roots institutions are no match for the tightening alliance of big business and big government. Taken together, however, the elements begin to form a coherent framework for a popular politics. Such a politics, by building on the reality of economic planning, will have an advantage over a corporate ideology that must maintain the illusion of free enterprise.

Over the short term, business-oriented policies may well grow, but the problems they bring—unemployment, high prices, resource waste—are also likely to grow, and to deepen citizen awareness of the need for a new direction.

Our modern political experience, from the New Deal to last night's confrontation with the city council, tells us that a realistic challenge to corporate ideology will not be brought in by the back door. A real alternative requires real, mass-based politics. And a commitment to those politics can be inspired only if immediate campaigns are linked to something beyond a single issue or the election of a congenial personality. That something more is a conscious political vision.

Because we are Americans our vision must be practical. It must show how jobs can be provided for all, how prices of necessities can be stabilized, how new values can be encouraged. These are the true needs of the vast majority of citizens, so our vision must demonstrate how the majority can, in fact, achieve its goals. It must also have an overriding premise: The major decisions in our economy are now or will soon become explicitly political; democracy, therefore, cannot stand still. If it is to survive, it must be extended to the economy.

37
EMPLOYMENT IMPACT OF THE SOLAR TRANSITION

Leonard Rodberg

Since World War II, American consumption of energy has tripled.[1] Total automotive horsepower increased seven-fold, home heating systems converted from coal to oil and then to natural gas, energy-consuming air conditioners and home appliances became commonly available, new commercial buildings incorporated artificial, energy-wasteful environments, airline travel expanded, and thousands of miles of highways were constructed. Overall energy consumption rose exponentially, climbing at a rate of 3.5 percent per year. Fossil fuels were consumed as if their supplies were limitless. Of course, they are not, and we now face the task of undoing the damage wrought in this 25-year binge.

AN END TO EXPONENTIAL GROWTH

Beginning in 1970, domestic production of oil and gas began to fall. The natural limits on such nonrenewable fuels began to make themselves felt.

Excerpted from Leonard Rodberg, *Employment Impact of the Solar Transition*, U.S. Congress, Joint Economic Committee, 1979.

The periodic winter gas shortages, the brown-outs, and the 1973 oil crisis are all symptoms of the dilemma we face, addicted to fuels whose supply is running out. With rapidly rising prices and diminishing reserves, we have to begin a comprehensive transition in the energy we use and the way we use it.

One approach which has strong support is through the expanded use of coal and nuclear energy, including the gasification and liquefaction of coal. However, both of these energy sources impose significant external costs. The extraction of coal, whether from underground mines or from the stripmining of near-surface veins, has serious deleterious effects on land, water, and agriculture; the conversion of coal to gas and liquid fuels consumes vast amounts of increasingly scarce water; and the burning of growing quantities of coal can have disastrous climatologic and health consequences.[2]

Likewise, the increasing use of nuclear energy poses a wide variety of serious social problems. With the growth of the nuclear power industry will come a significant likelihood of a reactor meltdown, with potentially catastrophic consequences for nearby population centers. Problems of waste disposal remain unsolved. Safety and environmental pollution difficulties are serious. The danger of nuclear weapons proliferation as a result of the widespread availability of plutonium and enriched uranium are fearsome. And, finally, the security measures necessary to avoid theft and sabotage could severely restrict our liberty.[3]

In the face of these mounting problems, an alternative must be sought. Such a policy would address the combined effects of declining supplies of oil and gas, higher fuel prices, dependence on imported oil, and worsening ecological problems in an environmentally benign and economically efficient manner. It would emphasize the conservation of energy and the replacement of the nonrenewable fuels with renewable energy sources, primarily solar energy. These so-called "soft technologies" would adapt energy production more closely to needs of the particular end use, rather than producing energy uniformly in a centralized facility.[4] They would include increased end-use efficiency, active and passive solar heating and cooling on individual buildings and neighborhood units, fuel production from biomass sources and wastes, and dispersed on-site photovoltaic and wind powered electric generation.

Advocates of the coal and nuclear route, with its implication of continued energy growth, argue that this approach, in spite of its potential costs, is essential for economic growth. As one advocacy group put it, "Growth in energy use is necessary to our national prosperity and to provide the jobs that are needed today . . . the relationship between energy availability and jobs is direct and inevitable."[5] Clearly, many people still believe that continued growth in our consumption of energy, and especially of the nonrenewable fuels—oil, gas, coal and uranium—is still essential if every American is to have a chance at the good life.

We will show in this paper that this view is not correct. We will demonstrate that it is possible to produce the same goods and services, and to achieve a higher GNP, by emphasizing the conservation of energy and conversion to renewable energy sources. Conservation and renewable energy can be major growth industries in the decades ahead, contributing both to the health of our economy and our citizenry. Introduction of a broad range of currently feasible conservation measures can simultaneously cut the consumption of rapidly depleting energy resources and create hundreds of thousands of new jobs. The expansion of solar energy programs can create a permanent substitute for declining reserves of nonrenewable fuels and add millions of new jobs, particularly in urban areas where they are desperately needed. It can also reduce the outflow of dollars for imported oil and curb the inflationary effects of rapidly rising fuel prices.[6]

THE CONTINUING SHORTAGE OF JOBS

The United States continues to experience a failure to provide enough jobs for its citizens, especially for minority groups who suffer the highest rates of unemployment. In 1978 the unemployment rate still stood at 6 percent, with black unemployment at 12 percent and teenage unemployment at 16 percent; "disguised unemployment" makes the real situation twice as bad. Economists do not see any prospect for an early improvement in this poor economic performance, and many foresee a downturn in the coming months which will make this situation even worse.

Many analysts argue that energy growth is crucial to a reduction in unemployment. In reality, the purpose of what we commonly call "energy" is to reduce the need for human labor, exacerbating the problem of providing jobs for a growing labor force. Industry has increased its output by drawing on the apparently limitless supplies of fossil fuels while shrinking its labor force. As the Congressional Office of Technology Assessment has commented, "The national energy policy of the last several decades has been to replace human labor as rapidly as possible with petroleum energy."[7] Thus the same practices which are creating the energy shortage have also been responsible for the shortage of jobs.

The ready availability of cheap energy has reduced employment opportunities in the energy-consuming industries and led to a continuing displacement of workers onto an uncertain job market. The energy industry itself cannot take up the slack; it employs a small proportion (historically, about 2 percent) of the labor force, and energy-related employment has not been growing. Both producers and users of energy have taken advantage of the ready availability of inexpensive energy supplies to introduce highly automated, energy-consuming production techniques, reducing employment per unit of output first in agriculture, then in manufacturing, and, most recently, in the service sector. The economy has not grown because of rising energy consumption, but in spite of it. Total employment has increased because the total output of goods and, especially, of services has increased and overcome the "labor-saving"— that is, employment-reducing—effects of rising energy usage.°[8]

The Nation thus faces two difficult but related problems, the continuing shortage of jobs and the coming shortage of energy. The purpose of this paper is to show, with a specific plan, how large-scale investment in conservation and solar energy can contribute to the resolution of both problems. Most projections show only slow growth for the renewable energy technologies. However, these projections tend to be self-fulfilling prophecies. By assuming slow growth, they inhibit investment and thus insure slow growth. We present a positive scenario that examines the implications of rapid growth, to stimulate discussion and interest in this possiblity.

The slow-growth scenario is favored by many economists who view the introduction of solar energy at this time as economically "inefficient." They argue that, at current fuel prices, interest rates, and lending terms, the average consumer would, in many cases, experience higher annual costs for energy through such a purchase. However, when viewed from the perspective of national resource use, such reasoning is shortsighted. The results of this study show that, within a few years after the onset of substantial conservation and solar investment, the savings from reduced use of nonrenewable fuels will far exceed the investment, allowing funds to be shifted from energy into the purchase of other goods and services. The solar transition *is* economically "efficient." . . .

Overview and Conclusions

1. Baseline Projections: Business as Usual

Conventional projections of energy consumption assume that the past relation between gross national product and energy consumption will continue into the future. Recently they have been assuming a rise in the price of the nonrenewable fuels and, as a consequence, a slightly less rapid rise in demand for energy.

°Economists often argue that such "labor-saving" measures increase economic "efficiency" by freeing workers to perform other necessary tasks. However, when the economy is not able to provide jobs for all who need them, and when energy supplies are limited, the opposite is true. If the workers who are displaced cannot find employment, they must be supported by unemployment insurance and welfare while being economically unproductive; those who do find employment will consume additional energy in their new jobs, thus accelerating the depletion of scarce energy resources.

Until about 4 years ago, most projections of energy demand envisioned an aggregate demand by the year 2000 of 190 quads° per year, 2 ½ times our current consumption. Now, with evident signs of a decline in the rate of energy growth, projections are beginning to show more moderate increases. A "consensus" prepared by the Edison Electric Institute calls for consumption of about 150 quads in the year 2000, twice our current usage.[9] They assume continuing growth at a rate of about 3.0 percent per year, somewhat less than the pre-1973 growth rate of 3.5 percent but still a continuation of exponential growth. In spite of clear signs of an approaching price and supply crunch, they continue to assume that energy consumption will grow exponentially out to the next century.[10]

These "business as usual" projections of energy consumption assume that past practices will continue into the future and that new supplies of the energy sources we use today—coal, oil, natural gas, and uranium—will be discovered as current sources are depleted. They assume that alternative sources of energy—solar heating and cooling, wind power, etc.—will play a small role during this period, and they foresee an ever-growing consumption of the nonrenewable energy sources. As oil and natural gas become increasingly scarce and expensive, they forecast a shift to coal and nuclear energy and, especially, to electricity produced by these fuels.

In this study we will use, as our reference base, an energy projection prepared by Data Resources, Inc., for the period 1977–90 using macroeconomic assumptions developed by the Bureau of Labor Statistics of the U.S. Department of Labor.[11] DRI assumes that oil prices will rise 7.5 percent per year to $1.31 per gallon by 1990, while natural gas prices rise 3.5 percent per year to $3.76 per thousand cubic feet.† They then forecast an energy growth rate of 2.98 percent per year and total consumption of primary fuels in 1990 of 110.7 quads. Extended to the year 2000, this yields a total annual consumption at that time of 148 quads. In the DRI projections, the consumption of energy by sector and fuel type is [shown in Table 1].

Consumption of every energy source increases, but coal and nuclear power meet most of the increased demand, largely through their use in electricity production. Nevertheless, petroleum and natural gas are assumed to be still available and, indeed, are consumed in even greater quantities than today. This is possible only because of the assumption that

---

° We use the common measure of energy output, the "quad," or one quadrillion (10^{15}) British thermal units (Btu). A quad is approximately equal to the energy supplied by 172 million barrels of oil, 42 million tons of bituminous coal, 0.98 trillion cubic feet of natural gas, or 293 billion kilowatt-hours of electricity. In 1977 the United States consumed 75.9 quads of primary fuels.

† Here, and throughout this study, we use 1978 dollars.

Table 1 *Energy Consumption [Quads per year]*

	Coal		Natural gas		Petroleum		Nuclear		Hydro		Total	
	1977	1990	1977	1990	1977	1990	1977	1990	1977	1990	1977	1990
Household and commercial	0.2	0.1	8.3	9.5	6.6	8.8					15.1	18.4
Industrial	4.2	6.1	7.2	7.9	7.3	11.3					18.7	25.3
Transportation					19.2	21.0					19.2	21.0
Electric Utilities	10.3	21.9	2.4	1.2	4.6	5.3	2.2	13.3	3.0	4.3	22.5	46.0
Total	14.7	28.1	17.9	18.6	37.7	46.4	2.2	13.3	3.0	4.3	75.5	110.7

increasing quantities of these fuels are imported (e.g., 57 percent of the petroleum is imported). However, U.S. demand will be competing with the increasing demand from other countries, including growing Third World economies, and many analysts foresee a shortfall in world supply between 1985 and 1995. For instance, the Report of the MIT Workshop on Alternative Energy Strategies concluded that, even in its moderate growth model, "energy demand growth quickly outpaces plausible projections of potential supply. It follows that historically high growth rates of energy use . . . projected into the future are simply not realistic."[10] As noted in the introduction, this is just one of a number of potential barriers to this scenario.

The Historic Relation of Jobs and Energy Over three-fifths of all energy use takes place in the industrial and commercial sectors, where goods and services are produced and workers employed. Yet, the major consumers of energy employ relatively few people. Between 1948 and 1970, energy use by the goods-producing sectors° rose 120 percent, while their employment declined 1.4 percent; by contrast, energy use in the provision of services increased 62 percent, but employment gained 75 percent.[12]

Six industries have historically consumed the lions' share of the energy used by industry. In 1968 (the year of the most recent detailed study of industrial energy use), the primary metals, chemical, food, paper, stone-clay-glass products, and the petroleum and coal processing industries used 68 percent of all energy used by industry, yet employed only 25 percent of all industrial workers and just 7 percent of the Nation's total work force.[13,1] Between 1950 and 1971, their work force increased only 2.5 percent, while their energy consumption increased 106 percent.[14]

These relationships will probably continue in a period when energy prices are rising. The response of business to rising energy prices and the prospect of shortages is difficult to forecast, since we have not encountered such a period before. Economic projections must be made on the basis of the past, but we have evidence only from a period in which energy prices were falling and supplies were plentiful.

Much will depend on the response of public policy to this new situation, as well as on the overall economic environment. Businesses may reduce output, and thus their demand for labor, in the face of higher energy prices (the "income effect"), or they may call upon more labor and capital resources to replace energy (the "substitution effect"). Studies

---

°In BLS categories, the goods-producing sectors are agriculture, forestry, fisheries, mining, construction, and manufacturing; the service-producing sectors are transportation, communication, utilities, wholesale and retail trade, finance, insurance, real estate, services, and government.

by Jorgenson and his coworkers suggest that the substitution effect will predominate, but only slightly. Using a model driven by cost-minimizing business behavior, they find that an average increase of 54 percent in energy prices will reduce energy consumption in the year 2000 by 38 percent and raise labor demand by 1.5 percent.[14,15]

The Bureau of Labor Statistics of the U.S. Department of Labor carries on a continuing program of economic projections, in order to provide forecasts of labor demand in particular industries and occupations.[16] These projections are based upon expected levels of employment and labor productivity, with price variables playing a secondary role. Thus, though they make use of the DRI projections to ensure that their predicted level of energy production is compatible with such "mainstream" energy forecasts, they do not incorporate the effects of rising energy prices on other categories of consumption. Nevertheless, since these effects are, at this point, uncertain but likely to be small—given sufficient time for adjustment to new patterns of consumption, new transportation modes, etc.—the BLS projections seem quite usable.

The BLS forecasts that the labor force will grow, between 1977 and 1990, from 99.5 million to between 113.5 and 125.6 billion.[17] This is an average growth rate of 1.4 percent, considerably slower than the 2.3 percent growth rate that characterized the 1970–77 period.

Within the BLS projections, the growing consumption of energy is not accompanied by a corresponding rise in employment in the energy industry or in the industries which use that energy. Rather, it leads to a continuing relative shift of employment away from these sectors to the more labor-intensive service sectors. [Table 2] shows the projected change in employment shares, as civilian employment rises from 90.5 million to a projected level of 114.0 million.

More than three out of every four workers entering the labor force in this period will have to find a job in the service sectors where, quite frequently, wages are low and jobs provide less than full-time work. In 1976 the average wage in the service-producing sectors was $4.45 per hour, only 79 percent of the average wage in the goods-producing sectors.[1]

Bullard has argued that escalating energy prices will make "planned obsolescence" more expensive and will favor the manufacture of more durable products.[18] Manufactured goods will become more expensive relative to less energy-intensive services, consumers will buy them less frequently, and they will have to last longer and be maintained better. This will result in fewer assembly-line jobs and more maintenance and repair jobs.

The new jobs in the energy industry, which are of primary interest to us in this study, are largely related to the expansion of electricity production. They are jobs constructing the needed electric plants, mining and refining coal and uranium, and operating powerplants. It is characteristic of

Table 2

	Increase in employment, 1977–90	Share of total employment (percent)	
		1977	1990
Goods-producing sectors[1]	4,797,000	26.8	25.5
Energy-intensive industries	(373,000)	(4.1)	(3.6)
Service-producing sectors[1]	18,352,000	71.2	72.6
Energy industry	351,000	2.0	1.9
Total	23,500,000	100.0	100.0

[1]The energy producing and distributing industries have been removed from these sectors and included with the "Energy industry."

these occupations that large-scale migrations of workers will be required, as fuel sources in particular locales are exploited and then depleted, and as health and safety requirements demand the remote location of power-plants. These can impose severe dislocations and social costs on workers and their communities.

In general, this "business as usual" projection envisions an economic environment in which it will be difficult to achieve high levels of employment. With energy prices rising relative to other costs, increasing portions of the consumer's dollar will be taken up with direct and indirect energy costs. Until energy conservation measures can be undertaken, or alternative living modes adopted which can reduce energy consumption, relatively less income will be available for the purchase of other goods and services having a low energy, and high job, content. In this setting, conservation and renewable energy become essential parts of any strategy for full employment.

2. Toward Conservation and Renewable Energy

To avoid the manifold deleterious consequences of continued reliance on nonrenewable fuels, we must undertake an active program stressing conservation and renewable energy (CARE). There would be a strong emphasis on conserving energy, that is, on making the most efficient possible use of the energy we do consume, and on conversion of an increasing portion of our energy consumption from nonrenewable fossil fuels and uranium to solar energy in its various direct and indirect forms (solar heating, wind, biomass). Total fuel consumption would be capped and ultimately reduced, and the mix of energy sources would be changed, with an increasing portion coming from renewable sources.

The Conservation of Energy   In general, energy consumption can be reduced by (i) performing the same activity in a more energy-efficient manner, (ii) using energy that is now wasted, and (iii) changing behavior to reduce the need for energy. All three should be undertaken, though the last—involving modifications in our housing patterns, our transportation systems, the way we produce goods and services—will require more time to implement and more sweeping social changes. Our present patterns have been developed in an era when energy was cheap and its supply thought to be endless. As we realize that these conditions no longer hold, we may begin making significant changes in the way society organizes its living and working activities.

Very large savings appear possible even without this. With relatively modest efforts in the first two categories, savings approaching one-half of current consumption can be made.[19] There are great opportunities for energy conservation, not just because we have been using energy wastefully, but also because we have been using it inappropriately. We have been using fuels and processes which produce very high temperatures (hundreds or even thousands of degrees) to heat our homes 10° or 20°, with excess heat simply thrown out into the atmosphere. By producing energy that is tailored to its use, and extracting all the useful work from it, we can make significant gains over our past inefficient practices. Furthermore, conservation is not expensive; estimates of the cost of conservation measures range from one-half to one-tenth the cost of adding an equivalent amount of energy from new sources. [20,21,22]

It should be emphasized that, as we (and most analysts) use the concept, "conservation" does not mean the curtailment of energy-using activities. Rather, as the CONAES Demand and Conservation Panel defined it, conservation includes "technological and procedural changes that allow us to reduce demand for energy (or specific scarce fuels) without corresponding reductions in the goods and services we enjoy."[23]

New Sources of Energy   We will need some additions to our current supply of energy, not just conservation of what we use, and we will soon have to begin replacing fossil fuels with renewable sources of energy. We have to create an entirely new industry to produce, install, and maintain solar energy units of all kinds—hot water and air collectors and storage units, photovoltaic generators, biomass converters, wind machines, and so on. In the 1950's, a national decision created the massive Federal highway system and, in the 1960's, the space program. Each involved investments of billions of dollars and hundreds of thousands of jobs. In the same way, we need to move toward a national program of solar energy production and conversion. Solar energy could be the technology that lifts the economy out of the doldrums of the 1970's into a more prosperous period in the 1980's.

We will look at projections to the year 1990, assuming that such a program is initiated. As a baseline, we use BLS projections for the economy in 1990. The year 1990 may be looked on as a typical year in a 50-year transition from dependence on nonrenewable fuels to nearly complete reliance on renewable energy sources, primarily energy from the sun. Most homes, office buildings, and factories have useful lives of the order of 50 years. Thus, about 50 years are required to replace this building convert it to energy-conserving, renewable resources.

One frequently hears expressions of concern for the employment impact of such alternative energy policies. These reflect doubts over the ability of the alternative approach to provide the energy that industry needs, in order to operate the machines on which many workers depend for their jobs. The approach adopted in this paper assumes that no policy will be adopted that does not provide sufficient energy to fuel the economy and, especially, its productive machinery. Thus the approach incorporates ways of substituting, step by step, renewable energy sources for nonrenewable ones. It assumes that there will be no reduction in the use of conventional energy sources, and no reduction in the supply of conventional fuels, at whatever price, until an alternative is available in sufficient quantity to meet the demand.

Elements of a CARE Strategy   An extensive range of measures can be encompassed within a CARE strategy. Those postulated to be installed and operational by 1990 include the following:

(1) For residential and commercial use:
Reduction of heat loss through additional insulation, efficiency improvements in the use of heating and cooling units, and careful attention to the flow of heat in the building and through its outer "envelope."

Improved energy efficiency of equipment and appliances.

Increased heat absorption from the sun through passive solar designs.

Solar water and space heating through active fluid collection and circulation.

(2) For industrial use:
More efficient industrial practices, recovery and reuse of waste heat, and use of recycled materials.

Generation of electricity as a byproduct of heat and steam production ("cogeneration").

Solar energy collectors and solar-powered heat engines.

(3) For transportation:
Increased automotive efficiency.

Increased use of urban mass transit and interurban rail and other energy-efficient modes of transportation.

(4) For portable fuels, production of methane and alcohol from agricultural and urban wastes.

(5) For electricity production:

Photovoltaic cells, including concentrators and cogeneration, on homes, commercial and industrial buildings.

Wind-powered electric generators.

Solar-powered heat engine-generator systems.

Other uses of solar energy, especially for cooling purposes, have not been included in the estimates made in this study because of the cost and underdeveloped nature of these systems. Similarly, capturing other forms of solar energy, such as ocean thermal energy, has been proposed, but such systems have not yet reached a sufficient stage of development to be able to estimate their energy and employment potential.

Energy Goals   The energy savings achieved, and the number of jobs produced by these measures, depend upon the scale of investment in them. For this study we assume a set of national goals, projecting the achievement of a specified level of implementation for each measure by the turn of the century. (With different goals, the results will be scaled up or down proportionately.) The goals we assume are [shown in Table 3].

These goals are ambitious but achievable with the vigorous support of public policy.

CARE-Related Employment   To meet them, we assume that investment in conservation and renewable energy builds up over a 5-year pe-

Table 3

Measure	Goal for year 2000
Residential use:	
Conservation	50 percent saving.°
Active and passive solar	100 percent of new homes; 50 percent of existing homes.
Commercial use:	
Conservation	50 percent saving.°
Active solar	50 percent of all buildings.
Industrial use:	
Conservation	40 percent saving by 1990.°
Cogeneration	100 percent of all usable sites.
Active solar	25 percent of all process heat.
Transportation	No specific goal.
Portable fuels	Conversion of 50 percent of waste products.
Solar electricity	25 percent of current electricity production.

°Energy saving goals refer to the consumption of delivered energy at the site of end use.

Table 4

	Annual investment (billions, 1978)	Number of jobs (thousands)		
		Direct	Indirect	Total
Residential:				
Building conservation	$5.7	125	74	199
Appliance conservation	1.4	29	23	52
Passive solar	.7	15	11	26
Active solar	14.8	266	244	510
Commercial:				
Conservation	2.4	52	34	86
Active solar	6.6	119	109	228
Industrial:				
Conservation	1.5	20	25	45
Cogeneration	3.8	51	62	113
Active solar	12.1	163	198	361
Transportation	—	—	—	—
Portable fuels	4.3	89	77	166
Electricity:				
Photovoltaics	3.6	69	53	122
Wind	5.3	91	81	172
Heat engines	3.4	31	59	90
Total	65.6	1,120	1,050	2,170

riod preceding 1985, with a constant level of investment thereafter.° This investment creates jobs which can be estimated using the input-output tables developed by the Bureau of Labor Statistics. These show the number of jobs in each industry required to produce a dollar of final output. . . . We find, for the year 1990 the . . . projections of investment and employment [shown on Table 4].

We distinguish the "direct" jobs involved in producing and installing the final products from the "indirect" employment involved in producing raw materials and components. The jobs projected here pay wages and salaries that are typical of the respective industries in 1990, especially manufacturing and construction. One-quarter of the investment and the jobs are in energy conservation, three-quarters in solar energy. About one-third of the investment is in the residential sector; the remainder of the investment must be made by business and government decisionmakers.

For comparison, the BLS projects the gross national product in 1990 to

°Because of the need for further advances in technology, we assume that implementation of photovoltaics does not begin until 1985.

be $3,241 billion, with gross private domestic investment equal to $510 billion. Total employment will be 114,000,000 and total unemployment 5,400,000, with the BLS assumption of an unemployment rate of 4.5 percent. Construction employment will be 5,574,000 and manufacturing employment 23,872,000. Thus, conservation and solar employment will impose relatively small pressure on the economy as a whole, but it can make a significant dent in unemployment.

Energy Savings   These investments lead to very significant savings of nonrenewable fuel. Rather than including solar energy in the national energy accounts as contributing positive amounts of energy, there is less ambiguity if it is viewed as a conservation measure, enabling the consumption of nonrenewable fuels to be curbed. (The recently-enacted National Energy Conservation Policy Act includes solar energy and wind power devices among the energy conservation measures it promotes.) This method of accounting is especially appropriate for on-site solar techniques, where the energy supplied by solar devices is not transmitted, marketed, or even measured, but simply permits less dependence on external energy sources powered by nonrenewable fuels.°

Assuming that a strong CARE program is begun in 1980, we find that the fuel consumed in 1990, compared with the DRI business-as-usual projection, is as [shown in Table 5].

The implementation of these CARE measures leads to a saving of 44.9 quads of nonrenewable fuels.† Projecting forward to the year 2000, with CARE measures implemented according to Table [4], we obtain a total fuel consumption of 52.7 quads, little more than a third of the 144 quads found if the conventional, business-as-usual path is followed. About half the savings are achieved through conservation measures, half through solar energy.

The conventional method of energy accounting would add to the energy sources shown in Table [5] the contribution of hydropower and various active solar systems envisioned in this scenario. Using this approach, we find for 1990 the [energy consumption shown in Table 6].

°Steve Baer has pointed out, for instance, that anyone who dries clothes on a clothesline will be using solar energy. As compared to the user of a gas or electric dryer, they will be using less fuel but not necessarily less energy. And the energy, of course, is not measured.

†It might be thought that we should add the fuel consumed in the course of manufacturing and installing the conservation and solar systems. However, we have no way of knowing whether this production is part of the production already included in the BLS projection, or is an addition to it. In any case, this energy "investment" is "paid back" by these systems in a year or two and thus represents 5–10 percent of their useful energy delivery.[24]

Table 5   Primary Fuel
           Consumption [Quads
           per year]

	DRI	CARE
Coal	28.1	14.2
Natural gas	18.6	11.5
Petroleum	46.4	33.6
Nuclear	13.3	2.2
Total	106.4	61.5

Total energy consumption in the CARE scenario is just about equal to total consumption in 1977; that is, there is zero energy growth between 1977 and 1990. Solar systems provide 10.2 quads or 13 percent of the energy in 1990, and they provide 22 quads or 28 percent of the energy in 2000. (This understates the significance of solar sources; to the extent they substitute for electricity produced from nonrenewable sources, 1 Btu of solar energy replaces 3.4 Btu of nonrenewable fuels.) For comparison, ERDA Report No. 49, the National Solar Energy Research, Development, and Demonstration Program, projected a solar contribution of the order of 10 quads by the turn of the century; the Stanford Research Institute found 15 quads in its "solar emphasis" scenario; the Mitre Corp. projected 6 quads; the Committee on Nuclear and Alternative Energy Systems (CONAES) of the National Academy of Sciences found a high-solar scenario yielding 14 quads; and the Council on Environmental Quality projected 15–25 quads.[23,25,26,27]

Net Job Creation   The savings achieved by introducing this wide range of conservation and renewable energy measures allows spending on nonrenewable fuels to be reduced by $118.8 billion compared to the BLS projection for 1990. We estimate that this will lead to 644,000 fewer jobs operating and supplying facilities that use and distribute nonrenewable

Table 6   Energy Consumption
           [Quads per year]

	DRI	CARE
Nonrenewable fuels	106.4	61.5
Hydropower	4.3	4.3
Solar systems		10.2
Total	110.7	76.0

fuels and 493,000 fewer jobs in electric powerplant manufacture and construction. Of the total of 1,137,000 jobs, 680,000 are directly in these industries; 457,000 are in industries that are indirectly affected by these
energy savings.

By 1990, the money saved by residential, commercial, and industrial
consumers from reduced fuel consumption greatly exceeds the amount
invested annually in CARE measures. These extra funds can be spent to
purchase additional goods and services. From the net spending of $53.2
billion ($118.8 billion less than the annual CARE investment of $65.6
billion), there will be an additional 1,870,000 jobs created. The BLS projections assume that the cost of energy rises no faster than the general rate
of inflation, which they project at 5.4 percent per year. Since the price of
these fuels will very likely rise faster than this, the dollar savings will
probably be greater and the number of jobs created by the shift in spending correspondingly larger. Also to the extent that CARE investments are
made out of borrowed funds rather than current income, there would be
more disposable income available and, consequently, more jobs produced.
On the other hand, if fuel prices are raised by their suppliers in response
to the drop in demand, there would be fewer additional jobs.

Keeping in mind these caveats regarding this estimate of the jobs created (and indeed, the approximate nature of all of the estimates in this
study), we then have the following net job creation:

Table 7

	Number of Jobs Created
Conservation	521,000
Solar energy	1,649,000
Nonrenewable fuels	−1,137,000
Added disposable income	1,870,000
Total	2,903,000

These figures do not include the additional jobs that would be created
through the multiplier effect (spending of the income earned through this
employment) and the accelerator effect (increased investment induced
through anticipated growth). Such effects result from a stimulus added to
an existing economic situation, whereas many of the jobs envisioned here
may be part of the employment growth projected by BLS. To the extent
they are not reflected in those projections, but represent additional investment beyond that in the BLS forecast, there would be a roughly equiv-

alent number of additional jobs created through the multiplier (re-spending) effect.

The CARE Employment Picture   It is now widely recognized that employment programs must be "targeted" to be effective, that is, they must place funds and jobs in the regions, and among the population groups, suffering the most from unemployment. Jobs in the fuel extraction industries (coal mining, oil and gas exploration, etc.) and in power-plant construction tend to be far from the areas suffering the most severe unemployment. On the other hand, energy conservation and solar energy system production and installation will take place largely in settled urban areas where the unemployed reside and where they can easily be trained and hired. Thus, the jobs created in this scenario can make a significant contribution to solving the chronic unemployment problem facing our urban areas. Some jobs, such as those involved in producing photovoltaic arrays and solar heat engines, will be in more centralized manufacturing facilities; these can replace the jobs displaced by the reduction in conventional energy investment and production.

The jobs will be dispersed as widely across the country as are the dwellings people live in and the sites of their work. Workers will not be required to move to remote or temporary construction sites. Energy conserving technologies tend to be decentralized, geographically distributed in roughly the same proportion as the population. Fuel supply technologies, on the other hand, tend to be centralized and located where the fuel sources are, e.g., in Alaska, offshore, in the Rocky Mountains or the northern plains.

Jobs will be created in insulating and retrofitting homes with solar units, manufacturing and installing more efficient heating and cooling systems, making office buildings more energy efficient, producing and operating mass transit systems, producing and installing cogeneration devices, and recycling valuable materials. The skills required will be similar to those required for conventional construction projects and heating system installation. Work will be provided for sheet metal workers, carpenters, plumbers, pipefitters, construction workers, and production line workers of all kinds. Energy management will be increasingly important and will be a new source of employment for engineers and designers. Also, solar energy technology is suited to community-based enterprise and small business. Expansion of this industry will open up opportunities for ownership and economic development by those who now have little or no role in the multinational energy industries.

As energy conservation and the use of renewable energy become guideposts for community planning, land use and housing density patterns will shift. Higher densities, with a reduction of suburban sprawl, will reduce transportation energy usage and allow more energy-efficient

housing construction.[28,29] Compact communities will facilitate the introduction of neighborhood-scale solar units for both heat and electricity
generation.[4] Such units have a number of significant advantages, including the possibility of utilizing shared community spaces with protected
access to the Sun and of incorporating very large storage tanks that can
store summer heat for winter usage. Very high densities (especially buildings of four or more stories) will be discouraged, since the solar resource is
relatively diffuse (requiring about 400 square feet per family) and on-site
energy supply would then become infeasible.

Commercial and industrial activities will require more energy planning
and more land for access to the Sun. (In a solarized society, land becomes
an energy resource.) Though these activities may occupy a small fraction
of a community's land, their solar energy needs will require several times
the space they occupy.[29] There will have to be community- and region-
wide planning to insure that the necessary space is available, whether on
buildings or on open spaces. There may also be a tendency for energy-
intensive industries to locate in areas having large amounts of annual solar
radiation, though increased transportation costs may tend to counter such
shifts.

In general, energy considerations will become a predominant consideration in land use planning, community organization, and the location of
jobs.

3. Financing the Solar Transition

Achievement of the scenario envisioned in this study, and of the job
creation it would generate, depends on political and economic decisions
which induce the necessary investment and make available the necessary
funds.

It seems likely that this will not occur unless mandatory Federal standards are established governing a broad range of energy conservation and
renewable energy measures (similar to the mileage requirements now imposed on automobile manufacturers). Even though price factors alone
would appear to impel the introduction of these measures today, in fact, a
great many of those with the ability to introduce them have not done so.
The builders of homes and commercial buildings want to keep their initial selling costs down even though, over the lifetime of the building, the
purchaser may well end up paying more through high energy usage for
heating, cooling, and lighting. Likewise, industrial decision makers have
been lukewarm to conservation and solar energy, insisting on twice as
large a return (about 30 percent per year) from an investment in energy
conservation as from an investment that increases productive output.[30]

Many conservation measures are relatively inexpensive and, even at
today's fuel prices, would pay for themselves in energy savings in just a

few months or years; as prices rise, they will become even more cost-effective. Many solar energy systems make economic sense today when compared with the cost of electricity, though not yet when compared with the cost of oil or gas.[31,32] In all cases, these financial benefits accrue in the future through some substantial investment in the present. Consumers and businesses may prefer other ways of spending their money. Generally, an energy-related investment will not markedly improve current living conditions for the individual consumer or expand sales for the businessman.

In addition, it is characteristic of most CARE measures that they are purchased by the users of energy, rather than by the current producers of energy. Whereas a powerplant is purchased, constructed, and operated by an electric utility, a solar heating unit is purchased by the individual homeowner or builder for installation on the individual home. The user's return on this investment depends on the cost of the energy saved, and thus on the average cost of all facilities then producing and distributing energy. A supplier's investment choice, on the other hand, is based on the comparative cost of new facilities currently being built.

New energy production plants tend to be increasingly expensive so that, in general, an investment in conservation or solar energy would save more energy than would be produced by the same expenditure on new facilities using nonrenewable fuels.[4,31] Cogeneration equipment costs industrial users more than what they are now paying for electricity, but less than what it would cost a utility to produce equivalent central powerplant capacity.[33] Since the user's investment is compared with the average cost of energy, while the supplier deals with replacement cost, the user's decision is weighted against the purchase. To overcome this, some alternative financing arrangement seems to be necessary.

One is to introduce some form of national subsidy, such as the recently approved tax credit for homeowners and businesses. However, this applies only to particular classes of taxpayers and will not address the general need for making CARE investments attractive to the energy user.

Another possibility would be to have the suppliers, especially the electric utilities, purchase (or loan the money for) conservation and solar installations. These investments would then be incorporated into the internal accounting of the energy producers. However, this would negate some of the main advantages of renewable energy systems, namely, their flexibility and amenability to control by the users. It would seem preferable to set up an alternative financing scheme which would accomplish the same end, that is, introducing a broad societal perspective into the financial arrangement, without transferring control to the current suppliers of energy. Since suppliers' investments will, in any case, be based on borrowed money which is repaid through payments by consumers, it should be possible, in principle, to devise mechanisms which would achieve this.

One would be an energy development bank which could borrow large sums at attractive rates on the private money market and loan these for CARE purchases, either directly or through local banking institutions, to users (including communities for shared, neighborhood-scale facilities). In effect, this federally backed bank would be borrowing the sums that would otherwise be drawn on by the utilities and other energy suppliers, and making them available to energy users. By loaning them out for long terms at low interest, the monthly cost to users can be reduced below what their energy spending would otherwise be. (Indeed, the San Diego Savings & Loan Association is already making available loans which are extensions of a homeowner's mortgage, so the homeowner may end up with no additional monthly cost for the CARE installation.)

With the introduction of a financing mechanism such as this, with a broad-based educational effort, and with the strong support of public officials, it should be possible to launch a national conservation and renewable energy program that would have the very great employment benefits identified in this study.

REFERENCES

1. Statistical Abstract of the United States, Bureau of the Census, U.S. Department of Commerce, Washington, D.C., 1977.

2. "Man's Impact on the Global Environment," Report of the Study of Critical Environmental Problems, MIT Press, Cambridge, 1970.

3. Alvin M. Weinberg, "Can We Do Without Uranium?," in "Future Strategies for Energy Development," Oak Ridge Associated Universities, Oak Ridge, Tenn., 1977.

4. Amory B. Lovins, "Soft Energy Paths," Ballinger, Cambridge, 1977, and "Soft Energy Technologies," Annual Review of Energy, 3, 477, 1978.

5. "Jobs and Energy: A Call for Action," Americans for Energy Independence, Washington, D.C., 1976.

6. For an excellent summary of the case for conservation and solar energy as an employment-producer, see the booklet "Jobs and Energy" prepared by Environmentalists for Full Employment, 1101 Vermont Ave. NW., Washington, D.C., 1977.

7. "Analysis of the Proposed National Energy Plan," Office of Technology Assessment, U.S. Congress, Washington, D.C., 1977.

8. For a more detailed examination of the relation between economic growth and energy consumption, see Leonard S. Rodberg, "Energy and Jobs: The Case for CARE," in "Energy and Equity: Some Social Concerns," Joint Center for Political Studies, Washington, D.C., to be published.

9. "Electric Perspectives," 77/6, Edison Electric Institute, New York, N.Y.

10. "Energy: Global Prospects, 1985–2000," Report of the Workshop on Alternative Energy Strategies, McGraw-Hill, New York, N.Y., 1977.

11. Energy Review, Summer 1977, Data Resources, Inc., and Maria Mahon, Bureau of Labor Statistics, U.S. Department of Labor, private communication.

12. Study by Jack Alterman, Bureau of Economic Analysis, U.S. Department of Commerce, 1975.

13. "Patterns of Energy Consumption in the United States," prepared by the Stanford Research Institute for the Office of Science and Technology, Executive Office of the President, Washington, D.C., 1972.

14. "A Time to Choose: America's Energy Future," by the Energy Policy Project of the Ford Foundation, Ballinger, 1974.

15. E. A. Hudson and D. W. Jorgenson, "U.S. Energy Policy and Economic Growth, 1975–2000," Bell Journal of Economics and Management Science, Autumn, 1974; K. C. Hoffman and D. W. Jorgenson, "Economic and Technological Models for Evaluation of Energy Policy," ibid., Autumn, 1977.

16. The projections used in this study for the period 1977–90 were preliminary results provided by the Office of Economic Growth of BLS, especially Charles T. Bowman. The author is grateful for the assistance of this Office. Summaries of the macroeconomic and industry final demand projections have now been published in Norman C. Saunders, "The U.S. Economy to 1990: Two Projections for Growth" and Arthur Andreassen, "Changing Patterns of Demand: BLS Projections to 1990," both appearing in the December 1978 issue of the Monthly Labor Review. The industry output and employment projections are scheduled for publication in the April 1979 issue of the Monthly Labor Review. These will incorporate some minor revisions from the preliminary results used in this study. For descriptions of earlier projections, see "The U.S. Economy in 1985: A Summary of BLS Projections" (Bulletin 1809), "The Structure of the U.S. Economy in 1980 and 1985" (Bulletin 1831), and "Factbook for Estimating the Manpower Needs of Federal Programs" (Bulletin 1832), all published by the Bureau of Labor Statistics, U.S. Department of Labor, Washington, D.C., 1975.

17. "New Labor Force Projections to 1990: Three Possible Paths," Bureau of Labor Statistics press release, August 16, 1978.

18. Clark W. Bullard, "Energy and Jobs," paper presented at the University of Michigan Conference on Energy Conservation—Path to Progress or Poverty, November 1–2, 1977.

19. Marc H. Ross and Robert H. Williams, "Energy and Economic Growth," prepared for the Joint Economic Committee, U.S. Congress, Washington, D.C., 1977.

20. Robert H. Williams (ed.), "The Energy Conservation Papers," Ballinger, 1975.

21. Denis Hayes, "Rays of Hope," Norton, N.Y., 1977.

22. Wilson Clark, in "Creating Jobs Through Energy Policy," Hearings before the Subcommittee on Energy of the Joint Economic Committee, U.S. Congress, Washington, D.C., March 16–18, 1978.

23. Demand and Conservation Panel of the Committee on Nuclear and Alternative Energy Systems, "U.S. Energy Demand: Some Low Energy Futures," Science, April 14, 1978, p. 142.

24. John P. Holdren, "Environmental Impacts of Alternative Energy Technologies for California," in "Distributed Energy Systems in California's Future," Interim Report, U.S. Department of Energy, Washington, D.C., May 1978.

25. "Solar Energy in America's Future: A Preliminary Assessment," Division of Solar Energy, ERDA, Washington, D.C., March 1977.

26. "Solar Energy: A Comparative Analysis to the Year 2000," Mitre Corp., McLean, Va., 1978.

27. "Solar Energy: Progress and Promise," Council on Environmental Quality, Washington, D.C., April 1978.

28. M. F. Fels and M. J. Munson, "Energy Thrift in Urban Transportation: Options for the Future," in reference 20.

29. Owen Carroll and Robert Nathans, "Land Use Configurations and the Utilization of Distributive Energy Technology," in "Distributed Energy Systems in California's Future," Interim Report, U.S. Department of Energy, Washington, D.C., May 1978; Robert Twiss, Pat Smith, and Peter Pollock, "Land Use Implications of a Dispersed Energy System," ibid.

30. G. N. Hatsopoulos, E. P. Gyftopoulos, R. W. Sant, and T. F. Widmer, "Capital Investment To Save Energy," Harvard Business Review, March-April 1978.

31. Denis Hayes, "The Solar Energy Timetable," Worldwatch Paper 19, Worldwatch Institute, Washington, D.C., 1978.

32. "The Economics of Solar Home Heating," study prepared for the Joint Economic Committee, U.S. Congress, Washington, D.C., March 13, 1977.

33. R. H. Williams, "Industrial Cogeneration," Annual Review of Energy, 3, 1978.

38
NO ROOM IN THE LIFEBOATS

Richard J. Barnet

Austerity, lowered expectations, and limits to what government can do have been the ascendant political slogans of the 1970's. Sluggish growth, inflation and high unemployment are no longer regarded as periodic problems to be remedied by swift governmental action but are now accepted by both parties as chronic conditions of our economic life.

In a little over 10 years the myth of abundance has been replaced by the myth of scarcity. The world is running out of oil; experts disagree only as to how fast. The United States' dependence on critical minerals is in-

From *The New York Times Magazine*, April 18, 1978. Copyright © 1978 by The New York Times Company. Reprinted by permission.

creasing dramatically, and so are prices. Crippling shortages of oil, natural gas, food and water, even breathable air, are now a familiar part of the worldwide political landscape. (In many poor countries there is even a grave shortage of firewood, their principal energy source.) Some scarce items seem almost inexhaustible but politics and economics conspire to keep them out of reach—at the right place, at the right time, at the right price. Each shortage tends to aggravate others. For example, the more dependent we are on foreign oil, the more food we must export and the higher the price of groceries in the supermarket. Because of drastically higher costs of producing and distributing critical resources, and of managing their ecological side effects, corporations are finding it ever harder to develop profitable investments. Thus, the worldwide "capital shortage."

The fear that we have come to the end of the ever-expanding frontier of economic growth challenges one of our most cherished political beliefs. The era that began in the New Deal was rooted in the Keynesian notion that unrestricted growth is the foundation for a democratic political system and a more or less egalitarian distribution of our national treasure. The bigger the pie, the bigger the crumbs for those who did not work but did get to the unemployment office. But the growing awareness of the physical and economic limits to growth has undermined the very basis of Keynesian liberalism and is calling into question the basic promises of the American system.

There has always been tension between America's economic and political systems. The promise of politics is one man, one vote—the chance for every voting American to participate in the basic decisions that affect his life. At the heart of the economic system, however, is the theory that inequality is a spur to progress. To stimulate economic growth, society should reward those who produce, and if non-producers vote themselves food, housing, or services that they have not "earned," sooner or later the economy will collapse from inflation.

The Age of Scarcity, it seems, is heightening the tension. In a survey of attitudes of United States corporate leaders, economist Leonard Silk and political scientist Davis Vogel find strong expressions of doubt about whether the United States can any longer afford a one-man, one-vote system. Samuel Huntington, a principal adviser to the National Security Council, warns against the "excesses" of government are too complex to accomodate the conflicts inherent in democratic rule. Elsewhere in the world, the collapse of democratic experiments and the rise of authoritarian regimes lend support to the increasingly fashionable view that strong rule, not democracy, is the wave of the future.

In an age of slow growth, the cost of natural resources is going up and the value placed on human life is going down. This, indeed, is the heart of the global human-rights problem. The expendability of human life and the waste of human potential are direct consequences of the sort of economic development being pursued in most parts of the world. An increasing proportion of the world's population is becoming irrelevant to the productive process. Automation has dramatically reduced the number of hands needed to make what the world wants, and because of the new mobility of the post-World War II multinational corporation, many of the jobs that remain are concentrated in low-wage enclaves in a few poor countries. The concentration and mechanization are drawing millions of people from subsistence farming into the international money economy in which they will have no role—either as producer or consumer—for without jobs they do not have the money to buy the food they once raised themselves.

Though it's fine to say that resources should go to those who produce, fewer and fewer have the chance to be regarded as productive. In large part because of resource scarcity and the population explosion, the reserve army of the unemployable is becoming so vast—perhaps as many as a billion—that it not only keeps wages depressed but also begins to create social instability. What to do about the surplus population, to use a phrase from Dickens's time, is the No. 1 problem for political leaders around the world, and in a condition of scarcity, managing societies made up of millions of people without jobs, money or hope invites Draconian economics and brutal politics.

So it is not hard to understand why a new antidemocratic, antihuman ideology is emerging under the banner of fiscal soundness. Intellectual careers are launched with metaphors that evoke the new realism, such as "triage," a strategy for spending limited resources on those who can be more productive and for consigning those who can't to various forms of "benign neglect," which for hundreds of millions means starvation. Others preach the "lifeboat ethic," a more modest proposal in which only the poorest billion are pushed out of "spaceship earth" to make room for the rest. Only a generation ago Americans were appalled by the genocidal mind-set behind Hitler's project for ridding the globe of inferior races. Now it is becoming almost fashionable here to suggest that too many people are getting in the way of society.

In the United States, the consequences of the "lifeboat ethic" are already visible: the vast wasteland of decay in every major city in which the poor are concentrated; the depressed rural areas no longer needed to produce the nation's food; the seven million Americans who cannot find work.

We are reaching the point where some of our most basic beliefs about human life will have to be tested. We will be forced either to bring our economic institutions into line with the fundamental humanist and democratic values we profess to or openly reject them in favor of the lifeboat ethic.

The lifeboat scenario is not hard to imagine. In the opening moments, "Looking out for No. 1" replaces "E Pluribus Unum" on our coins. The State Department once again reminds the world of what Lyle P. Schertz of the Department of Agriculture calls "the brutal facts of the world food market"—that the United States controls most of the spare grain that could be used to feed the hungry and that the United States aggressively uses its food, in the words of former Secretary of Agriculture Earl Butz, as "a tool in the kit of American diplomacy." American diplomats repolish those vague speeches about economic justice, while they continue to oppose any significant changes in the global distribution of wealth and power. The huge debt owed by third-world countries to international lending agencies and to private banks is used as leverage to control their internal development and keep them from becoming international troublemakers. The International Monetary Fund steps up what Arthur Burns called a "new assertiveness in monitoring the economic policies of its members" and offers its "certificate of good standing" only if the debtor countries practice the "responsible" economic policies that keep the poor hungry—by freezing wages, cutting imports and private consumption and eliminating social services and subsidies.

These policies can be practiced successfully only in an atmosphere of mounting repression, because there will be more than half a billion persons in the world actually starving or at the edge of starvation, and not all of them can be relied upon to die cheerfully. Death squads, mass-production torture chambers and military rule become indispensable aids to orderly government.

This scenario is in reality a continuing war of rich against poor. Sometimes it takes the form of conflict between the United States and the government of a third-world country. Sometimes it takes the form of a collaboration between the governments to prevent a poor majority from gaining access to resources or political power. In the future, it will take the form of hotter and hotter competition among the industrialized countries themselves, as they become more and more dependent upon the third world for raw materials. The turmoil offers, among other things, the chance to the Soviet Union to play a dangerous geopolitical game.

The strategy will of course require ever higher military budgets, for which we will continue to justify the starving of our cities, the lack of investment in basic human needs and the abandonment of the "unemployable"—the elderly, the young, the poor, the disadvantaged minorities and other nonproducers in the name of "national security."

The lifeboat ethic is by definition the abandonment of the goal of community, which Webster's New International Dictionary calls a body of people with common organization and common interests. The politics of community is based on the idea the everyone is a member to whom responsibilities are owed; the politics of austerity is a process for deciding who shall live. In a place like Chile and in many other countries in which national economic policy determines who shall eat, this is literally true. In advanced countries, including the United States, the politics of austerity determines at the very least who among us shall be sentenced to years without work or hope.

Will the strategy work? Can affluent and middle-class Americans survive in a world in which hundreds of millions of men, women and children starve to death each year, tens of thousands more are slaughtered in the interests of social peace, and tens of millions of Americans live in poverty? Military defense of a sort is possible. The world's poor who "want what we have," as Lyndon Johnson once put it, are unlikely to take over our skyscrapers, factories and suburbs. The fortresses can stand a long time.

But life inside will not be pleasant. We are already in the age of "monkey-wrench politics" in which a few terrorists can transform comfortable ways of life in the most advanced industrial societies—especially the most advanced. There is a greater degree of international anarchy now than at any time since World War II. Thirty-five nations have nuclear weapons or are in a position to acquire them rapidly. A new international economic order is coming into being to accommodate the new oil dynasties of the Middle East, but it is not the order the poor countries want. And the process by which the dead structure of colonialism is being replaced is already a form of warfare—struggles for power in the new states carved out of the old empires.

As tension and desperation mount abroad, the political struggles will be played out in the United States, whether it is by Cuban exiles, Iranians, Palestinians, Chileans, Ghanaians, South Moluccans or any one of a thousand armed groups contending for power somewhere in the world. Bombings, elaborate security precautions against bombings, kidnappings and sabotage of the extraordinarily vulnerable systems that keep our complex civilization going have in the last 10 years taken away some of the pleasure of living in the rich countries. The anger and fear that random violence elicits produce inevitable demands for less democracy and for more executions, as we have recently seen in West Germany and in New York City election rhetoric.

The recent export of cholera to developed countries in Europe is a taste of what we can expect here if famine and disease continue to overtake the people in vast areas of Africa, Asia and Latin America. The illegal immigration of millions of workers from Latin America and the Caribbean, which is already causing serious problems in parts of the United States, will increase as long as these poor countries are unable to feed and to employ their people. We do not have the technology to immunize the United States from the effects of world catastrophe—debt default, economic collapse, disease, refugees, terrorism. There is, it would seem, no way of inviting a billion or more people around the world out of the lifeboat without running great risks that they will rock it and sink the rest of us.

To try to keep the United States secure in such a world will lead to a loss of democracy. When an economic system cannot meet the goals of a democratic political system by supplying the needs of the majority, then either the one system or the other must change. In the 20th century, fascism in various guises—usually, in the West, taking the form of a marriage between Big Government and Big Business to promote the interests of a shrinking minority—has, indeed, been a conventional therapy for sick economies.

Instead of submitting to the seductive lifeboat ethic, we could instead affirm the basic beliefs on which the society was founded—respect for human life, respect for human dignity, democracy and justice—and resume the building of an American community which cannot be built except in the context of a world community. The idea of world community is meaningless unless it starts from the premise that every man, woman and child on earth is a member. This strategy would set forth a practical definition of the right to life and a commitment to support the political and economic institutions that would make that right real.

At the very least a worldwide definition of basic needs would include the following: (1) Right to minimum calories to maintain health—about 1,900 a day, 2,300 for an adult working male (by these criteria about half the world's population is seriously malnourished). (2) Right to clean drinking water (about 1.2 billion persons do not have access to sanitary water). (3) Basic health services, maternal and child care, instructions in elementary sanitation and nutrition (about 800 million have no access to such essential services). (4) Shelter, a decent minimum environment in which to live free of disease, vermin and exposure (about 800 million are without adequate shelter). (5) Basic education, a chance to learn enough to realize one's potential and to play a useful role in society (about 1.1 billion school-age children and adults in the world are illiterate). In 1944, Franklin Roosevelt proclaimed such basic economic rights as fundamental to American democracy, but the goal was abandoned a long time ago.

A strategy for economic justice in a time of scarcity cannot be a giant welfare program, because there is not enough money in the world to meet basic human needs unless human energies are mobilized in new ways. If the ethic of a modern zoo replaced the lifeboat ethic, more physical requirements would be met but not political and spiritual needs—especially the need for personal dignity and meaning to one's life and the chance for political participation in building society.

Thus, it is essential that the strategy must also offer a new vision of how political institutions can be created or regenerated to excite imagination, mobilize energies and encourage the contribution of free individuals to the common good. Fortunately, such ideas are percolating among a new generation of scholars and activists in the United States. The work of the Federal Budget Study of the Institute for Policy Studies, the Democratic Socialist Organizing committee, the New Democratic Coalition, the Conference on Alternative State and Local Public Policies, the Exploratory Project on Economic Alternatives and other groups experimenting with new organizational forms and technologies makes it possible to avoid the trap of the lifeboat ethic and to establish a new set of priorities and programs for re-creating an American community within a just order.

In the United States, we could start by redefining "national security" to make the security of local communities a prime national goal. Individuals derive their sense of personal security in large measure from the security that their city or town can provide. National security has little meaning if the local economy cannot provide jobs; if food, shelter, energy, health care and transportation are not available at prices people can afford; and if people are afraid to walk the streets. Youngstown, Ohio, was crippled last year when the board of directors of a distant corporation with no stake in the community suddenly decided to cease its steel operations there—a clear example of the lifeboat ethic. When businesses move on, the community is left to fend for itself. Legislation of the sort that exists in some European capitalist countries is essential to avoid this hardship on both the workers themselves and on the community taxpayers. Companies must be required to give notice, to negotiate the terms under which they leave, to bear a fair part of the cost of the dislocation they have caused. When a Youngstown disaster strikes, the city ought to be eligible for Federal funds with which to buy the facility and to convert it into an enterprise that can employ its citizens and finance essential public services.

Massive investment must be directed to underdeveloped areas of the United States. Not only vast rural areas, but also the burned-out and decayed centers of our major cities. Federal subsidies and tax policies now favor uneven development. Many communities—New York, for instance—pay more to the Federal Government than they receive. Luxury goods and nonessential military products are subsidized—the famous Lockheed bail-out is just one example—but the Government does little to create a market for essentials—low-cost housing, community health care, food, energy, and affordable transportation. An investment program to "balance" the American economy, as the economists Barry Bluestone and Bennett Harrison put it, is essential. This might be accomplished, in part, by developing land banks, as has been done in Western Europe, to assist communities in assembling land for low- and moderate-income people; and by a mortgage bank funded by tax dollars to make it possible to buy and to rehabilitate urban homes. There is no way to integrate wasted areas and wasted people into an American community without specifically directing capital to that end in such a way as to make it possible for people to become productive.

Providing useful work for every American should be the primary purpose of the economy. There are enormous national needs that require major investment and millions of jobs—rebuilding the railroads, developing urban mass transport, cleaning up the rivers, developing new energy sources and technologies. For many such needs a private market does not exist; but we must find the means of allocating private capital to them. The market could be created, as the weapons market is created, by Government policy—in this case, through a national development bank that, unlike the one recently proposed by President Carter, would have substantial funds and would promote community self-reliance and the development of alternative approaches to meet basic needs. However, as important as it is for job creation to allocate more credit to public needs, worldwide unemployment is so serious that it cannot be solved without a new concept of work itself. For one thing, the work week must be shortened. And we must begin to regard essential services that keep the society together, such as housework, raising children and caring for the elderly, as deserving of decent pay.

Inflation in basic necessities must be stopped. One way to keep energy prices down would be to increase competition in the highly concentrated energy industry through the establishment of Federal "yardstick" corporations that could develop and market publicly owned oil, coal and shale reserves. Another way could be to make funds available to local communities to develop municipally owned solar-energy systems. A third would be to use Federal funds directly to develop new energy sources and supplies, instead of using the funds as subsidies to private firms in the hope that they will do so. Past history suggests that tax incentives do not induce corporations to meet national needs because the financial interests of global companies and the national interest in energy development do not necessarily coincide. The development of more not-for-profit public utilites owned by municipalities would also keep prices down. (Municipally owned electric companies now deliver electricity at rates that are an average of 25 percent less than those of private companies.) There are similar ideas, as the economist Gar Alperovitz has demonstrated, for controlling inflation in the other basic necessities—food, transportation and housing—that take about 70 percent of the paycheck of most Americans.

There are other ways to finance or encourage appropriate economic development without spurring inflation. More long-term government bonds should be floated for public projects, increasing competition with private money-lending institutions; tax loopholes must be closed, creating needed Government revenue; wasteful Government programs should be cut, including many billions for weapons procurement and the maintenance of military facilities that add nothing to national security.

The United States should reverse policies that help to keep poor countries poor. Between 1950 and 1962 export prices of commodities, the mainstay of most third-world economies, declined 7 percent while the export prices of manufactured goods increased 27 percent. This process neatly guarantees that the poor continue to get poorer; to reverse it, the developed nations must lower the barriers they have erected around third-world trade; they must reduce the debt burden, as Sweden and Canada have done, support certain commodity prices, encourage self-sufficient agriculture—instead of subsidizing multinational corporations to use the land in poor countries for luxury-crop exports while people go hungry because they cannot afford imported food.

The enlightened self-interest of the American people dictates that they help integrate third-world countries into a new international economic order in which they are given a better chance to fulfill their own basic needs. Such an undertaking would, in turn, increase markets and jobs for Americans and would promote the global order necessary for American prosperity.

It would be naive to minimize the difficulty of reaching these goals. But it would be more naive to pretend that the United States can survive as a democracy without a massive effort to protect and stabilize its own cities and rural communities, without a serious commitment to redirecting the global economy toward full employment and without a new relationship with the world's desperately poor majority.

The next 25 years will not be like the last 25. In a time of scarcity, we can expect slower growth and declining productivity. The ideas of the last 25 years—more welfare, more debt, more subsidies to business to stimulate growth—will not do. They will not, they cannot, advance us toward either a vital American community or world community. The issue is not free market versus big government. The government is already deeply involved in our economy and will inevitably become more so. The issue is what kind of government—unwieldy, bureaucratic or responsive—and what kind of involvement—for whom, on whose behalf. Ways can be found to include citizens in making the crucial decisions about what we produce, what we consume, how we distribute the benefits and how we will relate to the rest of the world. But without a vision of what democracy in the last quarter of the 20th century requires and without the political will to make that vision real, we risk once again losing the last best hope of earth.

ABOUT THE EDITORS

ELLIOTT CURRIE has taught at Yale University and the University of California, Berkeley. He has been an assistant director of the Task Force on Protest and Confrontation of the National Commission on the Causes and Prevention of Violence and a consultant to the National Advisory Council on Economic Opportunity and other agencies, specializing in the issues of poverty, unemployment, crime, and violence. His articles have appeared in such publications as *Society, The Nation, The Progressive,* and *Working Papers.* He is continuing research on the social and psychological impact of economic policy and working on a book on American society in the 1980s.

JEROME H. SKOLNICK is a professor of law (Jurisprudence and Social Policy) and director of the Center for the Study of Law and Society at the University of California, Berkeley. He has done writing and research on crime and justice, legal processes, police, collective protest and violence, the family and family law, and race and race relations. His most recent book is *House of Cards: Legalization and Control of Casino Gambling.* As a Guggenheim Fellow in 1980, he studied the evolution and impact of libel and slander laws in England and the United States.